STECK-VAUGHN Spelling
Linking Words to Meaning™ LEVEL 3

John R. Pescosolido
Professor Emeritus
Central Connecticut State University
New Britain, Connecticut

Reviewers

Maria Driend
Literacy Coordinator
Cooperative Education Services
Trumbull, Connecticut

Terese D'Amico
Gifted Education Specialist for Grades 3–6
Thomas Jefferson Magnet School
Euclid City Schools
Euclid, Ohio

Patricia D'Amore
Assistant Reading Coordinator
Cooperative Educational Services
Trumbull, Connecticut

Dr. Donna Ronzone
Principal and Director of Special Education
Briggs Elementary School District
Santa Paula, California

STECK-VAUGHN
ELEMENTARY · SECONDARY · ADULT · LIBRARY

A Harcourt Company

www.steck-vaughn.com

Acknowledgments

Editorial Director Stephanie Muller
Senior Editor Amanda Sperry
Editor Meg E. Chrisler
Assistant Editor Julie M. Smith
Associate Director of Design Cynthia Ellis
Senior Design Manager Cynthia Hannon
Designer Deborah Diver
Media Researcher Sarah Fraser
Editorial Development, Design, and Production The Quarasan Group, Inc.
Cover Illustration Dale Verzaal
Senior Technical Advisor Alan Klemp

PHOTO CREDITS

3 ©James Darell/Stone; 5 ©Ron Austing/Frank Lane Picture Agency/Corbis; 6 ©Mary Kate Denny/Stone; 8 ©Jeff Smith/FOTOSMITH; 10 top (t) ©James Darell/Stone; bottom (b) ©David Young-Wolff/PhotoEdit, Inc.; 11 (juice and water) ©PhotoDisc, Inc; (fruit) ©Comstock, Inc.; (child) ©Ruth Anderson, Bruce Esbin/Photo Network/PictureQuest; 12 ©PhotoDisc, Inc.; 13 ©PhotoDisc, Inc.; 14 ©Myrleen Ferguson/PhotoEdit, Inc.; 15 ©David Young-Wolff/PhotoEdit, Inc.; 16 ©PhotoDisc, Inc.; 17 ©Lori Adamski Peek/Stone; 18 (t) ©Lori Adamski Peek/Stone; (b) ©Roy Morsch/The Stock Market; 20 ©Corbis; 21 ©PhotoDisc, Inc., 26 ©PhotoDisc, Inc.; 30 ©PhotoDisc, Inc.; 32 ©Mark E. Gibson/DRK Photo; 36 ©Bojan Brecelj/Corbis; 34 (t) ©Mark Richards/PhotoEdit, Inc.; (b) ©Michael Newman/PhotoEdit, Inc.; 34–35 ©PhotoDisc, Inc.; 35 ©CAROLCO/TRI-STAR/The Kobal Collection; 39 left (l) ©PhotoDisc, Inc.; right (r) ©C Squared Studios/PhotoDisc, Inc.; 41 ©Lori Adamski Peek/Stone ; 42 ©Corbis; 47 ©Corbis; 48 ©Mary Kate Denny/PhotoEdit, Inc.; 53 ©Quarto, Inc./Artville; 54 ©David Hanover/Stone; 56 (portrait) ©Myles Pinkney; (cup of brushes) ©PhotoDisc, Inc.; (brush) ©Joe Atlas/Artville; (pencils) ©Artville; 57 Sam and the Tigers published by Penguin Putnam, Home Place published by Simon & Schuster; 58 ©Myles Pinkney; 59 ©John Michael/International Stock; 60 ©Myrleen Ferguson/PhotoEdit, Inc.; 66 ©Bob Daemmrich/Stock Boston/PictureQuest; 72 ©Corbis; 73 ©PhotoDisc, Inc.; 75 ©Tim McGuire, Jim Cummins Studio/FPG International; 76 ©Comstock, Inc.; 82 ©Corbis; 84 (t) ©Hulton-Deutsch Collection/Corbis; (b) ©Museum of History & Industry/Corbis; 85 ©Ewing Galloway/Index Stock Imagery/PictureQuest; 86 ©Hulton-Deutsch Collection/Corbis; 88 ©Planet Earth Pictures/FPG International; 90 (t) ©SuperStock, Inc.; (b) ©Planet Earth Pictures/FPG International; 91 ©J. Sneesby & B. Wilkins/Stone; 92 (t) ©SuperStock, Inc.; (b) ©PhotoDisc, Inc.; 94 ©Otto Rogge/The Stock Market; 98 ©Corbis; 100 ©Telegraph Colour Library/FPG International; 106 ©PhotoDisc, Inc.; 107 ©SuperStock, Inc.; 108 ©Digital Studios; 109 ©Walter Bibikow/FPG International; 110 ©PhotoDisc, Inc.; 115 ©Corel Corporation; 116 ©Corbis; 122 ©Victoria Pearson/Stone; 126 ©Corel Corporation; 128 ©PhotoDisc, Inc.; 133 ©Digital Studios; 134 ©Comstock, Inc.; 136 (t) ©G.K. & Vikki Hart/PhotoDisc, Inc.; (b) ©Ryan McVay/PhotoDisc, Inc.; 137 ©Kathi Lamm/Stone; 138 ©G.K. & Vikki Hart/PhotoDisc, Inc.; 139 ©RubberBall Productions; 140 ©Image provided by MetaTools; 141 (l) ©Digital Studios; (r) ©PhotoDisc, Inc.; 143 ©Corbis; 144 ©Peter Cade/Stone; 145 ©PhotoDisc, Inc.; 148 ©PhotoDisc, Inc.; 149 ©PhotoDisc, Inc.; 150 ©Renee Lynn/Stone; 154 ©Roger Tidman/Corbis; 156 ©Digital Vision Photography/Eyewire, Inc.; 158 ©Bettmann/Corbis; 159 ©Hulton-Deutsch Collection/Corbis; 160 ©Bettmann/Corbis; 162 ©David Young-Wolff/PhotoEdit, Inc.; 168 ©Sonda Dawes/The Image Works; 173 ©Don Spiro/Stone; 174 ©PhotoDisc, Inc.; 175 ©Geostock/PhotoDisc, Inc.; 177 ©David Young-Wolff/PhotoEdit, Inc.; 178 ©PhotoDisc, Inc.; 184 ©Corbis; 185 ©PhotoDisc, Inc.; 186 (t) ©Paul Harris/Stone; middle (m) ©PhotoDisc, Inc.; (b) ©Felicia Martinez/PhotoEdit, Inc.; 187 (t) ©PhotoDisc, Inc.; (b) ©Lori Adamski Peek/Stone; 188 ©Paul Harris/Stone; 190 ©Corbis; 192 (t) ©Ron Austing/Frank Lane Picture Agency/Corbis; (bl) ©Joe McDonald/Corbis; (br) ©Wolfgang Kaehler/Corbis; 193 (l) ©W. Perry Conway/Corbis; (r) ©Kennan Ward/Corbis; 194 ©Wolfgang Kaehler/Corbis; 196 ©FPG International; 197 ©Quarto, Inc./Artville; 200 ©David Young-Wolff/PhotoEdit, Inc.; 202 ©PhotoDisc, Inc.; 206 ©PhotoDisc, Inc.; 208 (t) ©PhotoDisc, Inc.; (b) ©PhotoDisc, Inc.; 209 (l) ©Comstock, Inc.; (r) ©Image Farm; 211 ©PhotoDisc, Inc.; 219 ©Corbis; 224 ©Corbis; 225 ©Corbis; 229 ©iSwoop; 236 ©PhotoDisc, Inc.; 240 ©PhotoDisc, Inc. All Dictionary photos by Corbis, iSwoop, PhotoDisc, Steck-Vaughn Collection.

ART CREDITS

Bernard Adnet 155; Marilynn Barr 68–70, 204–206; Lynda Calvert–Weyant 123; Randy Chewning 152–154, 174, 191; David Austin Clar 151, 157, 175 (t); Mark Corcoran 28–30; Doug Cushman 163, 189; Karen Dugan 78–80, 129, 198–200; Cecile Duray–Bito 22–23; Allan Eitzen 44–46; Doris Ettlinger 55, 195; Peter Fasolino 38, 89; Cynthia Fisher 73 (t); Ruth Flanigan 27, 43, 101, 118–120, 170–172, 183; Susan Guevara 49, 99, 106; Laurie Hamilton 62–64, 107, 146–148; Laura Jacobsen 33, 83, 180–182; John Kanzler 72; Cheryl Kirk-Noll 50–52; John Lund 61, 164–166; Erin Mauterer 39, 96–98, 112–114, 169, 203; Michael Morris 140; Kathleen O'Malley 37, 102–104; Cary Pillo 9; Daniel Powers 77, 179; Stacey Schuett 111; Jeff Shelly 67, 117; Krystyna Stasiak 40, 73 (b); B.K. Taylor 95, 124–126; Jackie Urbanovic 135; Jason Wolff 130–132, 175 (b).

Pronunciation key and diacritical marks copyright © 1998 by Houghton Mifflin Company. Adapted and reproduced by permission from *The American Heritage Student Dictionary*.

Steck-Vaughn Spelling: Linking Words to Meaning is a trademark of Steck-Vaughn Company.

ISBN 0-7398-3617-X

The words *soil, worm, eggs, flower,* and *bird* are hidden on the cover. Can you find them?

Contents

Unit 1

Unit 2

Unit 3

Unit 4

Unit 5

Unit 6

Program Overview

In this age of instant electronic messaging and high standards for written communication, spelling is a skill students need to master more than ever. *Steck-Vaughn Spelling: Linking Words to Meaning*™ offers today's students and teachers a well-constructed, systematic program that builds spelling power, links spelling to word meaning, and connects spelling to the underlying purpose for learning it—the ability to write effectively.

> *"While children are studying words, they are also exploring word meaning and the connections between words."*
>
> Gay Su Pinnel and Irene C. Fountas,
> *Word Matters: Teaching Phonics and Spelling in the Reading/Writing Classroom*

Program Philosophy

Steck-Vaughn Spelling is based on three fundamental goals for students:

- to learn to spell common spelling patterns and troublesome words
- to learn strategies related to sounds and spelling patterns
- to link spelling and meaning

The majority of skill lessons in *Steck-Vaughn Spelling* focus on spelling patterns for vowel sounds in words derived from analysis of research on word frequency and spelling difficulty. Other skill lessons focus on word structure and content-area words.

Steck-Vaughn Spelling presents an integrated language-arts approach to the study of spelling for students in grades 1 through 6. Each of the Levels 2–6 student books consists of six instructional units, each containing five skill lessons and a unit review. Level 1 begins with two readiness units that focus on letter-sound relationships for consonants and short vowels. Skill lessons begin in Unit 3.

Skill lessons throughout the program follow a test-study-test structure. Students take a pretest on the lesson words to determine which words they know and which they need to study. Then they use prescribed Study Steps to Learn a Word and the lesson activities to practice the lesson words before they take a posttest. Research shows that this test-study-test approach is the most effective method of learning to spell. Throughout each lesson in the program, ample opportunities to write a word aid students in learning and retention.

Program Components

Student's Edition

Key features of the Student's Edition include

- **Study Steps to Learn a Word** that focus learning
- **Spelling Strategies** that provide ways to learn and remember troublesome words in real-world situations as well as in the classroom
- **Lessons** that build spelling competency
- a list of **Commonly Misspelled Words** that students can use as they write
- a **Spelling Table** that contains common spellings for consonant and vowel sounds
- a **Spelling Dictionary** that contains all lesson words and Challenge Words

Teacher's Edition

The Teacher's Edition for *Steck-Vaughn Spelling* contains everything in the Student's Edition—and more. Features include

- **Reduced, annotated student pages** for ease of use
- **Detailed lesson plans** including spelling strategy and reading comprehension activities, along with enrichment activities, activities for meeting individual needs, additional words for enrichment, and test-taking strategies
- **Pretests** and **posttest sentences** for dictation
- **Copying Masters,** including Home Activity Masters, Activity Masters, Review Test Masters, and Writer's Workshop Masters

Classroom Management

Each of the 36 *Steck-Vaughn Spelling* lessons per level in Levels 2–6 can be taught in one week, using three or five classroom periods per week. Suggested options for pacing are given below.

Levels 2 Through 6 Lesson Pacing

	Five-Day Plan	Three-Day Plan
• Pretest Word Sorting page	One Day	One Day
• Spelling and Meaning	One Day	
• Spelling in Context	One Day	One Day
• Spelling and Writing	One Day	
• Language Connection or Dictionary Skills • Challenge Yourself • Posttest	One Day	One Day
Review Lesson		
• Pretest	One Day	One Day
• Spelling patterns review	One Day	
• Review Sort	One Day	One Day
• Writer's Workshop	One Day	One Day
• Posttest	One Day	

The *Steck-Vaughn Spelling* Word List

At the heart of an effective spelling program lies its word list. The word list in *Steck-Vaughn Spelling: Linking Spelling to Meaning* is based on the philosophy that spelling instruction should focus on the words students misspell most often in their writing and on words that appear most often in print materials—that is, the words students are already attempting and those they need to know to participate in a variety of literacy communities. Because vowel sounds pose one of the greatest spelling challenges to students, *Steck-Vaughn Spelling* focuses strongly on the letter patterns used to spell those sounds.

To develop the initial word list, three types of research were consulted:
- studies of words students use most often in their writing
- analyses of words commonly appearing in print materials
- research on words children most frequently misspell

Research conducted for subsequent revisions has supported the initial analyses and preserved the integrity of a comprehensive and developmentally founded word list that parallels the natural development of written-language acquisition.

"Spelling instruction . . . requires systematic study of a well-researched list of words."

Ronald Cramer, "Making Better Spellers: Integrating Spelling, Reading, and Writing" in *Spelling Research and Information: An Overview of Current Research and Practices*

The Word List Sources

Writing Research

A Basic Vocabulary of Elementary School Children. Henry Rinsland, 1945.
"An Analysis of the Spelling Patterns of Children in Grades Two Through Eight." Roger Farr, C. Kelleher, K. Lee, and C. Beverstock, 1989.
"An Examination of the Writing Vocabulary of Children in Grades Two Through Eight." Roger Farr, C. Beverstock, and B. Robbins, 1988.
"Phoneme-Grapheme Correspondence as Clues to Spelling Improvement." Paul Hanna, Jean Hanna, Richard Hodges, and Edwin Ruddorf, Jr., 1976.
"Spelling." Edward Horn, 1960.
"The Basic Spelling Vocabulary List." Steve Graham, Karen Harris, and Connie Loynachan, 1993.

Reading Research

"220 Basic Sight Words." Edward Dolch, 1939.
Basic Reading Vocabularies. Albert J. Harris and Milton Jacobson, 1982.
Computational Analysis of Present-Day American English. Henry Kucera and W. Nelson Francis, 1967.
The American Heritage Word Frequency Book. John Carroll, Peter Davies, and Barry Richman, 1971.
The Living Word Vocabulary. Edgar Dale and Joseph O'Rourke, 1976.

Success-Rate Research

The New Iowa Spelling Scale. Harry Greene, 1954.

About the Author

Dr. John Pescosolido is Professor Emeritus at Central Connecticut State University, where he served as chairman of the department of reading and language arts and as associate dean and acting dean of the school of education. Dr. Pescosolido's research on different approaches to spelling instruction enabled him to create a spelling program that closely parallels a child's developmental acquisition of the sound-symbol relationships in printed language.

Steck-Vaughn Spelling was extensively researched in numerous classrooms during its development.

Dr. Pescosolido has served on the executive boards of the Connecticut Association for Reading Research and the New England Reading Association. He has also served as Connecticut chairperson of the International Reading Association and as a consultant to state education agencies and numerous school systems throughout the United States.

Meeting Individual Needs

Today's classrooms include students with a wide variety of abilities and needs. Each student in your classroom has a specific learning style. In addition, some students have limited English proficiency. Meeting each student's needs is not an easy task. *Steck-Vaughn Spelling* provides resources to appeal to a variety of learning styles and needs.

Addressing Students' Learning Styles

Because *Steck-Vaughn Spelling* recognizes that students learn in a variety of ways, the program addresses three different learning styles: visual, auditory, and kinesthetic.

- Some students are **visual** learners. They learn best by *seeing* how words are spelled. *Steck-Vaughn Spelling* contains a variety of activities designed to help visual learners see and practice the spelling patterns in words.
- Some students are **auditory** learners. They learn best by hearing sounds and the ways words are spelled. *Steck-Vaughn Spelling* allows auditory learners to hear themselves and their classmates say, chant, and sing word spellings and lesson words in oral sentences.
- Some students are **kinesthetic** learners. They learn best by *touching* and by *moving*. Suggested activities for kinesthetic learners in *Steck-Vaughn Spelling* involve manipulating letter cards and tiles to spell words, tracing letters in sand, sorting words on word cards by pattern, and acting out lesson words.

Helping ESOL Students

English Speakers of Other Languages (ESOL) students add an exciting dimension to the classroom. By sharing experiences from their country of origin, they enrich the lives of their classmates. Many ESOL students have limited English proficiency, however, and their needs must be met in specific ways. *Steck-Vaughn Spelling* provides a variety of activities to help these students learn the spellings and meanings of new words. The program activities incorporate the use of concrete objects and total physical response to help students understand the meanings of words before they learn to spell them.

Steck-Vaughn Spelling encourages ESOL students to pair with English-proficient students for peer support and modeling. Immersing ESOL students in the types of activities *Steck-Vaughn Spelling* suggests will expand their vocabulary, enhance their English fluency and comprehension, and strengthen their spelling skills.

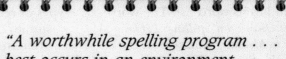

> *"A worthwhile spelling program . . . best occurs in an environment where both the teacher and the students recognize the students' spelling strengths and needs. . . ."*
>
> Diane Snowball and Faye Bolton,
> *Spelling K–8: Planning and Teaching*

Keeping Families Involved

Steck-Vaughn Spelling makes it easy for teachers to invite families to be an integral part of students' spelling progress. Home Activity Masters written in both English and Spanish offer specific activities for important at-home support. Designed to be sent home at the beginning of each unit, each master provides space for the dates of each weekly lesson. The master features the specific words for each lesson as well as interesting games and enjoyable activities for family members to do together to reinforce spelling skills. The master also provides suggestions for using the words in writing and for developing spelling strategies, providing families with the tools for interactive learning.

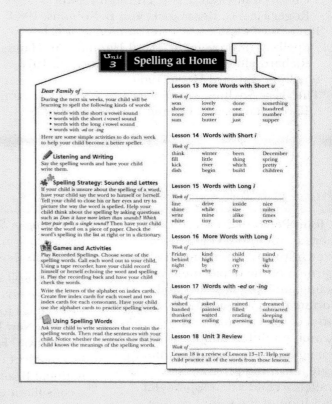

Assessing Students' Progress

Achieving spelling competency is a highly individual process. A responsible spelling program must provide ways for teachers and students to determine strengths and weaknesses on a regular basis. In Levels 1 through 6 of *Steck-Vaughn Spelling*, each lesson provides a pretest, student activities for a midweek informal self-assessment, and a posttest. The six review lessons at Levels 1 through 6 also provide for maintenance, diagnostic evaluation, and reinforcement.

> *"The single most effective technique in learning to spell is followed when the student . . . corrects his or her own errors immediately after taking a spelling test."*
>
> S. Graham and L. Miller, "Spelling Research and Practice: A Unified Approach" in *Spelling*, edited by W. Barbe, A. Francis, and L. Braun

Formal Assessment Opportunities

Steck-Vaughn Spelling features the test-study-test approach. At the beginning of each lesson, the teacher administers a **pretest,** which includes each lesson word in a sentence. The students spell only the lesson words and then have the opportunity to correct their spelling errors. The pretest can be found on the first page of each lesson in the Teachers' Edition.

When students score their performance on the pretest, they receive immediate feedback that reveals the words they do not yet know how to spell and which letters in the troublesome words give them difficulty. Students can follow the suggestions in Study Steps to Learn a Word on page 6 to practice the spelling of words they find difficult.

At the completion of the lesson, students take a teacher-directed **posttest** consisting of dictation sentences that contain lesson words. Students write the entire sentence. Posttest dictation sentences are found at the end of each lesson in the Teacher's Edition and are an important tool for helping teachers assess students' spelling progress.

Dictated pretests and posttests are also provided for review lessons. In addition, the Teacher's Edition provides **Review Test Masters in standardized test formats** as an alternative method of assessment for review lessons. Tips for how to administer these tests, as well as test-taking strategies for students, are imbedded in the Teacher's Edition lesson pages.

Informal and Student Self-Assessment Opportunities

Ongoing assessment of student progress includes **informal observation and questioning from the teacher.** *Steck-Vaughn Spelling* also provides ways for students to monitor their own progress and success. The **Cooperative Learning Activity** provides for an informal midweek self-assessment of mastery of lesson words. Students can compare the results of their performance in this activity to the results of their pretest to determine which words they still need to study.

The **Correcting Common Errors** feature in the Teacher's Edition provides helpful tips for teachers to use in helping students correct common spelling mistakes. Then, as students incorporate lesson words in the **Write to the Point** activity, both students and teachers can once again informally assess progress and success.

> *"Tests of any kind (observational, dictated, or writing analysis) generate information necessary to make good decisions about what to study."*
>
> Gladys Rosencrans, *The Spelling Book: Teaching Children How to Spell, Not What to Spell*

Writer's Workshop Scoring Rubric

A scoring rubric at the end of each review lesson in the Teacher's Edition provides an evaluation framework for teachers to use when evaluating their students' writing. With scores ranging from 1 through 3, the rubric is based on standards for idea development, organization, coherence, sentence structure, usage, punctuation, and spelling. The rubric may also be shared with students before they write.

Writer's Workshop Scoring Rubric: Friendly Letter

SCORE 3
The body of the letter contains developed ideas and specific details. Writing is organized and coherent and contains all the parts of a friendly letter. Contains a minimum of sentence-structure, usage, mechanics, and spelling errors.

SCORE 2
The body of the letter contains some developed ideas and specific details. Has some degree of organization and coherence. Contains most of the parts of a friendly letter. Contains some sentence-structure, usage, mechanics, and spelling errors.

SCORE 1
The body of the letter contains few or no developed ideas and specific details. Has minimal organization and coherence. Contains few if any parts of a friendly letter. Contains many sentence-structure, usage, mechanics, and spelling errors.

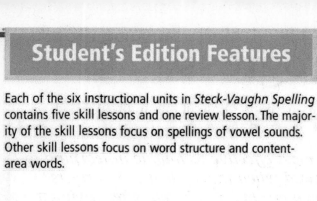

Student's Edition Features

Each of the six instructional units in *Steck-Vaughn Spelling* contains five skill lessons and one review lesson. The majority of the skill lessons focus on spellings of vowel sounds. Other skill lessons focus on word structure and content-area words.

The six pages of the skill lessons include a variety of activities to build students' spelling competency.

- Say and Listen • Think and Sort
- Spelling and Meaning
- Spelling in Context
- Spelling and Writing
- Language Connection • Dictionary Skills • Using the Spelling Table
- Challenge Yourself

Say and Listen helps students focus on the sound featured in the lesson.

Engaging **vocabulary activities** of the Spelling and Meaning page invite students to explore word meanings and use words in meaningful contexts.

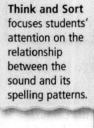

Think and Sort focuses students' attention on the relationship between the sound and its spelling patterns.

Spelling Patterns summary provides visual reinforcement.

Family Tree helps students explore words related to a lesson word, thereby building spelling power and expanding vocabulary.

Word Story provides students with the story behind a lesson word.

Study Steps to Learn a Word help students focus on the words they need to study after they take a pretest and before they take a posttest.

Lesson 15 — Words with Long *i*

1. *i*-consonant-*e* Words

alike
while
eyes
white
line
lion
size
miles
times
nice
drive
tiny
write
inside
mine
shine

2. *i* Words

3. eye Word

Say and Listen

Say each spelling word. Listen for the long *i* sound.

Think and Sort

Look at the letters in each word. Think about how long *i* is spelled. Spell each word aloud.

Long *i* can be shown as /ī/. How many spelling patterns for /ī/ do you see?

1. Write the **thirteen** spelling words that have the *i*-consonant-*e* pattern.
2. Write the **two** spelling words that have the *i* pattern.
3. Write the **one** spelling word that has the *eye* pattern.

Use the steps on page 6 to study words that are hard for you.

Spelling Patterns

i-consonant-*e*	*i*	*eye*
ni*c*e	t*i*ny	*eye* *eye*s

Spelling and Meaning

Clues Write the spelling word for each clue.

1. what people do with a car _____
2. belongs in a group with *feet* and *yards* _____
3. something that can be straight or crooked _____
4. a word meaning "at the same time" _____
5. a word that rhymes with *eyes* _____
6. what people do to some shoes _____

Analogies Write the spelling word that completes each analogy.

7. *Mean* is to _____ as *weak* is to *strong*.
8. *You* is to *me* as *yours* is to _____.
9. *Add* is to *plus* as *multiply* is to _____.
10. *Light* is to *dark* as _____ is to *black*.
11. *Hear* is to *ears* as *see* is to _____.
12. *Needle* is to *sew* as *pen* is to _____.
13. *Small* is to _____ as *big* is to *huge*.
14. *Different* is to *unlike* as *same* is to _____.
15. *Up* is to *down* as _____ is to *outside*.

Word Story One of the spelling words comes from the Greek word *leon*. *Leon* was the word for one of the big cats. The names Leona, Lenore, Leo, Leopold, and Lionel all come from this word. Write the spelling word that comes from *leon*.

16. _____

Family Tree: drive Think about how the *drive* words are alike in spelling and meaning. Then add another *drive* word to the tree.

driven
driver
17.
drives
drive

LESSON 15

Study Steps to Learn a Word

1. **Say** the word. What consonant sounds do you hear? What vowel sounds do you hear? How many syllables do you hear?

2. **Look** at the letters in the word. Think about how each sound is spelled. Find any spelling patterns or parts that you know. Close your eyes. Picture the word in your mind.

3. **Spell** the word aloud.

4. **Write** the word. Say each letter as you write it.

5. **Check** the spelling. If you did not spell the word correctly, use the study steps again.

Use the steps on this page to study words that are hard for you.

The **Spelling in Context** pages present lively reading passages in which students identify and write missing lesson words.

Lesson words are listed at point of use for convenience.

Students use lesson words in a meaningful context as they read high-interest **fiction, nonfiction, and functional passages** written at grade level.

Colorful photos and attractive art support the text and aid in comprehension.

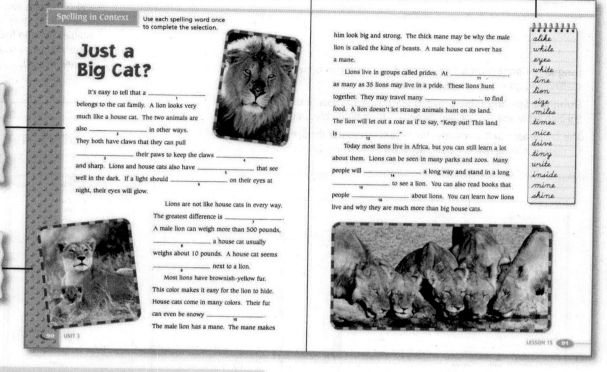

Spelling in Context

Use each spelling word once to complete the selection.

Just a Big Cat?

It's easy to tell that a _____1 belongs to the cat family. A lion looks very much like a house cat. The two animals are also _____2 in other ways. They both have claws that they can pull _____3 their paws to keep the claws _____4 and sharp. Lions and house cats also have _____5 that see well in the dark. If a light should _____6 on their eyes at night, their eyes will glow.

Lions are not like house cats in every way. The greatest difference is _____7. A male lion can weigh more than 500 pounds, _____8 a house cat usually weighs about 10 pounds. A house cat seems _____9 next to a lion. Most lions have brownish-yellow fur. This color makes it easy for the lion to hide. House cats come in many colors. Their fur can even be snowy _____10. The male lion has a mane. The mane makes him look big and strong. The thick mane may be why the male lion is called the king of beasts. A male house cat never has a mane.

Lions live in groups called prides. At _____11, as many as 35 lions may live in a pride. These lions hunt together. They may travel many _____12 to find food. A lion doesn't let strange animals hunt on its land. The lion will let out a roar as if to say, "Keep out! This land is _____13."

Today most lions live in Africa, but you can still learn a lot about them. Lions can be seen in many parks and zoos. Many people will _____14 a long way and stand in a long _____15 to see a lion. You can also read books that people _____16 about lions. You can learn how lions live and why they are much more than big house cats.

alike
while
eyes
white
line
lion
size
miles
times
nice
drive
tiny
write
inside
mine
shine

90 UNIT 3

LESSON 15 91

The **Spelling and Writing** page features activities that relate to the Spelling in Context passage in content and provide a natural link to writing skills.

Write to the Point invites students to respond to the Spelling in Context passage by using lesson words to write about a related topic.

The **Proofreading** activity provides real-world writing forms such as letters, newspaper articles, e-mail messages, and book reviews for students to proofread.

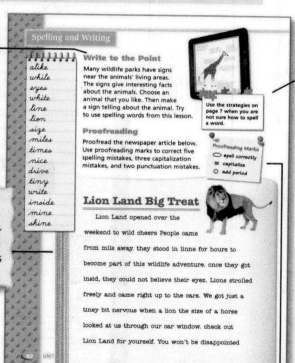

Spelling and Writing

alike
while
eyes
white
line
lion
size
miles
times
nice
drive
tiny
write
inside
mine
shine

Write to the Point

Many wildlife parks have signs near the animals' living areas. The signs give interesting facts about the animals. Choose an animal that you like. Then make a sign telling about the animal. Try to use spelling words from this lesson.

Proofreading

Proofread the newspaper article below. Use proofreading marks to correct five spelling mistakes, three capitalization mistakes, and two punctuation mistakes.

Use the strategies on page 7 when you are not sure how to spell a word.

Proofreading Marks
○ spell correctly
≡ capitalize
⊙ add period

Lion Land Big Treat

Lion Land opened over the weekend to wild cheers People came from mils away. they stood in linne for hours to become part of this wildlife adventure. once they got insid, they could not believe their eyez. Lions strolled freely and came right up to the cars. We got just a tiney bit nervous when a lion the size of a horse looked at us through our car window. check out Lion Land for yourself. You won't be disappointed

92 UNIT

Proofreading marks needed for each activity are listed at point of use for convenience.

Spelling Strategies provide students with ways to learn and remember troublesome words in real-world situations as well as in the classroom.

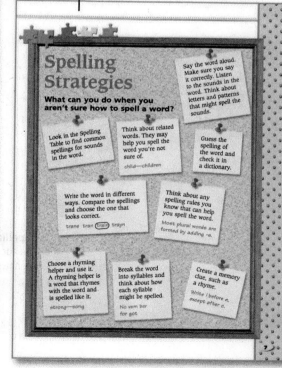

Spelling Strategies

What can you do when you aren't sure how to spell a word?

Say the word aloud. Make sure you say it correctly. Listen to the sounds in the word. Think about letters and patterns that might spell the sounds.

Look in the Spelling Table to find common spellings for sounds in the word.

Think about related words. They may help you spell the word you're not sure of.
child—children

Guess the spelling of the word and check it in a dictionary.

Write the word in different ways. Compare the spellings and choose the one that looks correct.
trane tran train trayn

Think about any spelling rules you know that can help you spell the word.
Most plural words are formed by adding -s.

Choose a rhyming helper and use it. A rhyming helper is a word that rhymes with the word and is spelled like it.
strong—song

Break the word into syllables and think about how each syllable might be spelled.
No vem ber for got

Create a memory clue, such as a rhyme.
Write i before e, except after c.

7

Each skill lesson concludes with an activity page that features
- Language Connection, Dictionary Skills, or Using the Spelling Table
- Challenge Yourself

The **Spelling Table** presents a number of spelling patterns for different vowel and consonant sounds. A valuable reference tool for students, the Spelling Table enables them to find spellings in the dictionary by using sounds they find problematic to spell.

Language Connection activities provide a connection between spelling and grammar, usage, or mechanics.

Using the Spelling Table activities teach students how to use the Spelling Table and the Spelling Dictionary to spell troublesome words.

The Dictionary Skills activities invite students to use the Spelling Dictionary to complete engaging activities that include lesson words.

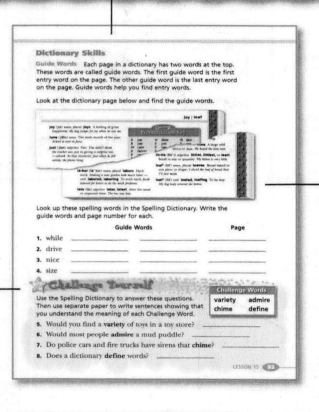

Challenge Yourself presents students with an opportunity to enrich vocabulary and extend spelling skills by focusing on words representing the sound, structural element, or content area featured in the lesson.

Spelling Table

Sound	Spellings	Examples	Sound	Spellings	Examples
/a/	a a_e ai au	ask, have, plaid, laugh	/ŏ/	o a	shop, was
/ā/	a a_e ai ay ea eigh ey	table, save, rain, gray, break, eight, they	/ō/	o o_e oa oe ou ow	both, hole, road, toe, boulder, slow
/ä/	a ea	father, heart	/oi/	oi oy	point, enjoy
/âr/	air are ere	chair, care, where	/ô/	o ea oo ou ough a au aw	off, coarse, door, four, brought, tall, autumn, draw
/b/	b bb	best, rabbit			
/ch/	ch tch	child, catch	/oŏ/	oo ou u u_e	book, could, pull, sure
/d/	d dd	dish, add	/ōō/	oo ou u u_e ue ew o	noon, you, June, blue, news, two
/ĕ/	e ea ie ue a ai ay	best, read, friend, guess, many, said, says	/ou/	ou ow	about, owl
/ē/	e e_e ea ee ei eo ey y	even, these, each, meet, receive, people, key, city	/p/	p pp	place, dropped
			/r/	r rr wr	rain, sorry, write
/f/	f ff gh	fly, off, laugh	/s/	s ss c	safe, dress, city
/g/	g gg	go, egg	/sh/	sh s	shook, sure
/h/	h wh	hot, who	/t/	t tt ed	take, matter, thanked
/ĭ/	i ui e ee u a	inside, build, pretty, been, busy, luggage	/th/	th	then
			/th/	th	third
/ī/	i i_e ie igh eye uy y	tiny, drive, pie, high, eyes, buy, fly	/ū/	u o oe	such, mother, does
/îr/	ear eer eir ere	year, deer, weird, here	/ûr/	ur ir er or ear err our	curl, girl, dessert, world, learn, worst, flourish
/j/	j g	jog, danger	/v/	v f	even, of
/k/	k c ck ch	keep, coat, kick, school	/w/	w wh o	walk, when, one
/ks/	x	six	/y/	y	year
/kw/	qu	quiet	/yōō/	u_e ew ue	use, few, Tuesday
/l/	l ll	late, tell	/z/	z zz s	sneeze, blizzard, says
/m/	m mb mm	much, comb, hammer	/ə/	a e i o u	along, misery, estimate, lion, subtract
/n/	n kn nn	need, know, beginning			
/ng/	n ng	thank, bring			

213

The **Spelling Dictionary** lists entries for all lesson words and Challenge Words.

T14

Review lessons present words from each unit lesson. In addition, students sort the review words according to vowel sound and/or spelling pattern and then compare words already sorted. Each review lesson concludes with a Writer's Workshop.

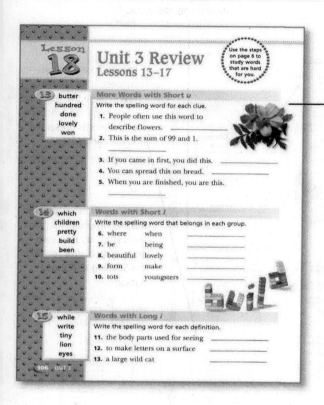

Review words representing the spelling patterns, structural element, or content area presented in each lesson are featured.

Engaging **vocabulary activities** help students review word meanings and use words in meaningful contexts.

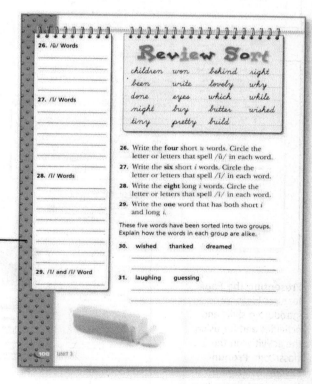

Review Sort helps students discriminate between vowel sounds and/or spelling patterns in the review words and then sort them accordingly.

Students also **analyze sorted words** to determine and explain their similarities and differences.

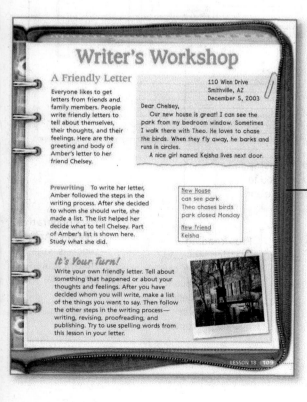

In **Writer's Workshop**, students participate in the **writing process** to write discourse with a variety of modes and aims.

A **model** provides students with an example of a specific kind of writing.

A **prewriting** activity, usually incorporating a graphic organizer, is explained and modeled. Copying masters presenting the steps in the writing process, a proofreading checklist, and graphic organizers are provided in the Teacher's Edition for duplication and distribution to students.

Teacher's Edition Features

An easy-to-use annotated Teacher's Edition with reduced pupil pages provides a wealth of activities to support and enrich all students' spelling development.

Word Story teaching notes present additional etymological information and ideas.

The **Pretest** provides a tool for determining words that students already know how to spell and those they need to learn.
Study Steps and **Home Activity Master icons** provide visual reminders for sequencing instruction.

Clear objectives state desired learning outcomes.

Family Tree activities suggest ways students can explore the spellings, meanings, and functions of the words presented in the Family Tree.

Reading Comprehension focuses on comprehension skills students can learn and practice after reading the Spelling in Context passage.

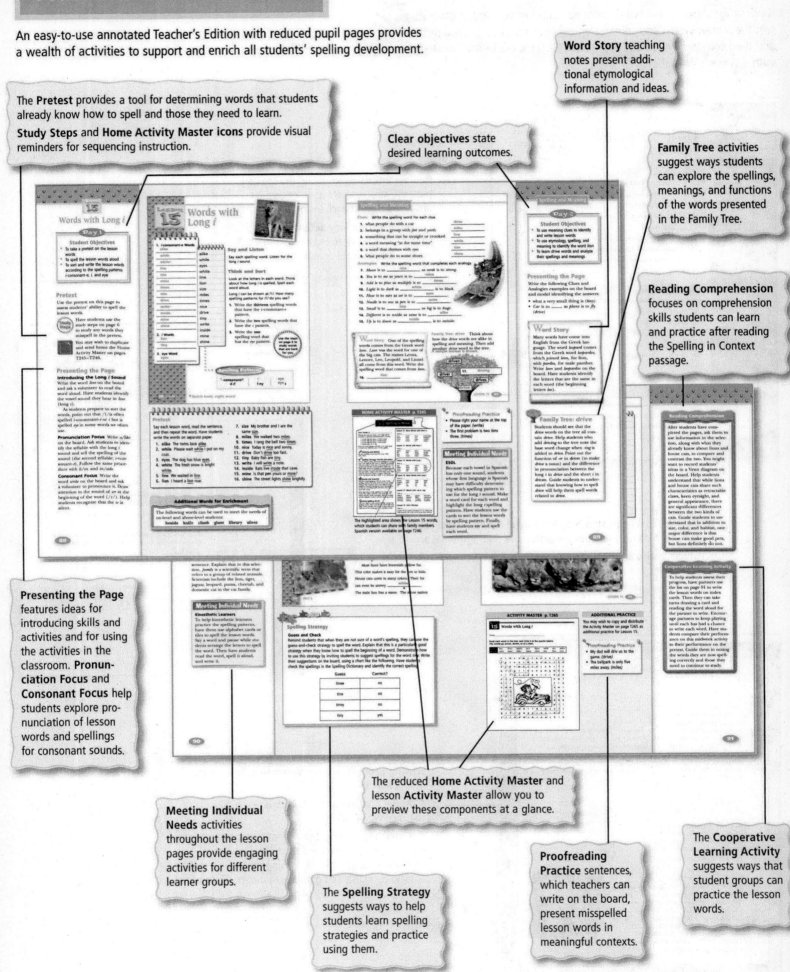

Presenting the Page features ideas for introducing skills and activities and for using the activities in the classroom. **Pronunciation Focus** and **Consonant Focus** help students explore pronunciation of lesson words and spellings for consonant sounds.

The reduced **Home Activity Master** and lesson **Activity Master** allow you to preview these components at a glance.

Meeting Individual Needs activities throughout the lesson pages provide engaging activities for different learner groups.

The **Spelling Strategy** suggests ways to help students learn spelling strategies and practice using them.

Proofreading Practice sentences, which teachers can write on the board, present misspelled lesson words in meaningful contexts.

The **Cooperative Learning Activity** suggests ways that student groups can practice the lesson words.

The **Pretest** provides a tool for determining words that students have mastered and those they need to continue to study.

Presenting the Pages provides suggestions for reviewing skills taught in the prior lessons of the unit.

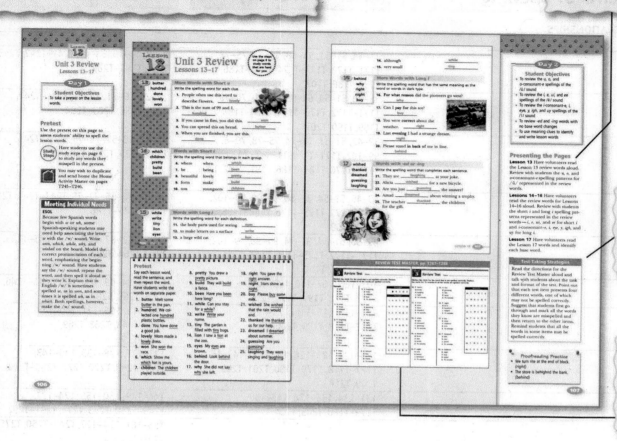

Test-Taking Strategies suggests ways for students to determine correct answers.

The **reduced Review Test Masters** allow you to preview the various standardized test formats.

Presenting the Page provides tips for guiding students through the writing process.

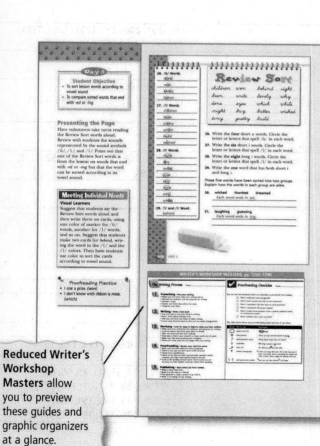

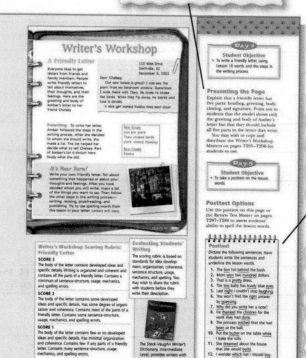

Reduced Writer's Workshop Masters allow you to preview these guides and graphic organizers at a glance.

Posttest sentences designed to be dictated to students are presented. Students write the sentences and underline the lesson words.

Writer's Workshop Scoring Rubric provides specific guidelines for reviewing and evaluating responses to the Writer's Workshop assignment.

Program Scope and Sequence

Elements of Spelling	Level 1	Level 2
SOUND-LETTER RELATIONSHIPS		
Vowel Sounds		
/ă/	31–34, 51–54, 55–58, 59–62, 75–78, T171–T172, T173–T174, T184–T186, T187, T188, T207	8–13, 14–19, 38–41, T241–T242, T253, T254, T283–T284
/ĕ/	35–38, 51–54, 63–66, 67–70, 75–78, T171–T172, T173–T174, T184–T186, T189, T190, T207	20–25, 26–31, 38–41, T241–T242, T255, T256, T283–T284
/ĭ/	39–42, 51–54, 71–74, 75–78, 79–82, 99–102, T171–T172, T173–T174, T175–T176, T184–T186, T191, T192, T207, T208	42–47, 48–52, 72–75, T243–T244, T258, T259, T285–T286
/ŏ/	43–46, 51–54, 83–86, 87–90, 99–102, T171–T172, T175–T176, T184–T186, T195, T208	54–59, 60–65, 72–75, T243–T244, T260, T261, T285–T286
/ŭ/	47–50, 51–54, 91–94, 95–98, 99–102, T171–T172, T175–T176, T184–T186, T195, T196, T208	76–81, 82–87, 106–109, T245–T246, T263, T264, T287–T288
/ā/	103–106, 107–110, 123–126, T177–T178, T197, T198, T209	88–93, 94–99, 106–109, T245–T246, T265, T266, T287–T288
/ē/	111–114, 115–118, 123–126, T177–T178, T199, T200, T209	110–115, 116–121, 140–143, T247–T248, T268, T269, T289–T290
/ī/	119–122, 123–126, 127–130, 147–150, T177–T178, T179–T180, T201, T202, T209, T210	122–127, 128–133, 140–143, T247–T248, T270, T271, T289–T290
/ō/	131–134, 135–138, 147–150, T179–T180, T203, T204, T210	144–149, 150–155, 174–177, T249–T250, T273, T274, T291–T292
/o͝o/		156–161, 174–177, T249–T250, T275, T291–T292
/o͞o/, /yo͞o/	139–142, 143–146, 147–150, T179–T180, T205, T206, T210	162–167, 174–177, T249–T250, T275, T291–T292
/âr/		
/ä/		196–201, 208–211, T251–T252, T281, T293–T294
/îr/		
/ô/		184–189, 190–195, 208–211, T251–T252, T279, T280, T293–T294
/oi/		
/ou/		178–183, 208–211, T251–T252, T278, T293–T294
/ûr/		
/ə/		
Consonant Sounds		
Consonants	7–10, 11–14, 15–18, 19–22, 23–26, 27–30, T169–T170, T181–T183	
VOCABULARY		
Definitions		39, 49, 72, 83, 89, 123, 140, 191
Etymologies		9, 15, 21, 27, 33, 43, 49, 55, 61, 67, 77, 83, 89, 95, 101, 111, 117, 123, 129, 135, 145, 151, 157, 163, 169, 179, 185, 191, 197, 203
Homographs		61

Level 3	Level 4	Level 5	Level 6
8–13, 38–41, T241–T242, T253, T283–T284	8–13, 38–41, T241–T242, T253, T283–T284	8–13, 38–41, T241–T242, T253, T283–T284	8–13, 38–41, T241–T242, T253, T283–T284
26–31, 38–41, 42–47, 72–75, T241–T242, T243–T244, T256, T258, T283–T284, T285–T286	20–25, 38–41, T241–T242, T255, T283–T284	20–25, 26–31, 38–41, T241–T242, T255, T256, T283–T284	20–25, 38–41, T241–T242, T255, T283–T284
82–87, 106–109, T245–T246, T264, T287–T288	48–53, 72–75, T243–T244, T259, T285–T286	54–59, 60–65, 72–75, T243–T244, T260, T261, T285–T286	76–81, 82–87, 106–109, T245–T246, T263, T264, T287–T288
110–115, 140–143, T247–T248, T268, T289–T290	76–81, 106–109, T245–T246, T263, T287–T288	82–87, 106–109, T245–T246, T264, T287–T288	110–115, 140–143, T247–T248, T268, T289–T290
60–65, 72–75, 76–81, 106–109, T243–T244, T245–T246, T261, T263, T285–T286, T287–T288	94–99, 106–109, 110–115, 140–143, T245–T246, T247–T248, T266, T268, T287–T288, T289–T290	110–115, 140–143, T249–T250, T268, T289–T290	48–53, 72–75, T243–T244, T259, T285–T286
14–19, 20–25, 38–41, T241–T242, T254, T255, T283–T284	14–19, 38–41, T241–T242, T254, T283–T284	14–19, 38–41, T241–T242, T254, T283–T284	14–19, 38–41, T241–T242, T254, T283–T284
48–53, 54–59, 72–75, T243–T244, T259, T260, T285–T286	26–31, 38–41, 42–47, 72–75, T241–T242, T243–T244, T256, T258, T283–T284, T285–T286	42–47, 48–53, 72–75, T243–T244, T258, T259, T285–T286	42–47, 72–75, T243–T244, T258, T285–T286
88–93, 94–99, 106–109, T245–T246, T265, T266, T287–T288	54–59, 60–65, 72–75, T243–T244, T260, T261, T285–T286	76–81, 106–109, T245–T246, T263, T287–T288	88–93, 106–109, T245–T246, T265, T287–T288
116–121, 122–127, 140–143, T247–T248, T269, T270, T289–T290	82–87, 88–93, 106–109, T245–T246, T264, T265, T287–T288	88–93, 94–99, 106–109, T245–T246, T265, T266, T287–T288	116–121, 140–143, T247–T248, T269, T289–T290
128–133, 140–143, T247–T248, T271, T289–T290	116–121, 140–143, T247–T248, T269, T289–T290		
144–149, 174–177, T249–T250, T273, T291–T292	122–127, 140–143, T247–T248, T270, T289–T290	122–127, 140–143, T247–T248, T270, T289–T290	
196–201, 208–211, T251–T252, T281, T293–T294	162–167, 174–177, T249–T250, T276, T291–T292	156–161, 174–177, T249–T250, T275, T291–T292	
156–161, 174–177, T249–T250, T275, T291–T292	162–167, 174–177, T249–T250, T276, T291–T292	156–161, 174–177, T249–T250, T275, T291–T292	156–161, 174–177, T249–T250, T275, T291–T292
196–201, 208–211, T251–T252, T281, T293–T294	178–183, 208–211, T251–T252, T278, T293–T294		
178–183, 184–189, 208–211, T251–T252, T278, T279, T293–T294	150–155, 156–161, 174–177, T249–T250, T274, T275, T291–T292	116–121, 140–143, 144–149, 174–177, T247–T248, T249–T250, T269, T273, T289–T290, T291–T292	122–127, 140–143, T247–T248, T270, T 289–T290
162–167, 174–177, T249–T250, T276, T291–T292	144–149, 174–177, T249–T250, T273, T291–T292	128–133, 140–143, T247–T248, T271, T289–T290	
190–195, 208–211, T251–T252, T280, T293–T294	128–133, 140–143, T247–T248, T271, T289–T290		144–149, 174–177, T249–T250, T273, T291–T292
150–155, 174–177, T249–T250, T274, T291–T292	178–183, 208–211, T251–T252, T278, T293–T294	150–155, 174–177, T249–T250, T274, T291–T292	150–155, 174–177, T249–T250, T274, T291–T292
	184–189, 208–211, T251–T252, T279, T293–T294	178–183, 184–189, 190–195, 196–201, 208–211, T251–T252, T278, T279, T280, T281, T293–T294	26–31, 38–41, 66–71, 72–75, 178–183, 184–189, 190–195, 208–211, T241–T242, T243–T244, T251–T252, T256, T262, T278, T279, T280, T283–T284, T285–T286, T293–T294
9, 33, 49, 55, 77, 95, 101, 106–107, 117, 123, 151, 157	9, 38, 43, 55, 61, 72, 107, 140–141, 157, 185, 209	9, 27, 38, 61, 72–73, 77, 107, 135, 163, 174, 179, 197, 208	15, 38, 61, 72–73, 83, 101, 106, 135, 140–141, 157, 175, 185, 203, 209
9, 15, 21, 27, 33, 43, 49, 55, 61, 67, 77, 83, 89, 95, 101, 111, 117, 123, 129, 135, 145, 151, 157, 163, 169, 179, 185, 191, 197, 203	9, 15, 21, 27, 33, 43, 49, 55, 61, 67, 77, 83, 89, 95, 101, 111, 117, 123, 129, 135, 145, 151, 157, 163, 169, 179, 185, 191, 197, 203	9, 15, 21, 27, 33, 43, 49, 55, 61, 67, 77, 83, 89, 95, 101, 111, 117, 123, 129, 135, 145, 151, 157, 163, 169, 173, 179, 185, 191, 197, 203	9, 15, 21, 27, 33, 43, 49, 55, 61, 67, 77, 83, 89, 95, 101, 111, 117, 123, 129, 135, 145, 151, 157, 163, 169, 179, 185, 191, 197, 203

Program Scope and Sequence, continued

Elements of Spelling	Level 1	Level 2
Homophones	146	95, 149, 163
Meaning Clues	123	9, 39, 43, 67, 72, 101, 107, 117, 135, 141, 151, 157, 163, 174, 179, 203, 208, 209
Meaning Relationships		15, 21, 27, 55, 61, 73, 77, 83, 89, 101, 107, 111, 117, 129, 140, 145, 155, 157, 169, 174, 185, 197, 208–209
Context Clues	56, 57, 60, 61, 64, 65, 68, 69, 72, 73, 77, 80, 81, 84, 85, 88, 89, 92, 93, 96, 97, 100, 101, 104, 105, 108, 109, 112, 113, 116, 117, 120, 121, 124, 128, 129, 132, 133, 136, 137, 140, 141, 144, 145, 149	10–11, 16–17, 22–23, 27, 28–29, 34–35, 38, 39, 44–45, 50–51, 56–57, 62–63, 68–69, 72–73, 78–79, 84–85, 90–91, 96–97, 102–103, 106, 107, 112–113, 118–119, 124–125, 129, 130–131, 136–137, 140, 146–147, 152–153, 158–159, 164–165, 170–171, 175, 180–181, 186–187, 192–193, 198–199, 204–205, 208
WORD STRUCTURE AND ANALYSIS		
Abbreviations		
Anagrams and Letter Order	99, 147	9, 25, 33, 38, 55, 67, 73, 106, 151, 179
Compound Words		
Confusing Word Pairs		
Contractions		
Inflectional Endings		100–105, 134–139, 168–173, 174–177, 202–207, T245–T252, T267, T272, T277, T282, T287–T294
Plural Forms		66–71, 72–75, T243–T244, T262, T285–T286
Possessives		
Related Words		9, 15, 21, 27, 33, 43, 49, 55, 61, 67, 77, 83, 89, 95, 101, 111, 117, 123, 129, 135, 145, 151, 157, 163, 169, 179, 185, 191, 197, 203
Rhyming Words	33, 37, 41, 45, 49, 53, 148	15, 33, 43, 49, 77, 123, 145, 197, 209
Suffixes		
Syllabication		
Vowel Patterns		8, 14, 20, 26, 40, 42, 48, 54, 60, 74, 76, 82, 88, 94, 108, 110, 116, 122, 128, 142, 144, 150, 156, 162, 176, 178, 184, 190, 196, 210
Word Building	34, 38, 42, 46, 50, 54, 75	21
DICTIONARY ELEMENTS		
Alphabetical Order	66, 74, 76, 82, 101, 124, 138, 149	37, 53, 93, 121, 207
Definitions	118	65, 99, 133, 201
Guide Words		121
Homographs		
Homophones	146	
Idioms		
Multiple Spellings		
Parts of a Dictionary Entry		71, 173

Level 3	Level 4	Level 5	Level 6
	15, 123, 163	202–207, 209	
27, 38–39, 61, 72–73, 83, 89, 106, 111, 129, 140, 145, 157, 175, 179, 185, 197, 208	27, 33, 39, 67, 72, 77, 83, 95, 107, 111, 141, 145, 174, 197, 203, 209	15, 33, 38, 55, 67, 72, 73, 83, 101, 106, 111, 123, 145, 157, 169, 174, 175, 185, 203, 208–209	9, 33, 39, 49, 61, 72, 77, 95, 106, 117, 123, 140, 151, 163, 169, 174, 179, 197, 208–209
9, 15, 21, 27, 33, 38, 43, 49, 55, 67, 72, 77, 89, 101, 106–107, 111, 117, 123, 127, 129, 135, 140–141, 145, 151, 155, 163, 169, 174–175, 179, 185, 197, 203	9, 21, 27, 38–39, 43, 49, 55, 67, 73, 77, 83, 89, 101, 106, 111, 117, 123, 129, 135, 140, 145, 151, 157, 163, 169, 175, 179, 185, 191, 197, 208	9, 21, 27, 38–39, 43, 49, 55, 61, 73, 77, 83, 89, 95, 100, 111, 117, 129, 135, 140–141, 145, 151, 157, 169, 174, 191, 197, 209	9, 15, 20, 27, 38–39, 43, 55, 67, 72–73, 77, 83, 89, 95, 101, 106, 117, 123, 129, 135, 140–141, 145, 151, 157, 163, 174–175, 179, 185, 191, 197, 209
10–11, 16–17, 19, 22–23, 28–29, 34–35, 39, 44–45, 50–51, 56–57, 62–63, 68–69, 73, 78–79, 84–85, 90–91, 96–97, 102–103, 107, 112–113, 118–119, 124–125, 130–131, 136–137, 139, 140–141, 146–147, 152–153, 158–159, 164–165, 170–171, 180–181, 186–187, 192–193, 198–199, 204–205, 209	10–11, 16–17, 21, 22–23, 28–29, 34–35, 38, 44–45, 50–51, 56–57, 62–63, 68–69, 78–79, 84–85, 90–91, 96–97, 102–103, 107, 112–113, 118–119, 124–125, 130–131, 136–137, 141, 146–147, 152–153, 158–159, 164–165, 170–171, 174–175, 180–181, 186–187, 192–193, 198–199, 204–205, 208	10–11, 16–17, 22–23, 28–29, 34–35, 39, 44–45, 50–51, 56–57, 62–63, 68–69, 72, 73, 78–79, 84–85, 89, 90–91, 96–97, 102–103, 107, 112–113, 118–119, 124–125, 130–131, 136–137, 140–141, 146–147, 152–153, 158–159, 164–165, 170–171, 179, 180–181, 185, 186–187, 192–193, 198–199, 204–205, 208	10–11, 16–17, 22–23, 28–29, 34–35, 38–39, 44–45, 50–51, 56–57, 62–63, 68–69, 78–79, 84–85, 90–91, 96–97, 102–103, 106–107, 112–113, 118–119, 124–125, 130–131, 136–137, 146–147, 152–153, 158–159, 164–165, 170–171, 175, 180–181, 186–187, 192–193, 198–199, 203, 204–205, 208
	196–201, 208–211, T251–T252, T281, T293–T294		
15, 61, 121, 133, 183, 191, 208			
	190–195, 208–211, T251–T252, T280, T293–T94	101, 162–167, 175–177, T249–T250, T276, T291–T292	32–37, 38–41, 128–133, 140–143, 169, T241–T242, T247–248, T257, T271, T283–T284, T289–T290
			134–139, 140–143, T249–T250, T272, T293–T294
66–71, 72–75, 168–173, 174–177, T243–T244, T249–T250, T262, T277, T285–T286, T291–T292	100–105, 106–109, T245–T246, T267, T287–T288		
100–105, 106–109, 134–139, 141–143, 202–207, 208–211, T245–T246, T247–T248, T251–T252, T267, T272–T282, T287–T288, T289–T290, T293–T294	134–139, 140–143, T249–T250, T272, T293–T294		
32–37, 38–41, T241–T242, T257, T283–T284	66–71, 72–75, 168–173, 174–179, T243–T244, T249–T250, T262, T277, T285–T286, T291–T292	66–71, 72–75, T243–T244, T262, T285–T286	60–65, 72–75, T243–T244, T261, T285–T286
	168–173, 174–177, T249–T250, T277, T291–T292	121, 167	183
9, 15, 21, 27, 33, 43, 49, 55, 61, 67, 77, 83, 89, 95, 101, 111, 117, 123, 129, 135, 145, 151, 157, 163, 169, 179, 185, 191, 197, 203	9, 15, 21, 27, 33, 43, 49, 55, 61, 67, 77, 83, 89, 95, 101, 111, 117, 123, 129, 135, 145, 151, 156, 163, 169, 179, 185, 191, 197, 203	9, 15, 21, 27, 33, 43, 49, 55, 61, 67, 77, 83, 89, 95, 101, 111, 117, 123, 129, 135,145, 151, 157, 163, 169, 179, 185, 191, 197, 203	9, 15, 21, 27, 33, 43, 49, 55, 61, 67, 77, 83, 89, 95, 101, 111, 117, 123, 129, 135, 145, 151, 157, 163, 169, 179, 185, 191, 197, 203
43, 67, 83, 95, 135, 191	15, 33, 61, 95, 101, 174	15, 21, 33, 49, 67, 123, 140, 151, 203	49, 89, 145
		197	162–167, 174–177, 196–201, 202–207, 208–211, T249–T250, T251–T252, T276, T281, T291–T292 T293–T294
	32, 202	32, 100, 134, 162, 168	32, 94, 100, 168, 176
8, 14, 20, 26, 40, 42, 48, 54, 60, 74, 76, 82, 88, 94, 108, 110, 116, 122, 128, 142, 144, 150, 156, 162, 176, 178, 184, 190, 196, 210	8, 14, 20, 26, 40, 42, 48, 54, 60, 74, 76, 82, 88, 94, 108, 110, 116, 122, 128, 142, 144, 150, 156, 162, 176, 178, 184, 210	8, 14, 20, 26, 40, 42, 48, 54, 60, 74, 76, 82, 88, 94, 108, 110, 116, 122, 128, 142, 144, 150, 156, 176, 178, 184, 190, 196, 210	8 ,14, 20, 26, 40, 42, 48, 54, 66, 74, 76, 82, 88, 108, 110, 116, 122, 142, 144, 150, 156, 176, 178, 184, 190, 210
	190, 191		141
13, 31, 37, 59, 99, 115, 189	13	13, 25	
31, 161	59	47, 161	71
93	25	25	13
		115	149
			149
81	127		201
		195	115
37	53		121

Program Scope and Sequence, continued

Elements of Spelling	Level 1	Level 2
Parts of Speech		
Pronunciation		31, 189
Syllabication		
GRAMMAR AND USAGE		
Adjectives		
Adverbs		
Nouns		167
Subjects and Predicates		81
Subject-Verb Agreement	98, 134	
Verbs		127, 139, 141, 183
MECHANICS		
Capitalization	62, 110, 114	13, 25, 59, 87, 115, 161
Punctuation	58, 86, 114	18, 25, 47, 87, 161, 195
Titles of Works		
WRITING SKILLS		
The Writing Process		41, 75, 109, 143, 177, 211, T295–T300
Forms of Writing		
Advertisements, Commercials		80
Book Reviews, Movie Reviews, Evaluations		
Descriptions		58, 143, 166, 200, 211, T295–T296, T299
Diary Entries, Journal Entries		30
Directions, Instructions, Explanations, Reports, News Articles		172, 194
Interviews, Interview Questions		
Jokes and Riddles		
Lists		64, 206
Messages, Letters, Notes		86, 109, 114, T295–T296
Opinions, Personal Reflections	78, 102, 126, 150	12, 18, 24, 36, 46, 52, 70, 104, 120, 126, 132, 154, 182, 188
Narratives		41, 75, 92, 98, 138, 148, 160, 177, T295–T296, T297, T298
Poems		138
Posters, Signs, and Announcements		
Sentences	70, 90, 94, 106, 122, 130, 142	
Speeches		
Modes and Aims of Writing		
Narrative	102	41, 75, 92, 98, 148, 160, 177, T295–T296, T297, T298
Descriptive		143, 166, 200, 211, T295–T296, T299
Expository	70, 90, 106, 122, 126, 130, 142	12, 18, 24, 36, 46, 64, 104, 126, 172, 182, 188, 194
Expressive	78, 94, 150	30, 52, 70, 86, 109, 114, 120, 132, 138, 154, 206
Persuasive		58, 80
Proofreading		
Spelling Errors	58, 62, 66, 70, 74, 75, 82, 86, 90, 94, 98, 99, 106, 110, 114, 118, 122, 123, 130, 134, 138, 142, 146, 147	12, 18, 24, 30, 36, 46, 52, 58, 64, 70, 80, 86, 92, 98, 104, 114, 120, 126, 132, 138, 145, 154, 160, 166, 172, 182, 188, 194, 200, 206
Capitalization Errors		12, 18, 24, 30, 36, 46, 52, 58, 64, 70, 80, 86, 92, 98, 104, 114, 120, 126, 132, 138, 145, 154, 160, 166, 172, 182, 188, 194, 200, 206
Punctuation Errors		12, 18, 24, 30, 36, 46, 52, 58, 64, 70, 80, 86, 92, 98, 104, 114, 120, 126, 132, 138, 145, 154, 160, 166, 172, 182, 188, 194, 200, 206
Missing Words		
Unnecessary Words		
Word Order		

Level 3	Level 4	Level 5	Level 6
25, 149, 195, 201	81, 149	99, 161	155
	19, 99, 115, 167, 189, 207	37, 127, 133, 149, 176, 207	47, 59, 207
	37		
87, 207	105	155	127, 167
		189	133, 195
53	65	31, 167, 173	31, 37
183	31, 71, 139	53, 87, 93	53, 93, 189
		71	
121, 173			
19, 47, 133, 167	32–37, 87, 121, 195	19, 59, 105	19, 37, 161, 173
19, 65, 105, 139	47, 93, 133, 161, 201	19, 65, 81, 121, 139, 201	19, 25, 81, 87, 99, 105, 139, 183
	155	183	65
41, 75, 109, 143, 177, 211, T295–T300	41, 75, 109, 143, 177, 211, T295–T300	41, 75, 109, 143, 177, 211, T295–T300	41, 75, 109, 143, 177, 211, T295–T300
36	46, 148	86, 114, 200	126, 154, 166
	154	166	177, T295–T296, T300
143, 154, T295–T296, T299	52, 92, 114, 120, 126, 143, 188, 211, T295–T296, T299	36, 46, 64, 143, 160, T295–T296, T299	98, 109, 160, T295–T296, T298
		80	92
64, 138, 154, 172, 177, 188, T295–T296, T300	166, 177, 200, T295–T296, T300	24, 30, 70, 104, 138, 148, 172, 177, 182, T295–T296	46, 143, 148, 172, 188, T295–T296, T299
		194	
120	160		
24, 30	98	98	30, 80
109, 132	86, 109, 132, T295–T296	58, 92, 109, 211, T295–T296	18, 86, 104, 194, 211, T295–T296
12, 52, 58, 70, 80, 86, 98, 104, 114, 126, 148, 160, 194	18, 24, 30; 36, 58, 64, 70, 80, 172, 182, 194, 206	18, 52, 104, 132, 166	12, 36, 52, 70, 98, 114, 120, 200, 206
41, 75, 166, 182, 211, T295–T296, T297, T298	12, 41, 75, 104, 138, T295–T296, T297, T298	12, 41, 70, 75, 120, 126, 154, 188, T295–T296, T297, T298	24, 41, 64, 75, 132, 138, T295–T296, T297
200			182
18, 46, 92, 206		200	
		206	
41, 75, 98, 166, 182, 211, T295–T296, T297, T298	12, 41, 70, 75, 104, 138, T295–T296, T297, T298	12, 41, 75, 126, 154, 188, T295–T296, T297, T298	18, 24, 41, 64, 75, 132, 138, T295–T296, T297
143, 154, T295–T296, T299, 211, T295–T296, T299	52, 92, 114, 120, 143, 160, 188,	46, 143, 160, T295–T296, T299	86, 98, 109, 160, T295–T296, T298
18, 24, 46, 64, 70, 92, 114, 138, 148, 154, 160, 172, 177, 188, 194, 206, T295–T296, T300	18, 30, 36, 46, 58, 64, 126, 148, 154, 166, 177, 198, 182, 200, T295–T296, T300	24, 30, 64, 138, 148, 166, 172, 177, 194, 200, T295–T296	30, 46, 52, 58, 70, 80, 143, 148, 172, 177, 188, 200, T295–T296, T299, T300
12, 30, 52, 58, 80, 86, 104, 109, 120, 126, 132, 200, T295–T296	24, 70, 80, 86, 109, 132, 172, 194, 206, T295–T296	18, 36, 52, 58, 70, 80, 92, 98, 109, 132, 206, T295–T296	12, 36, 92, 114, 120, 182, 194, 206, T295–T296, T300
36	148	86, 114, 182, 211, T295–T206	104, 126, 154, 166, 211
12, 18, 24, 30, 36, 46, 52, 58, 64, 70, 80, 86, 92, 98, 104, 114, 120, 126, 132, 138, 148, 154, 160, 166, 172, 182, 188, 194, 200, 206	12, 18, 24, 30, 36, 46, 52, 58, 64, 80, 86, 92, 98, 104, 114, 120, 126, 132, 138, 148, 154, 160, 166, 172, 182, 188, 194, 200, 206	12, 18, 24, 30, 36, 46, 52, 58, 64, 70, 80, 86, 92, 98, 104, 114, 120, 126, 132, 138, 148, 154, 160, 166, 172, 182, 188, 194, 200, 206	12, 18, 24, 30, 36, 46, 52, 58, 64, 70, 80, 86, 92, 98, 104, 114, 138, 148, 154, 160, 166, 172, 182, 188, 194, 200, 206
12, 18, 24, 30, 36, 46, 52, 58, 64, 70, 80, 86, 92, 98, 104, 114, 120, 126, 132, 138, 148, 154, 160, 166, 172, 182, 188, 194, 200, 206	18, 24, 36, 46, 52, 58, 80, 86, 92, 98, 104, 120, 126, 132, 138, 154, 160, 166, 172, 182, 188, 194, 200, 206	12, 18, 24, 36, 46, 52, 58, 64, 70, 86, 92, 98, 104, 114, 120, 126, 132, 138, 148, 160, 166, 172, 188, 194, 200, 206	12, 18, 30, 36, 46, 58, 64, 70, 86, 104, 114, 148, 154, 160, 166, 172, 182, 194, 200, 206
12, 30, 36, 46, 58, 64, 70, 80, 86, 92, 98, 114, 120, 126, 138, 148, 154, 160, 166, 188, 200, 206	12, 30, 52, 64, 80, 92, 98, 104, 114, 120, 126, 148, 154, 194, 200	12, 18, 30, 36, 58, 64, 70, 80, 98, 114, 120, 126, 148, 154, 166, 172, 194	18, 24, 46, 52, 58, 70, 86, 92, 98, 104, 114, 138, 166, 172, 182, 188, 200, 206
	12, 24, 30, 132, 160, 206	24, 114, 138	24, 98, 160
18, 24, 52, 104, 132, 172, 182, 194	18, 36, 46, 58, 64, 86, 114, 138, 148, 166, 172, 182, 188	30, 52, 80, 86, 132, 154, 182	12, 30, 52, 64, 80, 138, 148, 154, 194
		92, 104, 182, 188, 206	36, 92, 188

Word List *for Levels 2, 3, and 4*

Blue type indicates Dolch basic sight words (high-frequency words).
Red type denotes Challenge Words.
Lesson numbers are indicated in parentheses.

LEVEL 2

A
active (1)
add (1)
adjust (13)
admit (7)
admitting (23)
adopt (9)
advice (21)
after (1)
alerting (17)
all (32)
am (1)
amusing (29)
an (1)
and (1)
any (4)
are (34)
arm (34)
around (31)
art (34)
ask (2)
asked (17)
ate (15)
athlete (19)

B
baby (15)
baby sitter (35)
back (2)
backs (11)
bacon (15)
bake (15)
baked (29)
baker (35)
baking (29)
ball (32)
bamboo (28)
barber (34)
barn (34)
batches (11)
bed (3)
bees (19)
beggar (4)
beginner (35)
being (19)
belief (19)
bell (4)
bells (11)
best (4)
big (7)
bigger (35)
bike (21)
biked (29)
bitter (8)
black (2)
blank (1)
blizzard (7)
block (9)
blue (28)
blush (14)

boat (26)
bonnet (10)
bony (25)
book (27)
booth (28)
boulder (26)
box (10)
boys (5)
brave (15)
braver (35)
bravery (16)
bring (8)
brother (14)
brow (31)
buckle (13)
buddy (5)
bug (13)
bulletin (27)
bus (13)
bushel (27)
but (13)
by (22)

C
call (32)
came (15)
cannon (2)
car (34)
cat (1)
catch (2)
catching (17)
cats (11)
chain (16)
cheap (20)
cheat (20)
child (5)
children (5)
chop (10)
city (20)
claimed (17)
class (5)
classmate (5)
clean (20)
climate (21)
clock (10)
clover (26)
clown (31)
club (13)
coat (26)
cocoon (28)
cold (26)
colder (35)
come (14)
cook (27)
cookbook (27)
cookies (27)
corn (33)
could (27)
cow (31)
coward (31)

craft (2)
cry (22)
cut (13)
cutting (23)

D
dainty (16)
dark (34)
delay (15)
denying (17)
depart (34)
desk (5)
desks (11)
diet (22)
dipper (35)
disease (20)
disliked (29)
do (28)
dodge (10)
dog (32)
door (33)
dot (9)
dotted (23)
draw (32)
dream (20)
dress (5)
dresses (11)
dressing (17)
drop (10)
dropped (23)
dropping (23)
drought (31)
ducklings (11)

E
eat (20)
egg (5)
eggs (11)
eight (16)
end (4)
ended (17)
explode (25)
eye (21)

F
fade (15)
faithful (6)
false (32)
far (34)
farm (34)
farmer (34)
fast (3)
faster (35)
father (34)
faucet (32)
feet (19)
fill (7)
find (21)
fish (8)

fished (17)
fishing (17)
five (21)
flat (2)
flatter (35)
floor (33)
flower (31)
fly (22)
food (28)
foot (27)
for (33)
found (31)
four (33)
freeze (19)
frog (32)
from (13)
full (27)
fun (14)
funny (20)

G
gain (16)
game (15)
gave (15)
girls (5)
give (8)
giving (29)
glimpse (7)
go (25)
goat (26)
gold (26)
good (27)
got (9)
green (19)
grow (25)
guilt (8)

H
habit (1)
had (5)
hand (1)
handed (17)
hands (11)
happy (20)
harmful (34)
has (1)
haul (32)
have (2)
having (29)
he (19)
heat (20)
help (4)
helper (35)
helping (17)
her (5)
hid (7)
hide (21)
high (22)
hill (7)
him (5)

his (7)
hold (26)
hole (25)
home (25)
hop (9)
hope (25)
hoped (29)
hopeful (25)
hopped (23)
hopping (23)
horse (33)
hot (9)
house (31)
how (31)

I
ice (21)
inside (21)
insult (14)

J
jar (34)
jet (3)
jets (11)
job (9)
jobs (11)
jog (9)
jogged (23)
jogging (23)
joke (25)
joking (29)
jump (14)
jumper (35)
just (14)

K
keep (19)
kept (3)
know (25)

L
land (2)
last (2)
leap (20)
liberty (8)
license (21)
lie (22)
like (21)
liked (29)
lining (29)
lion (22)
live (8)
lived (29)
living (29)
lobster (9)
long (32)
longer (35)
look (27)
lost (32)

love (14)
loved (29)
lunch (14)

M
mail (16)
man (1)
many (4)
mark (34)
matter (2)
maybe (15)
mean (20)
melon (3)
memory (4)
men (11)
method (3)
mine (21)
mold (26)
monster (9)
moon (28)
more (33)
most (26)
mother (14)
mouse (31)
much (14)
mud (13)
my (22)

N
nail (16)
name (15)
named (29)
napkin (2)
new (28)
next (3)
nine (21)
no (25)
nose (25)
not (9)
now (31)
numb (13)

O
of (13)
off (32)
old (26)
older (35)
on (9)
one (14)
open (26)
or (33)
orange (33)
orchard (33)
organ (33)
other (14)
our (5)
out (31)
over (26)
owl (31)
ox (10)

P

pail (16)
paint (16)
painter (35)
party (34)
peach (20)
pedal (3)
penny (20)
people (19)
pick (7)
picking (17)
pie (22)
play (15)
please (20)
pond (10)
profit (10)
propped (23)
pull (27)
pupil (5)
puppy (20)
put (27)

R

rain (16)
recesses (11)
rest (4)
rhyme (22)
ride (21)
riding (29)
ring (8)

road (26)
rock (10)
roll (26)
room (28)
rope (25)
round (31)
run (13)
runner (35)
running (23)

S

said (3)
sail (16)
sang (2)
saw (32)
say (15)
says (3)
school (28)
see (19)
send (4)
seven (4)
she (19)
shelf (3)
ship (7)
ships (11)
shop (10)
shopped (23)
shopper (35)
shopping (23)
short (33)

should (27)
side (21)
sister (8)
six (7)
skunk (14)
sky (22)
small (32)
snail (16)
snore (33)
snow (25)
so (25)
sold (26)
song (32)
soon (28)
sound (31)
sponge (14)
spot (10)
spotted (23)
spring (8)
star (34)
stay (15)
stone (25)
stood (27)
stop (10)
stopped (23)
stopping (23)
store (33)
storm (33)
story (33)
street (19)
strutting (23)

such (14)
summer (13)
sun (13)
swim (8)

T

tail (16)
talk (32)
than (1)
thank (2)
thanked (17)
that (2)
the (5)
them (5)
these (19)
they (16)
thing (8)
think (8)
thinking (17)
this (7)
three (19)
tie (22)
tiger (22)
tiny (22)
to (28)
today (15)
told (26)
too (28)
took (27)

tooth (28)
top (9)
torch (33)
town (31)
train (16)
tread (4)
trick (7)
tricked (17)
truck (14)
try (22)
two (28)
tying (22)

U

under (13)
up (13)
us (13)

V

van (1)
vans (11)
very (20)
wait (16)

W

walk (32)
want (10)
was (9)
wash (10)

we (19)
week (19)
well (4)
went (3)
whale (15)
what (9)
when (3)
white (21)
who (28)
why (22)
will (7)
wind (7)
wish (8)
wished (17)
wishing (17)
with (8)
would (27)
write (21)
writer (35)
writing (29)

Y

yellow (25)
yes (3)
you (5)

Z

zoo (28)

Word List for Levels 2, 3, and 4, continued

LEVEL 3

A
able (3)
about (33)
add (1)
address (4)
addresses (5)
admire (15)
adobe (20)
afraid (3)
after (1)
again (3)
agent (3)
ago (21)
agony (3)
aid (3)
aim (3)
air (34)
alike (15)
almost (21)
alone (20)
along (31)
always (31)
apologize (19)
apple (1)
apples (5)
April (2)
arctic (14)
aren't (29)
arm (27)
around (33)
art (27)
artistic (27)
ask (1)
asked (17)
assure
ate (2)
athletic (4)
attempt (4)
August (32)
autumn (32)
away (2)

B
barbecue (27)
bark (27)
barn (27)
because (31)
been (14)
before (32)
begin (14)
beginning (23)
behind (16)
belong (31)
best (7)
better (7)
bird (26)
black (1)
blend (7)
block (19)
blow (20)
blue (25)
boat (21)

body (19)
boil (28)
book (22)
born (32)
both (21)
bottle (19)
bottom (19)
bough (33)
bought (31)
boy (28)
break (2)
broil (28)
broth (31)
brought (31)
brown (33)
build (14)
bureau (22)
busy (9)
butter (13)
buy (16)
buzzard (10)
by (16)

C
cable (2)
came (2)
can't (29)
card (27)
care (34)
careless (34)
carry (9)
carton (27)
casual (25)
catch (1)
caverns (5)
celebration (4)
cemetery (9)
cents (7)
chair (34)
change (2)
child (16)
children (14)
chime (15)
choice (28)
circular (26)
city (9)
clank (1)
class (1)
classes (5)
clock (19)
close (20)
closed (23)
clowns (5)
coarse (32)
coat (21)
coax (21)
cocoa (21)
coin (28)
comb (21)
comment (19)
consented (17)
console (20)

contain (3)
cook (22)
cookies (22)
corner (22)
corridor (32)
could (22)
could've (11)
couldn't (29)
count (33)
cover (13)
crinkled (23)
cry (16)
curl (26)
cycle (16)

D
dairy (34)
danger (3)
dark (27)
dawdle (31)
dear (34)
debate (2)
deceive (8)
December (14)
deer (34)
define (15)
deposit (19)
designer (16)
dessert (26)
devour (33)
didn't (29)
dirt (26)
dirtier (35)
dirtiest (35)
dish (14)
dismay (2)
dispute (25)
does (10)
doesn't (29)
dome (20)
don't (29)
done (13)
door (32)
doubtful (33)
down (33)
draw (31)
dream (8)
dreamed (17)
dreary (34)
dress (4)
dresses (5)
drive (15)
driving (23)
dropped (23)
dropping (23)

E
each (8)
ear (34)
earth (26)
egg (4)

eggs (5)
eight (3)
end (4)
ending (17)
endure (22)
enjoy (28)
enjoyment (28)
estimated (23)
even (9)
every (9)
eyes (15)

F
fable (3)
face (2)
faltering (17)
family (9)
father (27)
feat (8)
February (7)
few (25)
fill (14)
filled (17)
fire (34)
first (26)
floor (32)
flourish (26)
flower (33)
fly (16)
foot (22)
forget (4)
forgot (19)
fork (32)
found (33)
four (32)
fragile (1)
frail (3)
free (8)
Friday (16)
friend (7)
friendliness (7)
frog (31)
from (10)
front (10)
frontier (10)
fulfilling (17)
full (22)
funnier (35)
funniest (35)
funny (9)
fur (26)

G
garden (27)
genuine (4)
girl (26)
glider (16)
goes (20)
gold (21)
gourmet (22)
governed (17)

gray (2)
great (2)
greater (35)
greatest (35)
ground (33)
guess (7)
guessing (17)

H
hadn't (29)
hair (34)
half (1)
hammer (1)
hammers (5)
handed (17)
hands (5)
happy (9)
hard (27)
hasn't (29)
haven't (29)
he's (11)
head (4)
hear (34)
heart (27)
hello (21)
help (4)
here (34)
high (16)
hold (21)
hole (20)
hope (20)
hoped (23)
hopping (23)
hotter (35)
hottest (35)
hour (35)
house (33)
how'd (29)
huddle (10)
huge (25)
hundred (13)

I
I'd (11)
I'll (11)
I'm (11)
I've (11)
income (13)
index (7)
inside (15)
inspire (34)
install (31)
instruct (13)
isn't (29)
it's (11)

J
jabbing (23)
January (1)
jog (19)

jogged (23)
join (28)
joke (20)
joy (28)
June (25)
just (13)

K
kept (7)
key (9)
kick (14)
kind (16)
knew (25)
know (20)

L
labor (2)
late (2)
laugh (1)
laughing (17)
learn (26)
light (16)
liked (23)
line (15)
lion (15)
little (14)
loaf (21)
long (31)
longer (35)
longest (35)
losses (5)
lovely (13)
luggage (14)
lunch (10)

M
maintain (3)
mall (31)
many (7)
March (27)
market (27)
match (1)
matches (5)
matter (5)
May (2)
meat (8)
meet (8)
meeting (17)
meteors (5)
miles (15)
mind (16)
mine (15)
misery (9)
moisten (28)
Monday (10)
money (10)
month (10)
morning (32)
most (21)
mother (10)

move (25)
much (10)
must (13)
mustn't (29)

N

near (34)
neckties (5)
need (8)
never (7)
news (25)
next (4)
nice (15)
night (16)
noise (28)
none (13)
noon (25)
north (32)
nothing (10)
November (20)
number (13)

O

o'clock (19)
October (19)
off (31)
oil (28)
one (13)
only (9)
open (21)
ornament (32)
other (10)
our (33)
over (21)
owl (33)

P

page (2)
pages (5)
paint (3)
painted (17)
paints (5)
paper (3)
papers (5)
patrol (21)
pay (2)

penny (9)
people (8)
place (2)
places (5)
plaid (1)
please (8)
pleased (23)
point (28)
poisonous (28)
poor (22)
popcorn (32)
pour (32)
power (33)
pretty (14)
problem (19)
pull (22)
pursue (25)
put (27)

Q

quart (32)
queen (8)

R

rain (3)
rained (17)
read (4, 8)
reading (17)
ready (4)
rejoice (28)
right (16)
river (14)
road (21)
rodent (20)
rodeo (21)
royal (28)

S

safe (2)
said (4)
sail (3)
Saturday (1)
sausage (31)
save (2)
says (4)
scheme (9)

school (25)
sea (8)
seam (8)
second (4)
sent (7)
September (7)
shakier (35)
shakiest (35)
sharp (27)
sharper (35)
sharpest (35)
she'll (11)
she's (11)
shine (15)
shining (23)
shook (22)
shop (19)
shopping (23)
should (22)
shouldn't (29)
shove (13)
show (20)
shrewd (25)
size (15)
sketch (7)
sky (16)
skyline (16)
sleep (8)
sleeping (17)
sleepy (9)
slept (7)
slow (20)
slump (13)
smiling (23)
smudge (13)
sneeze (8)
sneezed (23)
snow (20)
socks (19)
soggy (9)
soil (28)
solo (21)
some (13)
somebody (10)
something (13)
sorry (19)
sound (33)
spent (4)
spinach (14)

spoil (28)
sport (32)
spring (14)
stairs (34)
star (27)
starch (27)
start (27)
stood (22)
stopped (23)
storm (32)
story (9)
street (8)
strong (31)
stronger (35)
strongest (35)
stunned (23)
subtract (1)
subtracted (17)
such (10)
sum (13)
summer (10)
sun (10)
Sunday (10)
sunny (9)
supper (13)
sure (22)
surgeon (26)

T

table (3)
tables (5)
taking (23)
talk (31)
tall (31)
taller (35)
tallest (35)
team (8)
teenager (8)
test (4)
tests (5)
thank (1)
thanked (17)
them (7)
then (7)
there'd (29)
there'll (29)
these (9)
they (3)

they'd (11)
they'll (11)
they've (11)
thing (14)
think (14)
third (26)
Thursday (26)
times (15)
tiny (15)
tire (34)
toast (21)
toe (20)
too (25)
took (22)
tooth (25)
tower (33)
town (33)
toy (28)
train (3)
trains (5)
true (25)
try (16)
Tuesday (25)
turn (26)
two (25)

U

under (10)
used (25)

V

variety (15)
very (9)
voice (28)

W

waffle (19)
wait (3)
waited (17)
walk (31)
was (19)
wash (19)
wasn't (29)
water (31)
we'd (29)
we'll (11)

we've (11)
Wednesday (7)
weigh (3)
weirder (35)
weirdest (35)
were (26)
weren't (29)
wharf (32)
what (19)
wheel (8)
when (7)
where (34)
where'd (11)
which (14)
while (15)
white (15)
who (25)
who'll (11)
whole (20)
why (16)
width (14)
wildflower (33)
winter (14)
wire (34)
wished (17)
won (13)
won't (29)
wood (22)
word (26)
work (26)
world (26)
worm (26)
would (22)
would've (11)
wouldn't (29)
write (15)
wrote (20)

Y

yard (27)
year (34)
yellow (20)
you'd (11)
you'll (11)
you've (11)

Word List for Levels 2, 3, and 4, continued

LEVEL 4

A
above (19)
absence (1)
accuse (21)
acknowledge (8)
acquaint (2)
acquire (10)
acrobat (1)
address (32)
adorn (27)
afraid (2)
afternoon (33)
again (3)
against (3)
air (28)
airborne (28)
alarm (28)
almost (14)
alone (15)
already (26)
among (19)
angry (7)
animal (32)
another (19)
answer (1)
anything (33)
apart (28)
applaud (26)
appoint (25)
appropriate (14)
apricot (13)
April (5)
aren't (17)
ask (1)
asked (23)
attorney (7)
auction (26)
audio (26)
August (5)
aunt (1)
author (26)
automobile (32)
autumn (26)
Ave. (34)
avoid (25)
awake (2)
awesome (27)
awhile (10)
axle (1)

B
babies (11)
balloon (21)
banana (1)
banish (8)
barrier (7)
basketball (33)
beach (4)
beacon (4)
beautiful (21)
because (26)
become (19)
before (27)
began (1)

begin (8)
beginning (23)
behind (10)
below (15)
beside (10)
betray (2)
between (4)
beyond (13)
binoculars (32)
birth (31)
birthday (33)
blind (10)
blizzard (32)
blood (19)
blouse (22)
Blvd. (34)
body (7)
bookstore (20)
boost (21)
bottom (13)
bought (26)
bouquet (15)
boxes (11)
branch (1)
branches (11)
bread (3)
break (2)
breakfast (3)
bridge (8)
bright (9)
broke (15)
brook (20)
brother (19)
brothers (11)
brought (26)
brush (16)
brushes (11)
building (8)
burglar (32)
buses (11)
bush (20)
busy (7)
button (16)
buy (10)

C
C (34)
c (34)
calendar (32)
Canada (32)
careful (28)
carrying (23)
cartoon (21)
caught (26)
cause (26)
caused (23)
changed (23)
chapter (32)
chase (2)
cheer (31)
cheeseburger (33)
chicken(8)
child (10)
child's (29)

children (29)
children's (29)
choice (25)
choose (21)
chorus (27)
chose (15)
circle (31)
circus (31)
cities (11)
city (7)
classes (11)
cleanse (3)
clear (31)
climb (10)
close (15)
closing (23)
clothes (14)
cloud (22)
cloud's (29)
cm (34)
coach (14)
coast (14)
coffee (26)
coin (25)
collage (28)
collide (10)
comb (14)
comet (35)
conceal (4)
constellation (35)
construct (16)
contest (13)
contribute (21)
convert (31)
cooked (20)
copied (23)
copy (7)
cotton (13)
cougar (21)
could (20)
couldn't (17)
counselor (22)
countdown (33)
counter (22)
country (16)
countryside (16)
couple (16)
coupon (21)
courtesy (31)
cover (19)
crack (1)
crawl (27)
cried (23)
crossroads (33)
crowd (22)
crowded (22)
crown (22)
curve (31)
customary (16)

D
daughter (26)
dawn (27)
deafen (3)
dear (31)

December (5)
defiant (10)
deliver (8)
deny (9)
desert (3)
destroy (25)
dewdrops (33)
didn't (17)
die (9)
different (8)
dinosaur (32)
dirty (31)
discover (19)
dishes (11)
dishwasher (33)
dismal (8)
dispose (15)
doctor (13)
does (16)
doesn't (17)
dollar (13)
don't (17)
done (19)
double (16)
downtown (33)
Dr. (5)
draperies (11)
dried (23)
drowsy (22)
drugstore (33)
dry (9)
during (20)
dwindle (32)

E
early (31)
earn (31)
Earth (35)
easy (7)
echo (3)
edge (3)
eight (2)
elbow (15)
employ (25)
employer (25)
enclosure (14)
encounter (22)
energy (3)
enjoy (25)
enough (16)
erupt (16)
evening (7)
ever (3)
every (7)
everybody (33)
everywhere (33)
exotic (13)
explode (15)
explore (27)
eyesight (9)

F
F (34)
fair (28)

families (11)
family (7)
fare (28)
farmland (33)
fatigue (7)
February (5)
feet (29)
fence (3)
festivities (11)
fight (9)
flight (9)
foe (14)
forever (33)
forgot (13)
fortified (23)
foxes (11)
freeze (4)
Friday (5)
friend (3)
front (19)
froze (15)
fruit (21)
ft (34)
fudge (16)
full (20)

G
g (34)
gal (34)
galaxy (35)
geese (29)
germ (31)
giant (10)
glad (1)
gloves (11)
goes (14)
gone (26)
good-bye (20)
goose (21)
Gov. (5)
grass (1)
gravity (35)
grew (21)
group (21)
growl (22)
guess (3)
guitar (8)
gym (8)
Gypsy (8)

H
hadn't (17)
half (1)
happen (1)
haven't (17)
health (3)
hear (31)
heard (31)
heart (28)
heavy (3)
here (31)
high (9)
highway (9)
hikes (11)

hoard (27)
hobby (13)
hollow (15)
hoping (23)
hospital (13)
host (14)
hotel (14)
hours (22)
hover (19)
hundred (16)
hungry (7)
hunt (16)
hustled (23)
Hwy. (34)

I
I'm (17)
important (27)
importing (23)
in (34)
inch (8)
inches (11)
inside (33)
interesting (8)
interior (31)
invited (23)
iron (10)
isn't (17)
it'd (17)
itch (8)

J
January (5)
jogging (23)
join (25)
Jr. (5)
July (5)
June (5)
jungle (16)
Jupiter (35)

K
kennel (3)
kg (34)
km (34)
knee (4)
knew (21)
knife (10)
knives (29)
knock (13)
knot (13)
knows (15)
knuckle (16)

L
l (34)
large (28)
larvae (29)
laugh (1)
lawn (27)
lb (34)
leaf (40)
learn (31)
let's (17)
life (10)

lightning (9)
lightweight (2)
loose (21)
loud (22)
loveliest (19)
loyal (25)
loyalty (25)

M

m (34)
magic (1)
man's (29)
marbles (28)
March (5)
Mars (35)
match (1)
May (5)
means (4)
meek (4)
men (29)
men's (29)
Mercury (35)
meteor (35)
mi (34)
mice (29)
middle (8)
midnight (9)
might (9)
mighty (9)
missile (32)
mistake (2)
misunderstood (20)
model (13)
moisture (25)
Monday (5)
money (19)
mongoose's (29)
monkey (19)
month (19)
morning (27)
motor (14)
mouth (22)
Ms. (5)
must've (17)

N

neighbor (2)
Neptune (35)
never (3)
new (21)
newspaper (33)
night (9)
nightmare (33)
noise (25)
north (27)
nose (15)
notebook (20)
nothing (19)
noun (22)
November (5)

O

o'clock (13)
oak (14)
obey (14)

object (13)
ocean (14)
October (5)
offer (26)
offerings (26)
office (26)
often (26)
once (19)
only (14)
orbit (27)
other (19)
ours (22)
outside (33)
overlapping (23)
own (15)
oxen (29)
oz (34)

P

package (8)
paid (2)
pass (1)
past (1)
patios (29)
pause (26)
peace (4)
peaches (11)
pennies (11)
people (7)
period (31)
physics (35)
piano (7)
picnic (8)
picture (8)
pillow (15)
pitch (8)
pizza (7)
plain (2)
plane (2)
planets (35)
plastic (1)
please (4)
pleased (23)
plenty (7)
Pluto (35)
pockets (11)
poem (14)
point (25)
pointless (25)
poise (25)
poison (25)
police (7)
pony (14)
popcorn (27)
powerful (22)
precaution (26)
Pres. (5)
problem (13)
program (14)
proud (22)
pt (34)
pudding (20)
pull (20)
purple (32)

Q

qt (34)
quart (27)
queen (4)
quick (8)
quiet (10)
quietness (9)

R

radio (7)
railroad (33)
Rd. (34)
ready (3)
reason (4)
regardless (28)
reign (2)
reply (9)
report (27)
retrieve (7)
revive (10)
revolve (35)
right (9)
rocks (11)
rotate (35)
rough (16)
route (21)
royal (25)
Rte. (34)
rural (20)

S

satellite (35)
Saturday (5)
Saturn (35)
saving (23)
scarf (28)
score (27)
scream (4)
season (4)
secret (7)
seem (4)
September (5)
shadow (15)
shape (2)
share (28)
sharp (28)
she'd (17)
sheep (29)
shelves (29)
sheriff (3)
shoot (21)
shore (27)
should (20)
should've (17)
shouldn't (17)
shower (22)
sight (9)
simple (32)
size (10)
ski (7)
skiers (11)
skirt (31)
slide (10)
slowly (15)

smart (28)
smile (10)
snack (1)
soap (14)
soil (25)
solar system (35)
solve (13)
somehow (22)
sometimes (33)
sorry (7)
soup (21)
sour (22)
south (22)
sow (15)
soybean (25)
space (2)
speak (4)
special (32)
speech (4)
spoil (25)
sponge (19)
spy (9)
squad (13)
square (28)
squeeze (4)
squirt (31)
St. (34)
stairs (28)
stamp (1)
stares (28)
state (2)
stole (15)
stomach (19)
stood (20)
stories (11)
stow (15)
straw (27)
stretch (3)
strong (26)
studied (23)
subject (16)
suddenly (16)
sugar (20)
summer (32)
Sunday (5)
sunshine (10)
supply (9)
surprise (10)
swallow (13)
sweater (3)
sweep (4)
sweet (4)
swimming (23)
swoosh (20)

T

takeoff (35)
taste (2)
tasted (23)
taught (26)
teach (4)
technology (35)
teeth (29)
that's (17)

their (28)
there (28)
there're (17)
they'll (17)
they're (28)
they've (17)
thick (8)
thieves (29)
third (31)
those (15)
though (15)
thought (26)
throat (14)
through (21)
Thursday (5)
tickle (32)
tie (9)
toe (14)
together (32)
toil (25)
tomorrow (15)
tonight (9)
too (21)
torture (27)
total (14)
touch (16)
tough (16)
toward (27)
towel (22)
tower (22)
trade (2)
traded (23)
tragic (1)
trail (2)
travel (1)
treason (4)
treat (4)
trees (11)
trouble (16)
truly (21)
truth (21)
trying (23)
Tuesday (5)
twice (10)
two (21)

U

under (16)
understood (20)
undiscovered (19)
United States of
    America (32)
universe (35)
until (16)
untimely (9)
upstairs (33)
Uranus (35)
utensils (11)

V

varnish (28)
vastness (35)
Venus (35)
village (8)

voice (25)
volcanic (13)
vowel (22)
voyage (25)

W

waist (2)
wait (2)
wallet (13)
wander (32)
warm (27)
wash (13)
wasn't (17)
waste (2)
watch (13)
water (27)
we're (17)
weather (3)
Wednesday (5)
weekend (33)
weight (2)
weren't (17)
where (28)
whether (32)
whistle (32)
wife's (29)
window (15)
winter (32)
wise (10)
without (33)
wives (29)
wolf (20)
woman (20)
woman's (29)
women (29)
women's (29)
won (19)
wonderful (19)
wondrous (19)
wooden (20)
wool (20)
world (31)
worthwhile (31)
would (20)
wouldn't (17)
wrinkle (32)
write (10)
writing (23)
written (8)
wrong (26)

Y

yawn (27)
yd (34)
yesterday (3)
you'd (17)
yours (20)

Z

zebra (7)
zero (14)

Study Steps to Learn a Word

1 **Say** the word. What consonant sounds do you hear? What vowel sounds do you hear? How many syllables do you hear?

2 **Look** at the letters in the word. Think about how each sound is spelled. Find any spelling patterns or parts that you know. Close your eyes. Picture the word in your mind.

3 **Spell** the word aloud.

4 **Write** the word. Say each letter as you write it.

5 **Check** the spelling. If you did not spell the word correctly, use the study steps again.

Use the steps on this page to study words that are hard for you.

Spelling Strategies

What can you do when you aren't sure how to spell a word?

Say the word aloud. Make sure you say it correctly. Listen to the sounds in the word. Think about letters and patterns that might spell the sounds.

Look in the Spelling Table to find common spellings for sounds in the word.

Think about related words. They may help you spell the word you're not sure of.

child—children

Guess the spelling of the word and check it in a dictionary.

Write the word in different ways. Compare the spellings and choose the one that looks correct.

trane   tran   (train)   trayn

Think about any spelling rules you know that can help you spell the word.

Most plural words are formed by adding -s.

Choose a rhyming helper and use it. A rhyming helper is a word that rhymes with the word and is spelled like it.

strong—song

Break the word into syllables and think about how each syllable might be spelled.

No vem ber
for got

Create a memory clue, such as a rhyme.

Write i before e, except after c.

Words with Short *a*

Student Objectives

- To take a pretest on the lesson words
- To spell the lesson words aloud
- To sort and write the lesson words according to the spelling patterns *a* and *au*

Pretest

Use the pretest on this page to assess students' ability to spell the lesson words.

 Study Steps Have students use the study steps on page 6 to study any words they misspell in the pretest.

 You may wish to duplicate and send home the Home Activity Master on pages T241–T242.

Presenting the Page

Introducing the Short *a* Sound
Explain that short *a* is the name for the /ă/ sound. Then say the following word pairs and have students raise their hand each time they hear a word with /ă/.

black–block	think–*thank*
matter–mutter	biscuit–*basket*

As students prepare to sort the words, point out that /ă/ is most often spelled *a* but is spelled *au* in some words that we often use.

Pronunciation Focus Point out the /f/ pronunciation for *gh* in *laugh*. Then write *Jan/u/ar/y* on the board. Say each syllable and ask which one has the short *a* sound (*Jan*). Point out that the *a* in the *ar* syllable has the /ĕr/ sound, not /ă/.

Consonant Focus Write *matter*, *add*, *class*, *apple*, and *hammer* on the board. Point out the double consonants in each word. Help students think of other short-vowel words that have double consonants, such as *rabbit*, *letter*, and *button*.

8

Words with Short *a*

catch

1. a Words

ask
matter
black*
add
match
Saturday
class
apple
subtract
thank*
catch
January
after*
hammer
half

2. *au* Word
laugh*

ask
matter
black
add
match
Saturday
class
apple
subtract
laugh
thank
catch
January
after
hammer
half

Say and Listen

Say each spelling word. Listen for the short *a* sound.

Think and Sort

Look at the letters in each word. Think about how short *a* is spelled. Spell each word aloud.

Short *a* can be shown as /ă/. How many spelling patterns for /ă/ do you see?

1. Write the spelling words that have the *a* pattern.
2. Write the spelling word that has the *au* pattern.

Use the steps on page 6 to study words that are hard for you.

Spelling Patterns

a	au
m**a**tch	l**au**gh

8 UNIT 1 *Dolch basic sight word

Pretest

Say each lesson word, read the sentence, and then repeat the word. Have students write the words on separate paper.

1. **ask** What did you ask me?
2. **matter** What's the matter?
3. **black** My cat is black.
4. **add** Can you add 14 and 21?
5. **match** Dad lit the fire with a match.
6. **Saturday** We have a game on Saturday.
7. **class** Our class has 29 students.
8. **apple** Would you like an apple?
9. **subtract** Can you subtract 13 from 19?
10. **laugh** She makes me laugh.
11. **thank** Say thank you.
12. **catch** Try to catch this ball.
13. **January** The coldest month is January.
14. **after** Wait until after dinner.
15. **hammer** Mom used a hammer and nails.
16. **half** He gave me half of his sandwich.

Additional Words for Enrichment

The following words can be used to meet the needs of on-level and above-level students:

aunt   magic   answer   happen   began   fasten

Spelling and Meaning

Definitions   Write the spelling word for each definition.
Use the Spelling Dictionary if you need to.

1. to find the sum — add
2. problem — matter
3. to look alike — match
4. group of students — class
5. following — after
6. to say one is grateful — thank
7. one of two equal parts — half
8. to request — ask

Classifying   Write the spelling word that belongs in each group.

9. banana   orange   pear — apple
10. add   multiply   divide — subtract
11. screwdriver saw   drill — hammer
12. white   green   yellow — black
13. chuckle   grin   smile — laugh
14. March   April   September — January
15. run   throw   pitch — catch

Word Story   One of the spelling words comes from two Old English words. The first is *Saeter*. The second is *daeg*. *Saeter* was the name for the Roman god Saturn. *Daeg* meant "day." Write the word.

16. ____Saturday____

Family Tree: *thank*   Think about how the *thank* words are alike in spelling and meaning. Then add another *thank* word to the tree. A sample answer is shown.

- thanks
- thanking
- 17. thanked
- thankful
- thankless
- thank

LESSON 1   9

HOME ACTIVITY MASTER p. T241

Unit 1 | Spelling at Home

Dear Family of _____

During the next six weeks, your child will be learning to spell the following kinds of words:
- words with the short *a* vowel sound
- words with the long *a* vowel sound
- words with the short *e* vowel sound
- plural words

Here are some simple activities to do each week to help your child become a better speller.

Listening and Writing
Say the spelling words and have your child write them.

Spelling Strategy: Shorter Words
If your child is unsure about the spelling of a word, have him or her write the word correctly on a sheet of paper. Study the word with your child and point out any shorter words in it. Then help your child find other list words that contain shorter words.

Games and Activities
Play Spelling Memory. Choose some spelling words. Have your child write each spelling word on two index cards. Turn each card face down. Take turns flipping over two cards to try to make a match. If the cards match, keep them. If they don't match, turn them face down. The person with more matches at the end of the game wins.

Have your child choose three colors of crayons. Ask him or her to use one color to write each spelling word. Then have your child trace each word with the other colors to create rainbow words.

Using Spelling Words
Ask your child to write sentences that contain the spelling words. Then read the sentences with your child. Notice whether the sentences show that your child knows the meanings of the spelling words.

Lesson 1 Words with Short a
Week of _____

ask	matter	black	add
match	Saturday	class	apple
subtract	thank	catch	January
after	hammer	half	laugh

Lesson 2 Words with Long a
Week of _____

ate	late	safe	page
face	save	place	came
change	gray	away	break
May	great	April	pay

Lesson 3 More Words with Long a
Week of _____

paint	rain	aid	wait
train	aim	sail	afraid
paper	danger	fable	able
table	weigh	eight	they

Lesson 4 Words with Short e
Week of _____

dress	address	end	second
forget	spent	egg	next
help	test	head	read
ready	said	again	says

Lesson 5 Plural Words
Week of _____

clowns	trains	tests	eggs
hammers	paints	hands	papers
tables	places	pages	apples
classes	addresses	dresses	matches

Lesson 6 Unit 1 Review
Week of _____

Lesson 6 is a review of Lessons 1–5. Help your child practice all of the words from those lessons.

The highlighted area shows the Lesson 1 words, which students can share with family members. Spanish version available on page T242.

Proofreading Practice
- I enjoy maath class. *(math)*
- I like to ad numbers. *(add)*

Meeting Individual Needs

ESOL
Some speakers of Asian languages may say /ă/ instead of /ă/. Have students look at your mouth as you pronounce both /ă/ and /ă/. Point out that the mouth opening for /ă/ is wider than for /ă/. Pair each student with a native speaker of English. Have the native speaker pronounce the lesson words for the partner to repeat and write.

Spelling and Meaning

Student Objectives
- To use meaning clues to identify and write lesson words
- To use etymology, meaning, and spelling to identify the word *Saturday*
- To learn *thank* words and analyze their spellings and meanings

Presenting the Page

Write the following Definitions and Classifying examples on the board and model identifying the answers:

- to make sounds to show joy *(laugh)*
- under beside before ____ *(after)*

Word Story

Many names for days of the week and months of the year are taken from the names of Greek and Roman gods and goddesses. *January* comes from Janus, a Roman god with two faces, one facing backward and one facing forward. Help students to understand that Janus is a fitting character to name a first month after because we often look back at the old year and ahead to the new one.

Family Tree: *thank*

Students should see that the *thank* words all contain *thank*. Have students find each word in a dictionary, write the meanings on the board, and talk about how the meanings of the words are alike and different. Point out that adding -*ful* to *thank* changes the meaning from "to express gratitude" to "full of gratitude." Have students identify another word part that changes the meaning of *thank* (-*less*).

9

Day 3

Student Objectives
- To use context to identify and write lesson words
- To identify a stated cause of an effect
- To identify author's purpose

Presenting the Pages

Have students take turns reading the paragraphs with a partner as both write the missing lesson words. Or read the selection aloud as students follow along. Have them write the missing words.

As an alternative, have students complete the pages independently by silently reading the selection and writing the missing words. Then have volunteers read the completed selection aloud.

Discuss with students different meanings for *catch*. Point out that in the selection *catch* means "to get a disease."

Meeting Individual Needs

Visual Learners
To help visual learners master the spelling patterns, have students write each lesson word on an index card. Have students use one color of marker to highlight the *a* spelling pattern and another color to highlight the *au* pattern on the cards. Then have students work in small groups to sort the lesson words by spelling pattern.

Spelling in Context   Use each spelling word once to complete the selection.

Cold Relief

Your head feels as if it is being pounded with a _____hammer_____.
1

Your eyes are so itchy and watery that you can't see well. You put on socks that do not _____match_____. Your throat
2

hurts. You sniffle and sneeze your way through every _____class_____ at
3

school. What is the _____matter_____?
4

You have a cold!

You may think that you _____catch_____ colds from cold,
5

wet weather. This is not true. Icy winds in _____January_____ or
6

February do not cause colds. You can _____thank_____ tiny
7

germs called cold viruses for your sniffles and sneezes.

Cold germs travel in the air and on people's hands, so you should wash your hands often. Washing your hands is especially important _____after_____
8

being around someone else who has a cold. You can also _____ask_____
9

people who sneeze to cover their mouth.

Unfortunately, there is no cure for the common cold. There are some things you can do, however, that will make you feel better.

10   UNIT 1

Spelling Strategy

Breaking a Word into Syllables
Invite students to read and discuss the spelling strategies on page 7. End the discussion with the strategy of breaking a word into syllables and thinking about how each syllable might be spelled. Review with students the syllabication rules below. Then have pairs of students break the seven multisyllable lesson words into syllables to complete a chart like the following.

	Two Syllables	Three Syllables	Four Syllables
VCV Pattern If the vowel sound is long, divide before the consonant, as in **ho tel**. If the vowel sound is short, divide after the consonant, as in **shad ow**.			Jan u ar y
VCCV Pattern Divide between the two consonants unless the consonants form a blend or digraph, as in **fath er**.	mat ter af ter ap ple ham mer	Sat ur day	
VCCCV Pattern Divide between the blend or digraph and the other consonant, as in **com plain**.	sub tract		

Drink lots of fruit juice and water. Drink at least ____half____ a glass every
10

hour. A full glass is even better.

People say that an ____apple____
11
a day keeps the doctor away. It is true
that apples and other good foods help
make your body strong. When you
have a cold, ____add____
12
extra fruits and vegetables to
your meals. At the same time,
____subtract____ potato chips,
13
candy, and other junk foods.

Some people think that chicken
soup is the best medicine for a cold.
Do not ____laugh____. Hot
14
soup really can make you feel better.
Some people say that adding a little
bit of ____black____ pepper
15
makes the soup work even better.

When you have a cold, stay in
bed and rest. This is true even if it
is a sunny ____Saturday____
16
morning. If you take good care of
yourself, you should feel better in
no time!

ask
matter
black
add
match
Saturday
class
apple
subtract
laugh
thank
catch
January
after
hammer
half

ACTIVITY MASTER p. T253

Lesson 1 Words with Short *a*

Name _____

Read each word in the box and circle it in the puzzle below.
The words go across, down, or at a slant.

Spelling Words	ask	matter	black	subtract	match	Saturday	class	apple
	add	thank	catch	January	after	hammer	half	laugh

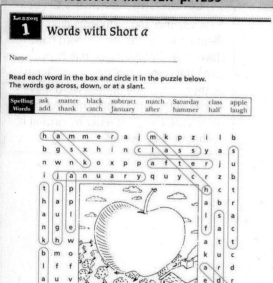

ADDITIONAL PRACTICE

You may wish to copy and distribute the Activity Master on page T253 as additional practice for Lesson 1.

Proofreading Practice
- Here's haf of my cookie. (half)
- You can eat it aftir school. (after)

Reading Comprehension

After students have completed the pages, ask them to find the sentence that states the cause of a common cold ("You can thank tiny germs called cold viruses for your sniffles and sneezes"). Remind students that getting a cold is the *effect* of coming into contact with cold viruses.

Discuss with students different purposes a writer may have for writing (to persuade, to entertain, to inform, to explain, etc.). Ask students to tell why the writer probably wrote this passage (to inform).

Cooperative Learning Activity

To help students assess their progress, have them work with a partner. Have one student say each word and the partner spell the word aloud and then write it. Have students reverse roles and repeat the activity. After both partners have written all of the words, have them compare their progress with their pretest results. Guide them in noting the words they are now spelling correctly and those they need to continue to study.

Day 4

Student Objectives
- To write an expressive paragraph, using lesson words
- To proofread an ad for spelling, capitalization, and punctuation

Presenting the Page

Have students recall a time when they had a bad cold. Suggest that they make a list of words and phrases that describe how they felt at the time. To jog memories, have students reread the beginning of the selection. Then have them look at the list of lesson words, along with the words and phrases on their list. Encourage them to use both sources to write their paragraph.

To assist students with the Proofreading activity, suggest that they read through the ad quickly for meaning. Then have them independently proofread it three times, once for spelling errors, once for capitalization errors, and once for punctuation errors. Invite students to discuss the errors they found.

Meeting Individual Needs

ESOL

Some speakers of Asian languages may have difficulty spelling the consonant cluster *tch* found in the lesson words *match* and *catch*, since this sound does not occur in most Asian languages. Say the words *match* and *catch*, emphasizing the /ch/ sound. Have students repeat the words aloud as you listen and reinforce correct pronunciation. Say the words again as you write them on the board. Have students write the words *match* and *catch*, spelling each word aloud as they write it.

---

ask
matter
black
add
match
Saturday
class
apple
subtract
laugh
thank
catch
January
after
hammer
half

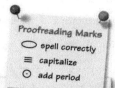

Write to the Point

Many people feel terrible when they have a cold. Have you ever had a cold? Write a paragraph about how you felt. Tell what you did to feel better. Try to use spelling words from this lesson in your paragraph. **Paragraphs will vary.**

Use the strategies on page 7 when you are not sure how to spell a word.

Proofreading

Proofread the ad for *Feelfine* apple juice below. Use proofreading marks to correct five spelling mistakes, three capitalization mistakes, and two punctuation mistakes.

Proofreading Marks
- ◯ spell correctly
- ≡ capitalize
- ⊙ add period

It's (Janary) You have the sniffles. did you (cach) a cold? to feel better fast, drink Feelfine.

It is the finest fruit

juice ever made.

Look for the (aple) on

the bottle. you will

feel great (affter) only

(haf) a glass⊙

(January, catch, apple, after, half marked as corrections)

12 UNIT 1

Proofreading Practice
- Will you share your appel? *(apple)*
- I will try to make you laf. *(laugh)*

✔ Correcting Common Errors

Note whether some students omit the silent letter *l* in the lesson word *half*. Have students who make this error write the correct spelling several times as they look at the printed word. Have them say the letters to themselves and emphasize the silent letter by circling it each time they write it.

12

Dictionary Skills

Alphabetical Order   When words are in alphabetical order, they are in **ABC** order.

This group of words is in alphabetical order.

bend	friend	horse

This group of words is <u>not</u> in alphabetical order.

egg	animal	chicken

Write the following groups of words in alphabetical order.

1. matter   January   hammer
   - hammer
   - January
   - matter

2. add   match   class
   - add
   - class
   - match

3. thank   ask   Saturday
   - ask
   - Saturday
   - thank

4. black   subtract   laugh
   - black
   - laugh
   - subtract

Challenge Yourself

Use the Spelling Dictionary to answer these questions. Then use separate paper to write sentences showing that you understand the meaning of each Challenge Word.
Sentences will vary.

Challenge Words	
plaid	agony
clank	fragile

5. Does a **plaid** shirt have one color or many colors?   _many colors_

6. Would you be in **agony** if you hit your thumb with a hammer?   _yes_

7. Could an old iron gate **clank** when you shut it?   _yes_

8. Would it be safe to play in a **fragile** tree house?   _no_

LESSON 1   **13**

Posttest

Dictate the following sentences. Have students use separate paper to write the sentences and underline the lesson words.

1. I will <u>ask</u> her what is the <u>matter</u>.
2. The <u>class</u> play is after school.
3. Do you <u>add</u> and <u>subtract</u> well?
4. Do the <u>black</u> socks <u>match</u>?
5. You can eat <u>half</u> of my <u>apple</u>.
6. My birthday is the first <u>Saturday</u> in <u>January</u>.
7. They <u>laugh</u> as they <u>catch</u> the ball.
8. I will <u>thank</u> him for the <u>hammer</u>.

Enrichment Activity

Have students work independently to search through newspaper recipes or cookbooks for short *a* words that name actions or ingredients. Suggest that they use the words they find to create funny recipes. They can share their completed recipes with classmates.

Student Objectives
- To write lesson words in alphabetical order
- To study the spellings and meanings of the Challenge Words
- To take a posttest on the lesson words

Presenting the Page

Review with students what the term *alphabetical order* means (Words are arranged in ABC order, according to the alphabet). Remind them that they need only use the first letters to arrange the words in ABC order if the first letter of each word to be alphabetized is different.

Challenge Yourself

To introduce the Challenge Words, write the following on the board:

plaid	ag/o/ny
clank	frag/ile

Pronounce the words for students and discuss the number of syllables in each. Ask students to identify the short *a* spelling pattern in each of the Challenge Words (*clank, agony,* and *agile* have the *a* pattern featured in the lesson, and *plaid* has a different pattern, *ai*).

Posttest

Use the posttest on this page to assess students' ability to spell the lesson words.

Lesson 2

Words with Long *a*

Day 1

Student Objectives
- To take a pretest on the lesson words
- To spell the lesson words aloud
- To sort and write the lesson words according to the spelling patterns *a-consonant-e*, *ay*, *ea*, and *a*

Pretest

Use the pretest on this page to assess students' ability to spell the lesson words.

 Study Steps Have students use the study steps on page 6 to study any words they misspell in the pretest.

 You may wish to duplicate and send home the Home Activity Master on pages T241–T242.

Presenting the Page

Introducing the Long *a* Sound
Write the words *at* and *ate* on the board. Help students distinguish between the long *a* and short *a* sounds. Read the following pairs of words and have students repeat the words that contain long *a*:

way–wax   brat–*break*
chat–*change*   *ate*–at

As students prepare to sort the words, point out that /ā/ is most often spelled as *a-consonant-e*, as *ay*, or as *a* at the end of a syllable but is spelled *ea* in some words that we often use.

Pronunciation Focus Write *A/pril* on the board. Have students identify the syllable that has the long *a* sound (the first) and the spelling pattern for the sound (*a*).

Consonant Focus Write *came*, *place*, and *face* on the board and point out the sound of *c* in each. Help students deduce that *c* followed by *e* has the /s/ sound. Explain that *c* usually has the /s/ sound when it comes before *e*, *i*, or *y*.

14

Lesson 2 Words with Long *a*

break

1. a-consonant-e Words
page
change
face
save
ate*
place
late
safe
came*

2. ay Words
gray
away*
pay
May*

3. ea Words
great
break

4. a Word
April*

gray
page
great
change
April
face
save
away
break
ate
place
pay
late
safe
May
came

Say and Listen

Say each spelling word. Listen for the long *a* sound.

Think and Sort

Look at the letters in each word. Think about how long *a* is spelled. Spell each word aloud.

Long *a* can be shown as /ā/. How many spelling patterns for /ā/ do you see?

1. Write the **nine** spelling words that have the *a-consonant-e* pattern.

2. Write the **four** spelling words that have the *ay* pattern.

3. Write the **two** spelling words that have the *ea* pattern.

4. Write the **one** spelling word that has the *a* pattern.

> Use the steps on page 6 to study words that are hard for you.

Spelling Patterns

a-consonant-e face	ay May	ea break	a April

14 UNIT 1   *Dolch basic sight word

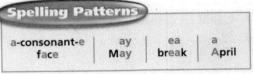

Pretest

Say each lesson word, read the sentence, and then repeat the word. Have students write the words on separate paper.

1. **gray** We saw a little gray mouse.
2. **page** Turn to page 96.
3. **great** I have great news!
4. **change** Go change your clothes.
5. **April** April comes after March.
6. **face** Meg washed her face.
7. **save** Please save me a seat.
8. **away** The bird flew away.
9. **break** Did Sam break his leg?
10. **ate** Rob ate bacon and eggs.
11. **place** Our team is in first place.
12. **pay** Who will pay the bill?
13. **late** Try not to be late!
14. **safe** A street is not a safe place to play.
15. **May** Tulips bloom in May.
16. **came** Victor came to my house.

Additional Words for Enrichment

The following words can be used to meet the needs of on-level and above-level students:
spray   holiday   mistake   steak   crayon   ache

Spelling and Meaning

Synonyms Synonyms are words that have the same meaning. Write the spelling word that is a synonym for each word below.

1. arrived   came
2. unhurt   safe
3. absent   away
4. put   place
5. messenger   page
6. wonderful   great
7. switch   change
8. silvery   gray

Anagrams An anagram is a word whose letters can be used to make another word. Write the spelling word that contains the letters of the underlined anagram in each sentence.

9. Jenna's birthday is in the month of ya<u>M</u>.   May
10. The team <u>tea</u> pizza after the game.   ate
11. Please do not <u>brake</u> my pencil.   break
12. Ten dollars is too much to <u>yap</u>.   pay
13. The bus was <u>tale</u> this morning.   late
14. Let's <u>vase</u> the best for last.   save
15. The baby had a big smile on her <u>cafe</u>.   face

Word Story Many English words come from other languages. One spelling word comes from the Latin word *Aprilis*. *Aprilis* was the name of the second month in the Roman calendar. It names one of the spring months. Write the spelling word.

16. _____ April

Family Tree: *pay* Think about how the *pay* words are alike in spelling and meaning. Then add another *pay* word to the tree. A sample answer is shown.

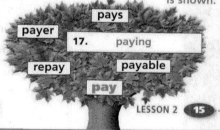

pays
payer
17. paying
repay
payable
pay

LESSON 2 **15**

HOME ACTIVITY MASTER p. T241

Unit 1 Spelling at Home

Dear Family of _____

During the next six weeks, your child will be learning to spell the following kinds of words:
- words with the short *a* vowel sound
- words with the long *a* vowel sound
- words with the short *e* vowel sound
- plural words

Here are some simple activities to do each week to help your child become a better speller.

Listening and Writing
Say the spelling words and have your child write them.

Spelling Strategy: Shorter Words
If your child is unsure about the spelling of a word, have him or her write the word correctly on a sheet of paper. Study the word with your child and point out any shorter words in it. Then help your child find other list words that contain shorter words.

Games and Activities
Play Spelling Memory. Choose some spelling words. Have your child write each spelling word on two index cards. Turn each card face down. Take turns flipping over two cards to try to make a match. If the cards match, keep them. If they don't match, turn them face down. The person with more matches at the end of the game wins.

Have your child choose three colors of crayons. Ask him or her to use one color to write each spelling word. Then have your child trace each word with the other colors to create rainbow words.

Using Spelling Words
Ask your child to write sentences that contain the spelling words. Then read the sentences with your child. Notice whether the sentences show that your child knows the meanings of the spelling words.

Lesson 1 Words with Short a			
Week of			
ask	matter	black	add
match	Saturday	class	apple
subtract	thank	catch	January
after	hammer	half	laugh

Lesson 2 Words with Long a			
Week of			
ate	late	safe	page
face	save	place	came
change	gray	away	break
May	great	April	pay

Lesson 3 More Words with Long a			
Week of			
paint	rain	aid	wait
train	aim	sail	afraid
paper	danger	fable	able
table	weigh	eight	they

Lesson 4 Words with Short e			
Week of			
dress	address	end	second
forget	spent	egg	read
help	test	head	says
ready	said	again	

Lesson 5 Plural Words			
Week of			
clowns	trains	tests	eggs
hammers	paints	hands	papers
tables	places	pages	apples
classes	addresses	dresses	matches

Lesson 6 Unit 1 Review
Week of
Lesson 6 is a review of Lessons 1–5. Help your child practice all of the words from those lessons.

The highlighted area shows the Lesson 2 words, which students can share with family members. Spanish version available on page T242.

Proofreading Practice
- The bird flew awae. *(away)*
- It will come back in Aypril. *(April)*

Meeting Individual Needs

ESOL

Spanish-speaking students may use *e* to spell the long *a* sound because the *e* spelling is a common one in their native language. Hold up a large index card on which you have written a lesson word and say the word aloud. Have children repeat the word, pointing to the long *a* spelling pattern as they say the word. Then have students write the word as they spell it aloud. Repeat with other lesson words.

Day 2

Student Objectives
- To use meaning clues to identify and write lesson words
- To use etymology, meaning, and spelling to identify the word *April*
- To learn *pay* words and analyze their spellings and meanings

Presenting the Page

Write the following Synonyms and Anagrams examples on the board and model identifying the answers:

- tardy _____ *(late)*
- It's time to <u>weak</u> up. *(wake)*

For the Anagrams items, point out that each sentence provides context clues for the scrambled word.

Word Story

Explain to students that like *January*, *April* comes from Latin. In Roman times the month of April was dedicated to the goddess known as Venus or Aphrodite. Have students discuss how *April* has changed from the original Latin. You may also wish to point out that *May* also comes from Latin, possibly from *Maja*, an earth goddess.

Family Tree: *pay*

Students should see that the *pay* words all contain *pay*. Have students find the meaning of each word in a dictionary. Write the meanings on the board and talk about them. Point out that the suffix *-er* changes *pay* from an action word, or verb, to a word that names, or noun. *Payer* means "a person who pays." Explain that the prefix *re-* means "again." Ask students what *repay* means ("to pay again").

15

Day 3

Student Objectives
- To use context to identify and write lesson words
- To summarize information from a nonfiction selection

Presenting the Pages

Read the selection aloud and invite volunteers to write the missing lesson words on the board as the rest of the class writes the words on their pages.

Alternatively, have students read the selection silently and write the missing words independently. Call on students to read the completed selection aloud.

Meeting Individual Needs

Auditory Learners
To help auditory learners, have them write the lesson words on the board, grouping them by spelling pattern. Then have them look at the words, spell them aloud, and clap as they say the letters that form the long *a* spelling patterns.

Spelling in Context Use each spelling word once to complete the selection.

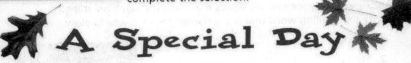

A Special Day

Arbor Day is a special holiday. The word *arbor* means "tree." Arbor Day helps people remember to plant new trees and to _____save_____ older ones. It can help _____change_____
        1   2
people's ideas about Earth and the environment.

Arbor Day was started by a Nebraska man named Sterling Morton in 1872. Mr. Morton loved trees. He asked everyone in the state to plant trees on a day he called Arbor Day. He wanted to give prizes to those who planted the most trees. A million trees were planted. Imagine the look on Mr. Morton's _____face_____! He
                                                                3
was very surprised and pleased. The day was a _____great_____
                                                          4
success.

Soon people in other states started to celebrate Arbor Day, too. In 1876 a man in Connecticut wanted to honor the nation's hundredth birthday. The man invited children to plant trees. He said he would _____pay_____ one dollar to each child who planted
              5
trees. He kept his promise.

Since that time children have always been part of Arbor Day celebrations. In 1882 almost 20,000 children in Cincinnati, Ohio, _____came_____ from many schools to the city's Eden Park. They
        6
planted new trees. They were careful not to _____break_____ any
                                                    7
leaves or branches. Then the children named each tree after a famous

---

Spelling Strategy

Related Words
Remind students that thinking about related words is a useful strategy to help them spell words they are unsure of. Demonstrate how to use this strategy to spell *payment*. First ask students to name a word they already know how to spell that is related to *payment* (pay). Write *pay* on the board to serve as the hub of a word web. Point out that students already know how to spell part of *payment* because they can spell *pay*. Ask what word part needs to be added to spell *payment* (-ment). Add *payment* to the web. Repeat the process for *repay*. Guide students to understand that knowing how to spell *pay* can help them spell *payment, repay, paying,* and so on.

person. Perhaps they _____ate_____ a picnic lunch.
8
They might even have read a _____page_____ from
9
a book about _____gray_____ squirrels.
10

Over the years Arbor Day celebrations have taken
_____place_____ in city parks, public squares, and schools.
11
Today both children and adults take part in Arbor Day
events. Many people celebrate Arbor Day in March,
_____April_____, or _____May_____. Others celebrate
12   13
in _____late_____ fall or winter. Japan, China, and other
14
countries far _____away_____ celebrate this holiday, too.
15

Arbor Day is an important day. It is a day to think about
trees and ways to help keep them _____safe_____. This
16
special day gives people a time to plant new life.

gray
page
great
change
April
face
save
away
break
ate
place
pay
late
safe
May
came

LESSON 2   **17**

ACTIVITY MASTER p. T254

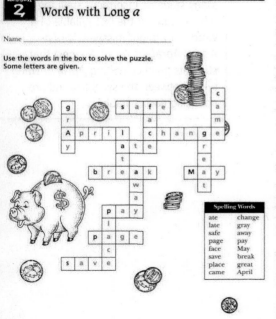

Lesson 2 Words with Long *a*

Name _____

Use the words in the box to solve the puzzle.
Some letters are given.

Spelling Words

ate	change
late	gray
safe	away
page	pay
face	May
save	break
place	great
came	April

ADDITIONAL PRACTICE

You may wish to copy and distribute
the Activity Master on page T254 as
additional practice for Lesson 2.

Proofreading Practice
- We ayt pizza last night.
  (ate)
- It tasted grayt. (great)

Reading Comprehension

After students have completed
the pages, help them to summarize a paragraph from the
selection. For example, help
them summarize the second
paragraph (Arbor Day began
when Sterling Morton promised to give prizes to people
who planted trees). Tell students that a summary of a
paragraph is short, usually one
or two sentences long. Then
invite volunteers to give summaries of other paragraphs.

Cooperative Learning Activity

To help students assess their
progress, have pairs of students write the lesson words
on index cards. Then tell students to put the cards face
down and take turns choosing
one, reading the word, turning the card face down again,
and then writing the word.
Repeat until each student has
written all of the lesson words.
Then have them check their
spelling and compare their
results with their pretest.
Guide students to note words
they are now spelling correctly and those they need to
continue to study.

Day 4

Student Objectives

- To create an informative poster, using lesson words
- To proofread directions for spelling, capitalization, and unnecessary words

Presenting the Page

Review with students some of the reasons why people plant trees in "A Special Day" on pages 16–17. Have them make notes about why trees are important. Suggest to students that they also consider lesson words when thinking of ideas for their poster.

To assist students with the Proofreading activity, you may wish to begin by having a student read the directions aloud. Then have students look for spelling errors by reading the passage backward, word by word. Have students complete the activity independently.

Meeting Individual Needs

Auditory Learners

Have students work in small groups to sort lesson-word cards according to where in each word they hear the long *a* sound—beginning, middle, or end. Have students then say each word and spell it aloud. Ask students to form generalizations about where the patterns appear (*a*: end of a syllable; *ea*, *a*-consonant-*e*: middle; *ay*: end).

---

gray
page
great
change
April
face
save
away
break
ate
place
pay
late
safe
May
came

Write to the Point

Posters help people learn about important events. Design a poster for Arbor Day. Use words that will make people want to help Earth by planting trees. Tell why trees are good for Earth and people. Try to use spelling words from this lesson in your poster.

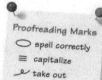

Use the strategies on page 7 when you are not sure how to spell a word.

Proofreading

Proofread these directions for planting a tree. Use proofreading marks to correct five spelling mistakes, three capitalization mistakes, and two unnecessary words.

Proofreading Marks
- ◯ spell correctly
- ≡ capitalize
- ℰ take out

How to Plant a Tree

To plant a tree, first choose a saif spot. it should

be a playce far from houses and awey from from

strong winds. Plant the tree laete in the day when

the sun is low. dig a deep hole and save the soil.

then put the tree in the hole and

water it well. Be careful not to to

brek any branches on the tree. Last,

pack the soil around the tree.

18 UNIT 1

Proofreading Practice
- Please saev some time for a trip. (save)
- I will pae for your ticket. (pay)

✓ Correcting Common Errors

Many students incorrectly spell the schwa sound in the last syllable of a word. They might misspell *April* as *Aprel*, *Apral*, or *Aprul*. Suggest that students practice writing *April*, drawing a line between the syllables, and pronouncing each syllable.

Language Connection

Sentences Begin the first word of each sentence with a capital letter.

| My sister collects postage stamps. |

Put a period at the end of a sentence that tells something.

| The first postage stamp was made in England**.** |

Use the spelling words in the boxes below to complete the story. Then use proofreading marks to correct mistakes in the use of capital letters and periods.

May   face   save   great   page   gray   away

heather likes to _____save_____ stamps⊙She must keep them _____away_____ from Scooter, her _____gray_____ puppy. last _____May_____ a _____page_____ fell out of Heather's stamp book⊙ She looked all over for it. then she looked at Scooter⊙ The fur on his _____face_____ was stuck together. he had a _____great_____ time eating her stamps.

Postage

⭐ Challenge Yourself

What do you think each Challenge Word means? Check the Spelling Dictionary to see if you are right. Then use separate paper to write sentences showing that you understand the meaning of each Challenge Word. **Definitions and sentences will vary.**

Challenge Words	
cable	debate
dismay	labor

1. A **cable** holds up the bridge.
2. She will **debate** whether to buy a new bike or fix her old one.
3. I watched in **dismay** as my hat fell in the mud.
4. Riding up the steep hill required a great deal of **labor**.

LESSON 2 **19**

Posttest

Dictate the following sentences. Have students use separate paper to write the sentences and underline the lesson words.

1. The jokes on this <u>page</u> are <u>great</u>.
2. My dog ran <u>away</u> in April.
3. She <u>came</u> back in <u>May</u>.
4. My cat has a <u>gray</u> <u>face</u>.
5. We ate baked eggs for a <u>change</u>.
6. Do I need to <u>pay</u> for the <u>late</u> book?
7. Please <u>save</u> my <u>place</u>.
8. Keep this <u>safe</u> so that it will not <u>break</u>.

Enrichment Activity

Have small groups of students use words with long *a* spelling patterns in the blanks of the following chant:

A, my name is _____, and my friend's name is _____. We come from _____, and we like _____.

Have groups list the long *a* words they use to complete the rhyme and then sort them by spelling pattern.

19

More Words with Long *a*

Student Objectives
- To take a pretest on the lesson words
- To spell the lesson words aloud
- To sort and write the lesson words according to the spelling patterns *ai, a, eigh,* and *ey*

Pretest

Use the pretest on this page to assess students' ability to spell the lesson words.

 Have students use the study steps on page 6 to study any words they misspell in the pretest.

 You may wish to duplicate and send home the Home Activity Master on pages T241–T242.

Presenting the Page

Introducing the Long a Sound
Write *ran* and *rain* on the board. Have a volunteer read the words aloud. Help students distinguish between the short *a* and long *a* sounds.

As students prepare to sort the words, point out that /ā/ is often spelled as *ai* or as *a* when it is the final sound in a syllable. It is spelled *eigh* or *ey* in some words we often use.

Pronunciation Focus Write *fable, table, able,* and *paper* on the board. Point out final /ā/ spelled *a* at the end of each first syllable.

Consonant Focus Point out that in the word *danger,* the letter *g* spells /j/. Explain that *g* usually spells the /j/ sound when it is followed by *i, e,* or *y.* Have students name other words in which *g* spells /j/ (*age, gym, orange*).

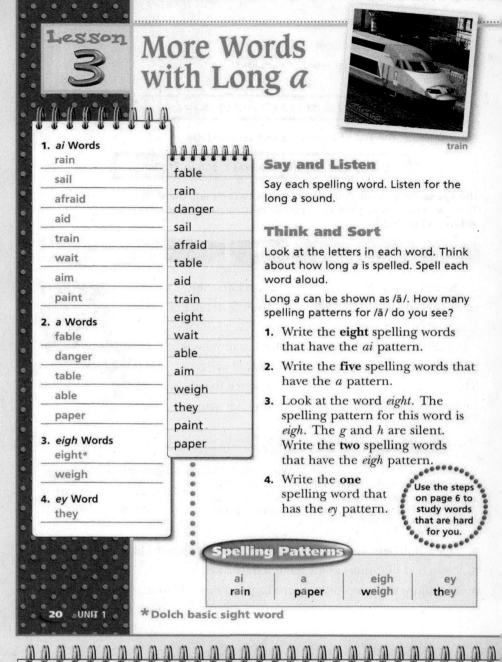

More Words with Long *a*

train

1. *ai* Words
rain
sail
afraid
aid
train
wait
aim
paint

2. *a* Words
fable
danger
table
able
paper

3. *eigh* Words
eight*
weigh

4. *ey* Word
they

fable
rain
danger
sail
afraid
table
aid
train
eight
wait
able
aim
weigh
they
paint
paper

Say and Listen
Say each spelling word. Listen for the long *a* sound.

Think and Sort
Look at the letters in each word. Think about how long *a* is spelled. Spell each word aloud.

Long *a* can be shown as /ā/. How many spelling patterns for /ā/ do you see?

1. Write the **eight** spelling words that have the *ai* pattern.
2. Write the **five** spelling words that have the *a* pattern.
3. Look at the word *eight.* The spelling pattern for this word is *eigh.* The *g* and *h* are silent. Write the **two** spelling words that have the *eigh* pattern.
4. Write the **one** spelling word that has the *ey* pattern.

Use the steps on page 6 to study words that are hard for you.

Spelling Patterns

ai	a	eigh	ey
rain	paper	weigh	they

*Dolch basic sight word

Pretest

Say each lesson word, read the sentence, and then repeat the word. Have students write the words on separate paper.

1. **fable** Do you know the fable of the rabbit and the turtle?
2. **rain** We walked in the rain.
3. **danger** Stay out of danger.
4. **sail** I want to sail in the boat.
5. **afraid** Are you afraid of mice?
6. **table** Please set the table.
7. **aid** Mom will aid the lost boy.
8. **train** That train has 64 cars.
9. **eight** She is eight years old.
10. **wait** Please wait for me.
11. **able** Mandy is able to play the harp.
12. **aim** Jon will aim the dart at the target.
13. **weigh** How much does your dog weigh?
14. **they** Do they live near us?
15. **paint** I will paint a picture.
16. **paper** Use both sides of your paper.

Additional Words for Enrichment

The following words can be used to meet the needs of on-level and above-level students:
explain   neighbor   flavor   remain   potato   obey

Spelling and Meaning

Antonyms Antonyms are words that have opposite meanings. Write the spelling word that is an antonym of each word below.

1. hurt ___aid___
2. fearless ___afraid___
3. go ___wait___
4. safety ___danger___
5. unable ___able___

Analogies An analogy shows that one pair of words is like another pair. Write the spelling word that completes each analogy.

6. *Bedspread* is to *bed* as *tablecloth* is to ___table___.
7. *Two* is to *four* as *four* is to ___eight___.
8. *Car* is to *road* as ___train___ is to *track*.
9. *Engine* is to *car* as ___sail___ is to *sailboat*.
10. *Story* is to ___fable___ as *animal* is to *dog*.
11. *Silk* is to *smooth* as ___rain___ is to *wet*.
12. *We* is to *us* as ___they___ is to *them*.
13. *Oven* is to *bake* as *scale* is to ___weigh___.
14. *Ink* is to *pen* as ___paint___ is to *brush*.
15. *Easy* is to *simple* as ___aim___ is to *point*.

Word Story   Long ago some people wrote on papyrus. Papyrus was made of dried grass. Today most people use another material to write on. It is made of finely cut wood. The name of this material comes from the word *papyrus*. Write the word.

16. ___paper___

Family Tree: *paint* Think about how the *paint* words are alike in spelling and meaning. Then add another *paint* word to the tree. A sample answer is shown.

paints
painter   17. painting
repaint   painted
paint

LESSON 3   **21**

HOME ACTIVITY MASTER p. T241

Unit 1 | **Spelling at Home**

Dear Family of ___
During the next six weeks, your child will be learning to spell the following kinds of words:
• words with the short *a* vowel sound
• words with the long *a* vowel sound
• words with the short *e* vowel sound
• plural words

Here are some simple activities to do each week to help your child become a better speller.

Listening and Writing
Say the spelling words and have your child write them.

Spelling Strategy: Shorter Words
If your child is unsure about the spelling of a word, have him or her write the word correctly on a sheet of paper. Study the word with your child and point out any shorter words in it. Then help your child find other list words that contain shorter words.

Games and Activities
Play Spelling Memory. Choose some spelling words. Have your child write each spelling word on two index cards. Turn each card face down. Take turns flipping over two cards to try to make a match. If the cards match, keep them. If they don't match, turn them face down. The person with more matches at the end of the game wins.

Have your child choose three colors of crayons. Ask him or her to use one color to write each spelling word. Then have your child trace each word with the other colors to create rainbow words.

Using Spelling Words
Ask your child to write sentences that contain the spelling words. Then read the sentences with your child. Notice whether the sentences show that your child knows the meanings of the spelling words.

Lesson 1 Words with Short a
Week of ___
ask, match, subtract, after | matter, Saturday, thank, hammer | black, class, catch, half | add, apple, January, laugh

Lesson 2 Words with Long a
Week of ___
are, face, change, May | late, save, gray, great | safe, place, away, April | page, came, break, pay

Lesson 3 More Words with Long a
Week of ___
paint, train, paper, table | rain, aim, danger, weigh | aid, sail, fable, eight | wait, afraid, able, they

Lesson 4 Words with Short e
Week of ___
dress, forget, help, ready | address, spent, test, said | end, egg, head, again | second, next, read, says

Lesson 5 Plural Words
Week of ___
clowns, hammers, tables, classes | trains, paints, places, addresses | tests, hands, pages, dresses | eggs, papers, apples, matches

Lesson 6 Unit 1 Review
Week of ___
Lesson 6 is a review of Lessons 1–5. Help your child practice all of the words from those lessons.

The highlighted area shows the Lesson 3 words, which students can share with family members. Spanish version available on page T242.

Proofreading Practice
• Don't get wet in the reyn. (*rain*)
• Would you like to salle a boat? (*sail*)

Meeting Individual Needs

ESOL
Some speakers of Asian languages may use /ĕ/ in place of long *a* as they speak and thus may make errors in writing long *a* words. Use the lesson words to write simple sentences on strips of paper, such as *I need paint and paper* and *Will they sail in the rain?* Have students repeat each sentence and point to the long *a* words. Then have students spell each lesson word aloud as they write it.

Spelling and Meaning

Day 2

Student Objectives
• To use meaning clues to identify and write lesson words
• To use etymology, meaning, and spelling to identify the word *paper*
• To learn *paint* words and analyze their spellings and meanings

Presenting the Page
Write these Antonyms and Analogies examples on the board and model identifying the answers. For the Analogies example, tell students to think about how the first two pairs of words in the sentence are related. Explain that the second pair is related in the same way.

• we   (*they*)
• *Happy* is to *cheerful* as *scared* is to ___. (*afraid*)

Word Story
Tell students that many English words come from other languages and cultures. The Latin word *papyrus* became the word *papier* in French. The English word *paper* came from *papier*. As students read the following pages on making a *papier-mâché* village, tell them that this French term literally means "mashed paper."

Family Tree: *paint*
Students should see that the *paint* words all contain *paint*. Read the words aloud and have students find them in a dictionary. Write the meanings on the board and explain that the prefix *re-* means "again." Ask students what *repaint* means ("to paint again"). Invite students to share the word they added to the tree.

21

Day 3

Student Objectives

- To use context to identify and write lesson words
- To sequence steps in a process
- To analyze graphic aids

Presenting the Pages

Invite volunteers to read the selection aloud. Tell them to pause for each missing lesson word so that everyone can write the word. Alternatively, have students read the selection silently and write the missing words. Then have volunteers read the completed selection.

Discuss the pronunciation and meaning of *wind* in the fourth paragraph. The word is pronounced /wīnd/. It means "to wrap around." Explain that *wind* can also be pronounced /wǐnd/, which means "moving air."

Meeting Individual Needs

Kinesthetic Learners
Write the lesson words on the board, omitting the spelling patterns for the long *a* sound, as in r_ _ n and _ _ _ _ t. Have students copy each item onto an index card and fill in the missing letter or letters. Then have them spell each word aloud and sort the cards by spelling pattern.

Spelling in Context Use each spelling word once to complete the selection.

Make Your Own Village

What can you do when you can't go outside and play because of ___rain___? Make your own village! It's fun and easy to do.
1

First, spread pieces of paper on top of a ___table___.
2
Newspaper is a good kind of paper to use. Then, cut more pieces of ___paper___ into strips.
3
Mix one cup of flour with enough water to make a thin paste. Gather seven or ___eight___
4
small boxes to use for buildings.

Next, get a towel and wet it. Keep it near you as you work with the paper and paste. The wet towel will ___aid___ you in
5
cleaning your sticky hands.

Dip the strips of paper into the paste. Don't be ___afraid___ to use a lot of
6
paste. Wind the paper strips around the boxes. You will be ___able___ to
7
make buildings of different shapes by using more strips in some places.

You should ___aim___ to work until you have covered all
8
your buildings with paper strips. Then, let the buildings dry. You will probably have to ___wait___ a day or two for all the wet
9
paper to dry.

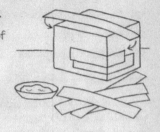

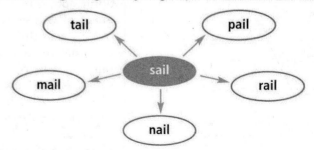

Spelling Strategy

Rhyming Helper

Remind students that using a rhyming helper can be a useful spelling strategy for remembering how to spell a troublesome word. Write the word *sail* on the board and invite students to suggest rhyming helpers. Remind students that rhyming helpers are spelled exactly like the original word, except for the beginning sound. Guide students in arriving at a good rhyming helper for *sail*, such as *mail*.

```
        tail              pail

  mail          sail            rail

             nail
```

Help students generate rhyming helpers for spelling words that they find difficult to spell.

Later, get some _____**paint**_____
₁₀
and brushes and paint your buildings. Then
you are ready to make the ground. Spread
the paste over wrinkled paper. Paint your
ground green after the paste dries. Then,
paint a lake. Make a boat to _____**sail**_____ on the lake.
₁₁
    Do you think your village needs a _____**train**_____? You
₁₂
can make one by using old matchboxes for the cars. Make
the train tracks out of toothpicks. For train wheels, buttons
work well because _____**they**_____ are small and round.
₁₃
    You can also add mountains and bridges to your village.
You can even add a sign that says "Falling Rock" to warn
of _____**danger**_____.
₁₄
    What is missing from your village? People! Make clay
people. If they don't _____**weigh**_____ too much, you can
₁₅
sit them in your boat without making it turn over. You can
also use the people to act out a _____**fable**_____ or other
₁₆
kind of story. Have fun playing with your village!

fable
rain
danger
sail
afraid
table
aid
train
eight
wait
able
aim
weigh
they
paint
paper

LESSON 3 **23**

ACTIVITY MASTER p. T255

Lesson **3** More Words with Long *a*

Name _____

Use the words in the box to complete the *ai* puzzle.
Some of the letters are given.

Spelling Words
rain   train
aid   aim
paint   wait
afraid sail

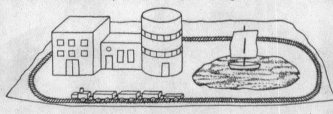

Find the word in the box that completes each sentence.
Write the word on the line.

Spelling Words table   paper   danger   eight   fable   weigh   able   they

9. Will you please set the ____**table**____ for dinner?
10. How many pounds does your dog ____**weigh**____?
11. Trees are used to make ____**paper**____.
12. Are you ____**able**____ to reach the top shelf?
13. My brother is ____**eight**____ years old.
14. Thin ice is a ____**danger**____ for ice skaters.
15. I stayed home, but ____**they**____ went to the zoo.
16. The teacher read a ____**fable**____ about a rabbit and a turtle.

ADDITIONAL PRACTICE

You may wish to copy and distribute the Activity Master on page T255 as additional practice for Lesson 3.

Proofreading Practice

- That fabel teaches a good lesson. *(fable)*
- The girls said thae liked reading it. *(they)*

Reading Comprehension

After students have completed the pages, explain that in order to successfully complete a project, it is important to pay attention to the order of the steps. Write various steps from the passage on strips of paper, using words such as *first, next, then, later,* and *also.* Then have students sequence the steps in order.

    Discuss how graphic aids enhance directions. Ask students to tell what information the illustrations on pages 22 and 23 provide (they show how to cut the strips, how to cover the box, etc.).

Cooperative Learning Activity

Have students work with a partner to study the word list on page 23 for a few minutes and then cover the list. Have each student write all the words that he or she can remember. Tell students to look at their partner's words and to say aloud any lesson words that are missing so the partner can write them. When they are finished, have students check their own spelling accuracy. Then they can compare these results with their pretest results. Guide them in noting the words they are now spelling correctly and those they need to continue to study.

Day 4

Student Objectives
- To write a list, using lesson words
- To proofread a paragraph for spelling, capitalization, and unnecessary words

Presenting the Page

Have students imagine that the village described in "Make Your Own Village" on pages 22–23 is a real place. What kinds of rules would be helpful for people who live there to follow? To get students started, suggest that they think of rules they follow in school or at home and write them in a list. Suggest that students use lesson words in their list of rules.

To assist students with the Proofreading activity, you may wish to read the paragraph aloud. Then review the proofreading marks. Suggest that students first find the misspelled words and then look for capitalization mistakes and unnecessary words. Have students complete the activity independently or with a partner.

Meeting Individual Needs

Visual Learners
Have students write the lesson words on cards and spread them face up on a table or the floor. Then have partners play a guessing game with the words. Have one student give a clue for a word and the partner name the word. As students guess the word, have them point to it, name the spelling pattern for the long *a* sound, and spell the word aloud.

Spelling and Writing

fable
rain
danger
sail
afraid
table
aid
train
eight
wait
able
aim
weigh
they
paint
paper

Write to the Point

Every village and town has rules to protect people, the things they own, and the environment. Make a list of rules for the people of a village to follow. Try to use spelling words from this lesson. **Rules will vary.**

Proofreading

Proofread the paragraph below. Use proofreading marks to correct five spelling mistakes, three capitalization mistakes, and two unnecessary words.

Please do not litter.

Use the strategies on page 7 when you are not sure how to spell a word.

Proofreading Marks
◯ spell correctly
≡ capitalize
↵ take out

Mr. sanchez is the art teacher at our school. He teaches the third grade once a week. each class is *able* (abel) to make many things. This week we are making things out of paper. our class has made a boat with ~~with~~ a large paper sail. Mrs. Digg's class has made a *train* (frane) that ~~that~~ is *eight* (aight) feet long. *They* (Thay) cannot *wait* (wate) to paint it.

24 UNIT 1

Proofreading Practice
- I like to wiegh fruit at the store. (weigh)
- I like to set the taible at home. (table)

✓ Correcting Common Errors

One common spelling error students may make is to transpose the *e* and *i* in *eight* and *weigh*. To help them spell these words correctly, have them memorize this rhyme:

I before *e*, except after *c*
And when sounding like /ā/,
As in *neighbor* and *weigh*.

Using the Spelling Table

Suppose that you need to find a word in a dictionary, but you're not sure how to spell one of the sounds. What can you do? You can use a spelling table to find the different ways that the sound can be spelled.

Let's say that you're not sure how to spell the last consonant sound in *sock*. Is it *k, c, ck,* or *ch*? First, find the pronunciation symbol for the sound in the Spelling Table on page 213. Then read the first spelling listed for /k/ and look up *soc* in the Spelling Dictionary. Look for each spelling in the dictionary until you find the correct one.

Sound	Spellings	Examples
/k/	k c ck ch	keep, coat, kick, school

Write the correct spelling for /k/ in each word below. Use the Spelling Table above and the Spelling Dictionary.

1. kable _____cable_____
2. karton _____carton_____
3. koarse _____coarse_____
4. blak _____black_____
5. blok _____block_____
6. skeme _____scheme_____
7. komb _____comb_____
8. subtrakt _____subtract_____
9. klok _____clock_____
10. kard _____card_____
11. korner _____corner_____
12. soks _____socks_____

⭐ Challenge Yourself

Use the Spelling Dictionary to answer these questions. Then use separate paper to write sentences showing that you understand the meaning of each Challenge Word.
Sentences will vary.

Challenge Words
frail   agent
maintain   contain

13. Would a bridge made of toothpicks be **frail**? _____yes_____
14. Could a secret **agent** work for a government? _____yes_____
15. Is it important to **maintain** a town's bridges and roads? _____yes_____
16. Are jars that **contain** jam empty? _____no_____

Posttest

Dictate the following sentences. Have students use separate paper to write the sentences and underline the lesson words.

1. What did that fable teach you?
2. We are not afraid of danger.
3. Are you able to aid me with my work?
4. This toy boat has a paper sail.
5. Wait for the paint to dry.
6. The rain got the bench and table wet.
7. I know they aim to be the best.
8. Let's wait for the train.
9. How much do eight apples weigh?

Enrichment Activity

Have students work with a partner to page through magazine ads and supermarket circulars for words with the *ai, a, eigh,* or *ey* spelling of long *a*. Then have students use the words to make a collage. Have them divide a piece of paper into four sections and write a spelling pattern in each section. Then have them glue or write the names of household products in the corresponding sections.

Student Objectives

- To use part of the Spelling Table and the Spelling Dictionary to write correct spellings
- To study the spellings and meanings of the Challenge Words
- To take a posttest on the lesson words

Presenting the Page

Explain that if students don't know how to spell a word, they may have trouble finding it in a dictionary. Using a spelling table can be helpful. Explain that a spelling table lists various ways a sound can be spelled. Write *sok, soc, sock,* and *soch* on the board. Have students study the Spelling Table excerpt. Then have them look up each spelling in the Spelling Dictionary to find the correct one.

⭐ Challenge Yourself

To introduce the Challenge Words, write the following on the board:

    frail   a/gent
    main/tain   con/tain

Pronounce the words for students and discuss the number of syllables in each. Have them note the long *a* spelling pattern for each word before they complete the activity (*frail, maintain,* and *contain* have the *ai* pattern; *agent* has the *a* pattern).

Posttest

Use the posttest on this page to assess students' ability to spell the lesson words.

Lesson 4
Words with Short *e*

Student Objectives
- To take a pretest on the lesson words
- To spell the lesson words aloud
- To sort and write the lesson words according to the spelling patterns *e*, *ea*, *ai*, and *ay*

Pretest

Use the pretest on this page to assess students' ability to spell the lesson words.

Have students use the study steps on page 6 to study any words they misspell in the pretest.

You may wish to duplicate and send home the Home Activity Master on pages T241–T242.

Presenting the Page

Introducing the Short *e* Sound
Read the following pairs of words and have students tell which word has the vowel sound in *pet*:

forgave–*forget*   head–had
said–sad   *end*–and

As students prepare to sort the words, point out that /ĕ/ is most often spelled *e* but is spelled *ea*, *ai*, or *ay* in some words that we often use.

Pronunciation Focus Explain that the word *address* is pronounced /ə **drĕs'**/ when used as a verb and either /ə **drĕs'**/ or /**ăd'** rĕs/ when used as a noun. Point out that *read* has a short *e* sound when it tells about the past, as in *I read this book last week.*

Consonant Focus Read *end*, *second*, and *spent* aloud and explain that the letters *nd* and *nt* are consonant blends. The sounds of the letters are blended together, but each letter is still pronounced. Have students name other words that end with *nd* and *nt*, such as *send*, *lent*, *dent*, and *went*.

26

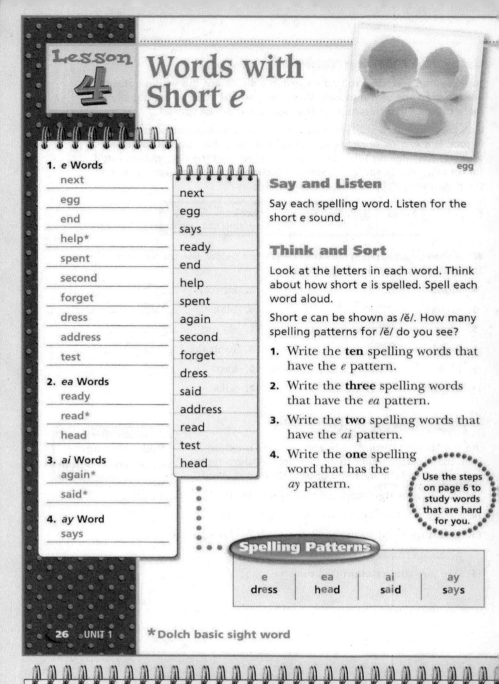

Lesson 4
Words with Short *e*

egg

1. *e* Words
next
egg
end
help*
spent
second
forget
dress
address
test

2. *ea* Words
ready
read*
head

3. *ai* Words
again*
said*

4. *ay* Word
says

next
egg
says
ready
end
help
spent
again
second
forget
dress
said
address
read
test
head

Say and Listen
Say each spelling word. Listen for the short *e* sound.

Think and Sort
Look at the letters in each word. Think about how short *e* is spelled. Spell each word aloud.

Short *e* can be shown as /ĕ/. How many spelling patterns for /ĕ/ do you see?

1. Write the **ten** spelling words that have the *e* pattern.
2. Write the **three** spelling words that have the *ea* pattern.
3. Write the **two** spelling words that have the *ai* pattern.
4. Write the **one** spelling word that has the *ay* pattern.

Use the steps on page 6 to study words that are hard for you.

Spelling Patterns

e	ea	ai	ay
dress	head	said	says

26 UNIT 1 *****Dolch basic sight word

Pretest

Say each lesson word, read the sentence, and then repeat the word. Have students write the words on separate paper.

1. **next** What will happen next?
2. **egg** I had an egg for breakfast.
3. **says** Alice says we should hurry.
4. **ready** I'll be ready soon.
5. **end** How does the movie end?
6. **help** I will help you study.
7. **spent** Kyle spent recess indoors.
8. **again** Sing that song again.
9. **second** Raul is in second grade.
10. **forget** Don't forget your homework.
11. **dress** I have a new red dress.
12. **said** Who said my name?
13. **address** Write your address here.
14. **read** Dad read us a funny story.
15. **test** The test is on Friday.
16. **head** Birds head south in winter.

Additional Words for Enrichment

The following words can be used to meet the needs of on-level and above-level students:
meant already yesterday mountain exit necklace

Spelling and Meaning

Clues Write the spelling word for each clue.

1. includes a ZIP code _____address_____
2. once more _____again_____
3. what is done to a book _____read_____
4. opposite of *remember* _____forget_____
5. used your money _____spent_____
6. all set _____ready_____
7. aid _____help_____
8. I say, you say, he ___ _____says_____

Classifying Write the spelling word that belongs in each group.

9. hour   minute   _____second_____
10. exam   quiz   _____test_____
11. spoke   told   _____said_____
12. first   then   _____next_____
13. stop   quit   _____end_____
14. blouse   skirt   _____dress_____
15. toast   juice   _____egg_____

W̱ord Story The phrase "raining cats and dogs" is called an **idiom**. In an idiom, the meanings of the words don't add up to the meaning of the phrase. Write the spelling word that completes each idiom below.

He **kept his** ___ when he got lost.

Don't **lose your** ___ during a storm.

16. _____head_____

Family Tree: *help* Think about how the *help* words are alike in spelling and meaning. Then add another *help* word to the tree. A sample answer is shown.

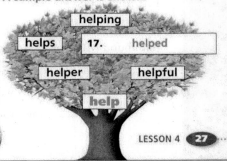

helping

helps   17. _____helped_____

helper   helpful

help

LESSON 4   **27**

The highlighted area shows the Lesson 4 words, which students can share with family members. Spanish version available on page T242.

Spelling and Meaning

Day 2

Student Objectives
• To use meaning clues to identify and write lesson words
• To use meaning to identify the word *head*
• To learn *help* words and analyze their spellings and meanings

Presenting the Page

Write these Clues and Classifying examples on the board and model identifying the answers:

• the time it takes to blink *(second)*
• tells   speaks ___ *(says)*

W̱ord Story

Head comes from the Old English word *heafod*, which meant "top of the body." It also meant "chief person" or "leader." Discuss with students the meanings of other *head* idioms, such as "off the top of my head" ("without preparation") and "hit the nail on the head" ("to make clear").

Family Tree: *help*

Students should understand that the *help* words all contain *help*, but each word ends differently. Have students find the words in a dictionary and write the meanings on the board. Tell students that a suffix is a word part added to the end of a word that changes the meaning of the word. Talk about how adding *-ful* changes the meaning of *help* (from "to be useful" to "giving help").

Proofreading Practice
• We rayd a good story today. *(read)*
• May we hear it agen? *(again)*

Meeting Individual Needs

ESOL
Some Spanish-speaking students may need extra practice with short *e* since *e* in Spanish is pronounced /ā/. Have these students play an echo game with native English speakers. First have the native speaker say the lesson words, emphasizing the short *e* sound, and have the partner repeat the words and write them. Then have students reverse roles and repeat the activity.

Day 3

Student Objectives
- To use context to identify and write lesson words
- To recognize science fiction

Presenting the Pages

Have students work in small groups to read the story aloud and write the missing lesson words. Suggest that students take turns reading paragraphs. As an alternative, have students complete the pages on their own by silently reading the story and writing the missing words.

Discuss with students the meaning of "She would lose her head if it was not screwed on" (she is very forgetful).

Meeting Individual Needs

Kinesthetic Learners
Have pairs of students make letter cards for lesson words. Then have them place the cards face up and take turns using the cards to spell words. Have one student say a lesson word while the partner manipulates the letters to make the word and spell it aloud.

Spelling in Context Use each spelling word once to complete the story.

ME-2

ME-2 was a little robot with a big problem. She had a very bad memory. On Friday morning ME-2 ate bread and a scrambled ___egg___₁. Then she forgot that she had eaten breakfast, so she ate it ___again___₂. On Saturday morning she put on blue jeans. Then she forgot what she had planned to wear, so she put on her best ___dress___₃, too.

Things were bad at home. They were no better at school. When her teacher asked her a question about a story, ME-2 forgot what she had ___read___₄. When the teacher gave the class a ___test___₅, ME-2 had forgotten to study for it. She couldn't find her pencil, either. She was never ___ready___₆ for gym because she always forgot her sneakers.

One day ME-2 forgot where she lived. She had forgotten her own ___address___₇! ME-2 ___spent___₈ the night with her best friend, US-2.

ME-2's mother was very worried. She found ME-2 at school early the very ___next___₉ day. ME-2's mother ___said___₁₀, "This won't happen a ___second___₁₁ time. You are going to the doctor."

28 UNIT 1

Spelling Strategy

Using the Spelling Table
Remind students that a spelling table is helpful for finding the correct way to spell words they are unsure of. Invite students to determine the correct way to spell *says* by using the /ĕ/ patterns in the Spelling Table on page 213. First, have them find the pronunciation symbol for the /ĕ/ sound in the Spelling Table. Then have students write the word, using a pattern, and look for that word in the Spelling Dictionary. If the word is not in the Spelling Dictionary, they should try another pattern for the word, look up that spelling, and continue in the same manner until they find the correct spelling.

/ĕ/ Spelling	Test Spelling	Found in Spelling Dictionary?
e	ses	no
ea	seas	no
ai	sais	no
ay	says	yes

Have students repeat the procedure for the words *ready* and *again*.

next
egg
says
ready
end
help
spent
again
second
forget
dress
said
address
read
test
head

The doctor gave ME-2 a checkup. Soon it was over. ME-2 told her mother, "The doctor _____**says**_____ ₁₂ I'm just fine. I wish I could remember why you brought me here."

"Doctor, how can ME-2 be fine?" asked her mother. "She would lose her _____**head**_____ ₁₃ if it was not screwed on her shoulders! Can't you _____**help**_____ ₁₄ her?"

The mother's words gave the doctor an idea. He looked at the screws in ME-2's head. Sure enough, one screw was loose. He fixed it. That put an _____**end**_____ ₁₅ to ME-2's bad memory.

"Oh, no! I just remembered something," cried ME-2. "We get report cards tomorrow. That is something I wish I could _____**forget**_____ ₁₆!"

LESSON 4 **29**

ACTIVITY MASTER p. T256

Lesson 4 Words with Short *e*

Name _____

Find the word in the box that matches each clue. Write the word. Then read down the squares to find the answer to the question.

Spelling Words	next	head	address	said
	read	dress	second	spent

WHAT DO YOU CALL A NICE DOE?

1. first, ___, third   s e c o n **d**
2. I am ___ in line after her.   **n** e x t
3. where you wear a hat   h e **a** d
4. where you live   a d **d** r e s s

5. say, ___, saying   s a **i** d
6. She ___ the chapter book.   **r** e a d
7. spend, ___, spending   s **p** e n t
8. She wore a nice ___ to the dance.   **d** r e s s

Find the word in the box that completes each sentence. Write the word on the line.

Spelling Words	end	help	says	forget	again	ready	egg	test

9. I will not _____**forget**_____ my lunch money.
10. He likes a scrambled _____**egg**_____ for breakfast.
11. Jesse needs some _____**help**_____ with his homework.
12. My favorite part of the movie was the _____**end**_____.
13. I will play my favorite video game _____**again**_____.
14. Are you _____**ready**_____ to go to the zoo?
15. Our teacher _____**says**_____ we are good listeners.
16. Reggie made a perfect score on her _____**test**_____.

ADDITIONAL PRACTICE

You may wish to copy and distribute the Activity Master on page T256 as additional practice for Lesson 4.

Proofreading Practice
• Pop ses it's time for dinner. *(says)*
• Is that what he sayd? *(said)*

Day 4

Student Objectives
- To write a "to do" list, using lesson words
- To proofread a journal entry for spelling, capitalization, and punctuation

Presenting the Page

Suggest that students review the lesson words for ideas about what they might include in their list.

To assist students with the Proofreading activity, you may wish to have a student read the directions and the journal entry aloud. Remind students to think about short *e* spelling patterns as they look for errors in spelling. Have students reread the entry and look for errors in capitalization and punctuation. Then have them complete the activity independently.

Meeting Individual Needs

Auditory Learners
Encourage students to work in small groups to make up rhymes and cheers like the following to help them spell the lesson words:

Ready, read, and *head*—
Don't use *e,* but *ea* instead.

Spelling and Writing

next
egg
says
ready
end
help
spent
again
second
forget
dress
said
address
read
test
head

Write to the Point

Sometimes it may be hard to remember all the things you have to do every day. You can help yourself remember by making a list. Make a list of things you have to do before and after school every day. Try to use spelling words from this lesson in your list. Lists will vary.

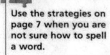

Use the strategies on page 7 when you are not sure how to spell a word.

Proofreading

Proofread the journal entry below. Use proofreading marks to correct five spelling mistakes, two capitalization mistakes, and three punctuation mistakes.

Proofreading Marks
◯ spell correctly
≡ capitalize
⊙ add period

October 18

Today I forgot to take my lunch to school.

I often ⟨forgit⟩ things Mom ⟨sezs⟩ that i need to
forget *says*

use my ⟨hed⟩ she gave me some string
head

and told me about a trick that

will ⟨healp⟩ I will use the string
help

to tie a bow around my

⟨secund⟩ finger The bow will help
second

me remember my lunch.

30 UNIT 1

Proofreading Practice
- The eg has a crack in it. *(egg)*
- I like to healp cook. *(help)*

Correcting Common Errors

Students often forget the double consonants in *address.* To correct this common spelling error, have them divide the word into syllables and pronounce each syllable separately as they look at the word. Then have them write the word and circle the double consonants.

Dictionary Skills

Multiple Meanings Many words have more than one meaning. If an entry word in a dictionary has more than one meaning, the different meanings are numbered. Read the dictionary entry below.

> **then** (thĕn) *adverb* **1.** At the time: *I used to sleep with a teddy bear, but I was only a baby then.* **2.** After that: *We saw lightning flash, and then we heard the thunder roar.* **3.** A time mentioned: *Go finish your homework, and by then dinner will be ready.*

1. What is the entry word? _____then_____

2. How many meanings does the word have? _____3_____

Write the words *egg, address, next,* and *help* in alphabetical order. Then look them up in the Spelling Dictionary. Write the page on which each entry appears. Then write the number of meanings each word has.

	Word	Page	Number of Meanings
3.	address	214	1
4.	egg	222	1
5.	help	225	1
6.	next	229	2

Challenge Yourself

What do you think each Challenge Word means? Check the Spelling Dictionary to see if you are right. Then use separate paper to write sentences showing that you understand the meaning of each Challenge Word. *Definitions and sentences will vary.*

Challenge Words
> genuine
> athletic
> attempt
> celebration

7. ME-2 was a **genuine** robot.

8. She liked gym class because she was **athletic**.

9. The doctor's first **attempt** to help ME-2 did not work.

10. They had a **celebration** when ME-2 got a good report card.

LESSON 4 **31**

Posttest

Dictate the following sentences. Have students use separate paper to write the sentences and underline the lesson words.

1. Did you forget about the test?
2. I am ready to help you.
3. She read the book a second time.
4. Mom says she likes my dress.
5. Tell me your address again.
6. The next chapter is the end of the book.
7. The man has an egg on his head!
8. They said they spent the day with you.

Enrichment Activity

Have partners use the yellow pages of a phone book to make a list of companies or their products that have the *e, ea, ai,* or *ay* spelling pattern for short *e*. For example, they might include a dentist, a place to buy eggs, and a dress shop. Partners can sort the words on their list by spelling pattern.

Student Objectives
- To analyze a dictionary entry and locate entries in the Spelling Dictionary
- To study the spellings and meanings of the Challenge Words
- To take a posttest on the lesson words

Presenting the Page

Review with students the different kinds of information they might find for an entry word in a dictionary. Explain that all of the meanings for a word may be found in one entry. Each separate definition may be numbered, as in the sample entry for *then*.

Challenge Yourself

To introduce the Challenge Words, write the following on the board:

> gen/u/ine   ath/le/tic
> at/tempt   cel/e/bra/tion

Pronounce the words for students and discuss the number of syllables in each. Have them identify the short *e* pattern in each of the words (all of them have the *e* pattern).

Have students write what they think each Challenge Word means, look up the words in the Spelling Dictionary, and write the correct definitions. Ask students to compare their definitions with those in the Spelling Dictionary.

Posttest

Use the posttest on this page to assess students' ability to spell the lesson words.

31

Plural Words

Lesson 5

Plural Words

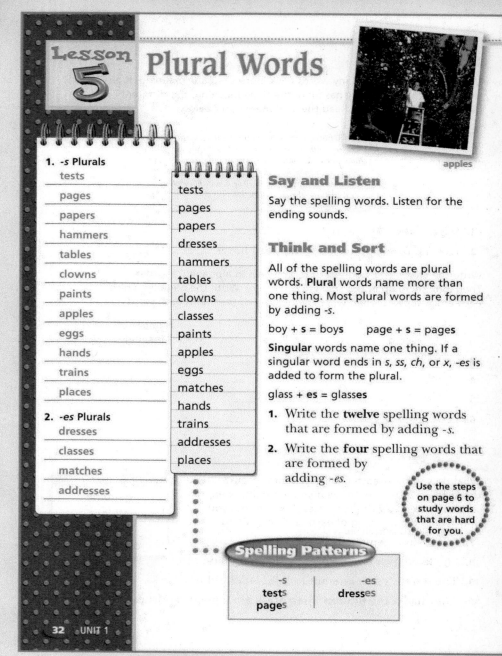

apples

Student Objectives
- To take a pretest on the lesson words
- To spell the lesson words aloud
- To sort and write the lesson words according to the plural endings -s and -es

Pretest

Use the pretest on this page to assess students' ability to spell the lesson words.

 Study Steps Have students use the study steps on page 6 to study any words they misspell in the pretest.

 You may wish to duplicate and send home the Home Activity Master on pages T241–T242.

Presenting the Page

Introducing Plural Words Write *egg* and *eggs* on the board. Have a volunteer read the words aloud. Explain that the -s ending changes the number of eggs from one to more than one. Then write *dress* and *dresses*. Explain that if a word ends in s, ss, ch, or x, -es is added to form the plural.

Pronunciation Focus Using the words *dresses, classes, matches,* and *addresses,* guide students to understand that when -es is added to form the plural of a word, the -es usually adds a syllable to the word.

Consonant Focus Point out to students that -s can have the /s/ or /z/ sound when used to form a plural, but s in -es always has the /z/ sound.

1. -s Plurals
tests
pages
papers
hammers
tables
clowns
paints
apples
eggs
hands
trains
places

2. -es Plurals
dresses
classes
matches
addresses

tests
pages
papers
dresses
hammers
tables
clowns
classes
paints
apples
eggs
matches
hands
trains
addresses
places

Say and Listen
Say the spelling words. Listen for the ending sounds.

Think and Sort
All of the spelling words are plural words. **Plural** words name more than one thing. Most plural words are formed by adding -s.

boy + **s** = boys   page + **s** = pages

Singular words name one thing. If a singular word ends in s, ss, ch, or x, -es is added to form the plural.

glass + **es** = glasses

1. Write the **twelve** spelling words that are formed by adding -s.
2. Write the **four** spelling words that are formed by adding -es.

Use the steps on page 6 to study words that are hard for you.

Spelling Patterns

-s	-es
test**s**	dress**es**
page**s**	

Pretest
Say each lesson word, read the sentence, and then repeat the word. Have students write the words on separate paper.

1. **tests** Jeff had three tests.
2. **pages** I read ten pages last night.
3. **papers** Jen passed out the papers.
4. **dresses** Those dresses are pretty.
5. **hammers** Dad has two hammers.
6. **tables** Our class has four lunch tables.
7. **clowns** The clowns had orange hair.
8. **classes** All classes will go on the trip.
9. **paints** Our paints are dried out.
10. **apples** Pete likes apples.
11. **eggs** Do you like boiled eggs?
12. **matches** Wet matches won't light fires.
13. **hands** My hands were cold.
14. **trains** Two trains stopped at the station.
15. **addresses** This book lists many addresses.
16. **places** Trade places with me.

Additional Words for Enrichment
The following words can be used to meet the needs of on-level and above-level students:
branches sisters sentences breezes beaches exercises

Making Connections
Complete each sentence with the spelling word that goes with the workers.

1. Artists use brushes and ___paints___.
2. Carpenters work with nails and ___hammers___.
3. Fruit farmers grow oranges and ___apples___.
4. Cooks work with milk and ___eggs___.
5. Teachers grade projects and ___papers___.
6. Writers work with ___pages___ in books.
7. Tailors sew skirts and ___dresses___.
8. Mail carriers work with names and ___addresses___.

Definitions
Write the spelling word for each definition. Use the Spelling Dictionary if you need to.

9. questions that measure knowledge — tests
10. small sticks of wood used to light fires — matches
11. connected railroad cars — trains
12. part of the arms below the wrists — hands
13. particular areas — places
14. circus performers who make people laugh — clowns
15. groups of students taught by the same teacher — classes

Word Story One spelling word comes from the Latin word *tabula*. A *tabula* was a board or plank. The spelling word that comes from *tabula* names things on which we set our food or play games. Write the word.

16. ___tables___

Family Tree: hands *Hands* is a form of *hand*. Think about how the *hand* words are alike in spelling and meaning. Then add another *hand* word to the tree. A sample answer is shown.

- handle
- hands
- 17. handed
- handful
- handy
- hand

LESSON 5 · 33

HOME ACTIVITY MASTER p. T241

Unit 1 — Spelling at Home

Dear Family of _____,

During the next six weeks, your child will be learning to spell the following kinds of words:

• words with the short a vowel sound
• words with the long a vowel sound
• words with the short e vowel sound
• plural words

Here are some simple activities to do each week to help your child become a better speller.

Listening and Writing
Say the spelling words and have your child write them.

Spelling Strategy: Shorter Words
If your child is unsure about the spelling of a word, have him or her write the word correctly on a sheet of paper. Study the word with your child and point out any shorter words in it. Then help your child find other list words that contain shorter words.

Games and Activities
Play Spelling Memory. Choose some spelling words. Have your child write each spelling word on two index cards. Turn each card face down. Take turns flipping over two cards to try to make a match. If the cards match, keep them. If they don't match, turn them face down. The person with more matches at the end of the game wins.
Have your child choose three colors of crayons. Ask him or her to use one color to write each spelling word. Then have your child trace each word with the other colors to create rainbow words.

Using Spelling Words
Ask your child to write sentences that contain the spelling words. Then read the sentences with your child. Notice whether the sentences show that your child knows the meanings of the spelling words.

Lesson 1 Words with Short a
Week of ____
ask   matter   black   add
match   Saturday class   apple
subtract thank   catch   January
after   hammer   half   laugh

Lesson 2 Words with Long a
Week of ____
ate   late   safe   page
face   save   place   came
change   gray   away   break
May   great   April   pay

Lesson 3 More Words with Long a
Week of ____
paint   rain   aid   wait
train   aim   sail   afraid
paper   danger   lable   able
table   weigh   eight   they

Lesson 4 Words with Short e
Week of ____
dress   address   end   second
forget   spent   egg   next
help   test   head   read
ready   said   again   says

Lesson 5 Plural Words
Week of ____
clowns   trains   tests   eggs
hammers paints   hands   papers
tables   places   pages   apples
classes addresses dresses   matches

Lesson 6 Unit 1 Review
Week of ____
Lesson 6 is a review of Lessons 1–5. Help your child practice all of the words from those lessons.

The highlighted area shows the Lesson 5 words, which students can share with family members. Spanish version available on page T242.

Proofreading Practice
• Mom will bring matchs on our camping trip. (matches)
• We will bring appels for a snack. (apples)

Meeting Individual Needs

ESOL
Speakers of Asian languages may be unfamiliar with the *-s* plural ending because Asian languages generally have only one noun form for both singular and plural. To provide practice with plural nouns, display concrete objects and give commands such as *Give me one egg. Give me two eggs.* Then have students write both forms of the lesson word.

Spelling and Meaning

Day 2

Student Objectives
• To use meaning clues to identify and write lesson words
• To use etymology, meaning, and spelling to identify the word *tables*
• To learn *hand* words and analyze their spellings and meanings

Presenting the Page
Write these Making Connections and Definitions examples on the board and model identifying the answers:

• Students study lessons and take _____ . *(tests)*
• tools used to drive nails *(hammers)*

For the Making Connections activity, remind students that the lesson word that completes a sentence goes with the workers mentioned in the sentence.

Word Story
The Old English word *tabele* comes from the Latin word *tabula*. *Tabele* was used to name a piece of furniture with a flat top on legs. Have students compare the spellings of *tabula*, *tabele*, and *table*. Invite students to list words that are related to *table* (*tablespoon*, *tablecloth*, *tabletop*, *table tennis*) and give their meanings.

Family Tree: hands
Students should see that each word contains *hand*. Have students find the words in a dictionary and discuss their meanings. Point out that *hand* can be both a noun and a verb. Allow students an opportunity to discuss the *hand* word they added to the tree.

Day 3

Student Objectives
- To use context to identify and write lesson words
- To identify stated main ideas

Presenting the Pages

Read the selection aloud and have students write the missing words. Remind students to use other words in the sentence for clues if they have difficulty figuring out a missing word. As an alternative, students can read the selection independently and write the missing words. Then call on students to read the completed selection.

Discuss the meaning of *set* in the selection. Point out that *set* is used as a noun and means "the setting for a scene in a play or a movie."

Meeting Individual Needs

ESOL
Spanish-speaking students will be familiar with the *-s* and *-es* construction of plural endings, so they should readily acquire new vocabulary in this lesson. Working with small groups, use photographs and concrete objects to help students learn the singular and plural forms of nouns in English.

34

Spelling in Context Use each spelling word once to complete the selection.

Behind the Scenes

makeup art

When many people think of movie artists, they think of actors. Actors are important movie artists. But other kinds of movie artists are important, too.

Makeup artists work on the actors. They make the actors look like the characters the actors are playing. Makeup artists brush face _____paints_____ onto actors
to make them look funny, scary, or old. These artists may also use
makeup on actors' arms and _____hands_____. They do this so that
all of the skin looks the same.

Costume artists plan and help make the clothes actors wear. These
include fancy gowns and other kinds of _____dresses_____ from the past.
Costume artists also make silly baggy pants for actors who play circus
_____clowns_____. They even make animal costumes for actors to wear.

Other movie artists make the movie sets, or
the _____places_____ where the stories take

set builder

place. They use saws, wood, _____hammers_____,
and nails to make rooms. They build the rooms
inside larger rooms called studios. They also build
_____tables_____, chairs, and other pieces of
furniture for the set.

34 UNIT 1

Spelling Strategy

Using a Spelling Rule
Tell students that thinking about spelling rules they already know can be a helpful strategy for spelling new words. Remind them that in this lesson they learned that when a singular word ends in *s*, *ss*, *ch*, or *x*, *-es* is added to form the plural. Invite students to use this rule to help them form the plural of *dress*, *class*, *match*, and *address*.

Rule: When a singular word ends in *s*, *ss*, *ch*, or *x*, *-es* is added to form the plural.	
Singular	**Plural**
dress	dresses
class	classes
match	matches
address	addresses

Prop artists find the objects actors need. For example, a movie script may say that actors eat fruit in one part of the movie. A prop artist must find shiny red **apples** .
8
In another part of the movie, an actor may have to light a fire. A prop artist must have wood and **matches**
9
on hand.

Other artists work with special sounds in movies. A movie may call for the sound of **eggs** frying. A sound
10
artist might crumple **papers** to make the sound.
11
Another part of the movie might call for the sound of two
trains racing down a railroad track. A sound
12
artist might use a recording of real trains. A sound artist puts all sounds through several different **tests** to
13
make sure they sound real.

Would you like to be a movie artist? You can start by working on school plays. You can take special
classes , too. You can also look in the yellow
14
pages of the telephone book. Find the
15
addresses and telephone numbers of
16
children's theaters near you. Get behind the scenes!

tests
pages
papers
dresses
hammers
tables
clowns
classes
paints
apples
eggs
matches
hands
trains
addresses
places

movie set

After students have completed the pages, help them identify the main idea of the selection, which is stated in the last sentence of the first paragraph. Then ask students to identify the stated main ideas in paragraphs 2–6. Point out that in each of these paragraphs, the first sentence states the main idea.

Cooperative Learning Activity

To help students assess their progress, have them scramble the letters in each word and give the words to a partner, who should unscramble the letters and rewrite the lesson words. Partners should check each other's spellings. Have students compare their performance on this midweek activity with their pretest performance to see which words they need to continue to study.

ACTIVITY MASTER p. T257

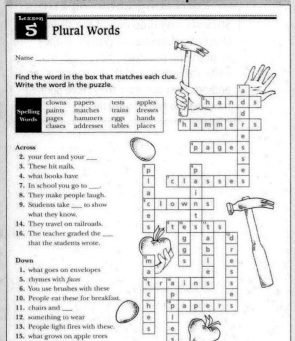

Lesson
5 Plural Words

Name _____

Find the word in the box that matches each clue.
Write the word in the puzzle.

Spelling Words	clowns	papers	tests	apples
	paints	matches	trains	dresses
	pages	hammers	eggs	hands
	classes	addresses	tables	places

Across
2. your feet and your ___
3. These hit nails.
4. what books have
7. In school you go to ___.
8. They make people laugh.
9. Students take ___ to show what they know.
14. They travel on railroads.
16. The teacher graded the ___ that the students wrote.

Down
1. what goes on envelopes
5. rhymes with *faces*
6. You use brushes with these
10. People eat these for breakfast.
11. chairs and ___
12. something to wear
13. People light fires with these.
15. what grows on apple trees

ADDITIONAL PRACTICE

You may wish to copy and distribute the Activity Master on page T257 as additional practice for Lesson 5.

Proofreading Practice
- The clownes did funny tricks. (*clowns*)
- They juggled with hamers. (*hammers*)

Day 4

Student Objectives

- To write a movie ad, using lesson words
- To proofread a movie review for spelling, capitalization, and punctuation

Presenting the Page

Discuss with students important features of a movie ad (title, plot, actors). Then review some important features of movies they have seen recently. Suggest that they use some of these ideas in their ad. Encourage students to use lesson words in their ads.

To assist students with the Proofreading activity, you may wish to ask a volunteer to read the directions and the review aloud. Then have students reread the review independently to find errors in spelling, capitalization, and punctuation.

Meeting Individual Needs

Auditory Learners

To assist auditory learners in practicing the lesson words, tell them to say the singular and plural forms of the words aloud, clapping for each syllable. Remind students that if they hear an extra syllable for the ending of a plural word, that word is spelled with the *-es* pattern, unless the word already ends in *e*. Students can work with partners to review the list words in this manner.

36

Spelling and Writing

tests
pages
papers
dresses
hammers
tables
clowns
classes
paints
apples
eggs
matches
hands
trains
addresses
place

Write to the Point

Many people enjoy movies. Write an ad telling people about a movie. The movie can be a real one or one you make up. Include details that will make people want to see the movie. Try to use spelling words from this lesson.
Ads will vary.

Use the strategies on page 7 when you are not sure how to spell a word.

Proofreading

Proofread the movie review below. Use proofreading marks to correct five spelling mistakes, three capitalization mistakes, and two punctuation mistakes.

Proofreading Marks
◯ spell correctly
≡ capitalize
⊙ add period

MOVIE REVIEW

Do you like funny movies? If you do, you will love

Pages

(Pagess) *from Our Lives.* it is the story of a group of

clowns   places

(clownes) as they travel to different (playces) all over

eggs

the world. They use apples and (egges) to teach

juggling to children at a school in France. they also

tables

dance on (tabels) at a park in China. you will have a

great time at this movie. Your parents will like it, too.

36   UNIT 1

Proofreading Practice

- What are your favorite clases in school? *(classes)*
- Be sure to hand in all your paperes. *(papers)*

✔ Correcting Common Errors

Students may drop one of the *s*'s in *dresses*, *addresses*, or *classes* as they form the plural. Have these students write the words and then cover the *-es* endings to make sure they have spelled the singular form correctly.

Dictionary Skills

Base Words A base word is a word from which other words are formed. For example, *apple* is the base word in *apples*, and *test* is the base word in *tests*.

Many entry words in a dictionary are base words. Different forms of a base word may be listed in the entry. The different forms are printed in dark type. Look up the word *dress* in the Spelling Dictionary. How many different forms of *dress* does the entry show? What are they?

Write the following words in alphabetical order. Write the base word for each word. Then find the base word in the Spelling Dictionary. Write the number of different forms given for the word.

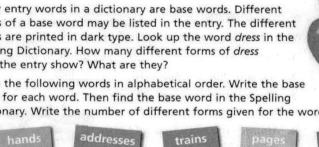

hands   addresses   trains   pages   paints

	Word	Base Word	Number of Word Forms
1.	addresses	address	1
2.	hands	hand	3
3.	paints	paint	3
4.	places	place	3
5.	trains	train	1

Challenge Yourself

Write the Challenge Word for each clue. Use the Spelling Dictionary to see if you are right. Then use separate paper to write sentences showing that you understand the meaning of each Challenge Word.
Sentences will vary.

Challenge Words

losses   meteors
caverns   neckties

6. These look like bright streaks of light in the sky. <u>meteors</u>

7. This word is made from two shorter words put together. <u>neckties</u>

8. These can make ball players sad. <u>losses</u>

9. You might find bats in these. <u>caverns</u>

LESSON 5 **37**

Posttest

Dictate the following sentences. Have students use separate paper to write the sentences and underline the lesson words.

1. The <u>clowns</u> jumped rope on the <u>tables</u>.
2. We have <u>tests</u> in all our <u>classes</u>.
3. They held the <u>hammers</u> in their <u>hands</u>.
4. The <u>trains</u> go many <u>places</u>.
5. That book has many <u>pages</u> of <u>addresses</u>.
6. You will need <u>papers</u> and <u>paints</u>.
7. Buy some <u>apples</u>, <u>eggs</u>, and <u>matches</u> at the store.
8. Those <u>dresses</u> look new.

Enrichment Activity

Have students work in small groups to scan newspaper headlines and magazine article titles for plural nouns that follow the *-s* and *-es* spelling patterns. Then they can cut out the words they find and use them to create a two-column chart on chart paper, organized by the spelling patterns.

Student Objectives
- To identify base words for lesson words
- To use the Spelling Dictionary to identify different forms of base words for lesson words
- To study the spellings and meanings of the Challenge Words
- To take a posttest on the lesson words

Presenting the Page

Review with students the meaning of base words. Have them identify the base word for each word on the spelling list. Then have them check the Spelling Dictionary for the number of forms of *dress* (there are four forms given: *dress, dresses, dressed,* and *dressing*).

Challenge Yourself

To introduce the Challenge Words write the following on the board:

los/ses   me/te/ors
cav/erns   neck/ties

Pronounce the words for students and discuss the number of syllables in each. Have students identify the plural ending for each word (*meteors, caverns,* and *neckties* have the *-s* ending; *losses* has the *-es* ending).

Posttest

Use the posttest on this page to assess students' ability to spell the lesson words.

Unit 1 Review
Lessons 1–5

Day 1

Student Objective

- To take a pretest on the lesson words

Pretest

Use the pretest on this page to assess students' ability to spell the lesson words.

Have students use the study steps on page 6 to study any words they misspell in the pretest.

You may wish to duplicate and send home the Home Activity Master on pages T241–T242.

Meeting Individual Needs

ESOL

Some students acquiring English may have difficulty with the correct pronunciation of short *e* words, since this sound does not exist in Spanish and has a slightly different pronunciation in some Asian languages.

Write the lesson words with short *e* on flash cards. Have students read the words aloud as you display them. For each word, ask which letters spell the short *e* sound. Underline these letters with markers in different colors. Then have students write each of the words, using one color for the vowel pattern and a second color for the other letters.

Lesson 6 — Unit 1 Review
Lessons 1–5

Use the steps on page 6 to study words that are hard for you.

1 subtract · catch · January · half · laugh

Words with Short a

Write the spelling word that completes each analogy.

1. *Grab* is to ___catch___ as *pitch* is to *throw*.
2. *Ten* is to *five* as *whole* is to ___half___.
3. *Chuckle* is to ___laugh___ as *cry* is to *sob*.
4. *Multiply* is to *divide* as *add* is to ___subtract___.
5. *Snow* is to ___January___ as *rain* is to *April*.

2 place · gray · break · great · April

Words with Long a

Write the spelling word that belongs in each group.

6. February, March, ___April___
7. put, set, ___place___
8. wonderful, excellent, ___great___
9. green, yellow, ___gray___
10. crack, split, ___break___

3 afraid · danger · table · weigh · they

More Words with Long a

Write the spelling word for each clue.

11. something you should try to avoid ___danger___
12. how people want you to feel when they yell "Boo!" ___afraid___

38   UNIT 1

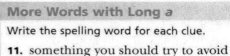

Pretest

Say each lesson word, read the sentence, then repeat the word. Have students write the words on separate paper.

1. **subtract** We can add and subtract.
2. **catch** Can you catch this?
3. **January** We had snow in January.
4. **half** My sister is half my age.
5. **laugh** I like to laugh.
6. **place** Is there a place for me to sit?
7. **gray** Mom has gray hair.
8. **break** Did she break the stick?
9. **great** We had a great weekend.
10. **April** His birthday is in April.
11. **afraid** I am not afraid of snakes.
12. **danger** Stay out of danger.
13. **table** Put the cup on the table.
14. **weigh** How much does the baby weigh?
15. **they** I said they could come.
16. **address** Tell me your home address.
17. **second** This is my second piece of pizza.
18. **ready** We are all ready to go.
19. **again** I hope to come here again.
20. **says** Dad says I'm smart.
21. **eggs** Some of the eggs were broken.
22. **hammers** These hammers are heavy.
23. **places** We looked in many places for the dog.
24. **apples** How many apples go into a pie?
25. **matches** We keep matches on a high shelf.

38

13. a word that can be used to name others
    __they__

14. what scales are used for _____ __weigh__

15. what you set before a meal and sit at to eat the meal _____ __table__

④ address
second
ready
again
says

Words with Short e

Write the spelling word that completes each sentence.

16. Are you _____ __ready__ _____ for school?

17. If my hair is still messy, I need to comb it _____ __again__ .

18. My mother _____ __says__ _____, "Clean up your room, please."

19. At the end of the race, Mario was in _____ __second__ _____ place.

20. Your street, town, and ZIP code are parts of your _____ __address__ .

⑤ eggs
hammers
places
apples
matches

Plural Words

Write the spelling word that answers each question.

21. What are red, round, and juicy? _____ __apples__

22. What do hens lay? _____ __eggs__

23. What tools are good for pounding nails? _____ __hammers__

24. Which word rhymes with *spaces*? _____ __places__

25. What can be used to light fires? _____ __matches__

LESSON 6   39

REVIEW TEST MASTER, pp. T283–T284

Unit 1 Review Test   Name _____

Darken the circle for the word that is spelled correctly.

Example
I hope that you can _____ and visit with me.
Ⓐ stey   Ⓒ stae
● stay   Ⓓ stai

1. The circus clown made Mario _____.
Ⓐ lagh   Ⓒ laf
Ⓑ lalf   ● laugh

2. Curtis found three _____ in the nest.
Ⓕ egs   Ⓗ egges
● eggs   Ⓙ egges

3. Please _____ the fruit on the scale.
Ⓐ waigh   ● weigh
Ⓑ wey   Ⓓ weagh

4. We are taking our class trip in _____.
Ⓕ January   Ⓗ Jenuary
● January   Ⓙ Januiry

5. Let's sit at this _____ and eat lunch.
Ⓐ teble   Ⓒ tayble
Ⓑ taible   ● table

6. Are you _____ to take the test?
● ready   Ⓗ raidy
Ⓖ redy   Ⓙ raydy

7. He used the _____ to light the candles.
Ⓐ maches   Ⓒ matchs
● matches   Ⓓ machses

8. Alex was _____ in line today.
Ⓕ seacond   Ⓗ sacond
Ⓖ secon   ● second

9. The sky looks cloudy and _____.
● gray   Ⓗ grai
Ⓑ greigh   Ⓙ graye

10. Kate wants to play that game _____!
Ⓕ agean   Ⓗ agayn
● again   Ⓙ agen

11. I like bananas and _____ in my fruit salad.
● apples   Ⓒ appels
Ⓑ appls   Ⓓ appleses

12. My puppy is _____ of thunder.
Ⓕ afrayd   ● afraid
Ⓖ afrade   Ⓙ afreid

13. The flowers bloomed in _____.
Ⓐ Aprel   ● April
Ⓑ Aipril   Ⓓ Aypril

Unit 1 Review Test   Name _____

Darken the circle for the word that is spelled correctly.

14. Will you give me your phone number and _____?
Ⓕ addrayss   Ⓗ addreass
Ⓖ adraiss   ● address

15. Ana won first _____ in the relay race.
Ⓐ plaice   ● place
Ⓑ plase   Ⓓ pleys

16. My little brother is learning how to add and _____.
● subtract   Ⓗ subtrauct
Ⓖ subtrac   Ⓙ subtrak

17. The vase will _____ if you drop it.
Ⓐ braik   ● break
Ⓑ breyk   Ⓓ breik

18. Tyrel has visited _____ all over the world.
Ⓕ placeses   ● places
Ⓖ placees   Ⓙ placs

19. My neighbor _____ hello to me every day.
Ⓐ seys   Ⓒ saiys
● says   Ⓓ seays

20. We could be in _____ if we go in the cave alone.
Ⓕ daingr   Ⓗ deingr
● danger   Ⓙ deyngr

21. She _____ the nail into the side of the tree house.
Ⓐ hamers   ● hammers
Ⓑ haummers   Ⓓ hammrs

22. We had a _____ time at the picnic!
Ⓕ grat   Ⓗ grayt
Ⓖ grait   ● great

23. Ling can _____ the football.
Ⓐ cach   Ⓒ cautch
● catch   Ⓓ cech

24. You can have _____ of my sandwich.
Ⓕ haf   Ⓗ haulf
Ⓖ hef   ● half

25. Do _____ want to go to the park with us?
Ⓐ thaiy   Ⓒ thay
Ⓑ thae   ● they

📌 **Day 2**

Student Objectives
• To review the *a* and *au* spellings of the short *a* sound
• To review the *a-consonant-e*, *ay*, *ea*, *a*, *ai*, *eigh*, and *ey* spellings of the long *a* sound
• To review the *e*, *ea*, *ai*, and *ay* spellings of the short *e* sound
• To review endings of plural words
• To use meaning clues to identify and write lesson words

Presenting the Pages

Lessons 1–3 Have volunteers read the review words for Lessons 1–3 aloud. Review with students the short and long *a* spelling patterns represented in the review words—*a* and *au* for short *a*; *a-consonant-e*, *ay*, *ea*, *a*, *ai*, *eigh*, and *ey* for long *a*.

Lesson 4 Have volunteers read the review words for Lesson 4 aloud. Review with students the short *e* spelling patterns they learned in Lesson 4—*e*, *ea*, *ai*, and *ay*.

Lesson 5 Have volunteers read the review words for Lesson 5 aloud. Have volunteers identify the base singular word in each plural word. Then review with students the *-s* and *-es* endings they learned for plural words.

Test-Taking Strategies

Read the directions for the Review Test Master aloud and discuss with students the format of the test. Suggest that students first mark all the words they know are spelled correctly and then return to the ones they are less sure of.

Proofreading Practice
• That will brayk if you drop it. (break)
• The boys said thay would be careful with it. (they)

Student Objectives
- To sort lesson words according to vowel sound
- To identify spelling patterns in lesson words
- To compare sorted plural words that end in -s or -es

Presenting the Page

Review with students the sounds represented by /ă/, /ā/, and /ĕ/. You may wish to point out that this activity asks students to sort one of the plural words *(eggs)* by vowel sound. For items 29 and 30, suggest that students look at the base words and think about what endings have been added.

Meeting Individual Needs

Kinesthetic Learners
Some students who have difficulty with handwriting will enjoy using a computer to practice the review words. The repetitive typing patterns will reinforce their use of correct spelling.

Proofreading Practice
- His birthday is in Jaunuary. *(January)*
- I'll be there in a secund. *(second)*

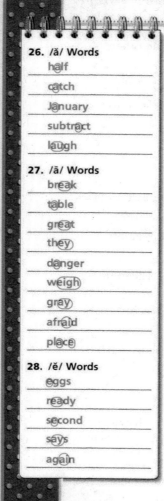

26. /ă/ Words
   half
   catch
   January
   subtract
   laugh

27. /ā/ Words
   break
   table
   great
   they
   danger
   weigh
   gray
   afraid
   place

28. /ĕ/ Words
   eggs
   ready
   second
   says
   again

Review Sort

half	they	second	afraid
break	danger	gray	place
table	catch	says	again
great	ready	January	laugh
eggs	weigh	subtract	

26. Write the **five** short *a* words. Circle the letters that spell /ă/ in each word.

27. Write the **nine** long *a* words. Circle the letters that spell /ā/ in each word.

28. Write the **five** short *e* words. Circle the letters that spell /ĕ/ in each word.

These four words have been sorted into two groups. Explain how the words in each group are alike.

29. hammers   places

   Both words are plurals that are formed by adding -s.

30. dresses   matches

   Both words are plurals that are formed by adding -es.

40 UNIT 1

WRITER'S WORKSHOP MASTERS, pp. T295–T297

The Writing Process   Name _____

1 Prewriting • Plan your writing.
- Make sure you know what your writing task is.
- Identify the audience and the purpose for writing.
- Choose a topic.
- Gather and write ideas about the topic.
- Organize your ideas.

2 Writing • Write a first draft.
- Use your plan to put your ideas in writing.
- Don't worry about mistakes now.
- Add any new ideas you think of while writing.
- Leave room between lines so that you can make changes later.

3 Revising • Look for ways to improve what you have written.
- Make sure your writing fits the audience and purpose for writing.
- Look for places that need more ideas or details.
- Take out sentences that don't belong.
- Find places where more colorful or exact words can be used.
- Make sure that your sentences are complete.
- Write and revise until you are happy with your writing.

4 Proofreading • Review your work for errors.
- Make sure you have indented each paragraph.
- Check to see that you have used words correctly.
- Check your capitalization.
- Check to see that you have used periods, question marks, commas, and other punctuation marks correctly.
- Look at the spelling of each word. Circle words you are not sure you have spelled correctly. Check their spelling.

5 Publishing • Share what you have written.
- Make a clean final draft.
- Read it to the class or a friend.
- Add pictures or make a poster to go with it.
- Make a recording of your writing.

✓ Proofreading Checklist   Name _____

You can use the questions below as a checklist to proofread your writing.
- ☐ Have I indented each paragraph?
- ☐ Have I used words correctly in every sentence?
- ☐ Have I capitalized the first word in each sentence?
- ☐ Have I capitalized all proper names?
- ☐ Have I ended each sentence with a period, question mark, or exclamation point?
- ☐ Have I spelled each word correctly?

The chart below shows some proofreading marks and how to use them.

Mark	Meaning	Example
◯	spell correctly	I liek dogs.
⊙	add period	They are my favorite kind of pet⊙
?	add question mark	What kind of pet do you have?
☰	capitalize	My dog's name is scooter.
✎	take out	He likes to to run and play.
¶	indent paragraph	¶ I love my dog, Scooter. He is the best pet I have ever had. Every morning he wakes me with a bark. Every night he sleeps with me.
⌄⌄	add quotation marks	You are my best friend, I tell him.

Chain of Events Chart   Name _____   Date _____

40

Writer's Workshop

A Personal Narrative

A personal narrative is a true story about the writer. This kind of writing contains words like *I*, *me*, *my*, and *mine*. Here is part of Maria's personal narrative about her first job.

Prewriting   To write her personal narrative, Maria followed the steps in the writing process. After she decided on a topic, she used a chain of events chart to list the things that happened. The chart helped Maria tell the story events in the right order. Part of Maria's chain of events chart is shown here. Study what Maria did.

My First Job

My first job taught me a big lesson. One day Ms. Chen offered me ten dollars. All I had to do was carry some magazines and newspapers from her basement to a trash can in her yard. "Great!" I said.

1
Ms. Chen offered me $10 to carry magazines.

2
She showed me her huge basement full of magazines.

3
The job took two weeks.

It's Your Turn!

Write your own personal narrative. It can be about the first time you did something, such as your first day of school or your first soccer game. After you have decided on your topic, make a chain of events chart. Then follow the other steps in the writing process—writing, revising, proofreading, and publishing. Try to use spelling words from this lesson in your personal narrative. **Narratives will vary.**

Writer's Workshop Scoring Rubric: Personal Narrative

SCORE 3
The narrative includes a clear beginning, middle, and end supported with much specific detail. Events are logically sequenced and often connected with time-order transition words such as *next* and *then*. Contains a minimum of sentence-structure, usage, mechanics, and spelling errors.

SCORE 2
One or more of the beginning, middle, and end of narrative is unclear or weak. Narrative is supported by some details. Sequence of events may not always be logical, and time-order transition words may not always be used. Contains some sentence-structure, usage, mechanics, and spelling errors.

SCORE 1
Narrative is incomplete or unclear and contains little or no detail. Few or no time-order transition words are used. Contains many sentence-structure, usage, mechanics, and spelling errors.

Evaluating Students' Writing

The scoring rubric is based on standards for idea development, organization, coherence, sentence structure, usage, mechanics, and spelling. You may wish to share the rubric with students before they write their description.

The *Steck-Vaughn Writer's Dictionary, Intermediate Level,* provides writers with a place to write words they want to remember.

Student Objective
- To write a personal narrative, using Lesson 6 words and the steps in the writing process

Presenting the Page

Read the first paragraph and the paragraph from "My First Job" with students. Guide students to see how the prewriting activity helped Maria plan her narrative.

You may wish to copy and distribute the Writer's Workshop Masters on pages T295–T297 for students to use as they write their personal narratives.

Day 5

Student Objective
- To take a posttest on the lesson words

Posttest Options

Use the posttest below or the Review Test Master on pages T283–T284 to assess students' ability to spell the lesson words.

Posttest

Dictate the following sentences. Have students write the sentences and underline the lesson words.

1. I am afraid of danger.
2. He is ready to catch the ball.
3. Did the plate break in half when it fell off the table?
4. How much does your gray cat weigh?
5. Mom will buy eggs and matches.
6. She had to laugh at my joke.
7. Dad says to come home this second.
8. What is the address of this place?
9. My favorite months are April and January.
10. Will you subtract that number again?
11. These apples taste great.
12. Where are some places that they can buy hammers?

Lesson 7

More Words with Short *e*

Student Objectives

- To take a pretest on the lesson words
- To sort and write the lesson words according to the spelling patterns *e*, *ie*, *a*, and *ue*

Pretest

Use the pretest on this page to assess students' ability to spell the lesson words.

Have students use the study steps on page 6 to study any words they misspell in the pretest.

You may wish to duplicate and send home the Home Activity Master on pages T243–T244.

Presenting the Page

Introducing the Short e Sound
Say each of the following word pairs and have students raise their hand when they hear a word with /ĕ/:

better–batter   sleep–*slept*
friend–fried   they–*them*

As students prepare to sort the words, point out that /ĕ/ is most often spelled *e* but is spelled *ie*, *a*, or *ue* in some words that we often use.

Pronunciation Focus Write *Feb/ru/ar/y* on the board and pronounce the word, emphasizing the *r* in the second syllable. Tell students that pronouncing *February* correctly will help them remember its spelling.

Consonant Focus Write the words *them* and *then* on the board. Have students say each word and identify the unvoiced and voiced sounds of *th*. Guide students to observe that the voiced and unvoiced sounds of *th* are spelled the same.

42

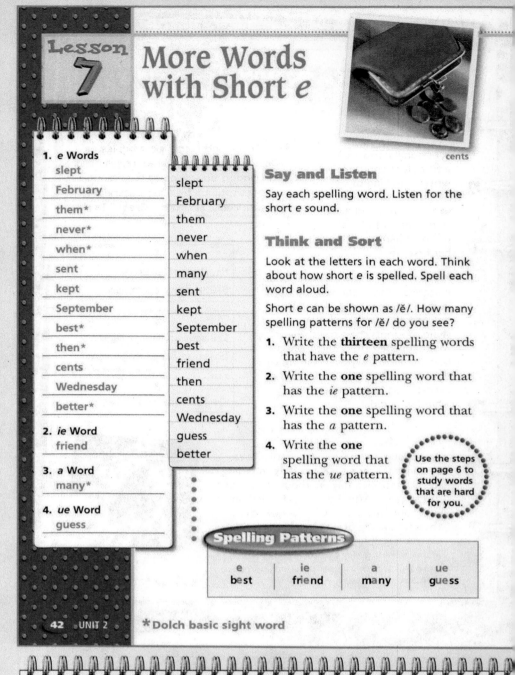

Lesson 7

More Words with Short *e*

cents

1. *e* Words

slept
February
them*
never*
when*
sent
kept
September
best*
then*
cents
Wednesday
better*

2. *ie* Word
friend

3. *a* Word
many*

4. *ue* Word
guess

slept
February
them
never
when
many
sent
kept
September
best
friend
then
cents
Wednesday
guess
better

Say and Listen

Say each spelling word. Listen for the short *e* sound.

Think and Sort

Look at the letters in each word. Think about how short *e* is spelled. Spell each word aloud.

Short *e* can be shown as /ĕ/. How many spelling patterns for /ĕ/ do you see?

1. Write the **thirteen** spelling words that have the *e* pattern.

2. Write the **one** spelling word that has the *ie* pattern.

3. Write the **one** spelling word that has the *a* pattern.

4. Write the **one** spelling word that has the *ue* pattern.

Use the steps on page 6 to study words that are hard for you.

Spelling Patterns

e	ie	a	ue
b**e**st	fr**ie**nd	m**a**ny	g**ue**ss

42 UNIT 2   *Dolch basic sight word

Pretest

Say each lesson word, read the sentence, and then repeat the word. Have students write the words on separate paper.

1. **slept** I <u>slept</u> late this morning.
2. **February** The shortest month is <u>February</u>.
3. **them** Dad washed the dishes, and I dried <u>them</u>.
4. **never** She has <u>never</u> flown in a plane.
5. **when** Tell us <u>when</u> to start.
6. **many** We saw <u>many</u> sheep.
7. **sent** My aunt <u>sent</u> flowers.
8. **kept** She <u>kept</u> pennies in a jar.
9. **September** School begins in <u>September</u>.
10. **best** Which story did you like <u>best</u>?
11. **friend** You are a good <u>friend</u>.
12. **then** I will see you <u>then</u>.
13. **cents** The pen cost sixty <u>cents</u>.
14. **Wednesday** We went to the zoo on <u>Wednesday</u>.
15. **guess** I will <u>guess</u> your name.
16. **better** I like red <u>better</u> than green.

Additional Words for Enrichment

The following words can be used to meet the needs of on-level and above-level students:

stretch   desert   edge   elephant   empty   energy

Spelling and Meaning

Classifying Write the spelling word that belongs in each group.

1. lots several **many**
2. pal buddy **friend**
3. July August **September**
4. Monday Tuesday **Wednesday**
5. rested napped **slept**
6. December January **February**
7. good better **best**
8. mailed shipped **sent**
9. who what **when**

Rhymes Write the spelling word that completes each sentence and rhymes with the underlined word.

10. If you don't have a <u>pen</u>, **then** I will lend you one.
11. No one <u>slept</u> because the dog **kept** us up.
12. Tell **them** to <u>hem</u> the curtains.
13. Have you ever read a **better** <u>letter</u>?
14. Let me **guess** who made this <u>mess</u>.
15. I **never** knew you were so <u>clever</u>.

Word Story The Latin word *centum* meant "hundred." Several English words come from *centum*. A *century* is one hundred years. A *centipede* is an animal with one hundred legs. Write the spelling word that means "hundredths of a dollar."

16. **cents**

Family Tree: *friend* Think about how the *friend* words are alike in spelling and meaning. Then add another *friend* word to the tree. A sample answer is shown.

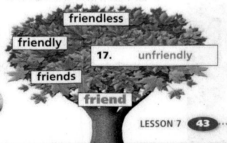

friendless
friendly
17. unfriendly
friends
friend

LESSON 7 **43**

Proofreading Practice
• My freynd lives in a big city. *(friend)*
• Can you gess my name? *(guess)*

Meeting Individual Needs

ESOL
To give speakers of other languages practice with present and past tenses, write *sent*, *slept*, and *kept* on the board. Then ask a present-tense question that contains *send*, *sleep*, or *keep*. For example, you might ask *Did you send your friend a card?* Have students use the past tense lesson word in a sentence that answers the question, as in *Yes, I sent my friend a card.*

Day 2

Student Objectives
• To use meaning clues to identify and write lesson words
• To use etymology, meaning, and spelling to identify the word *cents*
• To learn *friend* words and analyze their spellings and meanings

Presenting the Page

Write the following Classifying and Rhymes examples on the board and model identifying the answers:

• we   us   _____ *(them)*
• Of all the places I can <u>rest</u>, I like the couch _____ . *(best)*

For the Rhymes activity, tell students to read the sentence and to then find the lesson word that makes sense in the sentence and rhymes with the underlined word.

Word Story

Share with students that many languages besides English have words that come from the Latin word *centum*. In Spanish the equivalent of the English word *cents* is *centavos*. In French it is *centimes*.

Family Tree: *friend*

Students should see that all of the *friend* words contain *friend*. To help students explore the meanings of the words, have them locate the meanings in a dictionary, write their findings on the board, and talk about how the meanings are alike and different. Point out the change in function when *-ly* is added (to make *friend* an adverb). Guide students to understand that knowing how to spell *friend* will help them spell words related to *friend*.

Student Objectives
- To use context to identify and write lesson words
- To identify realistic fiction
- To make inferences

Presenting the Pages

Have students read the story silently and complete the pages on their own. Alternatively, read the story aloud as students write the missing words. Either way, have students take turns reading the completed story aloud.

Discuss with students the meanings of the words *clerk* and *sent* in the story. As they are used, *clerk* means "someone who sells items in a store," and *sent* means "ordered to go." Invite students to tell about any problems they may have had in taking care of someone else's pet.

Meeting Individual Needs

Kinesthetic Learners

To give kinesthetic learners additional practice with the lesson words, have students make cut-out words. Have them find and cut out from old magazines the letters that spell lesson words. Then direct them to build each word by gluing the letters onto a large piece of construction paper.

Spelling in Context Use each spelling word once to complete the story.

Lily

It was the month of ___February___,
1
so it was very cold in New Jersey. Lan and her family were going to sunny Florida on ___Wednesday___. Before they left, Lan took
2
her pet frog to Carlos. "I'm so glad you are going to take care of Lily for me," she told him. "This frog is the ___best___
3
pet I've ever had. Take her home in this shoebox. I'll pick her up on Saturday."

"This is great! I like frogs," said Carlos. He took the shoebox home. But when he opened it, Lily jumped out. Carlos looked for a long time, but he couldn't find Lily anywhere in the house. "I'll ___never___ find Lily," he groaned. "I guess I should
4
have ___kept___ the box closed."
5

Carlos went to bed worried about Lily. That night while he ___slept___, he dreamed about Lily. He woke up even more
6
worried. At school that day, he told his ___friend___ Cody
7
what had happened. "Lan is coming back in two days. I have to find Lily by ___then___," Carlos said in a shaky voice.
8

Cody said, "I have a ___better___ idea. Let's go to the
9
pet store and buy another frog. Lan will never ___guess___
10
that it's not Lily."

44 UNIT 2

Spelling Strategy

Guess and Check

Tell students that they can use the guess-and-check strategy for spelling a lesson word they find troublesome. Explain that this is a particularly good strategy when they know how to spell the beginning of a word. Demonstrate how to use this strategy by inviting students to suggest spellings for the word *friend*. Write their suggestions on the board. Then have students check each spelling in the Spelling Dictionary and identify the correct spelling on the board. Suggest that students try the same strategy with any lesson words they are having difficulty with.

Guess	Correct?
frand	no
frend	no
fruend	no
friend	yes

The pet store had _____ **many** _____ frogs. Carlos
_11_
and Cody looked at _____ **them** _____ all. They found
_12_
one that looked just like Lily.

"Five dollars," said the sales clerk.

"We have only sixty _____ **cents** _____," said Carlos
_13_
sadly. The clerk _____ **sent** _____ the boys away.
_14_

On Saturday morning Lan came to get Lily. Carlos
opened the door. He didn't know what to say. Suddenly
he heard a croak. Lily jumped out of his jacket pocket.

"Lily!" cried Lan happily. "Thanks for taking such
good care of her, Carlos. Would you take care of her
again _____ **when** _____ we visit my grandmother in
_15_
_____ **September** _____?"
_16_

Carlos looked at Lily and smiled.

slept
February
them
never
when
many
sent
kept
September
best
friend
then
cents
Wednesday
guess
better

LESSON 7 **45**

ACTIVITY MASTER p. T258

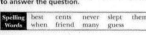

Lesson 7 More Words with Short *e*

Name _____

Find the word in the box that matches each clue.
Write the word. Then read down the squares
to answer the question.

Spelling Words best cents never slept them
when friend many guess

HOW CAN YOU SERVE TEN EGGS TO SEVEN PEOPLE?

Clues
1. to suppose   1. g u e s s
2. coins   2. c e n t s
3. at no time   3. n e v e r
4. a lot of   4. m a n y
5. those people   5. t h e m
6. most excellent   6. b e s t
7. sleep tonight, ___ last night   7. s l e p t
8. as soon as   8. w h e n
9. a pal   9. f r i e n d

Find the word in the box that completes each sentence.
Write the word on the line.

Spelling Words September then Wednesday better February kept sent

10. Keesha ___**sent**___ valentines in the month of ___**February**___.
11. His birthday is in ___**September**___.
12. Marcel is feeling ___**better**___ today.
13. The day that comes after Tuesday is ___**Wednesday**___.
14. We ___**kept**___ the secret.
15. The team practiced and ___**then**___ went out for pizza.

ADDITIONAL PRACTICE

You may wish to copy and distribute
the Activity Master on page T258 as
additional practice for Lesson 7.

Proofreading Practice
- Our team has won meny
  games. *(many)*
- We are playing much beter
  this year than last. *(better)*

Reading Comprehension

After students have completed
the pages, ask whether this
story could really happen.
Help students to understand
that the characters, problem,
and events help make the
story one that could indeed
happen. Explain that stories
with realistic characters, problems, and events are called
realistic fiction.

Ask students why they think
Carlos doesn't tell Lan that he
has lost Lily. If necessary,
prompt students to conclude
that Carlos probably doesn't
want to upset Lan. He wants
her to think he has taken
good care of Lily.

Cooperative Learning Activity

To help students assess their
progress, have pairs of students make word cards for
the lesson words. Suggest
they use different-color
markers to write or highlight
the letters that spell the short
e sound in each word. Then
have students sort the word
cards according to the *e, ie, a,*
and *ue* spelling patterns.
Students can then use the set
of cards to take turns dictating all of the lesson words to
each other. Have students
check their own work, using
the list on page 45. If possible, have students compare
their performance on this
midweek activity to their performance on the pretest.
Guide them in noting the
words they are now spelling
correctly and those they need
to continue to study.

45

Day 4

Student Objectives
- To make an informative sign, using lesson words
- To proofread an e-mail for spelling, capitalization, and punctuation

Presenting the Page

Ask students to give examples of additional information that might go on a "lost pet" sign, such as the pet's name and the location where it was lost. A picture of the pet could also go on such a sign. Then encourage students to use lesson words in their sign.

To assist students with the Proofreading activity, you may want to have a volunteer read the directions and e-mail aloud and then have students complete the activity independently. Then have partners compare and check their answers.

Meeting Individual Needs

ESOL

Spanish-speaking students, as well as some speakers of Asian languages, may pronounce the letter *e* with the long *a* sound, /ā/. These students will benefit from repeated opportunities to hear, say, and spell the lesson words. Say each word and have students repeat it. Then say a sentence with the word and have the students repeat the sentence. Finally, have students write the word, underlining the short *e* spelling pattern.

Spelling and Writing

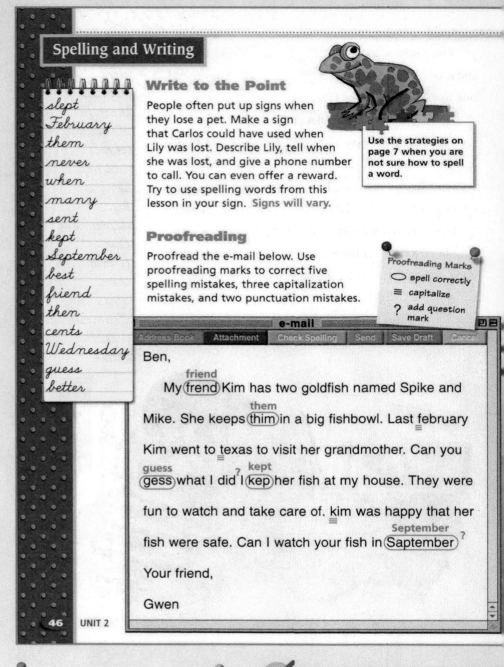

slept
February
them
never
when
many
sent
kept
September
best
friend
then
cents
Wednesday
guess
better

Write to the Point

People often put up signs when they lose a pet. Make a sign that Carlos could have used when Lily was lost. Describe Lily, tell when she was lost, and give a phone number to call. You can even offer a reward. Try to use spelling words from this lesson in your sign. Signs will vary.

> Use the strategies on page 7 when you are not sure how to spell a word.

Proofreading

Proofread the e-mail below. Use proofreading marks to correct five spelling mistakes, three capitalization mistakes, and two punctuation mistakes.

> **Proofreading Marks**
> ◯ spell correctly
> ≡ capitalize
> ? add question mark

e-mail

Address Book | Attachment | Check Spelling | Send | Save Draft | Cancel

Ben,

My (frend) Kim has two goldfish named Spike and [friend]

Mike. She keeps (thim) in a big fishbowl. Last february [them]

Kim went to texas to visit her grandmother. Can you

(gess) what I did I (kep) her fish at my house. They were [guess] [kept]

fun to watch and take care of. kim was happy that her

fish were safe. Can I watch your fish in (Saptember)? [September]

Your friend,

Gwen

46   UNIT 2

Proofreading Practice
- I take drum lessons on Wensday. (Wednesday)
- I started taking lessons last Febuary. (February)

✔ Correcting Common Errors

You may notice that some students drop the silent *d* or *e* in *Wednesday*. Suggest that these students say the silent letters as they practice pronouncing the word /Wĕd nĕs dā/ and writing it correctly.

46

Language Connection

Capital Letters Use a capital letter to begin the names of people and pets and to write the word *I*. Also use a capital letter to begin the first word of a sentence.

The following sentences have capitalization errors. Write each sentence correctly.

1. the book i like best was written by fred gibson.
   The book I like best was written by Fred Gibson.

2. it is about a dog called old yeller.
   It is about a dog called Old Yeller.

3. travis and old yeller have many adventures.
   Travis and Old Yeller have many adventures.

4. carl anderson wrote about a horse named blaze.
   Carl Anderson wrote about a horse named Blaze.

5. blaze was kept by a boy named billy.
   Blaze was kept by a boy named Billy.

6. a horse named thunderbolt became friends with billy and blaze.
   A horse named Thunderbolt became friends with Billy and Blaze.

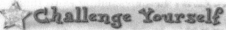 Challenge Yourself

Write the Challenge Word for each clue. Check the Spelling Dictionary to see if you are right. Then use separate paper to write sentences showing that you understand the meaning of each Challenge Word.
Sentences will vary.

Challenge Words
sketch
index
blend
friendliness

7. When you do this, you mix things.
   blend

8. This makes people feel liked. friendliness

9. You can use this to find something in a book. index

10. It helps to do this before you make a final drawing. sketch

LESSON 7 **47**

Posttest

Dictate the following sentences. Have students use separate paper to write the sentences and underline the lesson words.

1. You are my best friend.
2. He sent them a letter when he got home.
3. I slept better in my old bed.
4. Do you like February and September?
5. How many of you can guess my name?
6. She kept the ten cents she found on Wednesday.
7. Then she put it in her bank.
8. We were never late.

Enrichment Activity

Have students work independently to create riddles for the lesson words, such as *I start in the same way as* bag *and mean the opposite of* worst. *(best)* Suggest that each student write riddles for two or three words. Then have partners trade riddles and write the lesson word that answers each riddle.

Student Objectives
- To write sentences containing lesson words, using capital letters correctly
- To study the spellings and meanings of the Challenge Words
- To take a posttest on the lesson words

Presenting the Page

Review with students when to use capital letters: to begin the names of people and pets, to write the word *I*, and to begin the first word in a sentence. Before students complete the activity independently, you might have students volunteer to read the sentences aloud, pointing out words that are names.

 Challenge Yourself

To introduce the Challenge Words, write the words on the board in the following manner:

sketch	blend
in/dex	friend/li/ness

Pronounce the words for students and point out the /ĭ/ sound in the *-ness* suffix of *friendliness*. Then discuss the number of syllables in each word. Have students review the short *e* spelling patterns featured in this lesson. Ask students to identify the short *e* pattern in each of the Challenge Words (*sketch, index,* and *blend* have the *e* pattern; the first syllable in *friendliness* has the *ie* pattern).

Posttest

Use the posttest on this page to assess students' ability to spell the lesson words.

Lesson 8

Words with Long *e*

Day 1

Student Objectives

- To take a pretest on the lesson words
- To spell the lesson words aloud
- To sort and write the lesson words according to the spelling patterns *ee*, *ea*, and *eo*

Pretest

Use the pretest on this page to assess students' ability to spell the lesson words.

 Have students use the study steps on page 6 to study any words they misspell in the pretest.

 You may wish to duplicate and send home the Home Activity Master on pages T243–T244.

Presenting the Page

Introducing the Long e Sound

Write *met* and *meet* on the board. Have a volunteer read the words aloud. Help students to distinguish between the short *e* and long *e* sounds.

As students prepare to sort the words, point out that /ē/ is often spelled *ee* or *ea* but is spelled *eo* in *people*.

Pronunciation Focus
Point out that *read* can be pronounced two ways, /rĕd/ and /rēd/. Explain that /rĕd/ is a form of the word /rēd/. Stress that we usually do not know which word is intended unless it is used in a sentence.

Consonant Focus
Write the lesson words *please*, *free*, *sneeze*, *dream*, *sleep,* and *street* on the board and invite students to read them aloud. Point out that each word begins with two or more consonants and that each of these consonants can be heard when the word is pronounced. Explain that such consonant combinations are called consonant blends or consonant clusters. Help students identify the consonant cluster in each word.

48

Lesson 8

Words with Long *e*

read

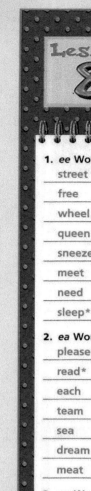

1. ee Words
street
free
wheel
queen
sneeze
meet
need
sleep*

2. ea Words
please*
read*
each
team
sea
dream
meat

3. eo Word
people

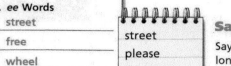

street
please
free
wheel
read
queen
each
sneeze
people
meet
team
sea
need
dream
sleep
meat

Say and Listen
Say each spelling word. Listen for the long *e* sound.

Think and Sort
Look at the letters in each word. Think about how long *e* is spelled. Spell each word aloud.

Long *e* can be shown as /ē/. How many spelling patterns for /ē/ do you see?

1. Write the **eight** spelling words that have the *ee* pattern.
2. Write the **seven** spelling words that have the *ea* pattern.
3. Write the **one** spelling word that has the *eo* pattern.

Use the steps on page 6 to study words that are hard for you.

Spelling Patterns

ee	ea	eo
m**ee**t	t**ea**m	p**eo**ple

48 UNIT 2   *Dolch basic sight word

Pretest

Say each lesson word, read the sentence, and then repeat the word. Have students write the words on separate paper.

1. **street** I live on this street.
2. **please** Wait for me, please.
3. **free** The tickets are free.
4. **wheel** The front wheel of my bike is bent.
5. **read** I will read my e-mail later.
6. **queen** We met the queen.
7. **each** Give a cap to each player.
8. **sneeze** Cats make me sneeze.
9. **people** Many people like dogs.
10. **meet** We will meet at two o'clock.
11. **team** She is on the soccer team.
12. **sea** We went swimming in the sea.
13. **need** We need more apples.
14. **dream** Last night I had a funny dream.
15. **sleep** Did you sleep well?
16. **meat** Dad grilled the meat.

Additional Words for Enrichment

The following words can be used to meet the needs of on-level and above-level students:

scream   reason   easy   agree   kneel   fifteen

Spelling and Meaning

Analogies Write the spelling word that completes each analogy.

1. *Sit* is to *chair* as ___sleep___ is to *bed*.
2. *Train* is to *track* as *car* is to ___street___.
3. *Hives* are to *bees* as *houses* are to ___people___.
4. *Cough* is to *mouth* as ___sneeze___ is to *nose*.
5. *Book* is to ___read___ as *movie* is to *watch*.
6. *Rectangle* is to *door* as *circle* is to ___wheel___.
7. *Bush* is to *shrub* as *ocean* is to ___sea___.

Definitions Write the spelling word for each definition. Use the Spelling Dictionary if you need to.

8. food from the flesh of animals — ___meat___
9. a group of people playing on the same side — ___team___
10. to think, feel, or see during sleep — ___dream___
11. to come together — ___meet___
12. without cost — ___free___
13. to give pleasure or happiness to — ___please___
14. every one — ___each___
15. must have — ___need___

Word Story The Old Saxon word *quan* meant "wife." Later it became the Old English word *cwen*, which meant "wife, woman, or wife of the king." What do we say today instead of *cwen*? Write the spelling word.

16. ___queen___

Family Tree: *read* Think about how the *read* words are alike in spelling and meaning. Then add another *read* word to the tree. A sample answer is shown.

- reread
- reader
- 17. ___reading___
- reads
- readable
- read

LESSON 8 **49**

HOME ACTIVITY MASTER p. T243

The highlighted area shows the Lesson 8 words, which students can share with family members. Spanish version available on page T244.

Proofreading Practice
- Give a flower to eech girl. *(each)*
- May I pleaze have one? *(please)*

Meeting Individual Needs

ESOL
Spanish-speaking students and some speakers of Asian languages may spell /ē/ with *i*. Have these students use letter cards to build lesson words. First have them use letters to make the *ee*, *ea*, and *eo* spelling patterns. Then have students take turns adding letters to build a lesson word, say the word, and write it.

Spelling and Meaning

Day 2

Student Objectives
- To use meaning clues to identify and write lesson words
- To use etymology, meaning, and spelling to identify the word *queen*
- To learn *read* words and analyze their spellings and meanings

Presenting the Page
Write the following Analogies and Definitions examples on the board and model identifying the answers. For the analogy, remind students that identifying the relationship represented by the first word pair will enable them to complete the last pair.

- *Husband* is to *wife* as *king* is to _____. *(queen)*
- the large body of salt water that covers most of the earth's surface *(sea)*

Word Story
Guide students to observe that the first two letters of *queen* changed from *qu* to *cw* and back to *qu*. Write *cwic* on the board and ask students what modern-day word they think this Old English word represents *(quick)*.

Family Tree: *read*
Students should see that the *read* words all contain *read*. To help students explore the meanings of the words, have them locate the meanings in a dictionary, write their findings on the board, and talk about how the meanings are alike and different. Point out the change in meaning and function when *-er* is added to the verb *read* to create a noun that means "one who reads." Explain that when *-able* is added to form *readable*, the result is an adjective that means "easy to read."

49

Day 3

Student Objectives
- To use context to identify and write lesson words
- To analyze a character's feelings

Presenting the Pages

Have volunteers read the story aloud paragraph by paragraph, supplying the missing words as another volunteer writes them on the board. Afterward, discuss the word choices, erase them, and have students complete the pages. Alternatively, have students read the story silently and complete the pages independently. Have students take turns reading the completed story aloud.

Invite students to tell about a time when they were bored and did something useful or helpful that made them feel better.

Meeting Individual Needs

Visual Learners
To help visual learners practice the spelling patterns, make a large chart with *ee*, *ea*, and *eo* written as column headings across the top. Then have students say a lesson word, spell it aloud, write it under the appropriate heading, and circle the letters that spell /ē/.

Queen of the Roads

Many years ago in a castle by the ___**sea**___, there lived
1

a wonderful ___**queen**___. She was a nice queen. All of the
2

___**people**___ in her kingdom loved her. But the queen was not
3

happy. No one at the castle would let her do any work. Every morning she

had to sit and ___**read**___ a book. Every afternoon she had to
4

___**meet**___ the kings and queens who came to visit. She even
5

had to eat roasted ___**meat**___ for every meal.
6

When she went to ___**sleep**___ at night, the queen would
7

often ___**dream**___ of a different life.
8

One morning she woke up early. She told a

servant, "I ___**need**___ to get away
9

from the castle. I want some time to think.

___**Please**___ get a carriage ready
10

for me."

The servant did as he was asked. In no

time at all, the queen was driving down the

main ___**street**___ of the city. "How
11

can I be useful?" she asked herself. "What

kind of work can I do?"

50   UNIT 2

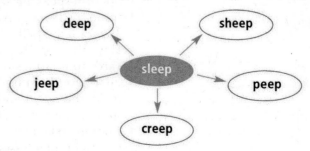

Spelling Strategy

Rhyming Helper
Remind students that they can use a rhyming helper to help them remember the spelling of a word. Write the word *sleep* on the board. Invite students to name rhyming helpers. If necessary, remind students that a rhyming helper must be spelled the same way as the word they are trying to spell, except for the beginning sound. Write all of students' appropriate rhyming helpers for *sleep* on the board.

```
        deep              sheep

jeep         sleep              peep

              creep
```

Then write *meet/street* and *please/sneeze* on the board. Point out that either *meet* or *street* could be a rhyming helper for the other, but that *please* and *sneeze* could not because these words do not have the same spelling pattern for /ē/.

The queen traveled far from the castle. The road became bumpy and dusty. She was thinking about being a farmer when her carriage hit a hole in the road. A ___wheel___ flew off
12
and got stuck between two large rocks. The queen tried and tried but couldn't get the wheel ___free___. It was getting
13
dark and cold. She began to shake and ___sneeze___.
14

At last two farmers came by. "Thank goodness you are here!" said the queen. "Will you help me?"

"Of course!" said the farmers. They helped the queen free the wheel and put it back on the carriage.

"We are a great ___team___!" said the happy queen.
15
She felt special inside. "How can I thank you?"

"We need new roads that are easy for everyone to travel on," said the farmers.

"New roads you shall have," answered the queen. "And I shall help build ___each___ and every one!"
16

The queen found a way to be useful. She made many new friends. She stayed busy building new roads with others. After a while everyone began to call her Queen of the Roads. She liked the new name, and she liked her new life. She was never unhappy again.

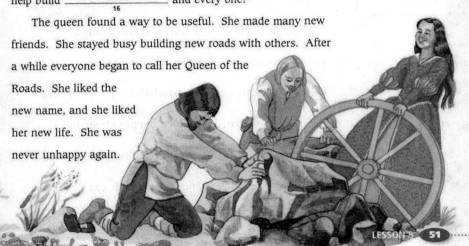

| street |
| please |
| free |
| wheel |
| read |
| queen |
| each |
| sneeze |
| people |
| meet |
| team |
| sea |
| need |
| dream |
| sleep |
| meat |

LESSON 8 **51**

Reading Comprehension

After students have completed the pages, ask them to tell how the queen's feelings about her life change from the beginning of the story to the end. Help students to understand that at the beginning of the story the queen is unhappy, bored, and frustrated. At the end of the story, she is happy.

Ask students why the queen is bored at the beginning of the story (every day is the same) and why she is happy at the end (she is doing something useful).

Cooperative Learning Activity

To help students assess their progress, have partners dictate the lesson words to each other. Then have students check their own work, using the list on page 51. If possible, have students compare their performance on this midweek activity to their performance on the pretest. Guide them in noting the words they are now spelling correctly and those they need to continue to study.

ACTIVITY MASTER p. T259

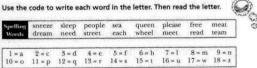

Lesson 8 Words with Long *e*

Name _____

Use the code to write each word in the letter. Then read the letter.

Spelling Words	sneeze	sleep	people	sea	queen	please	free	meat
	dream	need	street	each	wheel	meet	read	team

| 1 = a | 2 = c | 3 = d | 4 = e | 5 = f | 6 = h | 7 = l | 8 = m | 9 = n |
| 10 = o | 11 = p | 12 = q | 13 = r | 14 = s | 15 = t | 16 = u | 17 = w | 18 = z |

Dear Daniel,

Last night, I had a d r e a m when I went to s l e e p. I visited a kingdom near the s e a. The p e o p l e there loved hamburgers. The q u e e n was having a hamburger party. People took me to m e e t her. There was wonderful m e a t to eat. It was all f r e e. I started to eat and eat. Suddenly, I began to s n e e z e. I woke up with feathers tickling my nose. Now I n e e d a new pillow. Mine has three bites taken out of it!

Josie and I are playing stickball with our t e a m at the school on Main S t r e e t later today. Then we are going to the fair. We have money for e a c h of us to ride the Ferris w h e e l. P l e a s e write soon! I love to r e a d letters from my friends.

Love,
Brianna

ADDITIONAL PRACTICE

You may wish to copy and distribute the Activity Master on page T259 as additional practice for Lesson 8.

Proofreading Practice
- Mom bought meet at the market. *(meat)*
- We will meat Dad later. *(meet)*

Day 4

Student Objectives

- To write an expressive paragraph, using lesson words
- To proofread a book jacket for spelling, capitalization, and unnecessary words

Presenting the Page

To help students generate ideas for writing, have them work either as a group or individually to brainstorm a list of changes that would make their life more interesting or exciting, such as learning how to play chess or running errands for extra money. Then encourage students to use lesson words in their paragraphs.

To assist students with the Proofreading activity, ask a volunteer to read the directions and the book jacket aloud. Have students proofread the book jacket and then check their work by reading the sentences in reverse order.

Meeting Individual Needs

Kinesthetic Learners

To help kinesthetic learners practice the spelling patterns, have each student make three large cards, one with *ee*, one with *ea*, and one with *eo*. Then say a lesson word and have students hold up the card that shows the correct spelling pattern for long *e*. Invite a volunteer to say the word, spell it aloud, and then write it.

Spelling and Writing

street
please
free
wheel
read
queen
each
sneeze
people
meet
team
sea
need
dream
sleep
meat

Write to the Point

The queen was unhappy because she did not feel useful. She wanted a different kind of life. Write a paragraph about a different kind of life you would like to have. Use descriptive words and details to make your paragraph interesting. Try to use spelling words from this lesson. Paragraphs will vary.

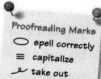

Use the strategies on page 7 when you are not sure how to spell a word.

Proofreading

Proofread the book jacket below. Use proofreading marks to correct five spelling mistakes, three capitalization mistakes, and two unnecessary words.

Proofreading Marks
- ⟋ spell correctly
- ≡ capitalize
- ✐ take out

The Teen Queen

Readers will love this new story about a young queen. one day she has a a strange dream. In the dream, she is on a baseball teme. [team] each time she gets up to bat, a sea of of peeple [people] cheer her. The queen hits four home runs. after the game, she wants to mete [meet] ech [each] fan. Rede [Read] this exciting tale to learn what happens when the queen wakes up.

52 UNIT 2

Proofreading Practice
- I love to swim in the see. (sea)
- Many poeple like to sail. (people)

✔ Correcting Common Errors

Some words present unique spelling problems. For example, some students may transpose the e and o or double the e and drop the o in *people*. Suggest that these students remember the order of the e and o in *people* by memorizing the clue "Most *people* know that e comes before o in the alphabet."

Language Connection

Nouns A noun is a word that names a person, place, thing, or idea. The following words are nouns.

Person	Place	Thing	Idea
boy	seashore	toy	beauty
girl	forest	dog	peace

Write the sentences below, completing them with the correct nouns from the boxes.

meat   wheel   sea   dream   people   street

1. I had a wonderful ___ last night.
   I had a wonderful dream last night.

2. All the ___ who live on my ___ were in it.
   All the people who live on my street were in it.

3. I used a big ___ to steer our big ship out to ___.
   I used a big wheel to steer our big ship out to sea.

4. We had a feast of fruit and roasted ___ on an island.
   We had a feast of fruit and roasted meat on an island.

Challenge Yourself

What do you think each Challenge Word means? Check the Spelling Dictionary to see if you are right. Then use separate paper to write sentences showing that you understand the meaning of each Challenge Word.
Definitions and sentences will vary.

Challenge Words

deceive   feat
seam   teenager

5. An honest queen does not **deceive** the people in her kingdom.
6. The young knight performed a brave **feat**.
7. I ripped the **seam** in my jacket.
8. I will be a **teenager** when I am thirteen.

LESSON 8   53

Posttest

Dictate the following sentences. Have students use separate paper to write the sentences and underline the lesson words.

1. We need more people for our team.
2. You dream when you sleep.
3. I want to meet the queen.
4. She likes to read books about the sea.
5. The wheel rolled down the street.
6. Will you please try not to sneeze?
7. I like each of my cats.
8. What kind of meat do you eat?
9. This pen is free.

Enrichment Activity

Have small groups of students look through magazines or newspapers to find and cut out long _e_ words with lesson spelling patterns. Then have students sort the words by the long _e_ pattern and make a word collage for each spelling pattern. Suggest that advanced students find and cut out all long _e_ words and use them to complete the activity.

Day 5

Student Objectives

- To identify noun lesson words that complete sentences and write the resulting sentences
- To study the spellings and meanings of the Challenge Words
- To take a posttest on the lesson words

Presenting the Page

Review with students that a noun is a word that names a person, a place, a thing, or an idea. Have students look at the examples. Help them to understand that _boy_ and _girl_ name people, _seashore_ and _forest_ name places, _toy_ and _dog_ name things, and _beauty_ and _peace_ name ideas.

Challenge Yourself

To introduce the Challenge Words, write the following on the board:

de/ceive   feat
seam   teen/a/ger

Pronounce the words for students and discuss the number of syllables in each. Then have students turn to page 48 and review the long _e_ spelling patterns featured in this lesson. Tell students that one of the Challenge Words contains another spelling pattern for long _e_. Ask students to identify the long _e_ spelling pattern in each of the Challenge Words (_deceive_ has a new pattern, _ei_; _seam_ and _feat_ have the _ea_ pattern; and _teenager_ has the _ee_ pattern).

Next, have students write what they think each Challenge Word means, look up the words in the Spelling Dictionary, and then write the correct definitions. Ask students to compare their definitions with those in the Spelling Dictionary.

Posttest

Use the posttest on this page to assess students' ability to spell the lesson words.

53

Lesson 9

More Words with Long *e*

Day 1

Student Objectives
- To take a pretest on the lesson words
- To spell the lesson words aloud
- To sort and write the lesson words according to the spelling patterns *e*, *y*, *e*-consonant-*e*, and *ey*.

Pretest

Use the pretest on this page to assess students' ability to spell the lesson words.

 Study Steps Have students use the study steps on page 6 to study any words they misspell in the pretest.

 You may wish to duplicate and send home the Home Activity Master on pages T243–T244.

Presenting the Page

Introducing the Long *e* Sound
Say the words *even*, *story*, *these*, and *key*. Ask students to identify the vowel sound present in all the words (/ē/).

As students prepare to sort the words, point out that /ē/ is often spelled as *e* at the end of a syllable and as *y* but is spelled *e*-consonant-*e* or *ey* in some words we often use.

Pronunciation Focus Write *ver/y*, *eve/ry*, *pen/ny*, and *e/ven* on the board. Guide students to observe that although the first three contain one or more *e*'s, none of these *e*'s is pronounced /ē/; help students to identify the *e* pronounced /ē/ in *even* (the first *e*).

Consonant Focus Have students identify the lesson words that have double consonants (*carry*, *sunny*, *funny*, *penny*, *happy*). Guide students to observe that the consonant is doubled to signal that the first vowel sound is short.

54

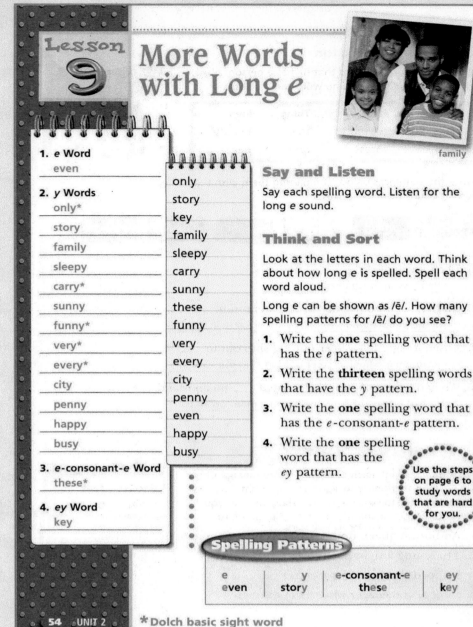

Lesson 9 More Words with Long *e*

family

1. *e* Word
even

2. *y* Words
only*
story
family
sleepy
carry*
sunny
funny*
very*
every*
city
penny
happy
busy

3. *e*-consonant-*e* Word
these*

4. *ey* Word
key

only
story
key
family
sleepy
carry
sunny
these
funny
very
every
city
penny
even
happy
busy

Say and Listen
Say each spelling word. Listen for the long *e* sound.

Think and Sort
Look at the letters in each word. Think about how long *e* is spelled. Spell each word aloud.

Long *e* can be shown as /ē/. How many spelling patterns for /ē/ do you see?

1. Write the **one** spelling word that has the *e* pattern.
2. Write the **thirteen** spelling words that have the *y* pattern.
3. Write the **one** spelling word that has the *e*-consonant-*e* pattern.
4. Write the **one** spelling word that has the *ey* pattern.

Use the steps on page 6 to study words that are hard for you.

Spelling Patterns

e	*y*	*e*-consonant-*e*	*ey*
even	story	these	key

54 UNIT 2   *Dolch basic sight word

Pretest

Say each lesson word, read the sentence, and then repeat the word. Have students write the words on separate paper.

1. **only** My sister is only two years old.
2. **story** Tell me a story.
3. **key** I keep my key in my pocket.
4. **family** My family likes to camp.
5. **sleepy** I yawn when I get sleepy.
6. **carry** Will you carry my bag?
7. **sunny** I hope today is sunny.
8. **these** Whose pencils are these?
9. **funny** I like funny movies.
10. **very** Hit the ball very hard.
11. **every** We visit my grandmother every week.
12. **city** A city is bigger than a town.
13. **penny** She tossed a penny into the pond.
14. **even** Even my brother likes to skate.
15. **happy** Good news makes people happy.
16. **busy** Are you busy today?

Additional Words for Enrichment

The following words can be used to meet the needs of on-level and above-level students:

angry   hungry   secret   really   county   forty

Spelling and Meaning

Definitions Write the spelling word for each definition. Use the Spelling Dictionary if you need to.

1. to take from one place to another _carry_
2. extremely _very_
3. the most important part _key_
4. laughable _funny_
5. each _every_
6. one cent _penny_
7. nearby items _these_
8. a telling of something that happened _story_
9. just _only_

Antonyms Write the spelling word that is an antonym of the underlined word.

10. Seth was <u>sad</u> when summer camp began. _happy_
11. We will go to the zoo on a <u>cloudy</u> day. _sunny_
12. Saturday was a <u>lazy</u> day for everyone. _busy_
13. Life in the <u>country</u> can be very exciting. _city_
14. Kara felt <u>lively</u> after reading a book. _sleepy_
15. Twelve is an <u>odd</u> number. _even_

Word Story Long ago in Rome, rich people had servants. The servants were called *familia*. As time passed, a husband, wife, their children, and their servants were called a *familia*. What spelling word comes from *familia*? Write the word.

16. _family_

Family Tree: *happy* Think about how the *happy* words are alike in spelling and meaning. Then add another *happy* word to the tree. A sample answer is shown.

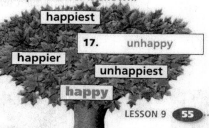

- happiest
- happier
- 17. unhappy
- unhappiest
- happy

LESSON 9 **55**

HOME ACTIVITY MASTER p. T243

Unit 2 **Spelling at Home**

Dear Family of _____,

During the next six weeks, your child will be learning to spell the following kinds of words:

- words with the short *e* vowel sound
- words with the long *e* vowel sound
- words with the short *u* vowel sound
- contractions

Here are some simple activities to do each week to help your child become a better speller.

Listening and Writing
Say the spelling words and have your child write them.

Spelling Strategy: Word Shape
If your child is unsure about the spelling of a word, ask your child to look at the correct spelling and to draw the shape of the word. Then have your child study the word shape. Tell your child that drawing a word's shape can help him or her remember how to spell it. k|e|y

Games and Activities
Play Invisible Writing. Ask your child to choose some spelling words. Write the words on a piece of paper. Then, using a finger, take turns writing a word on each other's back. Be sure to say each letter and the word aloud during the invisible writing.

Have your child go on a word search. Have your child find and circle spelling words in a magazine or newspaper.

Using Spelling Words
Ask your child to write sentences that contain the spelling words. Then read the sentences with your child. Notice whether the sentences show that your child knows the meanings of the spelling words.

Lesson 7 More Words with Short e
Week of ____
best / better / cents / February
never / kept / sent / September
slept / them / then / Wednesday
when / friend / many / guess

Lesson 8 Words with Long e
Week of ____
meet / need / sleep / street
queen / wheel / free / sneeze
dream / each / meat / read
sea / team / please / people

Lesson 9 More Words with Long e
Week of ____
happy / funny / very / busy
sleepy / carry / sunny / every
family / penny / only / city
these / even / key / story

Lesson 10 Words with Short u
Week of ____
mother / front / month / money
from / other / nothing / Monday
such / summer / much / lunch
sun / under / Sunday / does

Lesson 11 Contractions
Week of ____
they'll / she'll / I'll / we'll
you'll / I've / we've / you've
they've / he's / she's / it's
I'd / you'd / they'd / I'm

Lesson 12 Unit 2 Review
Week of ____
Lesson 12 is a review of Lessons 7–11. Help your child practice all of the words from those lessons.

The highlighted area shows the Lesson 9 words, which students can share with family members. Spanish version available on page T244.

Proofreading Practice
- Are theese your tickets? (*these*)
- We watched a verey good movie. (*very*)

Meeting Individual Needs

ESOL
Because Spanish-speaking students may use *i* instead of *y*, have these students cut a large rectangular "window" in the center of a sheet of paper and cut a wheel from another sheet of paper. Write *y* at the right of the "window." Write the first part of the *y* lesson words on the wheel. Attach the wheel behind the window. Have students read and spell the words formed by turning the wheel.

Spelling and Meaning

Day 2

Student Objectives
- To use meaning clues to identify and write lesson words
- To use etymology, meaning, and spelling to identify the word *family*
- To learn *happy* words and analyze their spellings and meanings

Presenting the Page

Write the following Definitions and Antonyms examples on the board and model identifying the answers. Remind students that antonyms are words with opposite meanings.

- having much sun (*sunny*)
- The clown made a <u>serious</u> face. (*funny*)

Point out that in the Antonyms activity, the sentences make more sense when the antonyms are read in place of the underlined words.

Word Story

Students may be able to identify the word *family* from the Latin word *familia*. Point out that the word came to refer to anyone who lived in the same house, whether they were related or not, and that today the word usually refers to people who are related, whether they live in same house or not.

Family Tree: *happy*

Students should see that the *y* in *happy* does not appear in the other Family Tree words. Guide students to conclude that the *y* is changed to *i* when an ending is added. Invite students to share the *happy* word they added to the tree.

55

Student Objectives
- To use context to identify and write lesson words
- To identify the features of biographical nonfiction
- To paraphrase information from a nonfiction selection

Presenting the Pages

If possible, display books illustrated by Jerry Pinkney and tell students that they are going to read about him. Have students work in pairs to read and complete the selection. Alternatively, have students read the selection silently and write the missing words independently.

Explain to students that some people—usually adults—go to school at night so they can work or take care of their children during the day. Discuss with students the phrase "the key to his later success." Be sure students understand that the meaning of *key* here is "the most important part."

Meeting Individual Needs

Kinesthetic/Visual Learners
Working with small groups of students, put a layer of sand in shoe box lids, one for each student. Have one student dictate a lesson word while the other students say each letter aloud and use their finger to write the word. Simply have them wipe the word away before writing the next word.

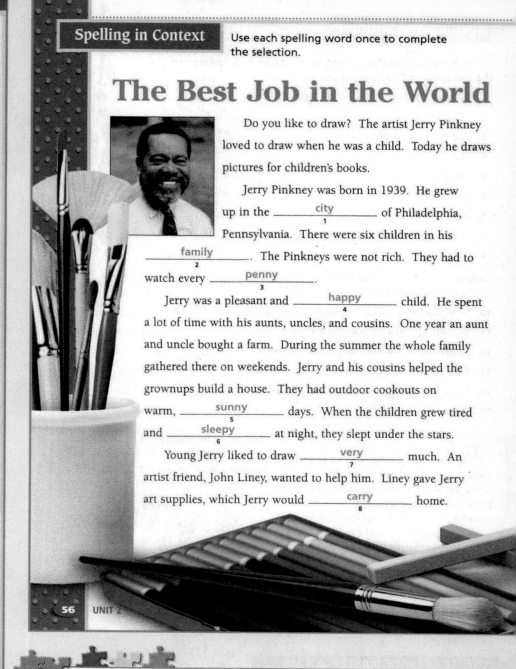

Spelling in Context   Use each spelling word once to complete the selection.

The Best Job in the World

Do you like to draw? The artist Jerry Pinkney loved to draw when he was a child. Today he draws pictures for children's books.

Jerry Pinkney was born in 1939. He grew up in the ____city____ of Philadelphia, Pennsylvania. There were six children in his ____family____. The Pinkneys were not rich. They had to watch every ____penny____.

Jerry was a pleasant and ____happy____ child. He spent a lot of time with his aunts, uncles, and cousins. One year an aunt and uncle bought a farm. During the summer the whole family gathered there on weekends. Jerry and his cousins helped the grownups build a house. They had outdoor cookouts on warm, ____sunny____ days. When the children grew tired and ____sleepy____ at night, they slept under the stars.

Young Jerry liked to draw ____very____ much. An artist friend, John Liney, wanted to help him. Liney gave Jerry art supplies, which Jerry would ____carry____ home.

Spelling Strategy

Using the Spelling Table
Remind students that a spelling table is helpful for finding the correct way to spell words they are unsure of. Invite students to determine the correct way to spell *very* by using the patterns for /ē/ in the Spelling Table. First, have them find the pronunciation symbol for the /ē/ sound in the Spelling Table. Then have students write the word, using a pattern given in the Spellings column, and look for that spelling in the Spelling Dictionary. If the spelling is not in the Spelling Dictionary, they should try another pattern for the word, look up that spelling, and continue in the same manner until they find the correct spelling. Have students record their work in a chart like the following.

/ē/ Spelling	Test Spelling	Found in Spelling Dictionary?
e	vere	no
ea	verea	no
ee	veree	no
ei	verei	no
ey	verey	no
y	very	yes

Have students repeat the procedure for other words they find difficult to spell.

Even though Jerry was _____only_____ 11 years old, he
⁹
knew he wanted to be an artist.

In high school Jerry took _____every_____ art class the
¹⁰
school offered. He _____even_____ went to night school. After
¹¹
high school Jerry studied art in college for more than two years.

After college Jerry worked as a truck driver and as a designer
in a flower shop. He knew that _____these_____ jobs were
¹²
not right for him. He kept drawing in his spare time. Jerry
never gave up his dream. Never giving up may have been the
_____key_____ to his later success.
¹³

Soon Jerry got a job designing greeting cards. Then he
got the chance to draw pictures for a book. The book was a
_____story_____ that retold an African folk tale. Jerry has been
¹⁴
_____busy_____ drawing for stories and books ever since.
¹⁵

Today Jerry Pinkney is a famous artist and lives in the state of
New York. He has drawn pictures for many books. Some are
serious books, such as *Home Place*. Others are
_____funny_____ books, such as *Sam and*
¹⁶
the Tigers. Pinkney also teaches young
people to draw. He likes sharing his talent
and skill with others. Some people think
he has the best job in the world.

only
story
key
family
sleepy
carry
sunny
these
funny
very
every
city
penny
even
happy
busy

LESSON 9 **57**

ACTIVITY MASTER p. T260

| Lesson 9 | More Words with Long *e* |

Name _____

Read the sentences. Cross out the misspelled words and write them correctly on the lines.

| Spelling Words | happy | funny | very | busy | carry | sunny |
| | family | penny | only | city | story | |

1. Ling ~~onle~~ had one more tooth to lose. ____only____
2. It was ~~sunnee~~ in the ~~citee~~. ____sunny____ ____city____
3. The whole ~~famly~~ went to the store. ____family____
4. The street was ~~vry bizy~~. ____very____ ____busy____
5. Alex was ~~happie~~ to ~~carre~~ the apples. ____happy____ ____carry____
6. Kyle thought the ~~storee~~ was ~~funy~~. ____story____ ____funny____
7. Eva gave Ruben a ~~peny~~. ____penny____

Use the words in the box to complete the *e* puzzle.

| Spelling Words |
| sleepy |
| every |
| these |
| even |
| key |

e v e n
k e y
e v e r y
s l e e p y
t h e s e

ADDITIONAL PRACTICE

You may wish to copy and distribute the Activity Master on page T260 as additional practice for Lesson 9.

Proofreading Practice
- My famly likes to work together. *(family)*
- We are bisy with yard work. *(busy)*

Reading Comprehension

After students have completed the pages, discuss what a biography is. Help students understand that a biography is the story of a real person's life written by somebody else. Have students underline words indicating that the selection is a biography, such as "born in," "grew up," "in high school," and "after college."

Next, call on volunteers to give information about Jerry Pinkney in their own words (example: *When Jerry was 11, an artist friend gave him some art supplies*).

Cooperative Learning Activity

Have pairs of students write the lesson words on index cards and place them face down. Then tell students to choose a card in turn and give a clue about that word without using the word, such as *When I am not well rested, I feel like this.* The partner should name the word, and both students should write it. Continue until both partners have written all words. Then have students check their own work, using the list on page 57. Encourage them to note words they are now spelling correctly and those they need to continue to study.

Day 4

Student Objectives
- To write an expressive paragraph, using lesson words
- To proofread a letter for spelling, capitalization, and punctuation

Presenting the Page

Review with students how Jerry Pinkney wanted to be an artist as a child and grew up to have "the best job in the world." With students, brainstorm a list of occupations, prompting them by asking what their parents or other adult family members do. Encourage students to use the lesson words in their paragraph.

To assist students with the Proofreading activity, direct them to read the directions and the letter aloud with a partner to find and correct the mistakes. Or have partners read the letter together and then complete the exercise independently. Identify the mistakes in the letter and have students check their work.

Meeting Individual Needs

ESOL

Because the /ĭ/ sound is more familiar than /ē/ for some speakers of Asian languages, they may pronounce y as /ĭ/ instead of /ē/. Have these students recite the lesson words aloud and use them in sentences.

58

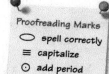

only
story
key
family
sleepy
carry
sunny
these
funny
very
every
city
penny
even
happy
busy

Write to the Point

Jerry Pinkney wanted to be an artist when he grew up. What would you like to be? Write a paragraph about a job that you would like to have someday. Use spelling words from this lesson. **Paragraphs will vary.**

Use the strategies on page 7 when you are not sure how to spell a word.

Proofreading

Proofread the letter below. Use proofreading marks to correct five spelling mistakes, three capitalization mistakes, and two punctuation mistakes.

Proofreading Marks
- ◯ spell correctly
- ≡ capitalize
- ⊙ add period

306 Maple Drive

Campbell, CA 95011

November 10, 2003

Dear Tina,

My mom got a new job. she is going to be a firefighter
                              ≡
            city   family   happy
in the big (citty) of Chicago, Illinois Our (familee) is very (hapy).
                                        ⊙
                   busy
we have been (buzy) packing since early thursday morning I will
≡   ≡   ⊙
            very
write again (verry) soon and tell you more.

Your cousin,

Tasha

58 UNIT 2

Proofreading Practice
- Cut the cake into an eaven number of pieces. *(even)*
- Give evry guest a piece of fruit. *(every)*

✔ Correcting Common Errors

Because silent letters often present spelling problems, some students may drop the silent e in *every*. Write the following sentence on the board, underlining the words as shown:

There's a <u>very</u> in every <u>every</u>.

Suggest that students recall this sentence before they spell the word.

Dictionary Skills

Alphabetical Order   The words in a dictionary are in alphabetical order. Use the Spelling Dictionary to complete the following sentences.

1. Words that begin with **A** start on page ____214____ and end on page ____216____.

2. Words that begin with **M** start on page ____228____ and end on page ____229____.

3. Words that begin with **W** start on page ____238____ and end on page ____240____.

Write the words below in alphabetical order. Then find each one in the Spelling Dictionary and write its page number.

funny   even   carry   key

	Word	Page
4.	carry	218
5.	even	222
6.	funny	224
7.	key	227

⭐ Challenge Yourself

What do you think each Challenge Word means? Check the Spelling Dictionary to see if you are right. Then use separate paper to write sentences showing that you understand the meaning of each Challenge Word. Definitions and sentences will vary.

Challenge Words
misery   scheme
soggy   cemetery

8. A headache can cause **misery**.

9. The children had a **scheme** for raising money to buy a gift.

10. Mia changed her **soggy** clothes after she fell in a puddle.

11. Some grave markers in this **cemetery** are very old.

LESSON 9   **59**

Posttest

Dictate the following sentences. Have students use separate paper to write the sentences and underline the lesson words.

1. They gave him the <u>key</u> to the <u>city</u>.
2. This <u>story</u> is about a lost <u>penny</u>.
3. I can <u>carry</u> <u>only</u> one more box.
4. You seem <u>very</u> <u>busy</u> today.
5. I get <u>sleepy</u> <u>every</u> day after lunch.
6. He was <u>happy</u> to go on a <u>family</u> trip.
7. I think <u>these</u> jokes are <u>funny</u>.
8. Today will be <u>sunny</u> but <u>even</u> colder.

Enrichment Activity

Have students work in pairs or independently to create an original poem containing at least four lesson words. Discuss rhyme schemes and write a sample such as the following on the board:

There once was a <u>sleepy</u> gray cat
Who was <u>happy</u> although <u>very</u> fat.
He'd eat <u>every</u> day,
Too <u>busy</u> to play,
And never would he chase a rat.

Day 5

Student Objectives
• To locate lesson words in the Spelling Dictionary
• To alphabetize lesson words
• To study the spellings and meanings of the Challenge Words
• To take a posttest on the lesson words

Presenting the Page

Review with students that dictionaries are organized alphabetically. Help them conclude that they must use alphabetical order to find words in a dictionary.

⭐ Challenge Yourself

To introduce the Challenge Words, write the following on the board:

mis/er/y   scheme
sog/gy   cem/e/ter/y

Pronounce the words for students and point out that a final *y* is sometimes a syllable by itself. Next, have students refer to page 54 and have them review the long *e* spelling patterns featured in this lesson. Ask students to identify the /ē/ spelling pattern for each word (*misery, soggy,* and *cemetery* have the *y* pattern; *scheme* has the *e-consonant-e* pattern).

Have students write what they think each Challenge Word means, look up the words in the Spelling Dictionary, and write the correct definitions. Ask students to compare their definitions with those in the Spelling Dictionary.

Posttest

Use the posttest on this page to assess students' ability to spell the lesson words.

Words with Short *u*

Student Objectives

- To take a pretest on the lesson words
- To spell the lesson words aloud
- To sort and write the lesson words according to the spelling patterns *u*, *o*, and *oe*

Pretest

Use the pretest on this page to assess students' ability to spell the lesson words.

 Have students use the study steps on page 6 to study any words they misspell in the pretest.

 You may wish to duplicate and send home the Home Activity Master on pages T243–T244.

Presenting the Page

Introducing the Short *u* Sound

Read the following word pairs and have students identify the words with /ŭ/:

| frame–*from* | money–many |
| match–*much* | simmer–*summer* |

As students prepare to sort the words, point out that /ŭ/ is most often spelled *u* but is spelled *o* or *oe* in some words that we often use.

Pronunciation Focus

Write the word *nothing* on the board. Review the two words that form this compound word (*no* and *thing*). Point out that when put together, the sound of *o* changes from /ō/ to /ŭ/.

Consonant Focus

Write *summer* on the board and demonstrate breaking a VCCV word into syllables by dividing between the double consonant (*sum/mer*). Write *Monday, under,* and *Sunday* on the board and have volunteers break them into syllables. Point out that consonants in consonant digraphs, such as *th*, need to stay together. Then show how to divide the words *moth/er* and *noth/ing*.

60

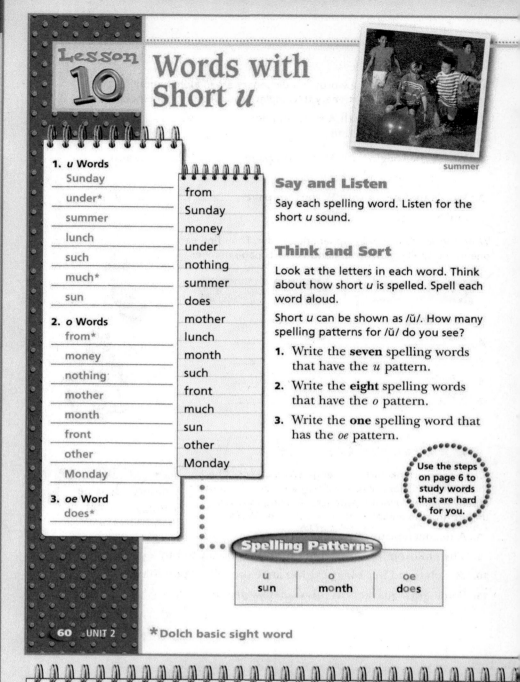

Words with Short *u*

summer

1. *u* Words
- Sunday
- under*
- summer
- lunch
- such
- much*
- sun

2. *o* Words
- from*
- money
- nothing
- mother
- month
- front
- other
- Monday

3. *oe* Word
- does*

from
Sunday
money
under
nothing
summer
does
mother
lunch
month
such
front
much
sun
other
Monday

Say and Listen

Say each spelling word. Listen for the short *u* sound.

Think and Sort

Look at the letters in each word. Think about how short *u* is spelled. Spell each word aloud.

Short *u* can be shown as /ŭ/. How many spelling patterns for /ŭ/ do you see?

1. Write the **seven** spelling words that have the *u* pattern.
2. Write the **eight** spelling words that have the *o* pattern.
3. Write the **one** spelling word that has the *oe* pattern.

Use the steps on page 6 to study words that are hard for you.

Spelling Patterns

u	o	oe
s**u**n	m**o**nth	d**oe**s

60 UNIT 2

*Dolch basic sight word

Pretest

Say each lesson word, read the sentence, and then repeat the word. Have students write the words on separate paper.

1. **from** The letter is from my cousin.
2. **Sunday** Let's go to a movie on Sunday.
3. **money** Grandpa gave me some money.
4. **under** The worm is under the rock.
5. **nothing** There was nothing in the box.
6. **summer** It is hot in summer.
7. **does** A juggler does funny tricks.
8. **mother** My mother is a nurse.
9. **lunch** When will we eat lunch?
10. **month** I was born in the month of November.
11. **such** We had never seen such a strange house.
12. **front** Who sits in front of you?
13. **much** I feel much better.
14. **sun** The sun is shining.
15. **other** Give me the other pen.
16. **Monday** We start a new lesson each Monday.

Additional Words for Enrichment

The following words can be used to meet the needs of on-level and above-level students:
button   hundred   uncle   brother   honey   jungle

Letter Scramble   Unscramble the underlined letters to make a spelling word. Write the word on the line.

1. Kelly was at the tronf of the line. _____front_____
2. We hid the keys drune the mat. _____under_____
3. How much noemy is in your pocket? _____money_____
4. We had never seen chus a mess. _____such_____
5. We could see honnitg in the dark. _____nothing_____
6. When osde the bus come? _____does_____

Clues   Write the spelling word for each clue.

7. The first one is January. _____month_____
8. This day comes before Tuesday. _____Monday_____
9. This word is the opposite of *to*. _____from_____
10. When it shines, you feel warmer. _____sun_____
11. This day comes after Saturday. _____Sunday_____
12. This person has at least one son or daughter. _____mother_____
13. If you have this, you have a lot. _____much_____
14. This season contains June, July, and August. _____summer_____
15. This word means "different." _____other_____

Word Story   You probably use this spelling word every day. It comes from the old English word *nuncheon*, which meant "a light meal." Later *nuncheon* changed to *luncheon* and also meant "a thick piece." The spelling word names the meal you eat at noon. Write the word.

16. _____lunch_____

Family Tree: does   *Does* is a form of *do*. Think about how the *do* words are alike in spelling and meaning. Then add another *do* word to the tree. A sample answer is shown.

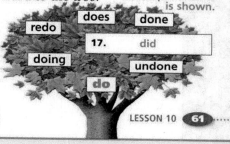

- redo
- does
- done
- 17. did
- doing
- undone
- do

LESSON 10   **61**

HOME ACTIVITY MASTER p. T243

Unit 2   Spelling at Home

Dear Family of ___,

During the next six weeks, your child will be learning to spell the following kinds of words:

- words with the short *e* vowel sound
- words with the long *e* vowel sound
- words with the short *u* vowel sound
- contractions

Here are some simple activities to do each week to help your child become a better speller.

Listening and Writing
Say the spelling words and have your child write them.

Spelling Strategy: Word Shape
If your child is unsure about the spelling of a word, ask your child to look at the correct spelling and to draw the shape of the word. Then have your child study the word shape. Tell your child that drawing a word's shape can help him or her remember how to spell it.

Games and Activities
Play Invisible Writing. Ask your child to choose some spelling words. Write the words on a piece of paper. Then, using a finger, take turns writing a word on each other's back. Be sure to say each letter and the word aloud during the invisible writing.

Have your child go on a word search. Have your child find and circle spelling words in a magazine or newspaper.

Using Spelling Words
Ask your child to write sentences that contain the spelling words. Then read the sentences with your child. Notice whether the sentences show that your child knows the meanings of the spelling words.

Lesson 7   More Words with Short e
Week of ___

best	better	cents	February
never	kept	sent	September
slept	them	then	Wednesday
when	friend	many	guess

Lesson 8   Words with Long e
Week of ___

meet	need	sleep	street
queen	wheel	free	sneeze
dream	each	meat	read
sea	team	please	people

Lesson 9   More Words with Long e
Week of ___

happy	funny	very	busy
sleepy	carry	sunny	every
family	penny	only	city
these	even	key	story

Lesson 10   Words with Short u
Week of ___

mother	front	month	money
from	other	nothing	Monday
such	summer	much	lunch
sun	under	Sunday	does

Lesson 11   Contractions
Week of ___

they'll	she'll	I'll	we'll
you'll	I've	we've	you've
they've	he's	she's	it's
I'd	you'd	they'd	I'm

Lesson 12   Unit 2 Review
Week of ___
Lesson 12 is a review of Lessons 7–11. Help your child practice all of the words from those lessons.

The highlighted area shows the Lesson 10 words, which students can share with family members. Spanish version available on page T244.

Proofreading Practice
- My muther cooked breakfast today. *(mother)*
- She is sutch a good cook! *(such)*

Meeting Individual Needs

ESOL

Spanish-speaking students may have difficulty recognizing the short *u* sound because it does not exist in Spanish. The letter *u* in Spanish is always pronounced /o͞o/. Make up sentences with the *u*-pattern lesson words. Write the sentences on the board and have students read them aloud. Then ask students to spell aloud and write each word that has the short *u* sound.

Day 2

Student Objectives
- To use meaning clues to identify and write lesson words
- To use etymology, meaning, and spelling to identify the word *lunch*
- To learn *do* words and analyze their spellings and meanings

Presenting the Page

Write the following Letter Scramble and Clues examples on the board and model identifying the answers:

- I want to eat my chuln. *(lunch)*
- This word is the opposite of *back*. *(front)*

For the Letter Scramble activity, remind students to use context clues in the sentence to help identify the scrambled words.

Word Story

Have students compare *nuncheon* and *luncheon* and guide them to conclude that *luncheon* was shortened to eventually become *lunch*. Explain that *luncheon* is still used today to describe lunch for a group of people.

Family Tree: do

Students should see that the *do* words all contain *do*. Point out that *does*, *done*, and *undone* contain the /ŭ/ sound spelled *oe* and *o*-consonant-*e*. Have students suggest a word that is the past tense of *do* but does not contain the word *do* (*did*). Then ask how adding *un*- to make *undone* changes the meaning of *done* (it means the opposite of *done*, or "not finished").

61

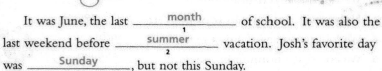

Student Objectives

- To use context to identify and write lesson words
- To identify the sequence of events
- To use context to identify each meaning of a multiple-meaning word

Presenting the Pages

Read the first two paragraphs of "Facing the Music" aloud. Then ask students to predict what will happen in the story. Write their predictions on the board. Continue reading the story aloud, stopping for students to write the missing words. Alternatively, have students complete the pages independently by silently reading the story and writing the missing words. Then have students take turns reading the completed story. Have students compare their predictions with the actual story events.

Meeting Individual Needs

Auditory Learners

A chant is a good mnemonic device for auditory learners. When students are having trouble with a particular word, suggest they make up a chant such as the following:

Under, under,
I can spell *under—*
U-n-d-e-r.

Facing the Music

It was June, the last _____month_____ of school. It was also the last weekend before _____summer_____ vacation. Josh's favorite day was _____Sunday_____, but not this Sunday.

On Saturday Josh found ten dollars in his jacket. He could not remember where the _____money_____ came _____from_____. But he knew how _____much_____ he wanted a compact disc, so he bought it with the money.

This morning he remembered how he got the money. The ten dollars was class money. The _____other_____ students had given him the money to buy a present for Mr. Farar, their music teacher. Josh didn't have any more money, and the compact disc had been on sale. He couldn't return it.

Josh was upset. His _____mother_____ asked what was wrong. "It's _____nothing_____," he told her. He couldn't bring himself to tell her about his mistake.

Then Petra called and asked, "How _____does_____ Mr. Farar's present look?"

Spelling Strategy

Memory Clue

Tell students that creating and using a memory clue can help them remember how to spell a word. Write the word *money* in a chart like the one shown. Explain that in one kind of memory clue, they can use a shorter word that is found inside a lesson word to help them remember how to spell the lesson word. Invite volunteers to find a shorter word within *money*, underline it, and write it. Then help students make up a memory clue containing both words to help them remember how to spell *money*. Do the same with *nothing* and *mother*.

Spelling Word	Shorter Word	Clue
money	one	one for the money
nothing	no	Nothing means "no thing."
mother	moth	Mother caught the moth.

"Well . . . ," Josh began.

"Remember to put a note on it. Don't forget all of our names."

Josh hung up the telephone. Petra's words had given him a great idea. He found his modeling clay ___under___ 11 his bed. He formed the clay into an egg shape and stuck a stick into it. Josh dried the whole thing outside in the ___sun___ 12. Then he painted it silver. When the paint was dry, he added all the students' names.

By ___Monday___ 13 morning all the names were dry. Josh wrapped the gift and took it to school. At noon he went to ___lunch___ 14. Petra asked, "Where are the present and the note?"

"You'll see," said Josh.

Mr. Farar opened his gift in ___front___ 15 of the class. "Wow! A compact disc and a silver music note with your names on it!" he exclaimed. "This note took ___such___ 16 a lot of work. Thank you! It's one note I'll hold forever!"

LESSON 10 **63**

Word list (notepad):
from
Sunday
money
under
nothing
summer
does
mother
lunch
month
such
front
much
sun
other
Monday

ACTIVITY MASTER p. T261

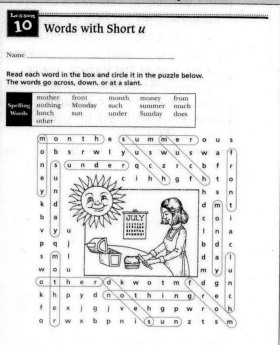

Lesson 10 Words with Short *u*

Name _____

Read each word in the box and circle it in the puzzle below. The words go across, down, or at a slant.

Spelling Words	mother	front	month	money	from
	nothing	Monday	such	summer	much
	lunch	sun	under	Sunday	does
	other				

ADDITIONAL PRACTICE

You may wish to copy and distribute the Activity Master on page T261 as additional practice for Lesson 10.

Proofreading Practice
- The wind is blowing frum that direction. (*from*)
- The sunn is bright today! (*sun*)

Reading Comprehension

After students have completed the pages, help them identify the sequence of events in the first two paragraphs by having them circle the word *Sunday* in the first paragraph and *Saturday* in the second paragraph. Then have students tell the events in the story in the order in which they really happened (On Saturday, Josh spends the money; on Sunday he remembers that he was supposed to buy a gift with it).

Then invite volunteers to give different meanings for the word *note* ("a written message," "a musical symbol," or "to notice"). Ask students to define *note* in each of the five sentences in which it is used on page 63.

Cooperative Learning Activity

Have pairs of students divide the lesson words evenly between them and write a sentence for each word, leaving a blank line for each letter in the word. Have them trade papers, complete the sentences, and check each other's work. If possible, have students compare their performance on this midweek activity with that on the pretest. Guide them in noting the words that need more study.

63

Day 4

Student Objectives

- To write an expository paragraph, using lesson words
- To proofread an e-mail for spelling, capitalization, and punctuation

Presenting the Page

Review with students the gift that Josh makes in "Facing the Music" on pages 62–63. Have students think of things they can make for someone else. Prompt them by asking who the present might be for, what kinds of gifts the person likes or needs, and what kinds of things they know how to make. Encourage students to look at the words in the spelling list and to use those words in their paragraph.

To assist students with the Proofreading activity, have a volunteer read the directions and e-mail aloud. Then have students complete the activity independently and work with a partner to check their work.

Meeting Individual Needs

ESOL

Although /ŭ/ occurs in some Asian languages, some speakers of Asian languages may substitute /o͞o/ for /ŭ/ in spoken English and write *oo* for *u*. Write sentences that contain /ŭ/ words on the board. Have students read the sentences and trace the /ŭ/ words with a finger. Examples:

We have *fun* in the *sun*.
Let's eat *lunch under* the tree.

---

from
Sunday
money
under
nothing
summer
does
mother
lunch
month
such
front
much
sun
other
Monday

Write to the Point

Josh made a gift for Mr. Farar out of clay. Think of a gift you can make out of things you have at home or school. Then write a paragraph telling what the gift is and how to make it. Try to use spelling words from this lesson. Paragraphs will vary.

Proofreading

Proofread the e-mail message below. Use proofreading marks to correct five spelling mistakes, three capitalization mistakes, and two punctuation mistakes.

Use the strategies on page 7 when you are not sure how to spell a word.

Proofreading Marks
○ spell correctly
≡ capitalize
? add question mark

e-mail

Address Book | Attachment | Check Spelling | Send | Save Draft | Cancel

Dear Grandpa,

      money
Thank you for the soccer ball and mony you gave

    Monday Summer
me for my birthday on Munday. Somer begins in only

one more month. Can you believe it? I am going to play

    front
soccer in our frunt yard every day. each sunday I will

come to your house. We can sit in the sun and eat

lunch
lonch. We'll have fun! does that sound good to you?

Josh

64 UNIT 2

Proofreading Practice
- That pie deos look good! *(does)*
- I do not have enough muney to buy it. *(money)*

Correcting Common Errors

The words *front* and *from* are sometimes misspelled as *frunt* and *frum* because *u* is the more common spelling for /ŭ/. Suggest that students making this error write these words several times, underlining the *o* and adding other lesson words with the same *o* spelling of /ŭ/.

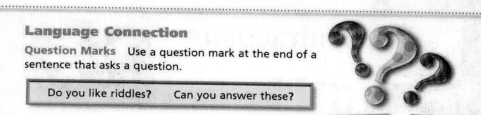

Language Connection

Question Marks Use a question mark at the end of a sentence that asks a question.

| Do you like riddles? Can you answer these? |

Write each riddle correctly. Then choose one of the answers in the boxes and write it in the space provided.

| your teeth | your lap |

| the letter m |

1. What comes once in a month, twice in a moment, but never in a hundred years

   What comes once in a month, twice in a moment, but never

   in a hundred years?

   Answer: _the letter m_

2. What do you lose whenever you stand up

   What do you lose whenever you stand up?

   Answer: _your lap_

3. What can you put into the apple pie you have for lunch

   What can you put into the apple pie you have for lunch?

   Answer: _your teeth_

Challenge Yourself

Write the Challenge Word for each clue. Check the Spelling Dictionary to see if you are right. Then use separate paper to write sentences showing that you understand the meaning of each Challenge Word. Sentences will vary.

| Challenge Words |
| huddle   buzzard |
| somebody frontier |

4. We use this word to talk about a person we don't know. _somebody_

5. This is a large bird with a beak. _buzzard_

6. This is a place where few people live. _frontier_

7. Football players make one of these to plan their next move. _huddle_

LESSON 10 **65**

Posttest

Dictate the following sentences. Have students use separate paper to write the sentences and underline the lesson words.

1. There is <u>nothing</u> <u>under</u> the bed.
2. Is this my <u>lunch</u> <u>money</u>?
3. I will study on <u>Sunday</u> and <u>Monday</u>.
4. I love the <u>summer</u> <u>sun</u>!
5. Mom <u>does</u> lots of cooking.
6. This has been <u>such</u> a nice <u>month</u>!
7. His <u>mother</u> is at the <u>front</u> door.
8. We have so <u>much</u> work to do!
9. Is this my <u>other</u> hat?
10. This is the letter <u>from</u> my dad.

Enrichment Activity

Have students work independently to find and cut out /ŭ/ words in magazines or newspapers. Have them make a column chart with headings showing the different spellings of /ŭ/. Have students glue the words under the correct headings. Encourage above-level students to look for words with patterns other than those on page 60 and to create columns for those words in the chart. Ask volunteers to share words they have found.

Student Objectives

- To write questions containing lesson words
- To use a question mark at the end of questions
- To study the spellings and meanings of the Challenge Words
- To take a posttest on the lesson words

Presenting the Page

Ask students if they like to solve riddles. Call on volunteers to name common "question" words used to begin riddles (*who, what, when, where, why*). Review the use of question marks at the end of questions. Then have students read the example questions and complete the page.

Challenge Yourself

To introduce the Challenge Words, write them on the board and have students tell you how to divide *huddle, buzzard,* and *frontier* into syllables (divide between the consonants in the VCCV pattern). Then identify the compound word *somebody* and help students divide first between the two words and then between the two syllables in *body.*

Next, have students refer to page 60 and have them review the short *u* spelling patterns featured in this lesson. Ask students to identify the short *u* spelling pattern in each of the Challenge Words (*huddle* and *buzzard* both have the *u* pattern, and *frontier* and *somebody* have the *o* pattern).

Posttest

Use the posttest on this page to assess students' ability to spell the lesson words.

65

Contractions

Lesson 11 Contractions

they'll

Day 1

Student Objectives

- To take a pretest on the lesson words
- To understand the function of the apostrophe in contractions
- To sort and write contractions according to the second of the two words from which they are made

Pretest

Use the pretest on this page to assess students' ability to spell the lesson words.

Study Steps Have students use the study steps on page 6 to study any words they misspell in the pretest.

You may wish to duplicate and send home the Home Activity Master on pages T243–T244.

Presenting the Page

Introducing Contractions Ask students to tell how *I will* and *I'll* are alike and different. Guide students to conclude that *I'll* is a contraction and that a contraction is two words that have been combined and shortened to form one word. Ask what punctuation mark is used in a contraction (an apostrophe). Tell students that the apostrophe usually comes after the first word of the contraction and that it indicates that one or more letters have been left out of the second word.

Pronunciation Focus Point out that there are no vowel sounds after the apostrophe in contractions, although there may be a silent *e*.

Consonant Focus Point out that *'d* can stand for both *would* and *had* and that *'s* can stand for both *is* and *has*. Have students identify the reason why one letter can stand for two words (both words end with the same letter).

66

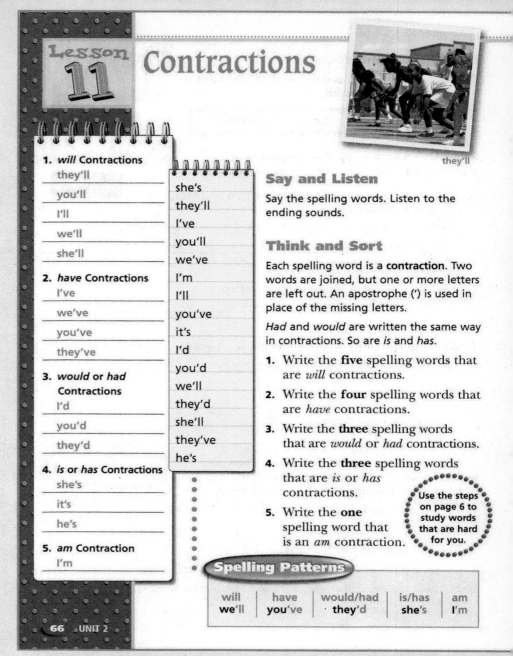

1. will Contractions
they'll
you'll
I'll
we'll
she'll

2. have Contractions
I've
we've
you've
they've

3. would or had Contractions
I'd
you'd
they'd

4. is or has Contractions
she's
it's
he's

5. am Contraction
I'm

she's
they'll
I've
you'll
we've
I'm
I'll
you've
it's
I'd
you'd
we'll
they'd
she'll
they've
he's

66 UNIT 2

Say and Listen

Say the spelling words. Listen to the ending sounds.

Think and Sort

Each spelling word is a **contraction**. Two words are joined, but one or more letters are left out. An apostrophe (') is used in place of the missing letters.

Had and *would* are written the same way in contractions. So are *is* and *has*.

1. Write the **five** spelling words that are *will* contractions.

2. Write the **four** spelling words that are *have* contractions.

3. Write the **three** spelling words that are *would* or *had* contractions.

4. Write the **three** spelling words that are *is* or *has* contractions.

5. Write the **one** spelling word that is an *am* contraction.

Use the steps on page 6 to study words that are hard for you.

Spelling Patterns

will	have	would/had	is/has	am
we'll	you've	they'd	she's	I'm

Pretest

Say each lesson word, read the sentence, and then repeat the word. Have students write the words on separate paper.

1. **she's** She says <u>she's</u> already met me.
2. **they'll** <u>They'll</u> be here later.
3. **I've** <u>I've</u> got a lot to learn.
4. **you'll** <u>You'll</u> know these words soon.
5. **we've** <u>We've</u> been to the beach.
6. **I'm** <u>I'm</u> glad to see you.
7. **I'll** Yes, <u>I'll</u> come to the party.
8. **you've** I heard that <u>you've</u> learned to dance.
9. **it's** <u>It's</u> time to play.
10. **I'd** <u>I'd</u> like to go swimming.
11. **you'd** <u>You'd</u> better study.
12. **we'll** <u>We'll</u> have to wait here.
13. **they'd** They said <u>they'd</u> be here.
14. **she'll** Do you think that <u>she'll</u> go?
15. **they've** <u>They've</u> been to the store.
16. **he's** I think <u>he's</u> in his room.

Additional Words for Enrichment

The following words can be used to meet the needs of on-level and above-level students:

we're   you're   they're   let's   that's   he'd

Language Connection

Contractions At least one letter and sound are missing from every contraction. An apostrophe (') shows where the letter or letters have been left out. For example, in the contraction *we've*, the apostrophe shows that the letters *ha* have been left out.

> I'm = I am   we've = we have

Write the contraction for each pair of words. Then write the letter or letters that are left out.

		Contraction	Letter or Letters Left Out
1.	I will	I'll	wi
2.	he is	he's	i
3.	it is	it's	i
4.	they have	they've	ha
5.	you had	you'd	ha
6.	I am	I'm	a
7.	you would	you'd	woul
8.	she has	she's	ha

⭐ Challenge Yourself

Use the Spelling Dictionary to look up each Challenge Word. Then answer the questions. Use separate paper to write sentences showing that you understand the meaning of each Challenge Word.
Sentences will vary.

Challenge Words
would've   could've
who'll   where'd

9. Is **would've** a contraction for *would have*? ___yes___

10. Is **could've** a contraction for *could give*? ___no___

11. Is **who'll** a contraction for *who all*? ___no___

12. Is **where'd** a contraction for *where did*? ___yes___

LESSON 11 **71**

Posttest

Dictate the following sentences. Have students use separate paper to write the sentences and underline the lesson words.

1. I've got to go, or I'll be late.
2. She's sure that she'll be able to help.
3. I'd like to know if they'll be here on time.
4. We'll be ready when it's time to go.
5. I'm sure you'll have a good trip.
6. They'd go with you if you'd ask them to.
7. He's glad that we've got the best team.
8. They've been here as long as you've been here.

Enrichment Activity

Find a comic strip in a newspaper or magazine. Cover the words in the speech bubbles and then make enough copies for each student. Have students work independently to use at least four lesson words to supply words for the speech bubbles.

Student Objectives
- To analyze contractions and identify letters omitted from them
- To study the spellings and meanings of the Challenge Words
- To take a posttest on the lesson words

Presenting the Page

Review with students that a contraction is a shortened form of two words and that an apostrophe takes the place of some letters that have been omitted. Have students look at the examples *I'm* and *we've*. Guide them to identify the missing letters (*a* for *I'm* and *ha* for *we've*).

⭐ Challenge Yourself

To introduce the Challenge Words, write them on the board and pronounce the words for students. Ask students to identify the letters that have been replaced by an apostrophe (the apostrophes in *could've* and *would've* replace the *ha* from *have*, the apostrophe in *who'll* replaces the *wi* from *will*, and the apostrophe in *where'd* replaces the *di* from *did*). Then have students complete the activity independently.

Posttest

Use the posttest on this page to assess students' ability to spell the lesson words.

Lesson 12

Unit 2 Review
Lessons 7–11

Student Objectives
- To take a pretest on the lesson words

Pretest

Use the pretest on this page to assess students' ability to spell the lesson words.

 Have students use the study steps on page 6 to study any words they misspell in the pretest.

 You may wish to duplicate and send home the Home Activity Master on pages T243–T244.

Meeting Individual Needs

Kinesthetic Learners
To give kinesthetic learners practice spelling the review words, give partners letter tiles and several counters. Have partners take turns putting one or more counters in place of the letters that spell the short *e*, long *e*, or short *u* sound. The other partner should replace the counters with letter tiles to show the correct spelling. Then that partner should say and spell the word aloud.

Lesson 12

Unit 2 Review
Lessons 7–11

Use the steps on page 6 to study words that are hard for you.

7

Wednesday
February
friend
many
guess

More Words with Short e
Write the spelling word that completes each analogy.

1. *Pal* is to _____friend_____ as *chilly* is to *cold*.
2. *Saturday* is to *end* as _____Wednesday_____ is to *middle*.
3. *Know* is to *understand* as *suppose* is to _____guess_____.
4. *Little* is to *few* as *much* is to _____many_____.
5. *Monday* is to *day* as _____February_____ is to *month*.

8

queen
meet
please
team
people

Words with Long e
Write the spelling word that belongs in each group.

6. duchess   princess   ___queen___
7. group   club   ___team___
8. persons   humans   ___people___
9. touch   join   ___meet___
10. delight   cheer   ___please___

9

even
every
family
these
key

More Words with Long e
Write the spelling word for each clue.

11. This has parents and children. ___family___
12. If a floor is flat, it is this. ___even___
13. You can use this word instead of *each*. ___every___

72 UNIT 2

Pretest

Say each lesson word, read the sentence, then repeat the word. Have students write the words on separate paper.

1. **Wednesday** Today is Wednesday.
2. **February** February comes after March.
3. **friend** I share with my friend.
4. **many** Dad has many hats.
5. **guess** Let me guess the answer.
6. **queen** The queen sat by the king.
7. **meet** Mom wants to meet the coach.

8. **please** Please open the door.
9. **team** I am on the hockey team.
10. **people** Lots of people have dogs.
11. **even** Cut the pie into even pieces.
12. **every** I eat breakfast every morning.
13. **family** My family is here.
14. **these** Are these pens mine?
15. **key** Where is the door key?
16. **lunch** I take my lunch to school.
17. **such** It was such a warm night!

18. **other** What is in your other hand?
19. **month** Which month do you like best?
20. **does** Dad does a good job.
21. **she'll** I hope she'll come.
22. **you've** I hear that you've moved.
23. **they'd** The team said that they'd win.
24. **it's** I know it's raining.
25. **I'm** I'm as happy as a lark.

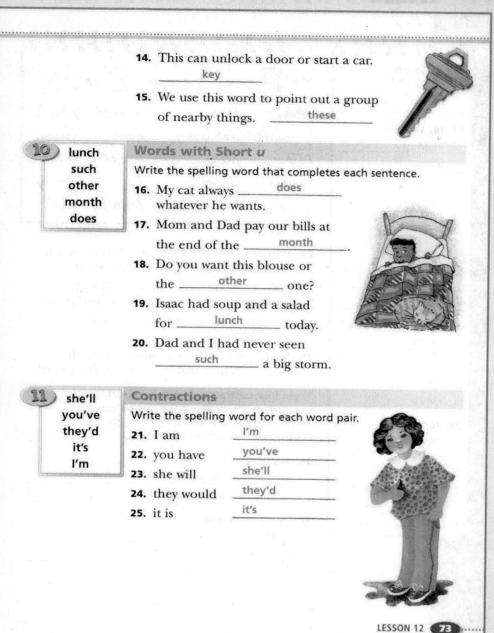

14. This can unlock a door or start a car.
   <u>key</u>

15. We use this word to point out a group of nearby things. <u>these</u>

10 Words with Short u

**lunch
such
other
month
does**

Write the spelling word that completes each sentence.

16. My cat always <u>does</u> whatever he wants.

17. Mom and Dad pay our bills at the end of the <u>month</u>.

18. Do you want this blouse or the <u>other</u> one?

19. Isaac had soup and a salad for <u>lunch</u> today.

20. Dad and I had never seen <u>such</u> a big storm.

11 Contractions

**she'll
you've
they'd
it's
I'm**

Write the spelling word for each word pair.

21. I am   <u>I'm</u>
22. you have   <u>you've</u>
23. she will   <u>she'll</u>
24. they would <u>they'd</u>
25. it is   <u>it's</u>

LESSON 12   **73**

Student Objectives

- To review the e, ie, a, and ue spellings of the /ĕ/ sound
- To review the ee, ea, and eo spellings of the /ē/ sound
- To review the e, y, e-consonant-e, and ey spellings of the /ē/ sound
- To review the u, o, and oe spellings of the /ŭ/ sound
- To review spelling patterns in contractions
- To use meaning clues to identify and write lesson words

Presenting the Pages

Lessons 7–9 Have volunteers read the review words for Lessons 7–9 aloud. Review with students the short e and long e spelling patterns represented in the review words— e, ie, a, and ue for /ĕ/; ee, ea, eo, e, y, e-consonant-e, and ey for /ē/.

Lesson 10 Have volunteers read the Lesson 10 review words aloud. Review with students the u, o, and oe spelling patterns for /ŭ/.

Lesson 11 Have volunteers read the review words for Lesson 11 aloud. Have students identify the spelling pattern on page 66 that each review word illustrates.

REVIEW TEST MASTER, pp. T285–T286

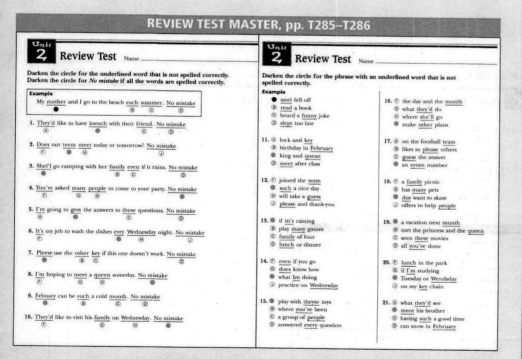

Test-Taking Strategies

Read the directions for the Review Test Master aloud and talk with students about the tasks on the test. Guide students to understand that the task on each page is the same—to identify misspelled words. Suggest that students scan each sentence or line, focusing only on the spelling of the underlined words unless they aren't sure what the word is, in which case they should read the sentence to determine the word.

Proofreading Practice

- Those books are about dogs, and theze are about cats. *(these)*
- I have meny books about pets. *(many)*

73

Student Objectives
- To sort lesson words according to vowel sound
- To compare sorted contractions

Presenting the Page

Point out that four of the words have both /ĕ/ and /ē/. Have a volunteer identify one of the words (*February*, *Wednesday*, *many*, or *every*) and the letters that spell /ĕ/ and /ē/.

Meeting Individual Needs

ESOL

To give speakers of other languages additional practice with the Review Sort words, have partners write the words on large sticky notes. Give partners four large sheets of construction paper and have them label the sheets *Short* e, *Long* e, *Both Short* e and *Long* e, and *Short* u. Then have partners sort the words, attaching each note to the appropriate sheet.

Proofreading Practice
- Lots of poeple ran the race. *(people)*
- You'v done well to finish first. *(you've)*

---

26. /ĕ/ Words

guess
friend

27. /ē/ Words

meet
team
please
queen
key
family
people
these
she'll

28. /ĕ/ and /ē/ Words

February
Wednesday
many
every

29. /ŭ/ Words

does
other
month
such
lunch

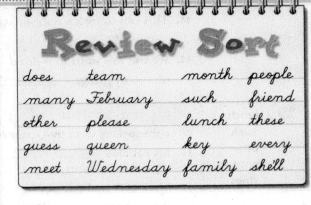

Review Sort

does	team	month	people
many	February	such	friend
other	please	lunch	these
guess	queen	key	every
meet	Wednesday	family	she'll

26. Write the **two** short e words. Circle the letter or letters that spell /ĕ/ in each word.

27. Write the **nine** long e words. Circle the letter or letters that spell /ē/ in each word.

28. Write the **four** words that have both /ĕ/ and /ē/.

29. Write the **five** short u words. Circle the letter or letters that spell /ŭ/ in each word.

These four contractions have been sorted into two groups. Think about the second word in each contraction. Then explain how the contractions in each group are alike.

29. it's   I'm

One letter is left out of the second word of each contraction.

30. she'll   they'd

More than one letter is left out of the second word of each contraction.

WRITER'S WORKSHOP MASTERS, pp. T295–T296, T298

The Writing Process   Name _____

1 Prewriting · Plan your writing.
- Make sure you know what your writing task is.
- Identify the audience and the purpose for writing.
- Choose a topic.
- Gather and write ideas about the topic.
- Organize your ideas.

2 Writing · Write a first draft.
- Use your plan to put your ideas in writing.
- Don't worry about mistakes now.
- Add any new ideas you think of while writing.
- Leave room between lines so that you can make changes later.

3 Revising · Look for ways to improve what you have written.
- Make sure your writing fits the audience and purpose for writing.
- Look for places that need more ideas or details.
- Take out sentences that don't belong.
- Find places where more colorful or exact words can be used.
- Make sure that your sentences are complete.
- Write and revise until you are happy with your writing.

4 Proofreading · Review your work for errors.
- Make sure you have indented each paragraph.
- Check to see that you have used words correctly.
- Check your capitalization.
- Check to see that you have used periods, question marks, commas, and other punctuation marks correctly.
- Look at the spelling of each word. Circle words you are not sure you have spelled correctly. Check their spelling.

5 Publishing · Share what you have written.
- Make a clean final draft.
- Read it to the class or a friend.
- Add pictures or make a poster to go with it.
- Make a recording of your writing.

✓ Proofreading Checklist   Name _____

You can use the questions below as a checklist to proofread your writing.
- ☐ Have I indented each paragraph?
- ☐ Have I used words correctly in every sentence?
- ☐ Have I capitalized the first word in each sentence?
- ☐ Have I capitalized all proper names?
- ☐ Have I ended each sentence with a period, question mark, or exclamation point?
- ☐ Have I spelled each word correctly?

The chart below shows some proofreading marks and how to use them.

Mark	Meaning	Example
◯	spell correctly	I liok dogs.
⊙	add period	They are my favorite kind of pet⊙
?	add question mark	What kind of pet do you have?
≡	capitalize	My dog's name is scooter.
℘	take out	He likes to to run and play.
¶	indent paragraph	¶ I love my dog, Scooter. He is the best pet I have ever had. Every morning he wakes me with a bark. Every night he sleeps with me.
᭝ ᭝	add quotation marks	You are my best friend, I tell him.

Story Map   Name _____   Date _____

Beginning

Middle

End

Writer's Workshop

A Narrative

A narrative is a story. Every good story has a beginning, a middle, and an end. In the beginning of a story, writers tell who or what the story is about. They often tell where and when the story takes place. Here is the beginning of Leo's story about an unusual giraffe.

> **The Mystery of the Talking Giraffe**
> Ryan looked at Jan. "Did you hear what I heard?" he asked in a trembling voice. Jan didn't answer. She just kept staring at the giraffe. Ryan and Jan lived a block from the Davis City Zoo. They came early every Friday morning, all summer long. The zoo workers knew them by name. Even the animals seemed to recognize them. Still, none of the animals had ever said hello to them before.

Prewriting   To write his narrative, Leo followed the steps in the writing process. After he decided on a topic, he completed a story map. The map helped him decide what would happen at the beginning, middle, and end of his narrative. Leo's story map is shown here. Study what Leo did.

Beginning
Ryan and Jan hear a giraffe say hello.

Middle
They see a wire and speaker.

End
They discover the zookeeper's trick.

It's Your Turn!

Write your own narrative. It can be a mystery like Leo's, an adventure story, or any kind of story you choose. After you have decided on your topic, make a story map. Then follow the other steps in the writing process — writing, revising, proofreading, and publishing. Try to use spelling words from this lesson in your narrative.
Narratives will vary.

LESSON 12   75

Writer's Workshop Scoring Rubric: Narrative

SCORE 3
Narrative has a clear beginning, middle, and end. Most events and ideas are well developed. Writing is coherent and contains a minimum of sentence-structure, usage, mechanics, and spelling errors.

SCORE 2
Narrative has a beginning, middle, and end, but one or more are not clear or are weak. Some events and ideas are not thoroughly developed. Writing has a degree of coherence but contains some sentence-structure, usage, mechanics, and spelling errors.

SCORE 1
Narrative is incomplete or unclear. Few or no events and ideas are developed. Writing has minimal or no coherence and contains many sentence-structure, usage, mechanics, and spelling errors.

Evaluating Students' Writing

The scoring rubric is based on standards for idea development, organization, coherence, sentence structure, usage, mechanics, and spelling. You may wish to share the rubric with students before they write their description.

The *Steck-Vaughn Writer's Dictionary, Intermediate Level*, provides writers with a place to write words they want to remember.

Presenting the Page

Read the first paragraph and the excerpt from "The Mystery of the Talking Giraffe" with students. Invite them to compare the model with the Beginning section of the story map. Point out that Leo used the idea in the Beginning section of the story map but that he added details and dialogue to make it more interesting.

You may wish to copy and distribute the Writer's Workshop Masters on pages T295–T296 and T298 for students to use as they write their narrative.

Day 5

Student Objective
- To take a posttest on the lesson words

Posttest Options

Use the posttest on this page or the Review Test Master on pages T285–T286 to assess students' ability to spell the lesson words.

Posttest

Dictate the following sentences. Have students write the sentences and underline the lesson words.

1. <u>Many</u> <u>people</u> in my <u>family</u> are tall.
2. Why <u>does</u> the <u>queen</u> wear <u>such</u> a big crown?
3. I think <u>it's</u> time to <u>meet</u> the <u>team</u>.
4. She gave the <u>key</u> to her <u>friend</u>.
5. Will you <u>please</u> take <u>these</u> boxes?
6. <u>They'd</u> help you <u>even</u> if it took all <u>month</u>.
7. I <u>guess</u> <u>you've</u> been to the store.
8. We will eat <u>lunch</u> here on the first <u>Wednesday</u> in <u>February</u>.
9. The sun came out <u>every</u> <u>other</u> day.
10. <u>I'm</u> not sure if <u>she'll</u> come with us.

More Words with Short *u*

Student Objectives
- To take a pretest on the lesson words
- To spell the lesson words aloud
- To sort and write the lesson words according to the spelling patterns *u*, *o*, and *o*-consonant-*e*

Pretest

Use the pretest on this page to assess students' ability to spell the lesson words.

Have students use the study steps on page 6 to study any words they misspell in the pretest.

You may wish to duplicate and send home the Home Activity Master on pages T245–T246.

Presenting the Page

Introducing the Short *u* Sound
Say each of the following word pairs and ask students to raise their hand when they hear a word with the short *u* sound:

butter–better	mist–*must*
none–nine	same–*some*

As students prepare to sort the words, point out that /ŭ/ is most often spelled *u* but is spelled *o* or *o*-consonant-*e* in some words we often use.

Pronunciation Focus Students should recognize that *one* and *won* are pronounced the same way, /wŭn/, but are spelled differently. Have students identify the letter or letters that spell /ŭ/ in each word (*o*-consonant-*e* and *o*, respectively). Follow a similar procedure for the words *some* and *sum*.

Consonant Focus Write *butter*, *supper*, and *number* on the board. Help students identify the VCCV pattern in each word and then divide the word into syllables.

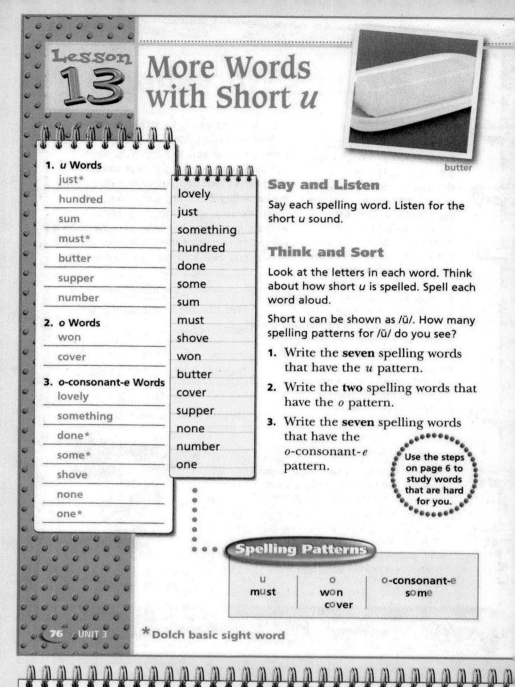

butter

1. *u* Words
just*
hundred
sum
must*
butter
supper
number

2. *o* Words
won
cover

3. *o*-consonant-*e* Words
lovely
something
done*
some*
shove
none
one*

lovely
just
something
hundred
done
some
sum
must
shove
won
butter
cover
supper
none
number
one

Say and Listen
Say each spelling word. Listen for the short *u* sound.

Think and Sort
Look at the letters in each word. Think about how short *u* is spelled. Spell each word aloud.

Short *u* can be shown as /ŭ/. How many spelling patterns for /ŭ/ do you see?

1. Write the **seven** spelling words that have the *u* pattern.
2. Write the **two** spelling words that have the *o* pattern.
3. Write the **seven** spelling words that have the *o*-consonant-*e* pattern.

Use the steps on page 6 to study words that are hard for you.

Spelling Patterns

u	o	o-consonant-e
m**u**st	w**o**n c**o**ver	s**o**me

76 UNIT 3

*Dolch basic sight word

Pretest

Say each lesson word, read the sentence, and then repeat the word. Have students write the words on separate paper.

1. **lovely** The roses are <u>lovely</u>.
2. **just** The king is a <u>just</u> ruler.
3. **something** I heard <u>something</u> drop.
4. **hundred** A <u>hundred</u> pennies are equal to a dollar.
5. **done** What have you <u>done</u>?
6. **some** She put <u>some</u> books on the table.
7. **sum** The <u>sum</u> of six and one is seven.
8. **must** I <u>must</u> leave now.
9. **shove** You can <u>shove</u> the boxes out of the way.
10. **won** We <u>won</u> the game.
11. **butter** Do you want <u>butter</u> on your toast?
12. **cover** Please <u>cover</u> the pan.
13. **supper** We ate <u>supper</u> early.
14. **none** She ate <u>none</u> of the grapes.
15. **number** What is your phone <u>number</u>?
16. **one** I have <u>one</u> apple.

Additional Words for Enrichment

The following words can be used to meet the needs of on-level and above-level students:
crumb   uncle   suddenly   wonder   become   tongue

Definitions Write the spelling word for each definition. Use the Spelling Dictionary if you need to.

1. gained a victory — won
2. to put or lay over — cover
3. a particular thing that is not named — something
4. a certain number of — some
5. the answer for an addition problem — sum
6. a number, written 1 — one
7. ten groups of ten — hundred
8. will have to — must
9. amount — number
10. not any — none

Synonyms Complete each sentence by writing the spelling word that is a synonym for the underlined word.

11. Tan's work will soon be finished. — done
12. Tasha is wearing a beautiful scarf. — lovely
13. I'll push Mother's surprise in the closet. — shove
14. No one could argue with the fair law. — just
15. Kevin ate fish and rice for dinner. — supper

Word Story Long ago the Greek language had the word *boutyron*. *Bous* meant "cow." *Tyros* meant "cheese." The first English spelling of the word was *butere*. Write the spelling that we use today.

16. ___butter___

Family Tree: *cover* Think about how the *cover* words are alike in spelling and meaning. Then add another *cover* word to the tree. A sample answer is shown.

- covered
- covering
- 17. uncover
- discover
- covers
- cover

LESSON 13 77

HOME ACTIVITY MASTER p. T245

Unit 3 Spelling at Home

Dear Family of _____,
During the next six weeks, your child will be learning to spell the following kinds of words:

- words with the short u vowel sound
- words with the short i vowel sound
- words with the long i vowel sound
- words with -ed or -ing

Here are some simple activities to do each week to help your child become a better speller.

Listening and Writing
Say the spelling words and have your child write them.

Spelling Strategy: Sounds and Letters
If your child is unsure about the spelling of a word, have your child say the following kinds of words to himself or herself. Tell your child to close his or her eyes and try to picture the way the word is spelled. Help your child think about the spelling by asking questions such as *Does it have more letters than sounds? What letter pair spells a single sound?* Then have your child write the word on a piece of paper. Check the word's spelling in the list at right or in a dictionary.

Games and Activities
Play Recorded Spellings. Choose some of the spelling words. Call each word out to your child. Using a tape recorder, have your child record himself or herself saying the word and spelling it. Play the recording back and have your child check the words.
Write the letters of the alphabet on index cards. Create five index cards for each vowel and two index cards for each consonant. Have your child use the alphabet cards to practice spelling words.

Using Spelling Words
Ask your child to write sentences that contain the spelling words. Then read the sentences with your child. Notice whether the sentences show that your child knows the meanings of the spelling words.

Lesson 13 More Words with Short u
Week of _____
won   lovely   done   something
shove some   one   hundred
none   cover   must   number
sum   butter   just   supper

Lesson 14 Words with Short i
Week of _____
think   winter   been   December
fill   little   thing   spring
lick   river   which   pretty
dish   begin   build   children

Lesson 15 Words with Long i
Week of _____
line   drive   inside   nice
shine   while   size   miles
write   mine   alike   times
white   tiny   fly   eyes

Lesson 16 More Words with Long i
Week of _____
Friday   kind   child   mind
behind   high   right   light
night   by   cry   sky
try   why   fly   buy

Lesson 17 Words with -ed or -ing
Week of _____
wished   asked   rained   dreamed
handed   painted   filled   subtracted
thanked   waited   reading   sleeping
meeting   ending   guessing   laughing

Lesson 18 Unit 3 Review
Week of _____
Lesson 18 is a review of Lessons 13–17. Help your child practice all of the words from those lessons.

The highlighted area shows the Lesson 13 words, which students can share with family members. Spanish version available on page T246.

Proofreading Practice
- Do not push or shuve. (*shove*)
- The clerk will call your nomber. (*number*)

Meeting Individual Needs

ESOL
Some Spanish-speaking students may need extra practice with the sound and spellings of short *u*, because Spanish contains only the /oo/ sound, as in *noon*, for the letter *u*. Have these students practice each lesson word by saying the word and then spelling it aloud as they write it.

Day 2

Student Objectives
- To use meaning clues to identify and write lesson words
- To use etymology, spelling, and meaning to identify the word *butter*
- To learn *cover* words and analyze their spellings and meanings

Presenting the Page

Write the following Definitions and Synonyms examples on the board and model identifying the answers. For the Synonyms item, point out to students that they should look for a lesson word that means the same as the underlined word.

- a yellow fat made from cream (*butter*)
- What total did you get when you added the numbers? (*sum*)

Word Story

The Greek word *boutyron* became *butyru* in Latin. The word then became *butere* in Old English. Invite students to compare the spellings for *butter* and *butere*.

Family Tree: *cover*

Students should see that the *cover* words all contain *cover*. Have students explore the meanings of the *cover* words by locating the meanings in a dictionary, writing the findings on the board, and discussing how the meanings are alike and different. Point out the change in meaning when *dis-* is added to create *discover*. Explain to students that knowing how to spell *cover* will help them spell related words.

Day 3

Student Objectives
- To use context to identify and write lesson words
- To identify a character's feelings

Presenting the Pages

Invite volunteers to read the story aloud. Tell them to pause for the missing lesson words so that they and their classmates can write them on the pages. Alternatively, have students complete the pages independently by silently reading the story and writing the missing words. Then have students take turns reading the completed story.

Discuss with students the meanings of the phrases "horse show" and "jumping course" in the story. Explain that a horse show is a kind of performance or competition. As it is used in this story, "jumping course" refers to the area on which the jumping contest in a horse show takes place.

Meeting Individual Needs

Kinesthetic Learners
To help kinesthetic learners practice the spelling patterns, have them copy each lesson word onto an index card or paper strip and prepare three paper bags labeled *u*, *o*, and *o*-consonant-*e*. Have students take turns sorting the word cards by short *u* spelling pattern. Suggest that they say and spell the word on the card and then drop the card into the appropriate bag.

Use each spelling word once to complete the story.

The First Horse Show

Simon rubbed his eyes and then looked out his bedroom window.

"What a _____lovely_____ day," he thought.
1

"Simon, you _____must_____ get up now. We will be late for the
2
show if you don't," his father called. "We've got a long way to drive, and we

won't be back until it's time for _____supper_____."
3

Simon began to feel funny. It felt as though _____something_____ was
4

caught in his throat. He heard his father walking toward his room. He

pulled the blanket up to _____cover_____ his head.
5

"Simon, why aren't you up yet?" his father asked from the door.

"I _____just_____ don't think I can do it," Simon replied.
6

"Sure you can," his father said. He smiled and gave Simon a gentle

_____shove_____. "Everyone is scared before a show. Even after a
7

_____hundred_____ shows, you'll still feel that way."
8

Spelling Strategy

Memory Clue
Remind students that they can use a memory clue to help them remember how to spell a troublesome word. Write the word *lovely* in a chart like the one shown. Explain that in one kind of memory clue, they can use a shorter word that is found inside the troublesome word to help them remember how to spell the word. Invite volunteers to find the shorter word within *lovely*, underline it, and write it. Then help students make up a memory clue that includes the shorter word to help them remember how to spell *lovely*. Do the same with and *none* and *cover*, guiding students to find each shorter word and create a clue for it.

Spelling Word	Shorter Word	Clue
lovely	love	We love lovely things.
none	one	You can find one in none.
cover	over	Put a cover over the pan.

Suggest to students that they try the memory clue strategy with any long word that is hard to remember.

Dad could always get Simon going. Simon dressed, grabbed a piece of warm toast, and spread some _____butter_____ on it. He knew he would be sorry later if he didn't eat.

Ryan watched his brother. "I want _____some_____ toast, too," he said. Ryan placed two slices of bread in the toaster. He was seven, and he wanted to do everything Simon did.

Simon, his dad, and Ryan loaded their truck and began the trip to the show. For Simon the three-hour trip flew by. After they arrived at the busy arena, Simon signed in. He would be rider _____number_____ ten. "Ten is a great number," he said to himself. "It's the _____sum_____ of nine, my age, and _____one_____, for first place."

Simon got on his pony, Rocket. They entered the big riding ring. Simon took a deep breath. He and Rocket went to work.

As he finished the jumping course, Simon hoped that _____none_____ of the others had _____done_____ as well as he and Rocket had.

Simon was still holding his breath when he heard the judge say, "In first place, Simon, riding Rocket."

"Rocket, we _____won_____!" Simon whispered to his horse. "We really won!"

Notepad list:
lovely
just
something
hundred
done
some
sum
must
shove
won
butter
cover
supper
none
number
one

ACTIVITY MASTER p. T263

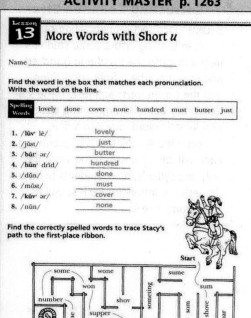
ADDITIONAL PRACTICE

You may wish to copy and distribute the Activity Master on page T263 as additional practice for Lesson 13.

Proofreading Practice
• Write the some of six and seven. *(sum)*
• I need a pen and sum paper. *(some)*

Reading Comprehension

After students have completed the pages, ask them to identify the main character in "The First Horse Show" (Simon). Explain that Simon's feelings change throughout the story. Ask students to describe how Simon feels as he talks with his father after he awakes on the morning of his horse show (frightened and nervous); when he signs in at the arena (excited and hopeful); and after the judge makes his announcement (happy and proud). Help students to recognize that a character's feelings can change during the course of a story.

Cooperative Learning Activity

To help students assess their progress, divide the class into groups of three. Have one student dictate the lesson words, a second spell them aloud, and a third write them on the board or a sheet of paper for the others to see. Encourage students to change roles so that each student can spell all the words. Guide students in noting the words they are spelling correctly and those they need to continue to study.

Day 4

Student Objectives

- To write an expressive paragraph, using lesson words
- To proofread a journal entry for spelling, capitalization, and punctuation

Presenting the Page

Remind students that in "The First Horse Show" on pages 78–79, Simon wins the jumping event. To help students clarify their view on whether doing their best is more important than winning, invite them to compare and contrast doing one's best and winning at any cost. On the board, list students' comments, perhaps in a chart. Encourage students to refer to the chart and the list of lesson words on page 80 as they write their paragraph.

To assist students with the Proofreading activity, invite a volunteer to read the journal entry aloud. Then have students complete the activity independently. Partners can compare their answers.

Meeting Individual Needs

ESOL

To give speakers of other languages additional practice with the spelling and pronunciation of the lesson words, say each word and use it in a question, such as *What did you eat for supper?* Have students repeat the word, use the word to answer your question, and then write the word.

lovely
just
something
hundred
done
some
sum
must
shove
won
butter
cover
supper
none
number
one

Write to the Point

Some people believe that doing your best is more important than winning. Do you agree? Write a paragraph about how important winning is to you. Give reasons why you think as you do. Try to use spelling words from this lesson in your paragraph. Paragraphs will vary.

> Use the strategies on page 7 when you are not sure how to spell a word.

Proofreading

Proofread the journal entry below. Use proofreading marks to correct five spelling mistakes, three capitalization mistakes, and two punctuation mistakes.

Proofreading Marks
- ◯ spell correctly
- ≡ capitalize
- ⊙ add period

December 15

    yesterday was the best day of my life. I (jest) *just*
cannot believe that I won something. rocket and I
were (nomber) *number* one in the show. now we have a (lovley) *lovely*
ribbon. There were more than two (hunderd) *hundred* people
watching.

    I must enter another horse show soon I've
never (dun) *done* anything as fun as riding in that show.

I think Rocket had fun, too. Dad says that he will
take us to any show in the state⊙

80 UNIT 3

Proofreading Practice

- Our team one the spelling bee. (won)
- We each got won free movie pass. (one)

Correcting Common Errors

Because incorrect pronunciation can result in spelling errors, some students may transpose the *r* and *e* in *hundred* and may drop the *g* from *something* and the *t* from *must* and *just*. These students may benefit from writing each problematic word, drawing a line between the syllables, and pronouncing each syllable distinctly. If the word has only one syllable, have students point to the letter or letters for each sound as they pronounce it.

Language Connection

Homophones Homophones are words that sound alike but have different spellings and meanings. Look at the homophone pairs in the boxes below. Think about what each homophone means.

| one | won | | some | sum |
| ate | eight | | son | sun | | sail | sale |

Use the homophones above to complete each sentence. Use the Spelling Dictionary if you need to.

1. The ship must _____ sail _____ at sunrise.
2. I bought this lovely jacket on _____ sale _____.
3. Jason _____ ate _____ some soup and a sandwich for supper.
4. My favorite number is _____ eight _____.
5. The hot _____ sun _____ made some of us thirsty.
6. We just met Mrs. Lee's daughter and her _____ son _____.
7. Jesse _____ won _____ two blue ribbons at the art contest.
8. Mr. Ono owns _____ one _____ car and two bicycles.
9. Mari found the _____ sum _____ of _____ some _____ numbers.

⭐ Challenge Yourself

What do you think each Challenge Word means? Check the Spelling Dictionary to see if you are right. Then use separate paper to write sentences showing that you understand the meaning of each Challenge Word. Definitions and sentences will vary.

Challenge Words	
income	slump
smudge	instruct

10. My allowance is my **income**.
11. The puppy's wet nose left a **smudge** on the window.
12. You will look taller if you don't **slump**.
13. I have a good teacher to **instruct** me in math.

LESSON 13 **81**

Posttest

Dictate the following sentences. Have students use separate paper to write the sentences and underline the lesson words.

1. Put the <u>cover</u> on the <u>butter</u>.
2. What is the <u>sum</u> of one <u>hundred</u> plus <u>one</u>?
3. He began to <u>shove</u> <u>some</u> toys into the box.
4. He <u>won</u> <u>something</u> at the fair.
5. She has <u>done</u> <u>none</u> of her work today.
6. I <u>must</u> eat <u>supper</u>.
7. What <u>number</u> did she <u>just</u> call?
8. The sky is <u>lovely</u> today.

Enrichment Activity

Have students work independently to make word scramble puzzles. Direct students to write a short clue for each lesson word, followed by the word in scrambled form. They can refer to the list of lesson words on page 76 if necessary. Make sure students put their clues and scrambled words in a different order from that of the word list. Have students trade papers with a classmate and solve each other's puzzles.

Student Objectives

- To use lesson words that are homophones to complete sentences
- To study the spellings and meanings of the Challenge Words
- To take a posttest on the lesson words

Presenting the Page

Review with students that homophones are words that sound alike but have different spellings and meanings. Invite volunteers to give the meanings of the homophones in each pair. Guide students to understand that in order to decide which homophone is correct, they need to rely on the rest of the sentence.

⭐ Challenge Yourself

To introduce the Challenge Words, write the following on the board:

| in/come | slump |
| smudge | in/struct |

Pronounce the words for students and discuss the number of syllables in each. Ask students to identify the short *u* spelling pattern in each of the Challenge Words (*income* has the o-consonant-e pattern; *slump*, *smudge*, and *instruct* have the *u* pattern).

Next, have students write what they think each Challenge Word means, look the words up in the Spelling Dictionary, and then write the correct definitions. Ask students to compare their definitions with those in the Spelling Dictionary.

Posttest

Use the posttest on this page to assess students' ability to spell the lesson words.

Words with Short *i*

Student Objectives

- To take a pretest on the lesson words
- To spell the lesson words aloud
- To sort and write the lesson words according to the spelling patterns *i*, *e*, *ui*, and *ee*

Pretest

Use the pretest on this page to assess students' ability to spell the lesson words.

Have students use the study steps on page 6 to study any words they misspell in the pretest.

You may wish to duplicate and send home the Home Activity Master on pages T245–T246.

Presenting the Page

Introducing the Short *i* Sound

Write *fill* and *fell* on the board. Have a volunteer read the words aloud. Help students distinguish between the short *i* and short *e* sounds.

As students prepare to sort the words, point out that /ĭ/ is often spelled *i* but is spelled *e*, *ui*, or *ee* in some words that we often use.

Pronunciation Focus Write the word *De/cem/ber* on the board and say the word aloud as you point to each syllable. Emphasize that the correct pronunciation for the word is Dĭ/sĕm/bər, not Dē/sĕm/bər. Ask students to identify the syllable with the short *i* sound and the spelling of the sound (the first syllable, *e*).

Consonant Focus Write *spring* on the board and draw attention to the *ng* at the end of the word. Repeat with the word *thing*. Help students think of other words that end with *ng*, such as *long*, *bring*, and *rang*.

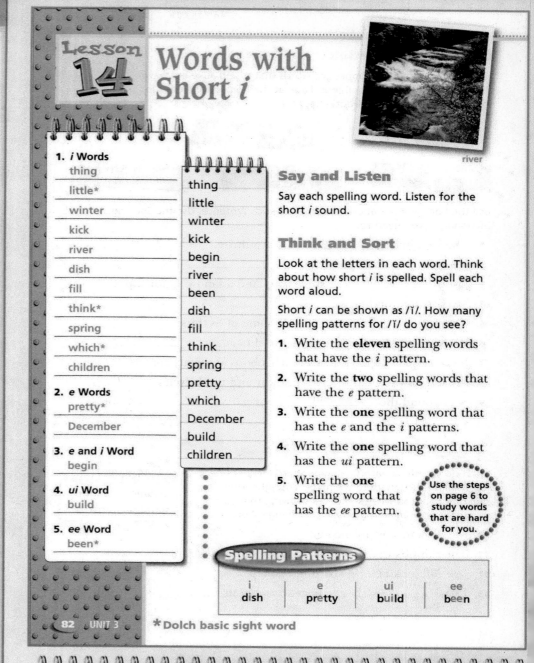

Lesson 14 Words with Short *i*

river

1. *i* Words
thing
little*
winter
kick
river
dish
fill
think*
spring
which*
children

2. *e* Words
pretty*
December

3. *e* and *i* Word
begin

4. *ui* Word
build

5. *ee* Word
been*

thing
little
winter
kick
begin
river
been
dish
fill
think
spring
pretty
which
December
build
children

Say and Listen
Say each spelling word. Listen for the short *i* sound.

Think and Sort
Look at the letters in each word. Think about how short *i* is spelled. Spell each word aloud.

Short *i* can be shown as /ĭ/. How many spelling patterns for /ĭ/ do you see?

1. Write the **eleven** spelling words that have the *i* pattern.
2. Write the **two** spelling words that have the *e* pattern.
3. Write the **one** spelling word that has the *e* and the *i* patterns.
4. Write the **one** spelling word that has the *ui* pattern.
5. Write the **one** spelling word that has the *ee* pattern.

Use the steps on page 6 to study words that are hard for you.

Spelling Patterns

i	e	ui	ee
dish	pretty	build	been

82 UNIT 3

*Dolch basic sight word

Pretest

Say each lesson word, read the sentence, and then repeat the word. Have students write the words on separate paper.

1. **thing** What is that blue thing on the shelf?
2. **little** I have a little sister.
3. **winter** Last winter it snowed a lot.
4. **kick** How far did the player kick the ball?
5. **begin** The movie will begin in five minutes.
6. **river** The river is deep.
7. **been** Have you been sleeping?
8. **dish** Put the fruit in a dish.
9. **fill** Please fill the pitcher.
10. **think** I think I lost my hat.
11. **spring** In spring the grass turns green.
12. **pretty** Pink is a pretty color.
13. **which** I wonder which jacket is mine.
14. **December** My birthday is in December.
15. **build** Let's build a boat.
16. **children** Some children ride a bus to school.

Additional Words for Enrichment

The following words can be used to meet the needs of on-level and above-level students:

different   whisper   guitar   important   swift   quick

Spelling and Meaning

Clues Write the spelling word for each clue.

1. what you do to a soccer ball — kick
2. young people — children
3. what you do with a hammer and nails — build
4. a big stream — river
5. a season that can be cold — winter
6. a word that rhymes with *fish* — dish
7. the opposite of *end* — begin
8. a word for *beautiful* — pretty
9. the opposite of *big* — little

Rhymes Write the spelling word that completes each sentence and rhymes with the underlined word.

10. I _____ think _____ I will wear my pink shirt.
11. The coach told the player _____ which _____ pitch was good.
12. If you have not _____ been _____ practicing, you will not win the music contest.
13. I will bring you flowers in the _____ spring _____.
14. Jill will climb the hill and _____ fill _____ the bucket.
15. Bring that little blue _____ thing _____ to me.

Word Story The Romans of long ago divided the year into ten months. The last Roman month was named *Decem*. *Decem* meant "ten." Write the spelling word that comes from *Decem*.

16. _____ December _____

Family Tree: children *Children* is a form of *child*. Think about how the *child* words are alike in spelling and meaning. Then add another *child* word to the tree. A sample answer is shown.

- childlike
- children
- childproof
- 17. childish
- childless
- child

LESSON 14 83

HOME ACTIVITY MASTER p. T245

Unit 3 Spelling at Home

Dear Family of _____,

During the next six weeks, your child will be learning to spell the following kinds of words:

- words with the short *u* vowel sound
- words with the short *i* vowel sound
- words with the long *i* vowel sound
- words with *-ed* or *-ing*

Here are some simple activities to do each week to help your child become a better speller.

Listening and Writing
Say the spelling words and have your child write them.

Spelling Strategy: Sounds and Letters
If your child is unsure about the spelling of a word, have your child say the word to himself or herself. Tell your child to close his or her eyes and try to picture the way the word is spelled. Help your child think about the spelling by asking questions such as *Does it have more letters than sounds?* Which *letter pair spells a single sound?* Then have your child write the word on a piece of paper. Check the word's spelling in the list at right or in a dictionary.

Games and Activities
Play Recorded Spellings. Choose some of the spelling words. Call each word out to your child. Using a tape recorder, have your child record himself or herself echoing the word and spelling it. Play the recording back and have your child check the word.

Write the letters of the alphabet on index cards. Create five index cards for each vowel and two index cards for each consonant. Have your child use the alphabet cards to practice spelling words.

Using Spelling Words
Ask your child to write sentences that contain the spelling words. Then read the sentences with your child. Notice whether the sentences show that your child knows the meanings of the spelling words.

Lesson 13 More Words with Short *u*

Week of _____

won	lovely	done	something
shove	some	one	hundred
none	cover	must	number
sum	butter	just	supper

Lesson 14 Words with Short *i*

Week of _____

think	winter	been	December
fill	little	thing	spring
kick	river	which	pretty
dish	begin	build	children

Lesson 15 Words with Long *i*

Week of _____

line	drive	inside	nice
shine	while	size	miles
write	mine	alike	times
white	tiny	lion	eyes

Lesson 16 More Words with Long *i*

Week of _____

Friday	kind	child	mind
behind	high	right	light
night	by	cry	sky
try	why	fly	buy

Lesson 17 Words with *-ed* or *-ing*

Week of _____

wished	asked	rained	dreamed
handed	painted	filled	subtracted
thanked	waited	reading	sleeping
meeting	ending	guessing	laughing

Lesson 18 Unit 3 Review

Week of _____
Lesson 18 is a review of Lessons 13–17. Help your child practice all of the words from those lessons.

The highlighted area shows the Lesson 14 words, which students can share with family members. Spanish version available on page T246.

Proofreading Practice

- Please help me bild a tower. (build)
- I have bin working on it all day. (been)

Meeting Individual Needs

ESOL

Spanish-speaking students may need more practice with the short *i* sound because this sound is not common in Spanish. Have students take turns using a lesson word or a group of words that contains a lesson word to complete the following sentence orally: *I am going on a trip, and I'm going to take a _____.* Encourage students to write the short *i* words on the board or a chart.

Day 2

Student Objectives

- To use meaning clues to identify and write lesson words
- To use etymology, spelling, and meaning to identify the word *December*
- To learn *child* words and analyze their spellings and meanings

Presenting the Page

Write the following Clues and Rhymes examples on the board and model identifying the answers:

- the season between winter and summer (*spring*)
- I gave the ball a quick _____. (*kick*)

Word Story

Share with students that other months of the Roman calendar were *Septem*, which meant "seven"; *Octo*, which meant "eight"; and *Novem*, which meant "nine." Ask students to use this information to identify the present months of the year that come from *Septem*, *Octo*, and *Novem* (September, October, and November).

Family Tree: *child*

Students should see that the *child* words all contain *child*. Have students locate the meanings of the *child* words in a dictionary and write their findings on the board. Then discuss with students the similarities and differences in meanings. Point out the change in meaning when *-less* is added to *child* to create *childless* and the /ĭ/ pronunciation of the *i* in children. Guide students to understand that knowing the spelling for *child* will help them spell *children* and other words related to *child*.

83

Day 3

Student Objectives
- To use context to identify and write lesson words
- To use stated information to compare and contrast lifestyles
- To draw a conclusion about life traveling west during the 1800s

Presenting the Pages

Write the title "Westward Adventures" on the board and ask a volunteer to read it aloud. Explain that this nonfiction selection tells about the lives of real people, including children, traveling west across the United States during the 1800s.

Have volunteers take turns reading the story aloud paragraph by paragraph and supplying the missing words. Then have students write the missing words independently. Or have students complete the pages on their own by silently reading the story and writing the missing words. Then have students take turns reading the completed story aloud.

Draw students' attention to the use of the word *dish* in the story. Have students use the Spelling Dictionary to discover which definition of *dish* is used in the story (definition 2).

Meeting Individual Needs

Visual Learners
To provide visual learners with additional practice, have them fold a sheet of paper into four sections and use a different color of marker to label the sections *i*, *e*, *ui*, and *ee*. Then have students write the lesson words in the squares where they belong. Suggest that students use the appropriate corresponding color of marker to write the letter or letters that spell the short *i* sound in each word. Students can write the word *begin* in both the *e* and the *i* sections, using the appropriate color of marker to highlight the corresponding letter.

Use each spelling word once to complete the selection.

WESTWARD ADVENTURES

Helen Scott and her family were pioneers. They traveled west across North America when Helen was only 11 years old. Helen and many other pioneers wrote about their adventures in journals, some of ____which____ we can read today. Their writings have ____been____ helpful because they tell us about life on the westward trail in the 1800s.

Pioneers traveled west in covered wagons. If a family lived in the middle of the country, the best time to ____begin____ their trip was in the ____spring____, after the rains. The trip took five to six months. A family that left in May could plan to arrive well before the month of ____December____. That was when the harsh ____winter____ began.

A covered wagon had very ____little____ room. Families had to ____think____ carefully about what they would pack. Young ____children____ could take few toys.

Meals on the trail were simple. Corn mush was a common ____dish____ that most pioneers ate. They also ate dried meat, eggs, and potatoes.

84 UNIT 3

Spelling Strategy

Different Spellings
Remind students that one strategy to use when they are not sure of a word's spelling is to spell the word in different ways and then choose the one that looks correct. Have students select a lesson word not yet mastered and use the spelling patterns featured in this lesson to write the word in different ways. Ask students to circle the spelling they think is correct.

i	*e*	*ui*	*ee*
bin	ben	buin	(been)

Before dinner, pioneers gathered sticks and branches to
_____build_____ a fire for cooking. After dinner, they sang
                 11
songs around the fire and danced to _____pretty_____ fiddle
                                                12
music. They told stories, too.

Horses and mules pulled the wagons. The ride was
bumpy and uncomfortable. Children often walked beside the
slow wagons. They had to be careful. They didn't want the
animals to bite or _____kick_____ them.
                            13
Children worked on the trail, too. Boys and girls helped get
the wagons ready to cross any stream or _____river_____.
                                                    14
Another _____thing_____ children did was to help make a
                    15
special wax paste to _____fill_____ cracks in the covered
                                16
wagons. Then they helped to fill the openings. Filling the
openings helped make the wagons waterproof.

Every day on the westward trail was an adventure.
Thanks to children like Helen Scott, we can share those
adventures.

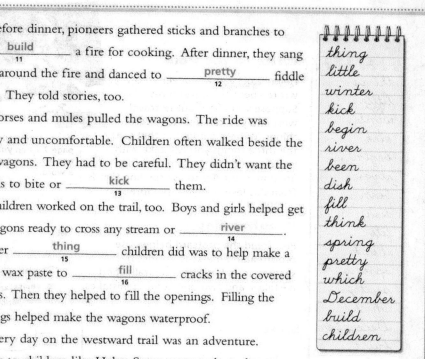

thing
little
winter
kick
begin
river
been
dish
fill
think
spring
pretty
which
December
build
children

LESSON 14 **85**

ACTIVITY MASTER p. T264

Lesson 14 Words with Short *i*

Name _____

Find the word in the box that matches each clue. Write the word in the puzzle.

Spelling Words	little	begin	pretty	river	build	which	spring	thing
	been	fill	think	winter	dish	children	kick	December

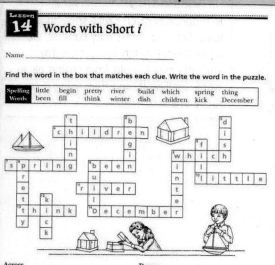

Across
4. Young people are called ___.
6. I didn't know ___ way to go.
7. Flowers bloom every ___.
9. I've already ___ to the zoo.
10. The opposite of *big* is ___.
11. They canoe on the ___.
13. ___ before you answer.
14. The last month of the year is ___.

Down
1. Half of the word *something* is ___.
2. The race will ___ at noon.
3. Jarrell put the ___ in the sink.
5. ___ the glass with water.
6. The season after autumn is ___.
8. That's a ___ picture.
9. Let's ___ a house with blocks.
12. She will ___ the soccer ball.

ADDITIONAL PRACTICE

You may wish to copy and distribute the Activity Master on page T264 as additional practice for Lesson 14.

Proofreading Practice
• Big boats travel down the reever. *(river)*
• In wuinter ice stops the boats. *(winter)*

Reading Comprehension

After students have completed the pages, have them describe the daily life of children traveling west, according to the selection. Then have them compare their life with that of the pioneer children. Help students to understand that on the westward trail, children generally had many responsibilities and worked hard.

Ask students why children had to work on the trip west. Guide students to conclude that it took many people, including children, working together every day to find and prepare food, to care for the wagons and animals, and to meet other basic needs.

Cooperative Learning Activity

To help students assess their progress, have partners dictate the lesson words to each other. Encourage students to call out the words in random order. Direct students to the list on page 85 to check their spelling. Have students compare their performance on this midweek activity to their performance on the pretest. Guide them to note which words they can now spell correctly and those they need to continue to study.

85

Day 4

Student Objectives

- To write an expressive paragraph, using lesson words
- To proofread a postcard for spelling, capitalization, and punctuation

Presenting the Page

Remind students that families had to limit what they could take in their small covered wagon. To help students decide what they would take, have them list all of the things they would like to take and then cross out items they could do without, one by one. When they get down to five items, have them number the top three *1, 2, 3.* Before students write, have them review the lesson word list on the page. Encourage students to use these words when possible.

To assist students with the Proofreading activity, have a volunteer read the directions and the postcard aloud. Then suggest that students complete the activity independently, proofreading the postcard once for spelling, once for capitalization, and once for punctuation.

Meeting Individual Needs

ESOL

To provide speakers of other languages with additional practice on the lesson words, have them use the words in an oral sentence game. The player who begins the game should choose a lesson word and write it on the board. The player should then select a volunteer to say the word and use it in a sentence. If that player uses the word correctly, he or she continues the game by choosing another lesson word to write on the board. If the player does not use the word correctly, the first player selects another volunteer to continue the game.

86

---

thing
little
winter
kick
begin
river
been
dish
fill
think
spring
pretty
which
December
build
children

Write to the Point

Helen Scott was a pioneer who wrote about her adventures. Suppose you are about to travel west and you can only take three things. Write a paragraph that tells the three things you will take with you on your trip. Explain why they are important. Try to use spelling words from this lesson in your paragraph. Paragraphs will vary.

Proofreading

Proofread the postcard below. Use proofreading marks to correct five spelling mistakes, three capitalization mistakes, and two punctuation mistakes.

Use the strategies on page 7 when you are not sure how to spell a word.

Proofreading Marks
- ⬭ spell correctly
- ≡ capitalize
- ⊙ add period

Hi, luke!

We had a great time at the pioneer
fair. i saw people build a barn I learned
that it was hard to be a pioneer in the
winter. The river freezes by December,
and then it is hard to fish. Life is easier
when spring comes. maybe you can
come to the fair with us next year

Dylan

Luke Babb

158 Beach Drive

Austin, TX 78739

86 UNIT 3

Proofreading Practice

- I asked wich flower you liked best. *(which)*
- I think the pink one is very pritty. *(pretty)*

Correcting Common Errors

Homophones often cause spelling problems. Some students may confuse the homophones *witch* and *which*. These students may benefit from saying each word, spelling it, and then using it correctly in a sentence.

Language Connection

Adjectives An adjective describes a noun or pronoun by telling which one, what kind, or how many.

| The **spotted** pony ate the **green** grass. | The **fresh** flowers are **lovely**. |

Use the adjectives in the boxes below to complete the sentences. Then circle all the adjectives in the sentences.

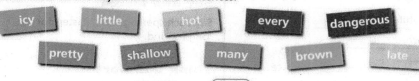

icy little hot every dangerous
pretty shallow many brown late

1. A river flows by the (simple) _____ little _____ cabin.
2. It travels for _____ many _____ miles through the (thick) forest.
3. In the winter the river is (cold) and _____ icy _____.
4. (Thin) ice in (some) places is _____ dangerous _____ for skaters.
5. (Many) _____ pretty _____ flowers line the banks in spring.
6. On _____ hot _____ (summer) days, people wade in the river.
7. They walk on (large) rocks in the _____ shallow _____ water.
8. In the fall, (red) and _____ brown _____ leaves float down the river.
9. The river changes with _____ every _____ season.

⭐ Challenge Yourself

Write the Challenge Word for each clue. Check the Spelling Dictionary to see if you are right. Then use separate paper to write sentences showing that you understand the meaning of each Challenge Word. *Sentences will vary.*

Challenge Words	
spinach	luggage
width	arctic

10. This word describes very cold air. _____ arctic _____
11. It is a green vegetable. _____ spinach _____
12. This can hold your clothes when you travel. _____ luggage _____
13. It is the distance from one side to another. _____ width _____

LESSON 14   **87**

Posttest

Dictate the following sentences. Have students use separate paper to write the sentences and underline the lesson words.

1. I like <u>winter</u> and <u>spring</u>.
2. The <u>children</u> like to <u>kick</u> the ball.
3. The <u>river</u> is cold in <u>December</u>.
4. We must <u>begin</u> to build our cabin.
5. Please <u>fill</u> the <u>little</u> cup.
6. I <u>think</u> this is a <u>pretty</u> dish.
7. That <u>thing</u> has <u>been</u> there all day.
8. Did you see <u>which</u> way he went?

Enrichment Activity

Have students work independently to write sentences containing lesson words written in a code such as that in which a=b, b=c, c=d, etc. Have students trade papers, decode the lesson words, and write them.

Student Objectives

- To use adjectives to complete sentences
- To identify adjectives in sentences containing lesson words
- To study the spellings and meanings of the Challenge Words
- To take a posttest on the lesson words

Presenting the Page

Review with students that an adjective describes a noun or a pronoun by telling which one, what kind, or how many. Draw students' attention to the examples, pointing out that adjectives do not necessarily appear beside the nouns or pronouns that they describe.

⭐ Challenge Yourself

To introduce the Challenge Words, write the following on the board:

spin/ach   lug/gage
width   arc/tic

Pronounce the words for students and discuss the number of syllables in each. Then have students refer to page 82 and review the short *i* spelling patterns featured in this lesson. Point out that *luggage* contains a different spelling pattern for the short *i* sound. Ask students to identify the short *i* spelling patterns in the Challenge Words, giving students the hint that one of the words contains two patterns (*width*, the first syllable in *spinach*, and *arctic* contain the *i* pattern; *luggage* and the second syllable in *spinach* contain the *a* pattern).

Posttest

Use the posttest on this page to assess students' ability to spell the lesson words.

Words with Long *i*

Student Objectives
- To take a pretest on the lesson words
- To spell the lesson words aloud
- To sort and write the lesson words according to the spelling patterns *i*-consonant-e, *i*, and *eye*

Pretest

Use the pretest on this page to assess students' ability to spell the lesson words.

 Have students use the study steps on page 6 to study any words they misspell in the pretest.

 You may wish to duplicate and send home the Home Activity Master on pages T245–T246.

Presenting the Page

Introducing the Long *i* Sound
Write the word *line* on the board and ask a volunteer to read the word aloud. Have students identify the vowel sound they hear in *line* (long *i*).

As students prepare to sort the words, point out that /ī/ is often spelled *i*-consonant-*e* or *i* but is spelled *eye* in some words we often use.

Pronunciation Focus Write *a/like* on the board. Ask students to identify the syllable with the long *i* sound and tell the spelling of the sound (the second syllable; *i*-consonant-*e*). Follow the same procedure with *li/on* and *in/side*.

Consonant Focus Write the word *write* on the board and ask a volunteer to pronounce it. Draw attention to the sound of *wr* at the beginning of the word (/r/). Help students recognize that the *w* is silent.

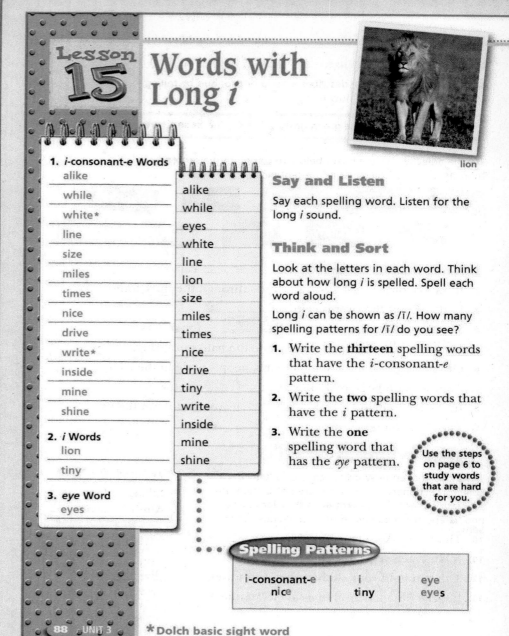

Words with Long *i*

lion

1. *i*-consonant-e Words
- alike
- while
- white*
- line
- size
- miles
- times
- nice
- drive
- write*
- inside
- mine
- shine

2. *i* Words
- lion
- tiny

3. *eye* Word
- eyes

alike
while
eyes
white
line
lion
size
miles
times
nice
drive
tiny
write
inside
mine
shine

Say and Listen

Say each spelling word. Listen for the long *i* sound.

Think and Sort

Look at the letters in each word. Think about how long *i* is spelled. Spell each word aloud.

Long *i* can be shown as /ī/. How many spelling patterns for /ī/ do you see?

1. Write the **thirteen** spelling words that have the *i*-consonant-*e* pattern.
2. Write the **two** spelling words that have the *i* pattern.
3. Write the **one** spelling word that has the *eye* pattern.

Use the steps on page 6 to study words that are hard for you.

Spelling Patterns

i-consonant-e nice	*i* tiny	eye eyes

*Dolch basic sight word

Pretest

Say each lesson word, read the sentence, and then repeat the word. Have students write the words on separate paper.

1. **alike** The twins look alike.
2. **while** Please wait while I put on my coat.
3. **eyes** The dog has blue eyes.
4. **white** The fresh snow is bright white.
5. **line** We waited in line.
6. **lion** I heard a lion roar.
7. **size** My brother and I are the same size.
8. **miles** We walked two miles.
9. **times** I rang the bell two times.
10. **nice** Today is nice and sunny.
11. **drive** Don't drive too fast.
12. **tiny** Baby fish are tiny.
13. **write** I will write a note.
14. **inside** Bats live inside that cave.
15. **mine** Is that pen yours or mine?
16. **shine** The street lights shine brightly.

Additional Words for Enrichment

The following words can be used to meet the needs of on-level and above-level students:

beside knife climb giant library silent

Spelling and Meaning

Clues Write the spelling word for each clue.

1. what people do with a car — drive
2. belongs in a group with *feet* and *yards* — miles
3. something that can be straight or crooked — line
4. a word meaning "at the same time" — while
5. a word that rhymes with *eyes* — size
6. what people do to some shoes — shine

Analogies Write the spelling word that completes each analogy.

7. *Mean* is to ____nice____ as *weak* is to *strong*.
8. *You* is to *me* as *yours* is to ____mine____.
9. *Add* is to *plus* as *multiply* is to ____times____.
10. *Light* is to *dark* as ____white____ is to *black*.
11. *Hear* is to *ears* as *see* is to ____eyes____.
12. *Needle* is to *sew* as *pen* is to ____write____.
13. *Small* is to ____tiny____ as *big* is to *huge*.
14. *Different* is to *unlike* as *same* is to ____alike____.
15. *Up* is to *down* as ____inside____ is to *outside*.

Word Story One of the spelling words comes from the Greek word *leon*. *Leon* was the word for one of the big cats. The names Leona, Lenore, Leo, Leopold, and Lionel all come from this word. Write the spelling word that comes from *leon*.

16. ____lion____

Family Tree: *drive* Think about how the *drive* words are alike in spelling and meaning. Then add another *drive* word to the tree.
A sample answer is shown.

- driven
- driver
- 17. driving
- drives
- drive

LESSON 15   89

HOME ACTIVITY MASTER p. T245

Unit 3 | Spelling at Home

Dear Family of ____

During the next six weeks, your child will be learning to spell the following kinds of words:
- words with the short *u* vowel sound
- words with the short *i* vowel sound
- words with the long *i* vowel sound
- words with *-ed* or *-ing*

Here are some simple activities to do each week to help your child become a better speller.

Listening and Writing
Say the spelling words and have your child write them.

Spelling Strategy: Sounds and Letters
If your child is unsure about the spelling of a word, have your child say the word to himself or herself. Tell your child to close his or her eyes and try to picture the way the word is spelled. Help your child think about the spelling by asking questions such as *Does it have more letters than sounds? Which letter pair spells a single sound?* Then have your child write the word on a piece of paper. Check the word's spelling in the list at right or in a dictionary.

Games and Activities
Play Recorded Spellings. Choose some of the spelling words. Call each word out to your child. Using a tape recorder, have your child record himself or herself echoing the word and spelling it. Play the recording back and have your child check the words.

Write the letters of the alphabet on index cards. Create five index cards for each vowel and two index cards for each consonant. Have your child use the alphabet cards to practice spelling words.

Using Spelling Words
Ask your child to write sentences that contain the spelling words. Then read the sentences with your child. Notice whether the sentences show that your child knows the meanings of the spelling words.

Lesson 13 More Words with Short *u*			
Week of ____			
won	lovely	done	something
shove	some	one	hundred
none	cover	must	number
sum	butter	just	supper

Lesson 14 Words with Short *i*			
Week of ____			
think	winter	been	December
fill	little	thing	spring
kick	river	which	pretty
dish	begin	build	children

Lesson 15 Words with Long *i*			
Week of ____			
line	drive	inside	nice
shine	while	size	times
white	mine	alike	lion
	tiny		eyes

Lesson 16 More Words with Long *i*			
Week of ____			
Friday	kind	child	mind
behind	high	right	light
night	by	cry	sky
try	why	fly	buy

Lesson 17 Words with *-ed* or *-ing*			
Week of ____			
wished	asked	rained	dreamed
handed	painted	filled	subtracted
thanked	waited	reading	sleeping
meeting	ending	guessing	laughing

Lesson 18 Unit 3 Review
Week of ____
Lesson 18 is a review of Lessons 15–17. Help your child practice all of the words from those lessons.

The highlighted area shows the Lesson 15 words, which students can share with family members. Spanish version available on page T246.

Proofreading Practice
- Please right your name at the top of the paper. (*write*)
- The first problem is two tims three. (*times*)

Meeting Individual Needs

ESOL
Because each vowel in Spanish has only one sound, students whose first language is Spanish may have difficulty determining which spelling pattern to use for the long *i* sound. Make a word card for each word and highlight the long *i* spelling pattern. Have students use the cards to sort the lesson words by spelling pattern. Finally, have students say and spell each word.

Spelling and Meaning

Spelling and Meaning

Day 2

Student Objectives
- To use meaning clues to identify and write lesson words
- To use etymology, spelling, and meaning to identify the word *lion*
- To learn *drive* words and analyze their spellings and meanings

Presenting the Page
Write the following Clues and Analogies examples on the board and model identifying the answers:
- what a very small thing is (*tiny*)
- *Car* is to _____ as *plane* is to *fly*. (*drive*)

Word Story
Many words have come into English from the Greek language. The word *leopard* comes from the Greek word *leopardos*, which joined *leon*, for lion, with *pardos*, for male panther. Write *leon* and *leopardos* on the board. Have students identify the letters that are the same in each word (the beginning letters *leo*).

Family Tree: *drive*
Students should see that the *drive* words on the tree all contain *drive*. Help students who add *driving* to the tree note the base word change when *-ing* is added to *drive*. Point out the function of *-er* in *driver* (to make *drive* a noun) and the difference in pronunciation between the long *i* in *drive* and the short *i* in *driven*. Guide students to understand that knowing how to spell *drive* will help them spell words related to *drive*.

Day 3

Student Objectives
- To use context to identify and write lesson words
- To use prior knowledge and stated information to compare and contrast lions and house cats

Presenting the Pages

Have students work with partners to take turns reading the selection aloud and supplying the missing words. Then have students write the missing words independently. Or have students complete the pages on their own by silently reading the selection and writing the missing words. Then have students take turns reading the completed selection. Invite students to share their observations about the behavior of either domestic or wild cats.

Draw students' attention to the use of the word *family* in the first sentence. Explain that in this selection, *family* is a scientific term that refers to a group of related animals. Scientists include the lion, tiger, jaguar, leopard, puma, cheetah, and domestic cat in the cat family.

Meeting Individual Needs

Kinesthetic Learners
To help kinesthetic learners practice the spelling patterns, have them use alphabet cards or tiles to spell the lesson words. Say a word and pause while students arrange the letters to spell the word. Then have students read the word, spell it aloud, and write it.

Use each spelling word once to complete the selection.

Just a Big Cat?

It's easy to tell that a _____lion_____ belongs to the cat family. A lion looks very
1

much like a house cat. The two animals are also _____alike_____ in other ways.
2

They both have claws that they can pull _____inside_____ their paws to keep the claws _____nice_____
3   4

and sharp. Lions and house cats also have _____eyes_____ that see
5

well in the dark. If a light should _____shine_____ on their eyes at
6

night, their eyes will glow.

Lions are not like house cats in every way.

The greatest difference is _____size_____.
7

A male lion can weigh more than 500 pounds,

_____while_____ a house cat usually
8

weighs about 10 pounds. A house cat seems

_____tiny_____ next to a lion.
9

Most lions have brownish-yellow fur.

This color makes it easy for the lion to hide.

House cats come in many colors. Their fur

can even be snowy _____white_____.
10

The male lion has a mane. The mane makes

90 UNIT 3

Spelling Strategy

Guess and Check
Remind students that when they are not sure of a word's spelling, they can use the guess-and-check strategy to spell the word. Explain that this is a particularly good strategy when they know how to spell the beginning of a word. Demonstrate how to use this strategy by inviting students to suggest spellings for the word *tiny*. Write their suggestions on the board, using a chart like the following. Have students check the spellings in the Spelling Dictionary and identify the correct spelling.

Guess	Correct?
tinee	no
tine	no
tiney	no
tiny	yes

him look big and strong. The thick mane may be why the male lion is called the king of beasts. A male house cat never has a mane.

Lions live in groups called prides. At _____ times _____, as many as 35 lions may live in a pride. These lions hunt together. They may travel many _____ miles _____ to find food. A lion doesn't let strange animals hunt on its land. The lion will let out a roar as if to say, "Keep out! This land is _____ mine _____."

Today most lions live in Africa, but you can still learn a lot about them. Lions can be seen in many parks and zoos. Many people will _____ drive _____ a long way and stand in a long _____ line _____ to see a lion. You can also read books that people _____ write _____ about lions. You can learn how lions live and why they are much more than big house cats.

alike
while
eyes
white
line
lion
size
miles
times
nice
drive
tiny
write
inside
mine
shine

ACTIVITY MASTER p. T265

Lesson 15 Words with Long *i*

Name _____

Read each word in the box and circle it in the puzzle below.
The words go across, down, or at a slant.

Spelling Words	line	drive	inside	nice	shine	while	size	miles
	write	mine	alike	times	white	tiny	lion	eyes

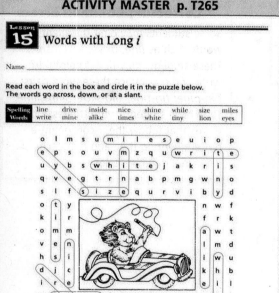

ADDITIONAL PRACTICE

You may wish to copy and distribute the Activity Master on page T265 as additional practice for Lesson 15.

Proofreading Practice
- My dad will driv us to the game. *(drive)*
- The ballpark is only five milez away. *(miles)*

Reading Comprehension

After students have completed the pages, ask them to use information in the selection, along with what they already know about lions and house cats, to compare and contrast the two. You might want to record students' ideas in a Venn diagram on the board. Help students understand that while lions and house cats share such characteristics as retractable claws, keen eyesight, and general appearance, there are significant differences between the two kinds of cats. Guide students to understand that in addition to size, color, and habitat, one major difference is that house cats make good pets, but lions definitely do not.

Cooperative Learning Activity

To help students assess their progress, have partners use the list on page 91 to write the lesson words on index cards. Then they can take turns drawing a card and reading the word aloud for the partner to write. Encourage partners to keep playing until each has had a chance to write each word. Have students compare their performance on this midweek activity to their performance on the pretest. Guide them in noting the words they are now spelling correctly and those they need to continue to study.

Day 4

Student Objectives
- To make an informative sign, using lesson words
- To proofread a newspaper article for spelling, capitalization, and punctuation

Presenting the Page

Remind students that in "Just a Big Cat?" on pages 90–91, they read that some lions live in parks and zoos. Invite students to describe signs they have seen in parks or zoos and tell what kind of information they have seen on the signs. Guide students to understand that informative signs provide facts and details about an animal, such as its scientific name, where it lives, how long it lives, what it eats, and what its habits are. Then encourage students to refer to the list of lesson words on the page as they make their sign. You might also want to provide animal encyclopedias or other reference sources for students to consult before they begin writing.

To assist students with the Proofreading activity, read the directions and newspaper article aloud as students follow along. Then have students reread the article silently and proofread it independently.

Meeting Individual Needs

ESOL
To provide speakers of other languages additional practice with the spelling, meaning, and pronunciation of the lesson words, have students study the words in context. Write the lesson word sentences from "Just a Big Cat?" on strips, leaving a space for each lesson word. Then write the lesson words on index cards. Read a sentence aloud. Have students choose the correct word or words for the sentence. Show the word card. Then have students practice saying the word, spelling it aloud, and writing it. Repeat for all sentences.

92

---

alike
while
eyes
white
line
lion
size
miles
times
nice
drive
tiny
write
inside
mine
shine

Write to the Point
Many wildlife parks have signs near the animals' living areas. The signs give interesting facts about the animals. Choose an animal that you like. Then make a sign telling about the animal. Try to use spelling words from this lesson. Signs will vary.

Use the strategies on page 7 when you are not sure how to spell a word.

Proofreading
Proofread the newspaper article below. Use proofreading marks to correct five spelling mistakes, three capitalization mistakes, and two punctuation mistakes.

Proofreading Marks
◯ spell correctly
≡ capitalize
⊙ add period

Lion Land Big Treat

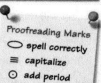

Lion Land opened over the

weekend to wild cheers People came ⊙
   miles   line
from (mils) away. they stood in (linne) for hours to
         ≡

become part of this wildlife adventure. once they got ≡
inside   eyes
(insid), they could not believe their (eyez). Lions strolled

freely and came right up to the cars. We got just a
tiny
(tiney) bit nervous when a lion the size of a horse

looked at us through our car window. check out
                                 ≡
Lion Land for yourself. You won't be disappointed ⊙

92 UNIT

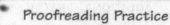

Proofreading Practice
- Wait in lin to see the animals. (line)
- Did you see the lione? (lion)

Correcting Common Errors
Some students may omit the silent e in words such as line, drive, and inside. These students may find it helpful to write and pronounce these word pairs: pin-pine; fin-fine; slid-slide; slim-slime. Then have students write the lesson words that follow the i-consonant-e pattern, writing the i and e in each word in a different color.

Dictionary Skills

Guide Words Each page in a dictionary has two words at the top. These words are called guide words. The first guide word is the first entry word on the page. The other guide word is the last entry word on the page. Guide words help you find entry words.

Look at the dictionary page below and find the guide words.

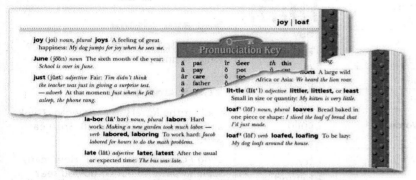

Look up these spelling words in the Spelling Dictionary. Write the guide words and page number for each.

		Guide Words		**Page**
1.	while	weird	wildflower	page 239
2.	drive	dirty	each	page 221
3.	nice	money	November	page 229
4.	size	size	spend	page 234

Challenge Yourself

Use the Spelling Dictionary to answer these questions. Then use separate paper to write sentences showing that you understand the meaning of each Challenge Word.
Sentences will vary.

Challenge Words	
variety	admire
chime	define

5. Would you find a **variety** of toys in a toy store? ___yes___

6. Would most people **admire** a mud puddle? ___no___

7. Do police cars and fire trucks have sirens that **chime**? ___no___

8. Does a dictionary **define** words? ___yes___

Posttest

Dictate the following sentences. Have students use separate paper to write the sentences and underline the lesson words.

1. She will <u>drive</u> for ten <u>miles</u>.
2. His <u>eyes</u> are the same color as <u>mine</u>.
3. The twins look <u>alike</u> and are the same <u>size</u>.
4. How many <u>times</u> did you <u>write</u> your name?
5. Do not cross the <u>white</u> <u>line</u>.
6. The <u>lion</u> is <u>inside</u> its den.
7. Please wait <u>while</u> I <u>shine</u> my shoes.
8. A <u>tiny</u> kitten makes a <u>nice</u> pet.

Enrichment Activity

Have students form small groups to play a dictionary game with spelling words. Players take turns being the scorekeeper. The scorekeeper calls out a lesson word. Players race to find the word in the Spelling Dictionary. The first player to find the word, spell it correctly, identify the long *i* spelling pattern, and read the definition wins points—one point for finding the word, a second point for spelling it correctly, a third point for correctly identifying the spelling pattern, and a fourth point for reading the definition. After a player earns four points, that player becomes the scorekeeper.

Student Objectives

- To use the Spelling Dictionary to locate and write guide words for lesson words
- To study the spellings and meanings of the Challenge Words
- To take a posttest on the lesson words

Presenting the Page

Review with students that guide words in a dictionary indicate the first and last entry words on a page. Write the guide words *joy* and *loaf* on the board and have students locate them in the Spelling Dictionary.

Challenge Yourself

To introduce the Challenge Words, write the following on the board:

va/ri/e/ty   ad/mire
chime   de/fine

Pronounce the words for students and discuss the number of syllables in each. Then have students refer to page 88 and review the long *i* spelling patterns featured in this lesson. Ask students to identify the long *i* spelling pattern in each of the Challenge Words (*variety* has the *i* pattern; *admire*, *chime*, and *define* have the *i*-consonant-e pattern).

Posttest

Use the posttest on this page to assess students' ability to spell the lesson words.

More Words with Long *i*

Day 1

Student Objectives
- To take a pretest on the lesson words
- To spell the lesson words aloud
- To sort and write the lesson words according to the spelling patterns *i*, *y*, *igh*, and *uy*

Pretest

Use the pretest on this page to assess students' ability to spell the lesson words.

Have students use the study steps on page 6 to study any words they misspell in the pretest.

You may wish to duplicate and send home the Home Activity Master on pages T245–T246.

Presenting the Page

Introducing the Long *i* Sound
Write the words *fly* and *flea* on the board. Help students distinguish between the long *i* and the long *e* sounds.

As students prepare to sort the words, point out that / ī / is often spelled *i* or *y* but is spelled *igh* or *uy* in some words we often use.

Pronunciation Focus
Write *Fri/day* on the board and say the word aloud as you point to each syllable. Ask students to identify the syllable with the long *i* sound and tell the spelling of the sound (the first syllable; *i*). Follow the same procedure with *be/hind* (second syllable; *i*).

Consonant Focus
Write *kind* on the board and draw attention to the sounds that the final consonant blend *nd* makes. Repeat the process with *mind* and *behind*.

---

night

1. *i* Words
Friday
kind*
child
mind
behind

2. *y* Words
fly*
why*
try*
sky
cry
by*

3. *igh* Words
high
right*
light*
night

4. *uy* Word
buy*

buy
Friday
fly
kind
why
child
mind
try
behind
sky
cry
high
right
by
light
night

Say and Listen
Say each spelling word. Listen for the long *i* sound.

Think and Sort
Look at the letters in each word. Think about how long *i* is spelled. Spell each word aloud.

Long *i* can be shown as /ī/. How many spelling patterns for /ī/ do you see?

1. Write the **five** spelling words that have the *i* pattern.

2. Write the **six** spelling words that have the *y* pattern.

3. Look at the word *high*. The spelling pattern for this word is *igh*. Write the **four** spelling words that have the *igh* pattern.

4. Write the **one** spelling word that has the *uy* pattern.

Use the steps on page 6 to study words that are hard for you.

Spelling Patterns

i	*y*	*igh*	*uy*
kind	try	high	buy

*Dolch basic sight word

Pretest

Say each lesson word, read the sentence, and then repeat the word. Have students write the words on separate paper.

1. **buy** I saved to buy a bike.
2. **Friday** The test is Friday.
3. **fly** Jet planes fly very fast.
4. **kind** What kind of pizza did you get?
5. **why** Do you know why bees buzz?
6. **child** Give each child a toy.
7. **mind** I don't mind walking.
8. **try** She will try to meet us.
9. **behind** My dog hid behind the bed.
10. **sky** The sky is cloudy.
11. **cry** The baby began to cry.
12. **high** Balloons floated high over the school.
13. **right** Raise your right hand.
14. **by** Sit by the window.
15. **light** Mom sat near the light.
16. **night** Most owls hunt at night.

Additional Words for Enrichment

The following words can be used to meet the needs of on-level and above-level students:

reply   bright   knight   delight   wind   myself

Spelling and Meaning

Definitions Write the spelling word for each definition. Use the Spelling Dictionary if you need to.

1. at the back of   behind
2. to move through the air   fly
3. day before Saturday   Friday
4. helpful   kind
5. next to   by

Rhymes Write the spelling word that completes each sentence and rhymes with the underlined word.

6. My ____right____ shoe feels too tight.
7. The big box of toys was quite ____light____.
8. The spy climbed ____high____ in the tree.
9. The young ____child____ chose a book about wild animals.
10. Wet or dry, these onions make me ____cry____.
11. Turn on the light to see at ____night____.
12. Here's a fork so you can ____try____ my apple pie.
13. What should I ____buy____ my mom for her birthday?
14. Do you ____mind____ if I close the blind?
15. Tell me ____why____ you used purple dye.

Word Story One spelling word comes from the Old English word *sceo*. *Sceo* meant "cloud." The spelling word names the place where we see clouds. Write the word.

16. ____sky____

Family Tree: *light* Think about how the *light* words are alike in spelling and meaning. Then add another *light* word to the tree. A sample answer is shown.

lights
lightly
17. lighting
lightning
lighten
light

LESSON 16   95

HOME ACTIVITY MASTER p. T245

Unit 3 Spelling at Home

Dear Family of ____,
During the next six weeks, your child will be learning to spell the following kinds of words:
- words with the short *u* vowel sound
- words with the short *i* vowel sound
- words with the long *i* vowel sound
- words with *-ed* or *-ing*
Here are some simple activities to do each week to help your child become a better speller.

Listening and Writing
Say the spelling words and have your child write them.

Spelling Strategy: Sounds and Letters
If your child is unsure about the spelling of a word, have your child say the word to himself or herself. Tell your child to close his or her eyes and try to picture the way the word is spelled. Help your child think about how the word is spelled. Help your child think about the spelling by asking questions such as *Does it have more letters than sounds? Which letter pair spells a single sound?* Then have your child write the word on a piece of paper. Check the word's spelling in the list at right or in a dictionary.

Games and Activities
Play Recorded Spellings. Choose some of the spelling words. Call each word out to your child. Using a tape recorder, have your child record himself or herself echoing the word and spelling it. Play the recording back and have your child check the words.

Write the letters of the alphabet on index cards. Create five index cards for each vowel and two index cards for each consonant. Have your child use the alphabet cards to practice spelling words.

Using Spelling Words
Ask your child to write sentences that contain the spelling words. Then read the sentences with your child. Notice whether the sentences show that your child knows the meanings of the spelling words.

Lesson 13 More Words with Short u
Week of ____
won, lovely, done, something
shove, some, one, hundred
none, cover, must, number
sum, butter, just, supper

Lesson 14 Words with Short i
Week of ____
think, winter, been, December
fill, little, thing, spring
kick, river, which, pretty
dish, begin, build, children

Lesson 15 Words with Long i
Week of ____
line, drive, inside, nice
shine, while, size, miles
write, mine, alike, times
white, tiny, lion, eyes

Lesson 16 More Words with Long i
Week of ____
Friday, kind, child, mind
behind, high, right, light
night, by, cry, sky
try, why, fly, buy

Lesson 17 Words with -ed or -ing
Week of ____
washed, asked, rained, dreamed
handed, painted, filled, subtracted
thanked, waited, reading, sleeping
meeting, ending, guessing, laughing

Lesson 18 Unit 3 Review
Week of ____
Lesson 18 is a review of Lessons 15–17. Help your child practice all of the words from those lessons.

The highlighted area shows the Lesson 16 words, which students can share with family members. Spanish version available on page T246.

Proofreading Practice
- I want to by a kite. *(buy)*
- I will fligh it in the park. *(fly)*

Meeting Individual Needs

Auditory Learners
Students sometimes omit *n* from the endings in words such as *mind* and *behind* because nasal sounds in final consonant blends can be hard to feel as separate segments in speech. Have students put one finger on each side of the nose and say *mid–mind, kid–kind,* and *hid–behind.* They should feel a slight vibration on the words with *-nd.* Have students say *mind, kind,* and *behind* again and spell them aloud.

Day 2

Student Objectives
- To use meaning clues to identify and write lesson words
- To use etymology, spelling, and meaning to identify the word *sky*
- To learn *light* words and analyze their spellings and meanings

Presenting the Page

Write the following Definitions and Rhymes examples on the board and model identifying the answers:
- anything that gives off energy by which we see *(light)*
- I will ____ my kite in the park. *(fly)*

Word Story

The Old English word *sceo* is related to another Old English word, *scua,* which meant "shadow" or "shade." Write *sceo, scua,* and *sky* on the board and ask students to compare and contrast the words. Prompt students to realize that the initial /sk/ sound has remained the same but that the spelling has changed from *sc* to *sk.*

Family Tree: *light*

Students should observe that the *light* words all contain *light.* To help students explore the meanings of the words, have them locate the meanings in a dictionary, write their findings on the board, and discuss how the meanings are alike and different. Write the words *lightning* and *lighting* on the board. Help students to recognize that even though both words are forms of the word *light,* their meanings and spellings differ. Guide students to understand that knowing how to spell *light* words will help them spell related words.

95

Day 3

Student Objectives

- To use context to identify and write lesson words
- To sequence story events
- To identify author's purpose

Presenting the Pages

Read the story aloud, having volunteers supply the missing words. Then ask students to complete the pages independently. Alternatively, have students complete the pages on their own by silently reading the story and writing the missing words. Then have students take turns reading the completed story aloud.

Meeting Individual Needs

ESOL

To help speakers of other languages practice the lesson words, say each word and use it in a sentence. Have students repeat the word and write it. Then ask a volunteer to make up another sentence, using the same lesson word. For example, you might say *Stars lit up the sky*. A volunteer might reply *The sky is blue today*.

Use each spelling word once to complete the story.

Living Room Circus

My family and I had planned to go to the circus last ____Friday____. It was a beautiful day. The sun was bright, and the ____sky____ was blue. But I got sick.
₁
₂

Mom made a bed for me on the couch. Then she opened the front door to let Tinker in. Tinker is our gray tabby cat. He sleeps all day in the warm ____light____ of the sun. He plays all ____night____. I ____try____ to talk Mom and Dad into letting me stay up all night, too. If the cat can, ____why____ can't I? They don't agree.

Well, that day Tinker dropped a fat pigeon ____by____ my dad's feet.

"Oh, no!" Mom cried. "Tinker, how could you bring that in the house? What were you thinking?"

Mom thinks she can talk to Tinker just as she can talk to a ____child____. She gets very angry when Tinker acts like a cat.

96 UNIT 3

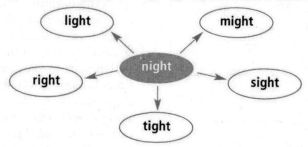

Spelling Strategy

Rhyming Helper

Remind students that they can use a rhyming helper to remember the spelling of a word. Write the word *night* on the board. Invite students to name rhyming helpers. Remind students that a rhyming helper must be spelled the same way as the word they are trying to remember, except for the beginning sound or sounds. Guide students in choosing a rhyming helper for *night*, such as *tight*, and write it on the board, along with other appropriate rhyming helpers students name.

```
light            might

        night

right            sight

        tight
```

Then write the words *sky*, *try*, *why*, *fly*, and *cry* on the board and help students observe that all of the words rhyme with each other and have the same spelling pattern. Explain that any of the words can be a rhyming helper for the others.

buy
Friday
fly
kind
why
child
mind
try
behind
sky
cry
high
right
by
light
night

Just then, the pigeon fluttered its wings. It wasn't hurt.
It began to _____fly_____ around the room.
9

Tinker saw the pigeon and hid _____behind_____ the
10
couch. He jumped out as the pigeon whizzed by.

Mom opened the door. Tinker chased the pigeon. Dad
chased Tinker. My baby brother began to _____cry_____.
11
And I began to laugh. You couldn't _____buy_____ a
12
ticket to a better show.

At last the pigeon flew out the door. Tinker was
_____right_____ behind it. But the pigeon got away.
13
It flew _____high_____ into the sky.
14

I was really glad that the pigeon was safe. And I didn't
_____mind_____ that I was sick. I got to see a circus after
15
all! It just wasn't the _____kind_____ of circus I expected
16
to see!

ACTIVITY MASTER p. T266

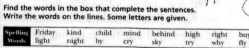

Lesson 16 More Words with Long *i*

Name _____

Find the words in the box that complete the sentences. Write the words on the lines. Some letters are given.

Spelling Words	Friday	kind	child	mind	behind	high	right	buy
	light	night	by	cry	sky	try	why	fly

1. A c h i l d saw a housefly f l y.

2. It flew b e h i n d the curtain and near the l i g h t.

3. It flew all day and into the n i g h t.

4. I saw a housefly fly b y me.

5. I watched it fly h i g h in the sky.

6. I once tried to b u y a housefly in a store.

7. On F r i d a y, a housefly flew down from the s k y.

8. The housefly flew r i g h t into the house.

9. It landed on my knee and began to c r y.

10. T r y to see a house fly.

11. What k i n d of house flies?

12. W h y do you ask?

13. Houses don't fly; it's all in your m i n d.

ADDITIONAL PRACTICE

You may wish to copy and distribute the Activity Master on page T266 as additional practice for Lesson 16.

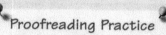

Proofreading Practice
- Our house is behighnd the trees. *(behind)*
- You walked rite by it. *(right)*

Day 4

Student Objectives

- To write a narrative paragraph, using lesson words
- To proofread an e-mail message for spelling, capitalization, and punctuation

Presenting the Page

Review with students the events that happen in the story "Living Room Circus," on pages 96–97. Prompt students to think of times when something exciting happened to them or someone they know. To spark thinking, suggest that students refer to the lesson words.

To assist students with the Proofreading activity, ask a volunteer to read the directions and the e-mail aloud as other students follow along. Then have students complete the activity independently. Have partners check each other's answers.

Meeting Individual Needs

ESOL

To help speakers of other languages build vocabulary and spelling skills, present clues such as *I'm thinking of a word that tells where clouds can be found.* Have students say the lesson word that fits the clue, spell the word aloud, and write it on the board.

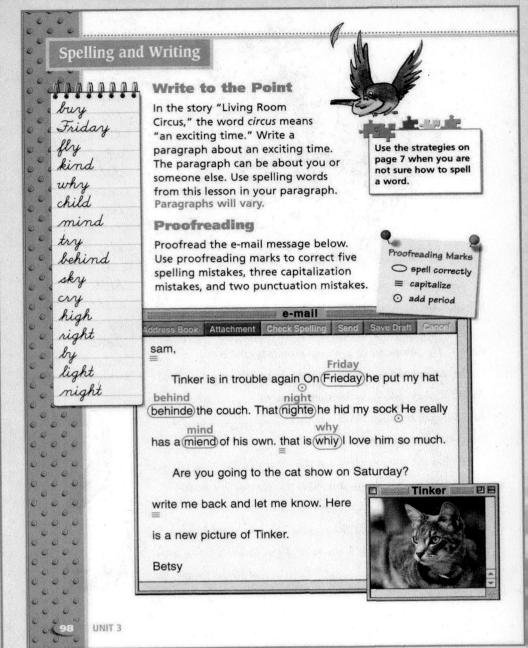

Spelling and Writing

buy
Friday
fly
kind
why
child
mind
try
behind
sky
cry
high
right
by
light
night

Write to the Point

In the story "Living Room Circus," the word *circus* means "an exciting time." Write a paragraph about an exciting time. The paragraph can be about you or someone else. Use spelling words from this lesson in your paragraph.
Paragraphs will vary.

Use the strategies on page 7 when you are not sure how to spell a word.

Proofreading

Proofread the e-mail message below. Use proofreading marks to correct five spelling mistakes, three capitalization mistakes, and two punctuation mistakes.

Proofreading Marks
- ⬭ spell correctly
- ≡ capitalize
- ⊙ add period

e-mail

Address Book | Attachment | Check Spelling | Send | Save Draft | Cancel

sam, [≡]

Tinker is in trouble again [⊙] On (Frieday) [Friday] he put my hat (behinde) [behind] the couch. That (nighte) [night] he hid my sock [⊙] He really has a (miend) [mind] of his own. that [≡] is (whiy) [why] I love him so much.

Are you going to the cat show on Saturday? write [≡] me back and let me know. Here is a new picture of Tinker.

Betsy

Tinker

Proofreading Practice

- The small chyld lay in his crib. *(child)*
- Soon he began to cruy. *(cry)*

Correcting Common Errors

A combination of silent letters often presents spelling problems. Some students may omit one or both of the silent letters *g* and *h* in *high, light, night,* and *right.* These students may benefit from repeated practice in saying each lesson word and then writing the word as they spell it aloud. Have students circle the *gh* in each word as a reminder to write *gh.*

Dictionary Skills

Alphabetical Order   Many words begin with the same letter. To arrange these words in alphabetical order, look at the second letter of each word. Look at the two words below. Then complete the sentences that follow.

sky	story

1. *Sky* and *story* both start with the letter *s*. To put them in alphabetical order, look at the ____second____ letter.

2. The second letter in <u>sky</u> is ____k____.

3. The second letter in <u>story</u> is ____t____.

4. In the alphabet, *k* comes before *t*, so the word ____sky____ comes before the word ____story____.

In each list below, the words begin with the same letter. Look at the second letter of each word. Then write the words in alphabetical order.

5. buy   behind   by

   behind
   buy
   by

6. fly   Friday   finish

   finish
   fly
   Friday

⭐ Challenge Yourself

Write the Challenge Word for each clue. Check the Spelling Dictionary to see if you are right. Then use separate paper to write sentences showing that you understand the meaning of each Challenge Word.
Sentences will vary.

Challenge Words	
designer	glider
cycle	skyline

7. It has big wings but is not a bird. ____glider____

8. A big city has one of these. ____skyline____

9. If you ride something with wheels, you may have this.
   ____cycle____

10. This is a person who makes drawings and plans. ____designer____

LESSON 16   **99**

Posttest

Dictate the following sentences. Have students use separate paper to write the sentences and underline the lesson words.

1. The <u>child</u> began to <u>cry</u>.
2. My party is on <u>Friday</u> night.
3. I am <u>right</u> <u>behind</u> you.
4. Please <u>try</u> to find out <u>why</u> he is late.
5. There is a <u>light</u> in the <u>sky</u>.
6. What <u>kind</u> of hat did you <u>buy</u>?
7. That bird cannot <u>fly</u> very <u>high</u>.
8. Do you <u>mind</u> if we walk <u>by</u> the park?

Enrichment Activity

Have each student write the lesson words on index cards or paper strips. Then have students sort the words by spelling pattern and put them in alphabetical order within each group. Afterward, students can work in pairs to check each other's groupings, spellings, and order.

Day 5

Student Objectives

- To arrange lesson words in alphabetical order
- To study the spellings and meanings of the Challenge Words
- To take a posttest on the lesson words

Presenting the Page

Review with students that alphabetical order is the order of the letters of the alphabet. Then have students look at the examples *sky* and *story*. Help students to understand that to arrange words that begin with the same letter in alphabetical order, they need to look at the second letter of each word.

⭐ Challenge Yourself

To introduce the Challenge Words, write the following on the board:

de/sign/er   glid/er
cy/cle   sky/line

Pronounce the words for students and discuss the number of syllables in each. Then have students refer to page 94 and review the long *i* spelling patterns featured in this lesson. Ask students to identify the long *i* spelling patterns in the Challenge Words (*designer* and *glider* have the *i* pattern; the first syllable in *cycle* and *skyline* have the *y* pattern; the second syllable in *skyline* has the *i*-consonant-e pattern).

Posttest

Use the posttest on this page to assess students' ability to spell the lesson words.

Lesson 17
Words with -ed or -ing

Day 1

Student Objectives
- To take a pretest on the lesson words
- To spell the lesson words aloud
- To sort and write the lesson words according to the -ed and -ing endings

Pretest

Use the pretest on this page to assess students' ability to spell the lesson words.

Study Steps
Have students use the study steps on page 6 to study any words they misspell in the pretest.

You may wish to duplicate and send home the Home Activity Master on pages T245–T246.

Presenting the Page

Introducing the -ed and -ing Endings Write *meet* and *meeting* on the board and say the words. Point out that because an ending can be added to *meet* to form another word, *meet* is a base word. Then write the word *asked* on the board and have students identify the base word and ending (*ask; -ed*).

Pronunciation Focus Write *dreamed* and *hand/ed* on the board, pointing out each syllable. Draw attention to the difference in pronunciation of the -ed ending. Guide students to observe that *painted, waited,* and *subtracted* are pronounced with -ed as a separate syllable.

Consonant Focus Write *laughing* on the board and point out the *gh* spelling for the /f/ sound. List additional words with the *gh* spelling for /f/, such as *rough, tough,* and *enough.* Have a volunteer say each word and circle the *gh* spelling for /f/.

laughing

Lesson 17
Words with -ed or -ing

1. -ed Words
- wished
- asked*
- dreamed
- rained
- handed
- painted
- filled
- subtracted
- thanked
- waited

2. -ing Words
- ending
- guessing
- laughing
- meeting
- sleeping
- reading

ending
wished
asked
guessing
laughing
dreamed
rained
meeting
sleeping
handed
painted
filled
reading
subtracted
thanked
waited

Say and Listen

Say the spelling words. Listen for the -ed and -ing endings.

Think and Sort

Each spelling word is formed by adding -ed or -ing to a base word. A **base word** is a word from which other words are formed. The base word for *wished* is *wish.* The base word for *ending* is *end.*

Look at each spelling word. Think about the base word and the ending. Spell each word aloud.

1. Write the **ten** spelling words that end in -ed.

2. Write the **six** spelling words that end in -ing.

Use the steps on page 6 to study words that are hard for you.

Spelling Patterns

-ed	-ing
paint**ed**	read**ing**

100 UNIT 3   *Dolch basic sight word

Pretest

Say each lesson word, read the sentence, and then repeat the word. Have students write the words on separate paper.

1. **ending** The play is ending now.
2. **wished** She wished for snow.
3. **asked** The driver asked for directions.
4. **guessing** I'm guessing that you're nine years old.
5. **laughing** Everyone started laughing.
6. **dreamed** I dreamed about a giant frog.
7. **rained** It rained last night.
8. **meeting** She is meeting me after school.
9. **sleeping** The baby is sleeping.
10. **handed** The clerk handed me the package.
11. **painted** The artist painted a picture.
12. **filled** The waiter filled the glasses.
13. **reading** He is reading a story.
14. **subtracted** I subtracted one from ten and got nine.
15. **thanked** I thanked my aunt for the gift.
16. **waited** The players waited for the rain to stop.

Additional Words for Enrichment

The following words can be used to meet the needs of on-level and above-level students:
followed   traveled   climbed   carrying   speaking   returning

Spelling and Meaning

Definitions Write the spelling word for each definition.
Use the Spelling Dictionary if you need to.

1. passed with one's hands   handed
2. said that one was pleased   thanked
3. stayed   waited
4. a coming together for some purpose   meeting
5. forming an opinion without all the facts   guessing
6. saw or thought during sleep   dreamed
7. fell in drops of water from the clouds   rained

Analogies Write the spelling word that completes each analogy.

8. *Taught* is to *instructed* as *hoped* is to ___wished___.
9. *Dress* is to *sewed* as *picture* is to ___painted___.
10. *Playing* is to *piano* as ___reading___ is to *book*.
11. *Chair* is to *sitting* as *bed* is to ___sleeping___.
12. *Told* is to *explained* as *questioned* is to ___asked___.
13. *Happy* is to ___laughing___ as *sad* is to *crying*.
14. *Beginning* is to *start* as ___ending___ is to *finish*.
15. *Out* is to *emptied* as *in* is to ___filled___.

Word Story One of the spelling words comes from two Latin words—*sub* and *trahere*. *Sub* meant "below or away." *Trahere* meant "to pull." *Subtrahere* meant "to pull away." Write the spelling word that comes from *subtrahere*.

16. ___subtracted___

Family Tree: *rained* *Rained* is a form of *rain*. Think about how the *rain* words are alike in spelling and meaning. Then add another *rain* word to the tree. A sample answer is shown.

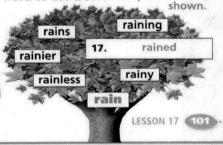

rains
raining
rainier
17. rained
rainless
rainy
rain

LESSON 17   101

HOME ACTIVITY MASTER p. T245

The highlighted area shows the Lesson 17 words, which students can share with family members. Spanish version available on page T246.

Proofreading Practice
- I dreamd I could fly. *(dreamed)*
- I woke up before the endin. *(ending)*

Meeting Individual Needs

ESOL

To give speakers of other languages practice with base words and endings, write each lesson word on the board and write the base word above it. Point to the base word and use it in a question such as *Did it rain?* Then point to the lesson word and have students use it in an answer such as *Yes, it rained.* Finally, have the students repeat the lesson word and write it.

Spelling and Meaning

Day 2

Student Objectives
- To use meaning clues to identify and write lesson words
- To use etymology, spelling, and meaning to identify the word *subtracted*
- To learn *rain* words and analyze their spellings and meanings

Presenting the Page

Write the following Definitions and Analogies examples on the board and model identifying the answers:

- bringing to a close *(ending)*
- *Stayed* is to ____ as *went* is to *left*. *(waited)*

Remind students that the key to solving an analogy is understanding the relationship between the given pair of words so that they can complete the other pair.

Word Story

Share with students additional English words that begin with the Latin *sub*, meaning "below or away," such as *suburb*, which means "away from a city." Then ask students to contribute other *sub* words such as *subway* and *submarine*.

Family Tree: *rain*

Students should see that the *rain* words all contain *rain*. To help students explore the meanings of the words, have them locate the meanings in a dictionary, write their findings on the board, and talk about how the meanings are alike and different. Explain the function of *y* in *rainy*—to change *rain* to an adjective. Guide students to understand that knowing how to spell *rain* can help them spell words related to *rain*.

Student Objectives
- To use context to identify and write lesson words
- To identify cause and effect

Presenting the Pages

Have students take turns reading the story paragraph by paragraph and supplying the missing words. Then have students reread the story silently and write the missing words. Alternatively, have students complete the pages on their own by silently reading the story and writing the missing words. Then have volunteers take turns reading the completed story aloud.

Call attention to the word *playoffs* in the title. Explain that in a sport such as ice hockey, the best teams play a series of games to see which team will be the champion. This series of games is called the playoffs. Also explain that even though "The Playoffs" is not a real story, the author used the name of a real hockey player, Wayne Gretzky, in the story.

Meeting Individual Needs

Kinesthetic Learners
To help kinesthetic learners practice with lesson words, have them write each base word on one index card and the ending on a second. Then have students shuffle the cards and build each word. Finally, have students say each word and write it.

Use each spelling word once to complete the story.

The Playoffs

When I left hockey practice yesterday, it was still raining. It had __rained__ all day. I __waited__ for Dad to pick me up.
1   2
Then I remembered that Mom and Dad were __meeting__ with
3
teachers and other parents. They were planning our fall festival, so I walked over to school to wait.

I tried not to think about the homework that I hadn't done yet. I had extra math problems to do because I added numbers on our last test when I should have __subtracted__ them. Oh, how I
4
__wished__ that I had done my homework before practice.
5
Then I would have been finished.

At school I ran into Ms. Ford, the art teacher. She was showing the parents some pictures that students had __painted__. Mr. Chan,
6
the librarian, was also at school. I __asked__ him if I could wait
7
in the library. He said yes.

I started doing my math homework. It was going pretty well. Then Mr. Chan __handed__ me a book that he was sure I would like. I
8
__thanked__ him and looked at the cover.
9
The book was about my favorite hockey player, Wayne Gretzky. It was __filled__ with pictures of him. I started __reading__.
10   11
The book was great. It started with his childhood. I could hardly wait to read the __ending__.
12

Spelling Strategy

Sound It Out
Remind students that they can use the sound-it-out strategy to help them spell a syllable or a one-syllable word. Remind them that in this strategy, they need to listen carefully to the sounds of the letters while saying each syllable correctly. Demonstrate the process with the word *subtracted*. Pronounce each syllable and write it on the board letter by letter, leaving space between the syllables. You may wish to cluster letters that spell consonant blends and digraphs, as is done below. Then say the word *handed* or *ending* and have students use the sound-it-out strategy to spell the word.

Sound It Out

s u b   tr a c t   e d
h a n d   e d
e n d   i ng

The next thing I knew, I was on the floor, swinging my arms and yelling. Mom and Dad were there in the library. They were _____laughing_____ at me. I shook my head and blinked.
13

"Was I _____sleeping_____?" I asked.
14

"I'm only _____guessing_____," Dad said, "but I would
15

say you _____dreamed_____ you were a hockey player.
16

The way you were swinging your arms around, I'm glad I wasn't on the other team!"

I grinned. Too bad it was just a dream.

ending
wished
asked
guessing
laughing
dreamed
rained
meeting
sleeping
handed
painted
filled
reading
subtracted
thanked
waited

Reading Comprehension

After students have completed the pages, ask them why the girl in the story fell asleep. Help students explore plausible causes. For example, she might have been tired after hockey practice, and/or the darkness and the sound of the rain may have lulled her to sleep. Remind students that the reasons why the girl fell asleep are *causes*. Falling asleep is the *effect* of one or more causes.

Cooperative Learning Activity

To help students assess their progress, have partners take turns dictating the *-ed* lesson words to each other and then the *-ing* lesson words. Have students check their own work, using the list on page 103. Have students compare their performance on this midweek activity to their performance on the pretest. Guide them in noting the words they are now spelling correctly and those they need to continue to study.

ACTIVITY MASTER p. T267

Lesson 17 Words with *-ed* or *-ing*

Name _____

Use the words in the box to solve the puzzle below. Some letters are given.

Spelling Words	wished	dreamed	rained	painted	filled
	handed	thanked	reading	guessing	ending
	waited	sleeping	meeting	laughing	asked
	subtracted				

ADDITIONAL PRACTICE

You may wish to copy and distribute the Activity Master on page T267 as additional practice for Lesson 17.

Proofreading Practice
- It raind all day. *(rained)*
- I stayed inside readen a book. *(reading)*

Spelling and Writing

Day 4

Student Objectives
- To write an expressive paragraph, using lesson words
- To proofread a movie review for spelling, capitalization, and unnecessary words

Presenting the Page

Review with students the story of the child who dreams of hockey in "The Playoffs" on pages 102–103. To encourage the use of the lesson words in their paragraph, have students think of ways one of their dreams might relate to some of the words on the spelling list on page 104. If students have trouble remembering a specific dream, suggest that they make up a dream that they would like to have.

To assist students with the Proofreading activity, you may wish to have a volunteer read the directions and the movie review aloud. Then have students complete the activity independently.

Meeting Individual Needs

ESOL
To give speakers of other languages practice with the lesson words, have students write the ending *-ed* on one sheet of paper and the ending *-ing* on another. Then say a lesson word aloud and have students hold up the appropriate word ending. Have students repeat the word and write it, underlining the *-ed* or *-ing* ending.

ending
wished
asked
guessing
laughing
dreamed
rained
meeting
sleeping
handed
painted
filled
reading
subtracted
thanked
waited

Write to the Point
You dream almost every time you sleep. Dreams can take you on great adventures. Sometimes dreams are happy. Other times they're silly. Write a paragraph about a dream you've had. Try to use spelling words from this lesson. Paragraphs will vary.

Use the strategies on page 7 when you are not sure how to spell a word.

Proofreading
Proofread the movie review below. Use proofreading marks to correct five spelling mistakes, three capitalization mistakes, and two unnecessary words.

Proofreading Marks
◯ spell correctly
≡ capitalize
✐ take out

The Winning Team ★★★★

Is a Winner!

this movie is about a losing hockey team. The

coach has tried everything to to help the team win.

he called a meating each day before practice. He
meeting

thankt the players for their hard work but told them
thanked

he wisht they would do better. He askt the players to
wished *asked*

run five miles a day, even when it it rained. the

surprise endin shows what really worked.
ending

104   UNIT 3

Proofreading Practice
- He handid me the ticket. *(handed)*
- Then I thankted him. *(thanked)*

✔ Correcting Common Errors
Students sometimes omit one of the double consonants in words such as *filled* and *guessing*. Help these students to understand that most one-syllable words ending with /l/ or /s/ sound are spelled with a double *l* or double *s*. Have them practice spelling and writing words such as *doll, pull, ball, miss, pass,* and *dress*. Conclude with the words *fill, guess, filled,* and *guessing*. Have students circle the double consonants in each word as a visual reminder.

Language Connection

End Punctuation   Use a period at the end of a sentence that tells or explains something. Use a question mark at the end of a sentence that asks a question. Use an exclamation point at the end of a sentence that shows strong feeling or surprise. In sentences that have quotation marks, place the end punctuation inside the quotation marks.

Matt said, "Here comes the team."	The police officer yelled, "Open that door!"

Write the following sentences, using periods, question marks, and exclamation points correctly.

1. Betsy asked Paul, "Who painted this picture"
   Betsy asked Paul, "Who painted this picture?"

2. She saw that Paul was sleeping
   She saw that Paul was sleeping.

3. Betsy shouted, "Boo"
   Betsy shouted, "Boo!"

4. Paul jumped up fast
   Paul jumped up fast.

5. "Oh, Betsy," he cried. "Now I'll never know the ending of my dream"
   "Oh, Betsy," he cried. "Now I'll never know the ending of my dream!"

6. They both started laughing
   They both started laughing.

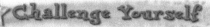
Challenge Yourself

What do you think each Challenge Word means? Check the Spelling Dictionary to see if you are right. Then use separate paper to write sentences showing that you understand the meaning of each Challenge Word. *Definitions and sentences will vary.*

7. He is **fulfilling** his promise.
8. A beginning skater may make **faltering** movements on the ice.
9. Mom **consented** to let us play.
10. The President **governed** the country for four years.

Challenge Words

fulfilling
faltering
consented
governed

LESSON 17   **105**

Posttest

Dictate the following sentences. Have students use separate paper to write the sentences and underline the lesson words.

1. I dreamed that it rained all week.
2. She asked me if he was sleeping.
3. I was laughing while the clown filled the balloon.
4. I wished that I had waited and painted my room red.
5. He thanked me when I handed him the book.
6. That book kept me guessing until the ending.
7. He subtracted the cost of the milk.
8. We are reading and will be meeting later.

Enrichment Activity

Have small groups of students write the lesson words on index cards and use the word cards in a game of charades. Players should take turns drawing a word card and acting out the lesson word for the other players to guess. The first player to guess the word, identify the word ending, and spell the word correctly draws the next card.

Student Objectives
- To write sentences containing the lesson words
- To use periods, question marks, and exclamation points correctly
- To study the spellings and meanings of the Challenge Words
- To take a posttest on the lesson words

Presenting the Page

Review with students the different kinds of end punctuation. Read the examples, pointing out each end mark and explaining why it is appropriate for the sentence in which it appears.

Challenge Yourself

To introduce the Challenge Words, write the following on the board:

ful/fill/ing   con/sent/ed
fal/ter/ing   gov/erned

Pronounce the words for students and discuss the number of syllables in each. Ask students to identify the Challenge Words with the *-ing* ending (*fulfilling* and *faltering*) and those with the *-ed* ending (*consented* and *governed*).

Next, have students write what they think each Challenge Word means, look up the words in the Spelling Dictionary, and then write the correct definitions. Ask students to compare their definitions with those in the Spelling Dictionary.

Posttest

Use the posttest on this page to assess students' ability to spell the lesson words.

Lesson 18

Unit 3 Review
Lessons 13–17

Use the steps on page 6 to study words that are hard for you.

Day 1

Student Objective
- To take a pretest on the lesson words.

Pretest

Use the pretest on this page to assess students' ability to spell the lesson words.

Have students use the study steps on page 6 to study any words they misspell in the pretest.

You may wish to duplicate and send home the Home Activity Master on pages T245–T246.

Meeting Individual Needs

ESOL

Because few Spanish words begin with *w* or *wh*, some Spanish-speaking students may need help associating the letter *w* with the /w/ sound. Write *won*, *which*, *while*, *why*, and *wished* on the board. Model the correct pronunciation of each word, emphasizing the beginning /w/ sound. Have students say the /w/ sound, repeat the word, and then spell it aloud as they write it. Explain that in English /w/ is sometimes spelled *w*, as in *won*, and sometimes it is spelled *wh*, as in *which*. Both spellings, however, make the /w/ sound.

Lesson 18

Unit 3 Review
Lessons 13–17

13
butter
hundred
done
lovely
won

More Words with Short *u*

Write the spelling word for each clue.

1. People often use this word to describe flowers. _____ **lovely**

2. This is the sum of 99 and 1. _____ **hundred**

3. If you came in first, you did this. _____ **won**

4. You can spread this on bread. _____ **butter**

5. When you are finished, you are this. _____ **done**

14
which
children
pretty
build
been

Words with Short *i*

Write the spelling word that belongs in each group.

6. where   when   _____ **which**
7. be   being   _____ **been**
8. beautiful   lovely   _____ **pretty**
9. form   make   _____ **build**
10. tots   youngsters   _____ **children**

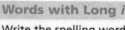

15
while
write
tiny
lion
eyes

Words with Long *i*

Write the spelling word for each definition.

11. the body parts used for seeing   _____ **eyes**
12. to make letters on a surface   _____ **write**
13. a large wild cat   _____ **lion**

106 UNIT 3

Pretest

Say each lesson word, read the sentence, and then repeat the word. Have students write the words on separate paper.

1. **butter** Melt some butter in the pan.
2. **hundred** We collected one hundred plastic bottles.
3. **done** You have done a good job.
4. **lovely** Mom made a lovely dress.
5. **won** She won the race.
6. **which** Show me which hat is yours.
7. **children** The children played outside.
8. **pretty** You drew a pretty picture.
9. **build** They will build a fence.
10. **been** Have you been here long?
11. **while** Can you stay for a while?
12. **write** Write your name.
13. **tiny** The garden is filled with tiny bugs.
14. **lion** I saw a lion at the zoo.
15. **eyes** My eyes are brown.
16. **behind** Look behind the door.
17. **why** She did not say why she left.
18. **right** You gave the right answer.
19. **night** Stars shine at night.
20. **buy** Please buy some milk.
21. **wished** She wished that the rain would end.
22. **thanked** He thanked us for our help.
23. **dreamed** I dreamed about summer.
24. **guessing** Are you guessing?
25. **laughing** They were singing and laughing.

14. although   _while_

15. very small   _tiny_

16
behind
why
right
night
buy

More Words with Long *i*

Write the spelling word that has the same meaning as the word or words in dark type.

16. **For what reason** did the pioneers go west?

     why

17. Can I **pay for** this toy?

     buy

18. You were **correct** about the weather.   _right_

19. Last **evening** I had a strange dream.

     night

20. Please stand **in back of** me in line.

     behind

17
wished
thanked
dreamed
guessing
laughing

Words with *-ed* or *-ing*

Write the spelling word that completes each sentence.

21. They are _____laughing_____ at your joke.

22. Alicia _____wished_____ for a new bicycle.

23. Are you just _____guessing_____ the answer?

24. Amad _____dreamed_____ about winning a trophy.

25. The teacher _____thanked_____ the children for the gift.

LESSON 18   **107**

REVIEW TEST MASTER, pp. T287–T288

Unit 3 Review Test   Name _____

Darken the circle for the word that is not spelled correctly. Darken the circle for *No mistakes* if all the words are spelled correctly.

Example
A pritty
B sky
C kick
D river
E *No mistakes*

1. A write
   B done
   C behind
   D iyes
   E *No mistakes*

2. F laughing
   G build
   H children
   J wch
   K *No mistakes*

3. A tiny
   B dreamed
   C lovly
   D lion
   E *No mistakes*

4. F been
   G wun
   H while
   J right
   K *No mistakes*

5. A laughing
   B write
   C childrin
   D lion
   E *No mistakes*

6. F nite
   G guessing
   H why
   J which
   K *No mistakes*

7. A been
   B right
   C while
   D thankd
   E *No mistakes*

8. F wished
   G hondred
   H buy
   J butter
   K *No mistakes*

9. A behind
   B tiny
   C guessng
   D which
   E *No mistakes*

Example
● Ⓑ Ⓒ Ⓓ Ⓔ

Answers
1. Ⓐ Ⓑ Ⓒ ● Ⓔ
2. Ⓕ Ⓖ Ⓗ ● Ⓙ
3. Ⓐ Ⓑ ● Ⓓ Ⓔ
4. Ⓕ ● Ⓗ Ⓙ Ⓚ
5. Ⓐ Ⓑ ● Ⓓ Ⓔ
6. ● Ⓖ Ⓗ Ⓙ Ⓚ
7. Ⓐ Ⓑ Ⓒ ● Ⓔ
8. Ⓕ Ⓖ ● Ⓙ Ⓚ
9. Ⓐ Ⓑ ● Ⓓ Ⓔ

Unit 3 Review Test   Name _____

Darken the circle for the word that is not spelled correctly. Darken the circle for *No mistakes* if all the words are spelled correctly.

10. F butter
    G lovely
    H laughig
    J right
    K *No mistakes*

11. A doen
    B write
    C been
    D thanked
    E *No mistakes*

12. F whyle
    G right
    H dreamed
    J guessing
    K *No mistakes*

13. A thanked
    B lieon
    C tiny
    D lovely
    E *No mistakes*

14. F night
    G eyes
    H butter
    J behined
    K *No mistakes*

15. A tiny
    B guessing
    C whi
    D been
    E *No mistakes*

16. F night
    G wich
    H hundred
    J wished
    K *No mistakes*

17. A buy
    B write
    C children
    D won
    E *No mistakes*

18. F dreamed
    G bild
    H eyes
    J pretty
    K *No mistakes*

19. A children
    B night
    C won
    D wishd
    E *No mistakes*

Answers
10. Ⓕ Ⓖ ● Ⓙ Ⓚ
11. ● Ⓑ Ⓒ Ⓓ Ⓔ
12. ● Ⓖ Ⓗ Ⓙ Ⓚ
13. Ⓐ ● Ⓒ Ⓓ Ⓔ
14. Ⓕ Ⓖ Ⓗ ● Ⓚ
15. Ⓐ Ⓑ ● Ⓓ Ⓔ
16. Ⓕ ● Ⓗ Ⓙ Ⓚ
17. Ⓐ Ⓑ Ⓒ ● Ⓔ
18. Ⓕ ● Ⓗ Ⓙ Ⓚ
19. Ⓐ Ⓑ Ⓒ ● Ⓔ

Day 2

Student Objectives

- To review the *u*, *o*, and *o*-consonant-*e* spellings of the /ŭ/ sound
- To review the *i*, *e*, *ui*, and *ee* spellings of the /ĕ/ sound
- To review the *i*-consonant-*e*, *i*, *eye*, *y*, *igh*, and *uy* spellings of the /ī/ sound
- To review -*ed* and -*ing* words with no base word changes
- To use meaning clues to identify and write lesson words

Presenting the Pages

Lesson 13 Have volunteers read the Lesson 13 review words aloud. Review with students the *u*, *o*, and *o*-consonant-*e* spelling patterns for /ŭ/ represented in the review words.

Lessons 14–16 Have volunteers read the review words for Lessons 14–16 aloud. Review with students the short *i* and long *i* spelling patterns represented in the review words—*i*, *e*, *ui*, and *ee* for short *i* and *i*-consonant-*e*, *i*, *eye*, *y*, *igh*, and *uy* for long *i*.

Lesson 17 Have volunteers read the Lesson 17 words and identify each base word.

Test-Taking Strategies

Read the directions for the Review Test Master aloud and talk with students about the task and format of the test. Point out that each test item presents four different words, one of which may not be spelled correctly. Suggest that students first go through and mark all the words they know are misspelled and then return to the other items. Remind students that all the words in some items may be spelled correctly.

Proofreading Practice

- We turn rite at the end of block. (right)
- The store is behighnd the bank. (behind)

107

Student Objectives
- To sort lesson words according to vowel sound
- To compare sorted words that end with -ed or -ing

Presenting the Page
Have volunteers take turns reading the Review Sort words aloud. Review with students the sounds represented by the sound symbols /ŭ/, /ĭ/, and /ī/. Point out that one of the Review Sort words is from the lesson on words that end with -ed or -ing but that the word can be sorted according to its vowel sound.

Meeting Individual Needs

Visual Learners
Suggest that students say the Review Sort words aloud and then write them on cards, using one color of marker for /ŭ/ words, another for /ĭ/ words, and so on. Suggest that students make two cards for *behind*, writing the word in the /ĭ/ and the /ī/ colors. Then have students use color to sort the cards according to vowel sound.

Proofreading Practice
- I one a prize. (won)
- I don't know wich ribbon is mine. (which)

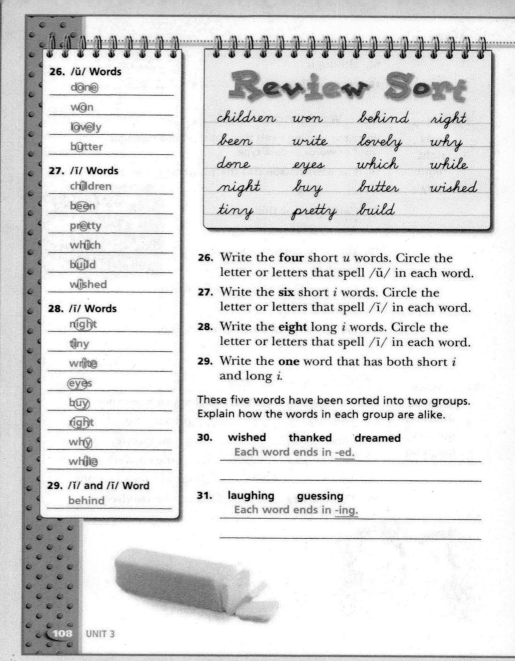

26. /ŭ/ Words
done
won
lovely
butter

27. /ĭ/ Words
children
been
pretty
which
build
wished

28. /ī/ Words
night
tiny
write
eyes
buy
right
why
while

29. /ĭ/ and /ī/ Word
behind

Review Sort

children   won   behind   right
been   write   lovely   why
done   eyes   which   while
night   buy   butter   wished
tiny   pretty   build

26. Write the **four** short *u* words. Circle the letter or letters that spell /ŭ/ in each word.

27. Write the **six** short *i* words. Circle the letter or letters that spell /ĭ/ in each word.

28. Write the **eight** long *i* words. Circle the letter or letters that spell /ī/ in each word.

29. Write the **one** word that has both short *i* and long *i*.

These five words have been sorted into two groups. Explain how the words in each group are alike.

30. **wished   thanked   dreamed**
Each word ends in -ed.

_____

31. **laughing   guessing**
Each word ends in -ing.

_____

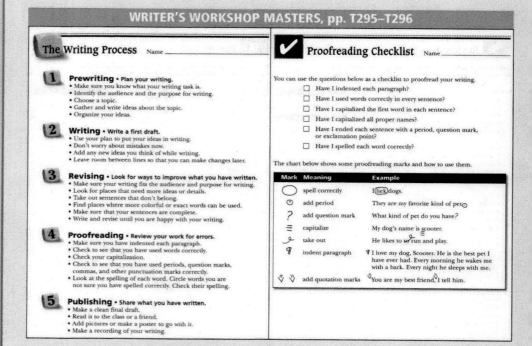

WRITER'S WORKSHOP MASTERS, pp. T295–T296

The Writing Process Name _____

1 **Prewriting** • Plan your writing.
- Make sure you know what your writing task is.
- Identify the audience and the purpose for writing.
- Choose a topic.
- Gather and write ideas about the topic.
- Organize your ideas.

2 **Writing** • Write a first draft.
- Use your plan to put your ideas in writing.
- Don't worry about mistakes now.
- Add any new ideas you think of while writing.
- Leave room between lines so that you can make changes later.

3 **Revising** • Look for ways to improve what you have written.
- Make sure your writing fits the audience and purpose for writing.
- Look for places that need more ideas or details.
- Take out sentences that don't belong.
- Find places where more colorful or exact words can be used.
- Make sure that your sentences are complete.
- Write and revise until you are happy with your writing.

4 **Proofreading** • Review your work for errors.
- Make sure you have indented each paragraph.
- Check to see that you have used words correctly.
- Check your capitalization.
- Check to see that you have used periods, question marks, commas, and other punctuation marks correctly.
- Look at the spelling of each word. Circle words you are not sure you have spelled correctly. Check their spelling.

5 **Publishing** • Share what you have written.
- Make a clean final draft.
- Read it to the class or a friend.
- Add pictures or make a poster to go with it.
- Make a recording of your writing.

Proofreading Checklist Name _____

You can use the questions below as a checklist to proofread your writing.
- ☐ Have I indented each paragraph?
- ☐ Have I used words correctly in every sentence?
- ☐ Have I capitalized the first word in each sentence?
- ☐ Have I capitalized all proper names?
- ☐ Have I ended each sentence with a period, question mark, or exclamation point?
- ☐ Have I spelled each word correctly?

The chart below shows some proofreading marks and how to use them.

Mark	Meaning	Example
◯	spell correctly	I liek dogs.
⊙	add period	They are my favorite kind of pet⊙
?	add question mark	What kind of pet do you have?
≡	capitalize	My dog's name is scooter.
﹃	take out	He likes to to run and play.
¶	indent paragraph	¶ I love my dog, Scooter. He is the best pet I have ever had. Every morning he wakes me with a bark. Every night he sleeps with me.
ᵛᵛ	add quotation marks	You are my best friend, I tell him.

Writer's Workshop

A Friendly Letter

Everyone likes to get letters from friends and family members. People write friendly letters to tell about themselves, their thoughts, and their feelings. Here are the greeting and body of Amber's letter to her friend Chelsey.

> 110 Winn Drive
> Smithville, AZ
> December 5, 2003
>
> Dear Chelsey,
>   Our new house is great! I can see the park from my bedroom window. Sometimes I walk there with Theo. He loves to chase the birds. When they fly away, he barks and runs in circles.
>   A nice girl named Keisha lives next door.

Prewriting To write her letter, Amber followed the steps in the writing process. After she decided to whom she should write, she made a list. The list helped her decide what to tell Chelsey. Part of Amber's list is shown here. Study what she did.

> New House
> can see park
> Theo chases birds
> park closed Monday
>
> New Friend
> Keisha

It's Your Turn!

Write your own friendly letter. Tell about something that happened or about your thoughts and feelings. After you have decided whom you will write, make a list of the things you want to say. Then follow the other steps in the writing process— writing, revising, proofreading, and publishing. Try to use spelling words from this lesson in your letter. Letters will vary.

LESSON 18 **109**

Writer's Workshop Scoring Rubric: Friendly Letter

SCORE 3
The body of the letter contains developed ideas and specific details. Writing is organized and coherent and contains all the parts of a friendly letter. Contains a minimum of sentence-structure, usage, mechanics, and spelling errors.

SCORE 2
The body of the letter contains some developed ideas and specific details. Has some degree of organization and coherence. Contains most of the parts of a friendly letter. Contains some sentence-structure, usage, mechanics, and spelling errors.

SCORE 1
The body of the letter contains few or no developed ideas and specific details. Has minimal organization and coherence. Contains few if any parts of a friendly letter. Contains many sentence-structure, usage, mechanics, and spelling errors.

Evaluating Students' Writing

The scoring rubric is based on standards for idea development, organization, coherence, sentence structure, usage, mechanics, and spelling. You may wish to share the rubric with students before they write their description.

The *Steck-Vaughn Writer's Dictionary, Intermediate Level,* provides writers with a place to write words they want to remember.

Day 4

Student Objective
- To write a friendly letter, using Lesson 18 words and the steps in the writing process

Presenting the Page

Explain that a friendly letter has five parts: heading, greeting, body, closing, and signature. Point out to students that the model shows only the greeting and body of Amber's letter but that they should include all five parts in the letter they write.

You may wish to copy and distribute the Writer's Workshop Masters on pages T295–T296 for students to use.

Day 5

Student Objective
- To take a posttest on the lesson words

Posttest Options

Use the posttest on this page or the Review Test Master on pages T287–T288 to assess students' ability to spell the lesson words.

Posttest

Dictate the following sentences. Have students write the sentences and underline the lesson words.

1. The <u>lion</u> hid <u>behind</u> the bush.
2. Mom <u>won</u> two <u>hundred</u> dollars.
3. That is a <u>pretty</u> dress.
4. The <u>tiny</u> baby has <u>lovely</u> blue <u>eyes</u>.
5. Last <u>night</u> I couldn't stop <u>laughing</u>.
6. You won't find the <u>right</u> answer by <u>guessing</u>.
7. <u>Why</u> did you <u>write</u> her a note?
8. He <u>thanked</u> the <u>children</u> for the work they had <u>done</u>.
9. The princess <u>wished</u> that she had <u>been</u> at the ball.
10. Put the <u>butter</u> on the table <u>while</u> I bake the rolls.
11. She <u>dreamed</u> about the house that she would <u>build</u>.
12. I wonder <u>which</u> hat I should <u>buy</u>.

Lesson 19
Words with Short *o*

Day 1

Student Objectives
- To take a pretest on the lesson words
- To spell the lesson words aloud
- To sort and write the lesson words according to the spelling patterns *o* and *a*

Pretest

Use the pretest on this page to assess students' ability to spell the lesson words.

Have students use the study steps on page 6 to study any words they misspell in the pretest.

You may wish to duplicate and send home the Home Activity Master on pages T247–T248.

Presenting the Page

Introducing the Short o Sound
Write *jog* on the board. Have a volunteer read the word and identify the sound of the *o* (/ŏ/). As students prepare to sort the words, point out that /ŏ/ is most often spelled *o* but is spelled *a* in some words we often use.

Pronunciation Focus Ask what punctuation mark is in *o'clock* (an apostrophe). Explain that *o'clock* is a contraction for "of the clock." Point out that the second *o* in *o'clock* has the short *o* sound. Write *Oc/to/ber*, *bot/tom*, and *for/got* on the board. Point out that each word has two *o*'s but that only one is pronounced /ŏ/. Call on students to say each word and to identify the syllable with /ŏ/ (*Oc*, *bot*, and *got*).

Consonant Focus Write the words *block*, *o'clock*, *clock*, and *socks* on the board. Underline the *ck* in each word. Ask students to identify the sound that the letters *ck* make (/k/). Point out that when the /k/ sound follows a short vowel sound, it is usually spelled *ck*.

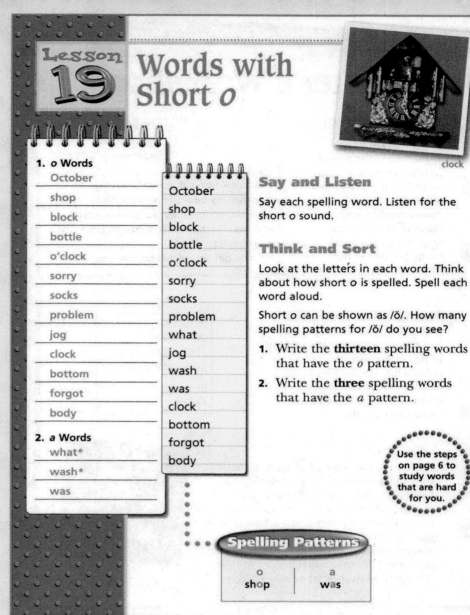

clock

Lesson 19
Words with Short *o*

1. *o* Words
October
shop
block
bottle
o'clock
sorry
socks
problem
jog
clock
bottom
forgot
body

2. *a* Words
what*
wash*
was

October
shop
block
bottle
o'clock
sorry
socks
problem
what
jog
wash
was
clock
bottom
forgot
body

Say and Listen
Say each spelling word. Listen for the short *o* sound.

Think and Sort
Look at the letters in each word. Think about how short *o* is spelled. Spell each word aloud.

Short *o* can be shown as /ŏ/. How many spelling patterns for /ŏ/ do you see?

1. Write the **thirteen** spelling words that have the *o* pattern.
2. Write the **three** spelling words that have the *a* pattern.

Use the steps on page 6 to study words that are hard for you.

Spelling Patterns

o	a
shop	was

110 UNIT 4   *Dolch basic sight word

Pretest

Say each lesson word, read the sentence, and then repeat the word. Have students write the words on separate paper.

1. **October** I found a red leaf in October.
2. **shop** Let's stop at this shop.
3. **block** I ran around the block.
4. **bottle** The glass bottle broke.
5. **o'clock** I go to bed at nine o'clock.
6. **sorry** He said that he was sorry.
7. **socks** I wore my black socks.
8. **problem** We solved the problem.
9. **what** I know what you need.
10. **jog** Can you jog up the hill?
11. **wash** Did you wash your hands?
12. **was** What was that noise?
13. **clock** The kitchen clock ticked loudly.
14. **bottom** We ran to the bottom of the hill.
15. **forgot** She forgot her jacket.
16. **body** Your body needs exercise.

Additional Words for Enrichment

The following words can be used to meet the needs of on-level and above-level students:
knock   hospital   dollar   swallow   cannot   odd

Spelling and Meaning

Clues   Write the spelling word for each clue.

1. clothes that belong on your feet _____ socks
2. has streets on all sides _____ block
3. in a group with *walk* and *run* _____ jog
4. feeling regret _____ sorry
5. a question word _____ what
6. opposite of *remembered* _____ forgot
7. means "of the clock" _____ o'clock

Analogies   Write the spelling word that completes each analogy.

8. *Have* is to *has* as *were* is to _____ was .
9. *Month* is to _____ October as *day* is to *Monday*.
10. *Bark* is to *tree* as *skin* is to _____ body .
11. *Top* is to _____ bottom as *up* is to *down*.
12. *Learn* is to *school* as _____ shop is to *store*.
13. *Solution* is to _____ problem as *answer* is to *question*.
14. *Soap* is to _____ wash as *towel* is to *dry*.
15. *Catsup* is to _____ bottle as *pickle* is to *jar*.

Word Story   One of the spelling words names an instrument for telling time. Many years ago, the instrument contained bells to sound out passing hours. The word comes from the Latin word *clocca*, which meant "bells." Write the word.

16. _____ clock

Family Tree: wash   Think about how the *wash* words are alike in spelling and meaning. Then add another *wash* word to the tree. A sample answer is shown.

washes   unwashed
washable   17. _____ washing
washer   rewash
wash

LESSON 19   **111**

HOME ACTIVITY MASTER p. T247

Unit 4   Spelling at Home

Dear Family of _____
During the next six weeks, your child will be learning to spell the following kinds of words:
• words with the short *o* vowel sound
• words with the long *o* vowel sound
• words with /ŏŏ/, as in *look*
• words with *-ed* or *-ing*

Here are some simple activities to do each week to help your child become a better speller.

Listening and Writing
Say the spelling words and have your child write them.

Spelling Strategy: Comparing Spellings
If your child is unsure about the spelling of a word, ask your child to write the word in different ways. Then have your child compare the spellings and choose the one that looks correct. Tell your child to check the spelling in a dictionary.

Games and Activities
Play Spelling Charades. Act out some spelling words for your child and ask your child to guess each word and spell it.

Write spelling words on index cards and have your child sort the words into groups. Ask your child to explain what all the words in each group have in common. For example, your child may explain that all the words in a group have the long *o* vowel sound spelled *oa*.

Using Spelling Words
Ask your child to write sentences that contain the spelling words. Then read the sentences with your child. Notice whether the sentences show that your child knows the meanings of the spelling words.

Lesson 19 Words with Short o
Week of _____
sorry   socks   clock   bottom
block   problem   jog   o'clock
October   forgot   shop   bottle
body   wash   what   was

Lesson 20 Words with Long o
Week of _____
hope   alone   whole   hole
close   joke   wrote   slow
know   yellow   blow   snow
how   goes   toe   November

Lesson 21 More Words with Long o
Week of _____
both   ago   almost   hold
comb   gold   hello   open
most   over   road   toast
loaf   boat   cocoa   coat

Lesson 22 Words with /ŏŏ/
Week of _____
book   cookies   took   stood
wood   poor   foot   cook
shook   put   full   pull
sure   should   could   would

Lesson 23 More Words with -ed or -ing
Week of _____
closed   hoped   liked   sneezed
pleased   stopped   jogged   dropped
taking   smiling   driving   shining
beginning   hopping   dropping   shopping

Lesson 24 Unit 4 Review
Week of _____
Lesson 24 is a review of Lessons 19–23. Help your child practice all of the words from those lessons.

The highlighted area shows the Lesson 19 words, which students can share with family members. Spanish version available on page T248.

Proofreading Practice
• What is Nathan's problim? (*problem*)
• The botle of milk broke. (*bottle*)

Meeting Individual Needs

Visual Learners
Write *jog* on the board and draw a box around each letter. Then erase the letters, leaving behind the word-shape boxes (☐☐☐). Explain that boxes show the shape of a word. Have students choose words from the spelling list and draw word-shape boxes for them without filling in the letters. Then have students trade with a partner, who can then write the matching lesson words.

Day 2

Student Objectives
• To use meaning clues to identify and write lesson words
• To use etymology, meaning, and spelling to identify the word *clock*
• To learn *wash* words and analyze their spellings and meanings

Presenting the Page

Write the following Clues and Analogies examples on the board and model identifying the answers:
• the month after September (*October*)
• *Gloves* is to *hands* as _____ is to *feet*. (*socks*)

Word Story

Students may be able to identify the word *clock* from the clue "an instrument for telling time" and the Latin word *clocca*. Ask if anyone has heard a grandfather clock chime, and call on volunteers to tell how the sound is made (usually a small hammer strikes a bell).

Family Tree: wash

Students should see that the *wash* words all contain *wash*. Have students locate the words in a dictionary, write the meanings on the board, and talk about how the meanings are alike and different. Point out that the spelling of *wash* does not change when other word parts are added. Then have students explain how the meaning is changed when *un-* is added to *washed* ("not washed") and *re-* is added to create *rewash* ("wash again"). Guide students to understand that knowing how to spell *wash* will help them spell related words.

111

Student Objectives
- To use context to identify and write lesson words
- To understand problem and solution

Presenting the Pages

Ask students to tell what a mystery story is and why they think some people like to read them. Read the story while the class listens and thinks about the missing words. Then have pairs of students reread the story and write the missing words. Alternatively, have students complete the pages independently by silently reading the story and writing the missing words. Then have students take turns reading the completed story.

Point out that in the last sentence of the message, *taste* means "a preference for; an attraction to."

Meeting Individual Needs

Auditory Learners

To help students hear the /ŏ/ sound in spelling words, especially those that have the *a* spelling pattern, say the sentences below. Have students identify and then spell the words that contain /ŏ/ as in *tock*.

Tick, tock, <u>wash</u> your <u>socks</u>.
Tick, tock, <u>what was</u> that?
Tick, tock, <u>what</u> is the <u>problem</u>?

Spelling in Context Use each spelling word once to complete the story.

The Problem with P.J.

The ____problem____ with P.J. was that she read too many
                1
mystery books. In September she read 15 mysteries. So far in the
month of ____October____, she had read 12.
              2
    P.J. had told Sonya all about every one of the books. Sonya
____was____ tired of hearing about P.J.'s mysteries. She
        3
decided to let P.J. know.

One afternoon when the hall
____clock____ struck four, P.J.
          4
started out on her daily two-mile
____jog____. She went around
        5
the ____block____ and into the
            6
center of town. Then she jogged past the
candy ____shop____ and headed
              7
down to the lake.

112 UNIT 4

Spelling Strategy

Breaking a Word into Syllables
Remind students that breaking a word into syllables and thinking about how each syllable is spelled is a helpful spelling strategy. Say the word *shop* and have students tell how many syllables they hear (one). Follow a similar procedure with *bot-tle* (two) and *October* (three). Have students work with a partner to sort the spelling words by number of syllables and write the words on a chart, drawing a line between syllables. Suggest that students use the Spelling Dictionary to check syllabication.

One Syllable	Two Syllables	Three Syllables
shop	bot/tle	Oc/to/ber

Have students circle the vowel in each syllable. Explain that *y* is often used as a vowel, as in *sorry* and *body*. Then call on volunteers to tell in their own words how breaking words into syllables can help them spell the words.

112

As she ran by the lake, something caught her eye. It looked like a ___bottle___ floating in the lake. She could see something white at the ___bottom___ of the bottle. It looked like a rolled-up piece of paper. She could hardly believe it. Here was her chance to solve a real mystery!

It was getting late. P.J. knew that she had to be home by five ___o'clock___. She was in such a hurry to get the bottle that she ___forgot___ to be careful. SPLASH! P.J.'s ___body___ was soaked from head to toe. But she had the bottle. She wondered ___what___ the message said. Quickly P.J. opened the bottle. She shook out the piece of paper and began to read.

"I am ___sorry___ you had to go through all this. I'll bet your shoes and ___socks___ are soaking wet. I hope the water will ___wash___ away your taste for mysteries. Guess who."

Suddenly P.J. heard a giggle. She knew that laugh anywhere! P.J. ran over to the big oak tree. Sonya jumped out from behind it, and both girls laughed. This mystery had been solved!

October
shop
block
bottle
o'clock
sorry
socks
problem
what
jog
wash
was
clock
bottom
forgot
body

LESSON 19 **113**

Reading Comprehension

After students have completed the pages, ask them to identify the sentence that tells the story's main problem ("Sonya was tired of hearing about P.J.'s mysteries").

Help students to understand that Sonya's solution to the problem is to let P.J. know how she feels. Ask students to list the three things that Sonya does to let P.J. know how she feels (she writes a note, places it in a bottle, and puts the bottle where P.J. will see it).

Cooperative Learning Activity

Have students work together to identify lesson words they have problems spelling correctly. Tell them to write these words on index cards. Then have students use the cards to dictate the words to each other. Have students check their own work, using the list on page 113.

ACTIVITY MASTER p. T268

Lesson **19** Words with Short *o*

Name _____

The underlined word in each sentence does not make sense. Find the word in the box that does make sense. Write the word on the line.

Spelling Words	sorry	socks	clock	bottom	block	problem	jog	o'clock
	October	forgot	shop	bottle	body	wash	what	was

1. My birds have holes in both heels. — socks
2. Set the bird for 7:00 A.M. — clock
3. Our houses are on the same bird. — block
4. The baby's mom gave her a bird of warm milk. — bottle
5. I found my ring at the bird of the drawer. — bottom
6. It's three bird, and all is well! — o'clock
7. Columbus Day is in the month of bird. — October
8. Maria bird to do her homework. — forgot
9. Would you like to bird around the track? — jog
10. Exercise is good for your bird. — body
11. Yesterday bird a beautiful day for a hike. — was
12. Did you bird your hands and face? — wash
13. Did you hear bird she said? — what
14. They worked together to solve the bird. — problem
15. I'm bird that you can't visit today. — sorry
16. Let's go to the bike bird to buy a helmet. — shop

ADDITIONAL PRACTICE

You may wish to copy and distribute the Activity Master on page T268 as additional practice for Lesson 19.

Proofreading Practice
- P. J. ran around the blok. (*block*)
- The bottim of the box fell out. (*bottom*)

113

Day 4

Student Objectives

- To write an expository paragraph, using lesson words
- To proofread a journal entry for spelling, capitalization, and punctuation

Presenting the Page

Remind students that Sonya grows tired of hearing about P. J.'s mysteries. Have the class brainstorm times when they had a problem with a friend. List their ideas on the board, using words from the spelling list, if possible. Generate a discussion on what they did to work out the problem.

To assist students with the Proofreading activity, have them read the directions and journal entry silently. Call on volunteers to identify mistakes they see. Then have students complete the activity independently.

Meeting Individual Needs

ESOL

In Spanish, the closest sound to /ŏ/ is /ä/ in *casa*. To help Spanish-speaking students associate the *o* spelling of /ŏ/ with /ä /, have them draw a picture of a house and label it *casa*. Next to the drawing, have them write the lesson words with the *o* spelling pattern: *October, shop, block, bottle, o'clock, sorry, socks, problem, job, clock, bottom, forgot* and *body*. Have students say each of these lesson words while looking at the *casa* picture to remind themselves of the sound of short *o*.

Spelling and Writing

October
shop
block
bottle
o'clock
sorry
socks
problem
what
jog
wash
was
clock
bottom
forgot
body

Write to the Point

Have you ever had a problem with a friend? Perhaps you had trouble agreeing about something. What did you do to make things better? Write a paragraph that tells the problem and what you did to solve it. Use spelling words from this lesson in your paragraph. **Paragraphs will vary.**

Use the strategies on page 7 when you are not sure how to spell a word.

Proofreading

Proofread the journal entry below. Use proofreading marks to correct five spelling mistakes, three capitalization mistakes, and two punctuation mistakes.

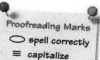

Proofreading Marks
- ◯ spell correctly
- ≡ capitalize
- ⊙ add period

October 18

today I have a mystery to solve. My running

socks
(sox) and hat were at the (botom) of the stairs
                                bottom

when I got home from school Now it is time for

jog   block
my (jogg) around the (blak), but there is a

problem
(problum). they are both missing. Mom says she

didn't move them Nobody is here but Mom

and me. Maybe sparky has moved them.

I haven't seen that dog since four o'clock.

114 UNIT 4

Proofreading Practice

- She wus writing a story. *(was)*
- My birthday is in Octobur. *(October)*

✔ Correcting Common Errors

The schwa sound often causes spelling problems. Students may misspell *bottom* as *bottem* or *bottum* and *problem* as *problum* or *problim*. Help these students by writing the schwa syllables (*tom, lem*) on the board and pronouncing each vowel with its short sound. Have students repeat this pronunciation. Then have them write the words and circle the vowels in the unstressed syllables.

Dictionary Skills

Alphabetical Order The words *block, bottle,* and *butter* begin with the same letter, *b*. To arrange words that begin with the same letter in alphabetical order, use the second letter.

| **bl**ock | **bo**ttle | **bu**tter |

Write each group of words in alphabetical order.

1. cover clock cap children

cap

children

clock

cover

2. shop salt sorry stack

salt

shop

sorry

stack

3. wash wonder west what

wash

west

what

wonder

4. forgot feed funny farmer

farmer

feed

forgot

funny

⭐ Challenge Yourself

What do you think each Challenge Word means? Check the Spelling Dictionary to see if you are right. Then use separate paper to write sentences showing that you understand the meaning of each Challenge Word.
Definitions and sentences will vary.

Challenge Words
deposit apologize
waffle comment

5. Marie decided to **deposit** a note in the bottle.

6. You should **apologize** when you hurt someone's feelings.

7. A hot **waffle** would taste good for breakfast.

8. What **comment** did his father make about Chen's grades?

LESSON 19 **115**

Posttest

Dictate the following sentences. Have students use separate paper to write the sentences and underline the lesson words.

1. I am <u>sorry</u> that I <u>forgot</u> the key.
2. Do you know <u>what</u> the <u>problem</u> is?
3. He must <u>wash</u> his <u>socks</u>.
4. I will <u>jog</u> at five o'<u>clock</u>.
5. The party <u>was</u> in <u>October</u>.
6. She saw a <u>bottle</u> at the <u>bottom</u> of the lake.
7. My dog has a long <u>body</u>.
8. The <u>clock</u> <u>shop</u> is on this <u>block</u>.

Enrichment Activity

Have students read independently several short stories or paragraphs from a favorite book. As they read, have them write down any short *o* words they find. Then after they've finished the selected pages, have them sort the words by /ŏ/ pattern.

Student Objectives
- To arrange words in alphabetical order
- To study the spellings and meanings of the Challenge Words
- To take a posttest on the lesson words

Presenting the Page

Have the students read the words *block, bottle,* and *butter* at the top of the page. Ask what letter these words all begin with (*b*) and how to arrange them in alphabetical order (use the second letter). Call on a volunteer to tell which of the letters in dark print comes first in the alphabet. Remind students that when words start with the same letter, they must use the second letter to put the words in alphabetical order.

⭐ Challenge Yourself

To introduce the Challenge Words, write the following on the board:

de/pos/it   a/pol/o/gize
waf/fle   com/ment

Pronounce the words and have students identify the number of syllables in each. Help students identify the syllable that has the short *o* sound (*pos, pol, waf,* and *com*).

Have students discuss what they think each Challenge Word means, look up the words in the Spelling Dictionary, and write the correct definitions. Ask students to compare their definitions with those in the Spelling Dictionary.

Posttest

Use the posttest on this page to assess students' ability to spell the lesson words.

Student Objectives
- To take a pretest on the lesson words
- To spell the lesson words aloud
- To sort and write the lesson words according to the spelling patterns o-consonant-e, ow, oe, and o

Pretest

Use the pretest on this page to assess students' ability to spell the lesson words.

Have students use the study steps on page 6 to study any words they misspell in the pretest.

You may wish to duplicate and send home the Home Activity Master on pages T247–T248.

Presenting the Page

Introducing the Long *o* Sound
Write *hop* and *hope* on the board. Have a volunteer read the words aloud. Help students distinguish between the short *o* and long *o* sounds.

As students prepare to sort the words, point out that /ō/ is often spelled as *o*-consonant-*e*, as *ow*, or as *o* at the end of a syllable but is spelled *oe* in some words we often use.

Pronunciation Focus Point out that *close* can be pronounced two ways, /klōz/ and /klōs/. Help students distinguish between the meanings of these words. Then write *No/vem/ber* on the board, pointing out each syllable. Ask students to identify the syllable with the long *o* sound and to identify the spelling of the sound (*No; o*).

Consonant Focus Read aloud *whole, wrote,* and *know* and make sure students recognize the initial consonants as silent consonants. Help students to think of other words that have silent *w* and *k*, such as *who, whose, wrist,* and *knot*.

116

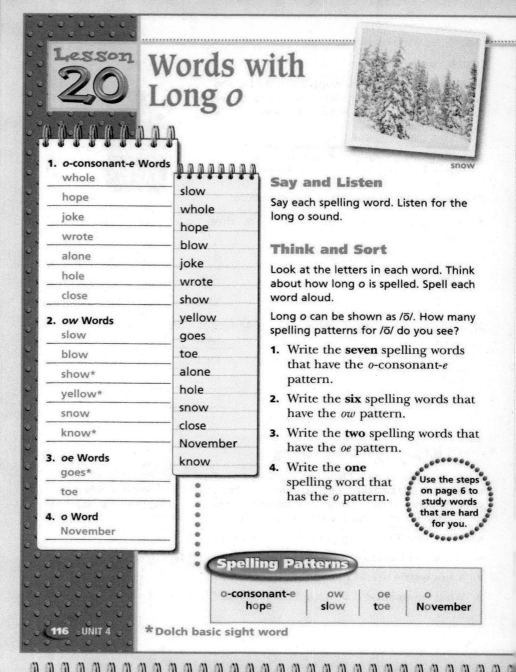

snow

1. o-consonant-e Words
whole
hope
joke
wrote
alone
hole
close

2. ow Words
slow
blow
show*
yellow*
snow
know*

3. oe Words
goes*
toe

4. o Word
November

slow
whole
hope
blow
joke
wrote
show
yellow
goes
toe
alone
hole
snow
close
November
know

Say and Listen
Say each spelling word. Listen for the long *o* sound.

Think and Sort
Look at the letters in each word. Think about how long *o* is spelled. Spell each word aloud.

Long *o* can be shown as /ō/. How many spelling patterns for /ō/ do you see?

1. Write the **seven** spelling words that have the *o*-consonant-*e* pattern.
2. Write the **six** spelling words that have the *ow* pattern.
3. Write the **two** spelling words that have the *oe* pattern.
4. Write the **one** spelling word that has the *o* pattern.

Use the steps on page 6 to study words that are hard for you.

Spelling Patterns

o-consonant-e hope	ow slow	oe toe	o November

116   UNIT 4   *Dolch basic sight word

Pretest

Say each lesson word, read the sentence, and then repeat the word. Have students write the words on separate paper.

1. **slow** This train is very slow.
2. **whole** We ate a whole pie.
3. **hope** I hope you feel better soon.
4. **blow** The wind began to blow.
5. **joke** He told us a joke.
6. **wrote** She wrote me a letter.
7. **show** Can you show me the way to class?
8. **yellow** A lemon is yellow.
9. **goes** She goes to school here.
10. **toe** I bumped my toe on a rock.
11. **alone** The boy was all alone.
12. **hole** My dog dug a hole in the yard.
13. **snow** The snow fell for two days.
14. **close** Please close the door.
15. **November** November is a cold month.
16. **know** Do you know that man?

Additional Words for Enrichment

The following words can be used to meet the needs of on-level and above-level students:
ocean   obey   tomorrow   explode   shadow   hollow

Spelling and Meaning

Definitions Write the spelling word for each definition. Use the Spelling Dictionary if you need to.

1. moves; travels — goes
2. made words with a pen — wrote
3. to wish for something — hope
4. the entire amount — whole
5. to be familiar with — know
6. by oneself — alone

Analogies Write the spelling word that completes each analogy.

7. *Shape* is to *square* as *color* is to ___yellow___ .
8. *Lose* is to *win* as ___close___ is to *open*.
9. *January* is to *February* as ___November___ is to *December*.
10. *Hand* is to *finger* as *foot* is to ___toe___ .
11. *Hot* is to *fire* as *cold* is to ___snow___ .
12. *Beat* is to *drum* as ___blow___ is to *whistle*.
13. *Write* is to *letter* as *dig* is to ___hole___ .
14. *Rabbit* is to *fast* as *tortoise* is to ___slow___ .
15. *Day* is to *night* as ___show___ is to *hide*.

Word Story Long ago Latin had the word *jocus*. The French changed the word to *jogleor*, which meant "juggler." A juggler does funny things. Later the English changed *jocus* to a word that means "something funny." Write the word.

16. ___joke___

Family Tree: *know* Think about how the *know* words are alike in spelling and meaning. Then add another *know* word to the tree. A sample answer is shown.

- knowledge
- known
- knows
- unknown
- 17. knowing
- knowingly
- know

LESSON 20 **117**

HOME ACTIVITY MASTER p. T247

Unit 4 Spelling at Home

Dear Family of ___
During the next six weeks, your child will be learning to spell the following kinds of words:
- words with the short *o* vowel sound
- words with the long *o* vowel sound
- words with /ŏŏ/, as in *book*
- words with *-ed* or *-ing*

Here are some simple activities to do each week to help your child become a better speller.

Listening and Writing
Say the spelling words and have your child write them.

Spelling Strategy: Comparing Spellings
If your child is unsure about the spelling of a word, ask your child to write the word in different ways. Then have your child compare the spellings and choose the one that looks correct. Tell your child to check the spelling in a dictionary.

Games and Activities
Play Spelling Charades. Act out some spelling words for your child and ask your child to guess each word and spell it.

Write spelling words on index cards and have your child sort the words into groups. Ask your child to explain what all the words in each group have in common. For example, your child might explain that all the words in a group have the long *o* vowel sound spelled *ow*.

Using Spelling Words
Ask your child to write sentences that contain the spelling words. Then read the sentences with your child. Notice whether the sentences show that your child knows the meanings of the spelling words.

Lesson 19 Words with Short o
Week of ___

sorry	socks	clock	bottom
block	problem	jog	o'clock
October	forgot	shop	bottle
body	wash	what	was

Lesson 20 Words with Long o
Week of ___

hope	alone	whole	hole
close	yellow	wrote	slow
know	goes	blow	snow
show		toe	November

Lesson 21 More Words with Long o
Week of ___

both	ago	almost	hold
comb	gold	hello	open
most	over	road	toast
loaf	boat	cocoa	coat

Lesson 22 Words with /ŏŏ/
Week of ___

book	cookies	took	stood
wood	poor	foot	cook
shook	put	full	pull
sure	should	could	would

Lesson 23 More Words with -ed or -ing
Week of ___

closed	hoped	liked	sneezed
pleased	stopped	jogged	dropped
taking	smiling	driving	shining
beginning	hopping	dropping	shopping

Lesson 24 Unit 4 Review
Week of ___
Lesson 24 is a review of Lessons 19–23. Help your child practice all of the words from those lessons.

The highlighted area shows the Lesson 20 words, which students can share with family members. Spanish version available on page T248.

Proofreading Practice
- I rote a story in class today. *(wrote)*
- The story was about a yello frog. *(yellow)*

Meeting Individual Needs

ESOL
Some Spanish-speaking students acquiring English may need extra practice with the different spellings of long *o* in English because Spanish contains only one long *o* spelling, *o*. Have these students use pencils and brightly colored markers to write the spelling words. Students should use the markers to write the letters that spell the long *o* patterns.

Spelling and Meaning

Day 2

Student Objectives
- To use meaning clues to identify and write lesson words
- To use etymology, meaning, and spelling to identify the word *joke*
- To learn *know* words and analyze their spellings and meanings

Presenting the Page
Write the following Definitions and Analogies examples on the board and model identifying the answers. For the analogy, point out to students that they should first determine the relationship between the given pair of words so that they can complete the other pair.

- an empty place in something *(hole)*
- *Smiles* is to *frowns* as *stops* is to ___. *(goes)*

Word Story
Students may be able to deduce that the English word *juggler* came from the French *jogleor*. Both *jogleor* and *juggler* existed before *joke*. Both *joke* and *juggler* ultimately derive from the Latin *jocus*. Invite students to compare and contrast *jocus*, *jogleor*, *juggler*, and *joke*.

Family Tree: *know*
Students should see that the *know* words all contain *know*. To help students explore the meanings of the words, have them locate the meanings in a dictionary, write their findings on the board, and talk about how the meanings are alike and different. Point out the change in meaning when *un-* is added to *known* to create *unknown* and the function of *-ledge* in *knowledge* (to make *know* a noun). You may also wish to point out the difference in the pronunciation of the *o* in *knowledge*.

117

Day 3

Student Objective
- To use context to identify and write lesson words
- To identify major story events
- To draw conclusions about a character

Presenting the Pages

Read the story aloud, having students write the missing spelling words as you read. You may wish to have volunteers supply the missing words for the class. Alternatively, have students complete the pages independently by silently reading the story and writing the missing words. Then have students take turns reading the completed story. Afterward, invite students to tell how they try to cheer up friends or family members.

Discuss with students the meanings of *pop* and *blow* in the story. As it is used, *pop* means "soda"; *blow* means "go."

Meeting Individual Needs

Auditory Learners
To help auditory learners practice the spelling patterns, group the words by pattern on the board. Have students say each lesson word and spell it aloud, stressing the letters of the pattern. For the *o*-consonant-*e* pattern, have them stress the *o* and the *e*.

118

Use each spelling word once to complete the story.

What Are Friends For?

Jacob wanted to go to Salvador's house on Saturday. Salvador ___wrote___[1] a note to Jacob. Salvador said he wanted to be ___alone___[2]. Jacob knew Salvador was sad because his dog had run away. Jacob decided to go to Salvador's house anyway.

Jacob had a plan. He would tell ___joke___[3] after joke. He would make Salvador laugh if it took the ___whole___[4] day to do it.

"Why did the boy ___close___[5] the door and leave his father outside in the month of ___November___[6]?" Jacob asked. Salvador didn't answer. He stared at his dog's picture.

"Because he wanted a cold pop." Jacob laughed. Salvador didn't even smile.

Jacob asked, "What kind of nail hurts when you hit it?" Salvador didn't look up.

"A ___toe___[7] nail." Jacob smiled. Salvador didn't.

Jacob tried again. "What comes after a snowstorm?" Salvador didn't answer.

Jacob said, "___Snow___[8] shovels. Here is another one. What ___goes___[9] away when you fill it up?"

Spelling Strategy

Rhyming Helper
Remind students that they can use a rhyming helper to remember how to spell a word. Write the word *hole* on the board. Invite volunteers to contribute rhyming helpers and write them on the board in a web like that below. Then review the helpers with students, emphasizing that to be a rhyming helper, the helper must be spelled the same as the word they are trying to spell, except for the beginning sound or sounds. Guide students in choosing a good rhyming helper for *hole*.

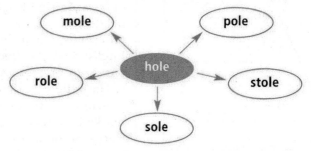

Then write *slow, blow, show,* and *know* on the board and guide students to observe that all of the words rhyme with each other. Point out that any of the words can be a rhyming helper for the others.

"I wish you would go away," Salvador said.

Jacob was hurt. He tried not to _____show_____ it. He knew Salvador was hurting, too. Jacob said, "A
10

_____hole_____. What did the north wind say to the
11

west wind?"

"I don't _____know_____," answered Salvador.
12

Jacob told him anyway. "It's time to _____blow_____."
13

"I _____hope_____ you don't have any more awful
14

jokes," Salvador said.

Jacob gave up. He ran out the door. Salvador yelled, "Jacob, _____slow_____ down!"
15

Jacob tripped on the steps. He flew up in the air and landed in a pile of bright red and _____yellow_____ leaves.
16
All Salvador could see was Jacob's nose. Salvador laughed and laughed.

Salvador wiped his eyes and said, "Thanks for cheering me up."

Jacob smiled and said, "That's what friends are for, Salvador!"

LESSON 20 119

slow
whole
hope
blow
joke
wrote
show
yellow
goes
toe
alone
hole
snow
close
November
know

Reading Comprehension

After students have completed the pages, ask them to identify the major events in the story. Help students understand that the way Jacob intended to make Salvador laugh was very different from what actually happened.

Ask students if they think Jacob was a good friend to Salvador and have them give reasons for their opinion.

Cooperative Learning Activity

To help students assess their progress, have pairs of students dictate the lesson words to each other. Then have students check their own work. If possible, have students compare their performance on this midweek activity to their performance on the pretest. Guide them in noting the words they are now spelling correctly and those they need to continue to study.

ACTIVITY MASTER p. T269

Lesson 20 Words with Long *o*

Name _____

Start with the word *blow*. Change one letter in each word to make a new one from the box.

Spelling Words	
slow	show
snow	know

1. blow
2. s l o w
3. s h o w
4. s n o w
5. k n o w

Find the word in the box that matches each clue. Write the word in the *o* puzzle.

Spelling Words	yellow	alone	joke	hole	close	toe
	whole	November	goes	wrote	hope	

6. part of the foot — t o e
7. I go, you go, she ___ — g o e s
8. I ___ I get it right. — h o p e
9. dig a ___ in the dirt — h o l e
10. tell a funny ___ — j o k e
11. We ate the ___ pizza. — w h o l e
12. without anyone else — a l o n e
13. Be sure to ___ the door. — c l o s e
14. write today, ___ yesterday — w r o t e
15. a month of the year — N o v e m b e r
16. the color of a lemon — y e l l o w

ADDITIONAL PRACTICE

You may wish to copy and distribute the Activity Master on page T269 as additional practice for Lesson 20.

Proofreading Practice
- How many days are in Noevember? *(November)*
- I don't kno. *(know)*

Student Objectives
- To write jokes, using spelling words
- To proofread a letter for spelling, capitalization, and punctuation

Presenting the Page

Review with students the jokes that Jacob tells Salvador in "What Are Friends For?" on pages 118–119. To encourage use of the spelling words in jokes, suggest that students start by looking at the list of spelling words on page 120. Then have students look at the jokes in the selection and think about jokes they have heard.

To assist students with the Proofreading activity, you may wish to have a volunteer read the directions and the letter aloud and then have students complete the activity independently.

Meeting Individual Needs

ESOL

Some speakers of Asian languages may have difficulty with long vowel sounds, many of which do not exist in those languages or are spelled differently. These students will benefit from repeated opportunities to hear and say the spelling words. Say each word and have students repeat the word. Then say a sentence with the word and ask students to repeat the sentence. Finally, have students write the word, underlining the long *o* spelling pattern.

120

---

slow
whole
hope
blow
joke
wrote
show
yellow
goes
toe
alone
hole
snow
close
November
know

Write to the Point

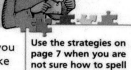

Jacob told Salvador jokes to make him laugh. They didn't work. Write a joke or riddle that makes you laugh. You may write one that you have heard before. You can also make up a new one of your own. Try to use spelling words from this lesson in your joke or riddle. Jokes will vary.

Use the strategies on page 7 when you are not sure how to spell a word.

Proofreading

Proofread the letter below. Use proofreading marks to correct five spelling mistakes, three capitalization mistakes, and two punctuation mistakes.

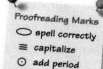

Proofreading Marks
- ◯ spell correctly
- ≡ capitalize
- ⊙ add period

Joe Jones
54321 Lone Oak Road
Soapstone Falls, OH 65432

214 Spring Street

Flint Hill, VA 22627

November
(Novemer) 29, 2003

Dear Joe,

    know   hope
I (kno) I haven't written lately. i (hoppe) you

are not mad. thanks for the (yello) sweater It
                       yellow

goes
(gose) great with my blue jacket.

    Here's a good joke. why did the pill wear a

blanket? It was a cold tablet

                        Moe

120 UNIT 4

Proofreading Practice
- The workers dug for a hole week. *(whole)*
- They dug a whole for a swimming pool. *(hole)*

✓ Correcting Common Errors

Homophones often cause spelling problems. Some students may confuse the homophones *whole* and *hole*. These students may benefit from writing sentences in which they use the words correctly.

Language Connection

Verbs Action words are called verbs. The spelling words in the boxes are verbs.

Unscramble the letters of the spelling words in the sentences below. Write each sentence and then circle the verb.

wrote	
	goes
know	

1. Jack hurt his oet.
   Jack (hurt) his toe.

2. Please wosh me your new shoes.
   Please (show) me your new shoes.

3. nows fell all night long.
   Snow (fell) all night long.

4. We ate the lewoh pizza.
   We (ate) the whole pizza.

5. Krista bought a loweyl skateboard.
   Krista (bought) a yellow skateboard.

6. Scooter dug a lohe in the yard.
   Scooter (dug) a hole in the yard.

7. Ming twore a story about a crow.
   Ming (wrote) a story about a crow.

8. Mrs. Sosa egos to lunch with our class.
   Mrs. Sosa (goes) to lunch with our class.

Challenge Yourself

Write the Challenge Word for each clue. Check the Spelling Dictionary to see if you are right. Then use separate paper to write sentences showing that you understand the meaning of each Challenge Word.
Sentences will vary.

Challenge Words	
console	dome
adobe	rodent

9. The roof of some buildings is one of these. _dome_

10. A mouse is this kind of animal. _rodent_

11. Some homes in the Southwest are made of this. _adobe_

12. You might do this to a friend who is sad. _console_

LESSON 20 **121**

Posttest

Dictate the following sentences. Have students use separate paper to write the sentences and underline the lesson words.

1. Did it <u>snow</u> in November?
2. Do you <u>know</u> who <u>wrote</u> this story?
3. I <u>hope</u> you will <u>show</u> me your room.
4. The rain will not <u>blow</u> in if you <u>close</u> the door.
5. Mom <u>goes</u> to work <u>alone</u>.
6. She has a <u>whole</u> box of <u>yellow</u> pens.
7. <u>Slow</u> down if you see a <u>hole</u> in the street.
8. It is no <u>joke</u> to break your <u>toe</u>.

Enrichment Activity

Have small groups of students use phone books to find and record names of people and businesses that have the *o*-consonant-*e, ow, oe,* and *o* spellings of long *o*. Suggest that students alphabetize their list.

Day 5

Student Objectives

- To write sentences containing lesson words in scrambled form
- To identify verbs in sentences
- To take a posttest on the lesson words
- To study the spellings and meanings of the Challenge Words

Presenting the Page

Review with students that a verb is a word that expresses action. Have students look at the examples *wrote, goes,* and *know.* Help students to understand that verbs can express actions that happen in the present, past, or future.

Challenge Yourself

To introduce the Challenge Words, write the following on the board:

con/sole   dome
a/do/be   ro/dent

Pronounce the words for students and discuss the number of syllables in each. Then have students review the long *o* spelling patterns featured in this lesson. Ask students to identify the long *o* spelling pattern in each of the Challenge Words (*dome* and *console* have the *o*-consonant-*e* pattern; *rodent* and *adobe* have the *o* pattern).

Posttest

Use the posttest on this page to assess students' ability to spell the lesson words.

121

Lesson 21

More Words with Long *o*

Day 1

Student Objectives

- To take a pretest on the lesson words
- To spell the lesson words aloud
- To sort and write the lesson words according to the spelling patterns *o* and *oa*

Pretest

Use the pretest on this page to assess students' ability to spell the lesson words.

 Have students use the study steps on page 6 to study any words they misspell in the pretest.

 You may wish to duplicate and send home the Home Activity Master on pages T247–T248.

Presenting the Page

Introducing the Long *o* Sound
Write *gold* and *boat* on the board. Call on a volunteer to read the words aloud and to tell how the words are alike (both have /ō/). Have students identify the letters that spell the long *o* sound in each word (*o* and *oa*).

As students prepare to sort the words, point out that /ō/ is often spelled *o* or *oa*.

Pronunciation Focus Point out that the *a* in *oa* is silent. Write *co/coa* on the board. Ask which syllable or syllables have the /ō/ sound (both). Write *hello* on the board and ask students to identify the double consonant (*ll*). Draw a line between the two *l*'s, identify the two syllables, and ask which syllable has long *o* (*lo*).

Consonant Focus Write the words *most*, *almost*, and *toast* on the board. Explain that when two consonants with different sounds are written together, they form a consonant blend. Call on volunteers to circle the *st* blend.

122

cocoa

Lesson 21 More Words with Long *o*

1. *o* Words
most
ago
hold*
hello
open*
over*
comb
almost
both*
gold

2. *oa* Words
coat
loaf
toast
boat
road

3. *o* and *oa* Word
cocoa

most
coat
ago
hold
hello
cocoa
open
loaf
over
comb
toast
almost
boat
both
road
gold

Say and Listen

Say each spelling word. Listen for the long *o* sound.

Think and Sort

Look at the letters in each word. Think about how long *o* is spelled. Spell each word aloud.

Long *o* can be shown as /ō/. How many spelling patterns for /ō/ do you see?

1. Write the **ten** spelling words that have the *o* pattern.
2. Write the **five** spelling words that have the *oa* pattern.
3. Write the **one** spelling word that has both the *o* and *oa* patterns.

Use the steps on page 6 to study words that are hard for you.

Spelling Patterns

o	oa
most	boat

122 UNIT 4   *Dolch basic sight word

Pretest

Say each lesson word, read the sentence, and then repeat the word. Have students write the words on separate paper.

1. **most** Which jar holds the <u>most</u> candy?
2. **coat** Wear your warm <u>coat</u>.
3. **ago** Dinosaurs lived long <u>ago</u>.
4. **hold** My mom will <u>hold</u> my glasses.
5. **hello** Say <u>hello</u> to my new friend.
6. **cocoa** Hot <u>cocoa</u> tastes good.
7. **open** Please <u>open</u> the door.
8. **loaf** Dad baked a <u>loaf</u> of bread.
9. **over** Geese flew <u>over</u> our house.
10. **comb** Please <u>comb</u> your hair.
11. **toast** Do you want <u>toast</u>?
12. **almost** We are <u>almost</u> done.
13. **boat** We sailed on the <u>boat</u>.
14. **both** Amy lost <u>both</u> her gloves.
15. **road** Is this the right <u>road</u>?
16. **gold** The ring was made of <u>gold</u>.

Additional Words for Enrichment

The following words can be used to meet the needs of on-level and above-level students:
zero   ocean   tomato   grocery   broken   approach

Spelling and Meaning

Definitions Write the spelling word for each definition.
Use the Spelling Dictionary if you need to.

1. to arrange the hair — comb
2. a precious metal — gold
3. in the past — ago
4. the one as well as the other — both
5. a greeting — hello
6. to keep in the hand — hold
7. the greatest amount — most
8. nearly — almost
9. to cause something to be no longer closed — open
10. above — over
11. bread baked in one piece — loaf

Classifying Write the spelling word that belongs in each group.

12. hat   scarf   gloves — coat
13. milk   eggs   cereal — toast
14. street   avenue   lane — road
15. car   train   airplane — boat

Word Story One of the spelling words was once spelled *cacao*, but many people misspelled it. They confused the word with *coco*, the name of the tree on which coconuts grow. Write the spelling word as it is spelled today.

16. cocoa

Family Tree: *toast* Think about how the *toast* words are alike in spelling and meaning. Then add another *toast* word to the tree.
A sample answer is shown.

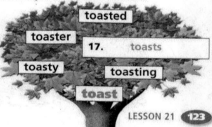

- toasted
- toaster
- 17. toasts
- toasty
- toasting
- toast

LESSON 21 **123**

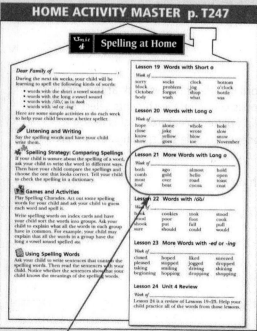
The highlighted area shows the Lesson 21 words, which students can share with family members. Spanish version available on page T248.

Proofreading Practice
- I am almos done with my story. (almost)
- Would you com my hair? (comb)

Meeting Individual Needs

ESOL
Speakers of Asian languages may need practice with the long *o* sound, since they usually pronounce it more like /ə/. Have these students make picture cards for picturable lesson words they have difficulty with. Then ask them to work with a partner to write each word under the picture, say the word aloud, and underline the long *o* spelling pattern.

Spelling and Meaning

Spelling and Meaning

Day 2

Student Objectives
- To use meaning clues to identify and write lesson words
- To use etymology, meaning, and spelling to identify the word *cocoa*
- To learn *toast* words and analyze their spellings and meanings

Presenting the Page
Write the following Definitions and Classifying examples on the board and model identifying the answers:
- to brown by heating (*toast*)
- silver copper tin ____ (*gold*)

Word Story
Tell students that *cacao* named the powder made from roasted cacao seeds. Even though the word was misspelled and became known as *cocoa*, the powder is still made from cacao leaves. Ask students what word we commonly use when talking about cocoa (*chocolate*).

Family Tree: *toast*
Students should see that the *toast* words all contain *toast*. To help students explore the meanings of the words, have them locate the meanings in a dictionary, write their findings on the board, and talk about how the meanings are alike and different. Point out that the spelling of *toast* does not change when word parts are added and that *toast* can be a noun or a verb. Guide students in understanding that knowing how to spell *toast* will help them spell related words.

123

Spelling in Context

Day 3

Student Objectives
- To use context to identify and write lesson words
- To identify stated details

Presenting the Pages

Have partners take turns reading the story aloud. Then have the partners work together to write the missing words. Alternatively, have students complete the pages independently by silently reading the story and writing the missing words. Then have students take turns reading the completed story.

Meeting Individual Needs

Visual Learners

Have students write the lesson words on index cards and sort them according to spelling pattern. Tell them to write the *o* with yellow or gold marker. Explain that the yellow or gold letters should remind them of the *o* spelling of long *o*.

Use each spelling word once to complete the story.

Gold Island

We spent last week at a lake that had an island in the middle of it. The island was tiny. It was called Gold Island. A legend says that a treasure was buried there many years ___ago___. The treasure was never found.
1

My sister, Jasmine, was excited about the legend. One day she packed a ___loaf___ of bread and some cheese. Then she got
2
into a small ___boat___ and rowed to the island. Jasmine
3
was going to search every inch of it until she found the treasure.

Jasmine had been gone ___almost___ three hours when a
4
storm came up. ___Both___ Mom and Dad were worried. So
5
was I. Jasmine can take care of herself ___most___ of the
6
time. But this was the worst storm I had ever seen.

Just then, Jasmine came running down the ___road___
7
to our cabin. "___Hello___!" she yelled as she came inside,
8
dripping water all ___over___ everything.
9

"You need to change those wet clothes and ___comb___
10
your hair," Dad said.

Spelling Strategy

Different Spellings

Remind students that they can write a word in different ways, look at the spellings, and then choose the spelling they think looks correct. Have students select lesson words not yet mastered and use the spelling patterns featured in this lesson to write the words in different ways. Ask students to circle the spellings they think are correct.

Spelled with o	Spelled with oa
(most)	moast
rod	(road)
(gold)	goald
lof	(loaf)
tost	(toast)

I said I would make some _____cocoa/toast_____ and
_____toast/cocoa_____.
        12

"Wait," said Jasmine. "The storm blew over a tree on the island. I found something interesting buried under it." She reached into her _____coat_____ pockets. "Please close
                      13
your eyes and then _____hold_____ out your hands." We
                      14
thought she was crazy. But we did it. Jasmine put rocks into our hands.

"Okay," she said, "_____open_____ your eyes."
                      15
The rocks looked just like _____gold_____. Then Mom
                      16
said, "Now I know why you are so excited. I hate to spoil your fun. These rocks only *look* like gold."

"It's easy to be fooled," Dad said. "That's why people call them fool's gold."

Jasmine hadn't found a treasure after all.
But now we know another reason why the island is called Gold Island.

most
coat
ago
hold
hello
cocoa
open
loaf
over
comb
toast
almost
boat
both
road
gold

LESSON 21 **125**

ACTIVITY MASTER p. T270

Lesson 21 More Words with Long *o*

Name _____

The underlined word in each sentence does not make sense. Find the word in the box that does make sense. Write the word on the line.

Spelling Words	both	ago	almost	hold	hello	open	most	over
	loaf	cocoa	comb	coat	gold	boat	toast	road

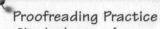

1. Tonya can goldfish reach the top shelf. _____almost_____
2. The judges gave prizes to goldfish Mei and Lee. _____both_____
3. My grandmother was born a long time goldfish. _____ago_____
4. Buy a goldfish of bread and a quart of milk. _____loaf_____
5. Tara's favorite drink is hot goldfish. _____cocoa_____
6. We had eggs and goldfish for breakfast. _____toast_____
7. They sailed a goldfish to the island. _____boat_____
8. The goldfish was icy after the storm. _____road_____
9. Wear your goldfish when it's cold. _____coat_____
10. When you meet someone, you say goldfish. _____hello_____
11. Can you jump goldfish that big puddle? _____over_____
12. The treasure chest was filled with goldfish. _____gold_____
13. Do you brush or goldfish your hair? _____comb_____
14. You can goldfish the door with this key. _____open_____
15. Sam asked Jetta to goldfish the door open. _____hold_____
16. This is the goldfish beautiful picture I've ever seen. _____most_____

ADDITIONAL PRACTICE

You may wish to copy and distribute the Activity Master on page T270 as additional practice for Lesson 21.

Proofreading Practice
- Rita drank a cup of coco. *(cocoa)*
- Please toste the bread for me. *(toast)*

Reading Comprehension

After students have completed the pages, have them discuss why the island is called Gold Island. Tell them to find and underline the parts of the story that give the two reasons for the island's name (legend says there was buried treasure; Jasmine finds gold rocks). Then have students underline the sentence that tells why the rocks are called fool's gold ("It's easy to be fooled," Dad said).

Cooperative Learning Activity

Have students work together to write the lesson words on index cards. Then have students use the cards to sort the words into one-syllable words and two-syllable words. To help students assess their progress, have pairs of students use the cards to dictate all of the lesson words to each other. Have students check their own work, using the list on page 125. If possible, have students compare their performance on this midweek activity to their performance on the pretest. Guide them in noting the words they are now spelling correctly and those they need to continue to study.

Day 4

Student Objectives

- To write an expressive paragraph, using lesson words
- To proofread an e-mail for spelling, capitalization, and punctuation

Presenting the Page

Review with students that Jasmine was excited about finding a treasure. Ask what kind of treasure she might have found other than gold rocks (examples: jewels, gold coins). Then have students brainstorm different kinds of treasures they would like to find. To encourage the use of lesson words in the paragraph, have students look over the list of lesson words on page 126.

To assist students with the Proofreading activity, have a volunteer read the directions and e-mail aloud. Then have students complete the activity independently.

Meeting Individual Needs

ESOL

Speakers of Asian languages may add a vowel sound between the *s* and *t*. These students will benefit from having words with *st* written on the board and the *st* consonant blend underlined as it is pronounced. Have students repeat each word, write it, and circle the *st*.

126

---

most
coat
ago
hold
hello
cocoa
open
loaf
over
comb
toast
almost
boat
both
road
gold

Write to the Point

Jasmine was excited by the legend of the buried treasure. Write a paragraph about a buried treasure you would like to find. What is the treasure? Where will you find it? Try to use spelling words from the lesson. **Paragraphs will vary.**

Use the strategies on page 7 when you are not sure how to spell a word.

Proofreading

Proofread the e-mail below. Use proofreading marks to correct five spelling mistakes, three capitalization mistakes, and two punctuation mistakes.

Proofreading Marks
- ◯ spell correctly
- ≡ capitalize
- ? add question mark

e-mail

Address Book | Attachment | Check Spelling | Send | Save Draft | Cancel

Hello
Helo, adam. We went to a lake last week. It

had an island in the middle. I thought I had found

gold
some goold, but it was only rocks. Are you ready

? comb
for our trip to the beach We'll combe the beach

for seashells early in the morning. we can eat

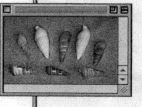

breakfast before we go. Mom

loaf
baked a lofe of bread. do you

toast
like toest with jam?

Jasmine

126 UNIT 4

Proofreading Practice

- We looked for the golde. *(gold)*
- The car is on a bumpy rood. *(road)*

Correcting Common Errors

Silent letters are often the cause of spelling problems. Some students may omit the *b* in *comb*. Suggest that these students think of a comb and brush, remembering that the *comb* ends with the same letter that begins the word *brush*, b.

Language Connection

Synonyms Synonyms are words that have the same meaning. The words *hello, howdy,* and *hi* are synonyms.

Use spelling words from this lesson to write synonym clues for the puzzle.

ACROSS

3. ___both___
4. ___cocoa___
6. ___road___
7. ___hold___

DOWN

1. ___over___
2. ___coat___
3. ___ago___
5. ___almost___
6. ___boat___

⭐ Challenge Yourself

Use the Spelling Dictionary to answer these questions. Then use separate paper to write sentences showing that you understand the meaning of each Challenge Word. *Sentences will vary.*

Challenge Words	
coax	solo
rodeo	patrol

8. Would a person **coax** cereal into a bowl? ___no___

9. Could one person go on a **solo** bicycle ride? ___yes___

10. Would you find a **rodeo** in the middle of a lake? ___no___

11. Do police officers go on **patrol**? ___yes___

LESSON 21 **127**

Posttest

Dictate the following sentences. Have students use separate paper to write the sentences and underline the lesson words.

1. Please <u>hold</u> my dog so I can <u>comb</u> him.
2. We <u>both</u> ate the <u>loaf</u> of bread.
3. The <u>boat</u> <u>almost</u> tipped <u>over</u>.
4. We like <u>toast</u> and <u>cocoa</u>.
5. I will <u>open</u> the door and say <u>hello</u>.
6. She got the <u>coat</u> a year <u>ago</u>.
7. The <u>road</u> in the story was made of <u>gold</u>.
8. Who has the <u>most</u> work to do?

Enrichment Activity

Have students choose lesson words and write clues for them. Then tell students to scramble the letters of the lesson words and put the scrambled letters beside the clues. Have students trade papers, unscramble the letters, and write the words correctly.

Presenting the Page

Review with students that synonyms are words that have the same meaning. Discuss how *hello, howdy, welcome,* and *hi* all have the same meaning. Then tell students that they will be writing the clues for a crossword puzzle.

⭐ Challenge Yourself

To introduce the Challenge Words, write the following on the board:

coax	so/lo
ro/de/o	pa/trol

Pronounce the words for students and discuss the number of syllables in each. Then have students review the long *o* spelling patterns featured in this lesson. Ask students to identify the long *o* spelling patterns in the Challenge Words (*coax* has the *oa* pattern; *solo* and *rodeo* have the *o* pattern in two different syllables; and *patrol* has the *o* pattern in one syllable).

Posttest

Use the posttest on this page to assess students' ability to spell the lesson words.

127

Words with /o͞o/

Student Objectives

- To take a pretest on the lesson words
- To spell the lesson words aloud
- To sort and write the lesson words according to the spelling patterns *oo*, *u*, *u-consonant-e*, and *ou*.

Pretest

Use the pretest on this page to assess students' ability to spell the lesson words.

Have students use the study steps on page 6 to study any words they misspell in the pretest.

You may wish to duplicate and send home the Home Activity Master on pages T247–T248.

Presenting the Page

Introducing the /o͞o/ Sound

Say the following word pairs and have students put up their thumb when they hear /o͞o/ as in *book*:

took–take   fruit–*foot*
pill–*pull*   feel–*full*
would–wide

As students prepare to sort the words, point out that /o͞o/ is most often spelled *oo*, *u*, or *ou* but is spelled *u-consonant-e* in some words that we often use.

Pronunciation Focus Write *shook*, *should*, and *sure* on the board and pronounce them. Point out that all of the words begin with the same /sh/ sound even though *shook* and *should* begin with the letters *sh*, and *sure* begins with *s*.

Consonant Focus Write *could*, *should*, and *would* on the board and point out that the *l* is silent. Then write the words *book*, *cookies*, *cook*, *shook*, and *could* on the board. Point out that /k/ at the beginning of a word is usually spelled *c*.

128

Words with /o͞o/

cook

1. *oo* Words

book
took
cook
stood
wood
poor
foot
shook
cookies

2. *u*, *u-consonant-e* Words

sure
put*
full*
pull

3. *ou* Words

should
would*
could*

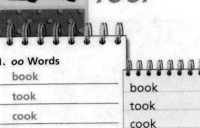

book
took
cook
sure
should
stood
wood
put
poor
foot
shook
would
full
cookies
pull
could

Say and Listen

Say each spelling word. Listen for the vowel sound you hear in *book*.

Think and Sort

Look at the letters in each word. Think about how the vowel sound in *book* is spelled. Spell each word aloud.

The vowel sound in *book* can be shown as /o͞o/. How many spelling patterns for /o͞o/ do you see?

1. Write the **nine** spelling words that have the *oo* pattern.

2. Write the **four** spelling words that have the *u* or *u-consonant-e* pattern.

3. Write the **three** spelling words that have the *ou* pattern.

Use the steps on page 6 to study words that are hard for you.

Spelling Patterns

oo	u	u-consonant-e	ou
book	put	sure	would

*Dolch basic sight word

Pretest

Say each lesson word, read the sentence, and then repeat the word. Have students write the words on a separate paper.

1. **book** How many pages are in this book?
2. **took** I took my jacket along.
3. **cook** Who will cook dinner?
4. **sure** Are you sure about that answer?
5. **should** We should visit soon.
6. **stood** We stood and waited for the bus.
7. **wood** He chopped wood for the fire.
8. **put** I will put the dishes away.
9. **poor** That poor plant needs water.
10. **foot** Don't step on my foot.
11. **shook** The leaves shook in the wind.
12. **would** He would be here if he could.
13. **full** The glass was full.
14. **cookies** Dad baked cookies.
15. **pull** You can pull the wagon.
16. **could** She could not open the door.

Additional Words for Enrichment

The following words can be used to meet the needs of on-level and above-level students:
understood football sugar handful push pudding

Spelling and Meaning

Antonyms Write the spelling word that is an antonym of each word.

1. push _____ pull
2. sat _____ stood
3. uncertain _____ sure
4. rich _____ poor
5. empty _____ full
6. gave _____ took

Clues Write the spelling word for each clue.

7. You put a shoe on this part of your body. _____ foot
8. This word means "ought to." _____ should
9. Logs are made of this. _____ wood
10. Most people like these sweet treats. _____ cookies
11. This word means "was able to." _____ could
12. You might do this to prepare food. _____ cook
13. This word means "to set." _____ put
14. This word sounds like *wood*. _____ would
15. This word is the past tense of *shake*. _____ shook

Word Story   Many years ago in England, people used the wood from beech trees to write on. One spelling word comes from *boece*, which meant "beech." Write the word.

16. _____ book

Family Tree: *cook* Think about how the *cook* words are alike in spelling and meaning. Then add another *cook* word to the tree. A sample answer is shown.

cooker   cookies
cooking   17. _____ cooks
cooked   uncooked
cook

LESSON 22 **129**

HOME ACTIVITY MASTER p. T247

| Unit 4 | Spelling at Home |

Dear Family of _____

During the next six weeks, your child will be learning to spell the following kinds of words:
- words with the short *o* vowel sound
- words with the long *o* vowel sound
- words with /o͞o/, as in *book*
- words with *-ed* or *-ing*

Here are some simple activities to do each week to help your child become a better speller.

Listening and Writing
Say the spelling words and have your child write them.

Spelling Strategy: Comparing Spellings
If your child is unsure about the spelling of a word, ask your child to write the word in different ways. Then have your child compare the spellings and choose the one that looks correct. Tell your child to check the spelling in a dictionary.

Games and Activities
Play Spelling Charades. Act out some spelling words for your child and have your child to guess each word and spell it.

Write spelling words on index cards and have your child sort the words into groups. Ask your child to explain what all the words in each group have in common. For example, your child may explain that all the words in a group have the long *o* vowel sound spelled *oo*.

Using Spelling Words
Ask your child to write sentences that contain the spelling words. Then read the sentences with your child. Notice whether the sentences show that your child knows the meanings of the spelling words.

Lesson 19 Words with Short *o*
Week of _____
sorry socks clock bottom
block problem jog o'clock
October forgot shop bottle
body wash what was

Lesson 20 Words with Long *o*
Week of _____
hope alone whole hole
close joke wrote slow
know yellow blow snow
show goes toe November

Lesson 21 More Words with Long *o*
Week of _____
both ago almost hold
comb gold hello open
most over road toast
loaf boat cocoa coat

Lesson 22 Words with /o͞o/
Week of _____
book cookies took stood
wood poor foot cook
shook put full pull
sure should could would

Lesson 23 More Words with *-ed* or *-ing*
Week of _____
closed hoped liked sneezed
pleased stopped jogged dropped
taking smiling driving shining
beginning hopping dropping shopping

Lesson 24 Unit 4 Review
Week of _____
Lesson 24 is a review of Lessons 19–23. Help your child practice all of the words from those lessons.

The highlighted area shows the Lesson 22 words, which students can share with family members. Spanish version available on page T248.

Proofreading Practice
- Could you carry the woud in the house? *(wood)*
- We shood have plenty for all winter. *(should)*

Meeting Individual Needs

ESOL
Because the /o͞o/ sound does not exist in the Spanish language, some Spanish-speaking students may substitute similar sounds in their language, such as /o͞o/ and /ō/. Say each lesson word and have students repeat it, spell it aloud, and then write it.

Spelling and Meaning

Day 2

Student Objectives
- To use meaning clues to identify and write lesson words
- To use etymology, meaning, and spelling to identify the word *book*
- To learn *cook* words and analyze their spellings and meanings

Presenting the Page

Write the following Antonyms and Clues examples on the board and model identifying the answers. Remind students that antonyms are words that have opposite meanings.

- Couldn't *(could)*
- If you tug, you do this. *(pull)*

Word Story

Tell students that thin sheets of beech wood were used before paper was perfected in England. Over time the name of the tree became the name of the tablets made from it.

Family Tree: *cook*

Students should see that the *cook* words all contain *cook*. Have students locate the words in a dictionary, write the meanings on the board, and talk about how the meanings are alike and different. Point out that the spelling of *cook* does not change when other word parts are added, even though the meaning and function change. Then ask a volunteer how *cook* changes when *un-* is added to make *uncooked* (it becomes an adjective that means "not cooked"). Guide students in understanding that knowing how to spell *cook* will help them spell related words.

129

Day 3

Student Objectives
- To use context to identify and write lesson words
- To identify the moral of a fable

Presenting the Pages

Ask students what a fable is. If necessary, explain that it is a made-up story, often with animals, that teaches a lesson. Call on volunteers to read the story "The Little Mouse" aloud. After it is read, have students suggest the missing words and write them in the story. Alternatively, have students complete the pages independently by silently reading the story and writing the missing words.

Discuss with students the meanings of *twitched* and *game* in the story. *Twitched* means "to move with a sudden, quick jerk" and *game* means "a wild animal hunted for food, or sport."

Meeting Individual Needs

Visual Learners
Visual learners can use a visual clue to remember the lesson words that are spelled with the *oo* pattern. Draw a pair of glasses on the board. Write the word *book* on the board, placing *b* and *k* on either side of the glasses. Continue this activity with other *oo* words, calling on volunteers to write the letters before and after the glasses to spell the words.

b◖◗k

Use each spelling word once to complete the story.

The Little Mouse

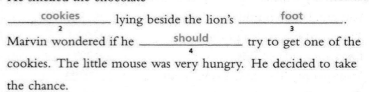

Marvin the mouse peeked over

a big pile of ___wood___ .
                  1

The lion was asleep. Then

Marvin's whiskers twitched.

He smelled the chocolate

___cookies___ lying beside the lion's ___foot___ .
    2   3

Marvin wondered if he ___should___ try to get one of the
                          4

cookies. The little mouse was very hungry. He decided to take

the chance.

Marvin tiptoed over to the lion. He slowly reached out to

___pull___ the cookies toward him.
   5

Whack! The lion ___put___ his big foot down on the
                     6

little mouse. Then the lion ___stood___ up and roared.
                                7

Marvin was scared. He ___shook___ like a leaf.
                          8

Marvin was afraid, but he was also smart. He did some fast

thinking. He said, "Mr. Lion, I'm just a ___poor___ little
                                            9

mouse. You would have to build a fire to ___cook___ me.
                                            10

Are you really ___sure___ I would be worth the trouble?"
                  11

The lion thought about it. He was still very ___full___
                                                12

from his last meal. The lion told Marvin to hurry away before he

changed his mind. Marvin thanked him and was gone.

130 UNIT 4

Spelling Strategy

Rhyming Helper
Remind students that they can use a rhyming helper to remember how to spell a word. Write the words *wood* and *could* on the board. Point out that *wood* and *could* rhyme, but that to be a rhyming helper, the helper must be spelled with the same spelling pattern as the word they are trying to spell. Have students suggest rhyming words for both *wood* and *could*.

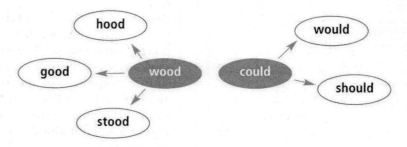

Guide students in arriving at good rhyming helpers for *wood* and *could*. Point out that any of the words can be a rhyming helper for the others.

The next day two hunters were looking for big game. They had read in a _____book_____ that there were lots
13
of lions nearby. The hunters saw the sleeping lion. They _____took_____ out a net and threw it over him.
14
There was nothing the lion _____could_____ do except
15
yell for help.

Marvin heard the lion's cry. He looked until he found the lion. He said he _____would_____ try to help. The
16
lion said, "You are too small to help."

Marvin didn't answer. He began to nibble on the net with his sharp teeth. Soon the little mouse had made a big hole. The lion slipped out of the net. He was free!

That is how the lion learned that good things often come in small packages.

book
took
cook
sure
should
stood
wood
put
poor
foot
shook
would
full
cookies
pull
could

LESSON 22 **131**

After students have completed the story, ask them what lesson the story teaches ("good things often come in small packages"). Ask what this lesson means to the lion. Then have students write a short response about what the saying means to them or write another fable that could be used to teach the same lesson. Call on volunteers to share their responses.

Cooperative Learning Activity

Have small groups of students write questions that can be answered by lesson words, such as "What makes a good snack?" (cookies). Then have groups trade questions and write the answers, checking the spelling of each lesson word as they go.

ACTIVITY MASTER p. T271

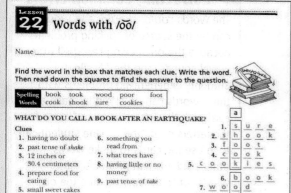

Lesson 22 Words with /o͝o/

Name _____

Find the word in the box that matches each clue. Write the word. Then read down the squares to find the answer to the question.

Spelling Words	book	took	wood	poor	foot
	cook	shook	sure	cookies	

WHAT DO YOU CALL A BOOK AFTER AN EARTHQUAKE?

Clues
1. having no doubt
2. past tense of *shake*
3. 12 inches or 30.4 centimeters
4. prepare food for eating
5. small sweet cakes
6. something you read from
7. what trees have
8. having little or no money
9. past tense of *take*

1. s u r e
2. s h o o k
3. f o o t
4. c o o k
5. c o o k i e s
6. b o o k
7. w o o d
8. p o o r
9. t o o k

Find the word in the box that completes each sentence. Write the word on the line.

Spelling Words	stood	put	full	pull	should	could	would

10. That bucket is _____full_____ of paint.
11. The dog _____stood_____ by the gate and barked.
12. What _____would_____ you do with the money if you won?
13. Many years ago that man _____could_____ sing very well.
14. It is time to _____put_____ on your hat and coat.
15. You _____should_____ not slam the door.
16. Jason will _____pull_____ weeds from the garden.

ADDITIONAL PRACTICE

You may wish to copy and distribute the Activity Master on page T271 as additional practice for Lesson 22.

Proofreading Practice
• They stoud by the front door. *(stood)*
• Where is the recipe for raisin cookees? *(cookies)*

Day 4

Student Objectives

- To write a thank-you note, using lesson words
- To proofread a story review for spelling, capitalization, and unnecessary words

Presenting the Page

Lead students in a discussion of times when someone helped them. Record their ideas on the board. Remind students that a thank-you note is similar to a friendly letter and begins with the date, an address, and a greeting, and ends with a closing, such as *Yours truly*. Tell students to look at the spelling list for ideas of words to use in the thank-you note.

To assist students with the Proofreading activity, call on one student to read the directions and the first sentence. Ask the class if they see any errors. Have students make the corrections. Have students complete the activity independently. Then have them work in small groups to check their work.

Meeting Individual Needs

Kinesthetic Learners

Have small groups of students use magnetic letters on cookie sheets to make lesson words. Distribute letters *b, t, c, o, o, k, s,* and *h.* Have students find the letters to make the word *book.* Then have them manipulate the letters to create new words as follows:

Change 1 letter to make *took.*
Change 1 letter to make *cook.*
Change 2 letters to make *shook.*

| book |
| took |
| cook |
| sure |
| should |
| stood |
| wood |
| put |
| poor |
| foot |
| shook |
| would |
| full |
| cookies |
| pull |
| could |

Write to the Point

A lion with good manners would thank the mouse for saving his life. Write a thank-you note to a person who has helped you. Include what the person did and why you are happy the person helped you. Try to use spelling words from this lesson in your thank-you note. Thank-you notes will vary.

Use the strategies on page 7 when you are not sure how to spell a word.

Proofreading

Proofread the story review below. Use proofreading marks to correct five spelling mistakes, three capitalization mistakes, and two unnecessary words.

Proofreading Marks
- ◯ spell correctly
- ≡ capitalize
- ✄ take out

Story Review

The Lion and the Mouse is an ~~an~~ old
story that has ⟨stod⟩ *stood* the test of time. ~~the~~
beginning will ⟨pul⟩ *pull* you into the story. ~~what~~
will happen to that ~~that~~ ⟨poer⟩ *poor* little mouse?
⟨Culd⟩ *Could* the lion be kind enough to let him go?

What lesson does the story teach? If you

have read the story before, then you know.

if not, read it soon. You are ⟨shure⟩ *sure* to enjoy it.

132 UNIT 4

Proofreading Practice
- Cuold you open the door? *(could)*
- The glass is foll of milk. *(full)*

✔ Correcting Common Errors

The words *could, should,* and *would* can be the source of spelling problems because the *ou* spelling can spell other vowel sounds, and the *l* is silent. Students experiencing problems with these words can be asked to make a card with the letters *ould* and cards for the letters *c, sh,* and *w.* One student can then use the cards to make words. The other students can pronounce the words, write them, underline the *ou,* and circle the *l.*

Language Connection

Capital Letters The names of cities and states always begin with a capital letter.

> **P**hoenix is the capital of **A**rizona.

Unscramble the spelling words in the sentences below. Then write the sentences, using capital letters correctly.

1. many dowo products come from maine.
   Many wood products come from Maine.

2. i am rues that the largest state is alaska.
   I am sure that the largest state is Alaska.

3. everyone dosluh visit chicago, illinois.
   Everyone should visit Chicago, Illinois.

4. dowlu you like to go to new orleans?
   Would you like to go to New Orleans?

5. san francisco ohsko during an earthquake.
   San Francisco shook during an earthquake.

6. my friend from toronto sent me some okecois.
   My friend from Toronto sent me some cookies.

Challenge Yourself

What do you think each Challenge Word means? Check the Spelling Dictionary to see if you are right. Then use separate paper to write sentences showing that you understand the meaning of each Challenge Word. Definitions and sentences will vary.

Challenge Words	
bureau	gourmet
assure	endure

7. A mouse was living in a drawer of my **bureau**.

8. It nibbled on the **gourmet** cheese Mom bought.

9. Can you **assure** me it has gone and won't come back?

10. I could not **endure** one more night of its noisy squeaks.

LESSON 22 **133**

Posttest

Dictate the following sentences. Have students use separate paper to write the sentences and underline the lesson words.

1. When <u>would</u> you like your <u>cookies</u>?
2. This <u>book</u> will help you <u>cook</u>.
3. He <u>put</u> his <u>foot</u> on the box.
4. She <u>took</u> the <u>wood</u> to her house.
5. This bottle <u>should</u> be <u>full</u> of milk.
6. I got a <u>poor</u> grade on the test.
7. We <u>stood</u> and began to <u>pull</u> the rope.
8. They were <u>sure</u> they <u>could</u> do the work.
9. They <u>shook</u> hands.

Enrichment Activity

Have students work in small groups to play a game of Concentration, using the lesson words. Make a word card for each lesson word except for one word with the *oo* pattern, one word with the *ou* pattern, the word *sure*, and one word with the *u* pattern. Put the fourteen cards face down and have players take turns turning over two cards, looking for two words with the same spelling pattern. If the words do not match, play passes to the next player. If the cards match, the player keeps the two cards. Play continues in this manner until all cards have been matched.

Day 5

Student Objectives
- To write sentences containing lesson words in scrambled form
- To capitalize the first word in a sentence, names of cities, and names of states correctly
- To study the spellings and meanings of the Challenge Words
- To take a posttest on the lesson words

Presenting the Page

Review with students that the names of cities and states begin with a capital letter. Write the name of your city and state on the board. Ask a student to draw a line under the capital letter in each word. Call on volunteers to write the names of other cities and states. Check to see that each city and state begins with a capital letter.

Challenge Yourself

To introduce the Challenge Words, write the following on the board:

bu/reau	gour/met
as/sure	en/dure

Pronounce each word and discuss the number of syllables. Point out that the final *t* in *gourmet* is silent. Then have students review the /o͞o/ spelling patterns. Ask students to identify the /o͞o/ spelling pattern in each of the Challenge Words (*bureau* has the *u* pattern; *assure* and *endure* have the *u*-consonant-*e* pattern; *gourmet* has the *ou* pattern).

Have students write what they think each Challenge Word means, look up the words in the Spelling Dictionary, and write the correct definitions. Ask students to compare their definitions with those in the Spelling Dictionary.

Posttest

Use the posttest on this page to assess students' ability to spell the lesson words.

133

More Words with -ed or -ing

Student Objectives

- To take a pretest on the lesson words
- To spell the lesson words aloud
- To sort and write the lesson words according to whether a final e in the base word is dropped or a final consonant is doubled

Pretest

Use the pretest on this page to assess students' ability to spell the lesson words.

 Have students use the study steps on page 6 to study any words they misspell in the pretest.

 You may wish to duplicate and send home the Home Activity Master on pages T247–T248.

Presenting the Page

Introducing the -ed and -ing Endings Write *drop, dropped, drive,* and *driving* on the board. Identify *drop* and *drive* as the base words in *dropped* and *driving* and underline *-ed* and *-ing*. Ask what changes are made to *drop* to form *dropped* (the *p* is doubled) and what changes are made to *drive* to form *driving* (the final *e* is dropped).

Pronunciation Focus Write *pleased, closed, hoped,* and *dropped* on the board and pronounce them. Point out that sometimes *-ed* has the /d/ sound, and sometimes it has the /t/ sound.

Consonant Focus Write *sn, sm, dr, st, pl,* and *cl* on the board, reminding students that although the two sounds in each are blended together, each sound is pronounced. Have students find the lesson words that begin with these blends.

134

Lesson 23
More Words with -ed or -ing

smiling

1. Final e Dropped
sneezed
smiling
hoped
shining
pleased
liked
taking
driving
closed

2. Final Consonant Doubled
beginning
dropping
stopped
dropped
jogged
hopping
shopping

sneezed
smiling
beginning
hoped
dropping
shining
stopped
pleased
dropped
liked
taking
driving
closed
jogged
hopping
shopping

Say and Listen

Say the spelling words. Listen for the *-ed* and *-ing* endings.

Think and Sort

Each spelling word is formed by adding *-ed* or *-ing* to a base word. Look at the letters in each spelling word. Spell each word aloud. Think about how the spelling of the base word changes.

1. If a base word ends in *e*, the *e* is usually dropped before *-ed* or *-ing* is added. Write the **nine** spelling words in which the final *e* of the base word is dropped.

2. If a base word ends in a single vowel and a single consonant, the consonant is often doubled before *-ed* or *-ing* is added. Write the **seven** spelling words in which the final consonant of the base word is doubled.

Use the steps on page 6 to study words that are hard for you.

Spelling Patterns

Final e Dropped	Final Consonant Doubled
take + ing = taking	begin + ing = beginning

134 UNIT 4

Pretest

Say each lesson word, read the sentence, and then repeat the word. Have students write the words on separate paper.

1. **sneezed** I sneezed loudly.
2. **smiling** We are smiling at you.
3. **beginning** It is beginning to rain.
4. **hoped** Mom hoped for a sunny day.
5. **dropping** Start dropping the seeds into the soil.
6. **shining** The sun was shining.
7. **stopped** The cars stopped.
8. **pleased** Was she pleased with the gift?
9. **dropped** I dropped my fork.
10. **liked** He liked dogs the best.
11. **taking** We were taking the books home.
12. **driving** Dad is driving to work.
13. **closed** The store closed early.
14. **jogged** I jogged in the park.
15. **hopping** She was hopping on one leg.
16. **shopping** They were shopping for shoes.

Additional Words for Enrichment

The following words can be used to meet the needs of on-level and above-level students:
swimming   saving   invited   used   writing   exciting

Spelling and Meaning

Synonyms Write the spelling word that is a synonym for each word.

1. trotted   jogged
2. starting   beginning
3. shut   closed
4. wished   hoped
5. enjoyed   liked
6. sparkling   shining
7. quit   stopped
8. grinning   smiling
9. jumping   hopping

Rhymes Write the spelling word that completes each sentence and rhymes with the underlined word.

10. The singer was not pleased when I _____ sneezed _____.
11. Are you _____ taking _____ the cake you are making?
12. The bus stopped, and my backpack _____ dropped _____.
13. To turn diving into _____ driving _____, add the letter r.
14. Mom was not _____ pleased _____ when I teased my brother.
15. I keep _____ dropping _____ the jelly and mopping up the mess.

Word Story Long ago in England, people sold things in places called *schoppes*. A *schoppe* was a booth in a marketplace. Write the spelling word you can make from this word plus -ing.

16. _____ shopping _____

Family Tree: pleased *Pleased* is a form of *please*. Think about how the *please* words are alike in spelling and meaning. Then add another *please* word to the tree. A sample answer is shown.

pleased
pleasing   17. pleasant
pleasure   unpleasant
please

LESSON 23 **135**

HOME ACTIVITY MASTER p. T247

Unit 4 Spelling at Home

Dear Family of _____,

Week of _____

During the next six weeks, your child will be learning to spell the following kinds of words:

• words with the short o vowel sound
• words with the long o vowel sound
• words with /ŏŏ/, as in *book*
• words with -ed or -ing

Here are some simple activities to do each week to help your child become a better speller.

Listening and Writing
Say the spelling words and have your child write them.

Spelling Strategy: Comparing Spellings
If your child is unsure about the spelling of a word, ask your child to write the word in different ways. Then have your child compare the spellings and choose the one that looks correct. Tell your child to check the spelling in a dictionary.

Games and Activities
Play Spelling Charades. Act out some spelling words for your child and have your child guess each word and spell it.

Write spelling words on index cards and have your child sort the words into groups. Ask your child to explain what all the words in each group have in common. For example, your child may explain that all the words in a group have the long o vowel sound spelled *ow*.

Using Spelling Words
Ask your child to write sentences that contain the spelling words. Then read the sentences with your child. Notice whether the sentences show that your child knows the meanings of the spelling words.

Lesson 19 Words with Short o
Week of _____

sorry	socks	clock	bottom
block	problem	jog	o'clock
October	forgot	shop	bottle
body	wash	what	was

Lesson 20 Words with Long o
Week of _____

hope	alone	whole	hole
close	joke	wrote	slow
know	yellow	blow	snow
show	goes	toe	November

Lesson 21 More Words with Long o
Week of _____

both	ago	almost	hold
comb	gold	hello	open
most	over	road	toast
loaf	boat	cocoa	coat

Lesson 22 Words with /ŏŏ/
Week of _____

book	cookies	took	stood
wood	poor	foot	cook
shook	put	full	pull
sure	should	could	would

Lesson 23 More Words with -ed or -ing
Week of _____

closed	hoped	liked	sneezed
pleased	stopped	jogged	dropped
taking	smiling	driving	shining
beginning	hopping	dropping	shopping

Lesson 24 Unit 4 Review
Week of _____
Lesson 24 is a review of Lessons 19–23. Help your child practice all of the words from those lessons.

The highlighted area shows the Lesson 23 words, which students can share with family members. Spanish version available on page T248.

Proofreading Practice
• We stoped to take a good look at the mountain. *(stopped)*
• The smileing boy looked happy. *(smiling)*

Meeting Individual Needs

ESOL

A common confusion for some speakers of other languages is the silent *e* in a long-vowel word. Write *smile, hope, shine, like, take,* and *drive* on the board. Have students underline the vowel and the *e* in colored chalk. Point out that when a vowel is followed by a consonant and a final *e*, the vowel is usually long, and the *e* is silent.

Spelling and Meaning

Day 2

Student Objectives

• To use meaning clues to identify and write lesson words
• To use etymology, meaning, and spelling to identify the word *shopping*
• To learn *please* words and analyze their spellings and meanings

Presenting the Page

Write the following Synonyms and Rhymes examples on the board and model identifying the answers:

• happy *(pleased)*
• The team was ___ to start winning games. *(beginning)*

Word Story

Students should be able to see the connection between the present day *shop* and the Old English word *schoppe*. *Schoppe* was a noun because it named a place. Explain that *shop* also became a verb meaning "to visit a shop."

Family Tree: *please*

Students should see that all of the *please* words are related in both spelling and meaning. Have students locate the meanings in a dictionary, write their findings on the board, and talk about how the meanings are alike and different. Write *please, pleased,* and *pleasing* in one column and *pleasure, pleasant,* and *unpleasant* in another. Help students to observe that in *please, pleased,* and *pleasing, ea* is pronounced /ē/, and in *pleasure, pleasant,* and *unpleasant, ea* is pronounced /ĕ/. Guide students to understand that knowing how to spell *please* will help them spell the /ĕ/ sound of *ea* in some words related to *please*.

135

Student Objectives

- To use context to identify and write lesson words
- To locate information in a nonfiction selection

Presenting the Pages

Read the selection while the class listens and thinks about the missing words. Then have students work in pairs to reread the selection and write the missing words. Alternatively, have students complete the pages independently by silently reading the selection and writing the missing words. Then have students take turns reading the completed selection.

Afterward, invite students to share experiences with caring for and training a pet.

Meeting Individual Needs

Visual Learners

To help students understand the concept of dropping final *e* before adding an ending, make cards for the base words that end in *e* and cards for the *-ing* and *-ed* endings. Have students work in pairs to match base-word cards and ending cards. They can cover the *e* on a base-word card with the ending card to form a lesson word. Partners should then write the word.

Spelling in Context   Use each spelling word once to complete the selection.

Puppy Love

Have you always _____liked_____ dogs? Have
                   1

you ever _____hoped_____ to own one? Suppose
            2

that you now have a new puppy. What do you need

to know?

At the _____beginning_____ of a young puppy's life, it needs three good
              3

meals a day. After it is five months old or so, your pup may need only two

meals a day. Be sure to feed your puppy only dog food. If you have been

_____dropping_____ leftovers from your dinner plate into your puppy's
     4

dish, you should stop. People food is not always good for

animals. Dogs need dog food. They also need lots

of water.

Handle your puppy gently. Be careful. It may

try to squirm and wiggle out of your arms. Your puppy

could get badly hurt if you _____dropped_____ it.
                     5

Do not get in the habit of _____taking_____ your
                    6

pup to bed with you. A puppy can sleep in your bedroom,

but it should stay in its own bed. Also, be sure your doors

are _____closed_____. This way, your
             7

puppy will not get out and hurt itself or

your things at night.

136   UNIT 4

Spelling Strategy

Using Spelling Rules

Explain to students that remembering and using spelling rules for adding endings is a helpful spelling strategy. Review with students the two spelling rules featured in this lesson. Have students restate them in their own words. Then have small groups of students make a chart like the following and sort the lesson words according to the spelling rules.

Rule: If a base word ends in *e*, the *e* is usually dropped before *-ed* or *-ing* is added.		Rule: If a base word ends in a single vowel and a single consonant, the consonant is often doubled before *-ed* or *-ing* is added.	
sneezed	smiling	stopped	beginning
hoped	taking	jogged	shopping

Teach your puppy good manners. It should not be jumping on everyone and ___**hopping**___ onto every lap. This kind of behavior must be ___**stopped**___. Put the puppy back on the floor. Say in a firm voice, "No, Scooter. No." Soon you will be ___**pleased**___ at how well your puppy behaves.

Pay attention to your puppy's health. If your pup has coughed or ___**sneezed**___ for several days, take it to a vet. Even if your pup is healthy, take it in for regular checkups and shots.

When your puppy is outdoors, keep it on a leash. A leash helps keep a dog away from people, other animals, and traffic. After you have played ball or ___**jogged**___ a few blocks with your puppy, give it some cool water. Let it rest or nap for a while, too.

Get your puppy used to riding in a car. Make sure it is in its carrier while the driver is ___**driving**___. Also make sure someone stays with your puppy when you or a family member is ___**shopping**___ in a store. Never leave your puppy alone in a closed car, especially when it is hot and the sun is ___**shining**___. This is dangerous!

Taking care of a puppy is a big job. Learn all you can about pet care. That way, both you and your pup can keep laughing and ___**smiling**___.

sneezed
smiling
beginning
hoped
dropping
shining
stopped
pleased
dropped
liked
taking
driving
closed
jogged
hopping
shopping

LESSON 23 **137**

ACTIVITY MASTER p. T272

Lesson 23 More Words with *-ed* or *-ing*

Name _____

Use the words in the box to solve the puzzle. Some letters are given.

Spelling Words

closed	taking
hoped	smiling
liked	driving
sneezed	shining
pleased	beginning
stopped	hopping
jogged	dropping
dropped	shopping

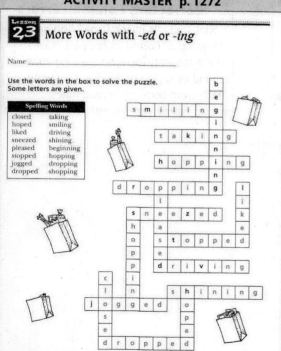

ADDITIONAL PRACTICE

You may wish to copy and distribute the Activity Master on page T272 as additional practice for Lesson 23.

Proofreading Practice
- My dad was pleassed with my grades. *(pleased)*
- My family went shoping at the mall. *(shopping)*

Reading Comprehension

After students have completed the pages, write on the board the title *How to Take Care of a New Puppy*. Then have students reread each paragraph to find information about taking care of a new puppy. List students' responses on the board in sentence form, such as *Feed a young puppy three meals a day* and *Feed your puppy only dog food*.

Cooperative Learning Activity

Have students work together to write each lesson word on one side of an index card and the base word on the other side. Then have students sort the words by the base word changes. To help students assess their progress, have pairs of students dictate the spelling words to each other. Have students check their own work. If possible, also have students compare their performance on this midweek activity to their performance on the pretest. Guide them in noting the words they are now spelling correctly and those they need to continue to study.

Student Objectives

- To write an expository paragraph, using the lesson words
- To proofread a letter for spelling, capitalization, and punctuation

Presenting the Page

Review "Puppy Love" and ask students to identify information that applies to any pet. Then have students list different types of pets that people have and ways in which each pet is fun. Remind students to review the lesson list to find words they can include in their paragraph.

To assist students with the Proofreading activity, have one student read the directions and letter aloud. Encourage students to look for mistakes. Tell students to complete the activity independently.

Meeting Individual Needs

ESOL

Speakers of other languages may not understand the concept of doubling the consonant before adding the -ed or -ing ending. Write the following base words on the board: *begin, drop, stop, jog, hop,* and *shop.* Call on volunteers to add the -ed or -ing ending to the word and remember to double the consonant. Then have them spell the word aloud, write it, and circle the doubled consonant.

Spelling and Writing

sneezed
smiling
beginning
hoped
dropping
shining
stopped
pleased
dropped
liked
taking
driving
closed
jogged
hopping
shopping

Write to the Point

Write a paragraph about something fun you can do with a pet. Tell where you can go and what you can do. Try to use spelling words from this lesson.
Paragraphs will vary.

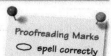

Use the strategies on page 7 when you are not sure how to spell a word.

Proofreading

Proofread the letter below. Use proofreading marks to correct five spelling mistakes, three capitalization mistakes, and two punctuation mistakes.

Proofreading Marks
◯ spell correctly
≡ capitalize
⊙ add period

2616 Lakeview Drive

Gilbert, AZ 85234

May 15, 2003

Dear Tyler,

    Last week we (stoped) [stopped] by the animal shelter. i [I]
(likd) [liked] the kittens a lot. my [My] parents said we could
get one I was so (pleaseed) [pleased] that I couldn't stop
(smiling). when [When] we were (driveing) [driving] home, I thought
of you. Please come see my new kitten soon ⊙

       Your friend,

       Samara

Proofreading Practice

- I hopt my present had arrived. *(hoped)*
- We missed the begining of the movie. *(beginning)*

Correcting Common Errors

Some students may misspell *hoping* as *hopping* or *hoped* as *hopped.* Have these students focus on the long vowel sound by saying it aloud as they write each word correctly several times.

Language Connection

Commas To make it easy to read a date, use a comma between the day and the year.

July 4, 1776	December 27, 1998

Decide which word from the boxes below completes each sentence. Then write the sentences, using commas correctly.

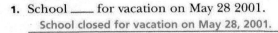

jogged	closed	dropped	hoped

1. School ____ for vacation on May 28 2001.
   School closed for vacation on May 28, 2001.

2. On June 25 1996, Ms. Padden ____ in a race.
   On June 25, 1996, Ms. Padden jogged in a race.

3. Old friends ____ in to visit us on February 4 2000.
   Old friends dropped in to visit us on February 4, 2000.

4. Ana ____ her party would be on May 17 2002.
   Ana hoped her party would be on May 17, 2002.

⭐ Challenge Yourself

What do you think each Challenge Word means? Check the Spelling Dictionary to see if you are right. Then use separate paper to write sentences showing that you understand the meaning of each Challenge Word. **Definitions and sentences will vary.**

5. I wasn't **jabbing** the window with a stick.

6. Straighten the **crinkled** paper.

7. We **estimated** that we picked up 500 cans.

8. The dog's huge size **stunned** me!

Challenge Words

jabbing
crinkled
estimated
stunned

LESSON 23 **139**

Posttest

Dictate the following sentences. Have students use separate paper to write the sentences and underline the lesson words.

1. The sun is <u>shining</u> today.
2. She is <u>driving</u> us to the <u>shopping</u> mall.
3. They <u>stopped</u> talking when I <u>sneezed</u>.
4. She <u>dropped</u> the yellow dish.
5. The show is <u>beginning</u>.
6. She was <u>hopping</u> down the road.
7. I <u>hoped</u> he was <u>pleased</u>.
8. I was <u>dropping</u> things as I <u>jogged</u>.
9. The store <u>closed</u> at five o'clock.
10. I am <u>taking</u> this book home.
11. He was <u>smiling</u> at me.
12. She <u>liked</u> her new coat.

Enrichment Activity

Have students write each lesson word in scrambled-letter form. Then have them trade papers and unscramble the words.

Student Objectives
- To use context to identify lesson words
- To write sentences, using commas in dates correctly
- To study the spellings and meanings of the Challenge Words
- To take a posttest on the lesson words

Presenting the Page

Write the date on the board without punctuation and ask students what is missing. Lead them to conclude that dates are easier to read when the day and the year are separated with a comma.

⭐ Challenge Yourself

To introduce the Challenge Words, write the following on the board:

jabbing	crinkled
estimated	stunned

Pronounce the words for the students and discuss the base word for each (*jab, crinkle, estimate, stun*). Have students identify the Challenge Words in which the final consonant is doubled (*jabbing* and *stunned*) and those in which the final *e* is dropped (*crinkled* and *estimated*).

Have students write what they think each Challenge Word means, look up the words in the Spelling Dictionary, and write the correct definitions. Ask students to compare their definitions with those in the Spelling Dictionary.

Posttest

Use the posttest on this page to assess students' ability to spell the lesson words.

Day 1

Student Objective
- To take a pretest on the lesson words

Pretest

Use the pretest on this page to assess students' ability to spell the lesson words.

Study Steps
Have students use the study steps on page 6 to study any words they misspell in the pretest.

You may wish to duplicate and send home the Home Activity Master on pages T247–T248.

Meeting Individual Needs

ESOL
Speakers of other languages often have difficulty deciding when to double the final consonant before adding -ed or -ing. Write *help*, *hop*, *droop*, and *drop* on the board. Guide students to see that only *hop* and *drop* end in a single vowel and a consonant and that the final consonant must be doubled in these words before -ed or -ing is added. Have students write the -ed and -ing forms of all the example words correctly.

Lesson 24
Unit 4 Review
Lessons 19–23

Use the steps on page 6 to study words that are hard for you.

19 socks
bottle
o'clock
wash

Words with Short o
Write the spelling word that belongs in each group.
1. time, watch, _____ o'clock
2. jar, can, _____ bottle
3. shoes, gloves, _____ socks
4. clean, scrub, _____ wash

20 wrote
hole
know
yellow
goes
November

Words with Long o
Write the spelling word for each clue.
5. This is something you might find in your sock. _____ hole
6. If your shirt is the color of butter, it's this color. _____ yellow
7. If you recorded your thoughts on paper, you did this. _____ wrote
8. Someone who travels does this. _____ goes
9. If you understand, you do this. _____ know
10. If it's the eleventh month, it's this month. _____ November

21 comb
hello
almost
road
toast

More Words with Long o
Write the spelling word that completes each sentence.
11. Would you like some eggs and _____ toast for breakfast?
12. The sun was setting, so it was _____ almost dark outside.

140 UNIT 4

Pretest

Say each lesson word, read the sentence, then repeat the word. Have students write the words on separate paper.

1. **socks** Put on your <u>socks</u> and shoes.
2. **bottle** The <u>bottle</u> was made of glass.
3. **o'clock** He must be home by five <u>o'clock</u>.
4. **wash** She will <u>wash</u> her dad's car.
5. **wrote** I <u>wrote</u> my name.
6. **hole** She has a <u>hole</u> in her shirt.
7. **know** Do you <u>know</u> where you are going?

8. **yellow** Lemons are <u>yellow</u>.
9. **goes** An elevator <u>goes</u> up and down.
10. **November** I will visit my aunt in <u>November</u>.
11. **comb** I forgot to <u>comb</u> my hair.
12. **hello** Did you say <u>hello</u> to him?
13. **almost** It is <u>almost</u> time to go home.
14. **road** They walked down the <u>road</u>.
15. **toast** I ate eggs and <u>toast</u>.
16. **poor** The <u>poor</u> little dog was lost.
17. **shook** The man <u>shook</u> my hand.

18. **cookies** Let's have some <u>cookies</u> and milk.
19. **sure** Are you <u>sure</u> you can go?
20. **should** We <u>should</u> eat our vegetables.
21. **hoped** She <u>hoped</u> she would find her lost dog.
22. **shining** The sun was <u>shining</u> at noon.
23. **stopped** The lady <u>stopped</u> her car.
24. **dropped** I <u>dropped</u> my books.
25. **hopping** A rabbit is <u>hopping</u> across our yard.

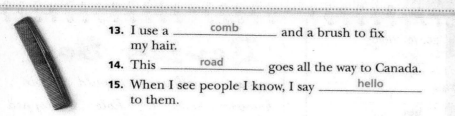

13. I use a ___comb___ and a brush to fix my hair.

14. This ___road___ goes all the way to Canada.

15. When I see people I know, I say ___hello___ to them.

---

22 poor
shook
cookies
sure
should

Words with /ŏŏ/

Write the spelling word that completes each analogy.

16. *Ice cream* is to *freeze* as ___cookies___ is to *bake*.

17. *Wake* is to *sleep* as *rich* is to ___poor___.

18. *Little* is to *small* as ___should___ is to *must*.

19. *Take* is to *took* as *shake* is to ___shook___.

20. *Thin* is to *skinny* as *certain* is to ___sure___.

---

23 hoped
shining
stopped
dropped
hopping

More Words with -ed or -ing

Write the spelling word that is a synonym for each underlined word.

21. The stars were <u>glowing</u> like diamonds.
___shining___

22. The temperature <u>fell</u> twenty degrees in three hours.
___dropped___

23. Cinderella <u>wished</u> she could go to the ball.
___hoped___

24. Our washing machine <u>quit</u> working yesterday.
___stopped___

25. My little brother was <u>jumping</u> on one foot.
___hopping___

LESSON 24 **141**

REVIEW TEST MASTER, pp. T289–290

Unit 4 Review Test Name _____

Darken the circle for the word that is spelled correctly.

Example
Please use this key to _____ the door.
A lok B lak C lock D locke

1. His house is at the end of this _____.
A road B rowd C roade D roed

2. Do you _____ the answer to her question?
F knoe G kno H know J knoaw

3. Rosa wore a bright red and _____ sweater.
A yelloe B yellow C yeloww D yello

4. My brother _____ to baseball practice twice a week.
F gows G goas H gose J goes

5. I like butter and jelly on my _____.
A toest B toast C tost D towst

6. Let's have some milk and _____.
F cuckies G coukies H cookies J cookeys

7. Don't forget to _____ your hair in the morning.
A comb B coem C combe D cowmb

8. She _____ her pencil on the floor.
F droppd G droped H dropt J dropped

9. Are you _____ that we have math homework?
A soor B sure C shur D shoure

10. My little sister can't find her _____ and shoes.
F sawks G socks H socs J saks

11. We _____ leave early so that we don't miss the bus.
A shood B shude C should D shoud

12. The coin sank to the _____ of the pond.
F bottom G batum H botom J bottum

Unit 4 Review Test Name _____

Darken the circle for the word that is spelled correctly.

13. The old jean jacket had a _____ in it.
A hoel B hoal C hole D howle

14. She waved to her friends and said _____.
F hellow G hello H heloww J helloe

15. I do not like to _____ dirty dishes.
A woush B wosh C wush D wash

16. The _____ little mouse was cold and wet.
F poor G por H poar J porr

17. She _____ that she would get her new puppy today.
A hopt B hoeped C hoped D hoppd

18. The men _____ hands and left the room.
F shooke G shook H shuk J shouck

19. The stars were _____ brightly in the sky.
A shineeng B shineing C shinning D shining

20. Is your birthday in _____ or December?
F Noavember G Nowvember H November J Noevember

21. I am _____ finished reading this book.
A almost B almoest C almowst D almoast

22. Please meet me here at two _____.
F oclock G o'clok H o'clock J oclak

23. My best friend _____ me a nice letter.
A wrot B wrote C wroat D roat

24. That traffic light _____ working this afternoon.
F stopped G stopt H stoped J stoppd

25. The rabbit is _____ across our lawn.
A hopng B hopeing C hawping D hopping

Example
Ⓐ Ⓑ ● Ⓓ
Answers
1. ● Ⓑ Ⓒ Ⓓ
2. Ⓕ Ⓖ ● Ⓙ
3. Ⓐ ● Ⓒ Ⓓ
4. Ⓕ Ⓖ Ⓗ ●
5. Ⓐ ● Ⓒ Ⓓ
6. Ⓕ Ⓖ ● Ⓙ
7. ● Ⓑ Ⓒ Ⓓ
8. Ⓕ Ⓖ Ⓗ ●
9. Ⓐ ● Ⓒ Ⓓ
10. Ⓕ ● Ⓗ Ⓙ
11. Ⓐ Ⓑ ● Ⓓ
12. ● Ⓖ Ⓗ Ⓙ

Answers
13. Ⓐ Ⓑ ● Ⓓ
14. Ⓕ ● Ⓗ Ⓙ
15. Ⓐ Ⓑ Ⓒ ●
16. ● Ⓖ Ⓗ Ⓙ
17. Ⓐ Ⓑ ● Ⓓ
18. Ⓕ ● Ⓗ Ⓙ
19. Ⓐ Ⓑ Ⓒ ●
20. Ⓕ Ⓖ ● Ⓙ
21. ● Ⓑ Ⓒ Ⓓ
22. Ⓕ Ⓖ ● Ⓙ
23. Ⓐ ● Ⓒ Ⓓ
24. ● Ⓖ Ⓗ Ⓙ
25. Ⓐ Ⓑ Ⓒ ●

Day 2

Student Objectives
- To review the *o* and *a* spellings of the /ŏ/ sound
- To review the *o*-consonant-*e*, *ow*, *oe*, *o*, and *oa* spellings of the /ō/ sound
- To review the *oo*, *u*, *u*-consonant-*e* and *ou* spellings of the /ŏŏ/ sound
- To review spelling patterns in -*ed* and -*ing* words containing base-word changes
- To use meaning clues to identify and write lesson words

Presenting the Pages

Lessons 19–21 Have volunteers read the review words for Lessons 19–21 aloud. Review with students the short *o* and long *o* spelling patterns represented in the review words—*o* and *a* for /ŏ/ and *o*-consonant-*e*, *ow*, *oe*, *o*, and *oa* for /ō/.

Lesson 22 Have volunteers read the Lesson 22 review words aloud. Review with students the /ŏŏ/ spelling patterns they learned in Lesson 22—*oo*, *u*, *u*-consonant-*e*, and *ou* for /ŏŏ/.

Lesson 23 Have volunteers read the Lesson 23 words and identify the spelling pattern on page 134 that each illustrates.

Test-Taking Strategies

Read the directions for the Review Test Master aloud and talk with students about the task and format of the test. Point out that in each test item, four spellings of one word are presented. Suggest that students quickly scan the answer choices to find the correctly spelled word.

Proofreading Practice
- You shuld play a game with us. (*should*)
- The sun is shinning today. (*shining*)

141

Student Objectives
- To sort spelling words according to vowel sound
- To compare sorted words that end with -ed or -ing

Presenting the Page

Have volunteers take turns reading the Review Sort words aloud. Point out that the activity asks students to classify four -ed or -ing words according to vowel sound. You may wish to have students work in small groups to complete the page.

Meeting Individual Needs

Kinesthetic Learners

To encourage spelling competence, supply students with letter tiles and have them use the tiles to spell the words. Ask students to tap the letter(s) that spell each vowel sound.

Proofreading Practice
- Look at my new yello hat. (yellow)
- I wosh my hair every night. (wash)

---

26. /ŏ/ Words
- socks
- bottle
- wash
- hopping
- stopped
- dropped

27. /ō/ Words
- know
- toast
- yellow
- road
- goes
- November
- hole
- comb
- wrote
- hello
- hoped

28. /o͞o/ Words
- shook
- sure
- should
- poor
- cookies

Review Sort

socks	yellow	should	wrote
know	road	hole	dropped
toast	sure	comb	hello
shook	hopping	stopped	cookies
bottle	goes	poor	hoped
wash	November		

26. Write the **six** short *o* words. Circle the letter that spells /ŏ/ in each word.

27. Write the **eleven** long *o* words. Circle the letter or letters that spell /ō/ in each word.

28. Write the **five** /o͞o/ words. Circle the letter or letters that spell /o͞o/ in each word.

These four words have been sorted into two groups. Explain two ways in which the words in each group are alike.

29. hoped   closed

Both have the long o vowel sound.

In both, the final e is dropped before -ed is added.

30. stopped   hopping

Both have the short o vowel sound.

In both, the final consonant is doubled before -ed or -ing is added.

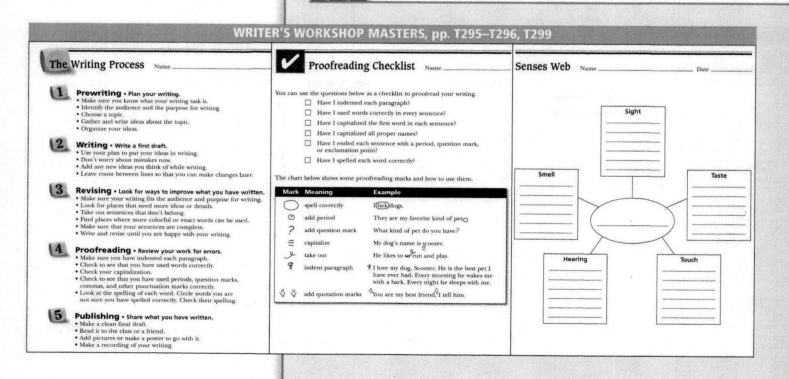

The Writing Process   Name _____

1. **Prewriting** • Plan your writing.
   - Make sure you know what your writing task is.
   - Identify the audience and the purpose for writing.
   - Choose a topic.
   - Gather and write ideas about the topic.
   - Organize your ideas.

2. **Writing** • Write a first draft.
   - Use your plan to put your ideas in writing.
   - Don't worry about mistakes now.
   - Add any new ideas you think of while writing.
   - Leave room between lines so that you can make changes later.

3. **Revising** • Look for ways to improve what you have written.
   - Make sure your writing fits the audience and purpose for writing.
   - Look for places that need more ideas or details.
   - Take out sentences that don't belong.
   - Find places where more colorful or exact words can be used.
   - Make sure that your sentences are complete.
   - Write and revise until you are happy with your writing.

4. **Proofreading** • Review your work for errors.
   - Make sure you have indented each paragraph.
   - Check to see that you have used words correctly.
   - Check your capitalization.
   - Check to see that you have used periods, question marks, commas, and other punctuation marks correctly.
   - Look at the spelling of each word. Circle words you are not sure you have spelled correctly. Check their spelling.

5. **Publishing** • Share what you have written.
   - Make a clean final draft.
   - Read it to the class or a friend.
   - Add pictures or make a poster to go with it.
   - Make a recording of your writing.

✔ Proofreading Checklist   Name _____

You can use the questions below as a checklist to proofread your writing.
- ☐ Have I indented each paragraph?
- ☐ Have I used words correctly in every sentence?
- ☐ Have I capitalized the first word in each sentence?
- ☐ Have I capitalized all proper names?
- ☐ Have I ended each sentence with a period, question mark, or exclamation point?
- ☐ Have I spelled each word correctly?

The chart below shows some proofreading marks and how to use them.

Mark	Meaning	Example
◯	spell correctly	I liek dogs.
⊙	add period	They are my favorite kind of pet⊙
?	add question mark	What kind of pet do you have?
≡	capitalize	My dog's name is scooter.
℘	take out	He likes to run and play.
¶	indent paragraph	¶ I love my dog, Scooter. He is the best pet I have ever had. Every morning he wakes me with a bark. Every night he sleeps with me.
⌄⌄	add quotation marks	You are my best friend, I tell him.

Senses Web   Name _____   Date _____

Sight

Smell

Taste

Hearing

Touch

Writer's Workshop

A Description

A description tells about a person, a place, or a thing. In description, writers use details that appeal to a reader's senses of sight, hearing, smell, touch, and taste. Here is a part of Ben's description of a baseball game.

The Game

My granddad took me to my first baseball game last summer. It was a perfect day. The sun was bright and yellow. I could smell the green, grassy field. Our seats were right behind home plate. I could hear the thump of the ball in the catcher's mitt. I could see the players' frowns when the umpire called, "You're out!"

Prewriting   To write his description, Ben followed the steps in the writing process. After he decided on a topic, he completed a senses web. On the web, he listed details that appealed to the five senses. The web helped Ben decide which details to include in his description. Part of Ben's senses web is shown here. Study what Ben did.

> Baseball Game
>
> **Hearing**
> thump of ball in catcher's mitt
> umpire's call
> crowd cheering

It's Your Turn!

Write your own description. It can be about a place, a person, or anything you can picture clearly in your mind. After you have decided on your topic, make a senses web. Then follow the other steps in the writing process—writing, revising, proofreading, and publishing. Try to use spelling words from this lesson in your description. **Descriptions will vary.**

LESSON 24   **143**

Writer's Workshop Scoring Rubric: Description

SCORE 3
Object of the description is clear, and ideas are well developed. Description contains clear, vivid sensory details. Writing is organized and coherent. Contains a minimum of sentence-structure, usage, mechanics, and spelling errors.

SCORE 2
Object of the description is clear, and some ideas are well developed. Description contains sensory details, but some are not vivid; some may not be clear. Has some degree of organization and coherence. Contains some sentence-structure, usage, mechanics, and spelling errors.

SCORE 1
Object of the description is not clear, or writing is not a description. Ideas are not well developed. Writing contains few or no sensory details, and most are not vivid or clear. Has minimal organization and coherence. Contains many sentence-structure, usage, mechanics, and spelling errors.

Evaluating Students' Writing

The scoring rubric is based on standards for idea development, organization, coherence, sentence structure, usage, mechanics, and spelling. You may wish to share the rubric with students before they write their description.

The *Steck-Vaughn Writer's Dictionary, Intermediate Level,* provides writers with a place to write words they want to remember.

Day 4

Student Objective
- To write a description, using Lesson 24 words and the steps in the writing process

Presenting the Page

Read the excerpt from "The Game" with students. Invite them to identify words that appeal to specific senses.

Allow students time to study the portion of Ben's senses web provided. Guide students to see how this prewriting activity helped Ben prepare to write his description.

You may wish to copy and distribute the Writer's Workshop Masters on pages T295–T296 and T299 for students to use as they write their description.

Day 5

Student Objective
- To take a posttest on the lesson words

Posttest Options

Use the posttest on this page or the Review Test Master on pages T289–T290 to assess students' ability to spell the lesson words.

Posttest

Dictate the following sentences. Have students write the sentences and underline the lesson words.

1. I need to <u>wash</u> my <u>yellow</u> <u>socks</u>.
2. We <u>should</u> find the green <u>bottle</u>.
3. She <u>hoped</u> she had her <u>comb</u>.
4. He <u>wrote</u> to say <u>hello</u>.
5. I <u>know</u> she <u>goes</u> to this school.
6. Are you <u>sure</u> this is the <u>road</u>?
7. The trees <u>shook</u> in the <u>November</u> wind.
8. I <u>dropped</u> the ball into the <u>hole</u>.
9. It is <u>almost</u> nine o'clock.
10. Do you want <u>toast</u> or <u>cookies</u>?
11. The <u>poor</u> mouse is <u>hopping</u> to his home.
12. The sun has <u>stopped</u> <u>shining</u>.

143

Words with /o͞o/ or /yo͞o/

Day 1

Student Objectives
- To take a pretest on the lesson words
- To spell the lesson words aloud
- To sort and write the lesson words according to the spelling patterns *oo*, *ue*, *ew*, *u-consonant-e*, *o*, and *o-consonant-e*

Pretest

Use the pretest on this page to assess students' ability to spell the lesson words.

 Have students use the study steps on page 6 to study any words they misspell in the pretest.

 You may wish to duplicate and send home the Home Activity Master on pages T249–T250.

Presenting the Page

Introducing the /o͞o/ and /yo͞o/ Sounds Write /o͞o/ and /yo͞o/ on the board and say them. Then read the following words and have students raise their hand when they hear a word with /o͞o/ or /yo͞o/:

teeth–*tooth*	fat–*few*
cute–cut	draw–*drew*

As students prepare to sort the words, point out that /o͞o/ and /yo͞o/ are most often spelled *oo*, *ue*, *ew*, or *u-consonant-e* but are spelled *o* or *o-consonant-e* in some words that we often use.

Pronunciation Focus Write *Tuesday*, *knew*, and *news* on the board. Guide students to recognize that these words may be pronounced as either /o͞o/ or /yo͞o/.

Consonant Focus Write *school* and *two* on the board. Ask students which consonants are silent (*h* and *w*). Then have students find other lesson words with silent consonants (*who*—*w*, *knew*—*k*).

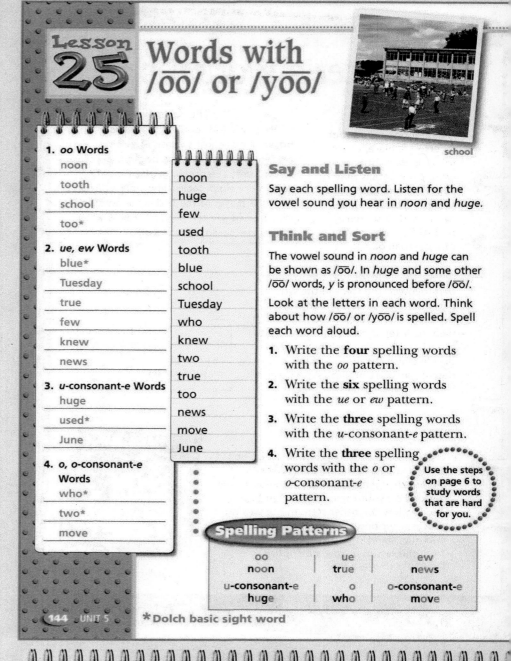

Lesson 25 Words with /o͞o/ or /yo͞o/

school

1. oo Words
- noon
- tooth
- school
- too*

2. ue, ew Words
- blue*
- Tuesday
- true
- few
- knew
- news

3. u-consonant-e Words
- huge
- used*
- June

4. o, o-consonant-e Words
- who*
- two*
- move

noon
huge
few
used
tooth
blue
school
Tuesday
who
knew
two
true
too
news
move
June

Say and Listen
Say each spelling word. Listen for the vowel sound you hear in *noon* and *huge*.

Think and Sort
The vowel sound in *noon* and *huge* can be shown as /o͞o/. In *huge* and some other /o͞o/ words, *y* is pronounced before /o͞o/.

Look at the letters in each word. Think about how /o͞o/ or /yo͞o/ is spelled. Spell each word aloud.

1. Write the **four** spelling words with the *oo* pattern.
2. Write the **six** spelling words with the *ue* or *ew* pattern.
3. Write the **three** spelling words with the *u-consonant-e* pattern.
4. Write the **three** spelling words with the *o* or *o-consonant-e* pattern.

> Use the steps on page 6 to study words that are hard for you.

Spelling Patterns

oo	ue	ew
noon	true	news
u-consonant-e	**o**	**o-consonant-e**
huge	who	move

*Dolch basic sight word

Pretest

Say each lesson word, read the sentence, and then repeat the word. Have students write the words on separate paper.

1. **noon** Class ended at noon.
2. **huge** We saw a huge van.
3. **few** A few of us played at the park.
4. **used** I used a new pencil.
5. **tooth** The boy lost a tooth.
6. **blue** The water is clear and blue.
7. **school** He taught at the high school.
8. **Tuesday** Your soccer game is Tuesday.
9. **who** I asked who called.
10. **knew** Mom knew what happened.
11. **two** Read two chapters.
12. **true** Is it true that you are going away?
13. **too** This room is too cold.
14. **news** The girls spread the news.
15. **move** We will move the piano.
16. **June** The weather grew warm in June.

Additional Words for Enrichment

The following words can be used to meet the needs of on-level and above-level students:

grew	stew	glue	goose	choose	loose

Spelling and Meaning

Classifying Write the spelling word that belongs in each group.

1. lunch time   twelve o'clock   **noon**
2. report   information   **news**
3. what   where   **who**
4. mouth   tongue   **tooth**
5. wiggle   walk   **move**
6. post office   library   **school**
7. red   green   **blue**

Clues Write the spelling word for each clue.

8. one of the summer months   **June**
9. not very many   **few**
10. the sum of one plus one   **two**
11. means the same as *also*   **too**
12. gigantic   **huge**
13. the opposite of *false*   **true**
14. not new   **used**
15. sounds like *new*   **knew**

Word Story The Vikings were people who came to England long ago. One spelling word comes from the word *Tiwesdaeg. Tiw* was the name of the Viking war god. *Daeg* meant "day." Write the spelling word that comes from *Tiwesdaeg.*

16. **Tuesday**

Family Tree: *move* Think about how the *move* words are alike in spelling and meaning. Then add another *move* word to the tree. A sample answer is shown.

- moveable
- moving
- remove
- 17. removed
- unmoved
- moves
- move

LESSON 25 **145**

Spelling and Meaning

Day 2

Student Objectives

- To use meaning clues to identify and write lesson words
- To use etymology, meaning, and spelling to identify the word *Tuesday*
- To learn *move* words and analyze their spellings and meanings

Presenting the Page

Write the following Classifying and Clues examples on the board and model identifying the answers:

- four   three   _____ (*two*)
- a day of the week   _____ (*Tuesday*)

Word Story

You may wish to explain that according to myth, Tiw was the only Viking brave enough to place his hand in the mouth of the giant wolf Fenris. He lost his hand, but the other warriors were able to tie up the wolf. You may also wish to point out that *June*, another lesson word, comes from *Juno*, the name of a Roman goddess.

Family Tree: *move*

Students should understand that all of the *move* words except *moving* contain *move*. Ask how *move* changes when *-ing* is added to form *moving* (the *e* is dropped). Have students write *moveable, remove, unmoved*, and *moves* on paper and circle the base word. Tell students that knowing how to spell *move* will help them spell related words.

HOME ACTIVITY MASTER p. T249

Unit 5   Spelling at Home

Dear Family of _____,
During the next six weeks, your child will be learning to spell the following kinds of words:

- words with /ōō/ or /yōō/, as in *noon* and *few*
- words with /ûr/, as in *fur*
- words with /ä/, as in *father*
- words with /oi/, as in *corn*
- contractions

Here are some simple activities to do each week to help your child become a better speller.

Listening and Writing
Say the spelling words and have your child write them.

Spelling Strategy: Rhyming Partner
If your child is unsure about the spelling of a word, help your child create a list of words that rhyme with the word and are spelled in the same way. Then ask your child to select one of the words as a rhyming partner. Then have him or her spell the word that he or she is having difficulty with.

Games and Activities
Play Easiest to Hardest. Choose a group of words from the list. Give yourself and your child a piece of paper. Next, write the easiest word from the list, the next two easiest words, the next three easiest words, and so on. Then compare the easiest-to-hardest word order with each other.

Choose five spelling words that are hard for your child to spell. Write each word on a separate sheet of paper, leaving space between the letters of the word. Then cut the words apart so that each letter is on a separate square of paper. Mix up the letters. Have your child put the letters together to form the different spelling words.

Using Spelling Words
Ask your child to write sentences that contain the spelling words. Then read the sentences with your child. Notice whether the sentences show that your child knows the meanings of the spelling words.

Lesson 25 Words with /ōō/ or /yōō/
Week of _____
noon   school   too   tooth
blue   true   Tuesday   who
move   two   news   knew
June   huge   few   used

Lesson 26 Words with /ûr/
Week of _____
girl   bird   first   dirt
third   world   work   word
worm   curl   fur   Thursday
turn   learn   earth   were

Lesson 27 Words with /ä/
Week of _____
father   market   barn   garden
star   sharp   bark   yard
dark   hard   card   start
March   arm   art   heart

Lesson 28 Words with /oi/
Week of _____
soil   broil   coin   point
boil   choice   noise   voice
spoil   oil   join   boy
toy   joy   enjoy   royal

Lesson 29 More Contractions
Week of _____
hasn't   aren't   couldn't   didn't
doesn't   hadn't   haven't   mustn't
shouldn't   wasn't   weren't   isn't
wouldn't   won't   don't   can't

Lesson 30 Unit 5 Review
Week of _____
Lesson 30 is a review of Lessons 25–29. Help your child practice all of the words from those lessons.

The highlighted area shows the Lesson 25 words, which students can share with family members. Spanish version available on page T250.

Proofreading Practice
- The music cost tou dollars. (*two*)
- I knue the song by heart. (*knew*)

Meeting Individual Needs

Auditory Learners
Have students work in small groups to create chants for the lesson words, such as the following:

> You asked how to spell it, and I was glad I knew— K-N-E-W.

> Blue is the color for me— B-L-U-E.

Invite students to share their chants with the class.

145

Student Objectives
- To use context to identify and write lesson words
- To identify the sequence of events

Presenting the Pages

Ask students to work with a partner to read the story and write the missing words. Alternatively, have students complete the page independently. Then have students take turns reading the completed story.

Discuss with students the context clues for the words related to time—*Tuesday, June,* and *noon.*

Meeting Individual Needs

Kinesthetic Learners
To help kinesthetic learners practice spelling patterns, provide modeling clay in different colors. Have students work in pairs to flatten out a "brick" of color for each spelling pattern and write that pattern in the clay with a dull pencil (red for *oo*, yellow for *ue*, and so forth). Then have students take turns calling out lesson words to each other. When one student calls out a word, the other student should choose the appropriate brick of color and write the word in it, under the pattern.

146

Use each spelling word once to complete the story.

The All-School Marathon

_____Tuesday_____ was a perfect day for the all-school marathon.
 1
The sun was out, but it wasn't _____too_____ hot to run. Jesse
 2
_____knew_____ he was in good shape. "I should be," he thought.
 3
"I've been training all through _____June_____, July, and August."
 4
 Jesse was new in town. He had moved to Green City late in the
_____school_____ year. He went to his new school for only two
 5
weeks. He didn't know anyone. He had met one boy, but it had
been too hard for them to talk. They had met at the dentist's office.
The boy was having a chipped _____tooth_____ fixed while Jesse
 6
was having his teeth cleaned. Jesse had
spent the summer by himself. He had
_____used_____ the summer to get
 7
in shape for the race.

 It was almost _____noon_____
 8
when Jesse saw the three-mile marker.
He was among the first ten runners.
He was the only one of them wearing
_____blue_____ and white, the
 9
colors of his school. "If I win," he
thought, "everybody will know
_____who_____ I am."
 10

146 UNIT 5

Spelling Strategy

Different Spellings
Remind students that one strategy for spelling a troublesome word is to write the word in different ways and then choose the spelling that looks correct. Ask volunteers to identify the six spelling patterns for /o͞o/ and /yo͞o/ and to write them in a chart on the board. Choose a lesson word and write it in the chart, using the various spelling patterns.

oo	ue	ew	u-consonant-e	o	o-consonant-e
troo	true	trew	truwe	tro	trowe

Tell students to choose the spelling that looks correct. Have students select other lesson words to write.

Jesse pushed on. Only _____two_____ runners were
                              11
in front of him now. He saw the finish line ahead. Then
Jesse made his _____move_____ on the leaders. For a
                        12
_____few_____ yards, they were all neck and neck.
        13
    Without warning, Jesse tripped. He fell and scraped his
knee. A _____huge_____ crowd gathered around him.
              14
"Did I win or lose?" he asked.

    "You finished second," a girl said. "But I've got some
good _____news_____ for you. That's the first time our
          15
school ever came close to winning."

    "It's _____true_____," said a boy. "You're the best
            16
runner we've ever had."

    Jesse looked up. It was the boy from the dentist's office.
"Remember me?" the boy asked. "My
name is Jack."

    Jesse smiled. He had
not won the race, but he
had won a new friend!

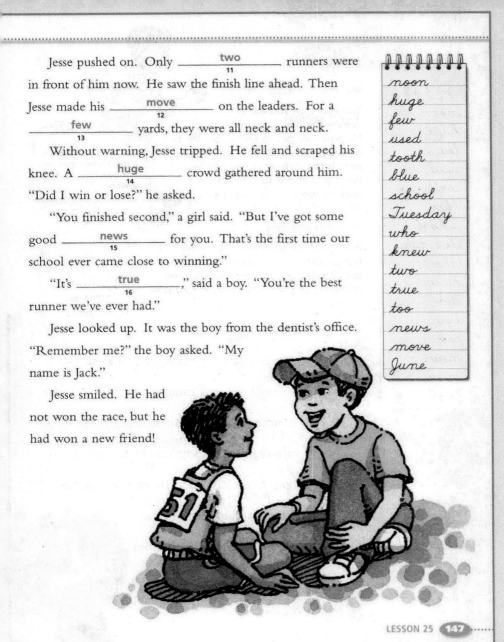

noon
huge
few
used
tooth
blue
school
Tuesday
who
knew
two
true
too
news
move
June

LESSON 25   **147**

ACTIVITY MASTER p. T273

Lesson **25** Words with /o͞o/ or /yo͞o/

Name _____

Use the code to solve the puzzle.

1 = b
2 = c
3 = d
4 = e
5 = f
6 = h
7 = k
8 = l
9 = n
10 = o
11 = r
12 = s
13 = t
14 = u
15 = w

t o o t h   k n e w
o   r   n   w
      u s e d   t
b l u e   w   w
        s c h o o l

Spelling Words
school   two
too   news
tooth   knew
blue   few
true   used

Across
3. 13 10 10 13 6
5. 7 9 4 15
7. 14 12 4 3
9. 1 8 14 4
10. 12 2 6 10 10 8

Down
1. 13 10 10
2. 5 4 15
4. 13 11 14 4
6. 9 4 15 12
8. 13 15 10

Find the word in the box that completes each sentence.
Write the word on the line.

Spelling Words	noon Tuesday who move June huge

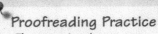

11. Do you know _____who_____ will be in the play?
12. Would you like to _____move_____ to another city?
13. The month after _____June_____ is July.
14. Twelve o'clock is also called _____noon_____.
15. I have a _____huge_____ pile of dirty socks under my bed.
16. Their book reports are due on _____Tuesday_____

ADDITIONAL PRACTICE

You may wish to copy and distribute
the Activity Master on page T273 as
additional practice for Lesson 25.

Proofreading Practice
- The room is a hoog mess.
  (huge)
- We will clean it on Tewsday.
  (Tuesday)

Reading Comprehension

After students have com-
pleted the pages, point out
that the story opens on race
day but then tells events that
happened before that day.
Guide students to observe
that the events in the first
two paragraphs are not told
in chronological order. Write
the following story events on
sentence strips:

Jesse moves to Green City.
Jesse meets a boy at the
    dentist's office.
Jesse trains for the race.
Jesse falls down at the race.

Distribute the strips to four
volunteers who stand before
the class. Have students tell
the volunteers where to stand
in order to put the strips in
correct chronological order.

Cooperative Learning Activity

To help students practice the
lesson words, have them work
in small groups to write the
words on index cards and sort
the words according to
spelling pattern. Then have
pairs of students dictate the
lesson words to each other.
Have students check their
work. If possible, have students compare their performance on this latter activity to
their performance on the lesson pretest. Guide them in
noting words that they should
continue to study.

147

Student Objectives

- To write a paragraph, using lesson words
- To proofread a journal entry for spelling, capitalization, and punctuation

Presenting the Page

To help students generate ideas for writing, encourage them to list things that they like and what they do for fun. Talk with students about a suitable way to open the paragraph, such as giving their name, age, or birthday and any family information they would like to share. Encourage students to use lesson words in their paragraph.

To assist students in the Proofreading activity, read the directions and the paragraph. Assign groups of students to proofread the paragraph together. Then put the uncorrected paragraph on the overhead projector. Call on volunteers to mark the paragraph, sentence by sentence.

Meeting Individual Needs

ESOL

Because /o͞o/ is always spelled *u* in Spanish, some Spanish-speaking students may have difficulty with other spelling patterns for this sound. To help these students practice the spelling patterns, have them write the spelling patterns on index cards, one pattern per card. Then have students dictate lesson words to each other. When one student says a word, the other student should hold up the correct spelling pattern and then write the word on the back of the card.

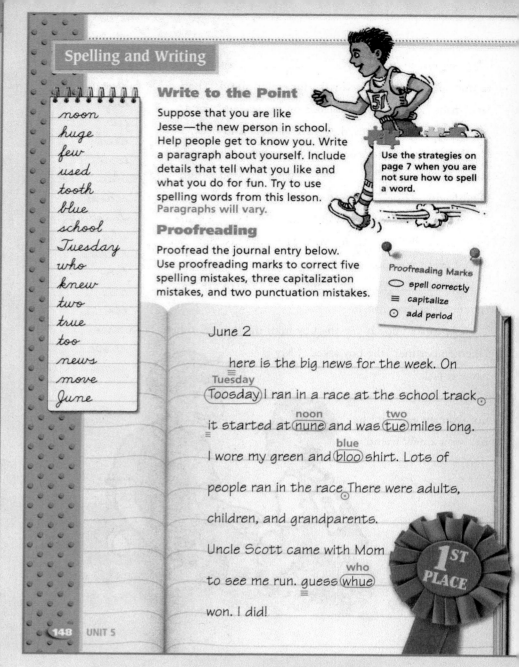

Spelling and Writing

noon
huge
few
used
tooth
blue
school
Tuesday
who
knew
two
true
too
news
move
June

Write to the Point

Suppose that you are like Jesse—the new person in school. Help people get to know you. Write a paragraph about yourself. Include details that tell what you like and what you do for fun. Try to use spelling words from this lesson. **Paragraphs will vary.**

Use the strategies on page 7 when you are not sure how to spell a word.

Proofreading

Proofread the journal entry below. Use proofreading marks to correct five spelling mistakes, three capitalization mistakes, and two punctuation mistakes.

Proofreading Marks
- ◯ spell correctly
- ≡ capitalize
- ⊙ add period

June 2

here is the big news for the week. On
Tuesday
(Toosday) I ran in a race at the school track⊙
noon   two
it started at (nune) and was (tue) miles long.
blue
I wore my green and (bloo) shirt. Lots of
people ran in the race⊙ There were adults,
children, and grandparents.
Uncle Scott came with Mom
who
to see me run. guess (whue)
won. I did!

1ST PLACE

148 UNIT 5

Proofreading Practice
- I yused to play piano. *(used)*
- I had a lesson every day at none. *(noon)*

✔ Correcting Common Errors

Some students may drop the *d* from *used* when writing *used* and *to* together. Suggest that these students write *used to* in a sentence, pronouncing each word individually and distinctly as they write. Then have the student circle the *d* for a visual reminder.

Dictionary Skills

Pronunciation Most dictionary entries show how a word is said. The way a word is said is called its pronunciation.

Entry Word ⟶ **noon** (nōōn) *noun* Midday; 12 o'clock in the middle of the day: *We'll eat at noon.*

Pronunciation

Letters and symbols are used to write pronunciations. These letters and symbols can be found in the pronunciation key.

Pronunciation Key

ă	pat	îr	deer	th	this
ā	pay	ŏ	pot	ŭ	cut
âr	care	ō	toe	ûr	urge
ä	father	ô	paw, for	ə	about,
ĕ	pet	oi	noise		item,
ē	bee	ŏŏ	took		edible,
ĭ	pit	ōō	boot		gallop,
ī	pie	ou	out		circus
		th	thin		

Use the pronunciation key to write the word from the boxes that goes with each pronunciation. Check your answers in the Spelling Dictionary.

tooth	move	few	huge

1. /fyōō/ ___few___
2. /tōōth/ ___tooth___
3. /mōōv/ ___move___
4. /hyōōj/ ___huge___

★ Challenge Yourself

Write the Challenge Word for each clue. Check the Spelling Dictionary to see if you are right. Then use separate paper to write sentences showing that you understand the meaning of each Challenge Word.

Challenge Words

pursue	shrewd
casual	dispute

Sentences will vary.

5. T-shirts and jeans are this type of clothing. ___casual___
6. Your teacher can help you with this. ___dispute___
7. A clever person is this. ___shrewd___
8. When you chase someone, you do this to them. ___pursue___

LESSON 25 **149**

Posttest

Dictate the following sentences. Have students use separate paper to write the sentences and underline the lesson words.

1. Is <u>school</u> over in <u>June</u>?
2. I will see you at <u>noon</u> on <u>Tuesday</u>.
3. Do you know <u>who used</u> my cup?
4. Is this <u>news true</u>?
5. There are <u>too few</u> of us to go.
6. He has <u>two blue</u> shirts.
7. She lost a <u>tooth</u>.
8. I <u>knew</u> you would <u>move</u> to this street.
9. We rode on a <u>huge</u> bus.

Enrichment Activity

Have small groups of students work together to create word search puzzles with words from the lesson and others that include the /ōō/ or /yōō/ sound. Then have groups trade puzzles to solve.

Day 5

Student Objectives
- To use a pronunciation key to identify and write the lesson words
- To study the spellings and meanings of the Challenge Words
- To take a posttest on the lesson words

Presenting the Page

Write the following on the board:
   (nōōn) (yōōzd) (trōō)
Point to each pronunciation and encourage students to use the pronunciation key on page 149 to identify the word. After each word is identified, have students complete the exercise.

★ Challenge Yourself

To introduce the Challenge Words, write the following on the board:

pur/sue	shrewd
ca/su/al	dis/pute

Pronounce the words for students and discuss the number of syllables in each. Then have students refer to page 144 and have them review the /ōō/ and /yōō/ spelling patterns featured in this lesson. Tell students that one Challenge Word has a new pattern (*casual* has the *u* pattern). Ask students to identify the /ōō/ or /yōō/ pattern in the other Challenge Words (*pursue* has *ue*, *dispute* has *u*-consonant-*e*, and *shrewd* has the *ew* pattern).

Posttest

Use the posttest on this page to assess students' ability to spell the lesson words.

Words with /ûr/

Student Objectives

- To take a pretest on the lesson words
- To spell the lesson words aloud
- To sort and write the lesson words according to the spelling patterns *ur, ir, or, ear,* and *ere*

Pretest

Use the pretest on this page to assess students' ability to spell the lesson words.

 Have students use the study steps on page 6 to study any words they misspell in the pretest.

 You may wish to duplicate and send home the Home Activity Master on pages T249–T250.

Presenting the Page

Introducing the /ûr/ Sounds
Write *fur* on the board and ask students to read it aloud and repeat the /ûr/ sound. Then say the following words and ask students to identify the words with /ûr/:

thread–*third* goal–*girl*
trim–*term* curl–cat

As students prepare to sort the words, point out that /ûr/ is most often spelled *ur, ir,* or *or* but is spelled *ear* or *ere* in some words that we often use.

Pronunciation Focus Point out that *ear* is often pronounced as long *e,* as in *hear.* Point out that when the sound of *ear* is /ûr/, the *r* is usually followed by a consonant.

Consonant Focus Write *curl* and *work* on the board. Ask students to identify the different spellings used for the sound /k/. Help students think of another spelling that produces the same sound, such as *ck* in *back.*

150

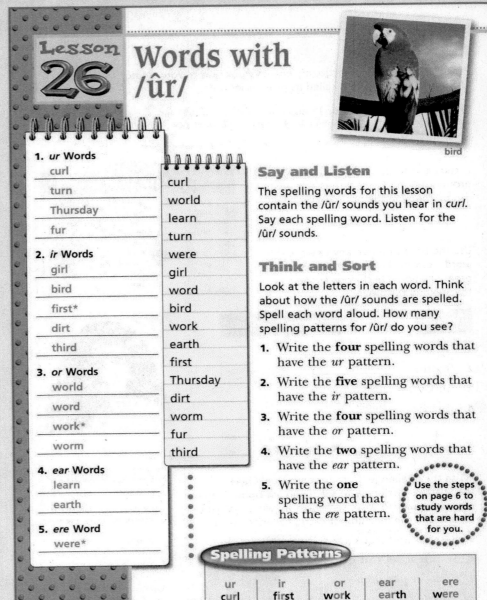

Words with /ûr/

bird

1. *ur* Words
curl
turn
Thursday
fur

2. *ir* Words
girl
bird
first*
dirt
third

3. *or* Words
world
word
work*
worm

4. *ear* Words
learn
earth

5. *ere* Word
were*

curl
world
learn
turn
were
girl
word
bird
work
earth
first
Thursday
dirt
worm
fur
third

Say and Listen

The spelling words for this lesson contain the /ûr/ sounds you hear in *curl.* Say each spelling word. Listen for the /ûr/ sounds.

Think and Sort

Look at the letters in each word. Think about how the /ûr/ sounds are spelled. Spell each word aloud. How many spelling patterns for /ûr/ do you see?

1. Write the **four** spelling words that have the *ur* pattern.
2. Write the **five** spelling words that have the *ir* pattern.
3. Write the **four** spelling words that have the *or* pattern.
4. Write the **two** spelling words that have the *ear* pattern.
5. Write the **one** spelling word that has the *ere* pattern.

Use the steps on page 6 to study words that are hard for you.

Spelling Patterns

ur	ir	or	ear	ere
curl	first	work	earth	were

*Dolch basic sight word

Pretest

Say each lesson word, read the sentence, and then repeat the word. Have students write the words on separate paper.

1. **curl** The kittens <u>curl</u> up in my lap.
2. **world** They are <u>world</u> champions.
3. **learn** We will <u>learn</u> about the moon.
4. **turn** The wheels <u>turn</u> around.
5. **were** They <u>were</u> singing loudly.
6. **girl** She was the only <u>girl</u> on the team.
7. **word** What does that <u>word</u> mean?

8. **bird** The <u>bird</u> flew away.
9. **work** He goes to <u>work</u> at nine o'clock.
10. **earth** The plants grew in sandy <u>earth</u>.
11. **first** I loved <u>first</u> grade.
12. **Thursday** Tomorrow is <u>Thursday</u>.
13. **dirt** Your shoes have <u>dirt</u> on them.
14. **worm** I used a <u>worm</u> as bait.
15. **fur** The cat licked its <u>fur</u>.
16. **third** He ran past <u>third</u> base.

Additional Words for Enrichment

The following words can be used to meet the needs of on-level and above-level students:

squirt **circle** **early** **burn** **thirsty** **disturb**

Definitions   Write the spelling word for each definition. Use the Spelling Dictionary if you need to.

1. a long, thin creature that crawls — worm
2. a young female child — girl
3. the third planet from the sun — earth or Earth
4. coming at the beginning — first
5. next after second — third
6. to move around — turn
7. the day between Wednesday and Friday — Thursday
8. a group of letters that has a meaning — word
9. soil or earth — dirt

Synonyms   Write the spelling word that is a synonym for the underlined word in each sentence.

10. Dinosaurs existed on Earth long ago. — were
11. Next year I hope to study French. — learn
12. We finished our task in the garden. — work
13. I will loop my hair around my finger. — curl
14. Wouldn't it be fun to go around the earth? — world
15. Our dog's hair is thick and black. — fur

Word Story   Sometimes the spelling of words changes to make them easier to say or sound nicer. One of the spelling words was once spelled *brid*. Over time, people switched the order of the *r* and *i*. Write the spelling word that shows how *brid* is spelled today.

16. _____ bird

Family Tree: *work*   Think about how the *work* words are alike in spelling and meaning. Then add another *work* word to the tree. A sample answer is shown.

- works
- rework
- 17. worked
- working
- worker
- work

LESSON 26 **151**

HOME ACTIVITY MASTER p. T249

Unit 5   Spelling at Home

Dear Family of _____
During the next six weeks, your child will be learning to spell the following kinds of words:

- words with /ōō/ or /yōō/, as in *noon* and *few*
- words with /ûr/, as in *fur*
- words with /ä/, as in *father*
- words with /oi/, as in *coin*
- contractions

Here are some simple activities to do each week to help your child become a better speller.

Listening and Writing
Say the spelling words and have your child write them.

Spelling Strategy: Rhyming Partner
If your child is unsure about the spelling of a word, help your child create a list of words that rhyme with the word and are spelled in the same way. Then ask your child to select one of the words as a rhyming partner. Ask your child to study the rhyming partner. Then have him or her spell the word that he or she is having difficulty with.

Games and Activities
Play Easiest to Hardest. Choose a group of words from the list. Give yourself and your child a piece of paper. Next, write the easiest word from the list, the next two easiest words, the next three easiest words, and so on. Then compare the easiest-to-hardest word order with each other.

Choose five spelling words that are hard for your child to spell. Write each word on a separate sheet of paper, leaving space between the letters of the word. Then cut the words apart so that each letter is on a separate square of paper. Mix up the letters. Have your child put the letters together to form the different spelling words.

Using Spelling Words
Ask your child to write sentences that contain the spelling words. Then read the sentences with your child. Notice whether the sentences show that your child knows the meanings of the spelling words.

Lesson 25 Words with /ōō/ or /yōō/
Week of _____

noon	school	too	tooth
blue	true	Tuesday	who
move	two	news	knew
June	huge	few	used

Lesson 26 Words with /ûr/
Week of _____

girl	bird	first	dirt
third	world	work	word
worm	curl	fur	earth
turn	learn	earth	Thursday
			were

Lesson 27 Words with /ä/
Week of _____

father	market	barn	garden
car	sharp	back	yard
dark	hard	card	start
March	arm	art	heart

Lesson 28 Words with /oi/
Week of _____

soil	broil	coin	point
boil	choice	noise	voice
spoil	oil	join	boy
toy	joy	enjoy	royal

Lesson 29 More Contractions
Week of _____

hasn't	aren't	couldn't	didn't
doesn't	hadn't	haven't	mustn't
shouldn't	wasn't	weren't	isn't
wouldn't	won't	don't	can't

Lesson 30 Unit 5 Review
Week of _____
Lesson 30 is a review of Lessons 25–29. Help your child practice all of the words from those lessons.

The highlighted area shows the Lesson 26 words, which students can share with family members. Spanish version available on page T250.

Proofreading Practice
- I want to lern about dogs. *(learn)*
- My dog has white fer. *(fur)*

Meeting Individual Needs

Kinesthetic Learners

Kinesthetic learners will benefit from spelling the lesson words in miniature sandboxes. For each pair of students, pour a thin layer of sand in the bottom of a shoe box. Have students use their index finger to spell a word in the sand, then smooth it over to spell the next word. Conclude by asking students to spell the words with paper and pencil.

Day 2

Student Objectives
- To use meaning clues to identify and write lesson words
- To use etymology and spelling to identify the word *bird*
- To learn *work* words and analyze their spellings and meanings

Presenting the Page

Write the following Definitions and Synonyms examples on the board and model identifying the answers. Remind students that synonyms are words that have the same meaning.

- to gain knowledge _____ *(learn)*
- Caterpillars <u>change</u> into butterflies. _____ *(turn)*

Word Story

The spelling of several lesson words is a result of changes in pronunciation. *Dirt* was originally *drit*, and *curl* was *crul*. Encourage students to compare the old spellings of *bird*, *dirt*, and *curl* with the new.

Family Tree: *work*

Students should understand that all the *work* words include the word *work*. To guide students in exploring the words, challenge them to tell what the words mean. Then have volunteers look up the words in a dictionary to confirm the meanings. Students should identify *work* as both noun and verb. Point out the change in meaning when *re-* is added to *work* ("to do again").

151

Spelling in Context Use each spelling word once to complete the story.

Day 3

Student Objectives
- To use context to identify and write lesson words
- To identify the setting of a story

Presenting the Pages

Ask students to skim the list of lesson words. Read the passage aloud, pausing for each missing word. Then have students complete the pages independently. Alternatively, have students complete the pages independently by silently reading the story and writing the missing words. Then have students read the completed story to a partner.

Explain that *bunting* is also a bright, colorful cloth used in decorating. Encourage students to consider reasons why the bird has the same name (because of its bright colors).

Meeting Individual Needs

ESOL

Speakers of other languages may find the /ûr/ sounds difficult. Have students draw or paste pictures for lesson words on index cards. Then have students write the /ûr/ spelling pattern used in the word in an upper corner of the card. For quick review of spelling patterns, choose a card and show the picture. After students pronounce and spell the word, have them identify the spelling pattern.

The Bunting

Last _____Thursday_____ my class went to Lone Pine State Park
₁
for a nature walk. We take these trips to _____learn_____ about
₂
nature. Each class trip seems as though it is a holiday.

At the park a _____girl_____ named Jane said she would be
₃
our guide. She told us that keeping the planet healthy is important

_____work_____. We learned lots of interesting facts about the
₄

_____earth_____ and sky. Then she told us what plants and
₅
animals to look for. Jane said that we might even see a painted

bunting. A painted bunting is a rare _____bird_____ with red,
₆
blue, and green feathers.

We _____were_____ only a little
₇
way down the trail when my friend
Elissa spotted a fawn. It had white

spots on its _____fur_____. If only
₈
I could find something special, too!

I kept my eyes and ears open as I
walked. The path turned once, twice,

Spelling Strategy

Guess and Check
Remind students that they can use the guess-and-check strategy for spelling a lesson word. Explain that this is a particularly good strategy when you know how to spell the beginning of a word. Demonstrate how to use this strategy by inviting students to suggest spellings for the word *learn*. Write their suggestions on the board. Then have students check the spelling in the Spelling Dictionary and identify the correct spelling on the board. Suggest that students try the same strategy with any lesson words they are having difficulty with.

Guess	Correct?
lern	no
lurn	no
learn	yes

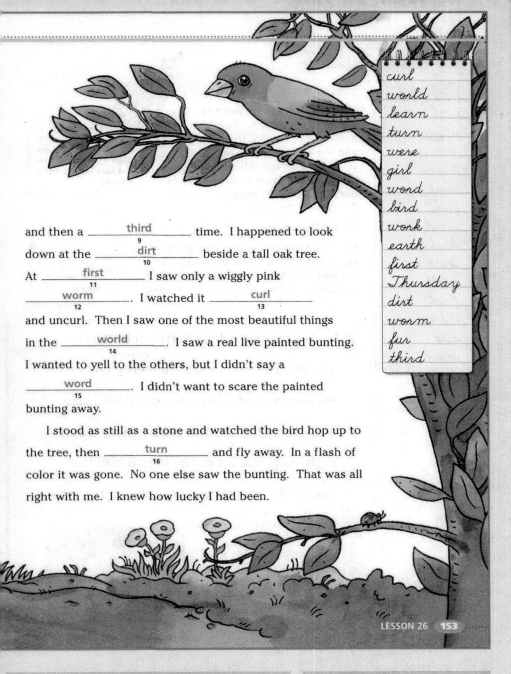

and then a ___third___ time. I happened to look
down at the ___dirt___ beside a tall oak tree.
At ___first___ I saw only a wiggly pink
___worm___. I watched it ___curl___
and uncurl. Then I saw one of the most beautiful things
in the ___world___. I saw a real live painted bunting.
I wanted to yell to the others, but I didn't say a
___word___. I didn't want to scare the painted
bunting away.

I stood as still as a stone and watched the bird hop up to
the tree, then ___turn___ and fly away. In a flash of
color it was gone. No one else saw the bunting. That was all
right with me. I knew how lucky I had been.

curl
world
learn
turn
were
girl
word
bird
work
earth
first
Thursday
dirt
worm
fur
third

LESSON 26 **153**

ACTIVITY MASTER p. T274

Lesson **26** Words with /ûr/

Name _____

Find the word in the box that matches each clue. Write the word.
Then read down the squares to find the answer to the question.

| Spelling Words | bird | first | dirt | third | world | work |
| | word | fur | Thursday | turn | learn | were |

WHAT IS *GIRL* IN THIS SENTENCE?

1. It's your ___ to play. — turn
2. first, second, ___ — third
3. We ___ at the zoo yesterday. — were
4. *A* is the ___ letter in the alphabet. — first
5. Friday comes after ___. — Thursday
6. Wipe the ___ off your shoes. — dirt
7. Did you ___ your spelling words? — learn
8. Each ___ in this lesson has the /ûr/ sound. — word
9. Cleaning the yard is hard ___. — work
10. A globe is a map of the ___. — world
11. The cat has soft black ___. — fur
12. A parrot is a ___. — bird

Find the word in the box that completes each sentence.
Write the word on the line.

| Spelling Words | girl | worm | curl | earth |

13. The ___girl___ wore her new cap.
14. She had a lot of ___curl___ in her hair.
15. She dug a hole in the ___earth___.
16. She found a ___worm___ to bait her hook.

ADDITIONAL PRACTICE

You may wish to copy and distribute the Activity Master on page T274 as additional practice for Lesson 26.

Proofreading Practice
- We went fishing last Thersday. *(Thursday)*
- I used a wurm for bait. *(worm)*

Reading Comprehension

Remind students that setting is the time and place in which story events occur. Point out that the story says the class went to Lone Pine State Park. Ask students to use story details to describe the region in which the park lies. Offer clues as needed to stir students' imaginations (mention of a pine tree, an oak tree, a fawn, a worm, and the bird suggests a forest). Then ask students to find time-of-year and time-of-day details in the story (the fawn suggests that it is probably spring; the fact that the children are on a school trip suggests school hours and therefore daytime).

After students describe the setting, have them draw the scene that they visualize. Invite students to share their drawings with the class and explain why they drew what they did.

Cooperative Learning Activity

To help students practice the spelling of the /ûr/ sounds, have pairs of students work together to see how many lesson words they can write without referring to the list. To help jog their memory, write the spelling patterns on the board, so that they can think of words with each pattern. Challenge students to generate a complete 16-word list. Then have them check their work, using the list on page 153. Ask students to make sure they have all 16 words and that all are spelled correctly.

153

Student Objectives

- To write an expository paragraph, using lesson words
- To proofread a paragraph for spelling, capitalization, and punctuation

Presenting the Page

Remind students of the walk through Lone Pine State Park in "The Bunting" on pages 152–153. To help students generate ideas for writing, brainstorm with the class things that they commonly see in nature, such as birds, trees, earth or dirt, and so on. Encourage student to use specific language such as *fresh* and *green* rather than general terms such as *pretty* to describe the natural element that they choose to write about.

To help students complete the Proofreading activity, suggest that they complete the task in three steps—reading the paragraph for spelling mistakes, then for capitalization mistakes, and then for punctuation mistakes. Then tell them to compare and check their answers with a partner.

Meeting Individual Needs

Kinesthetic Learners
Provide students with colorful strings of soft, bendable wax. Then write lesson words on an overhead with blanks where /ûr/ spelling patterns go. Have partners shape their wax strings into the letter combination and place them on the overhead where they belong in each word.

Spelling and Writing

curl
world
learn
turn
were
girl
word
bird
work
earth
first
Thursday
dirt
worm
fur
third

Write to the Point

You don't have to go into the woods to see nature. Look around you. The sky, the trees, and the animals are all part of nature. Write a paragraph telling about one thing you see often in nature. Try to use spelling words from this lesson. Paragraphs will vary.

> Use the strategies on page 7 when you are not sure how to spell a word.

Proofreading

Proofread this paragraph from a story. Use proofreading marks to correct five spelling mistakes, three capitalization mistakes, and two punctuation mistakes.

Proofreading Marks
- ◯ spell correctly
- ≡ capitalize
- ⊙ add period

Four young robins fluttered to the ground. The first bird ate a ◯werm◯ [worm] the second one ate a bug. The ◯therd◯ [third] bird said bugs made his feathers ◯kurl◯ [curl] he saw a berry in the ◯dert◯ [dirt] and ate it⊙ The fourth bird had work to do. For an hour she dug in the ◯erth◯ [earth]. the fifth bird slept late that morning⊙ He said it was his day off!

Proofreading Practice

- Our math team came in ferst. *(first)*
- I wurk hard to do well in math. *(work)*

Correcting Common Errors

Students sometimes confuse *were* and *where*. Assist students experiencing this problem by providing one or more of these memory aids:

> *Where* gives a location.
> *Here* tells *where*.
> *Here* is in *where*.

> *We're* tells about *we* today.
> *We were* tells about *we* yesterday.
> *We* is in *were*.

Language Connection

Synonyms and Antonyms Synonyms are words that have the same meaning. Antonyms are words that have opposite meanings.

small	little		thick	thin

Write the word from the boxes below that is an antonym of each word.

dir	add	huge	young

1. subtract ___add___
2. clean ___dirty___
3. tiny ___huge___
4. old ___young___

Each group of four words below has a pair of antonyms and a pair of synonyms. First write the antonyms. Then write the synonyms.

full	turn	empty	spin

5. Antonyms ___full, empty___
6. Synonyms ___turn, spin___

earth	first	world	last

7. Antonyms ___first, last___
8. Synonyms ___earth, world___

⭐ Challenge Yourself

Use the Spelling Dictionary to answer these questions. Then use separate paper to write sentences showing that you understand the meaning of each Challenge Word. **Sentences will vary.**

Challenge Words
circular	surgeon
dessert	flourish

9. Is the trunk of a pine tree **circular**? ___yes___
10. Would you expect to see a **surgeon** in a bird's nest? ___no___
11. Would you expect to find grass in a **dessert**? ___no___
12. Do some birds **flourish** in wooded areas? ___yes___

LESSON 26 155

Posttest

Dictate the following sentences. Have students use separate paper to write the sentences and underline the lesson words.

1. The <u>bird</u> ate the <u>worm</u>.
2. We will <u>learn</u> about the <u>world</u>.
3. We read the <u>first</u> and <u>third</u> pages.
4. The <u>earth</u> makes a <u>turn</u> every day.
5. The dog had <u>dirt</u> in its <u>fur</u>.
6. The new <u>girl</u> will <u>work</u> on <u>Thursday</u>.
7. My cat will <u>curl</u> up and go to sleep.
8. They <u>were</u> going home.
9. What does this <u>word</u> mean?

Enrichment Activity

Have students work in small groups to create a code to write lesson words. For example, students can write each word in reverse order or use a letter to represent the one that precedes it in the alphabet. Then have groups exchange coded words and decode them.

Day 5

Student Objectives
- To identify and write lesson words that are synonyms and antonyms
- To study the spellings and meanings of the Challenge Words
- To take a posttest on the lesson words

Presenting the Page

Write *earth, up, down,* and *dirt* on the board. Ask students to identify the two words that have the same meaning (*earth* and *dirt*). Then ask students which two words have opposite meanings (*up* and *down*). Remind students that words that have the same meaning are called *synonyms,* and words that have opposite meanings are called *antonyms.*

⭐ Challenge Yourself

To introduce the Challenge Words, write the following on the board:

cir/cu/lar	sur/geon
des/sert	flour/ish

Pronounce the words for students and discuss the number of syllables in each. Then have students review the /ûr/ spelling patterns featured in this lesson. Point out that two Challenge Words have new patterns. *Dessert* has the *er* pattern and *flourish* has the *our* pattern. Ask students to identify the /ûr/ pattern in the other Challenge Words (*ir* in *circular* and *ur* in *surgeon*).

Posttest

Use the posttest on this page to assess students' ability to spell the lesson words.

155

Lesson 27

Words with /ä/

Day 1

Student Objectives

- To take a pretest on the lesson words
- To spell the lesson words aloud
- To sort and write the lesson words according to the spelling patterns *a* and *ea*

Pretest

Use the pretest on this page to assess students' ability to spell the lesson words.

 Have students use the study steps on page 6 to study any words they misspell in the pretest.

 You may wish to duplicate and send home the Home Activity Master on pages T249–T250.

Presenting the Page

Introducing the /ä/ Sound

Write *father* on the board. Have students read the word and repeat the /ä/ sound. Then say the following word pairs and have students raise their hand when they hear /ä/:

barn–born	*hard*–heard
sharp–ship	stare–*star*

As students prepare to sort the words, point out that /ä/ is most often spelled *a* but is spelled *ea* in a few words that we often use.

Pronunciation Focus Write *dark* on the board next to *father* and call on volunteers to read both words aloud. Guide students to note that the /ä/ sound is slightly different when followed by *r*. Have students refer to the word list to find which lesson words include the /ä/ sound followed by *r* (all except *father*).

Consonant Focus Write *yard* and *card* on the board. Remind students that the final consonant sounds are blended together, but each can be heard. Ask students to find other lesson words that end with an *r* blend (*dark, art, hard, heart, arm, barn, start, sharp, bark*).

156

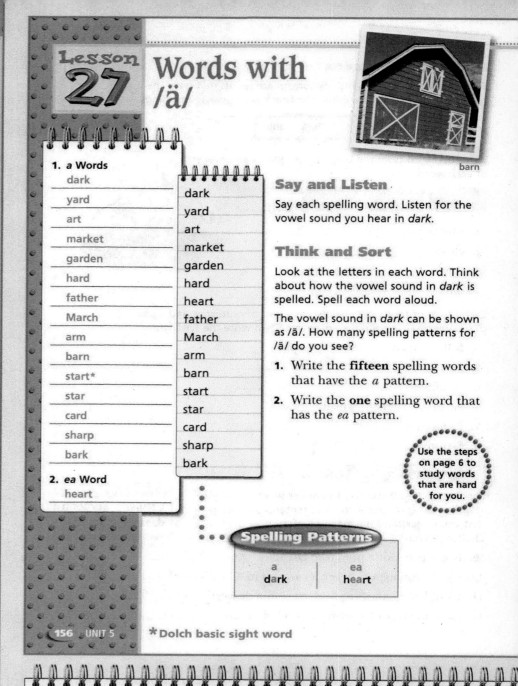

barn

Lesson 27 Words with /ä/

1. a Words

dark
yard
art
market
garden
hard
father
March
arm
barn
start*
star
card
sharp
bark

2. ea Word
heart

---

dark
yard
art
market
garden
hard
heart
father
March
arm
barn
start
star
card
sharp
bark

Say and Listen

Say each spelling word. Listen for the vowel sound you hear in *dark*.

Think and Sort

Look at the letters in each word. Think about how the vowel sound in *dark* is spelled. Spell each word aloud.

The vowel sound in *dark* can be shown as /ä/. How many spelling patterns for /ä/ do you see?

1. Write the **fifteen** spelling words that have the *a* pattern.

2. Write the **one** spelling word that has the *ea* pattern.

Use the steps on page 6 to study words that are hard for you.

Spelling Patterns

a	ea
dark	**heart**

156 UNIT 5   *Dolch basic sight word

Pretest

Say each lesson word, read the sentence, and then repeat the word. Have students write the words on separate paper.

1. **dark** It is dark by seven o'clock.
2. **yard** Snow covered the yard.
3. **art** I want to be an art teacher.
4. **market** The market sells fruit.
5. **garden** I have a vegetable garden.
6. **hard** The bug is hard to see.
7. **heart** We made a heart out of paper.
8. **father** My father will drive.
9. **March** Spring begins in March.
10. **arm** The girl broke her arm.
11. **barn** The horses are in the barn.
12. **start** When can we start?
13. **star** The first star is out.
14. **card** I made this card for you.
15. **sharp** Be careful with that sharp knife.
16. **bark** The dog will bark at strangers.

Additional Words for Enrichment

The following words can be used to meet the needs of on-level and above-level students:

smart	apart	hearth	large	artist	argue

Spelling and Meaning

Clues Write the spelling word for each clue.

1. where flowers grow
2. where to buy fruits and vegetables
3. month after February
4. what you send on someone's birthday
5. where farm animals sleep
6. a place to play near a house
7. what the inside of a cave is
8. what stones are
9. another word for *dad*
10. the kind of knife you need to cut things
11. what the car does when Mom turns the key
12. a drawing or painting

garden
market
March
card
barn
yard
dark
hard
father
sharp
start
art

Multiple Meanings Write the spelling word that has more than one meaning and completes each sentence below.

13. The movie ____ star ____ wished upon a shining ____ star ____

14. My ____ heart ____ pounded as I put all my ____ heart ____ into the final leg of the race.

15. I heard Scooter ____ bark ____ at the squirrel gnawing on the tree ____ bark ____.

Word Story Words that are spelled alike but have different meanings are called **homographs**. One spelling word is a homograph that means "a weapon." The word is also a homograph that names a part of the body. Write the spelling word.

16. ____ arm ____

Family Tree: *start* Think about how the *start* words are alike in spelling and meaning. Then add another *start* word to the tree. A sample answer is shown.

restart
starter
starts
17. started
start
starting

LESSON 27 **157**

HOME ACTIVITY MASTER p. T249

Unit 5 Spelling at Home

Dear Family of ____ ,
During the next six weeks, your child will be learning to spell the following kinds of words:
• words with /ōō/or /yōō/, as in *noon* and *few*
• words with /ûr/, as in *fur*
• words with /ä/, as in *father*
• words with /oi/, as in *coin*
• contractions

Here are some simple activities to do each week to help your child become a better speller.

✏ **Listening and Writing**
Say the spelling words and have your child write them.

✎ **Spelling Strategy: Rhyming Partner**
If your child is unsure about the spelling of a word, help your child create a list of words that rhyme with the word and are spelled in the same way. Then ask your child to select one of the words as a rhyming partner. Ask your child to study the rhyming partner. Then have him or her spell the word that he or she is having difficulty with.

🎲 **Games and Activities**
Play Easiest to Hardest. Choose a group of words from the list. Give yourself and your child a piece of paper. Next, write the easiest word from the list, the next two easiest words, the next three easiest words, and so on. Then compare the easiest-to-hardest word order with each other.

Choose five spelling words that are hard for your child to spell. Write each word on a separate sheet of paper, leaving space between the letters of the word. Then cut the words apart so that each letter is on a separate square of paper. Mix up the letters. Have your child put the letters together to form the different spelling words.

📖 **Using Spelling Words**
Ask your child to write sentences that contain the spelling words. Then read the sentences with your child. Notice whether the sentences show that your child knows the meanings of the spelling words.

Lesson 25 Words with /ōō/ or /yōō/
Week of
noon	school	too	tooth
blue	true	Tuesday	who
move	two	news	knew
June	huge	few	used

Lesson 26 Words with /ûr/
Week of
girl	bird	first	dirt
third	world	work	word
worm	curl	fur	Thursday
turn	learn	earth	were

Lesson 27 Words with /ä/
Week of
father	market	barn	garden
star	sharp	bark	yard
dark	hard	card	start
March	arm	art	heart

Lesson 28 Words with /oi/
Week of
soil	broil	coin	point
boil	choice	noise	voice
spoil	oil	join	boy
toy	joy	enjoy	royal

Lesson 29 More Contractions
Week of
hasn't	aren't	couldn't	didn't
doesn't	hadn't	haven't	mustn't
shouldn't	wasn't	weren't	isn't
wouldn't	won't	don't	can't

Lesson 30 Unit 5 Review
Week of
Lesson 30 is a review of Lessons 25–29. Help your child practice all of the words from those lessons.

The highlighted area shows the Lesson 27 words, which students can share with family members. Spanish version available on page T250.

Proofreading Practice
• My farther is away on business. (*father*)
• Mother and I are working in the guarden. (*garden*)

Meeting Individual Needs

Visual Learners
Students who see patterns and visual relationships will notice that there is only one word in the list that doesn't follow the *a* pattern. Ask students to come up with a way to help them remember that *heart* is the exception in the list. For example, students might draw a heart around *ea* or underline *ear* in *heart*.

Day 2

Student Objectives
• To use meaning clues to identify and write lesson words
• To use meanings of homographs to identify the word *arm*
• To learn *start* words and analyze their spellings and meanings

Presenting the Page

Write the following Clues and Multiple Meanings examples on the board and model identifying the answers:
• what the sun is (*star*)
• I found a ____ of ribbon in our front ____. (*yard*)

For the Multiple Meanings items, encourage students to look for a word that makes sense in the first blank and to then try it in the second blank.

Word Story

Students may not recognize *arm* as a word for a weapon because the plural form is more commonly used. Explain that sometimes *arm* can be used to mean "to defend against weapons." Write *armor* and point out that armor is used in battle with weapons, or arms, and it protects the body. Have students compare *armor* with *arm*.

Family Tree: *start*

Students should see that all of the *start* words include the word *start*. Ask students to explain what *-s* and *-ed* at the end of a word such as *start* tell about when the action occurs (*-s* indicates the action is happening now; *-ed* indicates the action happened in the past).

157

Use each spelling word once to complete the selection.

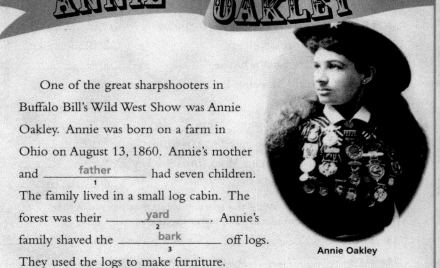

Annie Oakley

One of the great sharpshooters in Buffalo Bill's Wild West Show was Annie Oakley. Annie was born on a farm in Ohio on August 13, 1860. Annie's mother and _____father_____ had seven children. The family lived in a small log cabin. The forest was their _____yard_____. Annie's family shaved the _____bark_____ off logs. They used the logs to make furniture.

Life on the Oakley farm was _____hard_____. The family had to feed all of the animals that lived in the pens and in the _____barn_____. They had to pick the vegetables they grew in their _____garden_____. They could not afford to buy many things at a _____market_____. Annie learned to hunt to help feed her family. She became a sharpshooter on the family farm.

Annie put her whole _____heart_____ into her work. She often practiced shooting until it was _____dark_____. All her

158 UNIT 5

Spelling Strategy

Sound It Out

Tell students that saying words slowly and listening to the sounds in each syllable can help them spell many words. Ask students to sound out the word *father*. Start by having them say the word and tell how many syllables there are (two). Then have them think about the consonants and vowel sound they hear in each syllable. Remind students that every syllable has one vowel sound. Write the word on a chart by syllables, grouping the *th* digraph and the *er*. Then have students spell the word and write it. Help students see that most of the lesson words contain the letter combination *ar*. Encourage them to listen to the sounds they hear before and after *ar* and to write them in the chart.

Sound It Out	Spell It
f a th er	father
b ar n	barn
st ar t	start
m ar k e t	market
M ar ch	March

Point out that most words follow a spelling pattern as featured in the lesson but that there are some exceptions, such as *heart*. Help students devise ways to remember how to spell *heart*.

Day 3

Student Objectives

- To use context to identify and write lesson words
- To summarize information from a nonfiction selection

Presenting the Pages

Write each lesson word on an index card and distribute the cards to pairs or small groups of students. Ask students to think about where each word belongs in the selection as you read it, pausing for the missing words. Read the selection again, having volunteers hold up the correct cards as the class writes the words.

Alternatively, have students complete the pages independently by silently reading the selection and writing the missing words. Then have students take turns reading the completed selection.

Remind students that many words have more than one meaning, such as the word *sharp*. In the passage, *sharp* means "keen" or "precise."

Meeting Individual Needs

Kinesthetic Learners

Give small groups of students cookie sheets or shallow boxes filled with shaving cream. Have students take turns dictating a word from the spelling list as the others use a finger to write it in the shaving cream. Students should check their spelling and then smooth the surface to write the next word.

hard work helped her become a _____star_____. In 1875
10
Annie won a shooting contest against champion Frank E.
Butler. Annie and Frank later married.

In _____March_____ of 1884, Annie met Sitting Bull.
11
Sitting Bull was the chief of the Sioux tribe. Sitting Bull
liked Annie's _____sharp_____ eyesight and good aim.
12
He gave her the nickname Little Sure Shot.

Shortly after she got her nickname, Frank and Annie
joined Buffalo Bill's Wild West show. Buffalo Bill used Annie's
sharpshooting act to _____start_____ the show. One
13
of her most dangerous tricks was shooting the thin edge of a
playing _____card_____. She did this while holding a rifle
14
with only one _____arm_____.
15

Annie thought sharpshooting
was more than just quick, fancy
shooting. She believed it was an
_____art_____.
16

Buffalo Bill

BUFFALO BILL'S WILD WEST SHOW

dark
yard
art
market
garden
hard
heart
father
March
arm
barn
start
star
card
sharp
bark

Explain that a summary of a
piece of writing tells the most
important ideas in a few sentences. Ask students to reread
the selection and think about
the most important ideas.
Discuss ideas that students
feel are the most important.
Then tell students to use the
most important ideas to write
a two- or three-sentence summary of the passage. Invite
students to share completed
summaries.

Cooperative Learning Activity

Ask students to work in pairs.
Give each pair a set of alphabet cards. Tell students to
spread the cards on a table.
Then have each student take
a turn calling out a word
from the list on page 159.
The other student should
find the appropriate cards
and place them in the proper
order to spell the word. Have
students check the word
against the list. Guide them
in noting words that they
need to study further.

ACTIVITY MASTER p. T275

Lesson
27 Words with /ä/

Name _____

Read each word in the box and circle it in the puzzle below.
The words go across, down, or at a slant.

Spelling Words	father	market	barn	garden	star	sharp	bark	heart
	yard	dark	hard	card	start	March	arm	art

ADDITIONAL PRACTICE

You may wish to copy and distribute
the Activity Master on page T275 as
additional practice for Lesson 27.

Proofreading Practice
• I will steart playing tennis
  this summer. *(start)*
• We don't play tennis after
  durk. *(dark)*

Day 4

Student Objectives
- To write an expository paragraph, using lesson words
- To proofread an announcement for spelling, capitalization, and punctuation

Presenting the Page

Remind students that in "Annie Oakley" on pages 158–159, they learned that Annie became good at something because she "put her whole heart into her work." To help students plan what they will write, have them make a list of things they do well.

To assist students with the Proofreading activity, read aloud the directions and the announcement. Then have students complete the activity independently. Have students check their work by rereading the announcement, starting with the last sentence and ending with the first.

Meeting Individual Needs

ESOL

Since /ă/ is used in the Spanish language, encourage students to practice expanding their vocabulary without concern for pronunciation. Write the lesson words on cards. Hold up one card at a time and have students say the word on the card and use it in a sentence.

160

Spelling and Writing

dark
yard
art
market
garden
hard
heart
father
March
arm
barn
start
star
card
sharp
bark

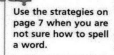

Write to the Point

Everyone is good at something. Annie Oakley was good at sharpshooting. Are you a good student? A good athlete? A great fisher? Maybe you are a good friend. Write a paragraph telling what you are good at. Try to use spelling words from this lesson in your paragraph. Paragraphs will vary.

Use the strategies on page 7 when you are not sure how to spell a word.

Proofreading

Proofread the announcement below. Use proofreading marks to correct five spelling mistakes, three capitalization mistakes, and two punctuation mistakes.

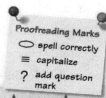
Proofreading Marks
◯ spell correctly
≡ capitalize
? add question mark

★ ★ Be a Star! ★ ★

Do you dance or sing? Can you do ⌍carde⌎ card

tricks? are you good at ⌍aret⌎? art The Near North

neighbors are having a talent show. We will

⌍steart⌎ start practicing next week. we also need

someone to paint signs. The show will end

with a parade around the Near North Park

flower ⌍gardin⌎ garden. Would you like to join us? Come

to mary Wu's ⌍yarde⌎ yard on Friday after school!

Proofreading Practice
- My aunt is showing me a new curd game. *(card)*
- Later, we will go to the farmers' markit. *(market)*

✔ Correcting Common Errors

An unstressed syllable at the end of a word often causes spelling problems. Some students may spell *garden* as *gardin*, *market* as *markit*, and *father* as *fathur*. To help these students remember the final vowel, have them practice writing these words, dividing them into syllables (*gar/den*, *mar/ket*, and *fa/ther*) and circling the vowel in each syllable.

Dictionary Skills

Multiple Meanings Some words have more than one meaning. Look at the entry for *heart* from the Spelling Dictionary. The word *heart* has two meanings. Each is numbered. Read the sample sentence for each meaning of *heart*. The words around the word *heart* give a clue to its meaning.

> **heart** (härt) *noun, plural* **hearts**
> **1.** The organ in the chest that pumps blood through the body: *The doctor listened to my heart.* **2.** Courage and enthusiasm: *He put his heart into winning the game.*

Write **Meaning 1** or **Meaning 2** to indicate which definition of *heart* is used in each sentence. Then write your own sentences showing you understand each meaning of *heart*.

1. Our class lost **heart** when we lost the game. _____ Meaning 2 _____
2. My **heart** beats fast after a race. _____ Meaning 1 _____
   Sentences will vary.

_____

_____

⭐ Challenge Yourself

What do you think each Challenge Word means? Check the Spelling Dictionary to see if you are right. Then use separate paper to write sentences showing that you understand the meaning of each Challenge Word. **Definitions and sentences will vary.**

Challenge Words	
carton	starch
artistic	barbecue

3. You can buy milk in a **carton** or a jug.
4. A lot of **starch** on your shirt will make it stiff.
5. Annie Oakley thought that sharpshooting was **artistic**.
6. My sister served **barbecue** at her wedding.

LESSON 27 **161**

Posttest

Dictate the following sentences. Have students use separate paper to write the sentences and underline the lesson words.

1. My father will start planting our garden.
2. She saw a star in the dark sky.
3. His dog gave a sharp bark.
4. I am going to the market.
5. March is art month at school.
6. My arm is a yard long.
7. Painting the barn was hard work.
8. Where is the card with the heart on it?

Enrichment Activity

Have students work in pairs with one partner facing the class and the other facing the chalkboard. Write one of the lesson words on the board. The partner facing the board should describe or define the word without using the word itself. The other partner should try to guess the word and then spell it aloud. Everyone should get a turn giving clues and guessing the word.

Student Objectives
- To distinguish between multiple meanings of a word
- To write sentences, using different meanings of a lesson word
- To study the spellings and meanings of the Challenge Words
- To take a posttest on the lesson words

Presenting the Page

Have students look at the dictionary entry on the page to determine how multiple meanings are shown. Challenge students to look for clues in sentence 1 to help them determine which meaning to use. Point out that the figure of speech "lost heart" is a clue because people cannot literally lose their heart.

⭐ Challenge Yourself

To introduce the Challenge Words, write the following on the board:

car/ton	starch
ar/tis/tic	bar/be/cue

Pronounce the words for students and discuss the number of syllables in each. Then have students review the /ä/ spelling patterns featured in this lesson and identify the /ä/ spelling pattern that appears in each of the Challenge Words (a). Have students write what they think the words mean, look up the words in the Spelling Dictionary, and write the correct definitions. Ask students to compare their definitions with those in the Spelling Dictionary.

Posttest

Use the posttest on this page to assess students' ability to spell the lesson words.

161

Lesson 28

Words with /oi/

Student Objectives
- To take a pretest on the lesson words
- To spell the lesson words aloud
- To sort and write the lesson words according to the spelling patterns *oi* and *oy*

Pretest

Use the pretest on this page to assess students' ability to spell the lesson words.

Have students use the study steps on page 6 to study any words they misspell in the pretest.

You may wish to duplicate and send home the Home Activity Master on pages T249–T250.

Presenting the Page

Introducing the /oi/ Sound
Write the words *bay* and *boy* on the board. Ask a volunteer to read the words and repeat the word that has the /oi/ sound (*boy*). Follow a similar procedure with *can* and *coin* (*coin*). Then say the following word pairs and ask students to repeat the words with /oi/:

toy–tea   *bay*–*boil*
point–paint   sail–*soil*

As students prepare to sort the words, point out that /oi/ is often spelled *oi* or *oy*.

Pronunciation Focus
Write *en/joy* and *roy/al* on the board, pointing out each syllable. Ask students to tell which syllables have the /oi/ sound (*joy* and *roy*).

Consonant Focus
Write the words *voice* and *choice* on the board. Ask students to say the sound of the *c* at the end of both of the words (/s/). Point out that soft *c* is often followed by *e*.

162

Lesson 28 Words with /oi/

1. *oi* Words
coin
choice
spoil
boil
voice
soil
noise
point
broil
join
oil

2. *oy* Words
boy
royal
toy
joy
enjoy

coin
boy
choice
spoil
royal
boil
voice
toy
soil
joy
noise
point
broil
enjoy
join
oil

boil

Say and Listen

Say each spelling word. Listen for the vowel sound you hear in *coin*.

Think and Sort

Look at the letters in each word. Think about how the vowel sound in *coin* is spelled. Spell each word aloud.

The vowel sound in *coin* can be shown as /oi/. How many spelling patterns for /oi/ do you see?

1. Write the **eleven** spelling words that have the *oi* pattern.

2. Write the **five** spelling words that have the *oy* pattern.

Use the steps on page 6 to study words that are hard for you.

Spelling Patterns

oi	oy
coin	toy

Pretest

Say each lesson word, read the sentence, and then repeat the word. Have students write the words on separate paper.

1. **coin** The book showed an old coin.
2. **boy** He is the youngest boy in our class.
3. **choice** I had no choice but to go.
4. **spoil** Don't spoil the party.
5. **royal** She is part of the royal family.
6. **boil** The water will boil soon.
7. **voice** He sang in a low voice.
8. **toy** He gave the toy to his sister.
9. **soil** The soil was dry and rocky.
10. **joy** I jumped for joy.
11. **noise** The alarm made a loud noise.
12. **point** That pencil has a sharp point.
13. **broil** We will broil our meat.
14. **enjoy** We will enjoy the show.
15. **join** I would like to join the computer club.
16. **oil** Mom changed the oil in the car.

Additional Words for Enrichment

The following words can be used to meet the needs of on-level and above-level students:
moisture   destroy   poison   voyage   avoid   disappoint

162

Spelling and Meaning

Classifying Write the spelling word that belongs in each group of words.

1. noble   kingly   _royal_
2. gas   coal   _oil_
3. doll   yo-yo   _toy_
4. happiness   pleasure   _joy_
5. sound   speech   _voice_
6. rot   decay   _spoil_
7. tie   connect   _join_
8. money   dollar bill   _coin_

Analogies Write the spelling word that completes each analogy.

9. *Man* is to *woman* as _boy_ is to *girl*.
10. *Laugh* is to _enjoy_ as *cry* is to *fear*.
11. *Lose* is to *loss* as *choose* is to _choice_.
12. *Soft* is to *whisper* as *loud* is to _noise_.
13. *Ocean* is to *sea* as _soil_ is to *dirt*.
14. *Cake* is to *bake* as *steak* is to _broil_.
15. *Finger* is to _point_ as *hand* is to *wave*.

Word Story This spelling word tells what happens when a liquid gets very hot. It comes from the Latin word *bulla. Bulla* meant "bubble." When a liquid gets very hot, we can see large bubbles in it. The bubbles move around very quickly. Write the word.

16. _boil_

Family Tree: *joy* Think about how the *joy* words are alike in spelling and meaning. Then add another *joy* word to the tree. A sample answer is shown.

- enjoyment
- enjoy
- 17. _joyfully_
- joyful
- joys
- joy

HOME ACTIVITY MASTER p. T249

Unit 5 Spelling at Home

Dear Family of _____
During the next six weeks, your child will be learning to spell the following kinds of words:

- words with /ōō/ or /yōō/, as in *noon* and *few*
- words with /ûr/, as in *fur*
- words with /ä/, as in *father*
- words with /oi/, as in *coin*
- contractions

Here are some simple activities to do each week to help your child become a better speller.

Listening and Writing
Say the spelling words and have your child write them.

Spelling Strategy: Rhyming Partner
If your child is unsure about the spelling of a word, help your child create a list of words that rhyme with the word and are spelled in the same way. Then ask your child to select one of the words as a rhyming partner. Ask your child to study the rhyming partner. Then have him or her spell the word that he or she is having difficulty with.

Games and Activities
Play Easiest to Hardest. Choose a group of words from the list. Give yourself and your child a piece of paper. Next, write the easiest word from the list, the next two easiest words, the next three easiest words, and so on. Then compare the easiest-to-hardest word order with each other.

Choose five spelling words that are hard for your child to spell. Write each word on a separate sheet of paper, leaving space between the letters of the word. Then cut the words apart so that each letter is on a separate square of paper. Mix up the letters. Have your child put the letters together to form the different spelling words.

Using Spelling Words
Ask your child to write sentences that contain the spelling words. Then read the sentences with your child. Notice whether the sentences show that your child knows the meanings of the spelling words.

Lesson 25 Words with /ōō/ or /yōō/
Week of _____

moon	school	too	tooth
blue	true	Tuesday	who
move	two	news	knew
June	huge	few	used

Lesson 26 Words with /ûr/
Week of _____

girl	bird	first	dirt
third	world	work	word
worm	curl	fur	Thursday
turn	learn	earth	were

Lesson 27 Words with /ä/
Week of _____

father	market	barn	garden
star	sharp	bark	yard
dark	hard	card	start
March	arm	art	heart

Lesson 28 Words with /oi/
Week of _____

soil	broil	coin	point
boil	choice	noise	voice
spoil	oil	join	boy
toy	joy	enjoy	royal

Lesson 29 More Contractions
Week of _____

hasn't	aren't	couldn't	didn't
doesn't	hadn't	haven't	mustn't
shouldn't	wasn't	weren't	isn't
wouldn't	won't	don't	can't

Lesson 30 Unit 5 Review
Week of _____
Lesson 30 is a review of Lessons 25–29. Help your child practice all of the words from those lessons.

The highlighted area shows the Lesson 28 words, which students can share with family members. Spanish version available on page T250.

Proofreading Practice
- The boi next door is my friend. *(boy)*
- His mother works for an oyl company. *(oil)*

Meeting Individual Needs

Auditory Learners
Ask small groups of students to use rhyming lesson words to create sentences. Examples:

I'd like to join the coin club.
The boy was full of joy when he saw the toy.

Then have students take turns reading the sentences and calling on others to spell each rhyming word.

Day 2

Student Objectives
- To use meaning clues to identify and write lesson words
- To use etymology, meaning, and spelling to identify the word *boil*
- To learn *joy* words and analyze their spellings and meanings

Presenting the Page
Write the following Classifying and Analogies examples on the board and model identifying the answers:

- simmer   bubble   _____ *(boil)*
- *Hammer* is to *tool* as *doll* is to _____. *(toy)*

Word Story
Write *bulla* on the board. Then write the Old French word *boilir* and explain that this word came from *bulla* and also meant "to bubble." Have students compare the spellings of *bulla* and *boilir*.

Family Tree: *joy*
Students should understand that the *joy* words all contain the word *joy*. To help students explore the words, have them locate the meanings in a dictionary, write their findings on the board, and talk about how the meanings are alike and different. Using the definitions, discuss with students how *en-* and *-ment* change the function of a word (*en-* changes *joy* from a noun to a verb; *-ment* changes *enjoy* from a verb to a noun).

163

Day 3

Student Objectives
- To use context to identify and write lesson words
- To predict story events

Presenting the Pages

Have a volunteer read the first paragraph aloud. Invite students to predict what will happen. Record their predictions on the board for later use. Then have students take turns reading sentences from the passage aloud and supplying the missing words as they read. Alternatively, have students complete the page independently by silently reading the story and writing the missing words. Then have students take turns reading the completed story.

Meeting Individual Needs

Kinesthetic Learners
Show kinesthetic learners how to play charades with the lesson words. Write the lesson words on index cards and give one to each student. Choose a student to act out his or her word. For example, the student can pantomime digging in the dirt for *soil*. The others should try to guess what the charade means. The player who guesses the word is the next presenter.

Spelling in Context   Use each spelling word once to complete the story.

A Camping Tale

Liza was full of _____joy_____ when she caught the fish. But soon after that, she realized that she was alone. She yelled until she almost lost her _____voice_____. But no one answered. She was lost. There was no one to _____point_____ the way back to camp. Her camping trip had become a nightmare.

"I might not _____enjoy_____ it," she thought, "but I guess I'll have to make it alone. I don't have any other _____choice_____!"

At first Liza jumped at every _____noise_____ in the woods. But soon she got used to the noises. She was very hungry. At least she had a few supplies in her backpack. She would be all right.

"The first thing I'll do," she thought, "is build a fire. It will keep me nice and warm. Then I'll _____boil_____ some water for cocoa. I don't have any _____oil_____ to fry the fish, but that's all right.

Spelling Strategy

Rhyming Helper
Students should observe that many of the rhyming words in this lesson contain the same spelling pattern. Write the word *boil* on the board. Ask volunteers to name rhyming helpers as you write them in a web on the board. Then review the helpers, making sure that they all have the same spelling pattern.

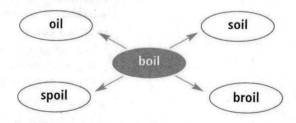

I think I can _____broil_____ it over the fire. I'll cook a

_____royal_____ feast!"

Liza gathered some wood and put it in a little pile. Then she

realized that she needed matches. She put her hand in her right

jeans pocket but found only an old _____coin_____. Then she

tried the other pocket. She found her yo-yo. "I don't think a

_____toy_____ will help me start a fire," she said aloud.

Then she looked through her backpack. She found the matches at

the bottom of it and lit the wood. Soon she had a little fire going.

Liza had just finished broiling the fish when it began to rain.

She didn't want the rain to _____spoil_____ her dinner. She

pushed a branch into the soft _____soil_____. Then she put

her jacket over it to make a kind of tent. She ate her fish and

listened to the rain. She began to yawn. Soon she was fast asleep.

When she woke up, a _____boy_____ was looking into

the tent. It was her brother. "Breakfast is

ready," he said. "Aren't you going

to _____join_____ us?"

Liza was in her family's

tent. It was a bright morning.

The birds were singing. She

laughed. Her nightmare

camping trip was only a dream.

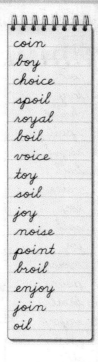

coin
boy
choice
spoil
royal
boil
voice
toy
soil
joy
noise
point
broil
enjoy
join
oil

LESSON 28 165

After students have completed the pages, discuss the predictions they made after reading the first paragraph and ask them to compare their predictions with the actual story outcome. Encourage discussion of surprise endings such as this one, and the appeal of such endings.

Cooperative Learning Activity

To help students assess their progress, have partners dictate the lesson words to each other. Then have students check their work. If possible, have students compare their performance on this midweek activity to their performance on the pretest. Guide them in noting words they are now spelling correctly and those they should continue to study.

ACTIVITY MASTER p. T276

Lesson 28 — Words with /oi/

Name _____

Find the word in the box that matches each clue. Write the word in the puzzle.

Spelling Words	soil	broil	coin	point	boil	choice	noise	voice
	spoil	oil	join	boy	toy	joy	enjoy	royal

Across
3. John is a name for a ___.
4. what a doll is
7. Milk can ___.
9. Use your ___ to sing.
12. used to fry food
14. You need to ___ water to make tea.
15. the sharp end of a pencil
16. Did you ___ the field trip?

Down
1. opposite of *quiet*
2. Dirt is ___.
5. a way to cook
6. Queens and kings are ___.
8. Let's ___ the club.
10. A nickel is a ___.
11. rhymes with *voice*
13. opposite of *sadness*

ADDITIONAL PRACTICE

You may wish to copy and distribute the Activity Master on page T276 as additional practice for Lesson 28.

Proofreading Practice
- I found a coyn on the street. (coin)
- I enjoi collecting things. (enjoy)

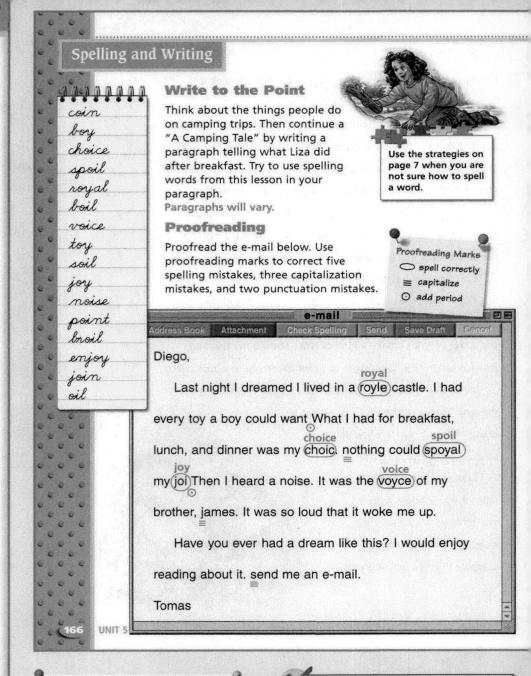

Day 4

Student Objectives
- To write a narrative paragraph, using lesson words
- To proofread a letter for spelling, capitalization, and punctuation

Presenting the Page

Since not all students have been camping, review "A Camping Tale" on pages 164–165 and ask for ideas about what a camper might do during the day. It might be helpful to discuss how people fish and what equipment they might use. Ask volunteers that have camping experience to tell what they know about camping and fishing.

To assist students with the Proof-reading activity, have a volunteer read the directions and e-mail aloud. Tell students to complete the activity independently. Then have partners check each other's work.

Meeting Individual Needs

ESOL

Speakers of other languages benefit from practicing words in the context of sentences. Challenge partners to find magazine pictures that represent the lesson words and glue each picture to a piece of paper. Then students should write a sentence, using the lesson word, to go with each picture. Have the partners exchange their papers with another pair who should read the sentences and identify the lesson words.

Spelling and Writing

coin
boy
choice
spoil
royal
boil
voice
toy
soil
joy
noise
point
broil
enjoy
join
oil

Write to the Point

Think about the things people do on camping trips. Then continue a "A Camping Tale" by writing a paragraph telling what Liza did after breakfast. Try to use spelling words from this lesson in your paragraph.
Paragraphs will vary.

Use the strategies on page 7 when you are not sure how to spell a word.

Proofreading

Proofread the e-mail below. Use proofreading marks to correct five spelling mistakes, three capitalization mistakes, and two punctuation mistakes.

Proofreading Marks
- ◯ spell correctly
- ≡ capitalize
- ⊙ add period

e-mail

Address Book Attachment Check Spelling Send Save Draft Cancel

Diego,

Last night I dreamed I lived in a (royle) royal castle. I had

every toy a boy could want What I had for breakfast,

lunch, and dinner was my (choic) choice nothing could (spoyal) spoil

my (joi) joy Then I heard a noise. It was the (voyce) voice of my

brother, james. It was so loud that it woke me up.

Have you ever had a dream like this? I would enjoy

reading about it. send me an e-mail.

Tomas

166 UNIT 5

Proofreading Practice
- He has a nice singing voyce. *(voice)*
- I want to make the right choece for the play. *(choice)*

✓ Correcting Common Errors

Mispronunciation of unstressed syllables often causes spelling problems. As a result, some students may spell *enjoy* as *injoy*. Encourage students to say the sentence "Then enjoy it." Have them note that th*en* will help them to remember that *enjoy* begins with *en*. Then tell students to write the word three times and circle the *en* in the word.

166

Language Connection

Capital Letters The following kinds of words begin with a capital letter:

> - the first word of a sentence
> - the names of people and pets
> - the names of streets
> - the names of cities and states

Write each sentence below, using capital letters correctly. Circle the spelling word in the sentence.

1. we will enjoy visiting minneapolis.
   We will (enjoy) visiting Minneapolis.

2. my dog max makes a lot of noise!
   My dog Max makes a lot of (noise)!

3. can you point out mallory street?
   Can you (point) out Mallory Street?

4. this coin was made in colorado.
   This (coin) was made in Colorado.

5. mrs. hays bought a toy for her baby.
   Mrs. Hays bought a (toy) for her baby.

6. kevin and I want to join the baseball team.
   Kevin and I want to (join) the baseball team.

Challenge Yourself

Use the Spelling Dictionary to answer these questions. Then use separate paper to write sentences showing that you understand the meaning of each Challenge Word. Sentences will vary.

Challenge Words
moisten
poisonous
rejoice
enjoyment

7. Do people ever **moisten** stamps?
    yes

8. Are **poisonous** snakes dangerous? ___yes___

9. Does Liza **rejoice** when she realizes she is lost? ___no___

10. Does a nightmare usually bring **enjoyment**? ___no___

LESSON 28 **167**

Posttest

Dictate the following sentences. Have students use separate paper to write the sentences and underline the lesson words.

1. That <u>boy</u> wants to <u>join</u> the club.
2. She found a <u>coin</u> in the <u>soil</u>.
3. The king has a loud <u>voice</u>.
4. I don't <u>enjoy</u> all this <u>noise</u>.
5. The baby played with the <u>toy</u>.
6. Please <u>point</u> to your <u>choice</u>.
7. Should we <u>boil</u> or <u>broil</u> this food?
8. The <u>royal</u> palace has many <u>oil</u> paintings.
9. Please do not <u>spoil</u> my <u>joy</u>.

Enrichment Activity

Have pairs of students play tic-tac-toe. Each student should pick a spelling pattern (either *oi* or *oy*) and play by writing lesson words with his or her chosen pattern on the tic-tac-toe grid. The student gets a square by correctly spelling a word with the appropriate pattern.

Student Objectives

- To use capital letters correctly in sentences
- To identify lesson words in sentences
- To study the spellings and meanings of the Challenge Words
- To take a posttest on the lesson words

Presenting the Page

Review the capitalization rules on page 167 with students. Ask volunteers to give an example for each kind of word.

Challenge Yourself

To introduce the Challenge Words, write the following on the board:

mois/ten   poi/son/ous
re/joice   en/joy/ment

Pronounce the words for students and discuss the number of syllables in each. Have students review the /oi/ spelling patterns featured in this lesson. Then ask students to identify the /oi/ pattern in each of the Challenge Words (*moisten, poisonous,* and *rejoice* have the *oi* pattern, and *enjoyment* has the *oy* pattern).

Posttest

Use the posttest on this page to assess students' ability to spell the lesson words.

More Contractions

Student Objectives

- To take a pretest on the lesson words
- To spell the lesson words aloud
- To sort and write the lesson words (contractions with *not*) according to the number of words from which they are formed

Pretest

Use the pretest on this page to assess students' ability to spell the lesson words.

Have students use the study steps on page 6 to study any words they misspell in the pretest.

You may wish to duplicate and send home the Home Activity Master on pages T249–T250.

Presenting the Page

Introducing the Contractions
Write *has not* and *hasn't* on the board and have students compare them. Call on a volunteer to explain what a contraction is. Explain that in most of the lesson words, the second word in the contraction is *not* and that the apostrophe represents the missing letter *o*.

Pronunciation Focus Write *weren't* on the board and ask volunteers to pronounce it. Point out that it can be pronounced with one syllable or with two (/wûrnt/ or /**wûr'** ənt/). Have students identify the lesson contractions that have one syllable and those that have two syllables.

Consonant Focus Write *mustn't* on the board and point out that when *must* is combined with *not*, the final *t* in *must* becomes silent. Write *wouldn't* on the board. Ask for a volunteer to name the letter that is silent (*l*). Point out that in the *ld* consonant pattern, the *l* is sometimes silent. Ask students to identify other lesson words that contain the same pattern (*couldn't, shouldn't*).

168

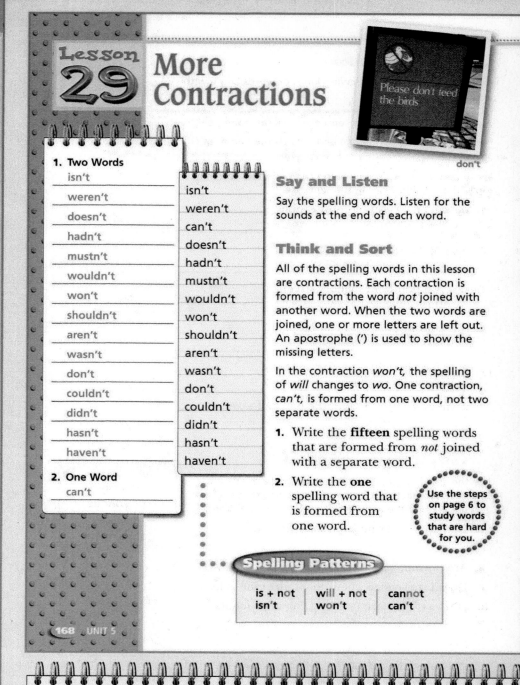

don't

1. Two Words
isn't
weren't
doesn't
hadn't
mustn't
wouldn't
won't
shouldn't
aren't
wasn't
don't
couldn't
didn't
hasn't
haven't

2. One Word
can't

isn't
weren't
can't
doesn't
hadn't
mustn't
wouldn't
won't
shouldn't
aren't
wasn't
don't
couldn't
didn't
hasn't
haven't

Say and Listen

Say the spelling words. Listen for the sounds at the end of each word.

Think and Sort

All of the spelling words in this lesson are contractions. Each contraction is formed from the word *not* joined with another word. When the two words are joined, one or more letters are left out. An apostrophe (') is used to show the missing letters.

In the contraction *won't*, the spelling of *will* changes to *wo*. One contraction, *can't*, is formed from one word, not two separate words.

1. Write the **fifteen** spelling words that are formed from *not* joined with a separate word.

2. Write the **one** spelling word that is formed from one word.

> Use the steps on page 6 to study words that are hard for you.

Spelling Patterns

is + not	will + not	cannot
isn't	won't	can't

168 UNIT 5

Pretest

Say each lesson word, read the sentence, and then repeat the word. Have students write the words on separate paper.

1. **isn't** The baby isn't asleep.
2. **weren't** They weren't at home.
3. **can't** I can't understand this word.
4. **doesn't** My father doesn't eat peas.
5. **hadn't** The team hadn't gone far.
6. **mustn't** You mustn't be noisy.
7. **wouldn't** The dog wouldn't sit.
8. **won't** The coach won't be at the game.
9. **shouldn't** We shouldn't be late.
10. **aren't** We aren't going if it rains.
11. **wasn't** There wasn't enough time.
12. **don't** I don't want this sandwich.
13. **couldn't** He couldn't see through the glass.
14. **didn't** I didn't see you there.
15. **hasn't** She hasn't been in school.
16. **haven't** We haven't finished packing.

Additional Words for Enrichment

The following words can be used to meet the needs of on-level and above-level students:

I'll   she'll   he'll   we'll   they'll   you'll

Spelling and Meaning

Either . . . or Write the spelling word that completes each sentence.

1. Either Wags will or he __won't__ .
2. Either you do or you __don't__ .
3. Either James could or he __couldn't__ .
4. Either Julie would or she __wouldn't__ .
5. Either Sara does or she __doesn't__ .
6. Either Ricky was or he __wasn't__ .

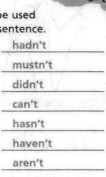

Trading Places Write the contraction that can be used instead of the underlined word or words in each sentence.

7. Marta <u>had not</u> seen the new puppy. __hadn't__
8. You <u>must not</u> touch the wet paint. __mustn't__
9. Lan <u>did not</u> bring his lunch. __didn't__
10. I <u>cannot</u> believe you ran five miles! __can't__
11. The mail <u>has not</u> come yet. __hasn't__
12. I <u>have not</u> finished my homework. __haven't__
13. Did you know that whales <u>are not</u> fish? __aren't__
14. We <u>were not</u> home on Saturday. __weren't__
15. "That <u>is not</u> my car," Ms. Ford said. __isn't__

Word Story One of the spelling words is a form of the word *shall*. First it was spelled *sceolde*. Then the spelling changed to *shollde*. Now it is spelled another way. Write the spelling word that is a form of this word plus *not*.

16. __shouldn't__

Family Tree: *haven't* *Haven't* is a contraction of *have* and *not*. Think about how the *have* words are alike in spelling and meaning. Then add another *have* word to the tree. A sample answer is shown.

```
        having
  had      17.  hadn't
  has          haven't
        have
```

LESSON 29 **169**

HOME ACTIVITY MASTER p. T249

Unit 5 **Spelling at Home**

Dear Family of _____ ,

During the next six weeks, your child will be learning to spell the following kinds of words:

• words with /ōō/ or /yōō/, as in *noon* and *few*
• words with /ûr/, as in *fur*
• words with /ä/, as in *father*
• words with /oi/, as in *coin*
• contractions

Here are some simple activities to do each week to help your child become a better speller.

✏ **Listening and Writing**
Say the spelling words and have your child write them.

✎ **Spelling Strategy: Rhyming Partner**
If your child is unsure about the spelling of a word, help your child create a list of words that rhyme with the word and are spelled in the same way. Then ask your child to select one of the words as a rhyming partner. Ask your child to study the rhyming partner. Then have him or her spell the word that he or she is having difficulty with.

🎲 **Games and Activities**
Play Easiest to Hardest. Choose a group of words from the list. Give yourself and your child a piece of paper. Next, write the easiest word from the list, the next two easiest words, the next three easiest words, and so on. Then compare the easiest-to-hardest word order with each other.

Choose five spelling words that are hard for your child to spell. Write each word on a separate sheet of paper, leaving space between the letters of the word. Then cut the words apart so that each letter is on a separate square of paper. Mix up the letters. Have your child put the letters together to form the different spelling words.

📖 **Using Spelling Words**
Ask your child to write sentences that contain the spelling words. Then read the sentences with your child. Notice whether the sentences show that your child knows the meanings of the spelling words.

Lesson 25 Words with /ōō/ or /yōō/
Week of _____
noon   school   too   tooth
blue   true   Tuesday   who
move   two   news   knew
June   huge   few   used

Lesson 26 Words with /ûr/
Week of _____
girl   bird   first   dirt
third   world   work   word
worm   curl   fur   Thursday
turn   learn   earth   were

Lesson 27 Words with /ä/
Week of _____
father market   barn   garden
star   sharp   bark   yard
dark   hard   card   start
March   arm   art   heart

Lesson 28 Words with /oi/
Week of _____
soil   broil   coin   point
boil   choice   noise   voice
spoil   oil   join   boy
toy   joy   enjoy   royal

Lesson 29 More Contractions
Week of _____
hasn't   aren't   couldn't   didn't
doesn't   hadn't   haven't   mustn't
shouldn't wasn't   weren't   isn't
wouldn't won't   don't   can't

Lesson 30 Unit 5 Review
Week of _____
Lesson 30 is a review of Lessons 25–29. Help your child practice all of the words from those lessons.

The highlighted area shows the Lesson 29 words, which students can share with family members. Spanish version available on page T250.

Proofreading Practice
• The mail hasent come yet. *(hasn't)*
• I cann't wait to read the letter! *(can't)*

Meeting Individual Needs

Auditory Learners
To help students become familiar with the proper contraction for each word pair, have them work in groups of three. The first two students should clearly say the two words, such as *do not*. The third student should say the contraction, in this case *don't*. Students should try to maintain a rhythm.

Day 2

Student Objectives
• To use meaning and structural clues to identify and write lesson words
• To use etymology, meaning, and spelling to identify the word *shouldn't*
• To learn *have* words and analyze their spellings and meanings

Presenting the Page

Write the following Either . . . or and Trading Places examples on the board and model identifying the answers:

• Either I have or I _____. *(haven't)*
• The letter <u>was not</u> for you. _____ *(wasn't)*

Word Story

Have students compare *shollde* and *should* and discuss their similar spellings. Then discuss what *shouldn't* means.

🌳 **Family Tree: *haven't***

Students should see that the *have* words contain some different forms. To help students explore the meanings of the words, have them locate the meanings in a dictionary, write their findings on the board, and talk about how the meanings are alike and different. Point out that *has* is used with *he*, *she*, or *it* and that *have* and *haven't* are used with *I* and with plural words. Ask students to identify the word that is in the past tense *(had)*.

169

Use each spelling word once to complete the story.

Day 3

Student Objectives
- To use context to identify and write lesson words
- To make inferences

Presenting the Pages

Ask students to work in small groups to supply the missing words. Because the words are similar, encourage students to test different words to see which is correct for each blank. Alternatively, have students complete the page independently by silently reading the story and writing the missing words. Then have students take turns reading the completed story.

Meeting Individual Needs

Kinesthetic Learners
Have students write the two words of each lesson contraction on a sentence strip. Then have students fold the right-hand end of the strip to cover the word *not*. On the exposed end of the folded strip, students should write *n't*. Have them read the open strip with the two words and then close the strip to read the contraction. Then have students spell the contraction aloud.

The Challenge

Max watched Hector nervously, waiting to see what Hector would do next. This was the first time he had faced Hector. Max _____wasn't_____ happy about it. "If only I _____hadn't_____
1   2
said yes to his challenge," he thought. "Then I _____wouldn't_____
3
be in this mess."

"You _____aren't_____ going to back down?" Hector asked.
4
Max knew in his heart that he could not back down now. He just
_____couldn't_____. A lot of his friends were watching him. They
5
_____weren't_____ going to leave until it was all over. They had
6
tried to tell him about Hector. "You _____haven't_____ heard?"
7
they had asked. "He's tough. He _____doesn't_____ ever lose."
8

Spelling Strategy

Guess and Check
Remind students that they can use the guess-and-check strategy for spelling a lesson word. Demonstrate how to use this strategy with contractions by inviting students to suggest spellings for the word *wouldn't*. Write their suggestions on the board. Then have students check the spellings in the Spelling Dictionary and identify the correct spelling on the board. Suggest that students try the same strategy with any lesson words they are having difficulty with.

Guess	Correct?
wooden't	no
woud'ent	no
would'nt	no
wouldn't	yes

Max _____didn't_____ like to lose. His hands were
9
sweaty. His knees were shaking. "I _____can't_____ help
10
it," he thought. "I want to beat this guy."

Max rubbed his hands on his jeans. "Calm down," he
told himself. "Whatever happens, I _____mustn't_____ look
11
scared. I _____don't_____ want to make it easy for Hector
12
to win. Besides, it really _____won't_____ be the end of
13
the world if I lose."

Then Hector made his move. Max knew that it was the
wrong one. "He _____hasn't_____ got a chance now!" he
14
thought. Max grinned. "You _____shouldn't_____ have done
15
that, Hector," he said. "I'm going to beat you. But don't
worry. It _____isn't_____ going to hurt for long."
16
In one move Max cleared the checkerboard of Hector's
pieces. The game was over.

Hector shook Max's
hand and smiled. "You play
a good game of checkers," he
said. "I think I like playing
with you."

Max smiled back. He had
met the challenge.

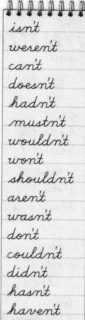

isnt
werent
cant
doesnt
hadnt
mustnt
wouldnt
wont
shouldnt
arent
wasnt
dont
couldnt
didnt
hasnt
havent

LESSON 29   **171**

ACTIVITY MASTER p. T277

Lesson 29 More Contractions

Name _____

Find the word in the box that matches each clue. Write the word.
Then read down the squares to find the answer to the question.
The lines for the letters include lines for apostrophes.

Spelling Words	hasn't	aren't	couldn't	didn't	hadn't
	wasn't	isn't	won't	don't	mustn't

WHY DOES AN ELEPHANT HAVE A TRUNK?
Because it has

1. did + not =   d i d n ' t
2. will + not =   w o n ' t
3. has + not =   h a s n ' t
4. must + not =   m u s t n ' t
5. is + not =   i s n ' t
6. do + not =   d o n ' t
7. could + not =   c o u l d n ' t
8. had + not =   h a d n ' t
9. was + not =   w a s n ' t
10. are + not =   a r e n ' t

Draw a line from each pair of words to its contraction.

11. have not   a. doesn't
12. cannot   b. haven't
13. would not   c. shouldn't
14. does not   d. weren't
15. should not   e. wouldn't
16. were not   f. can't

ADDITIONAL PRACTICE
You may wish to copy and distribute
the Activity Master on page T277 as
additional practice for Lesson 29.

Proofreading Practice
- I shoudn't stay out late.
  (*shouldn't*)
- You musn't go so soon.
  (*mustn't*)

Reading Comprehension

After students have com-
pleted the pages, ask them to
describe in one word how
Max feels at the beginning of
the story (nervous), in paragraph 3 (determined), and at
the end (happy or proud).
Have students underline specific words and phrases in the
story that indicate each of
these feelings. For example,
"nervously," "wasn't happy,"
and "in this mess" in the first
paragraph indicate that Max
is nervous about the challenge. You may wish to have
students create a chart that
displays the words and
phrases under column headings that name the feelings.

Cooperative Learning Activity

To help students practice the
lesson words, have them
work in small groups to write
a clue for each of the lesson
words. Tell them to divide
the list among themselves.
Explain that clues may
include beginning or ending
sounds, rhyming words,
meanings, and numbers of
letters. Then have students
take turns reading their clues
to the rest of their group.
The other students should
write the answer to the word
clue. The student giving
clues should then say and
spell the word, so that others
may check their answers.

Day 4

Student Objectives

- To write rules of a game, using lesson words
- To proofread a note for spelling, capitalization, and unnecessary words

Presenting the Page

Review with students what game Max and Hector are playing in "The Challenge" on pages 170–171. Brainstorm with students the rules for games they know. Remind them to try to use lesson words as they write their rules.

To assist students with the Proofreading activity, read the directions and note aloud and then have students complete the activity independently. To help students check their work, put the note on an overhead projector and call on volunteers to identify and correct the mistakes.

Meeting Individual Needs

ESOL

Contractions are less common in some languages than in others. To help speakers of other languages make the connection between two words and their contracted form, read a sentence aloud, using a lesson word. Have students restate and write the sentence, using individual words in place of contractions.

Spelling and Writing

isn't
weren't
can't
doesn't
hadn't
mustn't
wouldn't
won't
shouldn't
aren't
wasn't
don't
couldn't
didn't
hasn't
haven't

Write to the Point

Rules tell how to play a game and what players can and cannot do. For example, one soccer rule is "Don't touch the ball with your hands." Write three rules for a game you know. Try to use spelling words from this lesson in your rules.
Rules will vary.

Use the strategies on page 7 when you are not sure how to spell a word.

Proofreading

Proofread the note below. Use proofreading marks to correct five spelling mistakes, three capitalization mistakes, and two unnecessary words.

Proofreading Marks
◯ spell correctly
≡ capitalize
✗ take out

Chad,

     couldn't
I (couldnt) wait for you to see this game.

Open the box and look at the checkerboard. it
  hasn't
(has'nt) been used in ~~in~~ ten years. It's still in great
     Wouldn't
shape! (Wouldent) you like to play? Well, Aunt rose
won't
(won'nt) let anyone use it except me and one other

person. you are that person. I'll come to your
                 Doesn't
house tonight for a game. (Doesnt) that sound like

~~like~~ a great plan?

           Ling

172 UNIT 5

Proofreading Practice

- Tom and I wern't excited. (weren't)
- Tom dosen't get upset easily. (doesn't)

✓ Correcting Common Errors

Students sometimes misspell contractions by dropping silent letters. Some students may write *aren't* as *arn't*, *haven't* as *havn't*, and *weren't* as *wern't*. These students may benefit from writing the two words that make each contraction, crossing out the letter *o* in *not*, and then writing the contraction with the remaining letters.

Language Connection

Be Verbs There are many different forms of the verb *be*. Some tell what is happening now. Others tell what happened in the past. These forms of *be* are used in *not* contractions.

Present Tense		Contraction
is	The bus **is** late.	isn't
are	They **are** in a hurry.	aren't

Past Tense		Contraction
was	Bart **was** still here.	wasn't
were	Jill and Will **were** on the way.	weren't

Use the correct contraction above to complete each sentence.

1. Toni _____isn't_____ here every day.

2. Today the trains _____aren't_____ on time.

3. Paige and LaWanda _____weren't_____ here last Thursday.

4. Last month _____wasn't_____ the best month for planting a garden.

Challenge Yourself

Use the Spelling Dictionary to answer these questions. Then use separate paper to write sentences showing that you understand the meaning of each Challenge Word. *Sentences will vary.*

Challenge Words	
there'll	how'd
we'd	there'd

5. Is **there'll** a contraction for the words *there will*?

_____yes_____

6. Is **how'd** a contraction for the words *how did*? _____yes_____

7. Is **we'd** a contraction for *we did*? _____no_____

8. Is **there'd** a contraction for the words *there did*? _____no_____

Posttest

Dictate the following sentences. Have students use separate paper to write the sentences and underline the lesson words.

1. I wouldn't have gone if you hadn't.
2. They aren't going because they haven't saved any money.
3. I don't see why you can't come with us.
4. He doesn't care that he isn't ready.
5. You mustn't do that again.
6. She hasn't said why she didn't help.
7. They weren't happy because he wasn't there.
8. They couldn't tell us why they won't come.
9. We shouldn't forget to study.

Enrichment Activity

Have students work with partners to look through newspapers and magazines to find examples of contractions. Have them make a collage of contractions and phrases or sentences with contractions. Encourage students to display their collages and discuss the ways contractions are used.

Day 5

Student Objectives

- To identify and write present- and past-tense lesson words
- To study the spellings and meanings of the Challenge Words
- To take a posttest on the lesson words

Presenting the Page

Write the terms *present tense* and *past tense* on the board and discuss their meanings with students. Guide students to understand that some words describe things happening now *(isn't)*, while others describe events from the past *(wasn't)*. Encourage students to use these ideas to help them decide which contraction best fits each sentence.

Challenge Yourself

To introduce the Challenge Words, write the following on the board:

there'll	how'd
we'd	there'd

Point out that each contraction has one syllable. Then ask volunteers to tell what words each contraction is formed from (*there will, how did, we would* or *had,* and *there would* or *had*). Have students name the missing letters in each contraction (*wi, di, woul, ha*).

Posttest

Use the posttest on this page to assess students' ability to spell the lesson words.

Lesson 30

Unit 5 Review
Lessons 25–29

Student Objective

- To take a pretest on the lesson words

Pretest

Use the pretest on this page to assess students' ability to spell the lesson words.

Have students use the study steps on page 6 to study any words they misspell in the pretest.

You may wish to duplicate and send home the Home Activity Master on pages T249–T250.

Meeting Individual Needs

ESOL

Speakers of other languages may master the spelling of the words but still have difficulty using them in context. Ask students to work in pairs to choose a group of review words, such as words with /ûr/, write the words, and highlight each spelling pattern with a colored marker. Then have students write sentences containing the words. Encourage them to read their sentences aloud and spell the lesson words aloud.

Lesson 30

Unit 5 Review
Lessons 25–29

> Use the steps on page 6 to study words that are hard for you.

25 Words with /o͞o/ or /yo͞o/

too
true
knew
few
huge
used
two

Write the spelling word that can be used instead of the word or words in dark type in each sentence.

1. The story that we read was **real**. _____true_____
2. My father's car is **not new**. _____used_____
3. The sun is **very** hot in the summer. _____too_____
4. **One plus one** is less than three. _____Two_____
5. Malika **was certain** that she would win. _____knew_____
6. **Not very many** people stood in line. _____Few_____
7. Elephants and whales are **big**. _____huge_____

26 Words with /ûr/

curl
girl
worm
earth
were

Write the spelling word that belongs in each group.

8. lady   woman   _____girl_____
9. are   was   _____were_____
10. curve   coil   _____curl_____
11. soil   ground   _____earth_____
12. snake   eel   _____worm_____

174 UNIT 5

Pretest

Say each lesson word, read the sentence, and then repeat the word. Have students write the words on separate paper.

1. **too** The weather is <u>too</u> cold.
2. **true** Is it <u>true</u> that you won?
3. **knew** She <u>knew</u> my name.
4. **few** He invited a <u>few</u> friends.
5. **huge** They made a <u>huge</u> mess.
6. **used** We <u>used</u> all of the towels.
7. **two** I have <u>two</u> tests today.

8. **curl** The hamsters <u>curl</u> into a ball.
9. **girl** The <u>girl</u> watched the game.
10. **worm** A <u>worm</u> lives in the ground.
11. **earth** The <u>earth</u> was dry and cracked.
12. **were** They <u>were</u> digging a hole.
13. **garden** The <u>garden</u> was full of flowers.
14. **father** My <u>father</u> was proud of me.
15. **sharp** Those scissors are <u>sharp</u>.
16. **heart** My <u>heart</u> jumped.
17. **voice** Her <u>voice</u> was soft.

18. **soil** The <u>soil</u> here is sandy.
19. **enjoy** We <u>enjoy</u> going to the movies.
20. **royal** He is part of the <u>royal</u> family.
21. **weren't** They <u>weren't</u> in class today.
22. **won't** She <u>won't</u> say why.
23. **aren't** We <u>aren't</u> very happy.
24. **haven't** They <u>haven't</u> done the work.
25. **can't** We <u>can't</u> present our project.

27 garden / father / sharp / heart

Words with /ä/

Write the spelling word that completes each analogy.

13. *Scissors* is to _____sharp_____ as *feather* is to *soft*.

14. *Son* is to _____father_____ as *daughter* is to *mother*.

15. *Apple* is to *orchard* as *carrot* is to _____garden_____.

16. *Brain* is to *head* as _____heart_____ is to *chest*.

28 voice / soil / enjoy / royal

Words with /oi/

Write the spelling word for each clue.

17. People sing with this. _____voice_____

18. This is a synonym for *like*.
    _____enjoy_____

19. Kings and queens are this.
    _____royal_____

20. People plant seeds in this.
    _____soil_____

29 weren't / won't / aren't / haven't / can't

More Contractions

Write the contractions for the words.

21. cannot _____can't_____

22. are + not _____aren't_____

23. have + not _____haven't_____

24. will + not _____won't_____

25. were + not _____weren't_____

REVIEW TEST MASTER, pp. T291–T292

Unit 5 Review Test   Name _____

Darken the circle for the phrase with an underlined word that is not spelled correctly.

Example

A pull a loose <u>tooth</u>   C flowers in the <u>gardin</u>
B <u>move</u> near you   D <u>learn</u> how to swim

Example
Ⓐ Ⓑ ● Ⓓ

Answers

1. A a <u>wirm</u> in the apple   C not a <u>true</u> story
   B <u>enjoy</u> flying the kite   D <u>weren't</u> able to come
   1. ● Ⓑ Ⓒ Ⓓ

2. F has a loud <u>voice</u>   H <u>wo'nt</u> be home
   G mother and <u>father</u>   J a <u>sharp</u> pencil
   2. Ⓕ Ⓖ ● Ⓙ

3. A planted seeds in the <u>soil</u>   C <u>too</u> much noise
   B <u>havn't</u> seen your hat   D cat can <u>curl</u> up
   3. Ⓐ Ⓑ ● Ⓓ

4. F a <u>huge</u> smile   H <u>were</u> at the park
   G <u>knue</u> the answer   J <u>can't</u> hear a sound
   4. Ⓕ ● Ⓗ Ⓙ

5. A <u>few</u> pieces of gum   C the moon and the <u>earth</u>
   B found <u>two</u> frogs   D has a kind <u>hart</u>
   5. Ⓐ Ⓑ Ⓒ ●

6. F <u>can't</u> miss the bus   H a sweet <u>gurl</u>
   G the <u>royal</u> family   J very <u>sharp</u> claws
   6. Ⓕ Ⓖ ● Ⓙ

7. A <u>uesed</u> all the soap   C <u>true</u> or false
   B <u>voice</u> can be heard   D <u>weren't</u> in the room
   7. ● Ⓑ Ⓒ Ⓓ

8. F <u>arn't</u> in the play   H <u>few</u> more minutes
   G <u>enjoy</u> reading   J gave his <u>father</u> a gift
   8. ● Ⓖ Ⓗ Ⓙ

9. A <u>too</u> many people   C <u>won't</u> swim out too far
   B dug up the <u>soil</u>   D <u>cirl</u> her hair
   9. Ⓐ Ⓑ Ⓒ ●

Unit 5 Review Test   Name _____

Darken the circle for the phrase with an underlined word that is not spelled correctly.

10. F a <u>fue</u> more days   H <u>enjoy</u> the music
    G vegetable <u>garden</u>   J <u>aren't</u> coming
    10. ● Ⓖ Ⓗ Ⓙ

11. A <u>haven't</u> been there   C a <u>shearp</u> knife
    B <u>curl</u> around my finger   D a <u>true</u> story
    11. Ⓐ Ⓑ ● Ⓓ

12. F water the <u>soyal</u>   H <u>were</u> very happy
    G <u>used</u> the telephone   J a <u>huge</u> whale
    12. ● Ⓖ Ⓗ Ⓙ

13. A <u>won't</u> play with us   C little green <u>worm</u>
    B the <u>royal</u> castle   D <u>tew</u> pairs of shoes
    13. Ⓐ Ⓑ Ⓒ ●

14. F <u>girl</u> and boy   H all over the <u>earth</u>
    G in a soft <u>voyce</u>   J <u>knew</u> what to do
    14. Ⓕ ● Ⓗ Ⓙ

15. A <u>father</u> and son   C chocolate candy <u>heart</u>
    B weeds in the <u>garden</u>   D <u>wern't</u> outside
    15. Ⓐ Ⓑ Ⓒ ●

16. F <u>tue</u> much work   H <u>were</u> leaving today
    G <u>knew</u> how many   J <u>aren't</u> at their desk
    16. ● Ⓖ Ⓗ Ⓙ

17. A lost his <u>voice</u>   C <u>cant</u> find it
    B a sharp <u>nail</u>   D wasn't <u>true</u>
    17. Ⓐ Ⓑ ● Ⓓ

18. F her little <u>girl</u>   H <u>worm</u> on the leaf
    G <u>enjoi</u> swimming   J <u>used</u> more glue
    18. Ⓕ ● Ⓗ Ⓙ

19. A <u>huge</u> storm   C the sun and the <u>urth</u>
    B saw a <u>few</u> clouds   D <u>haven't</u> written the letter
    19. Ⓐ Ⓑ ● Ⓓ

Day 2

Student Objectives

- To review the *oo, ue, ew, u*-consonant-*e, o,* and *o*-consonant-*e* spellings of the /o͞o/ and /yo͞o/ sounds
- To review the *ur, ir, or, ear* and *ere* spellings of the /ûr/ sound
- To review the *a* and *ea* spellings of the /ä/ sound
- To review the *oi* and *oy* spellings of the /oi/ sound
- To review *not* contractions
- To use meaning clues to identify and write lesson words

Presenting the Pages

Lessons 25–26 Have volunteers read the review words for Lessons 25–26 aloud. Review with students the /o͞o/ and /yo͞o/ spelling patterns they learned in Lesson 25—*oo, ue, ew, u*-consonant-*e, o,* and *o*-consonant-*e*—and the /ûr/ spelling patterns they learned in Lesson 26—*ur, ir, or, ear,* and *ere.*

Lesson 27–28 Have volunteers read the review words for Lessons 27–28 aloud. Review with students the /ä/ and /oi/ spelling patterns represented by the review words—*a* and *ea* for /ä/ and *oi* and *oy* for /oi/.

Lesson 29 Have volunteers read the Lesson 29 words and explain how each contraction is formed.

Test-Taking Strategies

Read the directions for the Review Test Master aloud. Suggest to students that if they are unsure of the incorrect spelling, they can cross out the choices with underlined words that they know are spelled correctly and then make the best choice.

Proofreading Practice

- That gurl is a very good pitcher. (*girl*)
- I wont be able to go to the game. (*won't*)

Student Objectives
- To sort lesson words according to vowel sound
- To compare contractions sorted by verb

Presenting the Page

Have volunteers read the Review Sort words aloud. Review with students the sounds represented by /o͞o/, /yo͞o/, /ûr/, /ä/, and /oi/. Then have students complete the page with a partner.

Meeting Individual Needs

ESOL

Speakers of other languages may need extra practice with vowel sounds and their spelling patterns. Have small groups play the echo game: one student should pronounce one of the unit vowel sounds (example: /o͞o/); other students in the group should then say and spell a lesson word that contains the sound (*news*). Students should cite at least four words for each vowel sound.

Proofreading Practice
- My hart was beating fast. (*heart*)
- I knue all of the spelling words. (*knew*)

---

26. /o͞o/ or /yo͞o/ Words

tr(ue)
t(oo)
(us)(ed)
h(u)g(e)
kn(ew)
f(ew)

27. /ûr/ Words

w(or)m
g(ir)l
(ear)th
c(ur)l
w(er)e

28. /ä/ Words

sh(a)rp
h(ea)rt
g(a)rden
f(a)ther

29. /oi/ Words

s(oi)l
enj(oy)
r(oy)al
v(oi)ce

Review Sort

worm	girl	royal	knew
true	heart	huge	curl
sharp	enjoy	garden	were
soil	earth	father	few
too	used	voice	

26. Write the **six** /o͞o/ or /yo͞o/ words. Circle the letters that spell /o͞o/ or /yo͞o/ in each word.

27. Write the **five** /ûr/ words. Circle the letters that spell /ûr/ in each word.

28. Write the **four** /ä/ words. Circle the letter or letters that spell /ä/ in each word.

29. Write the **four** /oi/ words. Circle the letters that spell /oi/ in each word.

These six words have been sorted into two groups. Explain how the words in each group are alike.

30. hasn't   haven't   hadn't

All contain a form of the verb <u>have</u>.

31. doesn't   don't   didn't

All contain a form of the verb <u>do</u>.

The Writing Process   Name _____

1 Prewriting • Plan your writing.
- Make sure you know what your writing task is.
- Identify the audience and the purpose for writing.
- Choose a topic.
- Gather and write ideas about the topic.
- Organize your ideas.

2 Writing • Write a first draft.
- Use your plan to put your ideas in writing.
- Don't worry about mistakes now.
- Add any new ideas you think of while writing.
- Leave room between lines so that you can make changes later.

3 Revising • Look for ways to improve what you have written.
- Make sure your writing fits the audience and purpose for writing.
- Look for places that need more ideas or details.
- Take out sentences that don't belong.
- Find places where more colorful or exact words can be used.
- Make sure that your sentences are complete.
- Write and revise until you are happy with your writing.

4 Proofreading • Review your work for errors.
- Make sure you have indented each paragraph.
- Check to see that you have used words correctly.
- Check your capitalization.
- Check to see that you have used periods, question marks, commas, and other punctuation marks correctly.
- Look at the spelling of each word. Circle words you are not sure you have spelled correctly. Check their spelling.

5 Publishing • Share what you have written.
- Make a clean final draft.
- Read it to the class or a friend.
- Add pictures or make a poster to go with it.
- Make a recording of your writing.

✔ Proofreading Checklist   Name _____

You can use the questions below as a checklist to proofread your writing.
- ☐ Have I indented each paragraph?
- ☐ Have I used words correctly in every sentence?
- ☐ Have I capitalized the first word in each sentence?
- ☐ Have I capitalized all proper names?
- ☐ Have I ended each sentence with a period, question mark, or exclamation point?
- ☐ Have I spelled each word correctly?

The chart below shows some proofreading marks and how to use them.

Mark	Meaning	Example
◯	spell correctly	I liek dogs.
⊙	add period	They are my favorite kind of pet⊙
?	add question mark	What kind of pet do you have?
≡	capitalize	My dog's name is scooter.
✐	take out	He likes to to run and play.
¶	indent paragraph	¶ I love my dog, Scooter. He is the best pet I have ever had. Every morning he wakes me with a bark. Every night he sleeps with me.
ᵛ ᵛ	add quotation marks	You are my best friend, I tell him.

How-To Chart   Name _____   Date _____

1. _____
   ↓
2. _____
   ↓
3. _____
   ↓
4. _____

Writer's Workshop

A How-To Paragraph

A how-to paragraph tells how to do something. In a how-to paragraph, writers give step-by-step directions, using order words such as *first, second, next, then,* and *finally*. Here is part of Alicia's how-to paragraph. In it she tells how to make a kind of sandwich.

> **How to Make a Super Sandwich**
> A Super Sandwich is a tasty treat. Here's how to make it. First, get some bread, peanut butter, honey, and bananas. Second, cut the bananas into very thin slices. Next, spread the peanut butter on two slices of bread. Then, pour a little honey on the peanut butter.

Prewriting To write her how-to paragraph, Alicia followed the steps in the writing process. She began with a Prewriting activity. She used a how-to chart to list the steps for making her favorite snack. This helped her know the order in which to write the steps. Part of Alicia's how-to chart is shown here. Study what Alicia did.

1	Get two slices of bread, peanut butter, honey, bananas.
2	Cut the bananas.
3	Spread the peanut butter on the bread.

It's Your Turn!

Get ready to write your own how-to paragraph. Think of something you know how to do. After you have decided what to write about, make a how-to chart. Then follow the other steps in the writing process—writing, revising, proofreading, and publishing. Try to use spelling words from this lesson in your how-to paragraph. **Paragraphs will vary.**

Writer's Workshop Scoring Rubric: How-To Paragraph

SCORE 3 Topic of the paragraph is clearly indicated. Paragraph explains how to do something, and all necessary steps are presented in a logical order. Writing includes precise language and transitions to present the steps. Contains a minimum of sentence-structure, usage, mechanics, and spelling errors.

SCORE 2 Topic of the paragraph is clearly indicated. Paragraph explains how to do something, but some steps may be omitted. Writing includes some precise language, and transitions are occasionally used to present the steps. Contains some sentence-structure, usage, mechanics, and spelling errors.

SCORE 1 Topic of the paragraph is not clearly stated, or writing is not a how-to paragraph. Important steps are omitted, and ideas are not presented in a logical order. Writing includes little or no precise language and few or no transitions. Contains many sentence-structure, usage, mechanics, and spelling errors.

Evaluating Students' Writing

The scoring rubric is based on standards for idea development, organization, coherence, sentence structure, usage, mechanics, and spelling. You may wish to share the rubric with students before they write their description.

The *Steck-Vaughn Writer's Dictionary, Intermediate Level,* provides writers with a place to write words they want to remember.

Presenting the Page

Read the first paragraph, the excerpt from Alicia's paragraph, and her how-to chart with students. Ask students to name the words in *How to Make a Super Sandwich* that tell the order in which steps occur.

You may wish to copy and distribute the Writing Masters on pages T295–T296 and T300 for students to use as they write their paragraph.

Day 5

Student Objective
- To take a posttest on the lesson words

Posttest Options

Use the posttest on this page or the Review Test Master on pages T291–T292 to assess students' ability to spell the lesson words.

Posttest

Dictate the following sentences. Have students write the sentences and underline the lesson words.

1. My <u>father</u> won't weed the <u>garden</u>.
2. The <u>girl</u> <u>dug</u> in the <u>earth</u> with a <u>sharp</u> stick.
3. You <u>can't</u> dig in <u>soil</u> that is <u>too</u> wet.
4. I <u>enjoy</u> reading <u>true</u> stories.
5. The <u>royal</u> family gave away their <u>used</u> car.
6. The singer's <u>voice</u> made my hair <u>curl</u>.
7. I <u>haven't</u> seen the <u>huge</u> <u>worm</u>.
8. A <u>few</u> friends <u>knew</u> where we <u>were</u>.
9. The <u>two</u> babies <u>weren't</u> sleeping anymore.
10. The students <u>aren't</u> studying the <u>heart</u>.

Lesson 31
Words with /ô/

Student Objectives

- To take a pretest on the lesson words
- To spell the lesson words aloud
- To sort and write the lesson words according to the spelling patterns *o, a, ough, au,* and *aw*

Pretest

Use the pretest on this page to assess students' ability to spell the lesson words.

 Have students use the study steps on page 6 to study any words they misspell in the pretest.

 You may wish to duplicate and send home the Home Activity Master on pages T251–T252.

Presenting the Page

Introducing the /ô/ Sound Have students say the /ô/ vowel sound. Say the following word pairs. Ask students to raise their hand when they hear a word with /ô/:

draw–drew   tale–*tall*
lung–*long*   bite–*bought*

As students prepare to sort the words, point out that /ô/ is most often spelled *o, a, au,* or *aw* but is spelled *ough* in some words that we often use.

Pronunciation Focus Explain that some people say /ŏ/ instead of /ô/ in some words. Invite students to use the Spelling Dictionary to find lesson words such as *water* that are pronounced with /ŏ/.

Consonant Focus Write *tall, mall, walk, talk, always,* and *water* on the board and explain that in most of the words with the *a* pattern, the *a* precedes an *l* that may or may not be silent (/l/ is pronounced in *tall* and *mall* but not in *walk* and *talk*). Also point out that /ôl/ is usually spelled *all* at the end of a word.

178

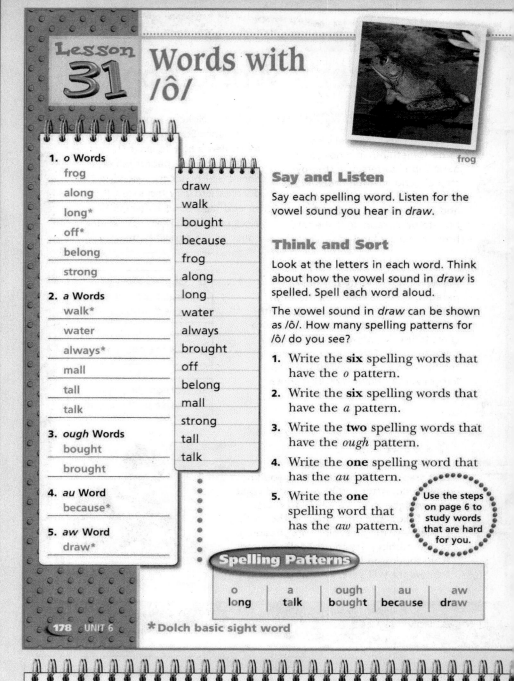

Lesson 31 Words with /ô/

frog

1. o Words
frog
along
long*
off*
belong
strong

2. a Words
walk*
water
always*
mall
tall
talk

3. ough Words
bought
brought

4. au Word
because*

5. aw Word
draw*

draw
walk
bought
because
frog
along
long
water
always
brought
off
belong
mall
strong
tall
talk

178 UNIT 6   *Dolch basic sight word

Say and Listen

Say each spelling word. Listen for the vowel sound you hear in *draw*.

Think and Sort

Look at the letters in each word. Think about how the vowel sound in *draw* is spelled. Spell each word aloud.

The vowel sound in *draw* can be shown as /ô/. How many spelling patterns for /ô/ do you see?

1. Write the **six** spelling words that have the *o* pattern.
2. Write the **six** spelling words that have the *a* pattern.
3. Write the **two** spelling words that have the *ough* pattern.
4. Write the **one** spelling word that has the *au* pattern.
5. Write the **one** spelling word that has the *aw* pattern.

Use the steps on page 6 to study words that are hard for you.

Spelling Patterns

o	a	ough	au	aw
long	talk	bought	because	draw

Pretest

Say each lesson word, read the sentence, and then repeat the word. Have students write the words on separate paper.

1. **draw** Please draw me a map.
2. **walk** We walk to school.
3. **bought** I bought a new pencil.
4. **because** I got wet because it was raining.
5. **frog** A frog jumped in the pond.
6. **along** Come along on our picnic.
7. **long** I read a long book.
8. **water** Pour me a cup of water.
9. **always** She always eats at noon.
10. **brought** Mom brought a salad.
11. **off** Please turn off the lights.
12. **belong** The books belong to us.
13. **mall** We shop at the mall.
14. **strong** My brother is strong.
15. **tall** The giraffe is tall.
16. **talk** Dad will talk to the coach.

Additional Words for Enrichment

The following words can be used to meet the needs of on-level and above-level students:
applause   claw   often   wrong   thought   chalk

Spelling and Meaning

Antonyms Write the spelling word that is an antonym of each underlined word.

1. That basketball player is very <u>short</u>. — tall
2. Please turn <u>on</u> the light. — off
3. Tina <u>never</u> eats breakfast. — always
4. Elephants are very large and <u>weak</u>. — strong
5. Mr. Good gave a <u>brief</u> speech. — long

Clues Write the spelling word for each clue.

6. what you do on the phone — talk
7. what people and animals drink — water
8. place to shop — mall
9. past tense of *bring* — brought
10. what artists do — draw
11. green thing that sits on a lily pad — frog
12. means "to be owned by" — belong
13. means almost the same as *beside* — along
14. rhymes with *talk* — walk
15. past tense of *buy* — bought

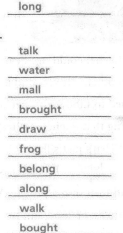

Word Story People used to say that a dish broke "by cause" it fell. Later, they made one word of *by* and *cause*. Write the word as it is spelled today.

16. _____ because

Family Tree: *talk* Think about how the *talk* words are alike in spelling and meaning. Then add another *talk* word to the tree. A sample answer is shown.

- talkative
- talks
- 17. talked
- talker
- talking
- talk

LESSON 31 **179**

HOME ACTIVITY MASTER p. T251

Spelling at Home Unit 6

Dear Family of _____
During the next six weeks, your child will be learning to spell the following kinds of words:
- words with /ô/, as in *draw*
- words with /ou/, as in *house*
- words with /îr/, /âr/, or /îr/, as in *hear, hair, and fire*
- words with *-er* or *-est*

Here are some simple activities to do each week to help your child become a better speller.

Listening and Writing
Say the spelling words and have your child write them.

Spelling Strategy: Guess and Check
If your child is having difficulty spelling a word, encourage him or her to guess the spelling. Then ask your child to check the list at right or a dictionary to see if his or her guess is correct.

Games and Activities
Play Spelling Chunks. Have your child choose some of the spelling words. Write the words on a piece of paper. Leave a space below each word. With your child, study the words. Then separate each word into smaller parts so that it is easy to remember. Divide each word into the "chunks" we hear when the word is read aloud. For example *isfhis/en*.

Write some of the spelling words on a piece of paper, leaving out some of the letters. Ask your child to complete each word. Taking turns, continue writing and completing as many spelling words as possible.

Using Spelling Words
Ask your child to write sentences that contain the spelling words. Then read the sentences with your child. Notice whether the sentences show that your child knows the meanings of the spelling words.

Lesson 31 Words with /ô/
Week of _____
frog   long   along   off
belong strong water always
mall   tall   talk   walk
bought brought draw   because

Lesson 32 More Words with /ô/
Week of _____
autumn August born   fork
morning sport popcorn before
north   corner before door
floor   pour   four   quart

Lesson 33 Words with /ou/
Week of _____
hour   sound ground about
house   around count our
found   owl   down   power
brown   tower town   flower

Lesson 34 Words with /îr/, /âr/, or /îr/
Week of _____
hear   dear   ear   near
year   here   deer stairs
air   chair hair care
where   tire   fire wire

Lesson 35 Words with -er or -est
Week of _____
stronger strongest taller tallest
greater greatest longer longest
sharper sharpest funnier funniest
dirtier dirtiest hotter hottest

Lesson 36 Unit 6 Review
Week of _____
Lesson 36 is a review of Lessons 31–35. Help your child practice all of the words from those lessons.

The highlighted area shows the Lesson 31 words, which students can share with family members. Spanish version available on page T252.

Proofreading Practice
- I spilled wauter on my shirt. *(water)*
- How lawng will it take to dry? *(long)*

Meeting Individual Needs

Visual Learners
Give each small group of students a set of index cards containing the spelling patterns for /ô/. Write the lesson words on the board, leaving out the letter or letters that represent /ô/. Have groups take turns holding up the card that shows the correct pattern for each word. Conclude by having volunteers write the missing letter or letters in the word on the board.

Day 2

Student Objectives
- To use meaning clues to identify and write lesson words
- To use etymology, meaning, and spelling to identify the word *because*
- To learn *talk* words and analyze their spellings and meanings

Presenting the Page

Write the following Antonyms and Clues examples on the board and model identifying the answers. Remind students that an antonym is a word that means the opposite of a given word.

- Dad <u>sold</u> the red car. *(bought)*
- _____ means "every time" *(always)*

Word Story

Focus students' attention on the pronunciation change that happened when *by* and *cause* were combined to make *because*. When the two words were combined, the *y* became unstressed and was spelled *e* according to the custom of the time.

Family Tree: *talk*

Students should see that each *talk* word contains *talk*. Have students find the words in a dictionary and discuss their meanings. Help students understand how adding the suffixes *-ative* and *-er* changes the meaning of the base word, *talk*. Guide students to understand that knowing how to spell *talk* can help them spell related words.

179

Day 3

Student Objectives

- To use context to identify and write lesson words
- To identify the sequence of events in a story
- To predict story events

Presenting the Pages

Have students read the first two paragraphs and predict what will happen in the story. Then have them work in pairs to complete the pages and read the completed story to be sure their choices make sense. Alternatively, have students complete the activity independently and then take turns reading the completed story.

Discuss with students the meaning of the word *signed* in the second paragraph. Point out that the girls in the story use sign language. You may wish to demonstrate or have a student demonstrate some signs for letters or words.

Meeting Individual Needs

Kinesthetic Learners

Write the lesson words on a chart, omitting the /ô/ spelling pattern in each. Have students write each spelling pattern (*o, a, ough, au, aw*) on a self-stick note. Then have students take turns using the self-stick notes to complete the lesson words on the chart, tracing the letters in the completed word, and spelling the word aloud.

The Frog Prince

Libby's older sister, Rachel, liked to
_____draw_____ pictures. One day she
1
drew a picture of a green _____frog_____.
2
It had a little gold crown on its head. Rachel
_____brought_____ the picture to Libby.
3

Rachel could not hear, so the two girls used their hands to talk to each other. "If you find a frog, it might turn into a prince," Rachel signed to Libby with her hands. Libby had a _____strong_____
4
feeling that Rachel was teasing her.

"That's just silly _____talk_____," Libby signed back. But not
5
_____long_____ after, she wondered what would happen if a frog
6
could turn into a prince. Would he be short or _____tall_____?
7
Would he be kind and fun? Libby thought about what she would say to a frog prince.

"Aren't you ready yet?" Mom called. Libby's daydream ended.
Sometimes Libby's mom spent Saturday afternoon shopping at the
_____mall_____. Libby _____always_____ went. Rachel usually
8   9
came _____along_____, too. Today at the mall, Mom and Rachel
10
just _____bought_____ a snack. Libby wanted to be by herself. She
11
decided to _____walk_____ around the mall.
12

It was warm, so Libby took _____off_____ her jacket. But
13
she was still hot. "Maybe it's cooler by the _____water_____," she
14

Spelling Strategy

Guess and Check

Remind students that they can use the guess-and-check strategy for words whose spelling they are not sure of. Model the use of this strategy by writing some logical guesses for *brought, always,* and *because*. Have students check the spellings in the Spelling Dictionary to determine which is correct.

Guess	Correct?
brawt	no
allways	no
because	yes

Invite students to use the guess-and-check strategy to spell lesson words that they find difficult to spell.

thought. Libby walked to the pond in the center of the mall. She sat down on the low wall around the pond. Suddenly a frog jumped to the wall and sat beside her.

"Could it be a prince?" Libby wondered. As she reached for the frog, a voice yelled, "Leave that frog alone! It doesn't ___belong___ to you!"
15

Mr. Muller, the pet store owner, rushed over. "What are you doing to my frog?" he asked. "I've been searching for him everywhere."

"Nothing at all," Libby replied. "I just wanted to help him ___because___ he might be . . ." She stopped. It
16
sounded so silly. She got up and quickly walked away.

"Now I'll never be sure," Libby thought as she went to look for her mom and Rachel.

draw
walk
bought
because
frog
along
long
water
always
brought
off
belong
mall
strong
tall
talk

LESSON 31 **181**

Reading Comprehension

After students have completed the pages, discuss the predictions they made before they read the entire story. Invite students to tell why they thought certain things might happen and to contrast their predictions with the story events.

Remind students that the sequence of events in a story is the order in which things happen in that story. Write events from the story in scrambled order on the board. Invite volunteers to number the events in the order they happened.

Cooperative Learning Activity

Invite students to work in pairs to practice spelling the lesson words. Have one partner say sentences that contain the lesson words. Have the other student identify the words and write them. Then have students reverse roles. Suggest that students use the list on page 181 to check their own work and that they compare their performance on this midweek activity with their performance on the pretest. Encourage students to practice the lesson words they still need to study.

ACTIVITY MASTER p. T278

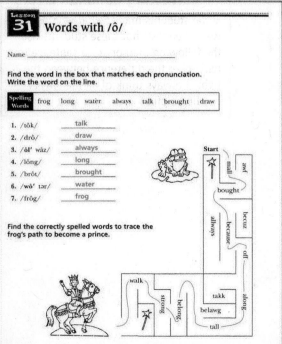

Lesson 31 Words with /ô/

Name _____

Find the word in the box that matches each pronunciation. Write the word on the line.

Spelling Words	frog	long	water	always	talk	brought	draw

1. /tôk/ — talk
2. /drô/ — draw
3. /ôl′ wāz/ — always
4. /lông/ — long
5. /brôt/ — brought
6. /wô′ tər/ — water
7. /frôg/ — frog

Find the correctly spelled words to trace the frog's path to become a prince.

ADDITIONAL PRACTICE

You may wish to copy and distribute the Activity Master on page T278 as additional practice for Lesson 31.

Proofreading Practice
• Does this coat beloung to you? (belong)
• I found it at the mal. (mall)

Day 4

Student Objectives

- To write a narrative, using lesson words
- To proofread an e-mail for spelling, capitalization, and unnecessary words

Presenting the Page

Before students work on their story ending, have them reread the story up to the point where Libby reaches for the frog. Suggest that students brainstorm ideas for a new ending and choose the best ending idea from their list.

To assist students with the Proofreading activity, suggest that they look for one type of error at a time. Direct students to complete the activity independently and work with a partner to check their answers.

Meeting Individual Needs

ESOL

The /ô/ sound does not occur in any language other than English. Use the spelling words in a question-and-answer format to help students recognize and spell the sound. For example, ask, "Is Pete <u>tall</u>?" and guide students to answer, "Yes, Pete is <u>tall</u>." Then ask students to write the lesson word featured in the sentence.

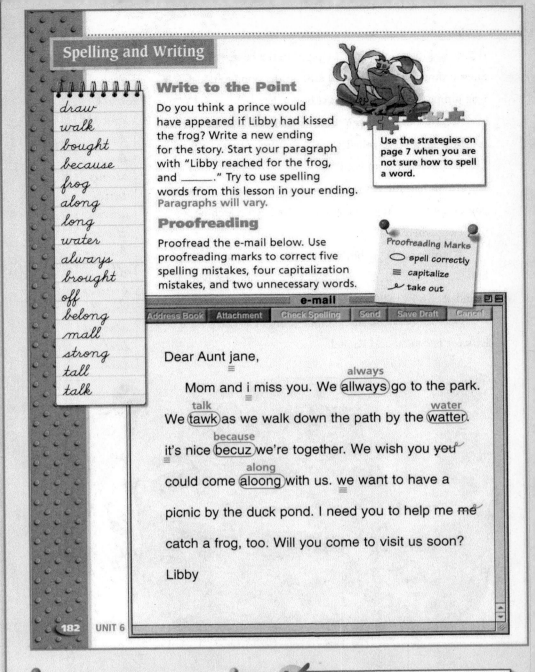

Spelling and Writing

draw
walk
bought
because
frog
along
long
water
always
brought
off
belong
mall
strong
tall
talk

Write to the Point

Do you think a prince would have appeared if Libby had kissed the frog? Write a new ending for the story. Start your paragraph with "Libby reached for the frog, and _____." Try to use spelling words from this lesson in your ending. **Paragraphs will vary.**

Use the strategies on page 7 when you are not sure how to spell a word.

Proofreading

Proofread the e-mail below. Use proofreading marks to correct five spelling mistakes, four capitalization mistakes, and two unnecessary words.

Proofreading Marks
- ⌒ spell correctly
- ≡ capitalize
- ℯ take out

e-mail

Address Book | Attachment | Check Spelling | Send | Save Draft | Cancel

Dear Aunt jane,

Mom and i miss you. We (allways) *always* go to the park.

We (tawk) *talk* as we walk down the path by the (watter) *water*.

it's nice (becuz) *because* we're together. We wish you you

could come (aloong) *along* with us. we want to have a

picnic by the duck pond. I need you to help me me

catch a frog, too. Will you come to visit us soon?

Libby

182 UNIT 6

Proofreading Practice

- I want to have a strawng body. (strong)
- I allways warm up before running. (always)

Correcting Common Errors

Some students may spell *always* as *all ways*. Suggest that these students use the following memory-clue sentence to remember the difference between the two: "I <u>always</u> think of <u>all</u> the <u>ways</u> I can be helpful."

Language Connection

Subject and Predicate   The subject of a sentence tells who or what is doing the action or being talked about. The predicate of a sentence tells what the subject does or did.

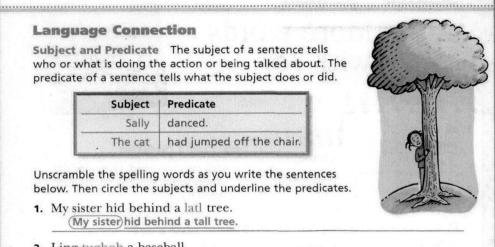

Subject	Predicate
Sally	danced.
The cat	had jumped off the chair.

Unscramble the spelling words as you write the sentences below. Then circle the subjects and underline the predicates.

1. My sister hid behind a latl tree.
   (My sister) hid behind a tall tree.

2. Ling tughob a baseball.
   (Ling) bought a baseball.

3. Mrs. Martinez took a nogl vacation.
   (Mrs. Martinez) took a long vacation.

4. I will wrad a picture of you.
   (I) will draw a picture of you.

5. The old clock fell fof the shelf.
   (The old clock) fell off the shelf.

⭐ Challenge Yourself

Use the Spelling Dictionary to answer these questions. Then use separate paper to write sentences showing that you understand the meaning of each Challenge Word.
Sentences will vary.

Challenge Words	
sausage	broth
dawdle	install

6. Should you comb your hair with a **sausage**? _____ no

7. Could you find **broth** in vegetable soup? _____ yes

8. If you were in a hurry, would you **dawdle**? _____ no

9. Should you **install** a stove before you turn it on? _____ yes

LESSON 31   **183**

Posttest

Dictate the following sentences. Have students use separate paper to write the sentences and underline the lesson words.
1. Is it a <u>long</u> <u>walk</u> to the <u>mall</u>?
2. Does this <u>frog</u> <u>belong</u> to you?
3. Wipe the <u>water</u> off the table.
4. He will <u>draw</u> a <u>tall</u> tree.
5. We <u>always</u> <u>talk</u> at lunch.
6. She won the race <u>because</u> she is <u>strong</u>.
7. I <u>brought</u> a book <u>along</u> to read.
8. He <u>bought</u> a hot dog.

Enrichment Activity

Invite students to look in newspapers and old magazines to find /ô/ words with the lesson patterns. Have students cut out the words, sort them, and glue the groups of words on construction paper.

Student Objectives

- To unscramble lesson words and write sentences containing them
- To identify complete subjects and predicates in sentences
- To study the spellings and meanings of the Challenge Words
- To take a posttest on the lesson words

Presenting the Page

Explain to students that one way to identify the predicate of a sentence is to look for the verb, which expresses action or a state of being, and often begins the predicate. Demonstrate for students that identifying the verb can help them separate the subject from the predicate. Point out that a verb can include a helper, as in Sentence 4, which contains the helping verb *will*.

⭐ Challenge Yourself

Write the following on the board:

sau/sage	broth
daw/dle	in/stall

Pronounce the words, having students repeat after you, and discuss the number of syllables in each word. Then have students review the spelling patterns for /ô/. Ask students to identify the spelling pattern for /ô/ in each Challenge Word (*sausage* has the *au* pattern; *dawdle* has the *aw* pattern; *broth* has the *o* pattern; *install* has the *a* pattern).

Posttest

Use the posttest on this page to assess students' ability to spell the lesson words.

Lesson 32

More Words with /ô/

Day 1

Student Objectives
- To take a pretest on the lesson words
- To spell the lesson words aloud
- To sort and write the lesson words according to the spelling patterns *au, o, oo, ou,* and *a.*

Pretest

Use the pretest on this page to assess students' ability to spell the lesson words.

 Have students use the study steps on page 6 to study any words they misspell in the pretest.

 You may wish to duplicate and send home the Home Activity Master on pages T251–T252.

Presenting the Page

Introducing the /ô/ Sound Write *August* and *morning* on the board. Say the words aloud, emphasizing the first vowel sound in each. Point out the slight difference when *r* follows /ô/. Then say the following word pairs and have students tap their foot when they hear /ô/:

pour–pear   quit–*quart*
behind–*before*   *autumn*–atom

As students prepare to sort the words, point out that /ô/ is often spelled as *au* and as *o* before *r* but is spelled as *a, oo,* or *ou* before *r* in some words that we often use.

Pronunciation Focus Write *popcorn* on the board and point out the two *o*'s in the word. Ask students to identify the sound of each (first *o*—/ŏ/, second *o*—/ô/). Point out that only one *o* in *popcorn* has the /ô/ sound.

Consonant Focus Write *autumn* on the board and ask what sound is heard at the end (/m/). Point out that the *n* is silent. Ask students to think of another word that ends with a silent *n,* such as *column.*

184

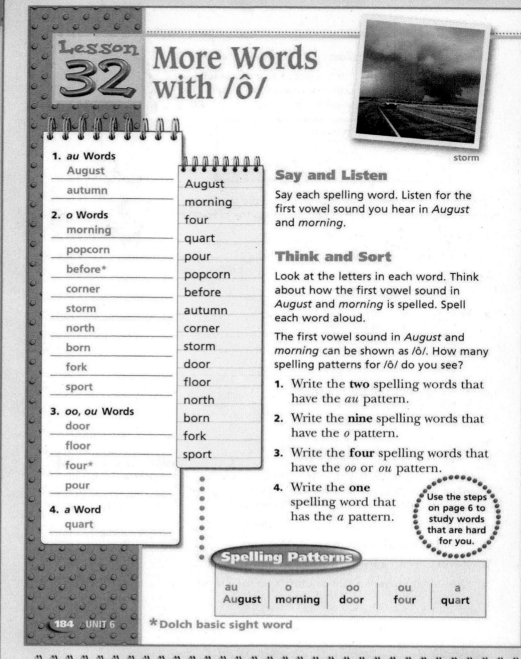

Lesson 32 More Words with /ô/

storm

1. au Words
August
autumn

2. o Words
morning
popcorn
before*
corner
storm
north
born
fork
sport

3. oo, ou Words
door
floor
four*
pour

4. a Word
quart

August
morning
four
quart
pour
popcorn
before
autumn
corner
storm
door
floor
north
born
fork
sport

Say and Listen

Say each spelling word. Listen for the first vowel sound you hear in *August* and *morning.*

Think and Sort

Look at the letters in each word. Think about how the first vowel sound in *August* and *morning* is spelled. Spell each word aloud.

The first vowel sound in *August* and *morning* can be shown as /ô/. How many spelling patterns for /ô/ do you see?

1. Write the **two** spelling words that have the *au* pattern.
2. Write the **nine** spelling words that have the *o* pattern.
3. Write the **four** spelling words that have the *oo* or *ou* pattern.
4. Write the **one** spelling word that has the *a* pattern.

Use the steps on page 6 to study words that are hard for you.

Spelling Patterns

au	o	oo	ou	a
August	morning	door	four	quart

184 UNIT 6   *Dolch basic sight word

Pretest

Say each lesson word, read the sentence, and then repeat the word. Have students write the words on separate paper.

1. **August** After July comes <u>August</u>.
2. **morning** We will leave in the <u>morning</u>.
3. **four** A year has <u>four</u> seasons.
4. **quart** Buy a <u>quart</u> of milk.
5. **pour** Please <u>pour</u> me some milk.
6. **popcorn** I love hot <u>popcorn</u>.
7. **before** Do your work <u>before</u> you play.
8. **autumn** Birds fly south in <u>autumn</u>.
9. **corner** Let's wait at the <u>corner</u>.
10. **storm** A <u>storm</u> is on the way.
11. **door** She closed the <u>door</u>.
12. **floor** Steve swept the <u>floor</u>.
13. **north** We drove <u>north</u>.
14. **born** I was <u>born</u> in June.
15. **fork** The <u>fork</u> goes at the right of the plate.
16. **sport** What is your favorite <u>sport</u>?

Additional Words for Enrichment

The following words can be used to meet the needs of on-level and above-level students:
important   explore   report   toward   warm   ignore

Spelling and Meaning

Clues Write the spelling word for each clue.

1. snack to eat at the movies   popcorn
2. spoon, knife, _____   fork
3. rain or snow and lots of wind   storm
4. where the walls in a room meet   corner
5. how to get milk into a glass   pour

Analogies Write the spelling word that completes each analogy.

6. *East* is to *west* as _____ north _____ is to *south*.
7. *Summer* is to *winter* as *spring* is to _____ autumn _____ .
8. *Evening* is to *dinner* as _____ morning _____ is to *breakfast*.
9. *Cool* is to *warm* as *after* is to _____ before _____ .
10. *Foot* is to *yard* as _____ quart _____ is to *gallon*.
11. *Above* is to *below* as *ceiling* is to _____ floor _____ .
12. *Lid* is to *jar* as _____ door _____ is to *house*.
13. *One* is to *two* as *three* is to _____ four _____ .
14. *Color* is to *blue* as _____ sport _____ is to *hockey*.
15. *Bird* is to *hatch* as *child* is to _____ born _____ .

Word Story Caesar Augustus was one of the greatest Roman emperors. *Augustus* meant "very great man." Caesar Augustus had the Romans name a month after him. This month still has his name. Write the spelling word that names this month.

16. _____ August _____

Family Tree: *north* Think about how the *north* words are alike in spelling and meaning. Then add another *north* word to the tree. A sample answer is shown.

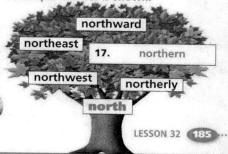

- northward
- northeast
- 17. _____ northern
- northwest
- northerly
- north

LESSON 32 **185**

HOME ACTIVITY MASTER p. T251

Unit 6 Spelling at Home

Dear Family of _____

During the next six weeks, your child will be learning to spell the following kinds of words:

- words with /ô/, as in *draw*
- words with /ou/, as in *house*
- words with /ir/, /âr/, or /îr/, as in *hear*, *hair*, and *fire*
- words with *-er* or *-est*

Here are some simple activities to do each week to help your child become a better speller.

Listening and Writing
Say the spelling words and have your child write them.

Spelling Strategy: Guess and Check
If your child is having difficulty spelling a word, encourage him or her to guess the spelling. Then ask your child to check the list at right or a dictionary to see if his or her guess is correct.

Games and Activities
Play Spelling Chunks. Have your child choose some of the spelling words. Write the words on a piece of paper. Leave a space below each word. With your child, study the words. Then separate each word into smaller parts so that it is easy to remember. Divide each word into the "chunks" we hear when the word is read aloud. An example is *pow/er*.

Write some of the spelling words on a piece of paper, leaving out some of the letters. Ask your child to complete each word. Taking turns, continue writing and completing as many spelling words as possible.

Using Spelling Words
Ask your child to write sentences that contain the spelling words. Then read the sentences with your child. Notice whether the sentences show that your child knows the meanings of the spelling words.

Lesson 31 Words with /ô/			
Work of _____			
frog	long	along	off
belong	strong	water	always
mall	tall	talk	walk
bought	brought	draw	because

Lesson 32 More Words with /ô/			
Work of _____			
autumn	August	born	fork
morning	sport	popcorn	storm
north	corner	before	door
floor	pour	four	quart

Lesson 33 Words with /ou/			
Work of _____			
hour	sound	ground	about
house	around	count	our
found	owl	down	power
brown	tower	town	flower

Lesson 34 Words with /ir/, /âr/, or /îr/			
Work of _____			
hear	dear	ear	near
year	here	deer	stairs
air	chair	hair	care
where	tire	fire	wire

Lesson 35 Words with *-er* or *-est*			
Work of _____			
stronger	strongest	taller	tallest
greater	greatest	longer	longest
sharper	sharpest	funnier	funniest
dirtier	dirtiest	hotter	hottest

Lesson 36   Unit 6 Review
Work of _____
Lesson 36 is a review of Lessons 31–35. Help your child practice all of the words from those lessons.

The highlighted area shows the Lesson 32 words, which students can share with family members. Spanish version available on page T252.

Proofreading Practice
- I dropped my fourk. *(fork)*
- Please pick it up off the flor. *(floor)*

Meeting Individual Needs

Auditory Learners
Have students work in pairs to practice spelling the lesson words. Have one student spell the word aloud for the partner to identify. Then have the partner spell the word aloud and write the word. Have students reverse roles and repeat the activity.

Spelling and Meaning

Day 2

Student Objectives
- To use meaning clues to identify and write lesson words
- To use etymology, meaning, and spelling to identify the word *August*
- To learn *north* words and analyze their spellings and meanings

Presenting the Page

Write the following Clues and Analogies examples on the board and model identifying the answers:

- the season after summer (*autumn*)
- *Pencil* is to *write* as _____ is to *eat*. (*fork*)

Word Story

Students may find it interesting to know that Caesar Augustus was not the only emperor of Rome named Augustus. All of the emperors after Julius Caesar, including Tiberius, Caligula, and Claudius, took the title *Augustus* to show their status and power. You may also wish to explain that although August is the eighth month on the calendar we use today, it was the sixth month of the ancient Roman calendar.

Family Tree: *north*

Students should see that the *north* words all contain *north*. Divide the class into four groups. Assign each group one word from the family tree to look up in a dictionary. Have groups share the meanings they find. Point out that the sound of *th* in *north* changes when the suffixes *-ern* and *-erly* are added. Guide students to understand that knowing how to spell *north* will help them spell words related to *north*.

185

Day 3

Student Objectives
- To use context to identify and write lesson words
- To identify stated main ideas and supporting details in a nonfiction selection

Presenting the Pages

Write the lesson words on the board. Then read the selection aloud, pausing for students to identify and write each missing word. As each word is used, cross it off the list to help students narrow their choices. Alternatively, have students work independently to read the selection silently and write the missing words. Suggest that students read the completed selection with a partner to check their work.

Discuss the meaning of "break in" in paragraph 2 ("to prepare something new for use or wear"). Explain that new boots are often stiff and need to be made softer and more flexible for hiking.

Meeting Individual Needs

ESOL
The lesson words *pour, four, popcorn, corner, door, floor, north,* and *fork* are concrete words whose meanings can be conveyed through demonstration of the action (as for *pour*) or through pairing each word with a corresponding object. Use these techniques to teach the meanings of the words. Invite speakers of other languages to repeat the words, use each word to identify the corresponding action or object, and write the words.

Use each spelling word once to complete the selection.

Happy Hiking

Hiking is a great _____sport_____ for families to enjoy together. Here are some easy tips to make hiking safe and fun for everyone.

Find and wear

good hiking boots. Remember that your legs and feet will be doing a lot of work. Break in brand new boots _____before_____ going hiking. Wear them around on your living room _____floor_____ first so that your feet won't hurt on the trail later.

Before you go out your front _____door_____ and head for the trail, make sure you and your family members pack plenty of supplies. You should also carry water. Each person will need one _____quart_____ of water for each _____four_____ or five miles you plan to hike.

Pack lots of healthful snacks as well. Fruit and granola bars make good snacks. Freshly popped and unsalted _____popcorn_____ is also good. You won't need a _____fork_____ or spoon to eat it, either.

186   UNIT 6

Spelling Strategy

Using the Spelling Table
Remind students that a spelling table is helpful for finding the correct way to spell words they are unsure of. Invite students to determine the correct way to spell *quart* by using the /ô/ patterns in the Spelling Table on page 213. First, have them find the pronunciation symbol for the /ô/ sound in the Spelling Table. Then have students write the word, using a pattern, and look for that word in the Spelling Dictionary. If the word is not in the Spelling Dictionary, they should try another pattern for the word, look up that spelling, and continue in the same manner until they find the correct spelling.

/ô/ Spelling	Test Spelling	Found in Spelling Dictionary?
o	quort	no
oa	quoart	no
oo	quoort	no
ou	quourt	no
ough	quoughrt	no
a	quart	yes

You and your family should also protect yourselves from the sun. Wear a hat with a wide brim. Remember to put on lots of sunblock. You can get a sunburn on cool days in the spring or in the __autumn__ as well as on hot
9
summer days in __August__ . You should also take a
10
raincoat in case rain starts to __pour__ . Remember
11
that a __storm__ can blow in at any time.
12

Learn how to use a compass. A compass needle always points to the __north__ . Keep in mind, too, that
13
in the __morning__ the sun is always in the east. If you
14
remember these two things, you will not get lost.

Be kind to any animals you see. Never back a wild animal into a __corner__ . Make noises to let animals know
15
where you are. It is especially important to avoid disturbing baby animals that have just been __born__ . Angry
16
animal parents can be dangerous!

Finally, stay with your family. Never go off by yourself. Stay together and help one another. Remembering these tips can help make your family hiking trip the best ever!

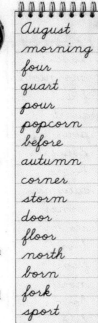

August
morning
four
quart
pour
popcorn
before
autumn
corner
storm
door
floor
north
born
fork
sport

LESSON 32 **187**

ACTIVITY MASTER p. T279

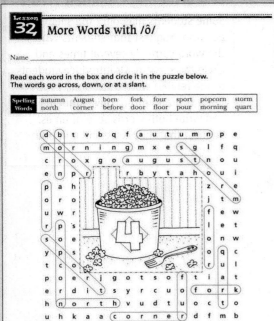

Lesson 32 More Words with /ô/

Name _____

Read each word in the box and circle it in the puzzle below.
The words go across, down, or at a slant.

Spelling Words	autumn	August	born	fork	four	sport	popcorn	storm
	north	corner	before	door	floor	pour	morning	quart

ADDITIONAL PRACTICE

You may wish to copy and distribute the Activity Master on page T279 as additional practice for Lesson 32.

Proofreading Practice
- We paddled naurth on our trip. *(north)*
- The foure of us love boating. *(four)*

Reading Comprehension

Once students have completed the pages, remind them that the main idea of a passage or a paragraph is the most important idea and that supporting details are pieces of information that tell more about the main idea. Model identifying the stated main idea and supporting details in paragraph 2 on page 186 (the first sentence tells the main idea; the other sentences contain supporting details). You may wish to point out how each supporting idea relates to the main idea.

Invite pairs or small groups to find the main idea and supporting details for paragraph 4 on page 186 and paragraph 3 on page 187. Suggest that students create webs to show main ideas and supporting details.

Cooperative Learning Activity

Students can work in pairs to assess their progress. Have one student give a clue for a word and the partner identify the word and write it. Then have students reverse roles and repeat the activity. When students are finished, have them compare their performance on this midweek activity to their performance on the pretest. Tell them to note which words they still need to study.

Day 4

Student Objectives
- To write an expository paragraph, using lesson words
- To proofread a paragraph for spelling, capitalization, and punctuation

Presenting the Page

Brainstorm with students different kinds of outdoor trips, such as such as hiking, boating, bicycling, and rafting. Encourage students who choose to write about hiking to refer to "Happy Hiking" on pages 186–187. Suggest ways for students to use lesson words in their paragraph.

Ask a volunteer to read the Proofreading directions and paragraph aloud. Then encourage students to work in pairs to complete the activity. Suggest focusing on one type of error at a time or working backward from the end to the beginning to spot spelling errors more easily.

Meeting Individual Needs

ESOL

Some speakers of Asian languages may have difficulty with the lesson words because of unfamiliarity with /ô/. Provide ample opportunities for these students to hear and say the words. First, say a lesson word and have students repeat it. Then, use the lesson word in a simple sentence and ask students to repeat the sentence. Finally, have students write the word and underline the letters that spell /ô/.

Spelling and Writing

august
morning
four
quart
pour
popcorn
before
autumn
corner
storm
door
floor
north
born
fork
sport

Write to the Point

Write a paragraph that tells younger children things that will help them prepare for a hiking or other outdoor trip. Tell what to bring and how to be safe. Try to use spelling words from this lesson. **Paragraphs will vary.**

Use the strategies on page 7 when you are not sure how to spell a word.

Proofreading

Proofread the paragraph below. Use proofreading marks to correct five spelling mistakes, three capitalization mistakes, and two punctuation mistakes.

Proofreading Marks
- ◯ spell correctly
- ≡ capitalize
- ⊙ add period

sport
Hiking is a great (spoort). It can be a lot of fun.

here are some things to remember when you go⊙
≡

Before
Make sure you are wearing good shoes. (Befour) you

go, put water and snacks in a backpack⊙ Trail mix and
popcorn
(popcawrn) are good snacks. also, bring rain gear in
≡
storm
case there is a (stourm). It's a good idea to start
morning
early in the (morening), when you have lots of energy.

As you hike along, remember to stop and rest⊙ you will
≡
have more fun if you don't get too tired.

Proofreading Practice
- Leaves fall in autum. *(autumn)*
- I'll paur you a glass of water. *(pour)*

Correcting Common Errors

Some students may omit the silent *n* in *autumn*. Suggest that students write the word correctly several times and circle the silent *n*. Or introduce students to the related word *autumnal*, in which the *n* is pronounced. Have students say and write both words several times. Suggest that they circle the *n* in both words.

Dictionary Skills

Alphabetical Order Many words begin with the same letter or the same two letters. To put these words in alphabetical order, use the third letter of each word. Look at the two words below.

train   trim

Both words start with the letters *tr*. To put them in alphabetical order, look at the third letter. The third letter in *train* is *a*. The third letter in *trim* is *i*. In the alphabet, *a* comes before *i*, so *train* comes before *trim*.

In each list below, the words begin with the same two letters. Look at the third letter of each word. Then write the words in alphabetical order.

1. autumn   aunt   August
   - August
   - aunt
   - autumn

2. porch   point   pour
   - point
   - porch
   - pour

3. fond   four   foggy
   - foggy
   - fond
   - four

4. money   morning   moon
   - money
   - moon
   - morning

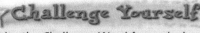 Challenge Yourself

Write the Challenge Word for each clue. Check the Spelling Dictionary to see if you are right. Then use separate paper to write sentences showing that you understand the meaning of each Challenge Word.
Sentences will vary.

> **Challenge Words**
> ornament   wharf
> coarse   corridor

5. You can expect to see water and boats at this.   wharf

6. You walk through this to get to another part of a building.
   corridor

7. This is a kind of decoration.   ornament

8. This word describes things that are not smooth.   coarse

Posttest

Dictate the following sentences. Have students use separate paper to write the sentences and underline the lesson words.

1. Please <u>pour</u> a <u>quart</u> of milk.
2. We love to make <u>popcorn</u> in <u>autumn</u>.
3. The <u>door</u> is on the <u>north</u> side of the house.
4. She was <u>born</u> in <u>August</u>.
5. The <u>storm</u> will come <u>before</u> <u>morning</u>.
6. What is on the <u>floor</u> in the <u>corner</u>?
7. Who eats soup with a <u>fork</u>?
8. Her <u>four</u> friends like the same <u>sport</u>.

Enrichment Activity

Have students form teams to play a story titles game. Ask students to use as many of the Lessons 31 and 32 words as they can to write titles for stories, such as "Because a Frog Came Along." After a set amount of time, have teams share their titles and point out the /ô/ words and spelling patterns in each.

> ### Student Objectives
> - To write words in alphabetical order
> - To study the spellings and meanings of the Challenge Words
> - To take a posttest on the lesson words

Presenting the Page

This activity focuses on words beginning with the same two letters; hence, students need to alphabetize by the third letter. Have students look at the three words in each list and cross out the beginning letters that are the same. Tell them that they can then use the third letter to alphabetize the words. Point out to students that knowing how to alphabetize words helps them locate words in a dictionary.

Challenge Yourself

> To introduce the Challenge Words, write the following on the board:
> ornament   wharf
> coarse   corridor
>
> Read the words aloud and have students repeat them after you. Have students identify the /ô/ spelling pattern in each word (*ornament, wharf,* and *corridor* have the o and a patterns featured in the lesson; *coarse* introduces a different pattern, *oa*).

Posttest

Use the posttest on this page to assess students' ability to spell the lesson words.

Words with /ou/

Student Objectives
- To take a pretest on the lesson words
- To spell the lesson words aloud
- To sort and write the lesson words according to the spelling patterns *ou* and *ow*

Pretest

Use the pretest on this page to assess students' ability to spell the lesson words.

 Have students use the study steps on page 6 to study any words they misspell in the pretest.

 You may wish to duplicate and send home the Home Activity Master on pages T251–T252.

Presenting the Page

Introducing the /ou/ Sound
Write *out* on the board and read the word aloud, emphasizing the /ou/ sound. Say the following word pairs, having students snap their fingers each time they hear a word with /ou/:

done–*down*   house–home
sound–sand   tin–*town*

Pronunciation Focus Remind students that homophones are words that sound exactly alike but have different spellings and meanings. Have students identify and define the two lesson words that are homophones (*our, hour*). Point out that the *h* at the beginning of *hour* is silent.

Consonant Focus Read aloud the words *sound* and *around*, focusing on the final *nd* blend. Ask students to identify other lesson words that end with this blend (*ground, found*).

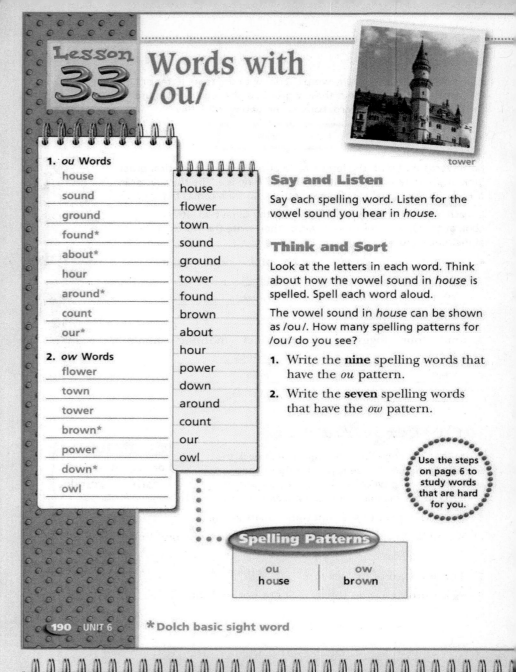

Lesson 33 Words with /ou/

tower

1. *ou* Words
- house
- sound
- ground
- found*
- about*
- hour
- around*
- count
- our*

2. *ow* Words
- flower
- town
- tower
- brown*
- power
- down*
- owl

house
flower
town
sound
ground
tower
found
brown
about
hour
power
down
around
count
our
owl

Say and Listen
Say each spelling word. Listen for the vowel sound you hear in *house*.

Think and Sort
Look at the letters in each word. Think about how the vowel sound in *house* is spelled. Spell each word aloud.

The vowel sound in *house* can be shown as /ou/. How many spelling patterns for /ou/ do you see?

1. Write the **nine** spelling words that have the *ou* pattern.

2. Write the **seven** spelling words that have the *ow* pattern.

Use the steps on page 6 to study words that are hard for you.

Spelling Patterns

ou	ow
h**ou**se	br**ow**n

*Dolch basic sight word

Pretest

Say each lesson word, read the sentence, and then repeat the word. Have students write the words on separate paper.

1. **house** Our <u>house</u> is blue.
2. **flower** A rose is a kind of <u>flower</u>.
3. **town** Our <u>town</u> is large.
4. **sound** Do you hear a <u>sound</u>?
5. **ground** Plant the seed in the <u>ground</u>.
6. **tower** The castle had a <u>tower</u>.
7. **found** I <u>found</u> a pretty shell.
8. **brown** She has a <u>brown</u> cat.
9. **about** The book is <u>about</u> whales.
10. **hour** Meet me in an <u>hour</u>.
11. **power** Moving a piano takes <u>power</u>.
12. **down** I walked <u>down</u> the stairs.
13. **around** The dog ran <u>around</u> the yard.
14. **count** Can you <u>count</u> all the stars?
15. **our** We're cooking <u>our</u> dinner.
16. **owl** The hoot <u>owl</u> sat in the tree.

Additional Words for Enrichment

The following words can be used to meet the needs of on-level and above-level students:
noun crowded towel powerful shower somehow

Spelling and Meaning

Hink Pinks Hink pinks are pairs of rhyming words that have funny meanings. Read each clue. Write the spelling word that completes each hink pink.

1. a place for mice to live   mouse ___house___
2. a beagle's bark   hound ___sound___
3. the time to bake   flour ___hour___
4. rain falling on a tall building   ___tower___ shower
5. a night bird's loud sound   ___owl___ howl

Letter Scramble Unscramble the letters in parentheses. Then write the spelling word to complete the phrase.

6. (wodn)   run ___down___ the hill
7. (repow)   ___power___ from electricity
8. (boaut)   books for and ___about___ children
9. (wolfer)   a ___flower___ in a vase
10. (ungord)   on the ___ground___ or in the air
11. (dnofu)   lost and ___found___
12. (nuoct)   ___count___ to ten
13. (wonrb)   ___brown___ hair and eyes
14. (ruodna)   in, ___around___, and through
15. (rou)   her, their, and ___our___

Word Story In Old English a fence or a wall was called a *toun*. A fence or wall became a sign that people lived nearby. The place where people lived became known as a *toun*. Write the spelling word that comes from *toun*.

16. ___town___

Family Tree: *power* Think about how the *power* words are alike in spelling and meaning. Then add another *power* word to the tree. A sample answer is shown.

powerless

powerfully

powered

17. powerful

powers

power

LESSON 33 **191**

HOME ACTIVITY MASTER p. T251

Unit 6 **Spelling at Home**

Dear Family of _____
During the next six weeks, your child will be learning to spell the following kinds of words:
• words with /ô/, as in *draw*
• words with /ou/, as in *house*
• words with /îr/, /âr/, or /ir/, as in *hear, hair,* and *fire*
• words with *-er* or *-est*

Here are some simple activities to do each week to help your child become a better speller.

Listening and Writing
Say the spelling words and have your child write them.

Spelling Strategy: Guess and Check
If your child is having difficulty spelling a word, encourage him or her to guess the spelling. Then ask your child to check the list at right or a dictionary to see if his or her guess is correct.

Games and Activities
Play Spelling Chunks. Have your child choose some of the spelling words. Write the words on a piece of paper. Leave a space below each word. With your child, study the words. Then separate each word into smaller parts so that it is easy to remember. Divide each word into the "chunks" we hear when the word is read aloud. An example is *pow/er*.
Write some of the spelling words on a piece of paper, leaving out some of the letters. Ask your child to complete each word. Taking turns, continue writing and completing as many spelling words as possible.

Using Spelling Words
Ask your child to write sentences that contain the spelling words. Then read the sentences with your child. Notice whether the sentences show that your child knows the meanings of the spelling words.

Lesson 31 Words with /ô/
Week of _____
frog   long   along   off
belong   strong   water   always
mall   tall   talk   walk
bought   brought   draw   because

Lesson 32 More Words with /ô/
Week of _____
autumn   August   born   fork
morning   sport   popcorn   storm
north   corner   before   door
floor   pour   four   quart

Lesson 33 Words with /ou/
Week of _____
hour   sound   ground   about
house   around   count   our
found   owl   down   power
brown   tower   town   flower

Lesson 34 Words with /îr/, /âr/, or /ir/
Week of _____
hear   dear   ear   near
year   here   deer   stairs
air   chair   hair   care
where   tire   fire   wire

Lesson 35 Words with -er or -est
Week of _____
stronger strongest taller   tallest
greater   greatest longer   longest
sharper   sharpest funnier   funniest
dirtier   dirtiest hotter   hottest

Lesson 36 Unit 6 Review
Week of _____
Lesson 56 is a review of Lessons 31–35. Help your child practice all of the words from those lessons.

The highlighted area shows the Lesson 33 words, which students can share with family members. Spanish version available on page T252.

Proofreading Practice
• Meet me at the bus stop in an our. (hour)
• The bus stop is doun the street. (down)

Meeting Individual Needs

Visual Learners
To help students visualize the spellings of the lesson words, write the spelling patterns *ou* and *ow* on the board. Have students write the lesson words on strips of paper and underline the spelling patterns. Then have them place each word under the correct spelling pattern on the board.

Spelling and Meaning

Student Objectives
• To use meaning clues to identify and write lesson words
• To use etymology, meaning, and spelling to identify the word *town*
• To learn *power* words and analyze their spellings and meanings

Presenting the Page

Write the following Hink Pinks and Letter Scramble examples on the board and model identifying the answers:

• a beagle that you find _____ hound (*found*)
• (rohu) drove sixty miles an _____ (*hour*)

Word Story

You may wish to explain that the word *town* is related to the French *ville,* which means "city" or "town." Ask students to think of or find town names that end in *-ville*. *Ville* comes from the Latin *villa,* which meant "farm" or "country house." We still use the word *villa* to describe a country house. *Village* also comes from *villa* and means "a small town."

Family Tree: *power*

Students should notice that all the *power* words contain *power.* Discuss the meanings of the words, encouraging students to look up definitions if necessary. Help students understand that the suffix *-less* changes *power* from a noun to an adjective. It also changes the meaning of the word: *-less* means "without," so *powerless* means "without power." Guide students to understand that knowing how to spell *power* will help them spell words related to *power.*

191

Student Objectives
- To use context to identify and write lesson words
- To identify facts and opinions in a nonfiction selection

Presenting the Pages

Read the first paragraph aloud, pausing for the missing word. Point out that the selection contains clues to help students determine which word to use. For example, in the first sentence the phrase "Of all the birds" is a clue that the missing word is *owl*. Continue the discussion by exploring the clues for other words, such as "Owls come in several colors," "Snowy owls are white," and "in color" for *brown*. Have students work independently or in pairs to complete the activity.

Explain that the word *rodents* in the second paragraph refers to small animals with strong front teeth that can gnaw hard objects. Mice, rats, and squirrels are rodents.

Meeting Individual Needs

ESOL
To help students understand the meanings of the lesson words, use total physical response. Write the word *owl* on the board and say, "Show me an owl." Lead students in acting like owls by opening your eyes wide, slowly moving your head back and forth, and hooting. As you perform the actions, point to the word, then spell it aloud. Repeat the process with other words.

Spelling in Context
Use each spelling word once to complete the selection.

Owls

Of all the birds, the ___owl___ is one of the easiest to recognize. An owl has a large, round head. It has big eyes that look straight ahead.

Owls come in several colors. Snowy owls are white. Owls of the deep rain forest are often dark ___brown___ in color. At last ___count___, there were ___about___ 130 different kinds of owls. Scientists think that some owls are in danger of becoming extinct. They feel it is ___our___ duty to protect the owl. Owls are not only beautiful. They are also useful to people. Owls help farmers. They eat rodents that hurt crops.

Owls can be ___found___ almost everywhere in the world. Some owls make their home in a tree or in a barn. Some

▲ long-eared owl

◄ crested owl

192 UNIT 6

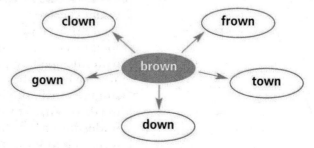

Spelling Strategy

Rhyming Helper
Remind students that they can use a rhyming helper to remember the spelling of a word. Write *brown* on the board. Invite volunteers to contribute rhyming helpers, reminding them if necessary that a rhyming helper must not only rhyme but also must have the same spelling pattern as the target word. Write students' ideas in web fashion around *brown*.

```
        clown              frown

  gown          brown           town

              down
```

Then write the lesson words *found, ground, sound,* and *around* on the board. Point out that any could be used as a rhyming helper for another.

owls have even nested on top of a water ___tower___
7

near a busy ___town___.
8

Most owls hunt for food at night. Their eyes are large,
so they see well in the dark. Owls also have very good
hearing. Using their sharp hearing and keen sight, they fly
above the ___ground___, looking for small animals
9

such as mice and rats. Owls are meat eaters. They never
nibble on leaves or the petals of a ___flower___.
10

An owl can swoop ___down___ without making
11

a ___sound___. Once caught, an animal has little
12

chance of getting away from the ___power___ of the
13

owl's grip. In one ___hour___ an owl can catch two
14

or three mice.

Owls are as good at catching mice as cats are. But owls
do not make good ___house___ pets. Owls need
15

room to fly ___around___. The best way to enjoy owls
16

is to watch them in the wild.

house
flower
town
sound
ground
tower
found
brown
about
hour
power
down
around
count
our
owl

snowy owl ▶

▲ great grey owl

LESSON 33 **193**

ACTIVITY MASTER p. T280

Lesson **33** Words with /ou/

Name _____

Use the words in the box to solve the puzzle below. Some letters are given.

Spelling Words

count	our
down	flower
owl	ground
tower	found
hour	around
power	about
brown	sound
town	house

ADDITIONAL PRACTICE

You may wish to copy and distribute the Activity Master on page T280 as additional practice for Lesson 33.

Proofreading Practice
• Please cownt to fifty.
(count)
• I see an animal track on the grownd. (ground)

Reading Comprehension

After students have completed the pages, point out that the selection is nonfiction. Tell students that nonfiction writing is writing that is based on facts, or statements that can be proven true, such as "A horse has four legs." Tell students to find facts in the selection and to underline two of them. Have students share their facts with the class.

Direct students' attention to the paragraph 2 sentence "Owls are not only beautiful" and help students distinguish this as an opinion.

Cooperative Learning Activity

Students can work in pairs to assess their spelling progress. Give students index cards and have them write each lesson word on a separate card. Then have them dictate the words to each other. After students have spelled the words and checked the spellings, have them compare their performance on this midweek activity with that on the pretest and note which words they still need to study. Conclude by asking students to sort the cards by spelling pattern for /ou/.

Day 4

Student Objectives
- To write an expository paragraph, using lesson words
- To proofread a journal entry for spelling, capitalization, and unnecessary words

Presenting the Page

To help students generate ideas for writing, assist them in brainstorming characteristics of an animal that makes a good pet, such as a cat, dog, or fish. Encourage them to look through the list of lesson words and use the words in their writing.

Read the journal entry aloud for students before they begin proofreading. Suggest that students first read the entry to find spelling errors, read it again to find capitalization mistakes, and read it a third time to find the unnecessary words. Have students complete the activity independently.

Meeting Individual Needs

ESOL

Some Spanish-speaking students may use *au* instead of *ow* or *ou* to spell the lesson words because the /ou/ sound in Spanish is spelled *au*. Encourage students to create a collection of words with the correct spellings for /ou/. Have students cut words from magazines or copy them from the spelling book or other resources. Reinforce the spelling by having students underline the letters that make the /ou/ sound.

Write to the Point

house
flower
town
sound
ground
tower
found
brown
about
hour
power
down
around
count
our
owl

An owl does not make a very good pet. Owls need space to fly and look for food. However, many other animals do make good pets. Write a paragraph telling which animal you think makes the best pet and why. Try to use spelling words from this lesson. **Paragraphs will vary.**

Use the strategies on page 7 when you are not sure how to spell a word.

Proofreading

Proofread the journal entry below. Use proofreading marks to correct five spelling mistakes, three capitalization mistakes, and two unnecessary words.

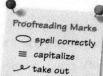

Proofreading Marks
- ◯ spell correctly
- ≡ capitalize
- ℯ take out

May 14

Today was a wild day! Dad and I heard a
strange (sownd) we looked around the inside of
the (howse) Then we looked outside. Finally we
climbed up on the roof. We found an (owel) stuck
in our ~~our~~ chimney. Dad got his gloves and a
fishing net. it took us an hour to free the big
(broun) bird, but it seemed all right as it flew
away. I can't wait to ~~to~~ tell chris (abuot) it.

(corrections above text: sound, house, owl, brown, about)

194 UNIT 6

Proofreading Practice
- The towir stands high on the hill. (tower)
- A pretty flowur grows nearby. (flower)

Correcting Common Errors

Students may have difficulty spelling lesson words with the /ər/ ending. Some students may spell the er at the end of *tower*, *flower*, and *power* as *ar*, *ir*, or *ur*. Students who make this error can practice the correct spelling by writing the words, dividing them into syllables, saying the words, and circling the e in *er*.

Using the Spelling Table

A spelling table can help you find the spelling of a word in a dictionary. Suppose you are not sure how the vowel sound in *should* is spelled. You can use a spelling table to find the different spellings for the sound. First, find the pronunciation symbol for the sound. Then read the first spelling listed for /o͝o/ and look up *shoold* in the dictionary. Look for each spelling in the dictionary until you find the correct one.

Sound	Spellings	Examples
/o͝o/	oo ou u u_e	book, could, pull, sure

Write the correct spelling for each word. Use the Spelling Table on page 213 and the Spelling Dictionary. One word has two correct spellings.

1. /brôth/   broth
2. /mān tān´/   maintain
3. /ăd mīr´/   admire
4. /dōm/   dome
5. /fīr/   fire
6. /wīr/   wire
7. /stärch/   starch
8. /dîr/   deer   dear

Challenge Yourself

What do you think each Challenge Word means? Check the Spelling Dictionary to see if you are right. Then use separate paper to write sentences showing that you understand the meaning of each Challenge Word. **Definitions and sentences will vary.**

Challenge Words

- doubtful
- devour
- bough
- wildflower

9. It is **doubtful** that an owl would be a good house pet.
10. A hungry owl will **devour** a big meal.
11. A little owl sat on the **bough** of a tree.
12. An owl would rather eat a mouse than a **wildflower**.

LESSON 33   **195**

Posttest

Dictate the following sentences. Have students use separate paper to write the sentences and underline the lesson words.

1. The <u>tower</u> is above the <u>ground</u>.
2. I picked a pretty <u>flower</u>.
3. The bird flew <u>around</u> the <u>house</u>.
4. The <u>owl</u> made a loud <u>sound</u>.
5. Please visit <u>our town</u>.
6. The sun goes <u>down</u> in an <u>hour</u>.
7. I <u>found</u> a book <u>about</u> rocks.
8. That <u>brown</u> car has a lot of <u>power</u>.
9. The boy will <u>count</u> the money.

Enrichment Activity

Students may enjoy pairing up to play spelling tic-tac-toe. In this version of the game, they should play with *ou* and *ow* words rather than *x*'s and *o*'s. The student who correctly writes three *ou* or *ow* words in a row vertically, horizontally, or diagonally, wins.

Day 5

Student Objectives

- To use the Spelling Table and Spelling Dictionary to locate correct spellings
- To study the spellings and meanings of the Challenge Words
- To take a posttest on lesson words

Presenting the Page

Point out to students that the Sound column of the Spelling Table contains pronunciation symbols for sounds. Explain that the symbols are in alphabetical order in the Spelling Table. Suggest that students use separate paper to spell each word as they use the Spelling Table's possible spellings for sounds.

Challenge Yourself

Introduce the Challenge Words by writing the following on the board:

   doubtful   devour
   bough   wildflower

Say the words aloud and have students repeat them after you. Point out that silent *b* in *doubtful* and silent *gh* in *bough*. Have students identify the /ou/ spelling pattern in each Challenge Word (*doubtful*, *devour*, and *bough* have the *ou* pattern; *wildflower* has the *ow* pattern). Have students write what they think each word means, look up the words in the Spelling Dictionary, and write the correct definitions. Then have students compare the two definitions.

Posttest

Use the posttest on this page to assess students' ability to spell the lesson words.

Words with /îr/, /âr/, or /īr/

Student Objectives
- To take a pretest on the lesson words
- To spell the lesson words aloud
- To sort and write the lesson words according to the /îr/, /âr/, and /īr/ sounds

Pretest

Use the pretest on this page to assess students' ability to spell the lesson words.

Study Steps Have students use the study steps on page 6 to study any words they misspell in the pretest.

You may wish to duplicate and send home the Home Activity Master on pages T251–T252.

Presenting the Page

Introducing the /îr/, /âr/, and /īr/ Sounds Write *here* on the board. Say the word aloud and then the /îr/ sounds. Then say the following pairs of words and have students raise their hand when they hear /îr/:

deer–door   never–*near*

Use the same process for /âr/, as in *care*, and for /īr/, as in *tire*:

/âr/: cheer–*chair*   hat–*hair*
/īr/: wear–*wire*   *fire*–four

Pronunciation Focus Write *hear* and *here* on the board and ask students what kind of words they are (homophones). Ask students to look for two other lesson words that are homophones (*deer, dear*).

Consonant Focus Make sure students understand that the *c* and *h* in *chair* have a sound, /ch/, that is totally different from the individual sounds of *c* and *h*. Help students think of other words that begin with /ch/ such as *church, chunk,* and *chill.*

Words with /îr/, /âr/, or /īr/

deer

1. /îr/ Words
near
hear
deer
ear
year
here*
dear

2. /âr/ Words
care
where*
stairs
chair
air
hair

3. /īr/ Words
fire
wire
tire

near	
care	
fire	
where	
hear	
wire	
stairs	
deer	
ear	
year	
tire	
here	
dear	
chair	
air	
hair	

Say and Listen

The spelling words for this lesson contain the /îr/, /âr/, and /īr/ sounds that you hear in *near, care,* and *fire.* Say the spelling words. Listen for the /îr/, /âr/, and /īr/ sounds.

Think and Sort

Look at the letters in each word. Think about how the /îr/, /âr/, or /īr/ sounds are spelled. Spell each word aloud.

1. Write the **seven** /îr/ spelling words. Circle the letters that spell /îr/ in each word.

2. Write the **six** /âr/ spelling words. Circle the letters that spell /âr/ in each word.

3. Write the **three** /īr/ spelling words. Circle the letters that spell /īr/ in each word.

Use the steps on page 6 to study words that are hard for you.

Spelling Patterns

/îr/			/âr/			/īr/
eer	ear	ere	are	air	ere	ire
deer	near	here	care	chair	where	fire

*Dolch basic sight word

Pretest

Say each lesson word, read the sentence, and then repeat the word. Have students write the words on separate paper.

1. **near** Sit near the front.
2. **care** A puppy needs good care.
3. **fire** Dad made a fire at camp.
4. **where** I know where he went.
5. **hear** Do you hear a noise?
6. **wire** He fixed the broken wire.
7. **stairs** Climb up the stairs.
8. **deer** The deer ran quickly.
9. **ear** He whispered in my ear.
10. **year** In what year were you born?
11. **tire** My bike has a flat tire.
12. **here** Let's stop here.
13. **dear** She is my dear friend.
14. **chair** This is a soft chair.
15. **air** The air smells fresh.
16. **hair** He has curly hair.

Additional Words for Enrichment

The following words can be used to meet the needs of on-level and above-level students:

cheer   appear   beware   admire   entire

Synonyms Write the spelling word that is a synonym of the underlined word.

1. Look at the long <u>fur</u> on that dog!

hair

2. These <u>steps</u> go to the attic.

stairs

3. Don't trip over that <u>cord</u>.

wire

4. The Rileys are <u>loved</u> family friends.

dear

Clues Write the spelling word for each clue.

5. You breathe this.

air

6. This animal can have antlers.

deer

7. When you listen, you do this.

hear

8. If you are concerned, you do this.

care

9. You hear with this.

ear

10. This equals 12 months.

year

11. This means the opposite of *far*.

near

12. This is a question word.

where

13. A car should have a spare one.

tire

14. Matches can start this.

fire

15. This means the opposite of *there*.

here

Word Story One spelling word started as the Greek word *cathedra*. *Cathedra* meant "seat." The French changed it to *chaiere*. The English changed it, too. Write the word.

16. _____ chair

Family Tree: *near* Think about how the *near* words are alike in spelling and meaning. Then add another *near* word to the tree. A sample answer is shown.

nearer
nearly
17. nearest
nearness
nearing
nearby
near

LESSON 34 **197**

HOME ACTIVITY MASTER p. T251

Unit 6 **Spelling at Home**

Dear Family of _____,
During the next six weeks, your child will be learning to spell the following kinds of words:

- words with /ô/, as in *draw*
- words with /ou/, as in *house*
- words with /îr/, /är/, or /âr/, as in *hear*, *hair*, and *tire*
- words with *-er* or *-est*

Here are some simple activities to do each week to help your child become a better speller.

🔲 **Listening and Writing**
Say the spelling words and have your child write them.

🔲 **Spelling Strategy: Guess and Check**
If your child is having difficulty spelling a word, encourage him or her to guess the spelling. Then ask your child to check the list at right or a dictionary to see if his or her guess is correct.

🔲 **Games and Activities**
Play Spelling Chunks. Have your child choose some of the spelling words. Write the words on a piece of paper. Leave a space below each word. With your child, study the words. Then separate each word into smaller parts so that it is easy to remember. Divide each word into the "chunks" we hear when the word is read aloud. An example is *paw/er*.

Write some of the spelling words on a piece of paper, leaving out some of the letters. Ask your child to complete each word. Taking turns, continue writing and completing as many spelling words as possible.

🔲 **Using Spelling Words**
Ask your child to write sentences that contain the spelling words. Then read the sentences with your child. Notice whether the sentences show that your child knows the meanings of the spelling words.

Lesson 31 Words with /ô/
Week of _____
frog / long / along / off
belong / strong / water / always
mall / tall / talk / walk
bought / brought / draw / because

Lesson 32 More Words with /ô/
Week of _____
autumn / August / born / fork
morning / sport / popcorn / storm
north / corner / before / door
floor / pour / four / quart

Lesson 33 Words with /ou/
Week of _____
hour / sound / ground / about
house / around / count / our
found / owl / down / power
brown / tower / town / flower

Lesson 34 Words with /îr/, /är/, or /âr/
Week of _____
hear / dear / ear / near
year / here / deer / stairs
air / chair / hair / care
where / tire / fire / wire

Lesson 35 Words with -er or -est
Week of _____
stronger / strongest / taller / tallest
greater / greatest / longer / longest
sharper / sharpest / funnier / funniest
dirtier / dirtiest / hotter / hottest

Lesson 36 Unit 6 Review
Week of _____
Lesson 36 is a review of Lessons 31–35. Help your child practice all of the words from those lessons.

The highlighted area shows the Lesson 34 words, which students can share with family members. Spanish version available on page T252.

Proofreading Practice
- Did you heer the news? (*hear*)
- A hero put out a large fir. (*fire*)

Meeting Individual Needs

Auditory Learners
Students who learn best by listening will have difficulty discerning the homophones simply by their sounds, because words like *hear* and *here* sound exactly alike. Have these students use the homophones to write sentences. Suggest that they read the sentences aloud to a partner. The partner should then spell each homophone aloud. Have students reverse roles so that each one can practice spelling the homophones.

Day 2

Student Objectives
- To use meaning clues to identify and write lesson words
- To use etymology, meaning, and spelling to identify the word *chair*
- To learn *near* words and analyze their spellings and meanings

Presenting the Page

Write the following Synonyms and Clues examples on the board and model identifying the answers. Remind students that synonyms are words that have the same meaning.

- They live <u>by</u> us. (*near*)
- This grows on your head. (*hair*)

Word Story

Write *cathedra* and *chair* on the board and invite students to compare the spellings. Explain that long ago *cathedra* was used to refer to a throne, or seat of power, held by an official or other important person, such as a teacher.

Family Tree: *near*

Students should see that the *near* words all contain *near*. Divide the class into five groups and assign each group a word related to *near*. Have each group find the meaning of their word in a dictionary and share it with the class. Point out that adding *by* to *near* makes it a compound word. Guide students to understand that knowing how to spell *near* will help them spell related words.

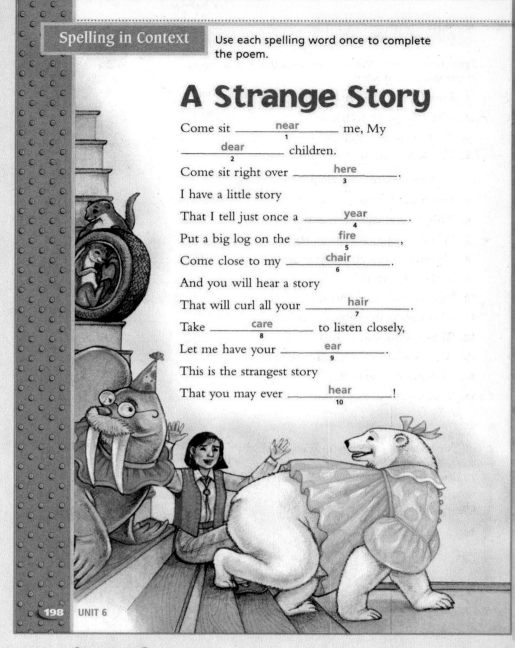

Use each spelling word once to complete the poem.

A Strange Story

Come sit _____near_____ me, My
1
_____dear_____ children.
2
Come sit right over _____here_____.
3
I have a little story
That I tell just once a _____year_____.
4
Put a big log on the _____fire_____,
5
Come close to my _____chair_____.
6
And you will hear a story
That will curl all your _____hair_____
7
Take _____care_____ to listen closely,
8
Let me have your _____ear_____.
9
This is the strangest story
That you may ever _____hear_____!
10

198   UNIT 6

Day 3

Student Objectives
• To use context to identify and write lesson words
• To identify and interpret idioms in a poem

Presenting the Pages

Tell students that this selection is a poem. Point out that it has patterns of rhythm and rhyme that may help students identify the missing lesson words. Read the poem aloud, pausing to let volunteers supply the missing words as all students write the missing words on their pages. When the missing word is a homophone (*hear-here, deer-dear*), have the volunteer spell the word aloud as well.

Alternatively, have students complete the pages with a partner. Have them read the poem aloud, decide on the correct words, and write them.

Meeting Individual Needs

ESOL

Have ESOL students work with native speakers of English to find magazine pictures that depict the lesson words for actions and concrete objects. Suggest that they glue each picture to a piece of paper, label the picture with its spelling word, and bind the resulting pages to make a book. Have students write the title *A Book with /îr/, /âr/, and /ir/ Words* on the cover.

Spelling Strategy

Memory Clue

Remind students that they can use a memory clue to help them remember how to spell a word. Write the word *stairs* in a chart like the one shown below. Explain that in one kind of memory clue, they can use a shorter word inside a lesson word. Invite students to find the shorter word in *hear*, underline it, and write it. Then help students make up a memory clue containing both words, such as "I hear with my ear." Guide students to create memory clues for any difficult lesson words.

Spelling Word	Shorter Word	Clue
hear	ear	I hear with my ear.
stairs	air	Stairs go high into the air.

198

I was on my way to go to bed,

I was halfway up the stairs,

When a herd of _____ deer _____ came dancing down,
_11_

Then fourteen polar bears!

Before I could catch a breath of _____ air _____,
_12_

Before I could go one step higher,

What do you think went walking by?

A walrus wearing glasses made of _____ wire _____.
_13_

And it was followed by two otters

That rode in an old _____ tire _____.
_14_

_____ Where _____ did those animals come from?
_15_

And where did all of them go?

I've asked myself a hundred times,

But still I do not know!

Some nights when it's time for bed,

And I start to climb the _____ stairs _____,
_16_

I think I hear a walrus and otters

And deer and polar bears!

near
care
fire
where
hear
wire
stairs
deer
ear
year
tire
here
dear
chair
air
hair

LESSON 34 **199**

Reading Comprehension

After students have completed the pages, call their attention to the phrase "curl all your hair" and ask what it means. Guide students to understand that it does not actually mean "to make the hair curly," but that it means, "scare you." Call students attention to "Let me have your ear" and ask what it means. Explain that it does not actually mean "Give away your ear"; instead, it means "Listen to me."

Cooperative Learning Activity

Have students work in pairs to write the lesson words on cards and then sort them by spelling pattern. Have students then shuffle the cards and use them to dictate the lesson words to each other. Suggest that students compare their performance on this midweek activity with that on their pretest. Encourage students to note any words they still need to study.

ACTIVITY MASTER p. T281

Lesson 34 Words with /îr/, /âr/, or /īr/

Name _____

Read the words in the box. Then sort them by vowel sound.
Write the words on the lines.

Spelling Words	chair	near	ear	wire	hair
	year	hear	fire	air	

wire	air	ear
fire	hair	near
	chair	hear
		year

Find the word in the box that completes each sentence in the letter.
Write the word on the line. Then read the letter.

Spelling Words	where	stairs	deer	care	here	tire	dear

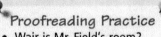

_____ Dear _____ Tom,

I like my new house. It has _____ stairs _____ going down to the back
_2_
yard. My dad made a swing for me out of an old _____ tire _____. I wish
_3_
you could come _____ here _____ and swing with me.
_4_

I also got a new puppy. He plays with me outside. I'm learning how to
take good _____ care _____ of him.
_5_

Do you know what I saw last night? I saw a _____ deer _____ walking
_6_
through the back yard. It was so neat!

I am really enjoying my new house. There is no _____ where _____ else
_7_
I would want to live but here!

Your friend,
Nick

ADDITIONAL PRACTICE

You may wish to copy and distribute the Activity Master on page T281 as additional practice for Lesson 34.

Proofreading Practice
- Wair is Mr. Field's room? *(Where)*
- It is at the top of the steares. *(stairs)*

199

Day 4

Student Objectives

- To write a narrative poem, using lesson words
- To proofread an ad for spelling, capitalization, and punctuation

Presenting the Page

As a prewriting activity, have students look at the lesson words and think of a story line that can contain some of the words. Then review the poem on pages 198–199 with students, having them point out the words that rhyme. Explain that not all poems rhyme, however.

Begin the Proofreading activity by reading the directions and ad aloud. Use inflection to convey that the first sentence is a question. Discuss what happens to your voice at the end of a question (it rises). Tell students to read the ad independently and correct the mistakes. Using an overhead projector, display the corrected ad, and have students check their answers.

Meeting Individual Needs

ESOL

Some Asian students may have less difficulty pronouncing /īr/ words than they do understanding them. Work in a small group to help students understand the meanings of these words. Say each word and tell what it means. Then invite students to say a sentence with each word and write the word.

200

---

near
care
fire
where
hear
wire
stairs
deer
ear
year
tire
here
dear
chair
air
hair

Write to the Point

Write a poem that tells a story. It can rhyme, but it doesn't have to. The story can be strange or simple. You may want to use one of the lines from "A Strange Story" to start your poem. Try to use spelling words from this lesson. **Poems will vary.**

Use the strategies on page 7 when you are not sure how to spell a word.

Proofreading

Proofread the ad for a Cozy Quilt below. Use proofreading marks to correct five spelling mistakes, three capitalization mistakes, and two punctuation mistakes.

Proofreading Marks
○ spell correctly
≡ capitalize
? add question mark

Cozy Quilt

are you toasty warm on cold winter nights? If not, try a Cozy Quilt. do you like to curl up in a chare and read? So do I! With a Cozy Quilt, I don't have to sit nere a the fire. The aire outside may be cold, but i don't caire. Even on the coldest night of the yeer, my Cozy Quilt keeps me as snug as a bug in a rug!

200 UNIT 6

Proofreading Practice

- Your haire is very long. *(hair)*
- I haven't cut it for a yier! *(year)*

✔ Correcting Common Errors

Some students may drop the *h* in *where* because the letter is silent. Offer the memory clue "Here is where" to these students and ask them to practice writing the word correctly.

Dictionary Skills

Pronunciation Letters and symbols are used to write pronunciations in a dictionary. The letters and symbols can be found in the pronunciation key.

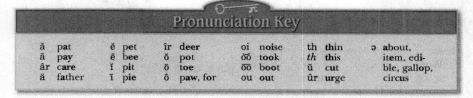

Pronunciation Key

ă	pat	ĕ	pet	îr	deer	oi	noise	th	thin	ə	about,
ā	pay	ē	bee	ŏ	pot	oŏ	took	th	this		item, edi-
âr	care	ĭ	pit	ō	toe	oō	boot	ŭ	cut		ble, gallop,
ä	father	ī	pie	ô	paw, for	ou	out	ûr	urge		circus

Write the three words from the boxes that go with each pronunciation.

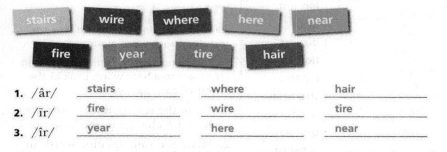

stairs   wire   where   here   near
fire   year   tire   hair

1. /âr/ ___stairs___ ___where___ ___hair___
2. /īr/ ___fire___ ___wire___ ___tire___
3. /îr/ ___year___ ___here___ ___near___

⭐ Challenge Yourself

Write the Challenge Word for each clue. Check the Spelling Dictionary to see if you are right. Then use separate paper to write sentences showing that you understand the meaning of each Challenge Word. Sentences will vary.

Challenge Words
careless   dreary
dairy   inspire

4. A beautiful sunset can often do this to an artist. ___inspire___

5. Cows are found at this. ___dairy___

6. If you do not pay attention to what you do, you are this. ___careless___

7. If a day is dark and cloudy, you can use this word to describe it. ___dreary___

LESSON 34 **201**

Posttest

Dictate the following sentences. Have students use separate paper to write the sentences and underline the lesson words.

1. Dad's <u>chair</u> is by the <u>fire</u>.
2. The <u>deer</u> jumped into the <u>air</u>.
3. Her <u>hair</u> covers one <u>ear</u>.
4. Did you <u>hear</u> <u>where</u> they are going?
5. Take <u>care</u> when you go up the <u>stairs</u>.
6. My <u>dear</u> friend is <u>here</u>.
7. The <u>wire</u> is <u>near</u> the wall.
8. Last <u>year</u> Mom gave me a new <u>tire</u> for my bike.

Enrichment Activity

Invite students to form small groups, choose one of the lesson sounds, and generate as many words with that sound as possible. Ask students to use highlighters to indicate the spelling patterns in the words.

Day 5

Student Objectives

- To translate pronunciations into lesson words
- To study the spellings and meanings of the Challenge Words
- To take a posttest on the lesson words

Presenting the Page

Review the pronunciation key with students. Explain that a symbol above a letter indicates how to pronounce the sound. Point out that the letter *a* can be pronounced /ă/ as in *cat,* /ā/ as in *pay,* /âr/ as in *care,* and /ä/ as in *father.* Guide students to understand that knowing what the symbols mean will help them pronounce words correctly.

⭐ Challenge Yourself

To introduce the Challenge Words, write the following on the board:

careless   dreary
dairy   inspire

Pronounce the words for students, emphasizing the /âr/, /îr/, or /īr/ sound in each. Ask students to repeat the words after you. Have students identify the /îr/, /âr/, or /īr/ spelling pattern in each word (*careless* has the *are* pattern; *dreary* has the *ear* pattern, *dairy* has the *air* pattern, and *inspire* has the *ire* pattern).

Posttest

Use the posttest on this page to assess students' ability to spell the lesson words.

201

Lesson 35

Words with -er or -est

Student Objectives
- To take a pretest on the lesson words
- To spell the lesson words aloud
- To sort and write the lesson words according to whether the base word changes when -er or -est is added and according to type of base word change

Pretest

Use the pretest on this page to assess students' ability to spell the lesson words.

 Have students use the study steps on page 6 to study any words they misspell in the pretest.

 You may wish to duplicate and send home the Home Activity Master on pages T251–T252.

Presenting the Page

Introducing the -er and -est Endings Write *long, longer,* and *longest* on the board. Explain that each word is an adjective, or describing word. Point out that we add -er to an adjective to compare two things and add -est to compare more than two things.

Pronunciation Focus Have students pronounce and write *funny* and *funnier.* Guide them to understand that even though the spelling changes in the second syllable, the /ē/ sound in the syllable does not.

Consonant Focus Write *hot, hotter,* and *hottest* on the board and point out the doubled final consonant of *hot* in *hotter* and *hottest.* Then write *hoter* on the board and explain that the function of doubling the consonant is to indicate the short vowel sound; without the doubled consonant we might think that the *o* should be pronounced as a long *o.*

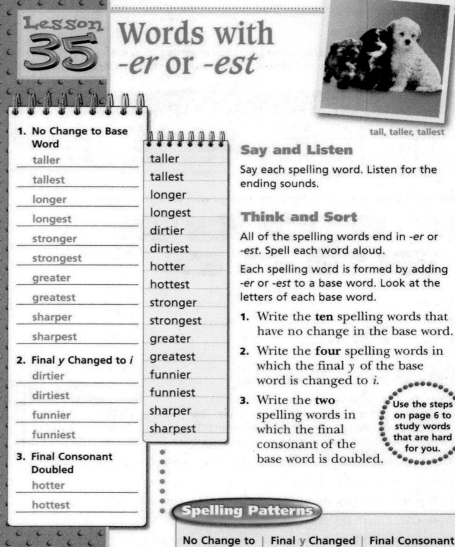

Lesson 35 Words with -er or -est

tall, taller, tallest

1. No Change to Base Word
- taller
- tallest
- longer
- longest
- stronger
- strongest
- greater
- greatest
- sharper
- sharpest

2. Final *y* Changed to *i*
- dirtier
- dirtiest
- funnier
- funniest

3. Final Consonant Doubled
- hotter
- hottest

taller
tallest
longer
longest
dirtier
dirtiest
hotter
hottest
stronger
strongest
greater
greatest
funnier
funniest
sharper
sharpest

Say and Listen

Say each spelling word. Listen for the ending sounds.

Think and Sort

All of the spelling words end in -er or -est. Spell each word aloud.

Each spelling word is formed by adding -er or -est to a base word. Look at the letters of each base word.

1. Write the **ten** spelling words that have no change in the base word.

2. Write the **four** spelling words in which the final *y* of the base word is changed to *i*.

3. Write the **two** spelling words in which the final consonant of the base word is doubled.

Use the steps on page 6 to study words that are hard for you.

Spelling Patterns

No Change to Base Word	Final *y* Changed to *i*	Final Consonant Doubled
tall**er**	funn**ier**	hot**ter**
tall**est**	funn**iest**	hot**test**

Pretest

Say each lesson word, read the sentence, and then repeat the word. Have students write the words on separate paper.

1. **taller** I am taller than she is.
2. **tallest** Giraffes are the tallest mammals.
3. **longer** A yard is longer than a foot.
4. **longest** Whose foot is longest?
5. **dirtier** This car is dirtier than that one.
6. **dirtiest** That car is the dirtiest of all.
7. **hotter** June is hotter than March.
8. **hottest** August is the hottest month.
9. **stronger** Which team is stronger?
10. **strongest** We have the strongest players.
11. **greater** Two is greater than one.
12. **greatest** He's the greatest poet in our class.
13. **funnier** Her costume is funnier than mine.
14. **funniest** His is the funniest joke of all.
15. **sharper** Your pencil is sharper than mine.
16. **sharpest** Mine is sharpest of all.

Additional Words for Enrichment

The following words can be used to meet the needs of on-level and above-level students:

angrier grayer sloppier mildest plumpest fluffiest

Spelling and Meaning

Antonyms Write the spelling word that is an antonym of the underlined word.

1. Turn on the fan if it gets <u>colder</u>. _____ hotter _____
2. I need the <u>dullest</u> knife for the steak. _____ sharpest _____
3. An owl's eyes are <u>duller</u> than a robin's. _____ sharper _____
4. The <u>weakest</u> wrestler is most likely to win. _____ strongest _____
5. I will put the <u>cleanest</u> clothes in the wash. _____ dirtiest _____

Comparisons Write the spelling word that completes each comparison.

6. An oak tree is _____ taller _____ than a person.
7. Her joke was the _____ funniest _____ one I ever heard.
8. Mt. Everest is the _____ tallest _____ mountain in the world.
9. Four is _____ greater _____ than three.
10. A mile is _____ longer _____ than a foot.
11. An elephant is _____ stronger _____ than a mouse.
12. The Nile River is the _____ longest _____ river in the world.
13. Summer is usually the _____ hottest _____ season of the year.
14. Who is the _____ greatest _____ basketball player of all time?
15. I thought the joke was _____ funnier _____ than the riddle.

Word Story Two spelling words come from a word that used to be spelled *dritti*. People began to change its spelling. They made the first *i* change places with the *r*. Then they changed the final *i* to *y*. Write the spelling word that is the -er form of the word.

16. _____ dirtier _____

Family Tree: *sharper* *Sharper* is a form of *sharp*. Think about how the *sharp* words are alike in spelling and meaning. Then add another *sharp* word to the tree. A sample answer is shown.

sharpen
sharpest
17. sharpening
sharper
sharpener
sharp

LESSON 35 **203**

HOME ACTIVITY MASTER p. T251

Unit 6 Spelling at Home

Dear Family of _____ ,
During the next six weeks, your child will be learning to spell the following kinds of words:
• words with /ô/, as in *draw*
• words with /ou/, as in *house*
• words with /îr/, /âr/, or /ìr/, as in *hear, hair,* and *tire*
• words with -er or -est

Here are some simple activities to do each week to help your child become a better speller.

Listening and Writing
Say the spelling words and have your child write them.

Spelling Strategy: Guess and Check
If your child is having difficulty spelling a word, encourage him or her to guess the spelling. Then ask your child to check the list at right or a dictionary to see if his or her guess is correct.

Games and Activities
Play Spelling Chunks. Have your child choose some of the spelling words. Write the words on a piece of paper. Leave a space below each word. With your child, study the words. Then separate each word into smaller parts so that it is easy to remember. Divide each word into the "chunks" we hear when the word is read aloud. An example is *pou/er*.

Write some of the spelling words on a piece of paper, leaving out some of the letters. Ask your child to complete each word. Taking turns, continue writing and completing as many spelling words as possible.

Using Spelling Words
Ask your child to write sentences that contain the spelling words. Then read the sentences with your child. Notice whether the sentences show that your child knows the meanings of the spelling words.

Lesson 31 Words with /ô/
Week of _____
frog   long   along   off
belong   strong   water   always
mall   tall   talk   walk
bought   brought   draw   because

Lesson 32 More Words with /ô/
Week of _____
autumn   August   born   fork
morning   sport   popcorn   storm
north   corner   before   door
floor   pour   four   quart

Lesson 33 Words with /ou/
Week of _____
hour   sound   ground   about
house   around   count   our
found   owl   down   power
brown   tower   town   flower

Lesson 34 Words with /îr/, /âr/, or /ìr/
Week of _____
hear   dear   ear   near
year   here   deer   stairs
air   chair   hair   care
where   tire   fire   wire

Lesson 35 Words with -er or -est
Week of _____
stronger strongest taller   tallest
greater   greatest   longer   longest
sharper   sharpest   funnier   funniest
dirtier   dirtiest   hotter   hottest

Lesson 36 Unit 6 Review
Week of _____
Lesson 36 is a review of Lessons 31–35. Help your child practice all of the words from those lessons.

The highlighted area shows the Lesson 35 words, which students can share with family members. Spanish version available on page T252.

Proofreading Practice
• Tomorrow will be hoter than today. *(hotter)*
• This has been the hotiest summer in ten years! *(hottest)*

Meeting Individual Needs

ESOL
The idea of adding -er and -est may not be intuitive to Spanish-speaking students. These students may benefit from using picture clues to practice saying and writing the words. Show a picture of three people of different heights, for example, to depict *tall, taller, tallest*. Have students underline the endings to reinforce the -er and -est endings.

Day 2

Student Objectives
• To use meaning clues to identify and write lesson words
• To use etymology, meaning, and spelling to identify the word *dirtier*
• To learn *sharp* words and analyze their spellings and meanings

Presenting the Page

Write the following Antonyms and Comparisons examples on the board and model identifying the answers. Remind students that the -er ending is used when two things are compared, and -est is used for three or more items.

• Zack is the <u>shortest</u> person in the class. *(tallest)*
• It is _____ in July than it is in November. *(hotter)*

Word Story

Share with students that the first *i* in *dritti* was once spelled as *y* and that another lesson word started as a word with a similar spelling. The Old English word *grytta* named a coarse meal that we now call grits. But *grytta* evolved to *great* to refer to something large in size. Later the word *great* also came to mean "admirable" and "excellent."

Family Tree: *sharp*

Students should see that the *sharp* words all contain *sharp*. Have students pronounce the words, look them up in a dictionary, and discuss their meanings. Point out that adding -en changes *sharp* from an adjective to a verb that means "to make sharp." Guide students to understand that knowing how to spell *sharp* will help them spell words related to *sharp*.

203

Day 3

Student Objectives
- To use context to identify and write lesson words
- To draw conclusions about story characters

Presenting the Pages

Preview with students the picture on page 205 and ask them to tell what the story is about. Then read the story aloud and have students write the missing words as you read. Ask students to identify the word that always appears before the *-est* words in the story *(the)*.

Point out that the story contains dialogue, or words characters say to each other, which is indicated by quotation marks. Have students work in groups of four to reread the story. Have one student read the nondialogue part (the part of the narrator) and the others read the parts of the characters, Ana, Mara, and Ty. Have students write the missing words as they read the story aloud.

204

Use each spelling word once to complete the story.

Big Splash

Ana, Mara, and Ty were playing in the park. Ana said, "Wow, it's hot today!"

Ty wiped his face and said, "It's _____hotter_____ than it's been all month."
1

"It's the _____hottest_____ it's ever been," cried Mara. She gave
2
a sharp whistle. Ana gave an even _____sharper_____ one. But both
3
girls had to cover their ears. Ty's whistle was the _____sharpest_____
4
of all.

"Oh, Ty. You think you're so great," said Mara.

"You think you're _____greater_____ than anyone," cried Ana.
5

"Well, my whistle was the _____greatest_____," boasted Ty. "But
6
let's have a real contest. Let's play tug-of-war."

Each one wanted to win. Mara was strong. But Ty thought he
was _____stronger_____ than Mara. And Ana thought she was the
7
_____strongest_____. You don't have to be tall to be strong. Ana
8
wasn't very tall. Mara was _____taller_____ than she was. And Ty
9
was the _____tallest_____.
10

"Let's put this mud puddle between us," said Ty. "The loser will fall and get dirty."

"I'll bet you'll get _____dirtier_____ than I will," said Mara.
11
"You'll be the _____dirtiest_____ of all," cried Ana.
12

204 UNIT 6

Spelling Strategy

Using Spelling Rules
Remind students that thinking about spelling rules is a helpful strategy for spelling words that end in *-er* or *-est*. In a chart like the one below, write the two spelling rules underlying many of the lesson words. Invite students to write the lesson words to complete the chart.

Rule:	Base Word	-er	-est
If a base word ends in a consonant and *y,* the *y* is changed to *i* when -er or -est is added.	dirty funny		
If a base word ends with a short vowel and a single consonant, the consonant is doubled when -er or -est is added.	hot		

Ty and Mara were first. They pulled the rope for a long time. Mara and Ana were next. They pulled for an even _____longer_____ time. Ty and Ana were the last to play.
13

Their tug-of-war contest was the _____longest_____.
14

Finally Ana pulled Ty into the mud. He fell with a big splash. The mud flew. There were big spots on Ana's face. Mara had mud on her sweater.

"You may be the winner, Ana, but you sure look funny," said Mara.

"No _____funnier_____ than you," said Ana.
15

Ty just sat in the puddle grinning. "And I'll bet I look the _____funniest_____ of all!" he laughed.
16

taller
tallest
longer
longest
dirtier
dirtiest
hotter
hottest
stronger
strongest
greater
greatest
funnier
funniest
sharper
sharpest

LESSON 35 **205**

Reading Comprehension

After students have completed the pages, tell them to think about what each character is like. Begin by inviting a volunteer to describe Ty (Ty is a bragger at first, but he is a good loser). Ask students to underline the information in the story that helps them figure out what Ty is like (Ty brags that his whistle is the greatest, but he laughs at himself when he ends up in the mud). Continue in the same manner to help students describe the other characters.

Cooperative Learning Activity

To provide students the opportunity to assess their progress, have them work in pairs to dictate the eight base words to each other. The partner should write both the *-er* and *-est* forms of each base word. They should then check their own work. Tell students to compare their performance on this activity with that on the pretest and to identify words they still need to study.

ACTIVITY MASTER p. T282

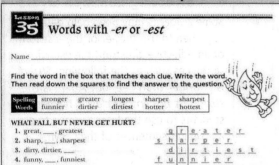

Lesson
35 Words with *-er* or *-est*

Name _____

Find the word in the box that matches each clue. Write the word.
Then read down the squares to find the answer to the question.

Spelling Words	stronger	greater	longest	sharper	sharpest
	funnier	dirtier	dirtiest	hotter	hottest

WHAT FALL BUT NEVER GET HURT?
1. great, ___, greatest   g r e a t e r
2. sharp, ___, sharpest   s h a r p e r
3. dirty, dirtier, ___   d i r t i e s t
4. funny, ___, funniest   f u n n i e r
5. dirty, ___, dirtiest   d i r t i e r
6. hot, ___, hottest   h o t t e r
7. strong, ___, strongest   s t r o n g e r
8. sharp, sharper, ___   s h a r p e s t
9. long, longer, ___   l o n g e s t

Find the word in the box that completes each sentence.
Write the word on the line.

Spelling Words	strongest	taller	tallest	greatest	longer	funniest	hottest

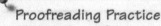

10. Anita told the ___funniest___ joke I ever heard.
11. August was the ___hottest___ month of the year.
12. Jacob is five feet tall, but Gilbert is ___taller___
13. The horse has ___longer___ legs than the pony.
14. The giraffe is the ___tallest___ animal at the zoo.
15. She is the ___strongest___ weight lifter at the gym.
16. Chocolate ice cream is the ___greatest___ ice cream ever made.

ADDITIONAL PRACTICE

You may wish to copy and distribute the Activity Master on page T282 as additional practice for Lesson 35.

Proofreading Practice
- That movie was funnyer than the book. *(funnier)*
- It was the gratest movie I have ever seen. *(greatest)*

Student Objectives

- To make an announcement sign, using lesson words
- To proofread a newspaper article for spelling, capitalization, and punctuation

Presenting the Page

Talk about the contest in "Big Splash" on pages 204–205. Have students brainstorm contest ideas they might use for their sign. Then discuss the information that the sign should contain: name of the contest, contest rules, the place, date, and time for the contest, and other important information, as well as words from the lesson.

Ask a volunteer to read the directions and excerpt from a newspaper article before students begin proofreading. Then have students work in pairs. Suggest that they focus on one type of error at a time until all errors are identified and marked.

Meeting Individual Needs

Visual Learners

For each pair of students, make a transparency on which you write some of the lesson words, omitting the endings. One student in each pair should say each lesson word, and the partner should add the correct ending to the transparency. Have students erase the endings and reverse roles.

206

taller
tallest
longer
longest
dirtier
dirtiest
hotter
hottest
stronger
strongest
greater
greatest
funnier
funniest
sharper
sharpest

Write to the Point

In "Big Splash" Ana, Mara, and Ty had a contest. Think of a contest you would like to have. Make a sign announcing the contest. Tell where and when it will be held and what the prize will be. Try to use spelling words from this lesson in your sign. **Signs will vary.**

Use the strategies on page 7 when you are not sure how to spell a word.

Proofreading

Proofread this paragraph from a newspaper article. Use proofreading marks to correct five spelling mistakes, three capitalization mistakes, and two punctuation mistakes.

Proofreading Marks
- ◯ spell correctly
- ≡ capitalize
- ⊙ add period

Gabby's Garden Tips

spring is the greatist season of them all. The sun shines
(greatest)

stronger than in winter. The days are longger. the trees and
(longer)

grass grow taler and faster. Early spring is the time to start
(taller)

a flower garden Digging in the earth might make your

hands dirtyer than watching TV, but it will also
(dirtier)

make you happier! A flower garden is

something everyone can enjoy. having

lots of bright, colorful flowers will

make your spring even grater!
(greater)

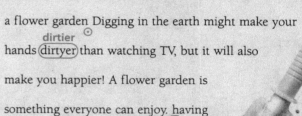

Proofreading Practice
- Jane's hair is launger than Mara's. *(longer)*
- Liz has the longist hair in the family. *(longest)*

Correcting Common Errors

Some students may need help determining when to use the *-er* or the *-est* form of an adjective. Illustrate the use with sentences such as the following: *Stuart is stronger than Lee, but Adam is the strongest boy in our class.* Challenge students to use the lesson words to create similar sentences of their own.

Language Connection

Adjectives An adjective describes a noun or pronoun. It tells which, what kind, or how many.

The **strong** man lifted the box.	Mike is **strong**.

Add *-er* to most adjectives to compare two people or things.
Add *-est* to compare more than two people or things.

Cliff is **stronger** than Mike.	Paul is the **strongest** of all.

Use the correct word from the boxes to write each sentence.

greater	hotter	funniest	tallest

1. Sharon tells the ___ jokes we've ever heard.
   Sharon tells the funniest jokes we've ever heard.

2. The sun is ___ today than it was yesterday.
   The sun is hotter today than it was yesterday.

3. Gigi is the ___ girl on the basketball team.
   Gigi is the tallest girl on the basketball team.

4. Twenty is ___ than ten.
   Twenty is greater than ten.

⭐ Challenge Yourself

What do you think each Challenge Word means? Check the Spelling Dictionary to see if you are right. Then use separate paper to write sentences showing that you understand the meaning of each Challenge Word. Definitions and sentences will vary.

Challenge Words

weirder	weirdest
shakier	shakiest

5. Which is **weirder** —blue hair or a green face?

6. The shadows made the **weirdest** shapes on the wall.

7. The chair with the short leg is **shakier** than the other.

8. My chair is the **shakiest** of all.

LESSON 35 **207**

Posttest

Dictate the following sentences. Have students use separate paper to write the sentences and underline the lesson words.

1. It is <u>hotter</u> this week than last.
2. She tells the <u>longest</u> and <u>funniest</u> stories I have ever heard.
3. His hair is <u>longer</u> than mine.
4. She is the <u>tallest</u> and <u>strongest</u> girl in school.
5. She is even <u>taller</u> and <u>stronger</u> than I am.
6. Your story is <u>funnier</u> than mine.
7. Five is <u>greater</u> than two.
8. The <u>hottest</u> day was the <u>greatest</u> day of the summer.
9. This is the <u>sharpest</u> pencil of all.
10. My shirt is <u>dirtier</u> than yours.
11. Her pencil was <u>sharper</u> than mine.
12. He wore the <u>dirtiest</u> shirt I have ever seen.

Enrichment Activity

Have students play a game of I Spy as a class. Tell them to choose an object in the classroom and to give clues for the object that contain lesson words, such as "I spy something that is longer than a yard." Invite the class to guess the object.

Day 5

Student Objectives
- To use context to identify lesson words that complete sentences
- To write sentences containing lesson words
- To study the spellings and meanings of the Challenge Words
- To take a posttest on the lesson words

Presenting the Page

Be sure that students realize that adjectives are describing words. If students need reinforcement, point to objects around the room, say their name, and ask students to say adjectives that describe each one. Focus students' attention on the four words in the activity, asking them to name the base words used to make the words (*great, hot, funny, tall*). Finally, point out that two of the sentences contain *the* before the blank. Ask students what this indicates about the missing word (the word ends with *-est*).

⭐ Challenge Yourself

Write the Challenge Words on the board. Pronounce the words for students and point out the ending in each. Ask students to identify the spelling rule that is illustrated by *shakier* and *shakiest* (if a base word ends in a consonant and *y*, the *y* changes to *i* when *-er* or *-est* is added).

Have students write what they think each Challenge Word means, look up the words in the Spelling Dictionary, and then write the correct definitions. Ask students to compare their definitions with those in the Spelling Dictionary.

Posttest

Use the posttest on this page to assess students' ability to spell the lesson words.

Lesson 36

Unit 6 Review
Lessons 31–35

Student Objectives
- To take a pretest on the lesson words

Pretest

Use the pretest on this page to assess students' ability to spell the lesson words.

Have students use the study steps on page 6 to study any words they misspell in the pretest.

You may wish to duplicate and send home the Home Activity Master on pages T251–T252.

Meeting Individual Needs

ESOL

Students acquiring English may need to review the meanings of the lesson words. To help them review the words, use gestures, encouraging students to join with you. For the word *autumn*, for example, say and write the word and then use your hands to show leaves falling from a tree. For *strong*, say and write the word and then flex and show a muscle. Have students write each word as well. Once students have reviewed the meanings of the words, have them work in pairs to complete the pages.

208

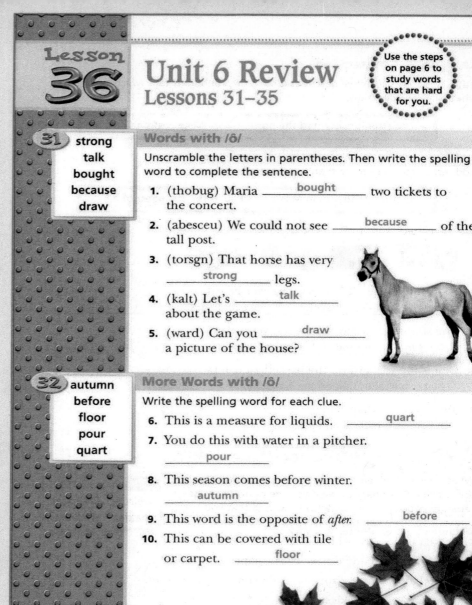

Lesson 36

Unit 6 Review
Lessons 31–35

Use the steps on page 6 to study words that are hard for you.

31
strong
talk
bought
because
draw

Words with /ô/

Unscramble the letters in parentheses. Then write the spelling word to complete the sentence.

1. (thobug) Maria _____ **bought** _____ two tickets to the concert.
2. (abesceu) We could not see _____ **because** _____ of the tall post.
3. (torsgn) That horse has very _____ **strong** _____ legs.
4. (kalt) Let's _____ **talk** _____ about the game.
5. (ward) Can you _____ **draw** _____ a picture of the house?

32
autumn
before
floor
pour
quart

More Words with /ô/

Write the spelling word for each clue.

6. This is a measure for liquids. _____ **quart** _____
7. You do this with water in a pitcher. _____ **pour** _____
8. This season comes before winter. _____ **autumn** _____
9. This word is the opposite of *after*. _____ **before** _____
10. This can be covered with tile or carpet. _____ **floor** _____

208 UNIT 6

Pretest

Say each lesson word, read the sentence, and then repeat the word. Have students write the words on separate paper.

1. **strong** My brother is <u>strong</u>.
2. **talk** We <u>talk</u> on the phone.
3. **bought** I <u>bought</u> new crayons.
4. **because** I am excited <u>because</u> it's my birthday.
5. **draw** Will you <u>draw</u> me a map?
6. **autumn** My favorite season is <u>autumn</u>.
7. **before** Wash your hands <u>before</u> dinner.
8. **floor** Don't slip on the wet <u>floor</u>.
9. **pour** Please <u>pour</u> me a glass of milk.
10. **quart** Two pints equal a <u>quart</u>.
11. **count** Can you <u>count</u> backwards?
12. **hour** The <u>hour</u> went by quickly.
13. **tower** The <u>tower</u> is very tall.
14. **owl** The <u>owl</u> sat in a tree.
15. **deer** I saw a <u>deer</u> in the woods.
16. **near** We live <u>near</u> the school.
17. **here** You can sit over <u>here</u>.
18. **care** I <u>care</u> about my friends.
19. **air** Living things need <u>air</u>.
20. **where** Do you know <u>where</u> the club meets?
21. **wire** Some <u>wire</u> is made from copper.
22. **greater** Four is <u>greater</u> than three.
23. **sharpest** She used her <u>sharpest</u> pencil to sketch.
24. **funnier** That joke is <u>funnier</u> than the first one.
25. **hottest** Which planet is the <u>hottest</u>?

33 count / hour / tower / owl

Words with /ou/

Write the spelling word that completes each analogy.

11. *Days* is to *week* as *minutes* is to ___hour___.

12. *Terrier* is to *dog* as ___owl___ is to *bird*.

13. *Read* is to *book* as ___count___ is to *money*.

14. *House* is to *garage* as *castle* is to ___tower___.

 34 deer / near / here / care / air / where / wire

Words with /îr/, /âr/, or /īr/

Write the spelling word that completes each sentence.

15. The smell of lilacs filled the ___air___.

16. The ___deer___ darted across the road.

17. Do you know ___where___ my keys are?

18. We can rest ___here___ in the shade.

19. The cage was made of wood and ___wire___.

20. Our hotel is ___near___ the park.

21. Heidi takes good ___care___ of her pet.

35 greater / sharpest / funnier / hottest

Words with -er or -est

Write the spelling word that belongs in each group.

22. sharp   sharper   ___sharpest___

23. great   ___greater___   greatest

24. hot   hotter   ___hottest___

25. funny   ___funnier___   funniest

LESSON 36 **209**

REVIEW TEST MASTER, pp. T293–T294

Unit 6 Review Test Name _____

Each underlined word in the story is misspelled. Darken the circle for the correct spelling.

Last week my dog, Max, needed a bath <u>becawse</u> he was so dirty. <u>Befour</u> I bathed him, I went to the pet store to <u>taulk</u> to Mr. Meng. "Max is really dirty. It will take at least a <u>quort</u> of soap to get him clean," I said.

Mr. Meng took a bottle of soap out of a <u>wier</u> basket. "<u>Porr</u> two drops of this on Max and scrub," he said. I <u>baught</u> the soap and went home.

Max is a very <u>straung</u> dog. When I started to wash him, he tried to jump on my head! Then he jumped to the <u>flor</u> and ran down the hall. I can't <u>cownt</u> how many towels I used to wipe up the soap and water. But I didn't <u>cair</u>. Max is <u>funier</u> than any other dog I know. I knew Max was hiding, and I knew just <u>whcare</u> to find him, too. Max wasn't mad at me, though. He gave me a big, wet kiss.

Answers

1. Ⓐ becouse	Ⓑ because	Ⓒ becase	Ⓓ becus
2. Ⓕ Befour	Ⓖ Befor	Ⓗ Before	Ⓙ Befour
3. Ⓐ tawk	Ⓑ tolk	Ⓒ toulk	Ⓓ talk
4. Ⓕ quart	Ⓖ qort	Ⓗ qart	Ⓙ quourt
5. Ⓐ wir	Ⓑ wire	Ⓒ wiur	Ⓓ wiyr
6. Ⓕ Por	Ⓖ Poar	Ⓗ Pour	Ⓙ Paur
7. Ⓐ bawght	Ⓑ bought	Ⓒ bawt	Ⓓ boght
8. Ⓕ strong	Ⓖ straung	Ⓗ stroung	Ⓙ strang
9. Ⓐ flaur	Ⓑ flore	Ⓒ floor	Ⓓ florr
10. Ⓕ coent	Ⓖ couent	Ⓗ coownt	Ⓙ count
11. Ⓐ cere	Ⓑ cear	Ⓒ care	Ⓓ ceer
12. Ⓕ funeer	Ⓖ funnier	Ⓗ funnyer	Ⓙ funnyier
13. Ⓐ wair	Ⓑ whair	Ⓒ whare	Ⓓ where

Unit 6 Review Test Name _____

Each underlined word in the story is misspelled. Darken the circle for the correct spelling.

Today was the <u>hotest</u> day of the summer! It was too hot to play outside, so I decided to stay <u>heere</u> in my room. At first I wanted to <u>dra</u> a picture of my cat. Then I decided I would paint a picture of a forest. I imagined a nice <u>autemn</u> day in the forest. I painted bright red and orange leaves. I also painted a mother <u>deere</u> and her baby standing <u>neer</u> some tall trees. I painted a large <u>owll</u> sitting on a tree branch, too. Then I added a stone <u>touwer</u> next to the trees. I could almost feel the cool <u>aer</u> on my face as I looked at the picture. I stayed in my room and painted for an <u>houer</u>.

I finished my painting, but something was missing. I needed to write a story about my picture. I found the <u>sharpst</u> pencil I could find and started to write. This story would be <u>greatr</u> than any other story I had ever written!

Answers

14. Ⓕ hottst	Ⓖ hottest	Ⓗ hottist	Ⓙ hotist
15. Ⓐ heer	Ⓑ heere	Ⓒ here	Ⓓ heir
16. Ⓕ drou	Ⓖ drow	Ⓗ drau	Ⓙ draw
17. Ⓐ autum	Ⓑ autumn	Ⓒ autimn	Ⓓ autem
18. Ⓕ deer	Ⓖ diir	Ⓗ deir	Ⓙ dere
19. Ⓐ nere	Ⓑ neir	Ⓒ niir	Ⓓ near
20. Ⓕ awl	Ⓖ ouwl	Ⓗ owl	Ⓙ owll
21. Ⓐ tower	Ⓑ tawer	Ⓒ towr	Ⓓ towir
22. Ⓕ ere	Ⓖ eer	Ⓗ ayr	Ⓙ air
23. Ⓐ howr	Ⓑ houir	Ⓒ hour	Ⓓ hower
24. Ⓕ sharpist	Ⓖ sharpest	Ⓗ sharppest	Ⓙ sharppist
25. Ⓐ graeter	Ⓑ greatr	Ⓒ grater	Ⓓ greater

Day 2

Student Objectives

- To review the *o*, *a*, *ough*, *au*, *aw*, *oo*, and *ou* spellings of the /ô/ sound
- To review the *ou* and *ow* spellings of the /ou/ sound
- To review the spellings of words with /îr/, /âr/, and /īr/
- To review words with *-er* and *-est*
- To use meaning clues to identify and write lesson words

Presenting the Page

Lessons 31–32 Ask volunteers to read aloud the review words for Lessons 31–32. Review the various patterns for /ô/: *o*, *a*, *ough*, *au*, *aw*, *oo*, and *ou*.

Lesson 33 Review with students the *ou* and *ow* representations of /ou/. Invite volunteers to read the review words for Lesson 33 aloud and identify the /ou/ spelling pattern in each.

Lessons 34–35 For Lesson 34, have students identify the /âr/, /îr/, or /īr/ sounds in each lesson word and tell how each sound is spelled. For Lesson 35, review the spelling rules that explain the formation of *funnier* and *hottest*.

Test-Taking Strategies

Read the directions for the Review Test Master aloud. Point out that each of the underlined words in the passage is misspelled and that the box at the bottom of the page contains four answer choices for each misspelled word. Make sure students understand that they should find and darken the circle for the correct spelling. Explain that one strategy to use in a test like this one is to read the passage first and then read it again, focusing on each misspelled word.

Proofreading Practice

- I like to cownt the deer near my home. *(count)*
- I know whair they like to play. *(where)*

209

Day 3

Student Objective

- To sort lesson words according to vowel sound
- To compare and contrast sorted words that have *-er* or *-est* endings

Presenting the Page

Invite volunteers to read the Review Sort words aloud. Have students name the sounds represented by /ô/, /ou/, /îr/, /âr/, and /īr/. For the last two items, guide students to focus on the endings of the words. You may wish to have students work with partners to complete the page.

Meeting Individual Needs

Kinesthetic Learners

Create a sorting chart on the board, using the sound spellings on the page as column headings. Have students work in small groups to write the Review Sort words on self-stick notes. Then have them say each word and place it under the correct heading.

Proofreading Practice

- I heard the oul in the tree. *(owl)*
- It hooted for almost an our. *(hour)*

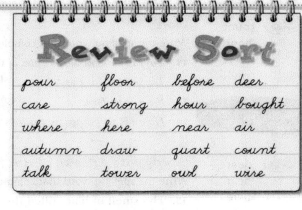

Review Sort

pour	floor	before	deer
care	strong	hour	bought
where	here	near	air
autumn	draw	quart	count
talk	tower	owl	wire

26. Write the **nine** /ô/ words.

27. Write the **four** /ou/ words.

28. Write the **three** /îr/ words.

29. Write the **three** /âr/ words.

30. Write the **one** /īr/ word.

26. /ô/ Words
pour
autumn
talk
floor
strong
draw
before
quart
bought

27. /ou/ Words
tower
hour
owl
count

28. /îr/ Words
here
near
deer

29. /âr/ Words
care
where
air

30. /īr/ Word
wire

These four words have been sorted into two groups. Explain how the words in each group are alike and how they are different.

31. greater funnier
Both words end in -er. In the word funnier, the y in funny changes to i when -er is added.

32. sharpest hottest
Both words end in -est. In the word hottest, the final consonant in hot is doubled when -est is added.

WRITER'S WORKSHOP MASTERS, pp. T295–T296, T298

The Writing Process Name ______

1 Prewriting • Plan your writing.
- Make sure you know what your writing task is.
- Identify the audience and the purpose for writing.
- Choose a topic.
- Gather and write ideas about the topic.
- Organize your ideas.

2 Writing • Write a first draft.
- Use your plan to put your ideas in writing.
- Don't worry about mistakes now.
- Add any new ideas you think of while writing.
- Leave room between lines so that you can make changes later.

3 Revising • Look for ways to improve what you have written.
- Make sure your writing fits the audience and purpose for writing.
- Look for places that need more ideas or details.
- Take out sentences that don't belong.
- Find places where more colorful or exact words can be used.
- Make sure that your sentences are complete.
- Write and revise until you are happy with your writing.

4 Proofreading • Review your work for errors.
- Make sure you have indented each paragraph.
- Check to see that you have used words correctly.
- Check your capitalization.
- Check to see that you have used periods, question marks, commas, and other punctuation marks correctly.
- Look at the spelling of each word. Circle words you are not sure you have spelled correctly. Check their spelling.

5 Publishing • Share what you have written.
- Make a clean final draft.
- Read it to the class or a friend.
- Add pictures or make a poster to go with it.
- Make a recording of your writing.

Proofreading Checklist Name ______

You can use the questions below as a checklist to proofread your writing.

- ☐ Have I indented each paragraph?
- ☐ Have I used words correctly in every sentence?
- ☐ Have I capitalized the first word in each sentence?
- ☐ Have I capitalized all proper names?
- ☐ Have I ended each sentence with a period, question mark, or exclamation point?
- ☐ Have I spelled each word correctly?

The chart below shows some proofreading marks and how to use them.

Mark	Meaning	Example
◯	spell correctly	I (liek) dogs.
⊙	add period	They are my favorite kind of pet⊙
?	add question mark	What kind of pet do you have?
≡	capitalize	My dog's name is scooter.
℘	take out	He likes to to run and play.
¶	indent paragraph	¶ I love my dog, Scooter. He is the best pet I have ever had. Every morning he wakes me with a bark. Every night he sleeps with me.
❛❛ ❜❜	add quotation marks	"You are my best friend," I tell him.

Story Map Name ______ Date ______

Beginning

Middle

End

Writer's Workshop

A Narrative

A narrative that continues another story is called a sequel. A sequel is a whole story with a beginning, middle, and an end. It usually has the same characters and setting as the original story. Here is part of Julio's sequel to "The Frog Prince" on pages 180 and 181.

Libby Returns

Libby could not forget about the frog, so the next time she was in the mall, she went to the pet shop. She looked for the frog, but it was not there. When she saw Mr. Muller, she asked, "Where has the frog gone?"

Prewriting To write his narrative, Julio followed the steps in the writing process. After he thought about his sequel, he completed a story map. The story map helped him decide what would happen at the beginning, middle, and end of his sequel. Julio's story map is shown here. Study what he did.

Beginning
Libby returns to the mall.

Middle
She can't find the frog.

End
She and Mr. Muller find a crown in the pond.

It's Your Turn!

Write your own sequel to a story. Choose any story that you have read or heard before. After you have chosen a story to continue, make a story map. Then follow the other steps in the writing process—writing, revising, proofreading, and publishing. Try to use spelling words from this lesson in your sequel.
Sequels will vary.

LESSON 36 **211**

Writer's Workshop Scoring Rubric: Narrative

SCORE 3
Narrative has a clear beginning, middle, and end. Most events and ideas are well developed. Writing is coherent and contains a minimum of sentence-structure, usage, mechanics, and spelling errors.

SCORE 2
Narrative has a beginning, middle, and end, but one or more are not clear or are weak. Some events and ideas are not thoroughly developed. Writing has a degree of coherence but contains some sentence-structure, usage, mechanics, and spelling errors.

SCORE 1
Narrative is incomplete or unclear. Few or no events and ideas are developed. Writing has minimal coherence and contains many sentence-structure, usage, mechanics, and spelling errors.

Evaluating Students' Writing

The scoring rubric is based on standards for idea development, organization, coherence, sentence structure, usage, mechanics, and spelling. You may wish to share the rubric with students before they write their description.

The *Steck-Vaughn Writer's Dictionary, Intermediate Level,* provides writers with a place to write words they want to remember.

Day 4

Student Objective
- To write a narrative, using Lesson 36 words and the steps in the writing process

Presenting the Page

Reread "The Frog Prince" on pages 180 and 181 aloud. Then invite a volunteer to read aloud the part of "Libby Returns" that is shown. Discuss how the sequel continues the story.

You may wish to copy and distribute the Writer's Workshop Masters on pages T295–T296 and T298 for students to use as they write.

Day 5

Student Objective
- To take a posttest on the lesson words

Posttest Options

Use the posttest on this page or the Review Test Master on pages T293–T294 to assess students' ability to spell the lesson words.

Posttest

Dictate the following sentences. Have students write the sentences and underline the lesson words.

1. A deer has strong legs.
2. An owl came near the camp where we stayed.
3. A wire ran across the floor.
4. I will draw a picture.
5. Let's talk about how to care for our air.
6. The clown on the tower was funnier than the other one.
7. Please count the students who were here last autumn.
8. I use my sharpest pencil because I want a thin line.
9. I bought my lunch an hour before the picnic.
10. This spring was the hottest in years.
11. Is that a quart jar?
12. At noon the rain began to pour.
13. Five is greater than four.

211

Commonly Misspelled Words

about	family	name	that's
above	favorite	nice	their
across	finally	now	then
again	friend	once	there
a lot	friends	one	they
always	from	our	though
another	get	out	today
baby	getting	outside	too
because	girl	party	two
been	goes	people	upon
before	guess	play	very
beginning	have	please	want
bought	hear	pretty	was
boy	her	read	went
buy	here	really	were
can	him	right	when
came	his	said	where
children	house	saw	white
color	into	scared	with
come	know	school	would
cousin	like	sent	write
didn't	little	some	writing
does	made	store	wrote
don't	make	swimming	your
every	many	teacher	you're

Spelling Table

Sound	Spellings	Examples
/ă/	a a_e ai au	ask, have, plaid, laugh
/ā/	a a_e ai ay ea eigh ey	table, save, rain, gray, break, eight, they
/ä/	a ea	father, heart
/âr/	air are ere	chair, care, where
/b/	b bb	best, rabbit
/ch/	ch tch	child, catch
/d/	d dd	dish, add
/ĕ/	e ea ie ue a ai ay	best, read, friend, guess, many, said, says
/ē/	e e_e ea ee ei eo ey y	even, these, each, meet, receive, people, key, city
/f/	f ff gh	fly, off, laugh
/g/	g gg	go, egg
/h/	h wh	hot, who
/ĭ/	i ui e ee u a	inside, build, pretty, been, busy, luggage
/ī/	i i_e ie igh eye uy y	tiny, drive, pie, high, eyes, buy, fly
/îr/	ear eer eir ere	year, deer, weird, here
/j/	j g	jog, danger
/k/	k c ck ch	keep, coat, kick, school
/ks/	x	six
/kw/	qu	quiet
/l/	l ll	late, tell
/m/	m mb mm	much, comb, hammer
/n/	n kn nn	need, know, beginning
/ng/	n ng	thank, bring

Sound	Spellings	Examples
/ŏ/	o a	shop, was
/ō/	o o_e oa oe ou ow	both, hole, road, toe, boulder, slow
/oi/	oi oy	point, enjoy
/ô/	o oa oo ou ough a au aw	off, coarse, door, four, brought, tall, autumn, draw
/o͝o/	oo ou u u_e	book, could, pull, sure
/o͞o/	oo ou u_e ue ew o	noon, you, June, blue, news, two
/ou/	ou ow	about, owl
/p/	p pp	place, dropped
/r/	r rr wr	rain, sorry, write
/s/	s ss c	safe, dress, city
/sh/	sh s	shook, sure
/t/	t tt ed	take, matter, thanked
/th/	th	then
/th/	th	third
/ŭ/	u o oe	such, mother, does
/ûr/	ur ir er or ear ere our	curl, girl, dessert, world, learn, were, flourish
/v/	v f	even, of
/w/	w wh o	walk, when, one
/y/	y	year
/yo͞o/	u_e ew ue	use, few, Tuesday
/z/	z zz s	sneeze, blizzard, says
/ə/	a e i o u	along, misery, estimate, lion, subtract

Spelling Dictionary

Major Parts of a Dictionary Entry

The **pronunciation** tells how to pronounce the word.

The **part of speech** is identified.

The **plural form** of a noun is given. Other major forms of a verb are given.

The **entry word** is divided into syllables.

One or more **definitions** tell you what the word means.

one (wŭn) *noun, plural* **ones** A number, written 1: *One plus two equals three.* —*pronoun* A particular person or thing: *One of my turtles is missing.* • **One** sounds like **won.**

A **sample sentence** helps to make the meaning clear.

Another **word with the same sound but different meaning** is sometimes shown.

a·ble (ā′ bəl) *adjective* **abler, ablest** Having enough skill to do something; capable: *Arnold, the circus elephant, is able to stand on his head.*

a·bout (ə bout′) *preposition* Of; concerning: *Do you know the story about Goldilocks and the three bears?* —*adverb* Almost; nearly: *This glass is about empty.*

add (ăd) *verb* **added, adding** To find the sum of: *When we add 2 and 6, we get a total of 8.*

ad·dress (ə drĕs′) or (ăd′ rĕs′) *noun, plural* **addresses** The place where a person lives or receives mail: *I want to mail a birthday card to Nina, but I don't know her address.*

ad·mire (ăd mīr′) *verb* **admired, admiring** **1.** To respect: *I admire your courage.* **2.** To look at or regard with pleasure and appreciation: *Our class admired the drawings of the animals.*

a·do·be (ə dō′ bē) *noun, plural* **adobes** **1.** Brick made of straw and clay that is dried in the sun. **2.** A building made out of these bricks: *Her house is made of adobe.*

a·fraid (ə frād′) *adjective* Frightened; full of fear: *I'm not afraid of the dark.*

af·ter (ăf′ tər) *preposition* Following; at a later time than: *I went to Rona's after dinner.*

a·gain (ə gĕn′) *adverb* Once more; another time: *It's time for a spelling test again.*

a·gent (ā′ jənt) *noun, plural* **agents** **1.** A person who acts for another person, company, or government: *His father is an insurance agent.* **2.** Something that produces or causes a certain effect: *Too much rain is the agent of a flood.*

a·go (ə gō′) *adverb* Past; before the time it is now: *The bus left five minutes ago.*

ag•o•ny (ăg′ ə nē) *noun, plural* **agonies**
Great pain or suffering: *I broke my leg and was in agony.*

aid (ād) *verb* **aided, aiding** To help or assist: *Carla will aid you in finding a seat.*

aim (ām) *verb* **aimed, aiming** **1.** To point at something: *Aim the dart at the target.* **2.** To have a goal or purpose: *We aim to please our teacher.*

air (âr) *noun* **1.** The mixture of gases surrounding the earth: *I like the cool air.* **2.** The space above the earth: *The air was full of kites.*

a•like (ə līk′) *adjective* Similar; like one another: *The goldfish in my fish tank are all alike.*

al•most (ôl′ mōst′) *or* (ôl mōst′) *adverb* Nearly: *It is almost time for lunch.*

a•lone (ə lōn′) *adverb* By oneself: *I like to walk by the sea all alone.*

a•long (ə lông′) *or* (ə lŏng′) *preposition* Beside the length of: *We walked along the beach.* —*adverb* Together; with someone: *When Calvin goes for a walk, his dog goes along.*

al•ways (ôl′ wāz) *or* (ôl′ wĭz) *adverb* At all times; every time: *Sonya always reads before she goes to bed.*

a•pol•o•gize (ə pŏl′ ə jīz′) *verb* **apologized, apologizing** To say one is sorry: *I apologize for being late to class.*

ap•ple (ăp′ əl) *noun, plural* **apples** A round fruit that is red, yellow, or green: *My favorite kind of fruit pie is apple.*

A•pril (ā′ prəl) *noun* The fourth month of the year: *April is a spring month.*

arc•tic (ärk′ tĭk) *or* (är′ tĭk) *adjective* Very cold: *The arctic air froze the water in the lake.*

aren't (ärnt) *or* (är′ ənt) The contraction of "are not": *Why aren't you coming to the playground with us?*

arm (ärm) *noun, plural* **arms** The part of the body between the hand and the shoulder: *Zelda's arm hurt from pitching.*

a•round (ə round′) *adverb* In a circle: *I saw the bird fly around.* —*preposition* About; here and there: *I travel around the country.*

art (ärt) *noun, plural* **arts** **1.** A painting, drawing, or sculpture. **2.** A skill or craft: *Dancing is an art.*

ar•tis•tic (är tĭs′ tĭk) *adjective* **1.** Having to do with art or artists: *He has artistic interests.* **2.** Showing talent, skill, or good taste.

ask (ăsk) *verb* **asked, asking** **1.** To put a question to: *I asked my father where he was born.* **2.** To request: *I asked for a small pizza.*

as•sure (ə shŏŏr′) *verb* **assured, assuring** **1.** To make sure or certain. **2.** To make less afraid: *Do you assure me that the dog will not bite?*

ate Look up **eat.** • **Ate** sounds like **eight.**

ath•let•ic (ăth lĕt′ ĭk) *adjective* **1.** Strong and active: *The athletic girl won every race.* **2.** Having to do with or for sports or athletes.

at•tempt (ə tĕmpt′) *noun, plural* **attempts** A try or effort: *I made an attempt to draw a picture of my cat.*

Au•gust (ô′ gəst) *noun* The eighth month of the year: *The weather is hot here in August.*

au•tumn (ô′ təm) *noun, plural* **autumns** The season of the year coming between summer and winter; fall: *Every autumn the leaves change color and then fall off the trees.*

a·way (ə wā') *adverb* **1.** In a different direction or place: *James is away from school.* **2.** From a place: *Take the dogs away.*

bar·be·cue (bär' bĭ kyo͞o') *noun, plural* **barbecues** A meal cooked outdoors over an open fire: *I like to eat barbecue.* —*verb* **barbecued, barbecuing** To cook over an open fire outdoors: *We will barbecue the meat.*

bark¹ (bärk) *noun, plural* **barks** The sharp, explosive sound made by a dog or fox: *I could hear my dog's bark.* —*verb* **barked, bark·ing** To make the sharp sound a dog makes: *Fido likes to bark at cats.*

bark² (bärk) *noun, plural* **barks** The outer covering of trees and other woody plants: *The bark of a birch tree is thin.*

barn (bärn) *noun, plural* **barns** A farm building used for storing grain and hay and for keeping livestock: *The horses ran into the barn.*

be (bē) *verb* **am, is, was** (wŏz) *or* (wŭz) *or* (wəz), **were** (wûr), **been** (bĭn), **being** **1.** To equal in identity or meaning: *That girl is my sister.* **2.** To have or show a certain quality or characteristic: *I am tall and thin.* **3.** To belong to a certain group or class: *Whales are mammals.* **4.** To occupy a certain place or position: *Your books have been here since yesterday.* **5.** To live; to exist: *Once upon a time, there were three bears.* **6.** To take place; to happen: *Thanksgiving is next week.* —*helping verb* (used with other verbs): *I am teaching my dog a new trick.*

bear (bâr) *verb* **bore, born** (bôrn), **bearing** **1.** To give birth to: *Some snakes lay eggs, and some bear their young.* **2.** To come into being: *George Washington was born on February 22, 1732.*
• **Bear** sounds like **bare.**

be·cause (bĭ kôz') *or* (bĭ kŭz') *conjunction* Since; for the reason that: *The class laughed because the cartoons were so silly.*

been Look up **be.**

be·fore (bĭ fôr') *conjunction* Earlier than; ahead of: *Liz did her chores before lunch.*

be·gin (bĭ gĭn') *verb* **began, begun, beginning** (bĭ gĭn' ĭng) To start: *The teams were ready to begin the game.*

be·gin·ning (bĭ gĭn' ĭng) *noun, plural* **beginnings** The first part: *At the beginning of the race, Carlos was ahead.*

be·hind (bĭ hīnd') *preposition* **1.** Following: *Ling and Trina were walking behind Jeff.* **2.** At the back of: *Maria hid behind a tree.*

be·long (bĭ lông') *or* (bĭ lŏng') *verb* **belonged, belonging** To be owned by: *These pencils belong to me.*

best (bĕst) *adjective* Most excellent, finest: *It was the best ice cream she had ever eaten.* Look up **good, well.**

bet·ter (bĕt' ər) *adjective* More excellent than another: *We have a better band than any other school.* Look up **good, well.**

bird (bûrd) *noun, plural* **birds** An animal with wings and feathers that lays eggs: *A cardinal is a bird with bright red feathers.*

black (blăk) *noun* The darkest color; the color of coal: *Black is the color of crows.* —*adjective* **blacker, blackest** Having this color: *Mom wore a black dress.*

blend (blĕnd) *verb* **blended, blending** To put together; mix: *Blend the eggs and sugar.* —*noun, plural* **blends** Something that has been mixed.

block (blŏk) *noun, plural* **blocks** Part of a city, often a square, with streets on all sides: *I live one block away.* —*verb* **blocked, blocking** To get in the way of: *The cow blocked the railroad track.*

blow (blō) *verb* **blew, blown, blowing** To be in motion, as the air: *Hold onto your hat, or the wind will blow it away.*

blue (blōō) *adjective* **bluer, bluest**
Having the color of the clear sky during
the day: *Benjamin wore a blue jacket.*
• **Blue** sounds like **blew**.

boat (bōt) *noun, plural* **boats** A vessel that
travels on water: *My sister and I went for a
ride on the boat.*

bod•y (bŏd′ē) *noun, plural* **bodies** All
of a person or animal except the mind:
The human body is very complex.

boil (boil) *verb* **boiled, boiling** To heat
a liquid until bubbles form and steam is
given off: *I boiled some water to make tea.*

book (bŏŏk) *noun, plural* **books** Printed
sheets of paper held together between two
covers: *Richie went to the library to get a book.*

born Look up **bear**.

both (bōth) *pronoun* The one as well as the
other: *Both of them can play the French horn.*
—*conjunction* (used with *and*): *Both Mom
and Dad were at work.*

bot•tle (bŏt′l) *noun, plural* **bottles** A
hollow container made of glass or plastic
that can be closed with a cap: *The children
drank juice from the bottles.*

bot•tom (bŏt′əm) *noun, plural* **bottoms**
The lowest part of anything: *I saw my dad at
the bottom of the hill.*

bough (bou) *noun, plural* **boughs** A large
or main branch of a tree: *The nest is on the
bough of the tree.*

bought Look up **buy**.

boy (boi) *noun, plural* **boys** A male child:
My dog chased the boy on the bike.

break (brāk) *verb* **broke, broken,
breaking 1.** To crack or damage; to
come apart: *Did you break the dish when you
dropped it?* **2.** To crack the bone of: *Rosa
fell off her bike and broke her arm.*

bring (brĭng) *verb* **brought** (brôt),
bringing To carry or take something to
a place or person: *He brought his photo
album to school.*

Pronunciation Key

ă	pat	îr	deer	*th*	this
ā	pay	ŏ	pot	ŭ	cut
âr	care	ō	toe	ûr	urge
ä	father	ô	paw, for	ə	about,
ě	pet	oi	noise		item,
ē	bee	ŏŏ	took		edible,
ĭ	pit	ōō	boot		gallop,
ī	pie	ou	out		circus
		th	thin		

broil (broil) *verb* **broiled, broiling** To
cook by holding directly over or under
heat: *Mia broiled the steaks for dinner.*

broth (brôth) *or* (brŏth) *noun, plural*
broths A thin clear soup made from the
water in which meat, fish, or vegetables have
been boiled: *We had chicken broth for lunch.*

brought Look up **bring**.

brown (broun) *adjective* **browner,
brownest** Having the color of coffee or
chocolate: *The dead leaves were brown.*

build (bĭld) *verb* **built, building** To make
something by putting materials or parts
together: *Many birds build nests in the spring.*

bu•reau (byŏŏr′ō) *noun, plural* **bureaus**
A chest of drawers: *Put it on the bureau.*

bus•y (bĭz′ē) *adjective* **busier, busiest**
At work; active: *She is busy doing her homework.*

but•ter (bŭt′ər) *noun* A soft, yellow fat
made from cream: *I like butter on corn.*

buy (bī) *verb* **bought** (bôt), **buying** To
get by paying a price: *He bought a model
rocket at the hobby shop.* • **Buy** sounds like **by**.

buz•zard (bŭz′ərd) *noun, plural*
buzzards A very large bird
with a sharp, hooked beak
and long, sharp claws; a
vulture: *The buzzard was
in the tree.*

by (bī) *preposition* Beside or
near: *Leave your boots by the door.*
• **By** sounds like **buy**.

ca•ble (**kā′** bəl) *noun, plural* **cables**
A strong, thick rope often made of steel
wire: *The boat is held to the dock by a cable.*

came Look up **come.**

can (kăn) *or* (kən) *helping verb* **could**
(kŏŏd) To be able to: *We could see that
the man was angry.*

can't (kănt) The contraction of "cannot":
I can't see any stars tonight.

card (kärd) *noun, plural* **cards** A small
rectangular piece of cardboard or plastic:
I sent my pen pal a birthday card.

care (kâr) *noun, plural* **cares** Close
attention: *The painter picked her colors with care.*
—*verb* **cared, caring** To be concerned:
Millie cared what people thought about her.

care•less (**kâr′** lĭs) *adjective* Not paying
attention to what one is doing: *I fell off
my bike because I was careless.*

car•ry (**kăr′** ē) *verb* **carries, carried,
carrying** To take from one place to
another: *Will you help me carry this box?*

car•ton (**kär′** tn) *noun, plural* **cartons**
A container or box made of cardboard,
paper, plastic, or other materials and used
for holding liquids or other objects: *We will
recycle the egg carton.*

ca•su•al (**kăzh′** ŏŏ əl) *adjective* Right for
informal wear: *Sam wears casual clothes.*

catch (kăch) *or* (kĕch) *verb* **caught,
catching** 1. To get hold of; capture: *Billy
tried to catch the cat.* 2. To reach or get to
in time: *I had to hurry to catch the train.*

cav•ern (**kăv′** ərn) *noun, plural* **caverns**
A large cave: *Raul likes to explore caverns.*

cel•e•bra•tion (sĕl′ ə **brā′** shən) *noun,
plural* **celebrations** A party or other
activity carried on to honor a special
occasion: *We had a celebration the last
day of school.*

cem•e•ter•y (**sĕm′** ĭ tĕr′ ē) *noun, plural*
cemeteries A place where dead people
are buried: *The class put flowers on the
graves in the cemetery.*

cent (sĕnt) *noun, plural* **cents** A coin that is
1/100 of a dollar; a penny: *Carlos bought the
notebook for 99 cents.* • **Cent** sounds like **sent.**

chair (châr) *noun, plural* **chairs** A seat for
one person, usually having four legs and a
back: *The chair was soft and comfortable.*

change (chānj) *verb* **changed, changing**
1. To make different: *Leaves change color in
the fall.* 2. To replace; exchange: *I'll change
this dress for a different one.* —*noun, plural*
changes A thing that has become
different: *We all noticed the change in
her hair.*

child (chīld) *noun, plural* **children**
(**chĭl′** drən) A young boy or girl: *Every
child in the school went on the picnic. All
children like fairy tales.*

chil•dren Look up **child.**

chime (chīm) *noun,
plural* **chimes**
1. A set of bells or
pipes that make
musical sounds.
2. A musical sound
made by bells or a similar
sound: *The chime of the doorbell woke me.*

choice (chois) *noun, plural* **choices** The
power or chance to choose: *They had their
choice of peanut butter sandwiches or tuna
salad for lunch.*

cir•cu•lar (**sûr′** kyə lər) *adjective* Shaped
like a circle; round: *The circular drawing
was well done.*

cit•y (**sĭt′** ē) *noun, plural* **cities** A large
or important town: *Mom goes to the city every
day to work.*

clank (klăngk) *verb* **clanked, clanking**
To make a sound like two pieces of metal
hitting each other: *The hammer clanked
against the iron bell.*

class (klăs) *noun, plural* **classes** A group of students taught by the same teacher or group of teachers: *Our class took a trip to the museum.*

clock (klŏk) *noun, plural* **clocks** An instrument that tells time: *According to the kitchen clock, I was late again.*

close (klōs) *adjective* **closer, closest** Near: *He is standing close to the door.* —*verb* (klōz) **closed, closing** To shut: *He closed the heavy suitcase.*

clown (kloun) *noun, plural* **clowns** A person who has a job in the circus or on stage making people laugh: *The clowns looked so funny.*

coarse (kôrs) *adjective* **coarser, coarsest 1.** Made of large bits: *The sand on the beach was coarse.* **2.** Rough: *Coarse wool makes me itch.*

coat (kōt) *noun, plural* **coats** A piece of clothing worn over other clothes to keep warm: *Keesha's new coat was too big.*

coax (kōks) *verb* **coaxed, coaxing** To try to persuade or convince by mild urging: *Mom had to coax me into going.*

co•coa (kō′ kō′) *noun* A drink made with chocolate, sugar, and milk or water: *We drink hot cocoa in winter.*

coin (koin) *noun, plural* **coins** A piece of round, flat metal stamped by the government, used for money: *I had a lot of coins in my pocket.*

comb (kōm) *noun, plural* **combs** A thin piece of hard material with teeth, used to arrange hair: *While Selena was untangling her hair, the comb broke.* —*verb* **combed, combing 1.** To arrange the hair. **2.** To look thoroughly: *I combed the house for my missing ring.*

come (kŭm) *verb* **came** (kām), **coming 1.** To draw near; approach: *The lion came closer and closer to the mouse.* **2.** To be available: *The toy robot came with two batteries.*

Pronunciation Key

ă	pat	îr	deer	*th*	this
ā	pay	ŏ	pot	ŭ	cut
âr	care	ō	toe	ûr	urge
ä	father	ô	paw, for	ə	about,
ĕ	pet	oi	noise		item,
ē	bee	ŏŏ	took		edible,
ĭ	pit	ōō	boot		gallop,
ī	pie	ou	out		circus
		th	thin		

com•ment (kŏm′ ĕnt′) *noun, plural* **comments** A remark or note that explains something or gives an opinion: *James made a comment about the news.*

con•sent (kən sĕnt′) *verb* **consented, consenting** To agree to; to give permission: *Michael consented to cleaning his room once a week.*

con•sole (kən sōl′) *verb* **consoled, consoling** To comfort: *When Kim's pet died, Belinda consoled her.*

con•tain (kən tān′) *verb* **contained, containing** To have in it; hold: *The bowl contains soup.*

cook (kŏŏk) *verb* **cooked, cooking** To prepare food for eating by using heat: *Cook the rice until it is fluffy.*

cook•ie (kŏŏk′ ē) *noun, plural* **cookies** A small, flat, sweet cake: *The cookies were shaped like hearts.*

cor•ner (kôr′ nər) *noun, plural* **corners** The place where two lines or sides meet: *My dog ate a corner of my homework paper.*

cor•ri•dor (kôr′ ĭ dər) *or* (kŏr′ ĭ dər) *noun, plural* **corridors** A long hall or passage in a building: *The corridor in the hotel was wide.*

could Look up **can.**

could•n't (kŏŏd′ nt) The contraction of "could not": *We couldn't go to the beach.*

could•'ve (kŏŏd′ əv) The contraction of "could have": *Lisa could've gone to the zoo, but she was sick.*

count (kount) *noun, plural* **counts**
The number reached by counting: *A count showed that one marble was missing.* —*verb* **counted, counting** To say numbers in order: *Ty's baby sister can count to 20.*

cov·er (kŭv' ər) *verb* **covered, covering**
To put or lay over: *I covered my bread with peanut butter.* —*noun, plural* **covers** Something that is put over another thing: *He hid the present under the covers on his bed.*

crin·kle (krĭng' kəl) *verb* **crinkled, crinkling** To wrinkle; crumple: *Betsy tried not to crinkle the wrapping paper.*

cry (krī) *verb* **cries, cried, crying**
1. To weep; shed tears: *Some people cry when they are happy.* **2.** To shout or call loudly: *If I need help, I'll cry out.*

curl (kûrl) *verb* **curled, curling** To twist into curves or coils: *The snake curled around the rock.* —*noun, plural* **curls** A coil of hair; a ringlet: *She wore her hair in curls.*

cy·cle (sī' kəl) *noun, plural* **cycles**
1. A bicycle, tricycle, or motorcycle: *My cycle is broken.* **2.** A series of events that happen over and over in the same order: *People enjoy the cycle of seasons.*

dair·y (dâr' ē) *noun, plural* **dairies**
A farm where cows are raised to produce milk: *Our class took a field trip to the dairy.*

dan·ger (dān' jər) *noun, plural* **dangers**
The chance that something harmful might happen: *A police officer faces danger every day.*

dark (därk) *adjective* **darker, darkest**
Having little or no light: *The cave was very dark inside.* —*noun* Nightfall: *The street lights come on after dark.*

daw·dle (dôd' l) *verb* **dawdled, dawdling** To take more time than necessary: *I often dawdle on my way home from school.*

dear (dîr) *adjective* **dearer, dearest**
Loved: *Billy is a dear friend of mine.*
• **Dear** sounds like **deer.**

de·bate (dĭ bāt') *verb* **debated, debating 1.** To think about in order to decide: *I debated which book to buy.*
2. To discuss or argue reasons for and against something.

de·ceive (dĭ sēv') *verb* **deceived, deceiving** To make a person believe something that is not true; mislead: *It was wrong to deceive my parents.*

De·cem·ber (dĭ sĕm' bər) *noun* The twelfth month of the year: *We are going skiing in December.*

deer (dîr) *noun, plural* **deer** A hoofed animal that can run very fast: *Look at the beautiful antlers on that male deer.*
• **Deer** sounds like **dear.**

de·fine (dĭ fīn') *verb* **defined, defining**
To give or explain the meaning of: *Our teacher told us to define the spelling words.*

de·pos·it (dĭ pŏz' ĭt) *verb* **deposited, depositing 1.** To put or place; set down: *I deposited my toys in the box.* **2.** To put money in the bank.

de·sign·er (dĭ zī' nər) *noun, plural* **designers** A person who makes the plan, pattern, or drawing for something: *The designer told us about her idea for a new doll.*

des·sert (dĭ zûrt') *noun, plural* **desserts** Food served last at a meal: *We had dessert after we finished dinner.*

de·vour (dĭ vour') *verb* **devoured, devouring** To eat in a hungry way: *The child will devour her lunch.*

did·n't (dĭd' nt) The contraction of "did not": *I didn't know who you were.*

dirt (dûrt) *noun* Loose earth or soil: *He drew a map in the dirt with a stick.*

dirt·y (dûr′ tē) *adjective* **dirtier, dirtiest**
Not clean: *Amy's shoes were dirtier than mine.
Eric's were the dirtiest.*

dish (dĭsh) *noun, plural* **dishes 1.** A plate
or bowl used for holding food: *The clown
balanced a dish on his nose.* **2.** A particular
food: *Barbara's favorite dish was spaghetti.*

dis·may (dĭs mā′) *noun* A feeling of fear
or loss of courage when danger or trouble
comes: *I felt dismay when my rabbit got out
of its pen.*

dis·pute (dĭ spyōōt′) *noun, plural*
disputes An argument or quarrel:
My friend and I had a dispute.

do (dōō) *verb* **does** (duz), **did, done**
(dun), **doing 1.** To perform; complete:
*Bibi, the circus monkey, is always doing
things that make people laugh.* **2.** To be
good enough: *No one had done as well on
the test as Valerie.* —*helping verb* (used to
ask questions): *Does she swim?*

does Look up **do.**

does·n't (dŭz′ nt) The contraction of
"does not": *She doesn't want to play the
game anymore.*

dome (dōm) *noun, plural*
domes A round roof or
top that looks like half of
a ball: *The building had a
dome at the top.*

done Look up **do.**

don't (dōnt) The contraction of "do not":
Don't sit on that wet bench.

door (dôr) *noun, plural* **doors 1.** A
movable panel that swings or slides to open
or close the entrance to a room, building, or
vehicle: *Raquel slammed the door behind her.*
2. A doorway: *Marta walked through the door.*

doubt·ful (dout′ fəl) *adjective* Feeling,
showing, or causing uncertainty; not sure:
Kim was doubtful that she could stay awake.

down¹ (doun) *adverb* From a higher to a
lower point on: *The ball rolled down the hill.*

Pronunciation Key

ă	pat	îr	deer	*th*	this
ā	pay	ŏ	pot	ŭ	cut
âr	care	ō	toe	ûr	urge
ä	father	ô	paw, for	ə	about,
ĕ	pet	oi	noise		item,
ē	bee	ŏŏ	took		edible,
ĭ	pit	ōō	boot		gallop,
ī	pie	ou	out		circus
		th	thin		

down² (doun) *noun* The soft under
feathers of birds: *The bird had soft down.*

draw (drô) *verb* **drew, drawn, drawing**
To make a picture with pen, pencil, crayon,
etc.: *I can draw great pictures of airplanes.*

dream (drēm) *noun, plural* **dreams**
Something felt, thought, or seen during
sleep: *I had a dream about a giant bee.*
—*verb* **dreamed** or **dreamt, dreaming**
To think, feel, or see during sleep; to have
dreams: *Amy dreamed that she could fly.*

drea·ry (drîr′ ē) *adjective* **drearier,
dreariest** Sad; gloomy: *The rainy day
was dreary.*

dress (drĕs) *noun, plural* **dresses** A piece
of clothing worn by women and girls, usually
having a top and skirt made in one piece:
Ella bought a new dress for the class party.
—*verb* **dressed, dressing** To put
clothes on: *Get dressed and we'll go shopping.*

drive (drīv) *verb* **drove, driven, driving**
1. To steer a vehicle: *Drive the car carefully.*
2. To carry in a vehicle: *My mom promised to
drive me to the rodeo.* —*noun, plural* **drives**
A ride in a vehicle: *Let's go for a drive.*

drop (drŏp) *verb* **dropped, dropping**
To fall or let fall: *I dropped the glass.*

each (ēch) *adjective* Every one of: *Each
student in the class gave me a report.*

ear (îr) *noun, plural* **ears** **1.** The part of the body with which animals and people hear: *An elephant's ears are big and floppy.* **2.** Attention: *This message is important, so give me your ear.*

earth (ûrth) *noun* **1.** The planet on which human beings live: *The earth is the third planet from the sun.* **2.** Soil; ground: *We planted a tree in the earth.*

eat (ēt) *verb* **ate** (āt), **eaten, eating** To take meals: *I ate dinner at home.*

egg (ĕg) *noun, plural* **eggs** The contents of a chicken egg, used as food: *I like to crack the shells of eggs.*

eight (āt) *noun* The number that follows seven: *Four plus four is eight.* —*adjective* Being one more than seven in number: *An octopus has eight tentacles.* • **Eight** sounds like **ate.**

end (ĕnd) *noun, plural* **ends** The finish of a thing: *The road comes to an end at the river.* —*verb* **ended, ending** To finish; to bring to an end: *The concert ended with a fireworks show.*

end•ing (ĕn' dĭng) *noun, plural* **endings** The last part: *The movie had a scary ending.*

en•dure (ĕn dŏŏr') *or* (ĕn dyŏŏr') *verb* **endured, enduring** **1.** To put up with: *The campers had to endure cold weather.* **2.** To continue; last. *The pyramids have endured a long time.*

en•joy (ĕn joi') *verb* **enjoyed, enjoying** To like to do: *I enjoy singing along with her.*

en•joy•ment (ĕn joi' mənt) *noun, plural* **enjoyments** Joy; pleasure: *We get enjoyment from a good book.*

es•ti•mate (ĕs' tə māt') *verb* **estimated, estimating** To guess by thinking about clearly: *We estimated that the trip would take five hours.*

e•ven (ē' vən) *adjective* Smooth; flat: *Willy likes to ride his bike on this road because it's so even.* —*adverb* **1.** Although it seems unlikely: *The boys were all dressed up, even Coby.*

eve•ry (ĕv' rē) *adjective* All in an entire group; each one: *Mr. Lee read every mystery book in the library.*

eye (ī) *noun, plural* **eyes** **1.** One of two round organs with which a person or animal sees: *My eyes followed the home run right out of the field.* **2.** A close watch: *Please keep an eye on my bike.*

fa•ble (fā' bəl) *noun, plural* **fables** A story that teaches a lesson: *My favorite fable is about the lion and the mouse.*

face (fās) *noun, plural* **faces** The front of the head: *Raymond had spots on his face from the measles.*

fal•ter (fôl' tər) *verb* **faltered, faltering** To act, speak, or move in an unsteady way: *My voice was faltering when I gave my speech.*

fam•i•ly (făm' ə lē) *or* (făm' lē) *noun, plural* **families** Parents and their children: *My family always goes on vacation together.*

fa•ther (fä' thər) *noun, plural* **fathers** The male parent of a child: *Gina's father took her to the doctor today.*

feat (fēt) *noun, plural* **feats** An act or deed that shows great bravery, skill, or strength: *Riding the bicycle ten miles was a feat.*

Feb•ru•ar•y (fĕb' rŏŏ ĕr' ē) *or* (fĕb' yŏŏ ĕr' ē) *noun* The second month of the year: *Groundhog Day comes in February.*

few (fyŏŏ) *adjective* **fewer, fewest** Not many: *There were only a few pieces left.*

fill (fĭl) *verb* **filled, filling** **1.** To make or become full: *I always fill the sugar bowl to the top.* **2.** To spread throughout: *My writing filled the pages of my diary.*

find (fīnd) *verb* **found** (found), **finding**
1. To look for and get: *I found my keys under my bed.* **2.** To meet with; come upon: *Polar bears are only found in the far north.*

fire (fīr) *noun, plural* **fires** Heat and light given off by burning something: *They saw the fire and ran for help.*

first (fûrst) *adjective* Coming before any other in time, place, or order: *This is my first pair of ice skates.* —*noun* Person or thing that is first: *Tyrel was first in line.*
Idiom. at first. In the beginning: *At first, Ellen was scared but then she got brave.*

floor (flôr) *or* (flōr) *noun, plural* **floors** The part of a room people walk on: *The floor squeaks when you walk on it.*

flour·ish (flûr′ ĭsh) *or* (flŭr′ ĭsh) *verb* **flourished, flourishing** To grow strongly and well: *The flowers flourish in the sunny garden.*

flow·er (flou′ ər) *noun, plural* **flowers** The part of the plant where seeds are made; the blossom: *This plant has yellow flowers.*

fly (flī) *verb* **flies, flew, flown, flying** To move through the air with wings: *I love to watch airplanes fly in and out of the airport.*

foot (fŏŏt) *noun, plural* **feet** The part of the leg on which a person or animal walks: *I put my shoe on the wrong foot.*

for·get (fər gĕt′) *or* (fôr gĕt′) *verb* **forgot** (fər gŏt′), **forgotten, forgetting** To be unable to remember: *Don't forget to study.*

for·got Look up **forget.**

fork (fôrk) *noun, plural* **forks** **1.** A tool used to pick up food: *I eat with a fork.* **2.** A place where something divides into more than one part: *When we came to the fork in the trail, we didn't know which way to go.*

found Look up **find.**

four (fôr) *noun* The number that follows three: *Two plus two is four.* —*adjective* Being one more than three in number: *There are four people in my family.*

frag·ile (frăj′ əl) *or* (frăj′ īl) *adjective* Easy to break or damage: *The glass is fragile.*

frail (frāl) *adjective* **frailer, frailest**
1. Easily broken or damaged: *The very old chair is frail.* **2.** Not having strength; weak: *I was frail after my illness.*

free (frē) *adjective* **freer, freest 1.** Not under someone else's control: *The cat was free to roam around the neighborhood.* **2.** Without cost: *We won two free tickets.*

Fri·day (frī′ dē) *or* (frī′ dā′) *noun, plural* **Fridays** The sixth day of the week: *Our teacher didn't give us homework on Friday.*

friend (frĕnd) *noun, plural* **friends** A person one knows and likes: *My friend and I write letters to each other in a secret code.*

friend·li·ness (frĕnd′ lē nĭs) *noun* The manner or actions of a friend: *Aaron's friendliness makes everyone feel welcome.*

frog (frôg) *or* (frŏg) *noun, plural* **frogs** A small animal with webbed feet and smooth skin: *Frogs have strong legs.*

from (frŭm) *or* (frŏm) *or* (frəm) *preposition* **1.** Having as an origin: *I got a letter from my cousin.* **2.** Starting at: *The boys raced from school to their house.*

front (frŭnt) *noun, plural* **fronts** The part of something that faces forward: *There was a crowd in front of the music store.*

fron•tier (frŭn tîr′) or (frŭn′ tîr′) noun, plural **frontiers** **1.** The border between countries: *The family crossed the frontier between Mexico and the United States.* **2.** The far edge of a country where people are just beginning to live. *Pioneers lived on the wild frontier of the West.*

ful•fill (fŏŏl fĭl′) verb **fulfilled, fulfilling** To carry out, finish, or do what is called for: *He is fulfilling his promise.*

full (fŏŏl) adjective **fuller, fullest** Holding all that it can hold: *My stomach was full after dinner.*

fun•ny (fŭn′ ē) adjective **funnier, funniest** Causing laughter; amusing: *Ty's jokes are funny. Brad's jokes are funnier than mine. Angela's are the funniest.*

fur (fûr) noun, plural **furs** Thick, soft hair that covers certain animals: *My dog's fur keeps him warm in the winter.*

gar•den (gär′ dn) noun, plural **gardens** A piece of land used for growing vegetables and flowers: *We plant beans in the garden.*

gen•u•ine (jĕn′ yŏŏ ĭn) adjective **1.** Real: *A genuine ruby costs a lot of money.* **2.** Sincere; honest: *My aunt showed a genuine interest in my story.*

girl (gûrl) noun, plural **girls** A female child: *Hannah was the only girl on the team.*

glid•er (glī′ dər) noun, plural **gliders** An aircraft that flies without a motor and moves easily on currents of air: *The ride in the glider was fun.*

go (gō) verb **goes** (gōz), **went, gone, going** To move; travel: *Mary goes to the dentist every year.*

goes Look up go.

gold (gōld) noun A heavy, precious, yellow metal used for making jewelry and coins: *Will has a watch that is made of gold.*

good (gŏŏd) adjective **better, best** **1.** Having high quality: *To hike, you need a good pair of boots.* **2.** Desirable; pleasing: *We had good weather for our picnic. The weather last month was better than now. The weather in the spring was the best all year.*

gour•met (gŏŏr mā′) or (gŏŏr′ mā′) noun, plural **gourmets** A person who loves fine food and knows a great deal about it. —adjective Having to do with fine food: *Mother cooked a gourmet dinner.*

gov•ern (gŭv′ ərn) verb **governed, governing** To rule, control, direct, or manage: *He governed the country for a year.*

gray (grā) noun, plural **grays** Any color that is a mixture of black and white: *Do you like the color gray?* —adjective **grayer, grayest** Having the color gray: *I have a gray cat.*

great (grāt) adjective **greater, greatest** Wonderful; very good: *It would be great to travel from zoo to zoo. Of the two zoos, which is greater? This is the greatest zoo in the world.*

ground (ground) noun Soil; land: *The ground was covered with snow after the storm.*

guess (gĕs) verb **guessed, guessing** **1.** To form an opinion without enough knowledge: *We were guessing what the surprise would be.* **2.** To think; suppose: *I guess I'll just stay here.*

had•n't (hăd′ nt) The contraction of "had not": *I hadn't known him long before he moved away.*

hair (hâr) noun, plural **hairs** The thin, threadlike strands that grow from a person's or animal's skin: *Nan wears her long hair in a braid.*

half (hăf) *noun, plural* **halves** One of two equal parts: *Jenna ate half of her sandwich.*

ham·mer (hăm′ ər) *noun, plural* **hammers** A tool with an iron head used to drive in nails: *I need a hammer to put the birdhouse together.*

hand (hănd) *noun, plural* **hands** The part of the arm below the wrist: *I held the baby chick in my hands.* —*verb* **handed, handing** To pass with the hands: *I handed the teacher my story.*

hap·py (hăp′ ē) *adjective* **happier, happiest** Feeling pleased or joyful: *She was happy when she won the award.*

hard (härd) *adjective* **harder, hardest** Not easy: *This math test is too hard.* —*adverb* **harder, hardest** With energy or effort: *Dennis worked hard.*

has·n't (hăz′ ənt) The contraction of "has not": *Joey hasn't gone yet.*

have·n't (hăv′ ənt) The contraction of "have not": *I haven't heard from Delyn since she went to camp.*

head (hĕd) *noun, plural* **heads** The top part of the body that contains the brain, eyes, ears, nose, and mouth: *Jane put the hat on her head.* —*verb* **headed, heading** To go toward: *The bird headed south for the winter.*

hear (hîr) *verb* **heard, hearing** **1.** To be aware of sound: *Do you hear a noise in the attic?* **2.** To be told: *Emily and her class were about to hear the story of Daniel Boone.* • **Hear** sounds like **here.**

heart (härt) *noun, plural* **hearts** **1.** The organ in the chest that pumps blood through the body: *The doctor listened to my heart.* **2.** Courage and enthusiasm: *He put his heart into winning the game.*

hel·lo (hĕ lō′) *or* (hə lō′) *interjection* A greeting: *Sharon always answers the phone with a cheery, "Hello."*

help (hĕlp) *verb* **helped, helping** To aid or assist; to be useful: *Will you help me hang this picture? I helped Dee buy new jeans.*

Pronunciation Key

ă	pat	îr	deer	*th*	this
ā	pay	ŏ	pot	ŭ	cut
âr	care	ō	toe	ûr	urge
ä	father	ô	paw, for	ə	about,
ĕ	pet	oi	noise		item,
ē	bee	ŏŏ	took		edible,
ĭ	pit	ōō	boot		gallop,
ī	pie	ou	out		circus
		th	thin		

here (hîr) *adverb* In this place or spot: *Cheri and I have been waiting here all afternoon.* —*noun* This place: *The ice cream truck is four blocks from here.* • **Here** sounds like **hear.**

he's (hēz) The contraction of "he is" or "he has": *He's the new music teacher.*

high (hī) *adjective* **higher, highest** Tall: *That pine tree is 25 feet high.* —*adverb* At or to a high point: *My balloon flew high up in the sky.*

hold (hōld) *verb* **held, holding** **1.** To have and keep in the hand; grasp: *I have to hold my sister's hand when we go shopping.* **2.** To keep in a certain position: *Hold your head still.*

hole (hōl) *noun, plural* **holes** A hollow or empty place in something solid: *The pirates dug a hole and buried a treasure chest.* • **Hole** sounds like **whole.**

hop (hŏp) *verb* **hopped, hopping** To move by taking small jumps or skips: *The rabbit was hopping across the field.*

hope (hōp) *verb* **hoped, hoping** To wish for something: *I hope my grandmother feels better soon. Julia hoped she wouldn't be late for school.*

hot (hŏt) *adjective* **hotter, hottest** Very warm: *It is hotter outside today than it was yesterday. Tomorrow may be the hottest day of the year.*

hour (our) *noun, plural* **hours** A period of time equal to 60 minutes: *The bread will take one hour to bake.* • **Hour** sounds like **our**.

house (hous) *noun, plural* **houses** (**hou**′ zĭz) A building that people live in: *The Scouts met at my house.*

how'd (houd) The contraction of "how did": *How'd you tie the knot?*

hud•dle (**hŭd**′ l) *noun, plural* **huddles** A group or crowd that is closely gathered or packed together: *Our team plans the next play when we are in a huddle.* —*verb* **huddled, huddling** To gather close together: *The campers huddled in the tent.*

huge (hyōōj) *adjective* **huger, hugest** Very large; enormous: *The circus parade was led by a huge elephant.*

hun•dred (**hŭn**′ drĭd) *noun, plural* **hundreds** The number that follows 99, written 100 in numerals: *Did you know that 100 is equal to 50 plus 50?* —*adjective* Being one more than 99 in number: *There are 100 pages in this book.*

I'd (īd) The contraction of "I had," "I would," or "I should": *I'd better get home before dark. I'd rather eat brownies than bake them.*

I'll (īl) The contraction of "I will" or "I shall": *I'll never remember everyone's name.*

I'm (īm) The contraction of "I am": *I'm sure I will make the team.*

in•come (**ĭn**′ kŭm′) *noun, plural* **incomes** Money that a person receives for work or from other things during a certain period of time: *Roderick wants to earn an income as a teacher.*

in•dex (**ĭn**′ dĕks′) *noun, plural* **indexes** An alphabetical list of names and subjects at the end of a book that gives the page or pages where each can be found: *Mary looked in the index to find the pages where butterflies are described.*

in•side (ĭn sīd′) *or* (**ĭn**′ sīd′) *noun, plural* **insides** The inner part: *We painted the inside of the house.* —*preposition* (ĭn sīd′) Into: *She put her hand inside the grab bag.*

in•spire (ĭn spīr′) *verb* **inspired, inspiring** 1. To move the mind, feelings, or imagination: *Nature may inspire the artist.* 2. To move to action: *He inspired me to try.*

in•stall (ĭn stôl′) *verb* **installed, installing** To put in place for use or service: *My father will install a new furnace.*

in•struct (ĭn strŭkt′) *verb* **instructed, instructing** To teach or show how to do something: *Will Bruce instruct the tennis class?*

is•n't (**ĭz**′ ənt) The contraction of "is not": *This isn't my lunch box.*

it's (ĭts) The contraction of "it is" or "it has": *It's time for lunch.*

I've (īv) The contraction of "I have": *I've never seen a movie that scared me so much.*

jab (jăb) *verb* **jabbed, jabbing** To poke with something pointed: *Why are you jabbing me with your finger?*

Jan•u•ar•y (**jăn**′ yōō ĕr′ ē) *noun* The first month of the year: *January has 31 days.*

jog (jŏg) *verb* **jogged, jogging** To run slowly: *My mom jogged one mile.*

join (join) *verb* **joined, joining** 1. To put together: *We joined hands and made a circle.* 2. To take part with others: *Will you join us for a swim across the lake?*

joke (jōk) *noun, plural* **jokes** Something funny said or done to make someone laugh: *Roberto makes everyone laugh with his elephant jokes.* —*verb* **joked, joking** To do or say something as a joke: *I was only joking.*

joy (joi) *noun, plural* **joys** A feeling of great happiness: *My dog jumps for joy when he sees me.*

June (jōōn) *noun* The sixth month of the year: *School is over in June.*

just (jŭst) *adjective* Fair: *Tim didn't think the teacher was just in giving a surprise test.* —*adverb* At that moment: *Just when he fell asleep, the phone rang.*

keep (kēp) *verb* **kept, keeping 1.** To have; own: *You may keep the picture.* **2.** To continue in a certain condition or place; to stay: *I kept the hamster in a cage.*

kept Look up **keep.**

key (kē) *noun, plural* **keys 1.** A piece of shaped metal used to open a lock: *I lost my key, so I couldn't get in the house.* **2.** The most important part: *Exercise is the key to good health.*

kick (kĭk) *verb* **kicked, kicking** To hit with the foot: *I saw the horse kick the door.*

kind¹ (kīnd) *adjective* **kinder, kindest** Thoughtful; helpful: *The nurse is very kind.*

kind² (kīnd) *noun, plural* **kinds** A type; variety: *What kind of music do you like?*

knew Look up **know.**

know (nō) *verb* **knew** (nōō) *or* (nyōō), **known, knowing 1.** To be certain of the facts: *I know you are hiding under the stairs.* **2.** To be familiar with: *Penny knew everyone.*

la•bor (lā′ bər) *noun, plural* **labors** Hard work: *Making a new garden took much labor.* —*verb* **labored, laboring** To work hard: *Jacob labored for hours to do the math problems.*

late (lāt) *adjective* **later, latest** After the usual or expected time: *The bus was late.*

Pronunciation Key

ă	pat	îr	deer	*th*	this
ā	pay	ŏ	pot	ŭ	cut
âr	care	ō	toe	ûr	urge
ä	father	ô	paw, for	ə	about,
ĕ	pet	oi	noise		item,
ē	bee	ōŏ	took		edible,
ĭ	pit	ōō	boot		gallop,
ī	pie	ou	out		circus
		th	thin		

laugh (lăf) *verb* **laughed, laughing** To make sounds and move your face to show joy or amusement: *I laugh at his jokes.*

learn (lûrn) *verb* **learned** or **learnt, learning** To gain knowledge or skill: *Erma wants to learn how to speak Spanish.*

light¹ (līt) *noun, plural* **lights** Anything that gives off the energy by which we see, such as a lamp: *Please turn off the light.*

light² (līt) *adjective* **lighter, lightest** Not heavy: *The box was light because it was empty.*

like¹ (līk) *verb* **liked, liking 1.** To be fond of someone or something: *I have always liked my cousin, Sal.* **2.** To enjoy: *Ida liked to dance.*

like² (līk) *preposition.* **1.** Similar to: *Harriet's coat is just like mine.* **2.** In the mood for: *I feel like going for a walk.*

line (līn) *noun, plural* **lines** A long row of people or things: *The line was too long.*

li•on (lī′ ən) *noun, plural* **lions** A large wild cat from Africa or Asia: *We heard the lion roar.*

lit•tle (lĭt′ l) *adjective* **littler, littlest,** or **least** Small in size or quantity: *My kitten is very little.*

loaf¹ (lōf) *noun, plural* **loaves** Bread baked in one piece or shape: *I sliced the loaf of bread that I'd just made.*

loaf² (lōf) *verb* **loafed, loafing** To be lazy: *My dog loafs around the house.*

long (lông) *or* (lŏng) *adjective* **longer, longest** Not short; great in length or time: *The school play was very long. Your fingers are longer than mine. That is the longest snake I have ever seen.* — *adverb* **longer, longest** For a great amount of time: *We worked on our math problems all day long.*

loss (lôs) *or* (lŏs) *noun, plural* **losses** The act or fact of not winning something: *Our hockey team has ten losses.*

love·ly (lŭv' lē) *adjective* **lovelier, loveliest** Beautiful: *The flowers look lovely.*

lug·gage (lŭg' ĭj) *noun* Suitcases and bags that a person takes on a trip: *The luggage is very heavy.*

lunch (lŭnch) *noun, plural* **lunches** The midday meal: *Ethan always has a sandwich for lunch.*

main·tain (mān tān') *verb* **maintained, maintaining 1.** To keep in good condition: *Mark will help maintain the garden.* **2.** To continue to have; keep.

mall (môl) *or* (mäl) *noun, plural* **malls** A shopping center: *Mom took me to the mall.*

man·y (mĕn' ē) *adjective* **more, most** A large number of: *Many animals live in this forest.*

March (märch) *noun* The third month of the year: *March is the best month for flying kites.*

mar·ket (mär' kĭt) *noun, plural* **markets** A place where goods are bought and sold: *We always go to the market for fresh vegetables.*

match¹ (măch) *verb* **matched, matching** To be alike; to look alike: *Socks need to match.*

match² (măch) *noun, plural* **matches** A small stick of wood or cardboard that bursts into flame when rubbed: *Dad lit the campfire with matches.*

mat·ter (măt' ər) *noun, plural* **matters** Problem or trouble: *What's the matter with your goldfish?* — *verb* **mattered, mattering** To be of importance: *Does it matter to you if we go to the store first?*

May (mā) *noun* The fifth month of the year: *Those flowers always bloom in May.*

meat (mēt) *noun* The flesh of animals used as food: *We had meat and salad for dinner.* • **Meat** sounds like **meet.**

meet (mēt) *verb* **met, meeting** To come together; come face to face: *Meet me on the corner after school.* • **Meet** sounds like **meat.**

meet·ing (mē' tĭng) *noun, plural* **meetings** A coming together for some common purpose: *The lion called a meeting of all the animals in his kingdom.*

me·te·or (mē' tē ər) *or* (mē' tē ôr') *noun, plural* **meteors** Matter from space that forms a bright trail or streak of light as it burns when it enters the earth's atmosphere: *We saw two meteors last night.*

mile (mīl) *noun, plural* **miles** A unit of distance equal to 5,280 feet or 1,609.34 meters: *The baseball field is two miles away.*

mind (mīnd) *noun, plural* **minds** The part of a person that thinks, feels, learns, etc.: *Mr. Sosa, my science teacher, says I have a good mind.* — *verb* **minded, minding** To object to: *Would you mind if I borrowed your pencil?*

mine (mīn) *pronoun* The thing or things belonging to me: *That's Bobby's bed, and this one is mine.*

mis·er·y (mĭz' ə rē) *noun, plural* **miseries** Great pain or unhappiness: *The tornado caused misery for everyone in its path.*

moist·en (moi' sən) *verb* **moistened, moistening** To make slightly wet or damp: *The rain moistened the garden.*

Mon·day (mŭn' dē) *or* (mŭn' dā') *noun, plural* **Mondays** The second day of the week: *Sometimes it's hard to wake up on Monday.*

mon•ey (mŭn′ ē) *noun* Coins and bills printed by a government and used to pay for things: *Judy is saving her money to buy a radio.*

month (mŭnth) *noun* One of the 12 parts that a year is divided into: *My birthday is this month.*

morn•ing (môr′ nĭng) *noun, plural* **mornings** The early part of the day: *I have cereal for breakfast every morning.*

most (mōst) *adjective* The greatest amount: *The team that gets the most runs will win.* —*noun* The larger part: *I like most of the people in this club.* Look up **many, much.**

moth•er (mŭ*th*′ ər) *noun, plural* **mothers** A female parent of a child: *Percy's mother writes articles for magazines.*

move (mōōv) *verb* **moved, moving** To change from one position to another: *Mom is always moving the furniture around.* —*noun, plural* **moves** The act of moving: *The frog made his move and caught the fly.*

much (mŭch) **more, most** *adjective* Great in amount: *I have much work to do.* —*adverb* Greatly; to a large degree: *Frank is much taller than his brother.*

must (mŭst) *helping verb* Will have to; should: *You must wear a smock in art class.*

must•n't (mŭs′ ənt) The contraction of "must not": *Carla mustn't have heard the dinner bell.*

near (nîr) *preposition* **nearer, nearest** Not far from; close to: *Ruben lives near his grandparents.*

neck•tie (nĕk′ tī′) *noun, plural* **neckties** A band of cloth worn around the neck and tied in a knot in front: *Nick wears neckties with all his shirts.*

need (nēd) *verb* **needed, needing** To require; must have: *I need a collar for my dog.*

nev•er (nĕv′ ər) *adverb* Not at any time: *Ben never gives up.*

news (nōōz) *or* (nyōōz) *noun* (used with a singular verb) Recent events or information: *The news about the earthquake is shocking.*

next (nĕkst) *adjective* **1.** Coming right after: *We'll get on the next train.* **2.** Nearest in position: *Mom is in the next room.*

nice (nīs) *adjective* **nicer, nicest** Pleasant; agreeable: *It was a nice evening for a walk.*

night (nīt) *noun, plural* **nights** The time between sunset and sunrise: *On a clear night, it's fun to look at the stars.*

noise (noiz) *noun, plural* **noises** A sound, especially if loud: *We heard a loud noise.*

none (nŭn) *pronoun* Not any; not one: *None of my friends can ski.*

noon (nōōn) *noun* Midday; 12 o'clock in the middle of the day: *We'll eat at noon.*

north (nôrth) *noun* The direction toward the North Pole: *A compass needle always points to the north.* —*adverb* Toward the north: *Clifton walked north to go into town.*

noth•ing (nŭth′ ĭng) *pronoun* **1.** Not anything: *Nothing the clown did made the child smile.* **2.** Of no importance: *It's nothing at all.*

No•vem•ber (nō vĕm′ bər) *noun* The eleventh month of the year: *We eat turkey in November.*

num·ber (**nŭm′** bər) *noun, plural* **numbers 1.** A figure or numeral that identifies something: *His football number is 12.* **2.** Amount: *Tell me the number of marbles you have.*

o'clock (ə **klŏk′**) *adverb* According to the clock: *My favorite TV show begins at 7 o'clock.*

Oc·to·ber (ŏk **tō′** bər) *noun* The tenth month of the year: *Halloween is the last day of October.*

off (ôf) *or* (ŏf) *adverb* Not on; removed: *He took his hat off.* —*preposition* Away from a place: *She dived off the pier.*

oil (oil) *noun* **1.** A greasy liquid or fat that easily becomes liquid: *We dropped the popcorn into the hot oil.* **2.** Petroleum: *They drill for oil.*

one (wŭn) *noun, plural* **ones** A number, written 1: *One plus two equals three.* —*pronoun* A particular person or thing: *One of my turtles is missing.* • **One** sounds like **won.**

on·ly (**ōn′** lē) *adjective* Sole; without others: *This is my only brother, Ricardo.* —*adverb* Just; merely: *Philip was 14, but he acted as if he were only 4.*

o·pen (**ō′** pən) *verb* **opened, opening** To cause something to be no longer closed: *I couldn't wait to open the box that was for me.*

or·na·ment (**ôr′** nə mənt) *noun, plural* **ornaments** An object that makes something more beautiful: *The tree ornament is blue and red.*

oth·er (**ŭth′** ər) *adjective* Different: *I have other things to do.* —*pronoun, plural* **others** The remaining people or things: *Mom carried the big box and I carried all the others.*

our (our) *adjective* Of or belonging to us: *Our dog followed us to school.* • **Our** sounds like **hour.**

o·ver (**ō′** vər) *preposition* **1.** Above; higher than: *It was raining, but at least we had a tent over our heads.* **2.** On the surface of; upon: *Teddy spilled raisins all over the floor.* —*adjective* Finished: *The play is over.*

owl (oul) *noun, plural* **owls** A kind of bird with a flat face, large eyes, and a short, hooked beak. Owls make a hooting sound: *The hoot of the owl scares some people.*

page¹ (pāj) *noun, plural* **pages** One side of a sheet paper in a book: *For homework I had to read pages 17 and 18 in my science book.*

page² (pāj) *noun, plural* **pages** A person who runs errands or delivers messages: *The page brought a message to my hotel room.* —*verb* **paged, paging** To call for someone in a public place: *When Tom got lost in the airport, his mother paged him on the loudspeaker.*

paint (pānt) *noun, plural* **paints** Coloring matter mixed with oil or water: *John made a picture with 12 different colors of paint.* —*verb* **painted, painting 1.** To cover or coat something with paint: *Alice painted her skateboard blue.* **2.** To make a picture using paint: *He liked to paint pictures of his dog, Igor.*

pa·per (**pā′** pər) *noun, plural* **papers 1.** A material made from wood pulp or rags. Paper is usually in the form of thin sheets. It is used for writing, drawing, printing, wrapping packages, and covering walls: *Tony used up all the paper in the house writing letters to his pen pal.* **2.** A newspaper: *I read about the parade in the paper.*

pa·trol (pə **trōl′**) *noun, plural* **patrols** A person or group of people who move about an area to make sure everything is all right: *The highway patrol makes sure people drive safely.*

pay (pā) *verb* **paid, paying 1.** To give money for something bought or for work done: *I had to pay 80 dollars for my new bicycle.* **2.** To give, make, or do: *I always pay attention in dance class.* —*noun* Money given for work done: *My pay was ten dollars.*

pen·ny (pĕn' ē) *noun, plural* **pennies** One cent: *This dollar equals 100 pennies.*

peo·ple (pē' pəl) *noun, plural* **people** Human beings: *Many people came to the party.*

place (plās) *noun, plural* **places** A particular spot: *People travel from many places to see the rodeo.* —*verb* **placed, placing** To put in a particular location or area: *I placed the toys on the shelf.* **Idiom. take place.** To happen: *When will the wedding take place?*

plaid (plăd) *noun, plural* **plaids** A design of stripes of different widths and colors that cross each other to make squares: *The plaid of his shirt was red, blue, and gold.*

please (plēz) *verb* **pleased, pleasing 1.** To give pleasure or happiness to; to be agreeable to: *He was pleased when I took him to the circus.* **2.** Be so kind as to: *Please close the door.*

point (point) *noun, plural* **points** Sharp or narrowed end of something; the tip: *I broke the point on my pencil.* —*verb* **pointed, pointing** To call attention to with the finger; to show.

poi·son·ous (poi' zə nəs) *adjective* Having poison in it or having the effects of poison: *We were careful not to step on a poisonous snake.*

poor (pŏŏr) *adjective* **poorer, poorest 1.** Having little or no money: *She was too poor to go to the movies with her friends.* **2.** Needing pity: *The poor kitten was lost.*

pop·corn (pŏp' kôrn') *noun* A kind of corn that pops open and puffs up when heated: *I like watching popcorn pop.*

pour (pôr) *verb* **poured, pouring 1.** To cause to flow in a stream: *I always pour maple syrup over my pancakes.* **2.** A heavy rain: *We opened our umbrellas as it started to pour.*

pow·er (pou' ər) *noun, plural* **powers** Strength or force: *This runner has plenty of power in her legs.*

pret·ty (prĭt' ē) *adjective* **prettier, prettiest** Pleasing; attractive; appealing: *The sunset was very pretty.*

prob·lem (prŏb' ləm) *noun, plural* **problems** Something or someone that is hard to understand or deal with: *Matt's problem was that he was tired.*

pull (pŏŏl) *verb* **pulled, pulling** To draw something toward oneself: *Pull on the rope.*

pur·sue (pər sōō') *verb* **pursued, pursuing 1.** To chase or follow in order to catch: *The cat pursued the mouse.* **2.** To keep trying to reach: *I will pursue my goals.*

put (pŏŏt) *verb* **put, putting** To place; to set: *Allen put the cookies in the cookie jar.*

Q

quart (kwôrt) *noun, plural* **quarts** A unit of measure equal to one quarter of a gallon: *I drank a quart of juice.*

queen (kwēn) *noun, plural* **queens 1.** A woman who rules over a country: *Queen Elizabeth rules Great Britain.* **2.** The wife of a king: *The queen lived in a castle.*

rain (rān) *noun* Drops of water that fall from the clouds: *The rain washed away the footprints in the dirt.* —*verb* **rained, raining** To fall in drops of water from the clouds: *It had rained all night.*

read (rēd) *verb* **read** (rĕd), **reading** To look at and get the meaning of something written or printed: *Every day I read the comics. I've already read the comics today.*

read•y (rĕd' ē) *adjective* **readier, readiest** Prepared to do something: *Tara was packed and ready to go.*

re•joice (rĭ jois') *verb* **rejoiced, rejoicing** To show or feel great joy: *We rejoice when our team wins.*

right (rīt) *adjective* **1.** Opposite the left side: *I throw a ball with my right arm.* **2.** Correct; true; just: *Being truthful is the right thing to do.* —*adverb* Straight on; directly: *I walked right into a wall.* • **Right** sounds like **write.**

riv•er (rĭv' ər) *noun, plural* **rivers** A large stream of water that flows into a lake, ocean, sea, or another river: *My dad and I go fishing in the river.*

road (rōd) *noun, plural* **roads** An open way for travel between two or more places: *Do you remember how Dorothy followed the yellow brick road to Oz?*

ro•dent (rōd' nt) *noun, plural* **rodents** Any of a large group of animals that have large front teeth used for gnawing, such as mice, rats, squirrels, and beavers: *We try to keep rodents out of the house.*

ro•de•o (rō' dē ō') *or* (ro dā' ō) *noun, plural* **rodeos** A show where people use their skill in contests such as riding horses and roping cattle: *It is fun to go to a rodeo.*

roy•al (roi' əl) *adjective* **1.** Of or having to do with kings or queens: *The prince was a member of the royal family.* **2.** Fit for a king or queen; splendid: *The queen lived in a royal palace.*

safe (sāf) *adjective* **safer, safest** Free from danger or harm: *Keep your money in a safe place.*

said Look up **say.**

sail (sāl) *noun, plural* **sails** A piece of strong material spread to catch the wind and make a boat move: *As the wind filled the sails, the sailboat moved faster.* —*verb* **sailed, sailing 1.** To travel across the water on a ship: *The ship is going to sail across the ocean to Europe.* **2.** To steer a boat: *I sailed the boat across the lake all by myself.*

Sat•ur•day (săt' ər dē) *or* (săt' ər dā') *noun, plural* **Saturdays** The seventh day of the week: *Mom took us to the baseball game on Saturday.*

sau•sage (sô' sĭj) *noun, plural* **sausages** Chopped meat that is mixed with spices and stuffed into a thin tube-shaped casing: *We had sausage for breakfast.*

save (sāv) *verb* **saved, saving 1.** To free from danger or harm: *Marie saved Ellen from falling off the swing.* **2.** To avoid wasting: *I took the bus instead of walking to save time.*

say (sā) *verb* **says** (sĕz), **said** (sĕd), **saying** To speak; to talk: *Grandma says it's time for dinner.*

scheme (skēm) *noun, plural* **schemes** A plan or plot for doing something: *Ling has a scheme for doing her homework.*

school¹ (skōol) *noun, plural* **schools** A place of teaching and learning: *We learned about Japan in school.*

school² (skōol) *noun, plural* **schools** A large group of fish that swim together: *While we were fishing, a school of minnows swam by.*

sea (sē) *noun, plural* **seas** The great body of water that covers about three-fourths of the earth's surface; ocean: *Whales live in the sea.*

seam (sēm) *noun, plural* **seams** A line or fold formed by sewing together two pieces of cloth or other material: *The seam on the shirt ripped.*

sec·ond¹ (sĕk′ ənd) *noun, plural* **seconds** A unit of time equal to ¹/₆₀ of one minute: *Janet finished the test in 3 minutes and 10 seconds flat.*

sec·ond² (sĕk′ ənd) *adjective* Next after the first: *Mike came in first in the race, and I came in second.*

send (sĕnd) *verb* **sent** (sĕnt), **sending** To cause or order to go: *Dad sent me to the store to buy ice cream for dessert.*

sent Look up **send**. • **Sent** sounds like **cent**.

Sep·tem·ber (sĕp tĕm′ bər) *noun* The ninth month of the year. September has 30 days: *In September we go back to school.*

shake (shāk) *verb* **shook** (shŏŏk), **shaken, shaking 1.** To tremble or quiver: *I was so scared that my whole body began to shake.* **2.** To cause to move: *The boys shook the tree, and all the leaves fell off.*

shak·y (shā′ kē) *adjective* **shakier, shakiest 1.** Trembling; quivering: *Her voice was shakier than mine.* **2.** Not firm; likely to break down: *Kevin's bike is the shakiest I have ever ridden.*

sharp (shärp) *adjective* **sharper, sharpest 1.** Something having a thin, cutting edge or point: *Anna needed a sharp pencil to do her homework. My pencil is sharper than Ben's. Taylor's pencil is the sharpest of all.* **2.** Quickly aware of things; keen: *Owls' sharp eyesight helps them to see in the dark.*

she'll (shēl) The contraction of "she will": *My mother says she'll pick us up after practice.*

she's (shēz) The contraction of "she is" or "she has": *She's going to the bookstore.*

shine (shīn) *verb* **shone** (shōn) **shined, shining 1.** To give off or reflect light: *Why are you shining the flashlight in my eyes?* **2.** To polish: *I shined my shoes today.*

shook (shŏŏk) Look up **shake**.

shop (shŏp) *noun, plural* **shops** A store; a place where goods are sold: *Don's favorite shop is Toy Joy.* —*verb* **shopped, shopping** To visit stores to buy things: *My brother and I are shopping for a pet frog.*

should (shŏŏd) *helping verb* Ought to; have a duty to: *I should practice the piano every day.*

should·n't (shŏŏd′ nt) The contraction of "should not": *You shouldn't tease your little sister.*

shove (shŭv) *verb* **shoved, shoving** To push roughly: *When Mom came into my room, I shoved the present under the bed.* —*noun, plural* **shoves** A push: *My dog wouldn't move, so I gave him a little shove.*

show (shō) *verb* **showed, shown, showing 1.** To make known; to reveal: *Please show me the way home.* **2.** To present for others to see: *Let's show everyone our bowling trophy.* —*noun, plural* **shows** Any kind of public performance, entertainment, or display: *Ms. Cook's class put on an art show at school.*

shrewd (shrōōd) *adjective* **shrewder, shrewdest** Clever and smart: *The shrewd buyer looked for the best price.*

size (sīz) *noun, plural* **sizes** The height, width, or length of a thing: *Billy and Vernon have always been the same size.*

sketch (skĕch) *noun, plural* **sketches** A rough, quick drawing: *The sketch showed a bare tree.* —*verb* **sketched, sketching** To make a sketch: *She sketched quickly.*

sky (skī) *noun, plural* **skies** The air high above the earth; the heavens: *I fly my kite high up in the sky.*

sky•line (skī′ līn′) *noun, plural* **skylines** **1.** The outline of buildings or other objects as seen against the sky: *We could see the city's skyline from the airplane.* **2.** The line at which the earth and sky seem to meet.

sleep (slēp) *noun* A natural rest of body and mind; state of not being awake: *I'm so tired that I could use a week of sleep.* —*verb* **slept** (slĕpt), **sleeping** To be in or to fall into a state of sleep: *My dad is sleeping in his chair.*

sleep•y (slē′ pē) *adjective* **sleepier, sleepiest** Ready for sleep; drowsy: *When I am sleepy, I start to yawn.*

slept Look up **sleep.**

slow (slō) *adverb* **slower, slowest** Not quick: *Bobby walks slower than a turtle.* —*verb* **slowed, slowing** To cause to move slow or slower: *Please slow down.*

slump (slŭmp) *verb* **slumped, slumping** To fall or sink down suddenly: *Mother told me not to slump in my chair at dinner.*

smile (smīl) *verb* **smiled, smiling** To show an expression of happiness by turning the corners of the mouth upward; grinning: *The boy was smiling at his new puppy.*

smudge (smŭj) *noun, plural* **smudges** A dirty mark or smear: *The birthday card had a black smudge on it.* —*verb* **smudged, smudging** To make dirty or smeared.

sneeze (snēz) *verb* **sneezed, sneezing** To force air to pass suddenly with force from the nose and mouth. A tickling inside the nose causes a person to sneeze: *When John caught a cold, he sneezed for two days.*

snow (snō) *noun, plural* **snows** Soft white flakes of frozen water vapor that form in the sky and fall to the earth: *Jeremy loved to ride his sled in the snow.* —*verb* **snowed, snowing** To fall as snow.

sock (sŏk) *noun, plural* **socks** A short stocking reaching no higher than the knee: *I stepped in a puddle and got my socks wet.*

sog•gy (sô′ gē) *or* (sŏ′ gē) *adjective* **soggier, soggiest** Very wet; soaked: *My shoes were soggy after I played in the rain.*

soil¹ (soil) *noun* The loose top layer of the earth's surface in which plants grow: *My class planted a little tree in the soil.*

soil² (soil) *verb* **soiled, soiling** To make dirty: *Jane soiled her clean shirt.*

so•lo (sō′ lō) *adjective* Done by one person alone: *The pilot made her first solo flight.* —*noun, plural* **solos** Music that one person plays or sings all alone.

some (sŭm) *adjective* A certain number of: *Some people like pizza, and some people don't.* • **Some** sounds like **sum.**

some•bod•y (sŭm′ bŏd′ ē) *pronoun* A person not known or named: *Somebody lost a hat.*

some•thing (sŭm′ thĭng) *pronoun* A particular thing that is not named or known: *I want something good to eat.*

sor•ry (sŏr′ ē) *adjective* **sorrier, sorriest** Feeling sadness, regret, or pity: *Ms. Kyoto was sorry that she lost her sister's book.*

sound (sound) *noun, plural* **sounds** Something that is heard; sensation made by vibrations in the air and picked up by the ear: *We were surprised to hear a thumping sound.*

spend (spĕnd) *verb* **spent** (spĕnt), **spending** **1.** To pay out money: *He spent a lot of money for a new bat.* **2.** To pass time: *Katy spent the whole day at the carnival.*

spent Look up **spend**.

spin•ach (spĭn' ĭch) *noun* A vegetable with dark green leaves. *I ate spinach for lunch.*

spoil (spoil) *verb* **spoiled** *or* **spoilt**, **spoiling 1.** To ruin or damage: *The rain spoiled the class picnic.* **2.** To become unfit for use: *Milk will spoil if it isn't kept cold.*

sport (spôrt) *noun, plural* **sports** A game or contest requiring physical activity: *My favorite sport is soccer.*

spring (sprĭng) *noun, plural* **springs 1.** The season before summer: *In the spring, flowers bloom.* **2.** A place where water flows to the surface: *Fish swim in the spring.*

stair (stâr) *noun, plural* **stairs** A step in a flight of steps: *Tom ran down the stairs.*

stand (stand) *verb* **stood, standing** To rise to be on one's feet: *He stood up and yawned.*

star (stär) *noun, plural* **stars 1.** Any heavenly body, other than the moon or planets, seen from Earth. *A star shown brightly.* **2.** A famous person in any field or profession: *She is a movie star.*

starch (stärch) *noun, plural* **starches 1.** White food matter that is made and stored in plants: *Corn has starch in it.* **2.** A product that is used to make cloth stiff.

start (stärt) *verb* **started, starting** To begin to go somewhere or do something: *Let's start a soccer club.*

stood Look up **stand**.

stop (stŏp) *verb* **stopped, stopping** To cease; to come to a halt: *When the rain stopped, Steven went out to play.*

storm (stôrm) *noun, plural* **storms** Strong winds accompanied by rain, hail, sand, or snow: *We saw a lot of lightning during the storm.*

Pronunciation Key

ă	pat	îr	deer	*th*	this
ā	pay	ŏ	pot	ŭ	cut
âr	care	ō	toe	ûr	urge
ä	father	ô	paw, for	ə	about,
ĕ	pet	oi	noise		item,
ē	bee	ŏŏ	took		edible,
ĭ	pit	ōō	boot		gallop,
ī	pie	ou	out		circus
		th	thin		

sto•ry (stôr' ē) *noun, plural* **stories 1.** An account of something that has happened: *I read a true story.* **2.** A tale of fiction: *Phil told his sister a story.*

street (strēt) *noun, plural* **streets** A road in a city or town that is usually lined with buildings: *My house is on this street.*

strong (strông) *adjective* **stronger, strongest** Having much power or strength: *Sled dogs are strong animals. Horses are stronger. Elephants are the strongest.*

stun (stŭn) *verb* **stunned, stunning 1.** To daze or make unconscious: *Jack was stunned when he bumped his head.* **2.** To shock: *Josh was stunned by the news.*

sub•tract (səb trăkt') *verb* **subtracted, subtracting** To take away: *I subtracted two cents from eight cents, and the total was six cents.*

such (sŭch) *adjective* Of this kind or that kind: *I knew you'd wear such shoes.* —*adverb* Especially: *That was such a nice party.*

sum (sŭm) *noun, plural* **sums** The number you get when you add two or more numbers: *The sum of 5 and 6 is 11.* • **Sum** sounds like **some**.

sum•mer (sŭm' ər) *noun, plural* **summers** The warmest season of the year. *Summer comes between spring and fall.*

sun (sŭn) *noun* The star around which Earth and other planets revolve. The sun is the source of Earth's light and heat: *I wake up when the sun rises in the morning.* • **Sun** sounds like **son**.

Sun·day (sŭn' dē) or (sŭn' dā') *noun, plural* **Sundays** The first day of the week: *On Sunday Inga went to church.*

sun·ny (sŭn' ē) *adjective* **sunnier, sunniest** Having much sun: *It was a sunny day at the beach.*

sup·per (sŭp' ər) *noun, plural* **suppers** The evening meal or the last meal of the day: *My family ate supper at a very special restaurant.*

sure (shŏŏr) *adjective* **surer, surest** Feeling certain; having no doubt: *Are you sure you don't want a piece of cake?*

sur·geon (sûr' jən) *noun, plural* **surgeons** A doctor who treats injuries and diseases by cutting into the body and removing or repairing parts of it: *The surgeon operated on my foot.*

ta·ble (tā' bəl) *noun, plural* **tables** A piece of furniture having a flat top supported by legs: *Lunch is on the table.*

take (tāk) *verb* **took** (tŏŏk), **taken, taking 1.** To get; accept: *Did you take the book on the table?* **2.** To carry to a different place: *I am taking your suitcase upstairs.*

talk (tôk) *verb* **talked, talking** To speak; say words: *We were talking about Mark when he walked in.* —*noun, plural* **talks 1.** An informal speech: *I gave a talk in my class.* **2.** A rumor: *There's talk that Tia is ill.*

tall (tôl) *adjective* **taller, tallest 1.** Of more than average height: *My dad says I am tall. My brother is taller than I am. Mom is the tallest one in our family.* **2.** Hard to believe; exaggerated: *Who would believe that tall story?*

team (tēm) *noun, plural* **teams 1.** Two or more animals harnessed together to work: *The team of horses pulled the plow.* **2.** A group of people playing on the same side in a game: *The whole school came to watch our team win.*

teen·ag·er (tēn' ā' jər) *noun, plural* **teenagers** A person who is between the ages of thirteen and nineteen: *My older sister is a teenager.*

test (tĕst) *noun, plural* **tests 1.** A series of questions that judge a person's skill or knowledge: *I studied hard to pass my spelling test.* **2.** A way to find out the quality of something: *Lifting weights is a test of your strength.* —*verb* **tested, testing** To put to a test; to try out: *I tested the yo-yo.*

thank (thăngk) *verb* **thanked, thanking** To say that one is grateful or pleased: *The boys and girls thanked the magician for the show.*

them (thĕm) or (thəm) *pronoun* Persons, things, or animals spoken or written about: *We ate the cookies after we baked them.*

then (thĕn) *adverb* **1.** At the time: *I used to sleep with a teddy bear, but I was only a baby then.* **2.** After that: *We saw lightning flash, and then we heard the thunder roar.* **3.** A time mentioned: *Go finish your homework, and by then dinner will be ready.*

there'd (thârd) The contraction for "there would" or "there had": *There'd be ten people at the party if they all came.*

there'll (thârl) The contraction for "there will": *There'll be a baseball game tomorrow.*

these Look up **this.**

they (thā) *pronoun* **1.** The people, animals, or things named before: *Mr. Martin gave us six arithmetic problems, and they were all hard.* **2.** People in general: *They used to think the world was flat.*

they'd (thād) The contraction of "they had" or "they would": *They'd already eaten.*

they'll (*th*āl) The contraction of "they will" or "they shall": *Gino and Bonnie said they'll bring the cake to the party.*

they've (*th*āv) The contraction of "they have": *The boys say they've never gone fishing.*

thing (thĭng) *noun, plural* **things 1.** Any object or substance that cannot be named exactly: *What is that green thing on the floor?* **2.** An act; a deed: *Hitting that home run was the best thing I ever did.*

think (thĭngk) *verb* **thought, thinking 1.** To use the mind to come to an opinion: *I think I should go home now.* **2.** To have in mind: *Julia thinks she would like to be a doctor.*

third (thûrd) *noun, plural* **thirds** One of three equal parts: *Roger ate a third of the pizza.* —*adjective* Next after second.

this (thĭs) *adjective, plural* **these** (thēz) Being a thing or person nearby or just mentioned: *Take these toys to your room.* —*pronoun, plural* **these** A thing or person nearby or just mentioned: *This is our secret clubhouse.*

Thurs•day (**thûrz'** dē) *or* (**thûrz'** dā') *noun, plural* **Thursdays** The fifth day of the week: *Art class meets every Thursday after school.*

time (tīm) *noun, plural* **times 1.** All the days that have been and will ever be; the past, present, and future. **2.** A period in which something happens or continues. *Idiom.* **at times.** Now and then; once in a while: *At times I wish I lived in a different country.*

times (tīmz) *preposition* Multiplied by: *Three times two equals six.*

ti•ny (tī' nē) *adjective* **tinier, tiniest** Very small: *The kitten was so tiny that it fit in my hand.*

tire¹ (tīr) *verb* **tired, tiring** To become weary: *Lee tired after hiking all day.*

tire² (tīr) *noun, plural* **tires** A band of rubber around the rim of a wheel: *My bicycle has a flat tire.*

toast (tōst) *verb* **toasted, toasting** To brown by heating: *We toasted marshmallows over the campfire.* —*noun* A slice of bread heated and browned on both sides: *I always have toast with my cereal.*

toe (tō) *noun, plural* **toes** One of the five separate divisions of the foot: *Ellen put her big toe into the bath water to see if it was too hot.*

too (tōō) *adverb* **1.** Also; besides: *Adam had to make the salad and set the table, too.* **2.** Very: *This soup is too hot.* • **Too** sounds like **two.**

took Look up **take.**

tooth (tōōth) *noun, plural* **teeth** Any of the hard, white, bony parts in the mouth used for biting and chewing: *Brittany's front tooth is ready to fall out.*

tow•er (**tou'** ər) *noun, plural* **towers** A high structure or a part of a building rising higher than the rest of it: *Rapunzel was hidden away in a tower so that no one could reach her.*

town (toun) *noun, plural* **towns** A group of houses or buildings that is larger than a village but smaller than a city: *My aunt is the new mayor of our town.*

toy (toi) *noun, plural* **toys** Something a child plays with: *Johnny's favorite toy is Robbie the Robot.*

train (trān) *noun, plural* **trains** Connected railroad cars pulled by an engine or powered by electricity: *The train left at 1:00 P.M.*

true (trōō) *adjective* **truer, truest** Not false; according to fact: *Only Marcel knows the true story.*

try (trī) *verb* **tries, tried, trying** To make an effort; to attempt: *Try to be brave.*

Tues·day (tōōz′ dē) *or* (tōōz′ dā′) *or* (tyōōz′ dē) *or* (tyōōz′ dā′) *noun, plural* **Tuesdays** The third day of the week: *I go to the library every Tuesday.*

turn (tûrn) *verb* **turned, turning** **1.** To move round; rotate: *The earth turns on its axis once every 24 hours.* **2.** To change direction or position: *The path turned into the woods.* —*noun, plural* **turns** A chance to do something after someone else.

two (tōō) *noun* One more than one: *The twins are two of my good buddies.* • **Two** sounds like **too.**

un·der (ŭn′ dər) *preposition* **1.** Below; beneath: *I put my shoes under my bed.* **2.** Less than: *Sue was under 12 years old.*

use (yōōz) *verb* **used, using** To put into service: *I used all the toothpaste.*
   Idiom. **used to.** Familiar with: *I was used to sleeping with the light on.*

used (yōōzd) *adjective* Not new: *Nick bought a used bike.*

va·ri·e·ty (və rī′ ĭ tē) *noun, plural* **varieties** **1.** A different kind within the same group: *We had a new variety of soup for lunch.* **2.** Change or difference: *I like variety in my day.*

ver·y (vĕr′ ē) *adverb* Much; extremely: *That joke was very funny.*

voice (vois) *noun, plural* **voices** The sound coming from the mouth: *Bernice has a wonderful voice.*

waf·fle (wŏf′ əl) *noun, plural* **waffles** A crisp cake made of batter: *Dad made waffles for breakfast.*

wait (wāt) *verb* **waited, waiting** To stay until someone comes or something happens: *We could hardly wait for the cartoon to start.* • **Wait** sounds like **weight.**

walk (wôk) *verb* **walked, walking** To go on foot at a steady pace: *The elephant walked slowly around the big circus tent.*

was (wŏz) *or* (wŭz) *or* (wəz) Look up **be.**

wash (wŏsh) *or* (wôsh) *verb* **washed, washing** To clean with water and sometimes soap: *I'll wash if you dry.*

was·n't (wŏz′ ənt) *or* (wŭz′ ənt) The contraction of "was not": *Bill wasn't ready when his friends arrived.*

wa·ter (wô′ tər) *or* (wŏt′ ər) *noun* **1.** The colorless, tasteless, odorless liquid that fills oceans, rivers, and ponds: *Water falls from the sky as rain.* **2.** A lake, river, pool, or any other body of this liquid: *We went for a swim in the water.* —*verb* **watered, watering** To sprinkle or provide with water: *The rain watered the grass for me.*

we'd (wēd) The contraction of "we had," "we should," or "we would": *We'd better call our parents before we walk home.*

Wednes·day (wĕnz′ dē) *or* (wĕnz′ dā′) *noun, plural* **Wednesdays** The fourth day of the week: *We will leave on Wednesday.*

weigh (wā) *verb* **weighed, weighing** **1.** To find out how heavy something is by using a scale: *Mom lets me weigh all the vegetables before she buys them.* **2.** To have a certain weight: *Jason's dog weighs only 11 pounds.*

weird (wîrd) *adjective* **weirder, weirdest**
1. Causing an uneasy feeling; mysterious:
*The noise from the cave was weirder today than
yesterday.* **2.** Strange; odd; unusual: *That is
the weirdest story I have ever read.*

we'll (wēl) The contraction of "we will" or
"we shall": *We'll go into the fun house with you.*

well (wĕl) *adverb* **better, best** In a way
that is good or correct: *I play the piano well.
Diego plays better than I do. Simon plays best
of all.*

were (wûr) Look up **be**.

were·n't (wûrnt) *or* (**wûr' ənt**) The
contraction of "were not": *My friends
weren't home when I stopped by.*

we've (wēv) The contraction of "we have":
We've still got a lot of work to do on the tree house.

wharf (wôrf) *noun, plural* **wharves** A
landing place for boats and ships built along
a shore; dock: *Five boats were at the wharf.*

what (wŏt) *or* (wŭt) *or* (wət) *pronoun*
1. Which thing or things: *What do you want
me to do?* **2.** The thing which: *I didn't know
what she wanted.* **3.** Which: *What color do
you want to paint your room?*

wheel (wēl) *noun, plural* **wheels**
A round frame supported by spokes on
which a vehicle moves: *Have you ever been
on the Ferris wheel?*

when (wĕn) *adverb* At what time: *When
will you be ready to go?* —*conjunction* At a
particular time: *Blink when I say your name.*

where (wâr) *adverb* **1.** At what place: *Where
are my mittens?* **2.** To what place: *Where are
we going on our class trip?*

where'd (wârd) The contraction of "where
did": *Where'd you leave your coat?*

which (wĭch) *pronoun* **1.** What one or
ones: *Which is mine?* **2.** The one or ones
mentioned: *I bought my mom a gift, which
I know she will like.* —*adjective* What one
or ones: *Pam couldn't tell which hat was hers.*

while (wīl) *noun* A period of time: *Please
stay for a while.* —*conjunction* **1.** At the same
time that: *Mom read the newspaper while I
did my homework.* **2.** Although: *Ron was
short while his brothers were tall.*

white (wīt) *noun* The lightest color; the
color of snow: *White is the color of clouds.*
—*adjective* **whiter, whitest** Having
the color white: *I have white shoes.*

who (hōō) *pronoun* What person or
persons: *Who is your best friend?*

whole (hōl) *adjective* **1.** Not broken;
complete: *Is this a whole deck of cards?*
2. Entire amount: *I ate the whole pie by myself.*
• **Whole** sounds like **hole.**

who'll (hōōl) The contraction of "who will"
or "who shall": *Who'll bring the games?*

why (wī) *adverb* For what reason: *Why is
your tongue green?*

width (wĭdth) *or* (wĭth) *or* (wĭtth) *noun,
plural* **widths** The distance from side to
side: *The width of the room is ten feet.*

wild·flow·er (wīld' flou' ər) *noun, plural*
wildflowers Flowers on a wild plant:
The wildflowers were pretty.

will (wĭl) *helping verb* **would** (wŏŏd) To intend to; to mean to: *I will go to the picnic. I knew you would come sooner or later.* • **Would** sounds like **wood**.

win (wĭn) *verb* **won** (wŭn), **winning** To gain a victory: *Who won the art contest?*

win•ter (wĭn' tər) *noun, plural* **winters** The coldest season of the year, coming between fall and spring: *I don't like to shovel snow in the winter.*

wire (wīr) *noun, plural* **wires** Metal drawn out into a thin thread: *The fence around the farm was made of wire.*

wish (wĭsh) *noun, plural* **wishes** A strong desire: *Renee's only wish was to be finished with her work.* —*verb* **wished, wishing** To have a desire for something: *Ken wished he could meet his favorite singing star.*

won Look up **win**.

won't (wōnt) The contraction of "will not": *I won't be at the park today.*

wood (wŏŏd) *noun* The hard material making up the trunk and branches of a tree: *The cabin was built of wood.* • **Wood** sounds like **would**.

word (wûrd) *noun, plural* **words** A sound or group of sounds having a certain meaning: *I missed only one word on my spelling test.*

work (wûrk) *noun* **1.** The effort made in doing or making something: *Mowing the lawn is hard work.* **2.** A task: *I can't go because I have too much school work to do.* —*verb* **worked, working** To have a job: *Joe worked at the supermarket every day after school.*

world (wûrld) *noun* The earth: *In history class we learn about the world.*

worm (wûrm) *noun, plural* **worms** A crawling creature with a long, slender body: *There are lots of worms in the backyard.*

would Look up **will**.

would•n't (wŏŏd' nt) The contraction of "would not": *Simone knew she wouldn't get home on time unless she ran.*

would•'ve (wŏŏd' əv) The contraction of "would have": *Jerrell would've cleaned his room, but he was late for school.*

write (rīt) *verb* **wrote** (rōt), **written, writing** To make letters or words with a pen, pencil, etc.: *Karen promised to write to*  *me when she went on vacation. I wrote my name on my paper.* • **Write** sounds like **right**.

wrote Look up **write**.

yard[1] (yärd) *noun, plural* **yards** A unit of length measuring 3 feet or 36 inches: *This room is 3 yards long.*

yard[2] (yärd) *noun, plural* **yards** A piece of land near a building: *My house has a big yard to play in.*

year (yîr) *noun, plural* **years** The length of time it takes the earth to go around the sun once; 365 days: *This year I will be 10 years old.*

yel•low (yĕl' ō) *noun* The color of gold or butter: *Yellow is the color of ripe lemons.* —*adjective* **yellower, yellowest** Having this color: *I wore my yellow shirt with my blue pants.*

you'd (yŏŏd) The contraction of "you had" or "you would": *You'd better go to bed before you fall asleep in the chair.*

you'll (yŏŏl) *or* (yŏŏl) *or* (yəl) The contraction of "you will" or "you shall": *You broke this vase, so you'll have to pay for it.*

you've (yŏŏv) The contraction of "you have": *You've got a turtle just like mine.*

Contents

Additional Resources

Dear Family of _____,

During the next six weeks, your child will be learning to spell the following kinds of words:

- words with the short *a* vowel sound
- words with the long *a* vowel sound
- words with the short *e* vowel sound
- plural words

Here are some simple activities to do each week to help your child become a better speller.

 Listening and Writing

Say the spelling words and have your child write them.

 Spelling Strategy: Shorter Words

If your child is unsure about the spelling of a word, have him or her write the word correctly on a sheet of paper. Study the word with your child and point out any shorter words in it. Then help your child find other list words that contain shorter words.

 Games and Activities

Play Spelling Memory. Choose some spelling words. Have your child write each spelling word on two index cards. Turn each card face down. Take turns flipping over two cards to try to make a match. If the cards match, keep them. If they don't match, turn them face down. The person with more matches at the end of the game wins.

Have your child choose three colors of crayons. Ask him or her to use one color to write each spelling word. Then have your child trace each word with the other colors to create rainbow words.

 Using Spelling Words

Ask your child to write sentences that contain the spelling words. Then read the sentences with your child. Notice whether the sentences show that your child knows the meanings of the spelling words.

Lesson 1 Words with Short *a*

Week of _____

ask	matter	black	add
match	Saturday	class	apple
subtract	thank	catch	January
after	hammer	half	laugh

Lesson 2 Words with Long *a*

Week of _____

ate	late	safe	page
face	save	place	came
change	gray	away	break
May	great	April	pay

Lesson 3 More Words with Long *a*

Week of _____

paint	rain	aid	wait
train	aim	sail	afraid
paper	danger	fable	able
table	weigh	eight	they

Lesson 4 Words with Short *e*

Week of _____

dress	address	end	second
forget	spent	egg	next
help	test	head	read
ready	said	again	says

Lesson 5 Plural Words

Week of _____

clowns	trains	tests	eggs
hammers	paints	hands	papers
tables	places	pages	apples
classes	addresses	dresses	matches

Lesson 6 Unit 1 Review

Week of _____

Lesson 6 is a review of Lessons 1–5. Help your child practice all of the words from those lessons.

Estimada familia de _____ ,

Durante las próximas seis semanas, su niño/a estará aprendiendo a escribir

- palabras que tienen la vocal *a* corta
- palabras que tienen la vocal *a* larga
- palabras que tienen la vocal *e* corta
- palabras en el plural

He aquí algunas actividades simples que puede hacer cada semana para ayudar a su niño/a a tener mejor ortografía.

Escuchar y escribir

Dicte las palabras de ortografía y pida a su niño/a que las escriba.

Estrategia de ortografía: Palabras más cortas

Si su niño/a no está seguro/a de cómo se escribe una palabra, estudie la palabra con su niño/a y señale las palabras más cortas que se hallen en esa palabra. Luego ayúdelo/a a hallar otras palabras de la lista que contengan palabras más cortas.

Juegos y actividades

Seleccione algunas palabras de ortografía y pida a su niño/a que escriba cada una sobre dos tarjetas. Revuelva las tarjetas y voltéelas boca abajo. Por turnos, volteen dos tarjetas para tratar de emparejarlas. Si las tarjetas son iguales, guárdenlas. Si no son iguales, pónganlas boca abajo. La persona que tenga más tarjetas al final del juego gana.

Pídale a su niño/a que seleccione tres diferentes lápices de color. Invítelo/a a utilizar un color para escribir cada palabra de ortografía. Luego pídale que trace cada palabra con los demás colores para crear un arco iris de palabras.

Emplear las palabras de ortografía

Pida a su niño/a que escriba oraciones con las palabras de ortografía. Lea las oraciones con su niño/a. Fíjese si demuestran que su niño/a entiende los significados de las palabras de ortografía.

Lesson 1 Words with Short *a*

Week of _____

ask	matter	black	add
match	Saturday	class	apple
subtract	thank	catch	January
after	hammer	half	laugh

Lesson 2 Words with Long *a*

Week of _____

ate	late	safe	page
face	save	place	came
change	gray	away	break
May	great	April	pay

Lesson 3 More Words with Long *a*

Week of _____

paint	rain	aid	wait
train	aim	sail	afraid
paper	danger	fable	able
table	weigh	eight	they

Lesson 4 Words with Short *e*

Week of _____

dress	address	end	second
forget	spent	egg	next
help	test	head	read
ready	said	again	says

Lesson 5 Plural Words

Week of _____

clowns	trains	tests	eggs
hammers	paints	hands	papers
tables	places	pages	apples
classes	addresses	dresses	matches

Lesson 6 Unit 1 Review

Week of _____

Lección 6 es un repaso de las Lecciones 1–5. Ayude a su niño/a a practicar todas las palabras de esas lecciones.

Dear Family of _____ ,

During the next six weeks, your child will be learning to spell the following kinds of words:

- words with the short *e* vowel sound
- words with the long *e* vowel sound
- words with the short *u* vowel sound
- contractions

Here are some simple activities to do each week to help your child become a better speller.

Listening and Writing

Say the spelling words and have your child write them.

Spelling Strategy: Word Shape

If your child is unsure about the spelling of a word, ask your child to look at the correct spelling and to draw the shape of the word. Then have your child study the word shape. Tell your child that drawing a word's shape can help him or her remember how to spell it.

`k e y`

Games and Activities

Play Invisible Writing. Ask your child to choose some spelling words. Write the words on a piece of paper. Then, using a finger, take turns writing a word on each other's back. Be sure to say each letter and the word aloud during the invisible writing.

Have your child go on a word search. Have your child find and circle spelling words in a magazine or newspaper.

Using Spelling Words

Ask your child to write sentences that contain the spelling words. Then read the sentences with your child. Notice whether the sentences show that your child knows the meanings of the spelling words.

Lesson 7   More Words with Short *e*

Week of _____

best	better	cents	February
never	kept	sent	September
slept	them	then	Wednesday
when	friend	many	guess

Lesson 8   Words with Long *e*

Week of _____

meet	need	sleep	street
queen	wheel	free	sneeze
dream	each	meat	read
sea	team	please	people

Lesson 9   More Words with Long *e*

Week of _____

happy	funny	very	busy
sleepy	carry	sunny	every
family	penny	only	city
these	even	key	story

Lesson 10   Words with Short *u*

Week of _____

mother	front	month	money
from	other	nothing	Monday
such	summer	much	lunch
sun	under	Sunday	does

Lesson 11   Contractions

Week of _____

they'll	she'll	I'll	we'll
you'll	I've	we've	you've
they've	he's	she's	it's
I'd	you'd	they'd	I'm

Lesson 12   Unit 2 Review

Week of _____

Lesson 12 is a review of Lessons 7–11. Help your child practice all of the words from those lessons.

Unit 2 Ortografía en casa

Estimada familia de _____ ,

Durante las próximas seis semanas, su niño/a estará aprendiendo a escribir

- palabras que tienen la vocal *e* corta
- palabras que tienen la vocal *e* larga
- palabras que tienen la vocal *u* corta
- contracciones

He aquí algunas actividades simples que puede hacer cada semana para ayudar a su niño/a a tener mejor ortografía.

Escuchar y escribir

Dicte las palabras de ortografía y pida a su niño/a que las escriba.

Estrategia de ortografía: La forma de la palabra

Si su niño/a no está seguro/a de cómo se escribe una palabra, pídale que mire la palabra escrita correctamente y que dibuje la forma—o contorno—de la palabra. Luego pídale que estudie la forma de la palabra. Explíquele que el dibujar la forma de una palabra puede ayudarle a recordar cómo escribirla.

k e y

Juegos y actividades

Pídale a su niño/a que seleccione algunas palabras de ortografía. Escriba las palabras sobre una hoja de papel. Luego, por turnos, escriban una palabra en la espalda del otro con el dedo índice. Asegúrense de decir cada letra y la palabra en voz alta durante la escritura invisible.

Pídale a su niño/a que halle y encierre en un círculo las palabras de ortografía en una revista o un periódico.

Emplear las palabras de ortografía

Pida a su niño/a que escriba oraciones con las palabras de ortografía. Luego lea las oraciones con su niño/a. Fíjese si las oraciones demuestran que su niño/a entiende los significados de las palabras de ortografía.

Lesson 7 More Words with Short *e*

Week of _____

best	better	cents	February
never	kept	sent	September
slept	them	then	Wednesday
when	friend	many	guess

Lesson 8 Words with Long *e*

Week of _____

meet	need	sleep	street
queen	wheel	free	sneeze
dream	each	meat	read
sea	team	please	people

Lesson 9 More Words with Long *e*

Week of _____

happy	funny	very	busy
sleepy	carry	sunny	every
family	penny	only	city
these	even	key	story

Lesson 10 Words with Short *u*

Week of _____

mother	front	month	money
from	other	nothing	Monday
such	summer	much	lunch
sun	under	Sunday	does

Lesson 11 Contractions

Week of _____

they'll	she'll	I'll	we'll
you'll	I've	we've	you've
they've	he's	she's	it's
I'd	you'd	they'd	I'm

Lesson 12 Unit 2 Review

Week of _____

Lección 12 es un repaso de las Lecciones 7–11. Ayude a su niño/a a practicar todas las palabras de esas lecciones.

Dear Family of _____ ,

During the next six weeks, your child will be learning to spell the following kinds of words:

- words with the short *u* vowel sound
- words with the short *i* vowel sound
- words with the long *i* vowel sound
- words with *-ed* or *-ing*

Here are some simple activities to do each week to help your child become a better speller.

Listening and Writing

Say the spelling words and have your child write them.

Spelling Strategy: Sounds and Letters

If your child is unsure about the spelling of a word, have your child say the word to himself or herself. Tell your child to close his or her eyes and try to picture the way the word is spelled. Help your child think about the spelling by asking questions such as *Does it have more letters than sounds? Which letter pair spells a single sound?* Then have your child write the word on a piece of paper. Check the word's spelling in the list at right or in a dictionary.

Games and Activities

Play Recorded Spellings. Choose some of the spelling words. Call each word out to your child. Using a tape recorder, have your child record himself or herself echoing the word and spelling it. Play the recording back and have your child check the words.

Write the letters of the alphabet on index cards. Create five index cards for each vowel and two index cards for each consonant. Have your child use the alphabet cards to practice spelling words.

Using Spelling Words

Ask your child to write sentences that contain the spelling words. Then read the sentences with your child. Notice whether the sentences show that your child knows the meanings of the spelling words.

Lesson 13 More Words with Short *u*

Week of _____

won	lovely	done	something
shove	some	one	hundred
none	cover	must	number
sum	butter	just	supper

Lesson 14 Words with Short *i*

Week of _____

think	winter	been	December
fill	little	thing	spring
kick	river	which	pretty
dish	begin	build	children

Lesson 15 Words with Long *i*

Week of _____

line	drive	inside	nice
shine	while	size	miles
write	mine	alike	times
white	tiny	lion	eyes

Lesson 16 More Words with Long *i*

Week of _____

Friday	kind	child	mind
behind	high	right	light
night	by	cry	sky
try	why	fly	buy

Lesson 17 Words with *-ed* or *-ing*

Week of _____

wished	asked	rained	dreamed
handed	painted	filled	subtracted
thanked	waited	reading	sleeping
meeting	ending	guessing	laughing

Lesson 18 Unit 3 Review

Week of _____

Lesson 18 is a review of Lessons 13–17. Help your child practice all of the words from those lessons.

Estimada familia de _____ ,

Durante las próximas seis semanas, su niño/a estará aprendiendo a escribir

- palabras que tienen la vocal *u* corta
- palabras que tienen la vocal *i* corta
- palabras que tienen la vocal *i* larga
- palabras que tienen *-ed* o *-ing*

He aquí algunas actividades simples que puede hacer cada semana para ayudar a su niño/a a tener mejor ortografía.

Escuchar y escribir

Dicte las palabras de ortografía y pida a su niño/a que las escriba.

Estrategia de ortografía: Letras y sonidos

Si su niño/a no está seguro/a de cómo se escribe una palabra, pídale que diga la palabra por sí mismo y trate de imaginarse la manera en que la palabra es escrita. Hágale las siguientes preguntas para ayudarlo/a a pensar en la ortografía de la palabra: *¿Tiene la palabra más letras que sonidos? ¿Qué par de letras representan un solo sonido?* Luego pídale a su niño/a que escriba la palabra en una hoja de papel y revise la ortografía.

Juegos y actividades

Seleccione algunas palabras de ortografía. Léale cada palabra en voz alta a su niño/a. Use una grabadora para grabar a su niño/a repitiendo la palabra y deletreándola. Luego escuchen la grabación y pídale a su niño/a que revise la ortografía de las palabras.

Escriba las letras del abecedario sobre tarjetas. Crea cinco tarjetas para cada vocal y dos tarjetas para cada consonante. Invite a su niño/a a utilizarlas para practicar a deletrear palabras.

Emplear las palabras de ortografía

Pida a su niño/a que escriba oraciones con las palabras de ortografía. Lea las oraciones con su niño/a. Fíjese si demuestran que su niño/a entiende los significados de las palabras de ortografía.

Lesson 13 More Words with Short *u*

Week of _____

won	lovely	done	something
shove	some	one	hundred
none	cover	must	number
sum	butter	just	supper

Lesson 14 Words with Short *i*

Week of _____

think	winter	been	December
fill	little	thing	spring
kick	river	which	pretty
dish	begin	build	children

Lesson 15 Words with Long *i*

Week of _____

line	drive	inside	nice
shine	while	size	miles
write	mine	alike	times
white	tiny	lion	eyes

Lesson 16 More Words with Long *i*

Week of _____

Friday	kind	child	mind
behind	high	right	light
night	by	cry	sky
try	why	fly	buy

Lesson 17 Words with *-ed* or *-ing*

Week of _____

wished	asked	rained	dreamed
handed	painted	filled	subtracted
thanked	waited	reading	sleeping
meeting	ending	guessing	laughing

Lesson 18 Unit 3 Review

Week of _____

Lección 18 es un repaso de las Lecciones 13–17. Ayude a su niño/a a practicar todas las palabras de esas lecciones.

Unit 4 — Spelling at Home

Dear Family of _____,

During the next six weeks, your child will be learning to spell the following kinds of words:

- words with the short *o* vowel sound
- words with the long *o* vowel sound
- words with /o͞o/, as in *book*
- words with *-ed* or *-ing*

Here are some simple activities to do each week to help your child become a better speller.

Listening and Writing

Say the spelling words and have your child write them.

Spelling Strategy: Comparing Spellings

If your child is unsure about the spelling of a word, ask your child to write the word in different ways. Then have your child compare the spellings and choose the one that looks correct. Tell your child to check the spelling in a dictionary.

Games and Activities

Play Spelling Charades. Act out some spelling words for your child and ask your child to guess each word and spell it.

Write spelling words on index cards and have your child sort the words into groups. Ask your child to explain what all the words in each group have in common. For example, your child may explain that all the words in a group have the long *o* vowel sound spelled *ow*.

Using Spelling Words

Ask your child to write sentences that contain the spelling words. Then read the sentences with your child. Notice whether the sentences show that your child knows the meanings of the spelling words.

Lesson 19 Words with Short *o*

Week of _____

sorry	socks	clock	bottom
block	problem	jog	o'clock
October	forgot	shop	bottle
body	wash	what	was

Lesson 20 Words with Long *o*

Week of _____

hope	alone	whole	hole
close	joke	wrote	slow
know	yellow	blow	snow
show	goes	toe	November

Lesson 21 More Words with Long *o*

Week of _____

both	ago	almost	hold
comb	gold	hello	open
most	over	road	toast
loaf	boat	cocoa	coat

Lesson 22 Words with /o͞o/

Week of _____

book	cookies	took	stood
wood	poor	foot	cook
shook	put	full	pull
sure	should	could	would

Lesson 23 More Words with *-ed* or *-ing*

Week of _____

closed	hoped	liked	sneezed
pleased	stopped	jogged	dropped
taking	smiling	driving	shining
beginning	hopping	dropping	shopping

Lesson 24 Unit 4 Review

Week of _____

Lesson 24 is a review of Lessons 19–23. Help your child practice all of the words from those lessons.

Estimada familia de _____ ,

Durante las próximas seis semanas, su niño/a estará aprendiendo a escribir

- palabras que tienen la vocal *o* corta
- palabras que tienen la vocal *o* larga
- palabras que tienen /o͝o/, como en *book*
- palabras que tienen *-ed* o *-ing*

He aquí algunas actividades simples que puede hacer cada semana para ayudar a su niño/a a tener mejor ortografía.

Escuchar y escribir

Dicte las palabras de ortografía y pida a su niño/a que las escriban.

Estrategia de ortografía: Comparar ortografías

Si su niño/a no está seguro/a de cómo se escribe una palabra, propóngale que escriba la palabra de distintas maneras. Luego pídale que compare las ortografías y que escoja la que se vea correcta. Pida a su niño/a que revise la ortografía en un diccionario.

Juegos y actividades

Juegen charadas, usando gestos para representar algunas de las palabras de ortografía y pídale a su niño/a que adivine cada palabra y que la escriba.

Escriba palabras de ortografía sobre tarjetas y pídale a su niño/a que las clasifique en grupos. Pídale que explique lo que tienen en común las palabras de cada grupo. Por ejemplo, su niño/a podría explicar que todas las palabras de un grupo tienen el sonido de la vocal *o* larga escrita *ow*.

Emplear las palabras de ortografía

Pida a su niño/a que escriba oraciones que contengan las palabras de ortografía. Luego lea las oraciones con su niño/a. Fíjese si las oraciones demuestran que su niño/a entiende los significados de las palabras de ortografía.

Lesson 19 Words with Short *o*

Week of _____

sorry	socks	clock	bottom
block	problem	jog	o'clock
October	forgot	shop	bottle
body	wash	what	was

Lesson 20 Words with Long *o*

Week of _____

hope	alone	whole	hole
close	joke	wrote	slow
know	yellow	blow	snow
show	goes	toe	November

Lesson 21 More Words with Long *o*

Week of _____

both	ago	almost	hold
comb	gold	hello	open
most	over	road	toast
loaf	boat	cocoa	coat

Lesson 22 Words with /o͝o/

Week of _____

book	cookies	took	stood
wood	poor	foot	cook
shook	put	full	pull
sure	should	could	would

Lesson 23 More Words with *-ed* or *-ing*

Week of _____

closed	hoped	liked	sneezed
pleased	stopped	jogged	dropped
taking	smiling	driving	shining
beginning	hopping	dropping	shopping

Lesson 24 Unit 4 Review

Week of _____

Lección 24 es un repaso de las Lecciones 19–23. Ayude a su niño/a a practicar todas las palabras de esas lecciones.

Dear Family of _____ ,

During the next six weeks, your child will be learning to spell the following kinds of words:

- words with /o͞o/ or /yo͞o/, as in *noon* and *few*
- words with /ûr/, as in *fur*
- words with /ä/, as in *father*
- words with /oi/, as in *coin*
- contractions

Here are some simple activities to do each week to help your child become a better speller.

 Listening and Writing

Say the spelling words and have your child write them.

 Spelling Strategy: Rhyming Partner

If your child is unsure about the spelling of a word, help your child create a list of words that rhyme with the word and are spelled in the same way. Then ask your child to select one of the words as a rhyming partner. Ask your child to study the rhyming partner. Then have him or her spell the word that he or she is having difficulty with.

Games and Activities

Play Easiest to Hardest. Choose a group of words from the list. Give yourself and your child a piece of paper. Next, write the easiest word from the list, the next two easiest words, the next three easiest words, and so on. Then compare the easiest-to-hardest word order with each other.

Choose five spelling words that are hard for your child to spell. Write each word on a separate sheet of paper, leaving space between the letters of the word. Then cut the words apart so that each letter is on a separate square of paper. Mix up the letters. Have your child put the letters together to form the different spelling words.

 Using Spelling Words

Ask your child to write sentences that contain the spelling words. Then read the sentences with your child. Notice whether the sentences show that your child knows the meanings of the spelling words.

Lesson 25 Words with /o͞o/ or /yo͞o/

Week of _____

noon	school	too	tooth
blue	true	Tuesday	who
move	two	news	knew
June	huge	few	used

Lesson 26 Words with /ûr/

Week of _____

girl	bird	first	dirt
third	world	work	word
worm	curl	fur	Thursday
turn	learn	earth	were

Lesson 27 Words with /ä/

Week of _____

father	market	barn	garden
star	sharp	bark	yard
dark	hard	card	start
March	arm	art	heart

Lesson 28 Words with /oi/

Week of _____

soil	broil	coin	point
boil	choice	noise	voice
spoil	oil	join	boy
toy	joy	enjoy	royal

Lesson 29 More Contractions

Week of _____

hasn't	aren't	couldn't	didn't
doesn't	hadn't	haven't	mustn't
shouldn't	wasn't	weren't	isn't
wouldn't	won't	don't	can't

Lesson 30 Unit 5 Review

Week of _____

Lesson 30 is a review of Lessons 25–29. Help your child practice all of the words from those lessons.

Estimada familia de _____ ,

Durante las próximas seis semanas, su niño/a estará aprendiendo a escribir

- palabras con /o͞o/ o /yo͞o/, como en *noon* y *few*
- palabras con /ûr/, como en *fur*
- palabras con /ä/, como en *father*
- palabras con /oi/, como en *coin*
- contracciones

He aquí algunas actividades simples que puede hacer cada semana para ayudar a su niño/a a tener mejor ortografía.

Escuchar y escribir

Dicte las palabras de ortografía y pida a su niño/a que las escriba.

Estrategia de ortografía: Pareja que rima

Si su niño/a no sabe escribir una palabra, ayúdelo/a a crear una lista de palabras que rimen con esa palabra y tengan la misma ortografía. Anímelo/a a seleccionar una de las palabras y estudiarla. Luego pídale que escriba la palabra con que tenía dificultad.

Juegos y actividades

Seleccione un grupo de palabras de la lista. A continuación, cada uno por su cuenta escribe en una hoja de papel la palabra más fácil de la lista, las siguientes dos más fáciles y así sucesivamente. Compare el orden de las palabras de sus listas.

Seleccione cinco palabras de ortografía que le son difíciles a su niño/a. Escriba cada palabra en distintas hojas de papel y luego recorte las palabras para que cada letra quede en un cuadro individual. Revuelva las letras y pídale a su niño/a que las ordene para formar las distintas palabras.

Emplear las palabras de ortografía

Pida a su niño/a que escriba oraciones con las palabras de ortografía. Lea las oraciones con su niño/a. Fíjese si demuestran que su niño/a entiende los significados de las palabras de ortografía.

Lesson 25 Words with /o͞o/ or /yo͞o/

Week of _____

noon	school	too	tooth
blue	true	Tuesday	who
move	two	news	knew
June	huge	few	used

Lesson 26 Words with /ûr/

Week of _____

girl	bird	first	dirt
third	world	work	word
worm	curl	fur	Thursday
turn	learn	earth	were

Lesson 27 Words with /ä/

Week of _____

father	market	barn	garden
star	sharp	bark	yard
dark	hard	card	start
March	arm	art	heart

Lesson 28 Words with /oi/

Week of _____

soil	broil	coin	point
boil	choice	noise	voice
spoil	oil	join	boy
toy	joy	enjoy	royal

Lesson 29 More Contractions

Week of _____

hasn't	aren't	couldn't	didn't
doesn't	hadn't	haven't	mustn't
shouldn't	wasn't	weren't	isn't
wouldn't	won't	don't	can't

Lesson 30 Unit 5 Review

Week of _____

Lección 30 es un repaso de las Lecciones 25–29. Ayude a su niño/a a practicar todas las palabras de esas lecciones.

Dear Family of _____ ,

During the next six weeks, your child will be learning to spell the following kinds of words:

- words with /ô/, as in *draw*
- words with /ou/, as in *house*
- words with /îr/, /âr/, or /īr/, as in *hear, hair,* and *tire*
- words with *-er* or *-est*

Here are some simple activities to do each week to help your child become a better speller.

Listening and Writing

Say the spelling words and have your child write them.

Spelling Strategy: Guess and Check

If your child is having difficulty spelling a word, encourage him or her to guess the spelling. Then ask your child to check the list at right or a dictionary to see if his or her guess is correct.

Games and Activities

Play Spelling Chunks. Have your child choose some of the spelling words. Write the words on a piece of paper. Leave a space below each word. With your child, study the words. Then separate each word into smaller parts so that it is easy to remember. Divide each word into the "chunks" we hear when the word is read aloud. An example is *pow/er.*

Write some of the spelling words on a piece of paper, leaving out some of the letters. Ask your child to complete each word. Taking turns, continue writing and completing as many spelling words as possible.

Using Spelling Words

Ask your child to write sentences that contain the spelling words. Then read the sentences with your child. Notice whether the sentences show that your child knows the meanings of the spelling words.

Lesson 31   Words with /ô/

Week of _____

frog	long	along	off
belong	strong	water	always
mall	tall	talk	walk
bought	brought	draw	because

Lesson 32   More Words with /ô/

Week of _____

autumn	August	born	fork
morning	sport	popcorn	storm
north	corner	before	door
floor	pour	four	quart

Lesson 33   Words with /ou/

Week of _____

hour	sound	ground	about
house	around	count	our
found	owl	down	power
brown	tower	town	flower

Lesson 34   Words with /îr/, /âr/, or /īr/

Week of _____

hear	dear	ear	near
year	here	deer	stairs
air	chair	hair	care
where	tire	fire	wire

Lesson 35   Words with *-er* or *-est*

Week of _____

stronger	strongest	taller	tallest
greater	greatest	longer	longest
sharper	sharpest	funnier	funniest
dirtier	dirtiest	hotter	hottest

Lesson 36   Unit 6 Review

Week of _____

Lesson 36 is a review of Lessons 31–35. Help your child practice all of the words from those lessons.

Estimada familia de _____ ,

Durante las próximas seis semanas, su niño/a estará aprendiendo a escribir

- palabras que tienen /ô/, como en *draw*
- palabras que tienen /ou/, como en *house*
- palabras que tienen /îr/, /âr/, o /īr/, como en *hear, hair* y *tire*
- palabras que tienen *-er* o *-est*

He aquí algunas actividades simples que puede hacer cada semana para ayudar a su niño/a a tener mejor ortografía.

Escuchar y escribir

Dicte las palabras de ortografía y pida a su niño/a que las escriba.

Estrategia de ortografía: Conjeturar y comprobar

Si la ortografía de una palabra le está causando dificultades a su niño/a, pídale que conjeture la ortografía y luego revise la ortografía consultando un diccionario.

Juegos y actividades

Pídale a su niño/a que seleccione algunas palabras de ortografía. Escriba las palabras en una hoja de papel. Deje espacio debajo de cada palabra. Con su niño/a, estudien las palabras. Luego separen cada palabra en partes más pequeñas para que sea más fácil de acordarse. Dividan y escriban cada palabra en "pedazos" que escuchamos cuando la palabra es leída en voz alta. Un ejemplo es *pow/er*.

Escriba algunas palabras de ortografía en una hoja de papel, omitiendo algunas de las letras. Pídale a su niño/a que complete cada palabra.

Emplear las palabras de ortografía

Pida a su niño/a que escriba oraciones que contengan las palabras de ortografía. Luego lea las oraciones con su niño/a. Fíjese si las oraciones demuestran que su niño/a entiende los significados de las palabras de ortografía.

Lesson 31 Words with /ô/

Week of _____

frog	long	along	off
belong	strong	water	always
mall	tall	talk	walk
bought	brought	draw	because

Lesson 32 More Words with /ô/

Week of _____

autumn	August	born	fork
morning	sport	popcorn	storm
north	corner	before	door
floor	pour	four	quart

Lesson 33 Words with /ou/

Week of _____

hour	sound	ground	about
house	around	count	our
found	owl	down	power
brown	tower	town	flower

Lesson 34 Words with /îr/, /âr/, or /īr/

Week of _____

hear	dear	ear	near
year	here	deer	stairs
air	chair	hair	care
where	tire	fire	wire

Lesson 35 Words with *-er* or *-est*

Week of _____

stronger	strongest	taller	tallest
greater	greatest	longer	longest
sharper	sharpest	funnier	funniest
dirtier	dirtiest	hotter	hottest

Lesson 36 Unit 6 Review

Week of _____

Lección 36 es un repaso de las Lecciones 31–35. Ayude a su niño/a a practicar todas las palabras de esas lecciones.

Name _____

Read each word in the box and circle it in the puzzle below.
The words go across, down, or at a slant.

Spelling Words	ask	matter	black	subtract	match	Saturday	class	apple
	add	thank	catch	January	after	hammer	half	laugh

```
h  a  m  m  e  r  a  j  m  k  p  z  i  l  b
b  g  s  x  h  i  n  c  l  a  s  s  y  a  s
n  w  n  k  o  x  p  p  a  f  t  e  r  j  u
i  j  a  n  u  a  r  y  q  u  y  c  r  z  b
t  l  p                          h  c  t
h  a  p                          a  b  r
a  u  l                          l  s  a
n  g  e                          f  a  c
k  h  w                          a  t  t
b  m  o                          k  u  c
l  f  f                          a  r  d
a  u  v                          e  d  r
c  a  t  c  h  u  o  e  d  h  r  l  t  a  d
k  l  e  m  a  t  t  e  r  r  d  k  c  y  d
```

Words with Long *a*

Name _____

**Use the words in the box to solve the puzzle.
Some letters are given.**

g				s		f						c
A				l		c				g		
				a								
b			a				M					
		p										
		p										
s												

Spelling Words	
ate	change
late	gray
safe	away
page	pay
face	May
save	break
place	great
came	April

More Words with Long *a*

Name _____

**Use the words in the box to complete the *ai* puzzle.
Some of the letters are given.**

Spelling Words	
rain	train
aid	aim
paint	wait
afraid	sail

1. ___ ___ ___ ___ **m**
2. ___ **r** ___ ___
3. **t** ___ ___
4. ___ **p** ___ ___ ___
5. ___ ___ **f** ___ ___
6. ___ ___ ___ ___ **d**
7. ___ **s** ___ ___
8. ___ ___ **w** ___ ___

**Find the word in the box that completes each sentence.
Write the word on the line.**

Spelling Words	table	paper	danger	eight	fable	weigh	able	they

9. Will you please set the _____ for dinner?

10. How many pounds does your dog _____?

11. Trees are used to make _____.

12. Are you _____ to reach the top shelf?

13. My brother is _____ years old.

14. Thin ice is a _____ for ice skaters.

15. I stayed home, but _____ went to the zoo.

16. The teacher read a _____ about a rabbit and a turtle.

Words with Short *e*

Name _____

Find the word in the box that matches each clue. Write the word. Then read down the squares to find the answer to the question.

Spelling Words	next	head	address	said
	read	dress	second	spent

WHAT DO YOU CALL A NICE DOE?

a

1. first, ____, third   __ __ __ __

2. I am ____ in line after her.   __ __ __ __ __ __

3. where you wear a hat   __ __ __ __

4. where you live   __ __ __ __ __ __ __

5. say, ____, saying   __ __ __ __

6. She ____ the chapter book.   __ __ __ __

7. spend, ____, spending   __ __ __ __ __

8. She wore a nice ____ to the dance.   __ __ __ __ __

Find the word in the box that completes each sentence. Write the word on the line.

Spelling Words	end	help	says	forget	again	ready	egg	test

9. I will not _____ my lunch money.

10. He likes a scrambled _____ for breakfast.

11. Jesse needs some _____ with his homework.

12. My favorite part of the movie was the _____.

13. I will play my favorite video game _____.

14. Are you _____ to go to the zoo?

15. Our teacher _____ we are good listeners.

16. Reggie made a perfect score on her _____.

Plural Words

Name _____

Find the word in the box that matches each clue. Write the word in the puzzle.

Spelling Words			
clowns	papers	tests	apples
paints	matches	trains	dresses
pages	hammers	eggs	hands
classes	addresses	tables	places

Across

2. your feet and your ___
3. These hit nails.
4. what books have
7. In school you go to ___.
8. They make people laugh.
9. Students take ___ to show what they know.
14. They travel on railroads.
16. The teacher graded the ___ that the students wrote.

Down

1. what goes on envelopes
5. rhymes with *faces*
6. You use brushes with these
10. People eat these for breakfast.
11. chairs and ___
12. something to wear
13. People light fires with these.
15. what grows on apple trees

More Words with Short *e*

Name _____

Find the word in the box that matches each clue. Write the word. Then read down the squares to answer the question.

Spelling Words	best	cents	never	slept	them
	when	friend	many	guess	

HOW CAN YOU SERVE TEN EGGS TO SEVEN PEOPLE?

Clues
 1. to suppose
 2. coins
 3. at no time
 4. a lot of
 5. those people
 6. most excellent
 7. sleep tonight, ___ last night
 8. as soon as
 9. a pal

1. __ __ __ __ __
2. __ __ __ __ __
3. __ __ __ __ __
4. __ __ __ __
5. __ __ __ __ __
6. __ __ __ __
7. __ __ __ __
8. __ __ __ __
9. __ __ __ __ __ __

Find the word in the box that completes each sentence. Write the word on the line.

Spelling Words	September	then	Wednesday	better	February	kept	sent

10. Keesha _____ valentines in the month of _____.

11. His birthday is in _____.

12. Marcel is feeling _____ today.

13. The day that comes after Tuesday is _____.

14. We _____ the secret.

15. The team practiced and _____ went out for pizza.

Words with Long *e*

Name _____

Use the code to write each word in the letter. Then read the letter.

Spelling Words	sneeze	sleep	people	sea	queen	please	free	meat
	dream	need	street	each	wheel	meet	read	team

1 = a	2 = c	3 = d	4 = e	5 = f	6 = h	7 = l	8 = m	9 = n
10 = o	11 = p	12 = q	13 = r	14 = s	15 = t	16 = u	17 = w	18 = z

Dear Daniel,

Last night, I had a ___ ___ ___ ___ ___ when I
3 13 4 1 8

went to ___ ___ ___ ___ ___. I visited a kingdom
14 7 4 4 11

near the ___ ___ ___. The ___ ___ ___ ___ ___ ___
14 4 1 11 4 10 11 7 4

there loved hamburgers. The ___ ___ ___ ___ ___
12 16 4 4 9

was having a hamburger party. People took me to

___ ___ ___ ___ her. There was wonderful ___ ___ ___ ___
8 4 4 15 8 4 1 15

to eat. It was all ___ ___ ___ ___. I started to eat and eat.
5 13 4 4

Suddenly, I began to ___ ___ ___ ___ ___ ___. I woke up with feathers
14 9 4 4 18 4

tickling my nose. Now I ___ ___ ___ ___ a new pillow. Mine has three
9 4 4 3

bites taken out of it!

Josie and I are playing stickball with our ___ ___ ___ ___ at the school
15 4 1 8

on Main ___ ___ ___ ___ ___ ___ later today. Then we are going to the fair.
14 15 13 4 4 15

We have money for ___ ___ ___ ___ of us to ride the Ferris ___ ___ ___ ___ ___.
4 1 2 6 17 6 4 4 7

___ ___ ___ ___ ___ ___ write soon! I love to ___ ___ ___ ___ letters from my friends.
11 7 4 1 14 4 13 4 1 3

Love,

Brianna

Name _____

Read the sentences. Cross out the misspelled words and write them correctly on the lines.

Spelling Words	happy	funny	very	busy	carry	sunny
	family	penny	only	city	story	

1. Ling onie had one more tooth to lose. _____
2. It was sunnee in the citee. _____ _____
3. The whole family went to the store. _____
4. The street was viry bizy. _____ _____
5. Alex was happie to carrey the apples. _____ _____
6. Kyle thought the storry was funy. _____ _____
7. Eva gave Ruben a peny. _____

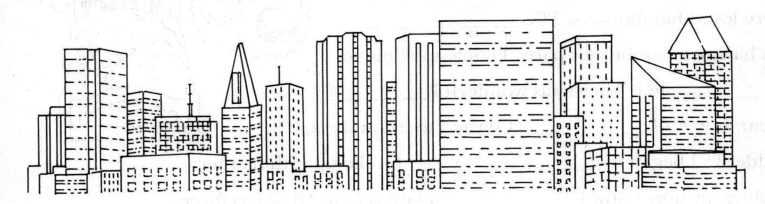

Use the words in the box to complete the e puzzle.

Spelling Words
sleepy
every
these
even
key

Words with Short *u*

Name _____

**Read each word in the box and circle it in the puzzle below.
The words go across, down, or at a slant.**

Spelling Words	mother	front	month	money	from
	nothing	Monday	such	summer	much
	lunch	sun	under	Sunday	does
	other				

```
m  o  n  t  h  e  s  u  m  m  e  r  o  u  s
o  b  s  r  w  l  y  u  s  w  u  s  w  a  f
n  s  u  n  d  e  r  q  c  z  r  c  b  f  r
e  u           c  i  h  h  g  f  h  t  o
y  n                          h  s  n
k  d                          d  m  t
b  a                          c  o  i
v  y  u                       l  n  a
p  q  j                       b  d  c
s  m  l                       d  a  l
w  o  u                       m  y  u
o  t  h  e  r  d  k  w  o  t  m  f  d  g  n
k  h  p  y  d  n  o  t  h  i  n  g  r  e  c
f  e  x  j  g  j  v  e  h  g  p  w  r  o  h
o  r  w  x  b  p  n  i  s  u  n  z  t  s  m
```

Name _____

Find the word in the box that matches each clue. Write the word in the puzzle. The puzzle includes boxes for apostrophes.

Spelling Words	they'll she'll I've they've he's it's they'd I'm she's

Across

1. she is
4. he is
7. they will
8. I have

Down

2. she will
3. I am
5. they have
6. it is
7. they would

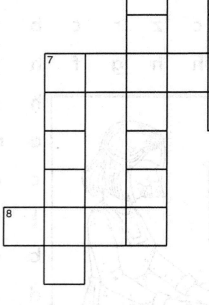

Draw a line from each pair of words to its contraction.

9. we will   a. I'll
10. you have   b. we'll
11. you would   c. you'll
12. I will   d. you've
13. we have   e. I'd
14. you will   f. you'd
15. I would   g. we've

More Words with Short *u*

Name _____

Find the word in the box that matches each pronunciation. Write the word on the line.

Spelling Words	lovely	done	cover	none	hundred	must	butter	just

1. /lŭv′ lē/ _____

2. /jŭst/ _____

3. /bŭt′ ər/ _____

4. /hŭn′ drĭd/ _____

5. /dŭn/ _____

6. /mŭst/ _____

7. /kŭv′ ər/ _____

8. /nŭn/ _____

Find the correctly spelled words to trace Stacy's path to the first-place ribbon.

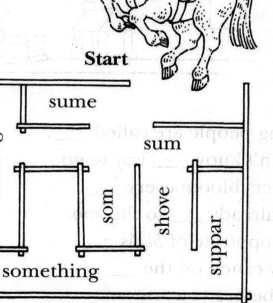

Start

some   wone   sume

won   sum

number   shov   someting

one   supper   som   shove   suppar

                 something

Words with Short *i*

Name _____

Find the word in the box that matches each clue. Write the word in the puzzle.

Spelling Words	little	begin	pretty	river	build	which	spring	thing
	been	fill	think	winter	dish	children	kick	December

Across

4. Young people are called ___ .
6. I didn't know ___ way to go.
7. Flowers bloom every ___ .
9. I've already ___ to the zoo.
10. The opposite of *big* is ___ .
11. They canoe on the ___ .
13. ___ before you answer.
14. The last month of the year is ___ .

Down

1. Half of the word *something* is ___ .
2. The race will ___ at noon.
3. Jarrell put the ___ in the sink.
5. ___ the glass with water.
6. The season after autumn is ___ .
8. That's a ___ picture.
9. Let's ___ a house with blocks.
12. She will ___ the soccer ball.

Words with Long *i*

Name _____

Read each word in the box and circle it in the puzzle below.
The words go across, down, or at a slant.

Spelling Words	line	drive	inside	nice	shine	while	size	miles
	write	mine	alike	times	white	tiny	lion	eyes

```
o  l  m  s  u  m  i  l  e  s  e  u  i  o  p
e  p  s  o  u  v  m  z  q  u  w  r  i  t  e
u  y  b  s  w  h  i  t  e  j  a  k  r  i  s
q  v  e  g  t  r  n  a  b  p  m  g  w  n  o
s  l  f  s  i  z  e  q  u  r  v  i  b  y  d
o  t  y                          n  w  f
k  i  r                          f  r  k
o  m  m                          a  w  t
v  e  n                          l  m  d
h  s  i                          i  w  u
d  j  c                          k  h  b
i  r  e                          e  i  l
w  l  i  o  n  d  r  t  d  c  g  x  o  l  j
g  x  h  v  p  q  p  p  i  n  s  i  d  e  i
y  l  i  n  e  m  s  h  i  n  e  r  h  i  h
```

Name _____

Find the words in the box that complete the sentences. Write the words on the lines. Some letters are given.

Spelling Words	Friday	kind	child	mind	behind	high	right	buy
	light	night	by	cry	sky	try	why	fly

1. A __ __ __ __ **d** saw a housefly **f** __ __ __.

2. It flew __ **e** __ __ __ __ the curtain and near the __ __ **g** __ __.

3. It flew all day and into the __ __ __ __ **t**.

4. I saw a housefly fly __ __ me.

5. I watched it fly __ **i** __ __ in the sky.

6. I once tried to __ **u** __ a housefly in a store.

7. On **F** __ __ __ __ __, a housefly flew down from the __ **k** __.

8. The housefly flew **r** __ __ __ __ into the house.

9. It landed on my knee and began to **c** __ __.

10. **T** __ __ to see a house fly.

11. What __ __ __ __ of house flies?

12. __ __ __ do you ask?

13. Houses don't fly; it's all in your __ __ __ __.

Words with -ed or -ing

Name _____

Use the words in the box to solve the puzzle below. Some letters are given.

Spelling Words	wished	dreamed	rained	painted	filled
	handed	thanked	reading	guessing	ending
	waited	sleeping	meeting	laughing	asked
	subtracted				

Name _____

The underlined word in each sentence does not make sense. Find the word in the box that does make sense. Write the word on the line.

Spelling Words	sorry	socks	clock	bottom	block	problem	jog	o'clock
	October	forgot	shop	bottle	body	wash	what	was

1. My <u>birds</u> have holes in both heels. _____

2. Set the <u>bird</u> for 7:00 A.M. _____

3. Our houses are on the same <u>bird</u>. _____

4. The baby's mom gave her a <u>bird</u> of warm milk. _____

5. I found my ring at the <u>bird</u> of the drawer. _____

6. It's three <u>bird</u>, and all is well! _____

7. Columbus Day is in the month of <u>bird</u>. _____

8. Maria <u>bird</u> to do her homework. _____

9. Would you like to <u>bird</u> around the track? _____

10. Exercise is good for your <u>bird</u>. _____

11. Yesterday <u>bird</u> a beautiful day for a hike. _____

12. Did you <u>bird</u> your hands and face? _____

13. Did you hear <u>bird</u> she said? _____

14. They worked together to solve the <u>bird</u>. _____

15. I'm <u>bird</u> that you can't visit today. _____

16. Let's go to the bike <u>bird</u> to buy a helmet. _____

Words with Long *o*

Name _____

Start with the word *blow*. Change one letter in each word to make a new one from the box.

Spelling Words	
slow	show
snow	know

1. blow
2. ___ ___ ___ ___
3. ___ ___ ___ ___
4. ___ ___ ___ ___
5. ___ ___ ___ ___

Find the word in the box that matches each clue. Write the word in the *o* puzzle.

Spelling Words	yellow	alone		joke	hole	close	toe
	whole	November		goes	wrote	hope	

6. part of the foot
7. I go, you go, she ___
8. I ___ I get it right.
9. dig a ___ in the dirt
10. tell a funny ___
11. We ate the ___ pizza.
12. without anyone else
13. Be sure to ___ the door.
14. write today, ___ yesterday
15. a month of the year
16. the color of a lemon

Name _____

The underlined word in each sentence does not make sense. Find the word in the box that does make sense. Write the word on the line.

Spelling Words	both	ago	almost	hold	hello	open	most	over
	loaf	cocoa	comb	coat	gold	boat	toast	road

1. Tonya can <u>goldfish</u> reach the top shelf. _____

2. The judges gave prizes to <u>goldfish</u> Mei and Lee. _____

3. My grandmother was born a long time <u>goldfish</u>. _____

4. Buy a <u>goldfish</u> of bread and a quart of milk. _____

5. Tara's favorite drink is hot <u>goldfish</u>. _____

6. We had eggs and <u>goldfish</u> for breakfast. _____

7. They sailed a <u>goldfish</u> to the island. _____

8. The <u>goldfish</u> was icy after the storm. _____

9. Wear your <u>goldfish</u> when it's cold. _____

10. When you meet someone, you say <u>goldfish</u>. _____

11. Can you jump <u>goldfish</u> that big puddle? _____

12. The treasure chest was filled with <u>goldfish</u>. _____

13. Do you brush or <u>goldfish</u> your hair? _____

14. You can <u>goldfish</u> the door with this key. _____

15. Sam asked Jetta to <u>goldfish</u> the door open. _____

16. This is the <u>goldfish</u> beautiful picture I've ever seen. _____

Words with /o͝o/

Name _____

Find the word in the box that matches each clue. Write the word. Then read down the squares to find the answer to the question.

Spelling Words	book	took	wood	poor	foot
	cook	shook	sure	cookies	

WHAT DO YOU CALL A BOOK AFTER AN EARTHQUAKE?

Clues

1. having no doubt
2. past tense of *shake*
3. 12 inches or 30.4 centimeters
4. prepare food for eating
5. small sweet cakes

6. something you read from
7. what trees have
8. having little or no money
9. past tense of *take*

a

1. __ __ __ __
2. __ __ __ __
3. __ __ __ __
4. __ __ __ __
5. __ __ __ __ __
6. __ __ __ __
7. __ __ __ __
8. __ __ __
9. __ __ __ __

Find the word in the box that completes each sentence. Write the word on the line.

Spelling Words	stood	put	full	pull	should	could	would

10. That bucket is _____ of paint.

11. The dog _____ by the gate and barked.

12. What _____ you do with the money if you won?

13. Many years ago that man _____ sing very well.

14. It is time to _____ on your hat and coat.

15. You _____ not slam the door.

16. Jason will _____ weeds from the garden.

More Words with -ed or -ing

Name _____

**Use the words in the box to solve the puzzle.
Some letters are given.**

Spelling Words	
closed	taking
hoped	smiling
liked	driving
sneezed	shining
pleased	beginning
stopped	hopping
jogged	dropping
dropped	shopping

Words with /o͞o/ or /yo͞o/

Name _____

Use the code to solve the puzzle.

1 = b	
2 = c	
3 = d	
4 = e	
5 = f	
6 = h	
7 = k	
8 = l	
9 = n	
10 = o	
11 = r	
12 = s	
13 = t	
14 = u	
15 = w	

Spelling Words

school	two
too	news
tooth	knew
blue	few
true	used

Across

3. 13 10 10 13 6

5. 7 9 4 15

7. 14 12 4 3

9. 1 8 14 4

10. 12 2 6 10 10 8

Down

1. 13 10 10

2. 5 4 15

4. 13 11 14 4

6. 9 4 15 12

8. 13 15 10

Find the word in the box that completes each sentence. Write the word on the line.

Spelling Words	noon	Tuesday	who	move	June	huge

11. Do you know _____ will be in the play?

12. Would you like to _____ to another city?

13. The month after _____ is July.

14. Twelve o'clock is also called _____.

15. I have a _____ pile of dirty socks under my bed.

16. Their book reports are due on _____.

Words with /ûr/

Name _____

**Find the word in the box that matches each clue. Write the word.
Then read down the squares to find the answer to the question.**

Spelling Words	bird	first	dirt	third	world	work
	word	fur	Thursday	turn	learn	were

WHAT IS *GIRL* IN THIS SENTENCE?

1. It's your ___ to play.
2. first, second, ___
3. We ___ at the zoo yesterday.

4. *A* is the ___ letter in the alphabet.
5. Friday comes after ___ .
6. Wipe the ___ off your shoes.
7. Did you ___ your spelling words?
8. Each ___ in this lesson has the /ûr/ sound.
9. Cleaning the yard is hard ___ .
10. A globe is a map of the ___ .
11. The cat has soft black ___ .
12. A parrot is a ___ .

**Find the word in the box that completes each sentence.
Write the word on the line.**

Spelling Words	girl	worm	curl	earth

13. The _____ wore her new cap.

14. She had a lot of _____ in her hair.

15. She dug a hole in the _____ .

16. She found a _____ to bait her hook.

Words with /ä/

Name _____

Read each word in the box and circle it in the puzzle below.
The words go across, down, or at a slant.

Spelling Words	father	market	barn	garden	star	sharp	bark	heart
	yard	dark	hard	card	start	March	arm	art

f a t h e r u f s b n w o g y
e r s m q i b a r n a s t a r
o m a r k e t b c g s r m r b
v x r   k d i
h b t   l e y
e k n   w n d
a w c   p s e
r o a   s h d
t r r   y a m
p y d   i r a
m a h p i v c b t e j a o p r
i r g a a t h a r d e t s a c
o d a r k r f t r a p k g r h
q u t k n a t z o s t a r t y
u p z a i l u y m o e s c s k

Name _____

Find the word in the box that matches each clue. Write the word in the puzzle.

Spelling Words	soil	broil	coin	point	boil	choice	noise	voice
	spoil	oil	join	boy	toy	joy	enjoy	royal

Across

3. John is a name for a ___.
4. what a doll is
7. Milk can ___.
9. Use your ___ to sing.
12. used to fry food
14. You need to ___ water to make tea.
15. the sharp end of a pencil
16. Did you ___ the field trip?

Down

1. opposite of *quiet*
2. Dirt is ___.
5. a way to cook
6. Queens and kings are ___.
8. Let's ___ the club.
10. A nickel is a ___.
11. rhymes with *voice*
13. opposite of *sadness*

Name _____

Find the word in the box that matches each clue. Write the word. Then read down the squares to find the answer to the question. The lines for the letters include lines for apostrophes.

Spelling Words	hasn't	aren't	couldn't	didn't	hadn't
	wasn't	isn't	won't	don't	mustn't

WHY DOES AN ELEPHANT HAVE A TRUNK?

Because it has

1. did + not = _ _ _ ☐ _ _ _
2. will + not = _ _ ☐ _ _
3. has + not = _ _ _ ☐ _ _
4. must + not = _ _ _ ☐ _ _ _
5. is + not = _ _ ☐ _ _
6. do + not = _ _ ☐ _ _
7. could + not = _ _ _ ☐ _ _ _
8. had + not = _ _ _ ☐ _ _
9. was + not = _ _ _ ☐ _ _
10. are + not = _ _ ☐ _ _

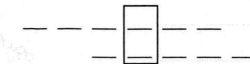
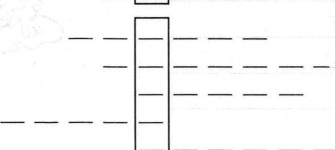
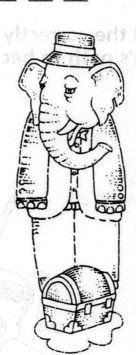

Draw a line from each pair of words to its contraction.

11. have not   **a.** doesn't
12. cannot   **b.** haven't
13. would not   **c.** shouldn't
14. does not   **d.** weren't
15. should not   **e.** wouldn't
16. were not   **f.** can't

Words with /ô/

Name _____

Find the word in the box that matches each pronunciation. Write the word on the line.

Spelling Words	frog	long	water	always	talk	brought	draw

1. /tôk/ _____

2. /drô/ _____

3. /ôl′ wāz/ _____

4. /lông/ _____

5. /brôt/ _____

6. /**wô′** tər/ _____

7. /frôg/ _____

Start

mall   awf

bought

allways   because   becuz   off

Find the correctly spelled words to trace the frog's path to become a prince.

walk

strong   belong   takk   along

belawg

tall

More Words with /ô/

Name _____

Read each word in the box and circle it in the puzzle below. The words go across, down, or at a slant.

Spelling Words	autumn	August	born	fork	four	sport	popcorn	storm
	north	corner	before	door	floor	pour	morning	quart

d b t v b q f a u t u m n p e
m o r n i n g m x e s g l f q
c r o x g o a u g u s t n o u
e n p r r b y t a h o u i
p a h z r e
o r o j t m
u w r f e w
r p s l e t
s o e o n w
y p s o q c
t c o r u l
p o e r j g o t s o f t i a t
e r d i t s y r c u o f o r k
h n o r t h v u d t u o c t o
u h k a a c o r n e r d f m b
l b e f o r e m a b r l y d x

Words with /ou/

Name _____

Use the words in the box to solve the puzzle below. Some letters are given.

Spelling Words	
count	our
down	flower
owl	ground
tower	found
hour	around
power	about
brown	sound
town	house

Words with /îr/, /âr/, or /īr/

Name _____

Read the words in the box. Then sort them by vowel sound. Write the words on the lines.

Spelling Words	chair	near	ear	wire	hair
	year	hear	fire	air	

_____   _____   _____

_____   _____   _____

_____

Find the word in the box that completes each sentence in the letter. Write the word on the line. Then read the letter.

Spelling Words	where	stairs	deer	care	here	tire	dear

_____ Tom,
          1

    I like my new house. It has _____ going down to the back
          2

yard. My dad made a swing for me out of an old _____. I wish
          3

you could come _____ and swing with me.
          4

    I also got a new puppy. He plays with me outside. I'm learning how to

take good _____ of him.
          5

    Do you know what I saw last night? I saw a _____ walking
          6

through the back yard. It was so neat!

    I am really enjoying my new house. There is no _____ else
          7

I would want to live but here!

Your friend,

Nick

Words with -er or -est

Name _____

Find the word in the box that matches each clue. Write the word. Then read down the squares to find the answer to the question.

Spelling Words	stronger	greater	longest	sharper	sharpest
	funnier	dirtier	dirtiest	hotter	hottest

WHAT FALL BUT NEVER GET HURT?

1. great, ___ , greatest

2. sharp, ___ , sharpest

3. dirty, dirtier, ___

4. funny, ___ , funniest

5. dirty, ___ , dirtiest

6. hot, ___ , hottest

7. strong, ___ , strongest

8. sharp, sharper, ___

9. long, longer, ___

Find the word in the box that completes each sentence. Write the word on the line.

Spelling Words	strongest	taller	tallest	greatest	longer	funniest	hottest

10. Anita told the _____ joke I ever heard.

11. August was the _____ month of the year.

12. Jacob is five feet tall, but Gilbert is _____ .

13. The horse has _____ legs than the pony.

14. The giraffe is the _____ animal at the zoo.

15. She is the _____ weight lifter at the gym.

16. Chocolate ice cream is the _____ ice cream ever made.

Unit 1 Review Test

Darken the circle for the word that is spelled correctly.

Example

I hope that you can _____ and visit with me.
- (A) stey
- ● stay
- (C) stae
- (D) stai

1. The circus clown made Mario _____.
   - (A) lagh
   - (B) lalf
   - (C) laf
   - (D) laugh

2. Curtis found three _____ in the nest.
   - (F) egs
   - (G) eggs
   - (H) egges
   - (J) eggses

3. Please _____ the fruit on the scale.
   - (A) waigh
   - (B) wey
   - (C) weigh
   - (D) weagh

4. We are taking our class trip in _____.
   - (F) Januery
   - (G) January
   - (H) Jenuary
   - (J) Januiry

5. Let's sit at this _____ and eat lunch.
   - (A) teble
   - (B) taible
   - (C) tayble
   - (D) table

6. Are you _____ to take the test?
   - (F) ready
   - (G) redy
   - (H) raidy
   - (J) raydy

7. He used the _____ to light the candles.
   - (A) maches
   - (B) matches
   - (C) matchs
   - (D) machses

8. Alex was _____ in line today.
   - (F) seacond
   - (G) secon
   - (H) sacond
   - (J) second

9. The sky looks cloudy and _____.
   - (A) gray
   - (B) greigh
   - (C) grai
   - (D) graye

10. Kate wants to play that game _____!
    - (F) agean
    - (G) again
    - (H) agayn
    - (J) agen

11. I like bananas and _____ in my fruit salad.
    - (A) apples
    - (B) appls
    - (C) appels
    - (D) appleses

12. My puppy is _____ of thunder.
    - (F) afrayd
    - (G) afrade
    - (H) afraid
    - (J) afreid

13. The flowers bloomed in _____.
    - (A) Aprel
    - (B) Aipril
    - (C) April
    - (D) Aypril

Name _____

Darken the circle for the word that is spelled correctly.

14. Will you give me your phone number and _____?
    - Ⓕ addrayss
    - Ⓗ addreass
    - Ⓖ adraiss
    - Ⓙ address

15. Ana won first _____ in the relay race.
    - Ⓐ plaice
    - Ⓒ place
    - Ⓑ plase
    - Ⓓ pleys

16. My little brother is learning how to add and _____.
    - Ⓕ subtract
    - Ⓗ subtrauct
    - Ⓖ subtrac
    - Ⓙ subtrak

17. The vase will _____ if you drop it.
    - Ⓐ braik
    - Ⓒ break
    - Ⓑ breyk
    - Ⓓ breik

18. Tyrel has visited _____ all over the world.
    - Ⓕ placeses
    - Ⓗ places
    - Ⓖ placees
    - Ⓙ placs

19. My neighbor _____ hello to me every day.
    - Ⓐ seys
    - Ⓒ saiys
    - Ⓑ says
    - Ⓓ seays

20. We could be in _____ if we go in the cave alone.
    - Ⓕ daingr
    - Ⓗ deingr
    - Ⓖ danger
    - Ⓙ deynger

21. She _____ the nail into the side of the tree house.
    - Ⓐ hamers
    - Ⓒ hammers
    - Ⓑ haummers
    - Ⓓ hammrs

22. We had a _____ time at the picnic!
    - Ⓕ grat
    - Ⓗ grayt
    - Ⓖ grait
    - Ⓙ great

23. Ling can _____ the football.
    - Ⓐ cach
    - Ⓒ cautch
    - Ⓑ catch
    - Ⓓ cech

24. You can have _____ of my sandwich.
    - Ⓕ haf
    - Ⓗ haulf
    - Ⓖ hef
    - Ⓙ half

25. Do _____ want to go to the park with us?
    - Ⓐ thaiy
    - Ⓒ thay
    - Ⓑ thae
    - Ⓓ they

Review Test   Name _____

Darken the circle for the underlined word that is not spelled correctly.
Darken the circle for *No mistake* if all the words are spelled correctly.

Example

My <u>muther</u> and I go to the beach <u>each</u> <u>summer</u>. <u>No mistake</u>
     ●   Ⓑ   Ⓒ   Ⓓ

1. <u>They'd</u> like to have <u>loench</u> with their <u>friend</u>. <u>No mistake</u>
  Ⓐ   Ⓑ   Ⓒ   Ⓓ

2. <u>Does</u> our <u>teem</u> <u>meet</u> today or tomorrow? <u>No mistake</u>
  Ⓕ   Ⓖ   Ⓗ   Ⓙ

3. <u>Shel'l</u> go camping with her <u>family</u> <u>even</u> if it rains. <u>No mistake</u>
  Ⓐ   Ⓑ   Ⓒ   Ⓓ

4. <u>You've</u> asked <u>many</u> <u>people</u> to come to your party. <u>No mistake</u>
  Ⓕ   Ⓖ   Ⓗ   Ⓙ

5. I'm going to <u>gess</u> the answers to <u>these</u> questions. <u>No mistake</u>
  Ⓐ   Ⓑ   Ⓒ   Ⓓ

6. It's my job to wash the dishes <u>evry</u> <u>Wednesday</u> night. <u>No mistake</u>
  Ⓕ   Ⓖ   Ⓗ   Ⓙ

7. <u>Pleese</u> use the <u>other</u> <u>key</u> if this one doesn't work. <u>No mistake</u>
  Ⓐ   Ⓑ Ⓒ   Ⓓ

8. I'm <u>hoping</u> to <u>meet</u> a <u>queen</u> someday. <u>No mistake</u>
  Ⓕ   Ⓖ   Ⓗ   Ⓙ

9. <u>Febuary</u> can be <u>such</u> a cold <u>month</u>. <u>No mistake</u>
  Ⓐ   Ⓑ   Ⓒ   Ⓓ

10. <u>They'd</u> like to visit his <u>family</u> on <u>Wednesday</u>. <u>No mistake</u>
  Ⓕ   Ⓖ   Ⓗ   Ⓙ

Review Test   Name _____

Darken the circle for the phrase with an underlined word that is not spelled correctly.

Example

- ● <u>weel</u> fell off
- Ⓑ <u>read</u> a book
- Ⓒ heard a <u>funny</u> joke
- Ⓓ <u>slept</u> too late

11.
- Ⓐ lock and <u>key</u>
- Ⓑ birthday in <u>February</u>
- Ⓒ king and <u>quean</u>
- Ⓓ <u>meet</u> after class

12.
- Ⓕ joined the <u>team</u>
- Ⓖ <u>soch</u> a nice day
- Ⓗ will take a <u>guess</u>
- Ⓙ <u>please</u> and thank-you

13.
- Ⓐ if <u>itt's</u> raining
- Ⓑ play <u>many</u> games
- Ⓒ <u>family</u> of four
- Ⓓ <u>lunch</u> or dinner

14.
- Ⓕ <u>even</u> if you go
- Ⓖ <u>does</u> know how
- Ⓗ what <u>Im</u> doing
- Ⓙ practice on <u>Wednesday</u>

15.
- Ⓐ play with <u>theyse</u> toys
- Ⓑ where <u>you've</u> been
- Ⓒ a group of <u>people</u>
- Ⓓ answered <u>every</u> question

16.
- Ⓕ the day and the <u>month</u>
- Ⓖ what <u>they'd</u> do
- Ⓗ where <u>she'll</u> go
- Ⓙ make <u>uther</u> plans

17.
- Ⓐ on the football <u>team</u>
- Ⓑ likes to <u>please</u> others
- Ⓒ <u>guess</u> the answer
- Ⓓ an <u>eyven</u> number

18.
- Ⓕ a <u>family</u> picnic
- Ⓖ has <u>many</u> pets
- Ⓗ <u>dus</u> want to skate
- Ⓙ offers to help <u>people</u>

19.
- Ⓐ a vacation next <u>munth</u>
- Ⓑ met the princess and the <u>queen</u>
- Ⓒ seen <u>these</u> movies
- Ⓓ all <u>you've</u> done

20.
- Ⓕ <u>lunch</u> in the park
- Ⓖ if <u>I'm</u> studying
- Ⓗ Tuesday or <u>Wendsday</u>
- Ⓙ on my <u>key</u> chain

21.
- Ⓐ what <u>they'd</u> see
- Ⓑ <u>meot</u> his brother
- Ⓒ having <u>such</u> a good time
- Ⓓ can snow in <u>February</u>

Review Test   Name _____

Darken the circle for the word that is not spelled correctly. Darken the circle for *No mistakes* if all the words are spelled correctly.

Example

- A pritty
- B sky
- C kick
- D river
- E *No mistakes*

1.
- A write
- B done
- C behind
- D iyes
- E *No mistakes*

2.
- F laughing
- G build
- H children
- J won
- K *No mistakes*

3.
- A tiny
- B dreamed
- C lovly
- D lion
- E *No mistakes*

4.
- F been
- G wun
- H while
- J right
- K *No mistakes*

5.
- A laughing
- B write
- C childrin
- D lion
- E *No mistakes*

6.
- F nite
- G guessing
- H why
- J which
- K *No mistakes*

7.
- A been
- B right
- C while
- D thankd
- E *No mistakes*

8.
- F wished
- G hondred
- H buy
- J butter
- K *No mistakes*

9.
- A behind
- B tiny
- C guessng
- D which
- E *No mistakes*

Example

● Ⓑ Ⓒ Ⓓ Ⓔ

Answers

1. Ⓐ Ⓑ Ⓒ Ⓓ Ⓔ

2. Ⓕ Ⓖ Ⓗ Ⓙ Ⓚ

3. Ⓐ Ⓑ Ⓒ Ⓓ Ⓔ

4. Ⓕ Ⓖ Ⓗ Ⓙ Ⓚ

5. Ⓐ Ⓑ Ⓒ Ⓓ Ⓔ

6. Ⓕ Ⓖ Ⓗ Ⓙ Ⓚ

7. Ⓐ Ⓑ Ⓒ Ⓓ Ⓔ

8. Ⓕ Ⓖ Ⓗ Ⓙ Ⓚ

9. Ⓐ Ⓑ Ⓒ Ⓓ Ⓔ

Darken the circle for the word that is not spelled correctly. Darken the circle for *No mistakes* if all the words are spelled correctly.

10. F butter
     G lovely
     H laughig
     J right
     K *No mistakes*

11. A doen
     B write
     C been
     D thanked
     E *No mistakes*

12. F whyle
     G right
     H dreamed
     J guessing
     K *No mistakes*

13. A thanked
     B lieon
     C tiny
     D lovely
     E *No mistakes*

14. F night
     G eyes
     H butter
     J behined
     K *No mistakes*

15. A tiny
     B guessing
     C whi
     D been
     E *No mistakes*

16. F night
     G wich
     H hundred
     J wished
     K *No mistakes*

17. A buy
     B write
     C children
     D won
     E *No mistakes*

18. F dreamed
     G bild
     H eyes
     J pretty
     K *No mistakes*

19. A children
     B night
     C won
     D wishd
     E *No mistakes*

Answers

10. Ⓕ Ⓖ Ⓗ Ⓙ Ⓚ
11. Ⓐ Ⓑ Ⓒ Ⓓ Ⓔ
12. Ⓕ Ⓖ Ⓗ Ⓙ Ⓚ
13. Ⓐ Ⓑ Ⓒ Ⓓ Ⓔ
14. Ⓕ Ⓖ Ⓗ Ⓙ Ⓚ
15. Ⓐ Ⓑ Ⓒ Ⓓ Ⓔ
16. Ⓕ Ⓖ Ⓗ Ⓙ Ⓚ
17. Ⓐ Ⓑ Ⓒ Ⓓ Ⓔ
18. Ⓕ Ⓖ Ⓗ Ⓙ Ⓚ
19. Ⓐ Ⓑ Ⓒ Ⓓ Ⓔ

Darken the circle for the word that is spelled correctly.

Example

Please use this key to _____ the door.

A lok   B lak   C lock   D locke

Example
Ⓐ Ⓑ ● Ⓓ

Answers

1. His house is at the end of this _____.

A road   B rowd   C roade   D roed

1. Ⓐ Ⓑ Ⓒ Ⓓ

2. Do you _____ the answer to her question?

F knoe   G kno   H know   J knoaw

2. Ⓕ Ⓖ Ⓗ Ⓙ

3. Rosa wore a bright red and _____ sweater.

A yelloe   B yellow   C yeloww   D yello

3. Ⓐ Ⓑ Ⓒ Ⓓ

4. My brother _____ to baseball practice twice a week.

F gows   G goas   H gose   J goes

4. Ⓕ Ⓖ Ⓗ Ⓙ

5. I like butter and jelly on my _____.

A toest   B toast   C tost   D towst

5. Ⓐ Ⓑ Ⓒ Ⓓ

6. Let's have some milk and _____.

F cuckies   G coukies   H cookies   J cookeys

6. Ⓕ Ⓖ Ⓗ Ⓙ

7. Don't forget to _____ your hair in the morning.

A comb   B coem   C combe   D cowmb

7. Ⓐ Ⓑ Ⓒ Ⓓ

8. She _____ her pencil on the floor.

F droppd   G droped   H dropt   J dropped

8. Ⓕ Ⓖ Ⓗ Ⓙ

9. Are you _____ that we have math homework?

A soor   B sure   C shur   D shoure

9. Ⓐ Ⓑ Ⓒ Ⓓ

10. My little sister can't find her _____ and shoes.

F sawks   G socks   H socs   J saks

10. Ⓕ Ⓖ Ⓗ Ⓙ

11. We _____ leave early so that we don't miss the bus.

A shood   B shude   C should   D shoud

11. Ⓐ Ⓑ Ⓒ Ⓓ

12. The coin sank to the _____ of the pond.

F bottom   G batum   H botom   J bottum

12. Ⓕ Ⓖ Ⓗ Ⓙ

Unit 4 Review Test

Name ______________________

Darken the circle for the word that is spelled correctly.

13. The old jean jacket had a _____ in it.
A hoel **B** hoal **C** hole **D** howle

14. She waved to her friends and said _____.
F hellow **G** hello **H** heloww **J** helloe

15. I do not like to _____ dirty dishes.
A woush **B** wosh **C** wush **D** wash

16. The _____ little mouse was cold and wet.
F poor **G** por **H** poar **J** porr

17. She _____ that she would get her new puppy today.
A hopt **B** hoeped **C** hoped **D** hoppd

18. The men _____ hands and left the room.
F shooke **G** shook **H** shuk **J** shouck

19. The stars were _____ brightly in the sky.
A shineeng **B** shineing **C** shinning **D** shining

20. Is your birthday in _____ or December?
F Noavember **G** Nowvember **H** November **J** Noevember

21. I am _____ finished reading this book.
A almost **B** almoest **C** almowst **D** almoast

22. Please meet me here at two _____.
F oclock **G** o'clok **H** o'clock **J** oclak

23. My best friend _____ me a nice letter.
A wrot **B** wrote **C** wroat **D** roat

24. That traffic light _____ working this afternoon.
F stopped **G** stopt **H** stoped **J** stoppd

25. The rabbit is _____ across our lawn.
A hopng **B** hopeing **C** hawping **D** hopping

Answers

13.	Ⓐ	Ⓑ	Ⓒ	Ⓓ
14.	Ⓕ	Ⓖ	Ⓗ	Ⓙ
15.	Ⓐ	Ⓑ	Ⓒ	Ⓓ
16.	Ⓕ	Ⓖ	Ⓗ	Ⓙ
17.	Ⓐ	Ⓑ	Ⓒ	Ⓓ
18.	Ⓕ	Ⓖ	Ⓗ	Ⓙ
19.	Ⓐ	Ⓑ	Ⓒ	Ⓓ
20.	Ⓕ	Ⓖ	Ⓗ	Ⓙ
21.	Ⓐ	Ⓑ	Ⓒ	Ⓓ
22.	Ⓕ	Ⓖ	Ⓗ	Ⓙ
23.	Ⓐ	Ⓑ	Ⓒ	Ⓓ
24.	Ⓕ	Ⓖ	Ⓗ	Ⓙ
25.	Ⓐ	Ⓑ	Ⓒ	Ⓓ

Darken the circle for the phrase with an underlined word that is not spelled correctly.

Example		Example
A pull a loose <u>tooth</u> C flowers in the <u>gardin</u>		Ⓐ Ⓑ ● Ⓓ
B <u>move</u> near you D <u>learn</u> how to swim		

Answers

1. A a <u>wirm</u> in the apple   C not a <u>true</u> story
   B <u>enjoy</u> flying the kite   D <u>weren't</u> able to come

     1. Ⓐ   Ⓑ   Ⓒ   Ⓓ

2. F has a loud <u>voice</u>   H <u>wo'nt</u> be home
   G mother and <u>father</u>   J a <u>sharp</u> pencil

     2. Ⓕ   Ⓖ   Ⓗ   Ⓙ

3. A planted seeds in the <u>soil</u>   C too much <u>noise</u>
   B <u>havn't</u> seen your hat   D cat can <u>curl</u> up

     3. Ⓐ   Ⓑ   Ⓒ   Ⓓ

4. F a <u>huge</u> smile   H <u>were</u> at the park
   G <u>knue</u> the answer   J <u>can't</u> hear a sound

     4. Ⓕ   Ⓖ   Ⓗ   Ⓙ

5. A <u>few</u> pieces of gum   C the moon and the <u>earth</u>
   B found <u>two</u> frogs   D has a kind <u>hart</u>

     5. Ⓐ   Ⓑ   Ⓒ   Ⓓ

6. F <u>can't</u> miss the bus   H a sweet <u>gurl</u>
   G the <u>royal</u> family   J very <u>sharp</u> claws

     6. Ⓕ   Ⓖ   Ⓗ   Ⓙ

7. A <u>uesd</u> all the soap   C <u>true</u> or false
   B <u>voice</u> can be heard   D <u>weren't</u> in the room

     7. Ⓐ   Ⓑ   Ⓒ   Ⓓ

8. F <u>arn't</u> in the play   H <u>few</u> more minutes
   G <u>enjoy</u> reading   J gave his <u>father</u> a gift

     8. Ⓕ   Ⓖ   Ⓗ   Ⓙ

9. A <u>too</u> many people   C <u>won't</u> swim out too far
   B dug up the <u>soil</u>   D <u>cirl</u> her hair

     9. Ⓐ   Ⓑ   Ⓒ   Ⓓ

Darken the circle for the phrase with an underlined word that is not spelled correctly.

	Answers

10. F a fue more days   H enjoy the music
     G vegetable garden   J aren't coming

10. F G H J

11. A haven't been there   C a shearp knife
     B curl around my finger   D a true story

11. A B C D

12. F water the soyal   H were very happy
     G used the telephone   J a huge whale

12. F G H J

13. A won't play with us   C little green worm
     B the royal castle   D tew pairs of shoes

13. A B C D

14. F girl and boy   H all over the earth
     G in a soft voyce   J knew what to do

14. F G H J

15. A father and son   C chocolate candy heart
     B weeds in the garden   D wern't outside

15. A B C D

16. F tue much work   H were leaving today
     G knew how many   J aren't at their desk

16. F G H J

17. A lost his voice   C cant find it
     B a sharp nail   D wasn't true

17. A B C D

18. F her little girl   H worm on the leaf
     G enjoi swimming   J used more glue

18. F G H J

19. A huge storm   C the sun and the urth
     B saw a few clouds   D haven't written the letter

19. A B C D

Each underlined word in the story is misspelled. Darken the circle for the correct spelling.

Last week my dog, Max, needed a bath <u>becawse</u> he was so dirty.
₁
<u>Befour</u> I bathed him, I went to the pet store to <u>taulk</u> to Mr. Meng. "Max
₂ ₃
is really dirty. It will take at least a <u>quort</u> of soap to get him clean," I said.
₄

Mr. Meng took a bottle of soap out of a <u>wier</u> basket. "<u>Porr</u> two drops
₅ ₆
of this on Max and scrub," he said. I <u>baught</u> the soap and went home.
₇

Max is a very <u>straung</u> dog. When I started to wash him, he tried to
₈
jump on my head! Then he jumped to the <u>flor</u> and ran down the hall. I
₉
can't <u>cownt</u> how many towels I used to wipe up the soap and water. But I
₁₀
didn't <u>cair</u>. Max is <u>funier</u> than any other dog I know. I knew Max was
₁₁ ₁₂
hiding, and I knew just <u>wheare</u> to find him, too. Max wasn't mad at me,
₁₃
though. He gave me a big, wet kiss.

Answers							
1.	Ⓐ becouse	Ⓑ because	Ⓒ becase	Ⓓ becus
2.	Ⓕ Befoor	Ⓖ Befor	Ⓗ Before	Ⓙ Befour
3.	Ⓐ tawk	Ⓑ tolk	Ⓒ toulk	Ⓓ talk
4.	Ⓕ quart	Ⓖ qort	Ⓗ qart	Ⓙ quourt
5.	Ⓐ wir	Ⓑ wire	Ⓒ wiur	Ⓓ wiyr
6.	Ⓕ Por	Ⓖ Poar	Ⓗ Pour	Ⓙ Paur
7.	Ⓐ bawght	Ⓑ bought	Ⓒ bawt	Ⓓ boght
8.	Ⓕ strong	Ⓖ straung	Ⓗ stroung	Ⓙ strang
9.	Ⓐ flaur	Ⓑ flore	Ⓒ floor	Ⓓ florr
10.	Ⓕ coent	Ⓖ couent	Ⓗ coownt	Ⓙ count
11.	Ⓐ cere	Ⓑ cear	Ⓒ care	Ⓓ ceer
12.	Ⓕ funeer	Ⓖ funnier	Ⓗ funnyer	Ⓙ funnyier
13.	Ⓐ wair	Ⓑ whair	Ⓒ whare	Ⓓ where

Each underlined word in the story is misspelled. Darken the circle for the correct spelling.

Today was the <u>hotest</u> day of the summer! It was too hot to play outside,
₁₄

so I decided to stay <u>heere</u> in my room. At first I wanted to <u>dra</u> a picture
₁₅ ₁₆

of my cat. Then I decided I would paint a picture of a forest. I imagined

a nice <u>autemn</u> day in the forest. I painted bright red and orange leaves.
₁₇

I also painted a mother <u>deere</u> and her baby standing <u>neer</u> some tall trees.
₁₈ ₁₉

I painted a large <u>owwl</u> sitting on a tree branch, too. Then I added a stone
₂₀

<u>touwer</u> next to the trees. I could almost feel the cool <u>aer</u> on my face as I
₂₁ ₂₂

looked at the picture. I stayed in my room and painted for an <u>houer</u>.
₂₃

I finished my painting, but something was missing. I needed to write

a story about my picture. I found the <u>sharpst</u> pencil I could find and started
₂₄

to write. This story would be <u>greatr</u> than any other story I had ever written!
₂₅

Answers

14.	Ⓕ hottst	Ⓖ hottest	Ⓗ hottist	Ⓙ hotist
15.	Ⓐ heer	Ⓑ heere	Ⓒ here	Ⓓ heir
16.	Ⓕ drou	Ⓖ drow	Ⓗ drau	Ⓙ draw
17.	Ⓐ autum	Ⓑ autumn	Ⓒ autimn	Ⓓ autem
18.	Ⓕ deer	Ⓖ diir	Ⓗ deir	Ⓙ dere
19.	Ⓐ nere	Ⓑ neir	Ⓒ niir	Ⓓ near
20.	Ⓕ awl	Ⓖ ouwl	Ⓗ owl	Ⓙ owll
21.	Ⓐ tower	Ⓑ tawer	Ⓒ towr	Ⓓ towir
22.	Ⓕ ere	Ⓖ eer	Ⓗ ayr	Ⓙ air
23.	Ⓐ howr	Ⓑ houir	Ⓒ hour	Ⓓ hower
24.	Ⓕ sharpist	Ⓖ sharpest	Ⓗ sharppest	Ⓙ sharppist
25.	Ⓐ graeter	Ⓑ greatr	Ⓒ grater	Ⓓ greater

The Writing Process

Name _____

Prewriting • Plan your writing.
- Make sure you know what your writing task is.
- Identify the audience and the purpose for writing.
- Choose a topic.
- Gather and write ideas about the topic.
- Organize your ideas.

Writing • Write a first draft.
- Use your plan to put your ideas in writing.
- Don't worry about mistakes now.
- Add any new ideas you think of while writing.
- Leave room between lines so that you can make changes later.

Revising • Look for ways to improve what you have written.
- Make sure your writing fits the audience and purpose for writing.
- Look for places that need more ideas or details.
- Take out sentences that don't belong.
- Find places where more colorful or exact words can be used.
- Make sure that your sentences are complete.
- Write and revise until you are happy with your writing.

Proofreading • Review your work for errors.
- Make sure you have indented each paragraph.
- Check to see that you have used words correctly.
- Check your capitalization.
- Check to see that you have used periods, question marks, commas, and other punctuation marks correctly.
- Look at the spelling of each word. Circle words you are not sure you have spelled correctly. Check their spelling.

Publishing • Share what you have written.
- Make a clean final draft.
- Read it to the class or a friend.
- Add pictures or make a poster to go with it.
- Make a recording of your writing.

Proofreading Checklist

Name_____

You can use the questions below as a checklist to proofread your writing.

☐ Have I indented each paragraph?

☐ Have I used words correctly in every sentence?

☐ Have I capitalized the first word in each sentence?

☐ Have I capitalized all proper names?

☐ Have I ended each sentence with a period, question mark, or exclamation point?

☐ Have I spelled each word correctly?

The chart below shows some proofreading marks and how to use them.

Mark	Meaning	Example
◯	spell correctly	I ⟨liek⟩ dogs.
⊙	add period	They are my favorite kind of pet⊙
?	add question mark	What kind of pet do you have?
≡	capitalize	My dog's name is s̲c̲o̲o̲t̲e̲r̲.
℘	take out	He likes to t̶o̶ run and play.
¶	indent paragraph	¶ I love my dog, Scooter. He is the best pet I have ever had. Every morning he wakes me with a bark. Every night he sleeps with me.
ⱽ ⱽ	add quotation marks	You are my best friend, I tell him.

Chain of Events Chart

Name _____ Date _____

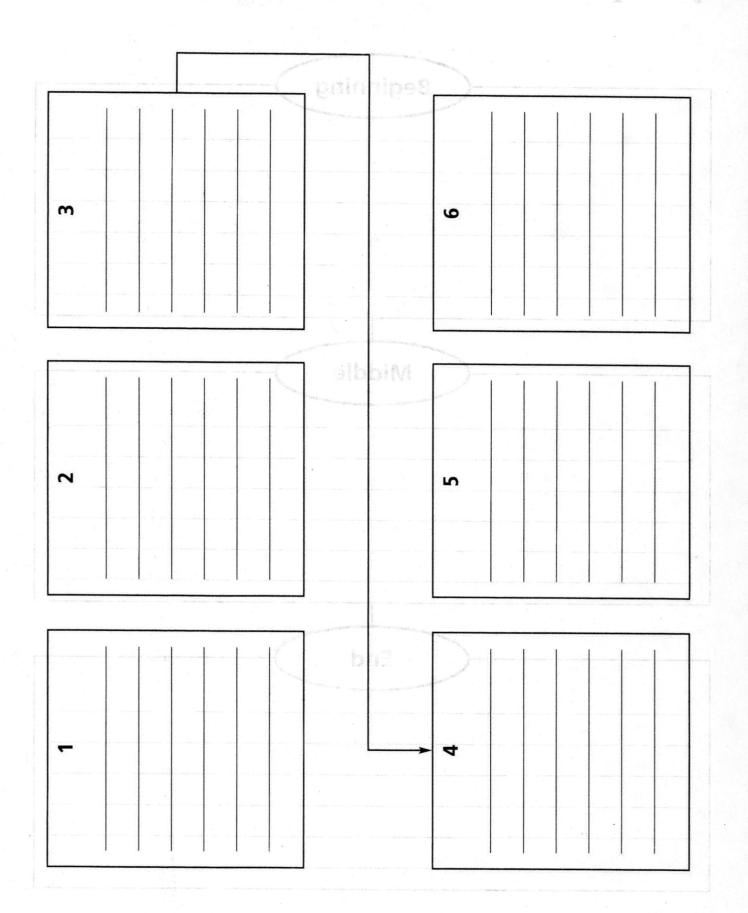

3

2

1

6

5

4

Story Map

Name _____ Date _____

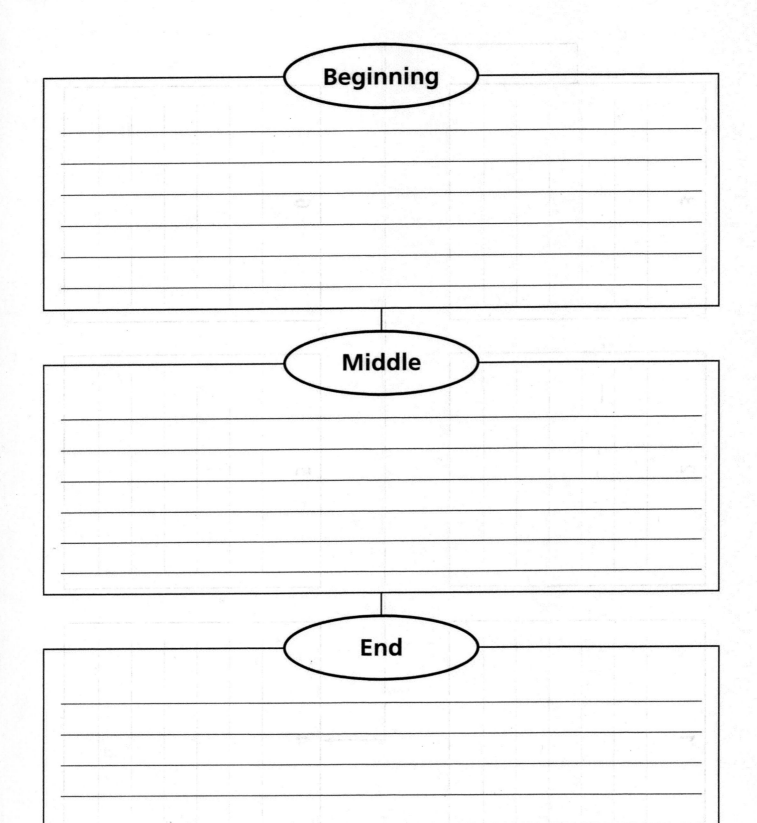

Beginning

Middle

End

Senses Web

Name _____ Date _____

Sight
_____
_____
_____
_____
_____

Smell
_____
_____
_____
_____
_____
_____

Taste
_____
_____
_____
_____
_____

_____

Hearing
_____
_____
_____
_____
_____

Touch
_____
_____
_____
_____
_____

How-To Chart

Name _____ Date _____

1 _____
_____
_____
_____
_____
_____

↓

2 _____
_____
_____
_____
_____
_____

↓

3 _____
_____
_____
_____
_____
_____

↓

4 _____
_____
_____
_____
_____